PENGUIN BUSINESS

EXPLORING MANAGEMENT AC

David J. Hickson is Professor of International Management and Organization at the University of Bradford Management Centre, England, and was founding Editor-in-Chief of the international journal *Organization Studies*. He has co-authored *Writers on Organizations* and *Management Worldwide* with Derek S. Pugh, both of which are published by Penguin.

Exploring Management across the World is a companion volume to *Management Worldwide*.

Exploring Management across the World

Selected Readings

Edited by David J. Hickson

PENGUIN BOOKS

PENGUIN BOOKS

Published by the Penguin Group
Penguin Books Ltd, 27 Wrights Lane, London W8 5TZ, England
Penguin Books USA Inc., 375 Hudson Street, New York, New York 10014, USA
Penguin Books Australia Ltd, Ringwood, Victoria, Australia
Penguin Books Canada Ltd, 10 Alcorn Avenue, Toronto, Ontario, Canada M4V 3B2
Penguin Books (NZ) Ltd, 182–190 Wairau Road, Auckland 10, New Zealand

Penguin Books Ltd, Registered Offices: Harmondsworth, Middlesex, England

First published in Penguin Books 1997
10 9 8 7 6 5 4 3 2 1

Typeset in Monotype Times and Univers
Typeset by Rowland Phototypesetting Ltd, Bury St Edmunds, Suffolk
Printed in England by Clays Ltd, St Ives plc

Contents

3. The Latins: Southern Europe and South America

4. The Northern Europeans and Israel

5. The East-Central Europeans

Acknowledgements

Permission to reprint the readings in this volume is acknowledged to the following sources.

1. Geert Hofstede 2. Geert Hofstede 3. Intercultural Press and Palmer & Dodge Agency 4. Monir Tayeb 5. Blackwell Publishers 6. Intercultural Press and Palmer & Dodge Agency 7. Seymour Martin Lipset, Canadian Journal of Sociology, and E. J. Brill 8. Jean-Louis Barsoux 9. Harper's Magazine 10. Pasquale Gagliardi 11. International Studies of Management and Organization 12. Malcolm Warner 13. Routledge 14. Stanley Thornes (Publishers) Ltd 15. Walter de Gruyter & Co 16. HarperCollins Publishers 17. Cassell plc 18. Magoroh Maruyama 19. John Child, Cambridge University Press, and The Economist 20. Walter de Gruyter & Co 21. Peter B. Smith 22. McGraw-Hill Book Company 23. Peter Wright 24. Macmillan Ltd 25. Monte Palmer 26. Management International Review 27. Routledge 28. Walter de Gruyter & Co 29. Monir Tayeb 30. Blackwell Publishers

Introduction: Managing Internationally

David J. Hickson

The modern student of management should not just study 'management', an unqualified, indiscriminate, amorphous notion. To be sure, management everywhere has a common core, a shared universal managerialism. Organization charts always show a hierarchical form with specialist sub-divisions recognizable to all. Everywhere the élite is the élite, a top management level where the main decisions are taken. Everywhere there are calculations of costings and capacities. And so on.

But this common core is surrounded by a diversity of practice on the part of managers, all of whom are steeped in the cultures of societies. From society to society, country to country, nation to nation, the approach to management differs. It differs in the way authority is used, in interpersonal relationships on the job, in communication style, in assertiveness, in speed of action, in bureaucratization, and much more. Even at the centre of what seems to be the common core, the formal structures of organizations can vary in terms of the number of layers and number of departmental specialisms.

Nevertheless, the student of management and organization should not panic. When he or she goes into, or returns to, a management job, there will be a recognizable common framework of structure and activities whatever the society. The newcomer is not entirely lost. Yes, there will be 'culture shock' over the way things are done if the society is an unfamiliar one, but that can be overcome and an effective adjustment can be attained with patience, and with sympathetic observation of others *and* of oneself. To help in this, prior understanding is an advantage, arguably even a necessity.

This book provides one means of gaining such understanding. It should aid both the study of academic subjects which are international in character, such as international management, international marketing, international business, and the like, and preparation for the world that is encountered after academia.

Useful Companions

This book is intended to save time and trouble and to evade frustration by giving easy access in one volume to a wide range of selected writings on management in various societies. It helps avoid the difficulties involved in finding the originals in libraries: searching for missing books and journals on incomplete shelves, waiting for others to return books borrowed, and delays caused by slow inter-library loan services. In addition, it gathers salient material together, so the student does not have to wade through less relevant material to find it.

In all of this, *Exploring Management* is similar in purpose to *Management Worldwide: the Impact of Societal Culture on Organizations around the Globe*, by David J. Hickson and Derek S. Pugh (Penguin, 1995). Though each book can be used separately, they are complementary and make ideal companion volumes. The text of *Management Worldwide* first describes prevailing societal cultures and their principal management-relevant elements, and then, chapter by chapter, the distinctive approaches to management which characterize the Anglos, the Latins, the Northern Europeans, the East-Central Europeans, the Asians, the Arabs, and developing countries in general, describing exemplifying societies in each chapter. *Exploring Management* follows the same sequence, presenting selections from the original source material which was the basis for writing *Management Worldwide*.

The cautions which apply to *Management Worldwide* therefore also apply to the present book. It is not possible to bring within a single cover everything that might be desirable. Only a selection of societies can be represented, and only a selection of readings, which inevitably vary in coverage and depth. These span a number of years, since the most recent are not always the most appropriate. If any readers do not find a portrayal of the management features in a particular society in which they are interested, then, hopefully, the general material on societal cultures, and the readings on societies that are similar in culture to the society whose approach to management they seek to understand, will give them some guidance.

Even if space permitted, which it does not, the lack of research evidence would prevent these books from dealing with anything more than the predominant cultures of the societies covered. The possible variations in management and organization that may be due to minority cultures have hardly been touched by research. The Basques in France and Spain, the Arabs in Israel, the people of Indian origin in Britain, the Turks in Germany, the Latin (Hispanic) Americans in the United States, people of black African origin in Brazil – these and countless others are not mentioned in either book.

Moreover, both books share a language limitation that is usually overlooked by those readers whose first language is English, and who take their language for granted. The great bulk of relevant research is published in English. The advantage is that this language is open to the widest international readership. But, as with all languages, it carries its own subtle idiosyncrasies and variations of meaning in relation to others. This book cannot avoid whatever limitations, even biases, English may have imposed upon the authors of many lands and languages whose work is included.

Coverage to Explore

The book begins with extracts that explore the nature of cultures in societies, especially as they are tied in with management and organization. Concepts of work-related values (notably Hofstede's well-known power distance, individualism versus collectivism, uncertainty avoidance, and masculinity versus femininity), of communication and language, and of time, are introduced.

Then Parts Two to Eight bring together selections from books and journals, culture by culture, as explained above. First come the Anglos, most widespread of all across the globe, showing in their approach to management direct influence from the British Empire which scattered them so far. Generally speaking, they decentralize managerial decisions and use the minimum of bureaucracy in a flexible manner, though the Americans are inclined to more paperwork and a more action-oriented style than the traditionally minded British. The Anglos are represented by extracts on the English (and British), the Americans and the Canadians.

Next come the Latins, both of Southern Europe and South America, with readings in particular on the French, the Italians and the Brazilians. They bear with them still the imprint of a much earlier empire, the Roman, and of the Spanish and Portuguese colonization which took this legacy to South and Central America. They tend to use management authority in a more centralized way, supporting it with more extensive and detailed formalized rules and regulations – but finding ways to avoid these when they need to.

The Northern Europeans are comparatively free of both British and Roman influence. They are represented by passages on management in Germany and Sweden, and (as in *Management Worldwide*) Israel is grouped with them. Their broadly democratic and open cultures result in decentralized management with minimal status distinctions, together, in the German case, with the careful attention to procedures and orderliness for which that country is known. Israel appears here because of its cultural similarity, though its approach has an especial informality and works on the basis of 'who knows who'.

East-Central Europe has a tortured history, and today the pace of change is so fast that it is difficult to choose material that will stay up to date. Russia and Poland are included, together with items on both the Communist-controlled, centrally planned, past and the current transformation to varying degrees of market economy. Management is changing from looking only upwards for instructions and permission from above, and devising ways of circumventing them, to looking outwards to customers and clients.

On the other side of the world, there are 'Alternative Concepts of Management', as the first extract on the Asians claims. These are well illustrated by material on China, together with Hong Kong and the 'overseas Chinese', and on Japan. Here collectivistic cultures are pronounced, with a view of management that, on the whole, gives greater value to creating and sustaining personal relationships than in the more individualistic West. This is apparent on examining how managerial hierarchies use authority in a consultative manner in Japan, where group affinities are more readily transferred into and developed within the work organization than seems to be the case in China.

Different again, the Arabs contribute an Islamic-influenced view of how to manage, represented – in greater or lesser degree – by selections on management in Saudi Arabia and Egypt. In the Middle East strong leadership is looked for from the top, combined with an 'open-door' to those below which derives both from Bedouin tradition and Koranic teachings. Personal loyalty is highly valued in a management style in which personal considerations matter more than they do to the Westerner trained to manage impersonally.

Then there is a section on developing countries in general, and Africa and India in particular. Here the strain between impersonal forms of organization brought from the West, and personal ways of working that harmonize with long-standing cultures and ways of life, is acute. Hierarchies staffed with personal obligations and relationships in mind can appear to be overstaffed by Western standards, and impersonal hiring and firing, as Western practice dictates, seems coldly inconsiderate and socially unacceptable.

The book concludes with an overall review, an 'Overview' by Peter Smith, of differences and similarities across the world, and the evidence for them.

These brief introductory characterizations are necessarily oversimplifications. They are general tendencies, to be seen always as comparative, of one society relative to another, and they should be taken as indications to entice the reader further.

This opening chapter must not end without a warning about its author. He is no more culture-neutral than is anyone else. He sees the world from an island off mainland Western Europe, an Englishman through and through, as unaware of his own latent cultural biases as any reader of this book will be. Fortunately, even if this should have influenced his choice of the items that make up this book, it cannot have influenced their content, written by many authors from many cultures.

1

Managing and the Cultures of Societies

Levels of Culture *and* National Cultures in Four Dimensions

Geert Hofstede

Chapter 1, pp. 4–13 in Geert Hofstede, *Cultures and Organizations: Software of the Mind* (London: McGraw-Hill, 1991) and Chapter 1, pp. 2–3 in David J. Hickson (ed.), *Management in Western Europe: Society, Culture and Organization in Twelve Nations* (Berlin and New York: Walter de Gruyter, 1993)

Levels of Culture

Culture as Mental Programming

Every person carries within him or herself patterns of thinking, feeling, and potential acting which were learned throughout their lifetime. Much of it has been acquired in early childhood, because at that time a person is most susceptible to learning and assimilating. As soon as certain patterns of thinking, feeling and acting have established themselves within a person's mind, (s)he must unlearn these before being able to learn something different, and unlearning is more difficult than learning for the first time.

Using the analogy of the way in which computers are programmed, this book will call such patterns of thinking, feeling, and acting *mental programs*, or, as the sub-title goes: '*software of the mind*'. This does not mean, of course, that people are programmed the way computers are. A person's behavior is only partially predetermined by her or his mental programs: (s)he has a basic ability to deviate from them, and to react in ways which are new, creative, destructive, or unexpected. The '*software of the mind*' this book is about only indicates what reactions are likely and understandable, given one's past.

The sources of one's mental programs lie within the social environments in which one grew up and collected one's life experiences. The programming starts within the family; it continues within the neighborhood, at school, in youth groups, at the work place, and in the living community. [. . .]

A customary term for such mental software is *culture*. This word has several meanings, all derived from its Latin source, which refers to the tilling of the soil. In most Western languages 'culture' commonly means 'civilization' or 'refinement of the mind' and in particular the results of such refinement, like education, art, and literature. This is 'culture in the narrow sense'; I sometimes call it 'culture one'. Culture as mental software, however, corresponds to a much broader use of the word which is common among social anthropologists: this is 'culture two', and it is the concept which will be used throughout this book.

Social (or cultural) anthropology is the science of human societies, in particular (although not only) traditional or 'primitive' ones. In social anthropology, 'culture' is a catchword for all those patterns of thinking, feeling, and acting referred to in the previous paragraphs. Not only those activities supposed to refine the mind are included in 'culture two', but also the ordinary and menial things in life: greeting, eating, showing or not showing feelings, keeping a certain physical distance from others, making love, or maintaining body hygiene. Politicians and journalists sometimes confuse culture two and culture one without being aware of it: the adaptation problems of immigrants to their new host country are discussed in terms of promoting folk dance groups. But culture two deals with much more fundamental human processes than culture one; it deals with the things that hurt.

Culture (two) is always a collective phenomenon, because it is at least partly shared with people who live or lived within the same social environment, which is where it was learned. It is *the collective programming of the mind which distinguishes the members of one group or category of people from another*.

Culture is learned, not inherited. It derives from one's social environment, not from one's genes. Culture should be distinguished from human nature on one side, and from an individual's personality on the other (see Figure 1), although exactly where the borders lie between human nature and culture, and between culture and personality, is a matter of discussion among social scientists.

Human nature is what all human beings, from the Russian professor to the Australian aborigine, have in common: it represents the universal level in one's mental software. It is inherited with one's genes; within the computer analogy it is the 'operating system' which determines one's physical and basic psychological functioning. The human ability to feel fear, anger, love, joy, sadness, the need to associate with others, to play and exercise oneself, the facility to observe the environment and to talk about it with other humans, all belong to

Figure 1 Three levels of uniqueness in human mental programming

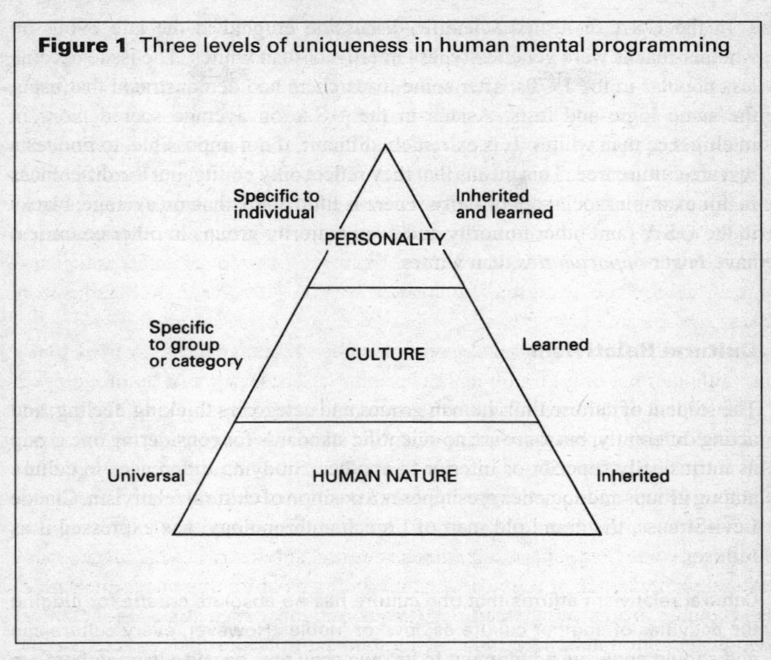

this level of mental programming. However, what one does with these feelings, how one expresses fear, joy, observations, and so on, is modified by culture. Human nature is not as 'human' as the term suggests, because certain aspects of it are shared with parts of the animal world.

The *personality* of an individual, on the other hand, is her/his unique personal set of mental programs which (s)he does not share with any other human being. It is based upon traits which are partly inherited with the individual's unique set of genes and partly learned. 'Learned' means: modified by the influence of collective programming (culture) *as well as* unique personal experiences.

Cultural traits have often been attributed to heredity, because philosophers and other scholars in the past did not know how to explain otherwise the remarkable stability of differences in culture patterns among human groups. They underestimated the impact of learning from previous generations and of teaching to a future generation what one has learned oneself. The role of heredity is exaggerated in the pseudo-theories of *race*, which have been responsible, among other things, for the Holocaust organized by the Nazis during the Second World War. Racial and ethnic strife is often justified by unfounded arguments of cultural superiority and inferiority.

In the USA, a heated scientific discussion erupted in the late 1960s on whether blacks were genetically less intelligent than whites. The issue became less popular in the 1970s, after some researchers had demonstrated that using the same logic and tests, Asians in the USA on average scored *more* in intelligence than whites. It is extremely difficult, if not impossible, to find tests that are culture free. This means that they reflect only ability, not the differences in, for example, social opportunity. There is little doubt that, on average, blacks in the USA (and other minority and even majority groups in other countries) have fewer *opportunities* than whites.

Cultural Relativism

The student of culture finds human groups and categories thinking, feeling, and acting differently, but there are no scientific standards for considering one group as intrinsically superior or inferior to another. Studying differences in culture among groups and societies presupposes a position of cultural relativism. Claude Lévi-Strauss, the grand old man of French anthropology, has expressed it as follows:

> Cultural relativism affirms that one culture has no absolute criteria for judging the activities of another culture as 'low' or 'noble'. However, every culture can and should apply such judgment to its own activities, because its members are actors as well as observers.

Cultural relativism does not imply normlessness for oneself, nor for one's society. It does call for suspending judgment when dealing with groups or societies different from one's own. One should think twice before applying the norms of one person, group or society to another. Information about the nature of the cultural differences between societies, their roots, and their consequences should precede judgment and action.

Even after having been informed, the foreign observer is still likely to deplore certain ways of the other society. If (s)he is professionally involved in the other society, for example as an expatriate manager or development assistance expert, (s)he may very well want to induce changes. In colonial days, foreigners often wielded absolute power in other societies and they could impose their rules on it. In these postcolonial days, foreigners who want to change something in another society will have to negotiate their interventions. Again, negotiation is more likely to succeed when the parties concerned understand the reasons for the differences in viewpoints.

Figure 2 The 'onion diagram': manifestations of culture at different levels of depth

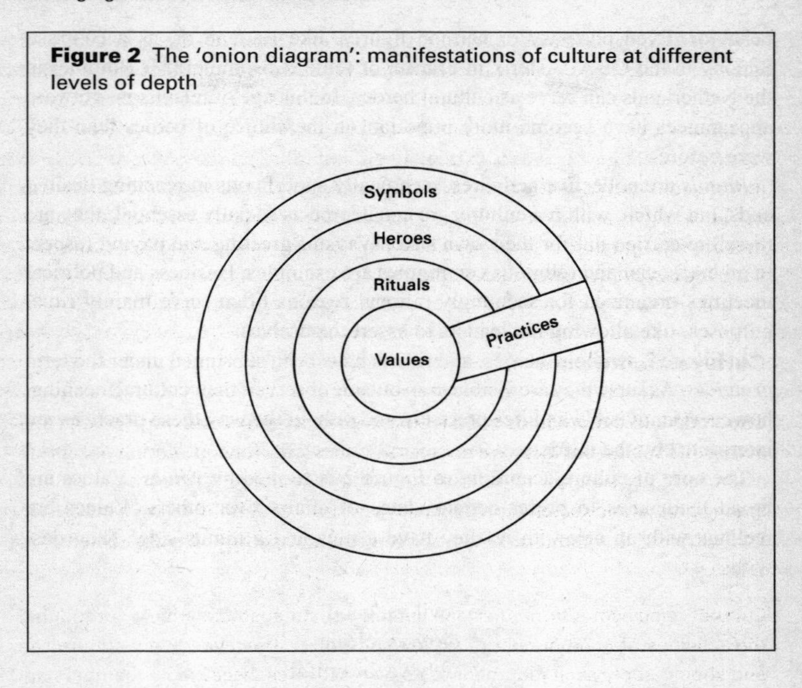

Symbols, Heroes, Rituals, and Values

Cultural differences manifest themselves in several ways. From the many terms used to describe manifestations of culture the following four together cover the total concept rather neatly: symbols, heroes, rituals, and values. In Figure 2 these are illustrated as the skins of an onion, indicating that symbols represent the most superficial and values the deepest manifestations of culture, with heroes and rituals in between.

Symbols are words, gestures, pictures or objects that carry a particular meaning which is only recognized by those who share the culture. The words in a language or jargon belong to this category, as do dress, hairstyles, Coca-Cola, flags, and status symbols. New symbols are easily developed and old ones disappear: symbols from one cultural group are regularly copied by others. This is why symbols have been put into the outer, most superficial layer of Figure 2.

Heroes are persons, alive or dead, real or imaginary, who possess characteristics which are highly prized in a culture, and who thus serve as models for behavior. Even phantasy or cartoon figures, like Batman or, as a contrast, Snoopy in the USA, Asterix in France, or Ollie B. Bommel (Mr Bumble) in the Netherlands can serve as cultural heroes. In this age of television, outward appearances have become more important in the choice of heroes than they were before.

Rituals are collective activities, technically superfluous in reaching desired ends, but which, within a culture, are considered as socially essential: they are therefore carried out for their own sake. Ways of greeting and paying respect to others, social and religious ceremonies are examples. Business and political meetings organized for seemingly rational reasons often serve mainly ritual purposes, like allowing the leaders to assert themselves.

In Figure 2 symbols, heroes, and rituals have been subsumed under the term *practices*. As such, they are visible to an outside observer; their cultural meaning, however, is invisible and lies precisely and only in the way these practices are interpreted by the insiders.

The core of culture according to Figure 2 is formed by *values*. Values are broad tendencies to prefer certain states of affairs over others. Values are feelings with an arrow to it: they have a plus and a minus side. They deal with:

evil vs. good
dirty vs. clean
ugly vs. beautiful
unnatural vs. natural
abnormal vs. normal
paradoxical vs. logical
irrational vs. rational

Values are among the first things children learn – not consciously, but implicitly. Development psychologists believe that by the age of ten, most children have their basic value system firmly in place, and after that age, changes are difficult to make. Because they were acquired so early in our lives, many values remain unconscious to those who hold them. Therefore they cannot be discussed, nor can they be directly observed by outsiders. They can only be inferred from the way people act under various circumstances.

For systematic research on values, inferring them from people's actions is cumbersome and ambiguous. Various paper-and-pencil questionnaires have been developed which ask for people's preferences among alternatives. The answers should not be taken too literally: in practice, people will not always act as they have scored on the questionnaire. Still the questionnaires provide useful information, because they show differences in answers between groups or categories of respondents. For example, suppose a question asks for one's preference for time off from work versus more pay. An individual employee who states (s)he prefers time off may in fact choose the money if presented with the actual choice, but if in group A more people claim preferring time off than in group B, this does indicate a cultural difference between these groups in the relative value of free time versus money.

In interpreting people's statements about their values it is important to distinguish between the *desirable* and the *desired*: how people think the world ought to be versus what people want for themselves. Questions about the desirable refer to people in general and are worded in terms of right/wrong, agree/disagree or something similar. In the abstract, everybody is in favor of virtue and opposed to sin, and answers about the desirable express people's views about what represents virtue and what corresponds to sin. The desired, on the contrary, is worded in terms of 'you' or 'me' and what we consider important, what we want for ourselves, including our less virtuous desires. The desirable bears only a faint resemblance to actual behavior, but even statements about the desired, although closer to actual behavior, should not necessarily correspond to the way people really behave when they have to choose.

What distinguishes the desirable from the desired is the nature of the *norms* involved. Norms are the standards for values that exist within a group or category of people. In the case of the desirable, the norm is absolute, pertaining to what is ethically right. In the case of the desired, the norm is statistical: it indicates the choices actually made by the majority. The desirable relates more to ideology, the desired to practical matters.

Interpretations of value studies which neglect the difference between the desirable and the desired may lead to paradoxical results. A case in which the two produced diametrically opposed answers was found in the IBM studies. Employees in different countries were asked for their agreement or disagreement with the statement 'Employees in industry should participate more in the decisions made by management.' This is a statement about the desirable. In another question people were asked whether they personally preferred a manager who 'usually consults with subordinates before reaching a decision'. This is a statement about the desired. A comparison between the answers to these two questions revealed that employees in countries where the manager who consults was less popular, agreed more with the general statement that employees should participate more, and vice versa; maybe the ideology served as a compensation for the day-to-day relationship with the boss.

Layers of Culture

As almost everyone belongs to a number of different groups and categories of people at the same time, people unavoidably carry several layers of mental programming within themselves, corresponding to different levels of culture. For example:

- a national level according to one's country (or countr*ies* for people who migrated during their lifetime)
- a regional and/or ethnic and/or religious and/or linguistic affiliation level, as most nations are composed of culturally different regions and/or ethnic and/or religious and/or language groups
- a gender level, according to whether a person was born as a girl or as a boy
- a generation level, which separates grandparents from parents from children
- a social-class level, associated with educational opportunities and with a person's occupation or profession
- for those who are employed, an organizational or corporate level according to the way employees have been socialized by their work organization

Additions to this list are easy to make. The mental programs from these various levels are not necessarily in harmony. In modern society they are often partly conflicting: for example, religious values may conflict with generation values; gender values with organizational practices. Conflicting mental programs within people make it difficult to anticipate their behavior in a new situation.

National Culture Differences

Human societies have existed for at least 10,000 years, possibly much longer. Archaeologists believe that the first humans led a nomadic existence as hunter-gatherers. After many thousands of years, some of them settled down as farmers. Gradually some farming communities grew into larger settlements, which became towns, cities, and finally modern megalopolises like Mexico City with over 25 million inhabitants.

Different human societies have followed this development to different extents, so that hunter-gatherers survive even today (according to some, the modern urban yuppy has reverted to a hunting-gathering state). As the world became more and more populated, an amazing variety of answers was found to the basic question of how people can live together and form some kind of a structured society.

In the fertile areas of the world large empires had already been built several thousand years ago, usually because the rulers of one part succeeded in conquering other parts. The oldest empire in existence within living memory is China. Although it had not always been unified, the Chinese Empire possessed a continuous history of about 4,000 years. Other empires disintegrated: in the eastern Mediterranean and southwestern part of Asia empires grew, flourished, and fell, only to be succeeded by others: the Sumerian, Babylonian, Assyrian, Egyptian, Persian, Greek, Roman, and Turkish states, to mention only a few. The South Asian subcontinent and the Indonesian archipelago had their empires, like the Maurya, the Gupta, and later the Moghul in India and the Majapahit on Java; in Central and South America the Aztec, Maya, and Inca empires have left their monuments. In Africa, Ethiopia and Benin are examples of ancient states.

Next to and often within the territory of these larger empires, smaller units survived in the form of tribes or independent small 'kingdoms'. Even now, in New Guinea most of the population lives in small and relatively isolated tribes, each with its own language, and hardly integrated into the larger society.

The invention of 'nations', political units into which the entire world is divided and to one of which every human being is supposed to belong – as manifested by her or his passport – is a recent phenomenon in human history. Earlier, there were states, but not everybody belonged to one of these or identified with one. The nation system was only introduced worldwide in the mid-twentieth century. It followed the colonial system which had developed during the preceding three centuries. In this colonial period the technologically advanced countries of Western Europe divided among themselves virtually all the territories of the globe which were not held by another strong political power. The borders between the ex-colonial nations still reflect the colonial legacy. In Africa, particularly, national borders correspond more to the logic of the colonial powers than to the cultural dividing lines of the local populations.

Nations, therefore, should not be equated to *societies*. Historically, societies are organically developed forms of social organization, and the concept of a common culture applies, strictly speaking, more to societies than to nations. Nevertheless, many nations do form historically developed wholes even if they consist of clearly different groups and even if they contain less integrated minorities.

Within nations that have existed for some time there are strong forces towards further integration: (usually) one dominant national language, common mass media, a national education system, a national army, a national political system, national representation in sports events with a strong symbolic and emotional appeal, a national market for certain skills, products, and services. Today's nations do not attain the degree of internal homogeneity of the isolated, usually nonliterate societies studied by field anthropologists, but they are the source of a considerable amount of common mental programming of their citizens.

On the other hand there remains a tendency for ethnic, linguistic, and religious groups to fight for recognition of their own identity, if not for national independence; this tendency has been increasing rather than decreasing in the latter part of the twentieth century. Examples are the Ulster Roman Catholics, the Belgian Flemish, the Basques in Spain and France, the Kurds in Iran, Iraq, Syria, and Turkey, and many of the ethnic groups in the Soviet Union.

In research on cultural differences nationality – the passport one holds – should therefore be used with care. Yet it is often the only feasible criterion for classification. Rightly or wrongly, collective properties are ascribed to the citizens of certain countries: people refer to 'typically American', 'typically German', or 'typically Japanese' behavior. Using nationality as a criterion is a matter of expediency, because it is immensely easier to obtain data for nations than for organic homogeneous societies. Nations as political bodies supply all kinds of statistics about their populations. Survey data, i.e., the answers of people on paper-and-pencil questionnaires related to their culture, are also mostly collected through national networks. Where it *is* possible to separate results by regional, ethnic or linguistic group, this should be done.

A strong reason for collecting data at the level of nations is that one of the purposes of the research is to promote cooperation among nations. The (over 200) nations that exist today populate one single world and we either survive or perish together. So it makes practical sense to focus on cultural factors separating or uniting nations.

National Cultures in Four Dimensions

Our empirical research on national culture differences at the Institute for Research on Intercultural Co-operation at Maastricht began with a study of the distribution of work-related *values* among 53 national subsidiaries of a large multinational business corporation. Values represent the most stable element in mental programming They are semi-conscious feelings about good and evil which are usually acquired in early childhood and are then difficult to change as adults. Values represent the stable core of culture. Measurements by skilful pencil-and-paper questionnaires of the values of similar people in these different national subsidiaries showed a strong national component. Comparison with studies by other people, comparing some or all of the same countries, confirmed the existence of such a national component. Statistical analysis showed that the differences between the dominant values in the national subsidiaries were linked to four different factors, four *dimensions of national culture*:

- individualism versus collectivism
- large versus small power distance
- strong versus weak uncertainty avoidance
- masculinity versus femininity

Each country could be given a score on each of these four dimensions.

In *individualist* cultures, people are supposed to look after their own interest and that of their immediate family (husband, wife and children). In *collectivist* cultures, on the other hand, people remain, throughout their lives, members of larger but close-knit in-groups which protect them in exchange for unquestioning loyalty, and which compete with other in-groups (families, tribes, clans or villages).

Power distance represents the extent to which the less powerful people in a culture accept and expect that power is distributed unequally.

Uncertainty avoidance represents the extent to which people in a culture become nervous in unstructured, ambiguous situations, and try to avoid such situations by strict rules of behaviour, intolerance of deviants, and a belief in absolute truths.

In *masculine* cultures, men are expected to be ambitious, assertive, concerned with money, and to admire whatever is big and strong. Women are supposed to care and serve. In *feminine* cultures, men and women are both expected to be non-competitive, modest, concerned with relationships, and to sympathize with whatever is small and weak.

The people in the 53 national subsidiaries studied varied considerably on these four dimensions, which occurred in virtually all possible combinations. The countries have been given scores on each dimension, and these scores can be shown to relate to phenomena in the various societies in which these subsidiaries operate, such as:

- political systems and political priorities
- educational systems and priorities
- management methods and objectives
- negotiation behaviour between individuals and organizations.

For example, individualism can be shown to relate to freedom of the press in a country; high power distance to income inequality among citizens; uncertainty avoidance to a belief in the competence of experts and the incompetence of lay people; and femininity to the percentage of its Gross National Product spent by a rich country on its development assistance to poor countries.

Key Concepts: Underlying Structures of Culture

Edward T. Hall and Mildred Reed Hall

Part 1, pp. 6–10 in Edward T. Hall and Mildred Reed Hall, *Understanding Cultural Differences* (Yarmouth, Maine: Intercultural Press, 1989)

High and Low Context: How Much Information is Enough?

Context is the information that surrounds an event; it is inextricably bound up with the meaning of that event. The elements that combine to produce a given meaning – events and context – are in different proportions depending on the culture. The cultures of the world can be compared on a scale from high to low context.

A high context (HC) communication or message is one in which *most* of the information is already in the person, while very little is in the coded, explicit, transmitted part of the message. A low context (LC) communication is just the opposite; i.e., the mass of the information is vested in the explicit code. Twins who have grown up together can and do communicate more economically (HC) than two lawyers in a courtroom during a trial (LC), a mathematician programming a computer, two politicians drafting legislation, two administrators writing a regulation. (Edward T. Hall, 1976)

Japanese, Arabs, and Mediterranean peoples, who have extensive information networks among family, friends, colleagues, and clients and who are involved in close personal relationships, are high-context. As a result, for most normal transactions in daily life they do not require, nor do they expect, much in-depth, background information. This is because they keep themselves informed about everything having to do with the people who are important in their lives. Low-context people include Americans, Germans, Swiss, Scandinavians, and other northern Europeans; they compartmentalize their personal relationships, their work, and many aspects of day-to-day life. Consequently, each time they interact with others they need detailed background information. The French are much higher on the context scale than either the Germans or the Americans. This difference can affect virtually every situation and every relationship in which the members of these two opposite traditions find themselves.

Within each culture, of course, there are specific individual differences in the need for contexting – the process of filling in background data. But it is helpful to know whether the culture of a particular country falls on the high or low side of the scale since every person is influenced by the level of context.

Contexting performs multiple functions. For example, any shift in the level of context is a communication. The shift can be up the scale, indicating a warming of the relationship, or down the scale (lowering the context), communicating coolness or displeasure – signaling something has gone wrong with a relationship. In the United States the boss might communicate annoyance to an assistant when he shifts from the high-context, familiar form of address to the low-context, formal form of address. When this happens the boss is telling the subordinate in no uncertain terms that she or he has stepped out of line and incurred disfavor. In Japan, moving the direction of the context is a source of daily feedback as to how things are going. The day starts with the use of honorifics, formal forms of address attached to each name. If things are going well the honorifics are dropped as the day progresses. First-naming in the United States is an artificial attempt at high-contexting; it tends to offend Europeans, who view the use of first names as acceptable only between close friends and family. With Europeans, one is always safe using a formal form of address, waiting for the other person to indicate when familiarity is acceptable.

Like their near relations the Germans, many Anglo-Americans (mostly those of northern European heritage) are not only low-context but they also lack extensive, well-developed information networks. American networks are limited in scope and development compared to those of the French, the Spanish, the Italians, and the Japanese. What follows from this is that Americans, unless they are very unsophisticated, will feel the need for contexting, for detailed background information, any time they are asked to make a decision or to do something. The American approach to life is quite segmented and focused on discrete, compartmentalized information; Americans need to know what is going to be in what compartment before they commit themselves. We experienced this in Japan when we were asked on short notice to provide names of well-placed Japanese and Americans to be participants in a small conference. Like most prudent Americans, we were reluctant to provide names until we knew what the conference was about and what the individuals recommended would be expected to do. This seemed logical and reasonable enough to us. Nevertheless, our reluctance was read as obstructionist by our Japanese colleagues and friends responsible for the conference. In Japan the mere presence of certain individuals endows the group and its activities with authority and status, which is far more important than the topic of the conference. It is characteristic of high-context, high-information societies that attendance at functions is as much a matter of the prestige associated with the function as anything else. This in turn means that, quite frequently, invitations to high-level meetings and conferences will be issued on short notice. It is taken for granted that those invited will eschew all previous commitments if the meeting is important enough. As a general rule Americans place greater importance on how long ago a commitment was made, on the agenda, and on the relevance of the expertise of different individuals to the agenda. (For an in-depth discussion of the Japanese, we refer the reader to the authors' *Hidden Differences: Doing Business with the Japanese*.)

Another example of the contrast between how high- and low-context systems work is this: consider a top American executive working in an office and receiving a normal quota of visitors, usually one at a time. Most of the information that is relevant to the job originates from the few people the executive sees in the course of the day, as well as from what she or he reads. This is why the advisors and support personnel who surround the presidents of American enterprises (as well as the president of the United States) are so important. They and they alone control the content and the flow of organizational information to the chief executive.

Contrast this with the office of virtually any business executive in a high-context country such as France or Japan, where information flows freely and from all sides. Not only are people constantly coming and going, both seeking and giving information, but the entire form and function of the organization is centered on gathering, processing, and disseminating information. Everyone stays informed about every aspect of the business and knows who is best informed on what subjects.

In Germany almost everything is low-context and compartmentalized. The executive office is both a refuge and a screen – a refuge for the boss from the distractions of day-to-day office interactions and a screen for the employees from continual supervision. Information communicated in the office is not shared except with a select few – the exact antithesis of the high-information cultures.

High-context people are apt to become impatient and irritated when low-context people insist on giving them information they don't need. Conversely, low-context people are at a loss when high-context people do not provide *enough* information. One of the great communications challenges in life is to find the appropriate level of contexting needed in each situation. Too much information leads people to feel they are being talked down to; too little information can mystify them or make them feel left out. Ordinarily, people make these adjustments automatically in their own country, but in other countries their messages frequently miss the target.

The other side of the coin when considering context level is the apparent paradox that high-context people, such as the French, want to see *everything* when evaluating a *new* enterprise to which they have not been contexted. Annual reports or tax returns are not enough. Furthermore, they will keep asking until they get the information they want. Being high-context, the French are driven to make their own synthesis of the meanings of the figures. Unlike Americans, they feel uncomfortable with someone else's synthesis, someone else's 'bottom line'.

Further Reading

Hall, Edward T., *The Silent Language*, Garden City, NY: Anchor Press/Doubleday, 1959.

— *The Hidden Dimension*, Garden City, NY: Anchor Press/Doubleday, 1966.

— *Beyond Culture*, Garden City, NY: Anchor Press/Doubleday, 1976.

— *The Dance of Life: The Other Dimension of Time*, Garden City, NY: Anchor Press/Doubleday, 1983.

Lewis, Flora, *Europe: A Tapestry of Nations*, New York: Simon & Schuster, 1987.

2

The Anglos Across the Continents

England

English Culture and Business Organizations

Monir Tayeb

Chapter 4, pp. 47 – 64 in David J. Hickson (ed.), *Management in Western Europe: Society, Culture and Organization in Twelve Nations* (Berlin and New York: Walter de Gruyter, 1993)

Introduction

This chapter is intended to demonstrate how the business climate of English organizations is influenced by their societal culture, political environment and economic context. The relationships between these parameters are of course interactive and very complex. The assumption here is that the political and economic factors interact with societal culture, and societal culture causes the business climate and approach to management.

The structure of the chapter follows the same sequence. The first section briefly discusses the salient societal cultural characteristics which are attributed to the English. The second section elaborates on those characteristics which are more likely to be relevant to business activities and business organizations. The third and fourth sections discuss England's political and economic systems. The last section details how the English business climate is shaped by these several influences.

Societal Culture

England – the Country

England is a part of the United Kingdom of Great Britain (England, Wales, Scotland) and Northern Ireland, an island nation to the west of the continental mainland of Europe. England is predominantly a lowland country and has a generally mild and temperate climate.

Britain emerged into recorded history with the arrival of the Celts in the British Isles. It was occupied by the Romans in the first century AD and an ordered civilization was established under their rule for about three hundred years. The Romans withdrew completely from Britain by the fifth century to be followed by a long period of increasing disorder caused by raids – mainly Angle, Saxon and Jute – on the island from northern Europe. In the following two centuries, the raiders established settlements and a number of small kingdoms were created. In the ninth century, further settlers arrived from Europe and the Vikings from Scandinavia pillaged the east coast and established settlements there. The last successful invasion of England took place in the eleventh century, when Normans from the coast of Northern France took complete control and imposed a full feudal system.

Immigration from Europe over the centuries has led to the establishment of Irish and Jewish communities in many of the larger cities. In the latter part of the twentieth century, immigrants from the South Asian countries and the Caribbean also formed distinctive urban communities. This chapter deals only with the English among the various peoples of Britain because it is their cultural characteristics and their political system which predominate and have the greatest influence on business performance. Nevertheless, the United Kingdom is a multi-cultural society and in Wales, Scotland, Northern Ireland and those parts of England where Asian and Afro-Caribbean communities predominate – or in companies elsewhere in the UK, whose entrepreneurial bases originate from them – the values of these communities fuse with those of the English to create nuances in business style and practice, which can be significant.

England – the Culture

A seminal and perhaps the first comprehensive empirical survey on the subject was conducted by Gorer (1955) among the readers of a popular national newspaper. His findings characterized the English as aggressive, shy, reserved, class conscious, and law-abiding, having high ideals of conduct both for themselves and for others.

This was followed by Terry (1979), who made an extensive survey of the literature on the English and their cultural values and attitudes written by both English and non-English writers, and other observers. He identified thirteen significantly English characteristics which go beyond those found by Gorer. These are conservatism, tenacity, compromise, rural focus, liberty and individualism, violence and aggression, class consciousness, love of sport and fair play, pragmatism, reserve, lack of ambition, chauvinism, and orderliness and discipline.

Later still, Tayeb (1984) identified, from her occupationally representative sample, thirty major characteristics attributed to the English, in order of significance. Table 1 lists these attributes from most significant to least, as seen by her 100 English respondents.

Table 1 Major English Characteristics

Characteristics	*Rank Order*
Strong sense of responsibility	1
Trustworthy	2
Cope well with set-backs	3
See things through	4
Honest	5
Self-control	6
Self-confidence	7
Independence	8
Law-abiding	9
Cope well with new and uncertain situations	9
Disciplined	10
Friendly	10
Not afraid of powerful people	11
Prefer to work on their own	12
Obedient to their seniors	13
Tolerant	14
Trusting	15
Rational	16
Not open to bribery	17
Interested in community affairs	18
Respect the law to the letter	19
Fair play	20
Aggressive	21
Prefer to be in a group	22
Respect powerful people	22
Reserved	23
Hate to be dictated to	24
Class conscious	24
Opposed to change	25
Prefer to merge with the crowd	26
Willing to take account of others' opinions	27
Play safe	28
Modest	29
Do not believe in fate	30

The characteristics that are most significantly present in English culture and which are more likely to have a bearing on English business climate and approach to management are individualism, deference and acceptance of inequality, self-control and reserve, conservatism, xenophobia, honesty and trust, regard for liberty, and class consciousness. These will be discussed below in some detail. However, given the stratified nature of English social structure, one needs to examine first if there is such a thing as English culture.

Social class differences are a well recognized feature of English life, and the literature on English culture shows that middle-class and working-class people are different from one another in terms of the degree to which they hold certain values and attitudes. Gorer (1955) argued that middle-class people participate in voluntary and charity activities and fund-raising functions to a greater extent than their working-class compatriots, because they have a guilty conscience about their poorer countrymen. Raynor (1969), commenting on working-class people, states that they like to exhibit their aggression and physical toughness. Tayeb (1984) found that working-class people seem to regard others in their walk of life as being less interested in community affairs, more modest, less rational, less law-abiding, and possessing less self-control.

On the whole, however, the similarities between working and middle classes are far greater than the differences between the two. Although members of the two classes experience a different family upbringing, they are more or less equally exposed to other social institutions such as school, religion, mass media and the like. The advanced communications systems within the society have also facilitated the fusion of values and attitudes among people. It may therefore be safe to assume for our purpose here that the two broad classes of English society are sufficiently alike to talk about an English culture.

Organizationally-Relevant Attitudes and Values

Individualism

Child-rearing practices and the religion of the English appear to be the major sources of their individualism. Although the present middle-class family in England is a loosely-knit and nuclear one, and the English working-class family is a network of comparatively closely-knit and dense relationships, autonomy and independence are inculcated in the children from an early age in both classes. Children in middle-class families are regarded as independent individuals and are 'pushed' towards independence at an age as early as two or three. Parents do not interfere with their children's affairs, at least not directly, especially after the age of puberty. Children have great freedom in matters like further education, marriage, social intercourse with people and the choice of a job, but parents very subtly and indirectly dissuade them from, say, becoming involved with partners of a lower class than their own, and engaging in jobs and general affairs considered undesirable and radically deviant from the norms of their own social class.

Life for the working-class child is harsher, on the whole, than that of his/her middle-class counterpart. Attitudes are more authoritarian, the father is the head of the household and demands obedience from the child. Even so, in common with middle-class practice, the independence of the children is valued and they are literally 'pushed' out of home at an early age (Rose, 1968; Roberts, 1978).

The main religion of the English is Christianity. A vast majority of those who claim any church membership (a minority of the population) belong to some organized Protestant Church, especially the Church of England, rather than to the Roman Catholic Church. Protestantism, which came to England during the reign of Henry VIII (1509–47), both as part of the wider protest against the interposition of the Church between God and the believer, and as an expression of nascent English nationalism, tended to replace those patterns of the society into which the institutions of the Church were integrated, with a more individualistic system.

Weber (1930) considered that the change from feudalism to capitalism and private ownership in English economic structure took place in the sixteenth century, and he saw Protestantism as the driving force behind capitalism. In Weber's view, Protestantism was instilled into the modern economic person from the cradle onwards, stressing personal responsibility, ability and initiative. Thus, although modern capitalism was derived from the peculiarities of Western social structure, it was inconceivable without it, for it 'had the psychological effect of freeing the acquisition of goods from the inhibitions of traditionalistic ethics' (p. 171).

It seems, however, that the origins of individualism and the 'capitalist ethic' in England can be identified long before the sixteenth century. Macfarlane (1978) argues that 'the majority of people in England from at least the thirteenth century were rampant individualists, highly mobile both geographically and socially, economically "rational", market-oriented and acquisitive, and ego-centred in kinship and social life' (p. 163), and from the thirteenth century onwards 'it is not possible to find a time when an Englishman did not stand alone. Symbolized and shaped by his ego-centred kinship system, he stood at the centre of his world' (p. 196). Protestantism appears to have encouraged and reinforced this individualism and the spirit of capitalism.

However, it has to be added that the 'Protestant ethic and the spirit of capitalism', which once were the major driving forces behind the Industrial Revolution, seem to have declined among the English since then (Barnett, 1972; Roderick and Stephens, 1978, 1981, 1982; Wiener, 1981). Nor do the English seem to be as highly individualistic as, say, the Americans (Jamieson, 1980; Wiener, 1981).

Deference and Inequality

Deference and obedience to seniors are held strongly as a virtue by the English. Further, English people are said to respect those in power. Yet at the same time, they do not like to be ordered about and hate to be dictated to. In effect, they respect authority when it is used well.

The English, wrote Bagehot a century ago, are a deferential nation.

> Certain persons are by common consent agreed to be wiser than others, and their opinion is, by consent, to rank for much more than its numerical value. We may in these happy nations weigh votes as well as count them . . . Instead of resenting the assumed superiority of a relative few, many Englishmen defer to those they regard as legitimately superior. (Bagehot, 1963: 141)

Although leaders enjoy special advantages in English politics by virtue of this deference to people in positions of authority, this same attitude also reflects the expectation that leaders will pay attention to the needs and the desires of their followers. Democratic elections are the main institutional restraints upon leaders, and regulate their activities. A sense of trust is also pervasive in the attitudes of the people towards political leaders and government. Rose (1965: 43) points out that 'the ancient legal maxim, "the Queen can do no wrong", suggests the viewpoint that the government is not a menace to English men [and women]' (see also Almond and Verba, 1963).

Self-Control and Reserve

The English are a disciplined people, with control over both themselves and their emotions. To me, as a person from an emotional culture (Iran), the English at first seemed unemotional and without feelings, but once I got to know them better, I found that they are indeed emotional, beneath the surface. The difference between the English and the Iranians is that the former refrain from expressing their emotions in public, which may have something to do with their love of privacy, whereas the latter are, in general, less inhibited in showing their finer feelings and emotions in the company of others.

Conservatism

The English are widely seen to be a nation with a love for the past, traditionalism and conservatism, and a reluctance to change. These characteristics are clearly manifested, for instance, in the careful preservation of old buildings and monuments, and in the detailed attention to public ceremonies such as the annual pageantry surrounding the opening of the Parliament, which has its roots in centuries-old traditions.

Xenophobia

The English are a tolerant, friendly people who believe in fair play, have a high public spirit and take an active interest in community affairs. These fine feelings, however, do not seem to be extended towards foreigners to the same extent as they are to fellow Englishmen and women.

England's geographical insularity has been a mixed blessing. As an island, the country has been sheltered to some extent from expansionist invaders. Also, because of this relative immunity, the country, unlike many landlocked countries, has never needed a strong standing army; as a result, the armed forces have not become a tool in the hands of rulers nor have they been used to suppress the people.

However, the other side of the insularity coin has meant that the English have developed relatively insular and xenophobic attitudes towards non-English people. The construction of the Channel tunnel linking England and France illustrates this point well. The English and French intended to build the tunnel as early as 1802, but whenever England seemed tempted to link itself physically with the Continent, history and xenophobia intervened (*Time*, 1990). For instance, in 1858, the then Prime Minister, Lord Palmerston, in response to renewed interest in the tunnel, said 'What! You pretend to ask us to contribute to a work, the object of which is to shorten a distance which we find already too short?' Lord Randolph Churchill, arguing against a Channel-tunnel bill in 1889, is reported as saying 'The reputation of England has hitherto depended upon her being, as it were, *virgo intacta*.' As recently as November 1990, the opening of the first minuscule connection in the tunnel to France brought out insulting headlines in one of the most popular English newspapers.

Honesty and Trust

The English are in general trustworthy, honest and trusting (Rowntree and Lavers, 1951; Almond and Verba, 1963). Having come from a different culture, Iran, where the state of trust among people in general is lower, and having conducted research in India, where the public administration is bedevilled by corruption, I personally perceive the English to be more honest and trusting than the Indians and Iranians. As a research student at Oxford in the mid-1970s, one of the things that struck me most at the Centre for Management Studies was the fact that students and fellows alike could use the photocopying machine as frequently as they wished without any control, counter key or supervision. All you had to do was to write down in a little book the number of the photocopies taken each time. I can think of many countries where this would be unthinkable!

Liberty

Among the rights of Englishmen and women, liberty is considered pre-eminent. Traditionally, individual liberty has been protected by Common law against Crown and State. As has already been pointed out, the absence of land frontiers has meant that the country has not needed a large standing army, and so she has avoided the threat posed to public liberty by the presence of an ever-ready agency for use by the executive power. Today, respect for the liberty to speak, act and travel where one pleases is so deeply inculcated in the individual that there are few statutory guarantees for liberty: it is taken for granted. However, the enjoyment of liberty may sometimes be curtailed by the activities of government departments, and in the conflict between the claims of an individual for libertarian rights and the claims of a government department, the individual is often the loser. It must be added, however, that one of the basic principles of the unwritten English constitution is the rule of law and the equality of individuals before the law.

Class Consciousness

The English are said to be obsessed with class differentiation (Terry, 1979). Almost everybody one speaks with can place themselves in one class or other. According to Gorer's survey in 1955, nine out of ten English people felt no hesitation in assigning themselves to a social class (Gorer, 1955). In 1971 he found that 35 per cent of the people whose attitudes he surveyed thought they belonged to the middle class and 65 per cent to the working class (Gorer, 1971).

Family background, education, and even accent, betray people's social class. The class hierarchy broadly consists of upper class (a very small proportion of the total population), middle class and working class, but there are subtle gradations within the classes rather than sharp and rigid divisions and, moreover, the structure is a dynamic one in that there is movement between classes. This stratified structure is not regulated by laws, as were the estates of medieval times, or by rituals, as are the castes in India, but is based on the way the different members of society regard their own position and that of others.

The values and attitudes of the society are dominated by those of the middle class, since, by definition, they occupy most of the positions of power and persuasion – in Parliament, the civil service, universities, mass communication media, financial and commercial institutions and the church.

How Do the English Compare with Other Western Europeans?

To put this sketch of the English into perspective, we can turn to Hofstede's (1980) massive study of cultural dimensions across 40 countries, which covers 11 of the EC countries, including Britain. The British sample may include also non-English respondents (Scots, Welsh, etc.), but given the size of English population as a whole (over 50m out of 56m), the majority will have been English. Table 2 was constructed using Hofstede's results. The nations are listed in alphabetical order.

Table 2 Comparison of Cultural Dimensions Across 11 EC Countries

Country	*Power Distance*	*Uncertainty Avoidance*	*Individualism*	*Masculinity*
Belgium	65	94	75	54
Britain	35	35	89	66
Denmark	18	23	74	16
Eire	28	35	70	68
France	68	86	71	43
Germany	35	65	67	66
Greece	60	112	35	57
Italy	50	75	76	70
Netherlands	38	53	80	14
Portugal	63	104	27	31
Spain	57	86	51	42

As the table shows, the British (and quite probably the English) perceive less power distance, are better able to cope with uncertainty, are more individualistic and more ambitious and aggressive (have a masculine culture) than most of their continental counterparts. Hofstede attributed the differences between his samples on these dimensions to cultural, historical and geographical factors.

Political System

The present political culture reflects a range of values and philosophies. Traditional Tories believe in a corporatist economy, managed by a technocratic élite, and moderated by the controls of party government and parliamentary democracy. The 'Thatcherite' Conservatives sought to move the burdens of social choice from government and politics to the market. Following 1979, the Conservative government pursued policies of free enterprise, competition and less state intervention and its top priority was to furnish a framework within which private business can succeed. Over the same period, the Labour Party abandoned many of its socialist policies, such as nationalization, unilateral nuclear disarmament and hostility to the European Community. It shifted its emphasis towards 'caring capitalism' with both private and 'social' ownership. The Liberal Democrats see their position as that of a party of the middle ground. The Greens place their emphasis on the overarching importance of the natural environment, and to some extent have succeeded in influencing public opinion and the policies of the major parties.

In the absence of an electoral system based on proportional representation, in the past sixty years or so governments have been formed either by the Conservative or Labour parties only.

Economic Context

England was the home of capitalism, which determined its evolution (Weber, 1930, 1961), even though capitalism developed slowly. As early as the end of the Middle Ages there was a system that could be called 'commercial capitalism'. This system changed to 'industrial capitalism' in the eighteenth century and for nearly two hundred years took on a *laissez faire* character, which implied opposition to government interference and a belief in free competition and the unrestricted liberty of the individual (Dore, 1973; Macfarlane, 1978).

The contemporary economy can hardly be called a pure version of capitalism since it is characterized by a mixture of freedom and control, and of private and state enterprise. The emphasis on freedom or control shifts from time to time depending on the policies of the government of the day. Since the 1920s, Labour governments have tended to use direct powers to control the economy, in addition to using fiscal measures to regulate growth. Conservative governments, on the other hand, have tended to rely mainly on fiscal policy, or what has recently been called 'monetarism', rather than direct intervention.

Since 1979 the economic scene has been dominated by 'Thatcherism', labelled after the former Prime Minister, Mrs Thatcher. In the pursuit of her policies, over two-thirds of the state-owned companies were privatized, control over foreign exchange was lifted, taxes were reduced, industry was deregulated and companies were left on their own to compete in a free market with domestic and foreign competitors. As a result, higher productivity and an 'enterprise culture' returned to the country and wealth creation became respectable. However, a price had to be paid for all this in terms of high interest rates, unemployment, companies going out of business, and strains in the state education and health services.

The Resulting Business Climate and Approach to Management

Attitudes Towards Industry and Business

On the surface, as some commentators (*Economist*, 1989) point out, the 1980s saw a resurgence in the desire of Britons to do well in business and to get rich. The so-called 'enterprise culture' made money-making more respectable. The City of London lured people from all classes to enjoy its telephone-number (i.e., six-figure) salaries, Porsche cars and insider-dealing trials. Something happened to revive the work ethic and pep up ambitious managers to work long hours, to stay sober at lunch, and to feel it was again possible to become rich through work. Nevertheless, the English display little love of business. This may be traced to the English educational system and its dominant values and priorities.

A major feature of the English educational institutions is their greater emphasis on arts and classics and the relatively low priority given to engineering and technology. This, as many writers have pointed out, betrays a significant influence of middle-class values in which arts subjects are still favoured, relatively speaking, and anything concerning industry and technology is disdained (see for instance, Barnett, 1972; Jamieson, 1980; Wiener, 1981; Roderick and Stephens, 1981).

Moreover, it is still not clear whether those with the best education want to go into business. In 1979 the proportion of new graduates from Cambridge University going into 'industry', a category which includes manufacturing, civil engineering and some services, but not the City or banking, was 16 per cent. By 1988 it had fallen to 9 per cent. On the other hand, the proportion going into 'commerce', which includes stockbroking, other financial services, advertising and management consultancy, rose from 8 per cent to 13 per cent, probably partly at industry's expense. Nevertheless, the combined total dropped from 24 per cent to 22 per cent. The picture is much the same using the figures for all university graduates (*Economist*, 1989).

Trade Unions

Although the origins of the trade union movement can be traced back to the craft guilds of the Middle Ages, the modern trade union is essentially a product of the Industrial Revolution (Irwin, 1976). Union membership is industry and craft based and cuts across firms and organizations. As a result, there are likely to be several unions in the same factory or office, bargaining not just with employers but against each other. Overall information on this is sketchy, but according to the latest Workplace Industrial Relations Survey, 35 per cent of manual workers and 61 per cent of non-manual workers still had more than one union at their place of work in 1984, compared with 35 per cent and 57 per cent, respectively, in 1980 (*Economist*, 1989). Most large plants are still organized by a cluster of separate, partly competing unions. There are some companies, especially those owned by Japanese multinationals, however, which have managed to sign single-union agreements with their workforce.

English unions, unlike their counterparts in some other European countries such as Poland and France, are more pragmatic in their approach and fight for better pay settlements and better working conditions within the present economic and social system rather than engaging in class struggles and ideological battles for the overthrow of the system. They see their role as one of representing the workforce, pushing for objectives that are consciously desired by the workers themselves.

Since the establishment of the Labour Party in 1906, which grew out of the trade union movement, unions have been able to use the Party to further their interests as well as themselves being its major source of finance. However, in recent years, a combination of decline in membership because of mass redundancies caused by economic recession and the introduction of new technology, and anti-union legislation (e.g. banning secondary picketing, ending closed shop practices, allowing the courts to seize unions' assets in cases of illegal action) has eroded the powers of the trade unions.

Them and Us

Tayeb (1988) in a study of a sample of English manufacturing companies found that the differences between shopfloor workers and white-collar employees, especially managers, inside the participating organizations appeared to reflect the social structures and systems of the society. The managers considered themselves to be members of the middle class, which shares in the ownership and participates in the control of the means of production, and the manual workers saw themselves as members of the working class, exploited by the former. In most cases, the relationship between management and workers was ridden with mistrust and hostility, emanating from a conflict of interests between the two classes.

The managers and other white-collar employees had great advantages over the manual workers in many respects, such as power, status, pay, physical working conditions, eating places, rules for lunch and tea breaks, and holidays. Shopfloor workers were subject to a tighter control at work. They had to clock in and out at specific times, and in some of the companies which produced chemicals and drugs, were subject to physical search every time they left the company premises.

It seems now though that there is a trend to diminish these differences. In a survey of British business, the *Economist* (1989) reported that many of the symbols of division between classes – between worker and manager, them and us – have been dismantled. Many firms have got rid of their ranks of corporate dining rooms and substituted one, modern single-status canteen. Some have got rid of their segmented car parks, where bosses were less likely than workers to get their hair wet in a rainstorm. This new trend, if trend it is, has affected most obviously the several thousand workers who work for Japanese firms operating in Britain.

English Business and 1992

The English have always been a trading people, and firms have developed considerable competence in dealing with export markets, responding to foreign competitors and to a flood of imports without going bust or requiring immediate trade protection.

The Channel tunnel and the fall of remaining non-tariff trade barriers in the EC after 1992 expose English business even further to international pressures. It remains to be seen how it will cope with the new situation. Various surveys conducted by the Confederation of British Industry showed that English firms were not prepared for 1992 and were reluctant to embrace this new and volatile market wholeheartedly. Of the 12,000 companies questioned, '10,000 companies appear to be sleepwalking towards 1992'. This may have something to do with English managers' conservatism. As the *Economist* (1989) points out,

> [English] firms are more comfortable spending their cash in buying American firms than European ones. Despite the hype about 1992, that is not necessarily a mistake; it is surely better to invest in a country you understand and where markets are open and transparent than in areas less well understood but temporarily fashionable.

The government, too, has customarily been closer to the United States and has been a 'reluctant European', opposing such proposals as the monetary and political union of the EC member states.

English Managers and Organizations

English managers are very polite, tenacious, resourceful, reserved, and self-disciplined (Terry, 1979); but at the same time, they have generally ethno-centric attitudes towards their foreign counterparts, and can hardly speak a foreign language – it doesn't matter, they all speak English, anyway!

Simon Newitt, a senior manager of a management consultancy firm, sums it all up thus: 'Purely and simply we still have an ignorant, arrogant, narrow minded colonial, nationalistic attitude . . . We were a great country once, ruling a fifth of the earth's surface and a quarter of the world's population . . . One Brit is worth 10 foreigners?' (*Executive Post*, No. 460, 27 Sept 89, p. 3).

As would be expected from their conservative individualism and xenophobic tendencies, English managers are said to have too short-term a perspective in their business planning (at least relative to the Japanese), to spend too little on R & D and on training, to have a conservative approach towards new technology, and to place more emphasis on the production rather than on the marketing side of their business, relative to their major competitors such as American, Japanese, German and French managers (see for instance, Jamieson, 1980; Locke, 1985; Handy, 1988; Reid, 1989; Gordon, 1990).

There are also non-cultural as well as cultural explanations for some of these attitudes. Take the managers' short-term perspective, for example. The City is one of the major sources of capital for most English companies. Above all, investors, both individuals and institutions, seek a quick return on their investment. This puts managers under immense pressure to go for a 'quick buck' (to use an Americanism). They do not have the luxury of the long-term financial support that their Japanese counterparts enjoy in their cosy relationships with banks and government. R & D is an obvious victim of this situation. Employee training is another. Product quality is the third. The list can go on.

Managers' reluctance to allocate a great deal of time and financial resources to employee training also has a foot in the societal culture. English employees, like many other individualistic people, and unlike the Japanese 'company man', pursue occupational advancement through their career rather than their work organization. Job-hopping and moving from company to company are the rules of the game, rather than life-time employment and cradle-to-grave commitment to one company. As a result, English managers see expenditure on training as a waste of their precious capital, and not as an investment in human resources.

The relatively poor quality of some English products (Trought, 1989) is not unexpected given the economic context of the firms. Within the decade between the early 1980s to the early 1990s, recession hit English firms twice. Moreover, the government's open-door policies subjected these firms to fierce competition from Japanese, German and American rivals, among others. Many managers were forced to go for lower quality in order to keep their prices down. A speech by the chairman of a large jewellery retail-chain firm, in which he told his audience that his company sells rubbish to customers at cheap prices (BBC Radio 4 news and commentary programmes, 23 April 1991), illustrates how some companies were left with precious little alternative.

Turning to the leadership style and management–employee relationships, one can also trace many of their features to the cultural, political and economic characteristics of English society. Deference to authority (culture) plus a high level of unemployment (economy), for instance, could together explain the absence of serious trade union challenge to management's prerogatives and right to manage. As was mentioned earlier, English unions pragmatically seek better working conditions and wage settlements, rather than engage in an ideologically based class struggle against their bosses (Gallie, 1978).

Love of privacy and individualism may be behind English managers' preference for formal and clearly defined job territories and regulations (Tayeb, 1988). The idea of territory is also present in the physical structures and designs of the buildings in which the organizations are housed. If you visit any English university, for instance, you will see that most lecturers have their own offices – little personal territories. In collectivist Iran, most university departments have only senior common rooms in which lecturers get together during the breaks between lecturing periods. The open-plan office is an imported phenomenon which has been adopted by only a few English firms whose managers are keen to learn lessons from their Japanese counterparts (Tayeb, 1990).

Individualism can also be expected to influence the relationships between employees, their bosses and their work organizations. English employees, unlike their collectivist counterparts, do not expect their superiors to look after them and to help them with their personal difficulties. This would be an invasion of their privacy. To them a manager who is concerned with the employee's well being is one who, for instance, provides them with updated equipment so that they can perform their tasks better. In other words, managers and workers have an impersonal and task-oriented relationship with one another (Tayeb and Smith, 1988).

Concluding Remarks

History, ecology and a long-drawn-out evolutionary process have created a culture and social climate in England which stand English managers and their companies in good stead in many respects, but handicap them in some others.

Their honesty, frankness, trust, self-control, self-discipline, and politeness are their major cultural assets. Their individualism, professionalism and reserve give an impersonal and formal air to business dealings, which are interpreted as what they are and respected as such by colleagues from similar Western cultures. This can be misunderstood, though, as arrogance, detachment and 'coolness' by businessmen and women from more emotional and group-oriented cultures, such as India and Japan. Also, the explicit xenophobic tendencies displayed by some English managers are bound to work against their business interests, especially when there are more receptive competitors across the Channel.

A vast majority of English firms, thanks to the economic climate and the government's open-door policies, are willing and quite competent to deal with competitive markets. At the same time, they are hampered in their efforts by unhelpful and sometimes downright harmful aspects of their culture and their society. These include capital market short-termism, less-than-favourable attitudes to business, traditionalism and reluctance to embrace new technology wholeheartedly, antipathetic industrial relations, and ill-prepared school leavers and university graduates. To an outside observer, the situation resembles a perfectly decent vehicle whose driver has put his feet on the accelerator and brake pedals simultaneously! It is a tribute to the resourcefulness and resilience of the English businessmen and women that, in spite of this, their country occupies such a high rank among the league of the industrialized nations.

References

Almond, G. A. and S. Verba, *The Civic Culture*, Princeton: Princeton University Press, 1963.

Bagehot, W., *The English Constitution*, London: Fontana/Collins, 1963.

Barnett, C., *The Collapse of British Power*, London: Eyre Methuen, 1972.

Dore, R., *British Factory – Japanese Factory*, London: George Allen and Unwin, 1973.

The *Economist*, 'Business in Britain' (a survey), 20 May 1989.

Gallie, D., *In Search of the New Working Class*, London: Cambridge University Press, 1978.

Gordon, C., 'The business culture in the United Kingdom', in C. Randlesome (ed.), *Business Cultures in Europe*, pp. 58–106, Oxford: Heinemann, 1990.

Gorer, G., *Exploring English Character*, London: The Crosset Press, 1955.

— *Sex and Marriage in England Today*, London: Nelson, 1971.

Handy, C., 'Great Britain', in C. Handy, C. Gordon, I. Gow and C. Randlesome, *Making Managers*, pp. 163–85, London: Pitman, 1988.

Hofstede, G., *Culture's Consequences*, Beverly Hills, CA: Sage, 1980.

Irwin, J., *Modern Britain*, London: George Allen and Unwin, 1976.

Jamieson, I., *Capitalism and Culture: A Comparative Analysis of British and American Manufacturing Organizations*, Farnborough: Gower, 1980.

Locke, B., 'The relationship between educational and managerial cultures in Britain and West Germany', in P. Joynt and M. Warner (eds.), *Managing in Different Cultures*, pp. 166–216, Oslo: Universitetsforlaget, 1985.

Macfarlane, A., *The Origins of English Individualism*, Oxford: Basil Blackwell, 1978.

Raynor, J., *The Middle Class*, London: Longman, 1969.

Reid, D. M., 'Operationalizing strategic planning', *Strategic Management Journal* 10/6, 1989, 553–67.

Roberts, K., *The Working Class*, New York: Longman, 1978.

Roderick, G. and M. D. Stephens, *Education and Industry in the Nineteenth Century: The English Disease*, London: Longman, 1978.

— *Where Did We Go Wrong?: Industry, Education and Economy of Victorian Britain*, London: The Falmer Press, 1981.

— *The British Malaise: Industrial Performance, Education and Training in Britain Today*, London: The Falmer Press, 1982.

Rose, G., *Politics in England*, London: Faber and Faber, 1965.

— *The Working Class*, London: Longman, 1968.

Rowntree, B. S. and G. R. Lavers, *English Life and Leisure: A Social Study*, London: Longman, 1951.

Tayeb, M. H., 'Nations and organizations', Ph.D. thesis, Aston University, 1984.

— *Organizations and National Culture: A Comparative Analysis*, London: Sage, 1988.

— 'Japanese management style', in C. Daily (ed.), *Organisational Behaviour*, pp. 257–82, London: Pitman, 1990.

Tayeb, M. H. and P. B. Smith, 'A survey of management styles in four capitalist countries', paper presented to the Fifth Workshop on Capitalist and Socialist Organizations, Brdo Pri Kranju, Yugoslavia, August 1988.

Terry, P., 'An investigation of some cultural determinants of English organization behaviour', unpublished Ph.D. thesis, University of Bath, 1979.

Time, '1066, 1993 and all that', 12 November 1990, p. 16.

Trought, B., 'A comparison of the work activity of quality assurance and production managers', *International Journal of Quality and Reliability Management* 6/2, 1989, 25–30.

Weber, M., *The Protestant Ethic and the Spirit of Capitalism*, London: George Allen and Unwin, 1930.

— *General Economic History*, New York: Collier, 1961.

Wiener, M. J., *English Culture and the Decline of the Industrial Spirit: 1850–1980*, London: Cambridge University Press, 1981.

Britain with the USA

Management in Britain – Impressions of a Visiting Professor

Robert Dubin

From *Journal of Management Studies*, Vol. 7, No. 2, 1970, 183–98

There is a tremendous demonstrated potential for industrial development and technical innovation in the UK today. Individual scientists, engineers, and technologists are as knowledgeable and well trained as any in the world. There are enough of them now to make a difference, and a substantial block of new recruits are in the university and college pipelines. If given the opportunity to work with the needed resources at their disposal, in an atmosphere that promotes opportunities for innovation, this cadre of the intellectual élite of the country could provide the substance of an economic miracle comparable to those achieved in Germany and Japan.

Why has this potential not been fully realized? Why is it necessary to cajole, push, or subsidize aspects of British industry into a new era of confident development? What, in short, are the road blocks that make British industry less effective than it might be?

I think that the analysis would lead inevitably to a consideration of the broad culture of British industry. This is, after all, the oldest industrial nation of the world. The ideas and practices that characterize industry in the UK have been developed and perfected over many decades. If the technological and scientific bases of business had continued to expand at the pre-World War II rate, there is a high probability that the culture of British industry would have adapted most effectively to the changes. But science and technology have had an unprecedented rate of growth in the past quarter century. Ideas and practices are revolutionary and change over much shorter time cycles. Effective industry must have a culture that is highly adaptive to the technical innovations undergirding it.

It is necessary, then, to search for influences dampening the thrust of innovation. Phenomena often become analytically clear when presented as contrasts. For that reason I have adopted the strategy of contrasting British and American industry in order to learn more about the former. Attention will focus particularly on several features of the industrial culture of each country to determine whether the contrast will reveal sources of resistance to change in British industry.

American industry is generally thought to be innovative and open to change. It is only this feature that is being modelled here by way of contrast with British industry. As a student of American industry I am fully aware of many shortcomings of its industrial culture. In this discussion a critique of British industry focuses only on reasons why it has failed to reach the level and rate of innovation that characterizes American industry.

Lagging response to the need for innovative management has its sources in three broad features of British industry: the attitudes of executives; the social structure of British industry; and the style of British management.

1. Two *attitudes* characterize certain fundamental ideas about innovation, and the qualifications of executives.
2. Three characteristics of the *social structure* of British industry affect the recruitment of executives, the movement upward in the ranks of management, and the sharing of innovative ideas among companies through the ability of their executives and managers to move between them.
3. Of comparable importance are three features of the *style of management* that emphasize status in the internal allocation of resources in the business firm, the dependence on personal trust of subordinates, and personalistic criteria for evaluating individuals.

In all there are eight separate features of the culture of British industry I will examine under the general headings of attitudes, social structure, and style of management. These observations are based on my impressionistic knowledge of British industrial practice gained through talking to and observing British managers and executives. These conclusions may be inaccurate in the individual instance. I am analyzing general tendencies and obviously do not mean to claim that *all* British industry is as I draw it, or *all* American industry has the contrasting characteristics set forth here. Moreover, some sectors of British industry, notably in electronics and computers, have already taken on the essential features of the American model so that there now exists in British industry 'two cultures' that I would predict will not freely intermingle, at least in the short run.

I. Executive Attitudes

Two broad attitudes color the thinking of typical British executives. The first affects the manner in which change is approached, and particularly ideas about perfectability and the risks entailed in undertaking unproven innovations. The second broad attitude has to do with the relative value placed on professional education and/or experience as qualification for executive positions.

These two underlying attitude sets are themselves enough to ensure a British orientation clearly distinguished from an American executive outlook. As we shall presently see, this distinctiveness is buttressed by features of the social structure of British industry and the style of management employed therein.

Perfectability

An essential contrast exists between British executives and their American counterparts with respect to their ideas about perfectability. In the American case there is a strong inclination to believe that present ways of doing things inevitably are to be replaced by even better ways. The assumption is generally favored that what now exists is simply a way station on the road to an improved mode of operation. This is essentially a forward-oriented outlook. History is important only to show what has been tried and proved unsuccessful. The future is considered to hold great promise because it contains unexplored and even, as yet, unknown options.

Among British executives there is likely to be greater emphasis upon the value of the present and the utility of existing conditions. The view of history is essentially to accept the present as a culmination of past developments and, therefore, as representing the highest achievements attainable. The past is taken as the confirmation of the adequacy, if not superiority, of the present.

Given these contrasting viewpoints, it seems relatively clear that attitudes towards innovation will differ in the two systems of thought. For American executives there is a lively inclination to value innovation on the assumption that it will prove, more times than not, to be valuable. This, of course, leads to experimentation with ideas and methods of operation that often fail. Operating from a probabilistic stance, the test of innovating is whether the proportion of successes exceeds the proportion of failures. Thus, American executives not only think change itself is desirable, but also are willing to accept the risks of changes being failures.

From a British point of view proposed changes are viewed more consistently as a threat to present stability and, therefore, potentially undesirable in their consequences. There is a greater likelihood to demand that proposals for innovation be proved before applied. Obviously, many innovations in business operations and practices can only be proved in application. Therefore, this attitude of expecting substantial support for a claim of improvement resulting from innovation is likely to have a dampening effect on wanting to improve because the outcome cannot be established in advance. Furthermore, information flows so slowly through a typical British industrial organization that rapid recovery from a mistaken course of action is hampered. This places a premium on 'doing it as usual' for fear that it will not be known for a long time whether a newly chosen direction will be good or bad.

Perhaps another way to characterize the difference respecting the views about perfectability is to suggest that American executives are perpetual optimists whose very optimism generates dissatisfaction with the present on the assumption that it may be improved. Among British executives there is greater scepticism about the probability that the future will be better than the present. Perhaps both orientations are historically relevant to the development of the two economies. There has been at least a whole generation during which the destiny of the British Empire, of the home country, and of British industry, has depended upon holding on and conserving a diminishing heritage. During this identical generation the American economy has had unprecedented growth and development. Optimism, therefore, may be historically confirmed in the latter case, while scepticism can well be a logical conclusion from experience in the former case.

Professionalization

A high percentage of candidates for managerial, professional, and executive positions in American industry have some sort of technical preparation for their future careers through their college and university education. In addition to technical preparation there is also a strong probability that entrants will have selected an area, if not an actual occupation, for their own specialization. Entry is made by a substantial portion of the future managers, executives, and professional personnel in American industry into career areas, or even technical specializations, for which the candidate is prepared and to which he is partially, if not wholly, committed.

What happens on the job in the way of further specialization and training is, therefore, often viewed as an intensification of professional or specialist training already received at the university or college level. The typical young man entering American industry is likely to know where he thinks he would like to go, and by virtue of his university and college education, has already signalled this choice to his employer. His subsequent business career usually confirms the high value placed on professionalization.

Until recently the situation has been quite different in British industry. Most managerial recruits to industry had little or no prior training or education directly relevant to their business employment. They, of course, are now the bulk of senior British executives. This has given rise to the popular image that industrial élites (as well as other élites in British society) were peopled by talented amateurs. It was assumed that talent overcame amateurishness in fulfilling executive roles. This pattern differed markedly from the career commitment and early training in American practice. Its consequences in executive performance were not viewed as less adequate than what obtained in the American situation.

The contemporary situation in British industry and commerce well illustrates the strong persistence of the talented amateur executive, exemplifying the traditional culture, contrasted with the specialist and professional executive personifying the new industrial culture. The latter are to be found in science-based industries like chemicals, electronics, and computers whose products and production technologies originated from highly sophisticated science applications. In traditional industry the non-professional executive is still a significant figure. There is no assurance that the culture of the new industries will influence or even supersede that of traditional business sectors.

It is important to raise some questions, not on the side of talent, but on the side of amateurishness. An amateur is on the road towards some kind of competence. In order to succeed, a great deal needs to be learned on the job, not only in practice, but also of underlying guiding principle. To the extent that only the practice is learned the amateur develops professional behaviors without comprehension of their reason for existence. This is the worst form of professionalism.

Another potential disadvantage of starting, and perhaps remaining, an amateur is the consequence this has for the level of commitment to the position occupied on an amateur basis. A professional has some degree of commitment to, and is dedicated towards, his professional practice. The amateur is more likely to be able to take it or leave it, depending on his mood, or the circumstances of operations. To the extent that commitment to a professional practice is a motivation to improve the quality of practice, the lack of commitment among amateurs may turn out to be dysfunctional.

It should also be pointed out that in direct contrast between professional and amateur, the latter is likely to feel not only at a disadvantage, but perhaps even inferior to his colleagues. The consequence of this may be either to demean ideas and recommendations of the professional on the assumption that they are too narrow and lacking in perspective or, at the opposite pole, to be intimidated by the professional because of the assumed profundity of his knowledge and competence.

Studies of British industry have indicated that there is a considerable misuse of professional talent by under-employing professionally trained individuals at their levels of highest competence and over-employing them at levels of performance for which there are less skilled substitutes. Thus, it may well be that another consequence of talented amateurs being in executive positions is that they fail to recognize the nature of specialist performance on the part of their staffs and are, therefore, quite insensitive to maximizing the utility of professionals' contributions to business organizations.

Perhaps the most devastating consequence of the amateur status of many British executives is their willingness to accept the *form* of 'good' business practices, very often defined as American business practices, on the assumption that they fit British conditions and that they will, therefore, produce American results. Emulating practice and form without understanding their application spreads across the entire spectrum of business operations. Some of the applications work, of course. Some do not. But the talented amateurs who decide which to employ are often incapable of evaluating technically their probable utility. The result has been a vast proliferation of consulting services to British industry in which the consultants literally take over the managerial functions of decision-making in the guise of recommending preferred practices and policies. The amateur in the end abdicates to the consultant who, while professing professional competence, may or may not possess it.

The amateur, therefore, lives with a number of disabilities that are the consequence of his amateurishness. It is simply not true that talent can make up for lack of training; that the talented amateur is equivalent to the less talented professional.

Put the other way round, an economy benefits more by professionalizing its average citizens than it does by permitting its talented citizens to remain amateurs in their functional performances. This is probably true because of the essential equality in the formula:

$$\text{talent} + \text{amateur} = \text{average} + \text{professional}.$$

As a matter of social and political policy, the combination of average talents and professional training will democratize personal opportunity and for that reason is presumably desirable. Far more important, however, is the impact on the entire economy of being able to mobilize more total manpower to produce goods and services by depending on professionalization of average citizens rather than on talented leaders with amateur knowledge. The attitudes sustaining the propriety of amateur direction of complex organizations constitute a genuine road block to the widespread professionalization of British industrial management. To the extent that professionals are innovative, this factor dampens the rate of industrial innovation.

II. Social Structure

British industry has characteristic structural features that are unlike those of American industry. I mean by 'structural features' the taken-for-granted ways of operating, not the more mundane aspects of organizational forms.

In British industry three operating features are traditional within the system. The primary reference point for selecting executive recruits is their fit with the class position of their predecessors. In addition, there is a strong tendency to equate organizational rank with age-grade. Finally, there is an expectation that business careers will be pursued exclusively within a single employing organization. These features of British industry are deeply rooted in its structure of operations.

Class Position

Of major significance in the operations of British industry is the way in which the class system has shaped recruits and limited recruitment to the ranks of management. This is a story already well told and understood in British society. I repeat the essential features of the situation in order to emphasize the loss of an important source of potential creative managers.

Recruitment of future executives in British industry is related to the educational system. Who is considered readily eligible for recruitment to the ranks of executives is revealed by the educational history of the individual. The institutionalization of distinctive educational systems has provided the readily identifiable marks of 'proper' qualifications. These educational qualifications have to do with the locale of education, and much less with its content. The essential qualification for entry into the executive ranks is where you went to school, not what you learned. This, of course, assumes the individual responds to the curricular offerings of the preparatory schools, the public schools, and the grammar schools which develop some learning and logical thinking together with a satisfactory content knowledge of culturally valued subjects.

Opportunities exist, and are expanding, to permit men of lower class origins to become eligible for managerial and executive positions. Those who are prepared as youths enter grammar schools and universities on scholarship.

There they are shaped and socialized so as to become almost indistinguishable from, and equally qualified with, colleagues of higher social origins. The point I am making is that lower-class children who move up are made over to a middle-class value pattern before they enter the market as recruits to management. This should not be confused with the argument about whether or how many mobility opportunities exist for lower-class boys.

The system of examinations at the immediate pre-university level is the final stage in the certification of the qualifications of recruits to executive ranks. The proportions of 'A' and 'O' level passes serve to discriminate within the group previously qualified by place of educational residence so that the more able examination-takers may be readily distinguished from their less able colleagues. On the basis of these examination results applicants are ranked in the hiring of future managers. For those who go on to university-level education a similar grading of aspirants is based upon the level of distinction achieved in the university degree.

The added dependence on educational performance in recruiting British managers suggests a belief that marks earned in school foreshadow performance in industry. The evidence is very clear-cut on this for the American experience. Study after study has shown that there is low or no correlation between university and college grades and success in business. This does *not* mean that education is valueless; it simply signifies that marks received in courses do not predict the level of 'real world' application of education. If American experience is guiding, then it seems rather unlikely that the selection of executive talent on the basis of school examination-taking ability leads to the recruitment of the best candidates for positions as executives.

Graduates of British technological universities and colleges, I have been told, most readily find their places in manufacturing operations, some eventually to rise to executive ranks. This is an interesting recognition of where professional skill is really most required in industry. It also reveals the explicit presumption that engineers and technologists are not qualified initially by their education for executive positions. In American industry discrimination is more likely to *favor* the engineer and business specialist as a candidate for executive positions.

A conclusion follows that continued use of (1) locale of schooling, and (2) academic performance, as the bases for selecting future executives results because the educational system is peculiarly adapted to qualifying and marking recruits who fit the social requirements of the executive role. Qualification results from social appropriateness to rule rather than skill or knowledge about ruling.

Those who are unable to gain entry into the schools of proper qualifications are very early foreclosed from achieving the socializing training that would make them acceptable recruits to the higher ranks of management. A man of ability who has a comprehensive school, or especially a secondary modern school, education has pretty early established for himself the impossibility of going back and acquiring, through schooling, the necessary qualifications for executive positions. There is a loss of ambitious and talented but socially unqualified candidates for executive and top managerial positions. (The current belief is that being consigned to a secondary modern and possibly even a comprehensive school is *prima facie* evidence of lack of talent, and consequently my conclusion does not hold. I am not convinced by this belief.)

What this adds up to is that it is not the content of education but the source of education that is essentially the qualifying mark of a potential candidate for the executive ranks of British industry. The existing British system cannot even, with certainty, be viewed as recruiting the best talent available for executive positions from an admittedly restricted source. The assumption that examination-taking ability in school ensures subsequent high level performance in business is not supported in American studies. British industry is unnecessarily hampered by a limited source of recruitment to management of men whose education and technical qualifications are not optimal for effective managerial performance.

Age-grading

A minor feature of British organizational practice is the firm conviction that age-grading is an appropriate device for allocating personnel to positions. Age-grading relates functional performance to chronological age. It is remarkable how prevalent this practice is in Britain's industry. With notable exceptions, job descriptions for any level of the professional, managerial, or executive ranks include a statement of age range within which the candidates should fall. This age criterion is surely not related to ability or skill in the performance of business functions. It is more likely related to a belief in the 'rightness' of age being correlated with rank and position in an hierarchical system. In recent years the age ranges specified have changed from earlier practice, but the use of the age-grading criterion is just as prevalent.

One consequence of age-grading in British industry is to discourage young men because the rewards of rapid promotion are not freely available to them for exceptional performance. However, to the extent that the young accept the age-grading system, it provides a high level of certainty that with age some progress up the hierarchy will be achieved. The relative certainty of moving up with chronological age may encourage willingness to defer the gratification of achieving promotion. Thus, the effects of age-grading as it influences the behavior of young recruits to industry may have compensating consequences that approximately balance out.

For those who did not achieve promotion at each approximate age there is a clear signal that they have 'had it'. They have reached their maximum level of advancement and, by virtue of being passed over for further promotion, are publicly recognized as being at their ceiling. For such individuals the incentives of further promotion have little or no motivational value. Indeed, there is a high probability that such individuals become the 'resters' who do a job with minimum enthusiasm and even indifference. This is most likely to happen in the middle age range.

The American practice is one in which age-grading is considerably less prevalent. There is wide opportunity for young men to move ahead rapidly. More significant is the continued opportunity for those in their middle years to look forward to the possibility of advancement. The American practice is to keep alive the opportunities for advancement for more people in management at older ages than is true in British industry. In so far as promotions provide incentives for work, this constitutes an advantage in maintaining the motivation for managers in their middle years for continued high performance in their positions. The practice also widens the range of still striving people from among whom executive and managerial recruits may be drawn.

Managerial Mobility

It is reasonably clear that managers and executives of American industry move much more readily than their British counterparts among organizations, and even between industries, in the course of their working lifetime.

The explanation of these differences may simply be that of scale. The number of business firms in the United States far exceeds that of Great Britain. Therefore, the sheer opportunity to move among organizations is correspondingly greater.

It should be relatively obvious that a higher degree of mobility among work organizations, and even between industries, produces interesting consequences for the diffusion of business practices and ideas. The manager and executive carries away with him what he has learned in his previous employment and, therefore, literally diffuses these ideas to his new employing organization. Indeed, it is often true that competition for executive and managerial talent by smaller companies is based exactly on the belief that those individuals hired away from large or more progressive organizations will bring to their new employment better ideas for doing things. Thus, mobility has as one of its unanticipated consequences the ready deployment of innovative ideas *throughout* industry and commerce.

One might go further and suggest that the competition in the goods market, which is considered so essential to a capitalist market economy, is now complemented by competition among business firms for innovative ideas that may improve business practices or products. The medium of exchange for the innovative ideas is the executive, professional, and managerial personnel for whom individual firms compete. Thus, a progressive capitalism requires that there be some ready source of innovative ideas and a market in which competition may resolve the distribution of the sources of innovation. This is the market of executive and professional talent, a highly competitive one in the American economy, and which continues very much throughout the major portion of the working lifetime of executives, professionals, and managers.

By way of contrast, it is clear that in British industry the mobility among organizations or between industries is very much less than in American industry. An individual is likely to feel that he is establishing a lifetime work career upon joining a work organization in Britain. Thoughts of moving to a new employer may be viewed as a break in, if not a disastrous termination of, a career. From the standpoint of the initial employer, voluntary resignation may be viewed as an act of utter disloyalty, not so much to be punished as sorrowed over. The recent warning by Peter Hall of ICL recognizes the situation: 'The days of lifelong loyalty to one firm are passing, and management must plan on this basis.'

By remaining with a single employer the individual enhances his opportunities to be socialized to the company orientation. This may become an important test of potentiality for advancement within the organization. There is, therefore, a pressure to conform to the company practices rather than to innovate them. Thus, one of the important consequences of immobility in the work careers of British management is what Thorstein Veblen once labelled 'trained incapacity'. For non-mobile British executives 'trained incapacity' is the inability to conceive of, or utilize, new ideas. This is obviously dysfunctional to innovation and can have as its consequence the further polishing of an already shiny system. The operating system itself is unlikely to be significantly modified, or changed, because of the trained incapacity of its directors to conceive adequate alternatives.

III. Style of Management

Just as there are distinctive British attitudes about business, and institutionalized practices that give structure to British organizations, so there is a style of management that is characteristically British. In particular, I want to draw your attention to three features of the British style of management that have special consequences for the culture of British industry.

The habits of giving pre-eminence to authority and power lead to the allocation of supporting resources favoring status rather than functional contribution. The presumed depth of attachment of follower to leader results in the extension of personal trust to subordinates. Finally, in the evaluation of individuals and their performance, there is a strong presumption that a man-to-man relation of leader to follower entitles the former to make judgements on personalistic grounds.

From the standpoint of organizational effectiveness, these three features of managerial style may prove dysfunctional. Together, these ways of governing produce dependency rather than foster initiative and autonomy among subordinates. The style of leadership is consistent with and supportive of existing structural arrangements.

Resource Allocation

In the best of all possible operating worlds the allocation of resources should be in direct proportion to the needs of the individual operating unit, and its relative contribution to the entire enterprise. Failure to make appropriate allocation of internal resources can result in inadequate performance in two ways: (1) enough total resources are not available and no amount of individual devotion and effort can overcome the lack; (2) the resources are unevenly allocated and individuals of skilled or professional ability are required to 'make do' by performing work that could well be done by less skilled and cheaper supporting staff. Inadequate total resources is a common problem in American and British industry and there is probably little difference in the manner in which the problem is treated in each country.

There is significant difference between industrial management in the two countries in the manner in which supporting services and equipment are provided for skilled and professional employees. In the American system there is a greater sensitivity to the relationship between functional requirements and adequate supply of services and equipment.

The explanation for this difference in treatment and in allocation of resources may be found in the status valuation of resources. In British industry there is a high probability that resources will be allocated in accordance with the relative status of the recipient of the resources. Status in hierarchy is not necessarily related to functional performance in the organization. Therefore, the allocation of scarce resources on the basis of status rank may result in dysfunctional distribution of resources. For example, when supervisors or department heads write a significant portion of their correspondence by hand in their first draft because adequate clerical help is not provided, while the executive suite may be over-populated with partially idle secretaries, then the distribution of clerical services is not in proper relation to the functional needs within the company.

The consequences of having inadequate resources with which to carry out a function can be a strong deterrent to innovation. Lack of resources is too easy an excuse for not trying. This then makes even more critical the need for ensuring that the resources distributed within a firm be managed with exceptional prudence to ensure their most effective utilization. The status system of British industry is an important barrier to achieving this desirable outcome.

Personal Trust

A characteristic feature of the style of management among British executives is their emphasis upon personal trust in their subordinates. The basic idea is that the first criterion for valuing subordinates is whether you can trust them. The meaning of trust may be rather diffuse. It may mean you can trust a man to think like the boss; you can trust him to anticipate the boss's way of thinking or acting; or you can trust him to do the 'right thing', even in the boss's absence. It is clear that this sense of trust does not relate to the matter of fiscal responsibility but rather to the personal reliability and dependability to know what the right thing is, and do it. This is often designated 'character' in trusted subordinates.

Extending trust to subordinates places a tremendous pressure upon them to conform to the expectations of those according the trust. The pressure to conform is very pervasive and has the consequence of making the recipient of trust extremely cautious to ensure his behaviors, and even his thoughts, merit the trust extended by his superior. The primary effect of trust, then, is to place a premium on conforming thinking and conforming behavior, with obvious consequences for the introduction of innovating ideas and practices. The most trusted subordinates of principal executives are least likely to be the source of innovating ideas and practices. Put another way, trustworthy subordinates never surprise their superiors with innovative thoughts or behaviors.

American executives also depend upon a relationship of trust with their subordinates. What differentiates the two groups of executives is the extent of the circle of trusted subordinates. The American executive tends to operate in a relationship of trust largely with his personal staff. The range of relationship of trust for a British executive is likely to be broader and may even extend over the entire organization. The demands of a trusting relationship may even intrude upon functional relationships to the distinct detriment of the latter's effectiveness.

One method for lessening the need to have a trusting relationship with subordinates is to substitute universalistic criteria of evaluation. I simply mean that objective criteria of performance are applied uniformly as grounds for evaluating. These criteria are known by those to whom they apply and performance is, therefore, against the objective standard rather than in conformance with the expectations of being trustworthy.

As suggested in the next paragraphs, there is a marked tendency among British executives to prefer personalistic relations to universalistic criteria of evaluation. This practice is consistent with the belief in the importance of personal trust and buttresses continued dependence upon a trusting relationship in the style of British management.

Personalistic Relations

An essential feature of recruitment in large-scale organizations is that the characteristics of positions, and the corresponding criteria for selection of recruits to the positions, be stated in universalistic terms. These criteria should be independent of the idiosyncratic features of present incumbents of the positions, or their successors. The extent to which the universalistic criteria are set aside or ignored in favor of personalistic criteria for evaluating individuals, or selecting them, will lead to deviations from objective standards. These deviations may be in either direction, for it is possible to choose exceptionally talented men by personalizing the selection criteria, as well as to choose or retain less than adequate individuals.

The general effect of using personalistic criteria is to make exceptions of poor performance, poor potential, or eccentricities rather than recognize exceptions at the high end of the scale. The reason for this is clear. The need to consider extenuating circumstances or idiosyncratic characteristics arises only when there is some questioning of past performance or future capabilities. The resolution of such dilemmas, when the individual is favored, is to use personalistic criteria to justify a decision that cannot meet universalistic criteria. This encourages subordinates to 'butter up' the boss through behaviors towards him that may not be relevant to job or position performance. Personalizing bases for evaluation also relieves the boss of having to make the hard decision to get rid of people with lesser competence.

Finally, the personalistic criteria of evaluation deter the subordinate from demanding payoffs he considers appropriate to his level of performance. For the subordinate to go in and demand of the boss exceptional rewards for outstanding performance might very well lead to the boss evaluating such demands as representing 'ungentlemanly pushiness', or even the subordinate's fundamental distrust that his boss can be expected to 'look after' his people.

Thus, the personalistic criteria for evaluation, which are controlled by the superior, bring considerable pressure upon the subordinate to conform to the boss's image of him in ways that may modify, if not eliminate, the potential for 'being himself' and all that may imply in the way of effective performance.

The balance between personalistic and universalistic criteria in evaluating performance and potential is different in American industry than in British industry. In American industry there is a greater probability that universalistic criteria will prevail or, put most crudely, that the balance sheet and P and L statement will govern. It is not uncommon for British executives who visit their American counterparts to comment upon the pervasiveness of evaluating almost everything in money terms. This is taken as evidence of American materialism. What is overlooked is that very effective universalistic measures of performance are grounded in a single medium of exchange – money. All means of costing, and measures of profitability, as well as rewards, can be measured in a common currency, thus encouraging substitution of universal for personal criteria of evaluation.

IV. British Industrial Culture

There is a great fund of scientific and technological creativity locked up in British society. For the further progress of the society, towards whatever social goals its citizens choose, it will be necessary to provide maximum opportunity for this creativity to emerge.

I believe that a major barrier to the rapid and full flowering of industrial creativity is the culture of British industry. For that reason this analysis has been limited to a consideration of the climate and form of executive behavior in British industry, ignoring shop-floor workers and unions. Contemporary interest has focused on making British industry more productive. A major effort in this direction has been to improve shop-floor efficiency by improving worker effort and union cooperation. The former has even been institutionalized in the grounds for granting extraordinary wage increases under the policy of the Prices and Incomes Board. The latter is the subject of the recent White Paper, 'In Place of Strife'.

It is perfectly easy to attribute the sources of trouble to 'the other fellow'. In so far as the working man and labor unions can be blamed as the source of industrial productivity problems, there is less need for self-analysis among British executives. In American industrial folklore, however, an old saying declares that 'management gets the kind of union (or work force) it deserves'.

With this in mind it may very well be that the shop-floor problems of British industry have some relationship to what goes on in the executive offices.

The attitudes towards innovation analyzed above are clearly not conducive to achieve the potential for change (and, hopefully, improvement) made possible by existing scientific and technical knowledge. The faith in the adequacy of the amateur executive almost guarantees that existing attitudes towards innovation will change slowly and painfully. Thus, there is an attitudinal climate which thwarts innovative decisions and ensures that successor decision-makers will likely foster the same climate.

In so far as differing perspectives resulting from unlike social origins may be a source of innovative ideas, the structure of British industry is peculiarly adapted to minimizing this influence. A restricted recruitment system for executives makes the direct circulation of lower-middle-class and working-class men into executive ranks rather improbable. More than that, the young, and potentially innovative members of management, are likely to have to wait their turn, because of age-grading, before succeeding to crucial decision-making positions. This simply utilizes the 'generation gap' to emasculate innovation. Too early in their work careers men in their middle years may be accepted as at their ceiling, losing their incentives to be creative, and minimizing their potential to be a bridge over the generation gap. Finally, the strictures against inter-company mobility serve to dampen another potential source of innovation. These three structural aspects of British industry seem almost deliberately designed to ensure an unhurried, discreet rate of innovation.

At the more personal level, the allocation of supporting services and equipment is another means by which the more hardy who fail to bend to the attitudinal climate, or who don't quite fit the structural practices, are presented with additional barriers to their own creativity. It takes extraordinary ability, or exceptional luck, to exceed the levels of average productivity with only limited resources at one's disposal. In addition, the hierarchy of the organization may be clogged up with individuals who qualify for their present positions because of less than adequate performance, excused on the grounds of personalistic evaluating criteria. Finally barriers to creativity may be further sustained by the style of management which demands that subordinates be trustworthy and, therefore, non-innovative.

I have obviously overdrawn the picture in order to make eight simple points about the form and operations of British industrial management. The caricature does bear some relationship to the reality, and like a proper caricature emphasizes prominent features so that they may be more readily identified.

The purpose of this exercise has been to demonstrate that the culture of British industry is distinctly different from that in American industry. In the process I have also demonstrated that the culture of British industry is remarkably consistent among the eight features analyzed here.

The fact of cultural difference from the American model is enough to establish that British industry is not now 'Americanized'. Whether British culture will ever be modified in the American direction rests on the internal unity of the British culture, and the tenacity with which these cultural patterns persist. I am convinced of the unity of the cultural patterns, and remain reasonably certain that they will change only very slowly. Furthermore, I have repeatedly heard from British executives the proud assertion that they do not want to 'go American' because of the miserable values this entails adopting. What all this may mean for the future of the British economy could be the subject of some very interesting and informed speculation.

The Americans

Edward T. Hall and Mildred Reed Hall

Part 4, pp. 139–54 in Edward T. Hall and Mildred Reed Hall, *Understanding Cultural Differences* (Yarmouth, Maine: Intercultural Press, 1989)

American Culture

The U.S. is not a melting pot: ethnic groups persist. Nonetheless, Americans feel a bond to other Americans that transcends differences in ethnic origins.

Jackson Toby, 'America Works Despite All the Odds', *Wall Street Journal*

Like people all over the world, Americans take their culture for granted. Indeed, it's only in juxtaposition with other cultures that Americans begin to understand the influence of their own culture on their behavior. Only when we can see that there is more than one approach to life and many different ways of behaving can we begin to experience the strong, pervasive influence of our own culture.

It is more difficult to describe American culture than German or French culture because the United States is not just another country; it spans a continent, and has a population of over 250,000,000 people whose ancestors came from virtually every country in the world. American culture is a rich mix of Anglo-Saxon, French, German, Scandinavian, Spanish, Italian, Latin American, Native American, African, Polish, Russian, Japanese, Chinese, Korean, Filipino, Vietnamese, and Arab influences, just to name a few. In its early days the country was strongly influenced by the British and other people from northern Europe; its laws are based on British common law and American English has absorbed many northern European words.

Since this book focuses on business between the United States, Germany, and France, we have concentrated on the culture of the majority of American business executives, which can best be described as that of Americans whose forebears came from northern Europe. In a recent Gallup survey made for the

Wall Street Journal, 65 per cent of Fortune 500 executives as well as 68 per cent of small-business executives were in this category. While the US is a nation of immigrants and there are many people in American business who are not of northern European heritage, for the purposes of our discussion of American culture, it is the American-European culture we refer to and not the many other cultures represented in the American population. This dominant or mainstream business culture is the norm to which people with other cultural backgrounds are expected to conform, particularly in large corporations.

Despite its ethnic diversity, the US has managed to absorb bits and pieces of many cultures and weave them into a unique culture that is strikingly consistent and distinct. You can pick out Americans any place in the world, often very quickly, because of their behavior. Among their most observable traits are openness, friendliness, informality, optimism, creativity, loudness, and vitality.

In common with others, Americans tend to be ethnocentric, in part because of the great size and economic power of the United States. Unlike the Germans and the French, Americans do not have close foreign neighbors with whom they interact constantly. The country shares borders with Canada and Mexico, but relatively few Americans have dealings with or know much about either country.

While the United States has absorbed millions of people from countries around the globe, the *core culture of the United States has its roots in northern European or Anglo-Saxon culture*. As a result, it is a predominantly monochronic, low-context culture. To succeed in the American economic system, people must adapt to schedules and the other conventions of doing business in a monochronic, low-context environment. It also means their approach to life is compartmentalized and they need detailed background information because they do not have well developed information networks.

Time: One Thing at a Time

The majority of Americans are monochronic, especially in business. This means that for them time is scheduled and compartmentalized so that people can concentrate on one thing at a time. Schedules are sacred and time commitments are taken very seriously. There are polychronic Americans, usually from families with origins in Latin America, the Mediterranean countries, or the Middle East. They handle time differently and are neither prompt nor necessarily scrupulous in observing deadlines. There are also regional variations in the handling of time. In the Northwest, South, and Southwest, for instance, the rules governing punctuality are more relaxed.

In their business and professional lives, however, most Americans adhere to the monochronic norms of Anglo-Saxon culture. Promptness is sacred, especially where business appointments are concerned. Being five minutes late calls for a brief apology; ten or fifteen minutes needs a more elaborate apology, or, if possible, a telephone call warning of the delay.

American time and consciousness are fixed in the present. Americans don't want to wait; they want results now. They move at a rapid pace; everything about their business lives is hurried. Wanting quick answers and quick solutions, they are not used to waiting long periods of time for decisions and become anxious when decisions are not made promptly. This attitude puts them at a disadvantage in dealing with people such as the Germans, the Japanese, and Latin Americans, all of whom, for different reasons, take more time to reach decisions.

American planning intervals are shorter than those in Germany and many other countries as well. Since most American companies are publicly owned and must report all financial details quarterly for use by banks, security analysts, and the government, American businesspeople tend to think in short-term intervals. When Americans talk about the 'long term', they usually mean no more than two or three years.

Space: Keeping Your Distance

The size and scale of the United States and the feeling of open spaces are overpowering to visitors who are accustomed to the smaller scale of Europe. There is an expansiveness to the American character that is undoubtedly related to the geographical size of the country and to the lively frontier spirit that runs through American history.

Many Europeans comment on how large American apartments and homes are. The separate bedrooms Americans provide for each of their children and the other special rooms set aside for adult use often surprise Europeans and attest to the value Americans place on individuality and personal privacy. Americans are proud of the amount and kind of living space they have and will show visitors around the entire house, something unheard of in France and Germany.

Like Germans, Americans avoid close physical contact and keep their distance when conversing, automatically adjusting their chairs to a comfortable range. French conversational distance is closer than either the German or the American, which causes discomfort to the latter two. During conversation Americans maintain eye contact while listening but shift their eyes away and back when they speak; this level of eye contact is much less intense than that of the French.

Americans gesture only moderately with their hands and arms, but their faces tend to be quite animated. Americans smile a lot in greetings and during formal introductions; except in large cities, they occasionally even smile at strangers they pass in the street. A strong handshake is the norm among American men and is associated with masculinity.

Although some American business executives have an 'open door' policy to encourage the idea of accessibility, they do prefer private offices to working together in large open spaces, which they find distracting. Remember that monochronic, low-context Americans are vulnerable to interruptions.

Education in a Changing Society

One of the great differences between the US and its European counterparts is the quality of public education. Critics of American schools have described them as training grounds for taking standardized tests and claim that education in the fundamentals of literacy is relegated to a secondary function. They also say that the average American public school curriculum overemphasizes memorization and that it encourages verbal expression but provides little training in written expression. It is generally agreed that the quality of public education has declined markedly over the last few decades. There are many reasons for this decline, which we discuss at some length because they reflect larger problems in American society and culture.

Americans want to provide the same basic education for all children from the first through the twelfth grades. This is a difficult goal because many students come from families where English is not the primary language or where the importance of education as a requirement for success is not understood. American schools also offer more extracurricular activities and more time is devoted to sports, clubs, music, and drama (and hence less to studies) than in European schools. Most important, in the authors' opinion, in American public schools there is no strong tradition of hard work and regularly assigned homework. Studies indicate that American children spend more hours per year watching television than they spend in school. The American school year is short compared to that of West Germany and France. Finally, the standard American curriculum is much less demanding than the German or the French, especially in mathematics, sciences, and languages (only 15 per cent of American high school students study a foreign language). The results of American public-school training are shown in studies and comparisons. Among twenty industrialized countries, American students ranked as low as eighteenth in some mathematical tests and no higher than tenth in any others. A study in the state of Illinois found 90 per cent of high school graduates scientifically and technologically illiterate. Sixteen per cent of all white adults, 44 per cent of blacks, and 56 per cent of native Hispanics are either functionally or marginally illiterate. Most shocking to us, the US ranks forty-ninth among the 158 members of the United Nations in literacy levels.

Unfortunately, there is a nationwide shortage of qualified, experienced teachers. Teachers are poorly paid compared to other professionals, and their social status is low compared to their counterparts in Europe. Low salaries and the overwhelming bureaucratic demands made on teachers have made teaching unattractive as a career for many Americans; the results are over-large classes and little individual attention to each pupil.

Another very serious problem in the American school system is the use of drugs. In junior high and high schools, drug use is common. There are some community and government programs designed to combat drug use, but it remains a major problem.

Dissatisfaction with public schools in the US has driven many middle-class families to send their children to private or church-supported schools in the hope of providing them a better education. Most private and parochial schools have higher academic standards and insist on daily homework. Their student bodies are smaller and entrance standards usually more selective.

The authors recommend two recent books on the crisis in the US educational system: *The Closing of the American Mind* by Allan Bloom and *Cultural Literacy* by E. D. Hirsch. Both offer useful insight into American culture.

Mobility: a Nation on the Move

Americans are highly mobile. Statistics indicate that the average American family moves every four to five years; many American business firms transfer employees every two years. This frequency of moving means that Americans are forced to meet and interact with strangers and learn to make new friends easily. It also helps explain why many Americans form superficial relationships more often than deeper and more lasting ones. Sometimes the surface friendliness of Americans creates expectations among non-Americans that close friendships will develop, but more often than not, these expectations are disappointed.

In the suburbs and in small towns, being a good neighbor means maintaining your property; lending tools, supplies and assistance; visiting across the fence; working together on projects; and sometimes trading invitations for coffee or dinner. Newcomers are generally welcomed with gifts of food, offers of assistance, and invitations to meet other neighbors.

In a society of ethnic diversity and high mobility, a 'nation of strangers', many Americans suffer from an absence of roots. Perhaps this is one reason why many Americans find their identity in business or professions and in the civic organizations to which they belong – organizations such as the Rotary, Kiwanis, Elks, Lions, Jaycees, PTA, Junior League, Garden Club, and the Chamber of Commerce. These civic and business organizations perform a variety of community services but they also provide their members with a feeling of community, rituals of recognition, and rewards for outstanding performance. Americans like the feeling of belonging to a group that works together toward the achievement of common goals.

Work Ethic

Many Americans are still motivated by a strong work ethic which the early settlers from northern Europe brought with them when they came to the American continent. Europeans often observe that Americans schedule everything except time for relaxation. This is particularly true of American executives, who drive themselves hard, often at the expense of their families and their health. Americans have fewer holidays and take shorter vacations than do Europeans. Senior American executives often work fifty-six hours a week and take only fourteen days of vacation per year. In the opinion of many German and French executives, American executives are obsessed with work; 'they're workaholics' was a comment we heard often. Like most Europeans who do not accept working on weekends or holidays, the Germans and the French reserve these times for themselves and their families.

Immigrants from East and Southeast Asia and elsewhere have also brought with them their own culture-based work ethic. However, in the American population as a whole today, the work ethic as a motivation appears to be diminishing, especially among younger Americans, while a stronger orientation toward material or other social and personal rewards is becoming more evident.

Communication Style

Americans do prefer directness in communication, although they are not as frank or blunt as Germans are. Americans are often uncomfortable with indirectness and sometimes miss nonverbal cues: subtle shifts in voice; slight, almost imperceptible changes in body posture or breathing. This failure to perceive or understand nonverbal cues means that Americans often miss a build-up of tension in people such as the French, and, as a consequence, fail to realize that something is wrong until a crisis develops.

Bragging and boastfulness are common among Americans, and there's a lot of informal jockeying for position in American groups. They tend to exaggerate, much to the distress of the Germans, and they enjoy writers who tell 'tall tales'.

In manner, Americans are not as serious as Germans and often use humor to diffuse tensions on the job and in social situations. Jokes are relished and a good sense of humor is much admired. Most Americans keep their social conversations light, rather than engaging in serious, intellectual or philosophical discussions, a trait which especially bothers Europeans. Generally, Americans have little interest in discussing philosophy – either traditional philosophy or political philosophy. They consider philosophy too theoretical or abstract.

American Psychology

I respect the American frontier spirit. Recently I met someone who drove 3,000 miles to find a job.

Japanese automobile executive

The American dream is often a very private dream of being the star, the uniquely successful and admirable one, the one who stands out from the crowd of ordinary folk who don't know how.

Habits of the Heart

The American and European cultures focus on the individual, in contrast to other cultures such as the Japanese, where the focus is on the group. Americans are outwardly oriented; concerned with appearances; preoccupied with what other people think, do, and say about them; and eager to be liked and accepted. Above all, they are individualists. Many are ambitious, hardworking, competitive, confident, and direct. They are usually egalitarian to the point of being quite casual in their manner and are pragmatic and sometimes simplistic in their approach to problems.

Americans pride themselves on being fiercely individualistic. They want to be 'their own person'. They are much more concerned about their own careers and their personal success than about the welfare of the organization or group. For Americans, it's 'every man for himself'.

Their strong bent toward individualism is directly tied to the value Americans place on freedom in all things, not just political freedom to vote as they wish, or religious freedom, or freedom of assembly, or freedom of the press but a vast array of individual rights protected by the American Constitution and the Bill of Rights. In addition, Americans expect freedom of choice in virtually everything. They are free to marry the person of their choice with little or no interference from their parents, free to choose whatever job or profession they wish, free to attend the college of their choice if they are accepted and can afford it. Individualism and freedom pervade every segment of American society and explain why for anything one can say or write about Americans, there are bound to be many exceptions. The great degree of freedom in the United States extends to all aspects of an individual's behavior. For young people there has never been a time of greater choice in terms of careers or lifestyles, which presents problems for some, who have so many choices it often takes them years to settle on a career.

Many Americans have little actual faith in political ideologies beyond the basic tenets of democracy. Nevertheless, they are patriotic, proud of their country, and believe strongly in democracy. Too much power and authority is considered unwise or even dangerous by Americans. Politicians who appear to seek power for its own sake are even more suspect than those seeking office for economic gain. As a result, politicians are especially adept at presenting an image of a 'good old boy' – a submissive posture that diffuses the voter's hostility toward anyone with power and influence. For the same reason, Americans like to poke fun at symbols of power, and they tell jokes about their political leaders incessantly.

Government is viewed as a necessary evil and is generally disliked and disparaged. Most Americans think their government is too large and that control over people is immoral; they like to quote Lord Acton: 'All power corrupts and absolute power corrupts absolutely'. This distrust of authority leads to a certain ambivalence since Americans also admire decisive leaders. Given their attitude toward government, it is not surprising that many Americans take a dim view of politics and politicians. In fact, many Americans want nothing to do with political life, the result being a kind of apathy on the part of the American electorate. In a 1984 article, columnist Flora Lewis pointed out that in West Germany's last election, 89.1 per cent of voters cast ballots; in France, 85.8 per cent; in Britain, 72.7 per cent; in Spain, 79.6 per cent; in Italy, 89 per cent. In the American presidential election of 1984, however, only 52.9 per cent of eligible voters cast their ballots; and in 1988, only 50.16 per cent voted.

Basically, Americans are practical people who like challenges and enjoy solving problems. They pride themselves on being pragmatic. They like to handle their own problems and they chafe at authority. In business and professional life Americans are ambitious, competitive, and hard-driving. Once they reach a goal, they set another. In negotiations they like to win, which explains the popularity of books such as *Looking Out for Number One* by Robert J. Ringer.

Most Americans admire hard work and success, and they don't feel ambivalent or hesitant about enjoying it. Their strong drive for recognition – as evidenced in their stance, dress, posture, attitude, voice level, and possessions – is one of the reasons why Americans are readily identifiable anywhere in the world. Their heroes are public figures who frequently appear in the press and on television: outstanding athletes, Hollywood actors, television stars, even business leaders.

One of the terms most often used by German and French business people to describe American business executives is 'self-confident'. Overseas Americans feel confident that their ways are the best ways and often demonstrate messianic zeal about imposing them on other cultures and then fail to understand why they encounter resistance and resentment. In addition to an overconfident attitude, Americans suffer from a tendency to dichotomize, to see things as 'all black' or 'all white' and therefore are either 'for' or 'against' something, often without fully examining the alternatives. In general, they tend to oversimplify and to look for instant solutions, which in part accounts for the American reputation for naïvety in the rest of the world. They are often more interested in the headlines and the bottom line than in what comes between.

Many foreigners comment on the American low-context, legalistic approach to things; everything is spelled out and put on paper. Two-thirds of all the lawyers in the world are practicing in the United States; there is one lawyer for every 355 Americans, and litigation has become a way of life. Consumers are increasingly inclined to sue for damages when they feel they have been harmed by a product.

Within the American system of justice, there has been a preoccupation with protecting the rights of the individual, especially those accused of a crime. Critics of the system say the victim is too often forgotten, and American lawmakers and the courts are moving slowly to rectify this imbalance.

Americans value fairness, which means treating people impartially and without favoritism. They believe in equal opportunity for all and in equality before the law, that is, justice for every person regardless of social or economic circumstances. However, while most Americans profess a belief in tolerance and democratic ideals, women and minorities still face enormous barriers to achieving acceptance of their rights despite some progress in the past forty years.

Consistent with their egalitarianism, most Americans are friendly, outgoing and informal. They dislike being made to feel inferior and bristle at any system of arbitrary social ranking independent of achievement. They are uncomfortable with class systems such as those in France or England. The American belief in equality makes Americans dislike those who act superior or condescending or who attempt to 'pull rank'. Even influential people usually make an effort to appear approachable. For example, the manager who puts his feet on the desk, works in his shirt-sleeves, and invites everyone to call him by his first name is trying to show that he too is a member of the team. These efforts to create an egalitarian atmosphere are often offensive to foreigners, who decry the American lack of formality and manners.

American informality is partly a reflection of the egalitarian society and the absence of a formalized class system. The frequent use of the first name in addressing others is an example of this informality. The use of the last name, preceded by Mr, Ms, Mrs, or Miss, is a sign of respect reserved for older people, new acquaintances, or those to whom one wishes to show deference (a customer being served by a clerk, for example). Many Americans use the first name before they even know the other person, a habit most Europeans deplore.

This constant use of first names extends to business organizations at all levels – among peers and with subordinates – including secretaries, assistants, clerks, and service personnel. Titles are seldom used; the only people who are routinely addressed as 'Doctor' are physicians, dentists and veterinarians. Most Ph.D.s, unless they are very well-known, are only called 'Doctor' in academic settings. This is not true in Europe.

In formal introductions Americans shake hands; they do not shake hands with co-workers at the office every day, as Germans do. In social situations, some Americans shake hands; others hug or kiss friends of the opposite sex by way of greeting; women often embrace; and men sometimes clap each other on the back. Most Americans do not, however, touch other people unless they are friends or relatives.

Even though Americans are very informal, they do value good manners and proper social behavior. They say 'please' and 'thank you' frequently or sometimes just 'thanks' with a smile. It is considered polite for American acquaintances and friends to inquire about each other's families when they meet. Recently, there has been renewed interest in etiquette books and newspaper columns that offer advice on social courtesies after a decade of relaxed rules during the 1960s and a gradual move toward formality during the 1970s (see *Time* article, 'Minding Our Manners Again', in Further Reading). Good manners are more highly esteemed in some social circles and geographic areas than in others. Cities such as Boston, Washington, Charleston and Atlanta – and in the South in general – tend to be more formal because, although there are no formal class distinctions, there are 'old families' that emphasize polite behavior. However, some Americans prominent in business, politics, and the professions lack the manners Europeans expect of individuals in these positions.

Although Americans are informal, they do react strongly to being corrected or reprimanded in public. They prefer that this be done in private, if at all. The German propensity toward correcting strangers is shocking and offensive to most Americans.

There are a number of paradoxes in the American character that puzzle foreigners. For instance, hand in hand with their individualism is a competing drive to conform. Despite the surface appearance of easy informality, egalitarianism, and great freedom, there are very strong pressures to conform in certain areas of American culture. The rules are not always explicit but they do exist, and, as in every culture, social pressure reinforces conformity.

Appearances are important to Americans, both personal appearance and the outside appearance of their homes, especially in middle-class suburbs. Neighbors become very upset if property is not well maintained and cared for. They think indifference to the appearance of one's house implies an anti-social attitude and a lack of concern for one's neighbors, not to mention the fear that unsightliness may also bring down property values. Americans become disturbed when neighbors don't cut the grass, shovel the snow on the sidewalk or driveway, or attend to outside painting and repairs.

There is also strong pressure on Americans to be team players, to go along with the majority. In business, this means not rocking the boat or making waves, and in politics it all too often means supporting a leader at the expense of telling the truth or of doing the right thing. The pressure to get along well with others means individualism is less appreciated than conformity on the job.

Approval and popularity are strong motivators for Americans, who have a deep need to be accepted and liked. There are numerous books on how to make friends and how to persuade people to accept your thinking. The American drive to be liked, accepted, and approved of by a wide circle of friends and associates means they must inevitably sacrifice some of their individuality. The French are less likely to hide their real selves and hence the French are equally less likely to be good team players in business or elsewhere.

Another of the great paradoxes in American culture is the conflict between the individual's drive for acceptance and popularity and the drive for success and achievement. People who value getting ahead in a career more than getting along with others often find themselves isolated (American women particularly face this problem when they enter fields heretofore reserved for men). They may be admired but not generally liked.

However strong the American need to conform and to be a team player, the American's first loyalty is still to self, family, and career, not the company. In order to advance in salary or rank, the individual may move from one company to another. A person may work for many different companies in one lifetime. This is normal and accepted in American business and is not considered an indication of disloyalty and unreliability.

Americans also have little personal loyalty in their business dealings. Being pragmatic, they do business where they 'get the best deal', which usually means the best price. In their personal life, individuals often prefer to do business with someone they know is reliable, whom they've dealt with for years. Their personal relationship overrides their desire for the lowest price.

American friendship depends more on common interests and congeniality than on shared philosophical beliefs. In contrast to people from other cultures, Americans maintain friendships with people of differing philosophies and beliefs. Another difference is that American friends do not always discuss deep personal problems with each other; often they go to professionals for counseling instead. However, friends are important to Americans and despite the mobility that characterizes the society, they do form some deep, lasting relationships. Some even maintain links with childhood friends, including classmates from school and college.

Keeping up the standard of living in the United States leaves most people with little money for savings. While Americans are not traditionally savers, many families do save money to pay for their children's education. Since higher education in the US is expensive compared to Europe, this leaves little for other needs in the future. Nevertheless, Americans can be extraordinarily generous to others. They contribute billions of dollars to charity each year (nearly $90 billion in recent years) and are easily moved to respond to the misfortunes of others, both at home and abroad. This generosity is matched by no other country we know. Business leaders are among the many Americans who spend a great deal of time and money on charitable and civic activities. As one American banker said, 'The sense of altruism and its concomitant commitment of time runs through all levels of U.S. industry.'

Many Americans are involved in civic and community affairs or are active in political parties at the local, state, and national level. Others work in organizations such as the League of Women Voters, dedicated to informing the public about elections and candidates running for office, as well as in groups concerned with environmental issues and social problems. Most communities abound in civic organizations. In addition, many families belong to churches with programs for social welfare to which they devote considerable time.

Further Reading

Bloom, Allan, *The Closing of the American Mind*, New York: Simon & Schuster, Inc., 1987.

Hirsch, E. D., Jr., *Cultural Literacy*, Boston: Houghton-Mifflin Company, 1987.

Peters, Thomas J. and Robert H. Waterman, Jr., *In Search of Excellence: Lessons from American's Best-Run Companies*, New York: Harper & Row, 1982.

Ringer, Robert J., *Looking Out for Number One*, New York: Fawcett Books, 1978.

Time, 'Immigrants: the changing face of America', special issue, 8 July 1985.

— 'Minding our manners again', 8 November 1984.

Tocqueville, Alexis de, *Democracy in America* 1835–1840, 1945 (numerous editions).

Whyte, William H., Jr., *The Organization Man*, New York: Touchstone Books, 1972.

Canada with the USA

Historical Traditions and National Characteristics: a Comparative Analysis of Canada and the United States

Seymour Martin Lipset

From *Canadian Journal of Sociology*, Vol. 11, No. 2, 1986, 113–37

There is much to be gained, both in empirical and analytic terms, from a systematic comparative study of Canada and the United States. They have many of the same ecological and demographic conditions, approximately the same level of economic development, and similar rates of upward and downward social mobility. And alongside the obvious distinctiveness of francophone Quebec, anglophone Canadians and Americans have much in common in cultural terms as well. Yet, although overall these two peoples probably resemble each other more than any other two nations on earth, there are consistent patterns of difference between them. To discover and analyze the factors which create and perpetuate such differences among nations is one of the more intriguing and difficult tasks in comparative study.[1]

In this essay I shall focus on value differences between the two countries, that is, differences in that set of attitudes which tends to characterize and permeate both the public and private ethos in each country. The central argument of the paper is that Canada has been a more élitist, law-abiding, statist, collectivity-oriented, and particularistic (group-oriented) society than the United States,[2] and that these fundamental distinctions stem in large part from the defining event which gave birth to both countries, the American Revolution. The social effects of this division have been subsequently reinforced by variations in religious traditions, political and legal institutions, and socio-economic structures, among other factors.

A brief characterization of the essential core, or organizing principles, of each society may help clarify the type of difference being referred to here. With respect to the United States, the emphases on individualism and achievement orientation by the American colonists were an important motivating force in the launching of the American Revolution, and were embodied in the Declaration of Independence. The manifestation of such attitudes in this historic event and their crystallization in an historic document provided a basis for the reinforcement and encouragement of these orientations throughout subsequent American history. Thus, the United States remained through the nineteenth and early twentieth centuries the extreme example of classically liberal or Lockean society which rejected the assumptions of the alliance of throne and altar, of ascriptive élitism, of mercantilism, of *noblesse oblige*, of communitarianism. Friedrich Engels, among other foreign visitors, noted that as compared to Europe, the United States was 'purely bourgeois, so entirely without a feudal past' (Engels, 1942: 467).

By contrast, both major Canadian linguistic groups sought to preserve their values and culture by reacting against liberal revolutions. English-speaking Canada exists because she opposed the Declaration of Independence; French-speaking Canada, largely under the leadership of Catholic clerics, also sought to isolate herself from the anti-clerical, democratic values of the French Revolution.[3] The leaders of both, after 1783 and 1789, consciously attempted to create a conservative, monarchical and ecclesiastical society in North America. Canadian élites of both linguistic groups saw the need to use the state to protect minority cultures, English Canadians against Yankees, French Canadians against anglophones. In the United States, on the other hand, the Atlantic Ocean provided an effective barrier against the major locus of perceived threat – Britain – which helped sustain the American ideological commitment to a weak state that did not have to maintain extensive military forces. As with the United States, however, these initial 'organizing principles' in Canada served to structure subsequent developments north of the border. Although the content and extent of the differences between the two countries have changed over time, the contemporary variations still reflect the impact of the American Revolution. Before presenting empirical findings which sustain these general arguments, I would first like to address a number of questions related to comparative social science in general, and to the study of national value systems in particular, illustrating the points raised with examples drawn from the Canadian and American cases.

Basically, all social science is comparative. Social scientists seek to formulate generalizations which apply to all human behavior; to do this involves specifying the conditions under which a given relationship among two or more variables holds true. In attempting to account for a specific pattern of behavior which has occurred in a given part of the world – for instance, the causal relationship (if any) between the emergence of Protestantism and the rise of capitalism – it is clearly necessary to engage in comparative research. Without examining social relations in different nations it is impossible to know to what extent a given factor actually has its suggested effect. For example, if it is true that the German *Standesstaat* (rigid status system) has played an important role in determining the authoritarian tradition of German politics, how does it happen that a similar structure in Sweden has been associated with a very different political culture?

In seeking to develop an answer to such a question, the social scientist, guided by a set of theoretical suppositions concerning the phenomenon under study, can turn to a comparative analysis of other variables (such as the educational system or family structure) to determine whether they mediate the impact of the status system on political culture. Perhaps variations along these dimensions, or, possibly, consequences associated with differences in potential military power, will explain why comparable status systems in Germany and Sweden have been linked to varying political outcomes. A complementary line of inquiry might involve studying these various aspects of society in countries which have a political culture similar to that of Sweden, to determine whether the same set of factors is associated with a comparable political culture in a variety of contexts.

If this sounds vaguely reminiscent of the natural scientist's behavior in the laboratory – for instance, observing the properties of different gases at a constant temperature and volume, then examining the impact of changing the temperature, or the volume, or both – it is because the two research endeavors do share an underlying logic of inquiry. However, the social scientist is simply not free to manipulate variables which are of theoretical interest in the same way as the laboratory scientist. Statistical methods, such as those used in the analysis of large scale surveys of voting behavior and political attitudes, do permit an approximation of the laboratory practice of holding all variables constant except those whose relationship is being investigated. However, such methods are suitable only where the quantification of relevant variables is both possible and appropriate, and where the number of cases is large enough to satisfy statistical requirements.

When the social scientist wants to explain a particular difference among a limited number of cases – for instance, the prevailing political values in two or three countries – the problem of 'too few cases, too many variables' can be mitigated somewhat by the selection of countries for analysis. That is, by choosing countries for comparison so that the range of variables on which the chosen cases are similar is maximized, the researcher can increase the certainty with which the variation in the phenomenon being studied can be attributed to those variables on which the two cases differ from each other. While obviously not as stringent as laboratory procedures, a careful selection of cases can allow the investigator to control for a large number of variables, and hence greatly enhance the analytic rigor of the research. This set of considerations renders Canada and the United States a promising combination for the purposes of comparative analysis.

It is important to note that any effort to specify the values, ethos, or national character of nations confronts the problem that such statements are necessarily made in a comparative context. Thus the assertion that the United States or Canada is a materialistic nation, that it is egalitarian, that its family system is unstable, obviously does not refer to these characteristics in any absolute sense. The statement that a national value system is egalitarian clearly does not imply the absence of severe differences in power, income, wealth or status. Generally this statement means that from a comparative perspective, nations classified as egalitarian tend to place more emphasis on universalistic criteria in judging others, and tend to de-emphasize the institutionalization of hierarchical differences.

The key words here are 'tend', 'more than' and 'comparative'. No one suggests that any given complex social structure is in fact egalitarian in any absolute sense. Macroscopic sociology employs polarity concepts when it compares core aspects of societies – *Gemeinschaft-Gesellschaft*, organic solidarity-mechanical solidarity, inner-directed-other-directed, diffuseness-specificity, achievement-ascription, traditional-modern, and this approach purposely exaggerates such differences for analytic purposes.

Related to this point is a second one concerning the frame of reference within which specific comparisons are made. It may seem a truism, but is nonetheless worth stating, that what appear as significant differences when viewed through one lens may seem to be minor variations viewed through another. For example, an American political scientist, Louis Hartz, has argued that Canada, the United States and other countries settled by groups emigrating from Europe are all 'fragment cultures', since the upper and lower strata did not move. As a result, they lacked the privileged aristocratic class and its institutions such as were found in the European 'whole'. The North American states were formed as predominantly 'middle-class' liberal societies. Hence traditional European conservatism, which emphasized a strong monarchical state, was not present in the settler societies. Over time, the very absence of a traditional right transmuted the original liberal or radical doctrines into conservative dogmas of the 'fragment'. It is impossible to build an ideological left in the fragment cultures because there is no hereditary aristocracy against whom to rebel, and because the philosophical bases on which an ideological left might be founded are already institutionalized as part of the received liberal and radical tradition of the society (Hartz, 1964: 1–48).

Hence, for Hartz the American Revolution is not, and cannot be seen as, a watershed event signalling a radical distinction between the value system developing in post-revolutionary America and that emerging in counter-revolutionary Canada. The minor differences between the two are of far less significance than the traits they share in common, which sharply set them off from European societies. By contrast, the perspective that I have emphasized sees a greater degree of continuity between the communitarian and élitist aspects of Imperial Britain and the character of Canadian value orientations than Hartz's analysis suggests. My analysis indicates that the survival of these attitudes in Canada and their relative absence in the United States is an important distinction between the two countries which has resulted, in the first instance, from the Revolution south of the border and its rejection to the north.[4]

One aspect of this distinction is a greater conservatism in Canada – in the European sense of the word – than in the United States. This political orientation, with its emphasis on the values of *noblesse oblige* and state responsibility, has meant, ironically, that Canada has provided a more favorable political and social climate for the development of welfare state policies than is found south of the border.

The effort to relate variations in the value systems and institutions of nations to the differences in their key formative experiences provides a good illustration of Max Weber's methodological dictum that current differences among social structures may often be linked to specific historical events which set one process in motion in one nation or unit, and a different one in a second. Weber, in fact, used the analogy of a dice game in which each time the dice came up with a certain number they were loaded in the direction of coming up with that number again. That is, a decision in a certain direction tends to reinforce those elements which are congruent with it. In other words, historical events establish values and predispositions, and these in turn affect later events (Weber, 1949: 182–5).

One illustration of how, in concrete terms, this process can unfold can be seen by looking at the broad sweep of Canadian history from the time of the American Revolution through to the establishment of Canadian independence in 1867. It was not just in 1776 that those to the north opted for the more conservative path. Canadian historians have noted that the democratic or populist elements lost their battle on many occasions. As Frank Underhill summed up that history:

Our forefathers made the great refusal in 1776 when they declined to join the revolting American colonies. They made it again in 1812 when they repelled American invasions. They made it again in 1837 when they rejected a revolution motivated by ideals of Jacksonian democracy, and opted for a staid moderate respectable British Whiggism which they called 'Responsible Government'. They made it once more in 1867 when the separate British colonies joined to set up a new nationality in order to preempt [American] expansionism . . . [It] would be hard to overestimate the amount of energy we have devoted to this cause. (Underhill, 1960: 222)

This sequence is understandable in view of the fact that as a result of the American Revolution, many Loyalists – those most opposed to the populist egalitarianism of the Revolution – emigrated to Canada. As J. M. S. Careless, another Canadian historian, has noted, they formed the 'backbone of . . . resistance' to American invasion in 1812 (Careless, 1963: 113). The dice were loaded in this instance in the direction of a more conservative posture in Canada than in the United States by virtue of the Revolution and the subsequent migration north by those opposed to the values embodied in this historic event. Interestingly enough, as suggested earlier, it may be argued that the values inherent in a monarchically rooted conservatism such as those which developed in Canada and much of Europe give rise in the modern world to support for social democratic redistributive and welfare policies. Conversely a dominant *laissez-faire* Lockean tradition which has been characteristic of the United States for much of its history is antithetical to such programs. Northrop Frye, Canada's leading literary critic, called attention to this alliance of opposites when he stated in 1952: 'The Canadian point of view is at once more conservative and more radical than Whiggery [the liberal ideology of the American Revolution], closer both to aristocracy and to democracy [equality] . . .' (Frye, 1953: 273).

The attitudes and values characteristic of a people do not exist in a vacuum, however. It is important to recognize that one of the major factors explaining the persistence of particular orientations is that they become embodied in institutions which help perpetuate them. An illustration of this interaction between values and institutions can be found by comparing religious institutions and attitudes in Canada and the United States, which have consistently differed (see Lipset, 1970: 37–75; 1979: 140–70; 1985: 109–60; Clark, 1948). The American tradition and law have placed much more emphasis on separation of church and state than have the Canadian. A large majority of Americans have adhered to Protestant sects, which had opposed the established state Church in England. These largely have a congregational structure, and foster the idea of an individual relationship with God. Most Canadians have belonged to either the Roman Catholic or the Anglican churches, both of which have been hierarchically organized state religions in Britain and Europe. While efforts to sustain church establishment ultimately failed in Canada, state support of religious institutions, particularly schools, has continued into the present. Hence religious institutions have both reflected and contributed to anti-élitist and individualist orientations in the United States and countered them in Canada.

It should be noted that a great deal of debate has been generated over the question of the relative significance of Canadian-American value differences. The argument essentially has been between those, like myself, who emphasize the distinctiveness of the *values* of the two countries, and the ways these in turn affect behavior, beliefs and institutional arrangements, and those who place primary importance on various *structural* differences, particularly geographic, economic, and political factors. It should be stressed, however, that a concern with the influence of economic, ecologic, and value elements in determining given national developments or traits is not a matter of dealing with alternative mutually exclusive hypotheses. Rather, as in the case of Weber's discussion of the relative contribution of economic and value factors in the rise of capitalism, one may conclude that different variables are each necessary but not sufficient to produce the results sometimes credited to one of them alone.

And, in fact, when the arguments of those identified as adhering to one or the other interpretation of the sources of Canadian-American differences (values or structure) are carefully examined, it becomes apparent that most of the distinctions really are ones of emphasis. For example, my own analysis takes into account that the two nations do vary in their ecology, demography and economy, and that these differences have exerted an important influence on the development of values and attitudes on both sides of the border. Canada controls an area which, while larger than her southern neighbor's, is much less hospitable to human habitation in terms of climate and resources. Her geographical extent and weaker population base have contributed to an emphasis on direct government involvement in the economy to provide various services, for which sufficient private capital or a profitable market have not been available (Bryce, 1921: 471). South of the border, the anti-statist emphasis subsumed in the revolutionary ideology was not challenged by the need to call upon the state to intervene economically to protect the nation's independence against a powerful neighbor.[5]

In a similar way, those whose analysis emphasizes the significance of structural factors also acknowledge the role that values play in affecting the development of political and economic differences across the border. A good example can be found in the writing of Friedrich Engels, the co-founder of the most influential structural approach of all. He was one of the first writers to contend that Canada's economic backwardness compared to the United States is primarily a function of her value system. Following a visit to both countries in 1888, he wrote: 'Here one sees how necessary the *feverish speculative spirit* of the

Americans is for the rapid development of a new country' and looked forward to the abolition of 'this ridiculous boundary line' separating the two countries (Engels, 1953: 204, emphasis mine). More recently, Harold Innis, Canada's preeminent economic historian who has strongly emphasized structural factors, such as the 'hard' character of the Canadian frontier in affecting national orientations, has also noted the importance of 'the essentially counter-revolutionary traditions, represented by the United Empire Loyalists and by the Church in French Canada, which escaped the influences of the French Revolution' (Innis, 1956: 406).

A comparison of the frontier experiences of the two countries encapsulates the ways in which values and structural factors can interact to produce different outcomes. Inasmuch as Canada had to be on constant guard against the expansionist tendencies of the United States, it could not leave its frontier communities unprotected or autonomous. 'It was in the established tradition of British North America that the power of the civil authority should operate well in advance of the spread of settlement' (McInnis, 1942: 306–7). Law and order in the form of the centrally controlled North West Mounted Police moved into the frontier before and along with the settlers. This contributed to the establishment of a much greater tradition of respect for the institutions of law and order on the Canadian frontier as compared with the American, meant the absence of vigilante activity in Canada, and enabled Canada to avoid the Indian Wars which were occurring south of the border.

The pervasiveness of government legal controls on the Canadian frontier seriously undermined the development of an excessive emphasis on individualism which characterizes the United States. The development of the Canadian frontier, in fact, did not simply follow on population movements impelled by natural social pressures, as occurred in the United States. Rather, the Canadian government felt the need deliberately to plan for the settlement of the West. As S. D. Clark has put it:

> Canada maintained her separate political existence but only by resisting any movement on the part of her population, which had the effect of weakening the controls of central political authority. The claims to the interior of the continent were staked not by advancing frontiersmen, acting on their own, but by advancing armies and police forces, large corporate economic enterprises and ecclesiastical organizations, supported by the state. The Canadian political temper, as a result, has run sharply counter to the American. Those creeds of American political life – individual rights, local autonomy, and limitation of executive power – which have contributed so much to the political strength of the American community have found less strong support within the Canadian political system. (Clark, 1962: 214)

And this history of active state involvement in the political and economic development of the country is reinforced by the population and geographic factors that today encourage a continued state role in economic investment and the provision of industrial infrastructure. Thus it may be argued with Weber that the appropriate structural environment for a given development requires the emergence of facilitating values, or that necessary values will not result in the anticipated changes unless the structural conditions are propitious.

Given all of the differences distinguishing the Canadian historical experience from the American, it is not surprising that the peoples of the two countries formulated their self-conceptions in sharply different ways. As an ideological nation whose left and right *both* take sustenance from the American Creed, the United States is quite different from Canada, which lacks any founding myth, and whose intellectuals frequently question whether the country has a national identity. Sacvan Bercovitch has well described America's impact on a Canadian during the conflict-ridden sixties.

> My first encounter with American consensus was in the late sixties, when I crossed the border into the United States and found myself inside the myth of America . . . of a country that despite its arbitrary frontiers, despite its bewildering mix of race and creed, could believe in something called the True America, and could invest that patent fiction with all the moral and emotional appeal of a religious symbol . . . Here was the Jewish anarchist Paul Goodman berating the Midwest for abandoning the promise; here the descendant of American laves, Martin Luther King, denouncing injustice as a violation of the American Way; here, an endless debate about national destiny, . . . conservatives scavenging for un-Americans, New Left historians recalling the country to its sacred mission . . .
>
> Nothing in my Canadian background had prepared me for that spectacle . . . To a Canadian skeptic . . . it made for a breathtaking scene: a pluralistic pragmatic people openly living in a dream, bound together by an ideological consensus unmatched by any other modern society.
>
> Let me repeat that mundane phrase: *ideological consensus* . . . It was a hundred sects and factions, each apparently different from the others, yet all celebrating the same mission . . . (Bercovitch, 1981: 5–6, emphasis in original)

Although interpreted in a variety of ways by different groups and individuals, the ideology of the American Revolution provides for each of them a *raison d'être* for the Republic – it explains why the United States came into being, and what it means to be American.

The contrast with Canada is a sharp one. Canada could not offer her citizens 'the prospect of a fresh start . . . because (as the Canadian poet Douglas Le Pan put it) Canada is ''a country without a mythology'' ' (Bercovitch, 1981: 24). To justify her separate existence, both linguistic cultures deprecated American values and institutions. As Frank Underhill once noted, Canadians are the world's oldest and most continuing anti-Americans (Underhill, 1960: 222; for an elaboration, see Kendall, 1974: 20–36). This stance was reflected in the writings of various Canadian observers in the 1920s, who 'discerned and condemned an excessive egalitarian quality derived from notions of independence and democracy that had been set free during the [American] Revolution' (Weaver, 1973: 80). Further evidence of such attitudes was gathered during the 1930s when the first efforts at a systematic sociological investigation of opinions in Canada concerning themselves and Americans were launched. One of the most important and prolific contributors to the research was S. D. Clark, then starting his scholarly career. He summarized the findings in the following terms:

> Canadian national life can almost be said to take its rise in the negative will to resist absorption in the American Republic. It is largely about the United States as an object that the consciousness of Canadian national unity has grown up . . .
>
> Constantly in the course of this study we shall come across the idea that Canadian life is simpler, more honest, more moral and more religious than life in the United States, that it lies closer to the rural virtues and has achieved urbanization without giving the same scope to corrupting influences which has been afforded them in the United States. (Clark, 1938: 243, 245)[6]

As Clark suggests in this passage, Canadians have tended to define themselves, not in terms of their own national history and tradition, but rather by reference to what they are *not*: American.

These differences between Canada and the United States can be seen, not just in history or in the findings of social science research, but also in the novels, poems, and stories created by writers in each country. In fact, of all artefacts, the art and literature of a nation should most reflect, as well as establish, her basic myths and values. And many analysts of North American literature have emphasized the continuing effects of the 'mythic and psychic consequences of founding a country on revolution or out of the rejection of revolution' (Brown, n.d.: 2).

Russell Brown, who has studied Canadian and American literature in a comparative context, argues that a revolt against tradition and authority, against king and ancestral fatherland, is at some deepest level an Oedipal act (Brown, n.d.: 2). He notes with respect to this that critics have identified the writings of a number of American authors as reflecting Oedipal themes. In elaborating this point, Brown argues:

> The American desire to free oneself from the father is also a desire to escape the past, its tradition and authority. It is no surprise that the American hero par excellence is that man without fathers, Adam . . . The American flight from history is the root of the American dream, the Horatio Alger myth, the self-made man. (Brown, n.d.: 17)

If American literature is pervaded by a mood, it is one of optimism.

By contrast, Canadian literary critics tend to see their own country and their literature as reflecting defeat, difficult physical circumstances, and abandonment by Britain. According to Robert L. McDougall, the representative images in Canadian writing 'are those of denial and defeat rather than fulfilment and victory' (McDougall, 1963: 10–11). Russell Brown, quoted above, couches the distinction between the two national literatures in terms of alternate Greek myths. It is not the Oedipal theme of generational conflict that one finds reflected in literature written north of the border, but rather the myth of Telemachus. This Greek character has grown up without his father who, for reasons unfathomable to the young man, left the family home while the boy was still young. Thus, Telemachus sets out at the beginning of the Odyssey to find his father, trying to discover the events which took him away (Brown, n.d.: 8). This concern with the past and with the roots of identity is prototypically Canadian. The contrast between the conservatism of this historically oriented, backward-looking perspective and the prospects for radical 'newness' conveyed by the themes and images of American literature is striking.

One of Canada's foremost novelists, Margaret Atwood, has vividly captured this distinction in discussing what she sees as the central symbol of each of these two countries and their cultures. She suggests that the symbol for America is 'The Frontier', which implies 'a place that is *new*, where the old order can be discarded' and which 'holds out a hope, never fulfilled but always promised, of Utopia, the perfect human society'. She notes that most twentieth-century American literature is about the 'gap between the promise and the actuality, between the imagined ideal . . . and the actual squalid materialism, dotty small town, nasty city, or redneck-filled outback' (Atwood, 1972: 31–2). Such an image both reflects and encourages a belief that one ought to *strive*, to seek out the better in life.

The central symbol for Canada, by contrast, based on numerous examples of its appearance in French and English Canadian literature, is 'Survival, *la Survivance*'. The main meaning of survival in Canadian literature is the most basic one, 'hanging on, staying alive'. Atwood notes the continued Canadian concern with Canada: does it exist? will it last? what does it mean to be a Canadian? do we have an identity? etc. As she puts it: 'Canadians are forever taking the national pulse like doctors at a sickbed; the aim is not to see whether the patient will live well but simply whether he will live at all' (Atwood, 1972: 33).

Atwood points out other national differences which are reflected in the literature of the two countries; one of the most important of these is the difference in the way the two societies look at authority. She argues that Canadians, unlike Americans, do not see authority or government as an enemy. 'Canada must be the only country in the world where a policeman [the Mountie] is used as a national symbol.' It is not surprising, then, to find that rebels and revolutionists are not heroes in Canadian literature (Atwood, 1972: 171).

The study of a nation's arts and literature is important to any effort to *understand* her values. But as Ronald Sutherland has suggested, literature also helps *form* national values: 'The greatest writers of a nation . . . respond to the forces that condition a nation's philosophy of life, and they in turn condition that philosophy' (Sutherland, 1982: 402). Literature is, of course, not alone or even predominant in these respects. As we turn now to a systematic comparison of a number of facets of the two societies, ranging from law and crime to center-periphery relations, we shall continue to observe this mutual interaction between the values predominant in a nation and the institutions which both reflect and shape them.

Religion

One sphere of life in which this relationship is clearly observable is that of religion. As far as understanding the ways in which religious tradition in Canada differs from that in the United States is concerned, Harold Innis may have said it all when he wrote that a 'counter-revolutionary tradition implies an emphasis on ecclesiasticism' (Innis, 1956: 385). As previously mentioned, the majority of Canadians adhere to the Roman Catholic or Anglican churches, both of which are hierarchically organized and continued until recently to have a strong relationship to the state. On the other hand, most Americans have belonged to the more individualist 'nonconformist' Protestant sects.[7] Sutherland sums up the differences as follows:

> American Puritanism, developing as it did from the peculiar notions of a small and persecuted sect, underlined self-reliance and the responsibility of the individual . . . Canada, by contrast, had relatively sophisticated church systems among both Catholics and Protestants. New England Puritanism and subsequent evangelical movements called for personal seeking of God, working out one's own salvation through 'fear and trembling'. Canadians, on the other hand, had the security of reliance upon a church establishment, detailed codes of behaviour, a controlling system; and in general, *until very recently*, Canadians have tended

to depend upon and to trust systems which control their lives . . . (Sutherland, 1977: 2–3)

The abolition of established religion in the United States fostered a strong commitment to voluntarism which, as Tocqueville argued, has been an important factor strengthening religion in the United States. In his view, voluntary competitive institutions which rely on their membership for funds and support are likely to be stronger than institutions supported by the state. Moreover, this commitment to voluntarism, together with the considerable strength of the dissenting and anti-statist Methodist and Baptist denominations, meant that religion not only contributed to the economic orientations of the people, but also reinforced the egalitarian and democratic ethos. Tocqueville pointed out that all American denominations were minorities and hence had an interest in liberty and a weak state (Tocqueville, 1945: 312).

By contrast, as John Webster Grant points out, Canadians have

never succeeded in drawing with any precision a line between areas in which the state has a legitimate interest and those that ought to be left to the voluntary activities of the churches . . . [F]ew Canadians find 'the separation of Church and State' an acceptable description either of their situation or of their ideal for it. (Grant, 1973: 34)

Both the Church of England and the Roman Catholic Church received overt government support and, in return, gave strong support to the established political and social order. Hence one found mutually reinforcing conservative forces at the summits of the class, church and political structures (Clark, 1950: 388). In comparing French and English Canada, Roger O'Toole emphasizes that until recently in Quebec the Roman Catholic Church has retained the informal role of the state church of French Canada. And, although the Anglican Church failed in its efforts to become a 'national' church in English Canada, it helped establish the founding ethos of the country and to legitimate 'monarchy, aristocracy, and British constitutionalism [as] part of a sacred scenario . . . [I]ts condemnation of mass democracy, egalitarianism, republicanism, and revolution as the work of the devil, left an indelible mark on English-Canadian political life' (O'Toole, 1982: 184–5).

Just as religious practices and institutions can reinforce general value orientations prevalent in a national community, so too can the latter influence the former, as is demonstrated in Kenneth Westhues' comparative study of the American and Canadian Catholic churches. He suggests that there has been an 'acceptance by the American [Church] of the role of voluntary association . . . as the most it could hope for' (Westhues, 1978: 251). Thus, the Catholic Church in the United States has taken over many of the characteristics of Protestantism, including a strong emphasis on individual moralism (see Bruckberger, 1960: 45–7). As a result, the Vatican has frowned on the American church and has, in fact, not treated it as well as the Canadian affiliate. The conflict between the Catholic Church and its American branch is a result of the difference

> between that world-view, espoused by the American state, which takes the individual as the basic reality of social life, and the church's world-view, which defines the group as primary. American non-recognition of the church is thus not merely a political matter . . . It is instead a genuinely sociological issue, resting as it does on a fundamental conflict of values. (Westhues, 1978: 256)

And Westhues argues, the 'major question always before the Catholic church in the United States has been how far to assimilate to the American way of life'. This question 'has never arisen in Canada, basically for the lack of a national ideology for defining what the Canadian way of life is or ought to be' (Westhues, 1978: 254–5).

Religion in both countries has become more secularized in tandem with increased urbanization and education. For instance, Canadian Catholicism, particularly in Quebec, has modified the nature of its corporatist commitment from a link to agrarian and élitist anti-industrial values to a tie to leftist socialist beliefs. These variations, of course, parallel the changes in French Canadian nationalism. Public opinion research suggests that francophone Catholics have given up much of their commitment to Jansenist puritanical values, particularly as they affect sexual behavior and family size. This secularizing trend, although generally observable in both countries, has been less noticeable in the United States, particularly among evangelical Protestants. Americans, according to data from sample surveys presented below, are much more likely to attend church regularly than Canadians, and to adhere to fundamentalist and moralistic beliefs. And the continued strength of Protestant evangelical, sectarian and fundamentalist religion south of the border has meant that traditional values related to sex, family and morality in general are stronger there than in Canada.

A large body of public opinion data gathered in the two countries bears on these issues. Most findings are not precisely comparable because of variations in question wording. Fortunately, a research organization linked to the Catholic Church, CARA, has conducted a systematically comparative study of values in 22 countries, including Canada and the United States, where the data were collected by the Gallup Poll at the start of the eighties.[8] The two tables which follow present some of the relevant CARA findings.

There is a consistent pattern in these data: Americans far outnumber Canadians generally in giving expression to Protestant fundamentalist beliefs, with

Table 1 Religious beliefs and values 1980–81, in per cent

	Americans	*English Canadians*	*French Canadians*
How important is God in your life? (1 = not at all; 10 = very important) Percentage choosing 9 or 10	59	44	47
Believe 'there is a personal God'	65	49	56
Believe the ten Commandments apply fully to themselves	83	76	67
Believe the ten Commandments apply fully to others as well	36	28	23
Believe in 'the Devil'	66	46	25
Believe in 'Hell'	67	45	22
Believe in 'Heaven'	84	73	58
Believe in life after death	71	61	63
Believe in a soul	88	80	80

Source: CARA, Center for Applied Research in the Apostolate, *Values Study of Canada* (code book) Washington, DC: May 1983.

Table 2 Social values 1980–81, in per cent

	Americans	*English Canadians*	*French Canadians*
Agree that 'marriage is an outdated institution'	7	11	19
Believe that 'individuals should have a chance to enjoy complete sexual freedom without being restricted'	18	18	24
Disapprove of idea of a woman wanting a child but not a stable relationship with one man	58	53	34
Agree that sexual activity must subscribe to certain moral rules	51	49	34

Source: CARA, Center for Applied Research in the Apostolate, *Values Study of Canada* (code book) Washington, DC: May 1983.

anglophones more likely to hold such views than francophones. And, congruent with the variation in religious practice and belief, Americans appear to be more puritanical than Canadians, with francophones the most tolerant with respect to sexual behavior.

Institutionally, national values should be clearly expressed in a nation's system of laws and the way individuals are treated under and react to them and, in fact, this is what we find in examining these aspects of Canadian and American society.

Law and Deviance

The difference in the role of law in the two countries is linked to the historical emphases on the rights and obligations of the community as compared to those of the individual. The explicit concern of Canada's founding fathers with 'peace, order, and good government' implies control and protection. The American stress on 'life, liberty, and the pursuit of happiness' suggests upholding the rights of the individual. This latter concern for rights, including those of people accused of crime and of political dissidents, is inherent in the 'due process' model, involving various legal inhibitions on the power of the police and prosecutors, characteristic of the United States. The 'crime control' model, more evident in Canada, as well as Europe, emphasizes the maintenance of law and order, and is less protective of the rights of the accused and of individuals generally.[9] As John Hagan and Jeffrey Leon note:

> [T]he due-process model is much concerned with exclusionary rules of evidence, the right to counsel, and other procedural safeguards thought useful in protecting accused persons from unjust applications of criminal sanctions . . .
>
> [T]he crime-control model places heavy emphasis on the repression of criminal conduct, arguing that only by insuring order can individuals in a society be guaranteed personal freedom. It is for this reason that advocates of crime control are less anxious to presume the innocence of accused persons and to protect such persons against sometimes dubious findings of guilt. (Hagan and Leon, 1978: 182; see also Griffiths, Klein, and Verdun-Jones, 1980; Tepperman, 1977)

Property rights and civil liberties are also under less constitutional protection in Canada than in the United States. John Mercer and Michael Goldberg note:

> In Canada . . . property rights are not vested with the individual but rather with the Crown, just the opposite of the US where the Fifth and Fourteenth Amendments to the US Constitution guarantee property rights. Interestingly, in the [recently

enacted] Canadian Charter of Rights and Freedoms property rights (as distinct from human rights) were explicitly not protected . . . Such a state of affairs would be unacceptable in the United States where individual rights and particularly those related to personal and real property are sacrosanct. (Mercer and Goldberg, 1982: 22)

The Canadian government has greater legal power to restrict freedom of speech and to invade personal privacy. Acting through an order-in-council, it may limit public discussion of particular issues and, as in 1970 during the Quebec crisis, impose a form of military control (see Callwood, 1981: 333–4, 341–2; Bell and Tepperman, 1979: 83–4; Smith, 1971). Comparing American and Canadian public reactions to violations of privacy by the government, Alan Westin writes:

[I]t is important to note that in Canada there have been some incidents which, had they happened in the United States, would probably have led to great *causes célèbres*. Most Canadians seem to have accepted Royal Canadian Mounted Police break-ins without warrants between 1970 and 1978, and also the RCMP's secret access to income tax information, and to personal health information from the Ontario Health Insurance Plan. If I read the Canadian scene correctly, those did not shock and outrage most Canadians. (Westin, 1983: 41)

That Canadians and Americans differ in the way they react to the law is demonstrated strikingly in the aggregate differences between the two with respect to crime rates for major offenses. Americans are much more prone than Canadians to commit violent offenses like murder, robbery, and rape and to be arrested for the use of serious illegal drugs such as opiates and cocaine. They are also much more likely to take part in protest demonstrations and riots, as the following table shows. Although the United States population outnumbers the Canadian by about ten to one, the ratios for political protest activities have ranged from twenty to one to forty to one.

Table 3 Political protest and violence in Canada and the United States

	United States		*Canada*	
	48–67	*68–77*	*48–67*	*68–77*
Number of protest demonstrations	1179	1005	27	33
Number of riots	683	149	29	5
Deaths from political violence	320	114	8	4

Source: Calculated from data in Taylor and Jodice (1983: 19–25, 33–6, 47–51).

Evidence from national opinion surveys in the two countries indicates that lower rates of crime and violence in Canada are accompanied by greater respect for police, public backing for stronger punishment of criminals, and a higher level of support for gun control legislation. For example, when asked by the Canadian Gallup poll in 1978 to rate the local, provincial, and Royal Canadian Mounted Police, a large majority (64 per cent, 64 per cent, and 61 per cent, respectively) said 'excellent or good'. The corresponding percentages reported by the Harris survey for local, state and federal law enforcement officials in 1981 were 62, 57, and 48.[10] In the early eighties, the CARA surveys conducted by Gallup found more Canadians (86 per cent) than Americans (76 per cent) voicing a great deal or quite a lot of confidence in the police. There was no significant difference between the two Canadian linguistic groups on this item.

In the United States, gun ownership has been regarded as a 'right', one linked to a constitutional guarantee established to protect the citizen. Canada's policy is based on the belief that 'ownership of "offensive weapons" or "guns" is a privilege, not a right' (Thomas, 1983: 40). It is not surprising, then, that Canadians have consistently been much more supportive of gun control legislation than Americans and have been much less likely to own guns (Thomas, 1983: 6).[11] When asked by the Gallup Polls in 1975, 'Would you favor or oppose a law which would require a person to obtain a police permit before he or she could buy a gun?' 83 per cent of Canadians voiced support compared to 67 per cent of Americans (Michalos, 1980: 147, also 58–9).[12]

The lesser respect for the law, for the 'rules of the game' in the United States, may be viewed as inherent in a system in which egalitarianism is strongly valued and in which diffuse élitism is lacking. Generalized deference is not accorded to those at the top; therefore, in the United States there is a greater propensity to redefine the rules or to ignore them. The decisions of the leadership are constantly being questioned. While Canadians incline toward the use of 'lawful' and traditionally institutionalized means for altering regulations which they believe are unjust, Americans seem more disposed to employ informal and often extralegal means to correct what they perceive as wrong.

The greater lawlessness and corruption in the United States may be attributed in part to the greater strength of the achievement value in the more populous nation. As Robert Merton has pointed out, a strong emphasis on achievement means that '[t]he moral mandate to achieve success thus exerts pressure to succeed, by fair means if possible and by foul means if necessary' (Merton, 1957: 169). Merton accounts for the greater adherence to approved means of behavior in much of Europe compared to the United States as derivative from variations in the emphasis on achievement for all. And the same logic implies that since Americans are more likely than their Canadian neighbors to be concerned with the achievement of ends – particularly pecuniary success – they will be less concerned with the use of the socially appropriate *means*; hence we should expect a higher incidence of deviations from conventional norms in politics and other aspects of life south of the forty-ninth parallel.

Although the cross-national behavioral and attitudinal variations with respect to law and crime have continued down to the present, Canada has been involved since 1960 in a process of changing her fundamental rules in what has been described as American and due process directions. The adoption of a Bill of Rights in 1960, replaced by the more comprehensive Charter of Rights and Freedoms in 1982, was designed to create a basis, absent from the British North American Act, for judicial intervention to protect individual rights and civil liberties.

While these changes are important, it is doubtful that they will come close to eliminating the differences in legal cultures. Canadian courts have been more respectful than American ones of the rest of the political system. As Kenneth McNaught concluded in 1975,

> our judges and lawyers, supported by the press and public opinion, reject any concept of the courts as positive instruments in the political process . . . [P]olitical action outside the party-parliamentary structure tends automatically to be suspect – and not least because it smacks of Americanism. This deep-grained Canadian attitude of distinguishing amongst proper and improper methods of dealing with societal organization and problems reveals us as being, to some extent, what Walter Bagehot once called a 'deferential society'. (McNaught, 1975: 138; see also Whyte, 1976: 656–7; Swinton, 1979: 91–3)

Beyond these general distinctions there are specific provisions in the new Charter of Rights and Freedoms which set it apart from the American Bill of Rights. For example, to protect parliamentary supremacy, the Canadian constitution provides that Parliament or a provincial legislature may 'opt out' of the constitutional restrictions by inserting into any law a clause that it shall operate regardless of any part of the Charter. In addition, the new rights do not include any assurance that an accused person shall have a lawyer, nor that he has the right to remain silent, nor that he need not answer questions which may tend to incriminate him in civil cases or in investigatory proceedings (Pye, 1982: 221–48; McWhinney, 1982: 55–7, 61; Westin, 1983: 27–44; see also McKercher, 1983).

Just as the legal system has aspects which are relevant both to our private lives and the public realm, so too does the economy. Thus the next task is to examine the relationship between values and structure in the two North American states in this sphere of activity.

The Economy: the Private Sector

The United States, born modern, without a feudal élitist corporatist tradition, could create, outside of the agrarian South, what Engels described as the purest example of a bourgeois society. Canada, as we have seen, was somewhat different, and that difference affected the way her citizens have done business. As Herschel Hardin puts it:

It was . . . rough egalitarianism, practical education . . . and the relentless psychic push to keep up in the 'Lockian [*sic*] race' that made the exceptional United States go.

[T]o expect that on this side of the border, out of a French Canada tied to its clerical, feudal past, and out of an English-speaking Canada, which, although it inherited much of the spirit of liberal capitalism, was nevertheless an elitist, conservative, defensive colony – to expect it *without an intense ideological revolution* – was to dream a derivative impossibility. (Hardin, 1974: 62, emphasis in original)

And as a result, according to Hardin, Canadian entrepreneurs have been less aggressive, less innovating, less risk-taking than Americans.[13] Hardin seeks to demonstrate that private enterprise in Canada 'has been a monumental failure' in developing new technology and industry, to the extent that Canadian business has rarely been involved in creating industries to process many significant inventions by Canadians, who have had to go abroad to get their discoveries marketed (see also Brown, 1967; Bourgault, 1972; Hardin, 1974: 102–5).

This has been partly due to traditional management values and organizational processes (McMillan, 1978: 45).[14] Also important is the fact that, compared to Americans, Canadian investors and financial institutions are less disposed to provide venture capital. They 'tend consistently to avoid offering encouragement to the entrepreneur with a new technology-based product . . . [or to] innovative industries' (Science Council of Canada, 1972: 123).

The thesis has been elaborated by economists. Jenny Podoluk found that 'investment is a much more significant source of personal income in the United States than in Canada . . . When Canadians have invested, the risky new Canadian enterprise has not been as attractive as the established American corporation.'[15] Kenneth Glazier, in explaining the Canadian tendency to invest in the US rather than in Canada, argues that

One reason is that Canadians traditionally have been conservative, exhibiting an inferiority complex about their own destiny as a nation and about the potential of their country . . .

Thus, with Canadians investing in the 'sure' companies of the United States, Canada has for generations suffered not only from a labor drain and a brain drain to the United States, but also from a considerably larger capital drain. (Glazier, 1972: 61)

Data drawn from opinion polls reinforce the comparative generalizations about the greater economic prudence of Canadians. Studies of English and French speaking Canadians indicate that on most items, anglophones fall between Americans and francophones. When asked by the American and Canadian Gallup Polls in 1979 (US) and 1980 (Canada) about usage of credit cards, 51 per cent of Canadians said they never used one, as compared to 35 per cent of Americans. The latter were more likely than Canadians to report 'regular' usage, 32 per cent to 16 per cent. Francophones made less use of credit cards (64 per cent, never) than anglophones (44 per cent, never). English speakers were also more likely to be regular users than French speakers.[16]

These national differences in the degree of risk generally accepted by actors in the economic sphere are accompanied by differences in attitudes toward, or the absorption of, the values of the business-industrial system. The following table shows responses to a number of questions dealing with feelings about work asked in the CARA surveys referred to earlier. On the first three questions, Americans were more disposed to give the 'business' answer, English Canadians were second and French Canadians third. But Americans were least likely to score high with regard to job satisfaction. This response pattern, the inverse of those reported for pride in the job and feelings of exploitation, may reflect a greater interest by Americans in achieving upward mobility through a change in job.

If Canadians have been more conservative than Americans in their behavior in the private sector, they have been much more prone to rely on the state to handle economic and other matters, as the next section indicates.

The Economy: the Public Sector

As mentioned earlier, and as will be further elaborated below, the stronger conservative orientation north of the border historically has meant a larger role for the state in the Canadian economy. For example, the proportion of the Canadian GNP in government hands as of the mid-seventies was 41 per cent, compared to 34 per cent in the United States; as of 1982 the ratio was 44 to 38 per cent (Nelles, 1980: 132, 143 n. 28; United Nations, 1983: 22). Subtracting defense spending, roughly 2 per cent for Canada, and 5 to 6 per cent for the

Table 4 Attitudes toward work

Percentage of respondents who:	*Americans*	*English Canadians*	*French Canadians*
Express a great deal of pride in the work they do	84	77	38
Say they never feel exploited	37	44	56
Say employees should unquestioningly follow their superior's instructions on a job	68	57	45
Score high (8, 9, 10) on a 10 point scale of job satisfaction	63	69	74

Source: CARA, Center for Applied Research in the Apostolate, *Values Study of Canada* (code book). Washington, DC: May 1983.

United States, widens the gap between the two countries considerably (see US Arms Control and Disarmament Agency, 1982: 42, 71). Taxes as a share of total domestic product were 35 per cent in Canada as compared to 30 per cent in the United States in 1982 (*US News and World Report*, 1984: 65).[17] Unlike 'the United States, [Canada] has never experienced a period of pure unadulterated *laissez-faire* market capitalism' (McLeod, 1976; Aitken, 1959). The period since 1960 has witnessed a particularly rapid expansion in the number of crown corporations: fully 70 per cent of them were created in the past quarter of a century (Chandler, 1983: 187). Mercer and Goldberg have summed up the magnitude of government involvement in the Canadian economy as of 1982:

Of 400 top industrial firms, 25 were controlled by the federal or provincial governments. Of the top 50 industrials, all ranked by sales, 7 were either wholly-owned or controlled by the federal or provincial governments. For financial institutions, 9 of the top 75 were federally or provincially owned or controlled . . . Canadian governments at all levels exhibit little reticence about involvement in such diverse enterprises as railroads, airlines, aircraft manufacture, financial institutions, steel companies, oil companies, and selling and producing atomic reactors for energy generation. (Mercer and Goldberg, 1982: 27)

Research based on opinion poll interviews indicates that Canadians, at both élite and mass levels, are more supportive than Americans of state intervention. Summarizing surveys of high level civil servants and federal, state and provincial legislators, Robert Presthus reports:

[a] sharp difference between the two [national] elites on 'economic liberalism', defined as a preference for 'big government' . . . Only about 17 percent of the American legislative elite ranks high on this disposition, compared with fully 40 percent of their Canadian peers . . . [T]he direction is the same among bureaucrats, only 17 percent of whom rank high among the American sample, compared with almost 30 percent among Canadians. (Presthus, 1974: 463)

Differences related to party affiliation in both countries emphasize this cross-national variation. Canadian Liberal legislators score much higher than American Democrats on economic liberalism and Canadian Conservatives score much higher than Republicans. Conservatives and Republicans in each country are lower on economic liberalism than Liberals and Democrats, but *Canadian Conservatives are higher than American Democrats* (Presthus, 1977: 15).

Table 5 Attitudes toward government (in per cent)

Items	*Mean level of agreement:*	
	Americans	*Canadians*
The government in Ottawa (Washington) is too big and powerful	54	40
The government should guarantee everyone at least $3,000 per year whether he works or not	14	36

Source: Arnold and Tigert (1974: 80).

Mass attitudinal data reinforce the thesis that Canadians are more collectivity oriented than Americans and therefore are more likely to support government intervention. In the 1968–70 studies of American and English Canadian attitudes discussed earlier, Stephen Arnold and Douglas Tigert found that, compared to Canadians, Americans are more opposed to big government and less likely to believe that government should guarantee everyone an income (see Table 5). They also reported that Americans are more likely than Canadians to take part in voluntary communitarian activities which, according to the authors, contradicts my assumption that Canadians are more collectivity oriented (Arnold and Tigert, 1974: 80–81). However, I would argue that the findings support this contention, since they demonstrate that Americans are more likely to take part in voluntary activity to achieve particular goals, while Canadians are more disposed to rely on the state.[18] And in fact, a subsequent article by Stephen Arnold and James Barnes dealing with the same findings concluded: 'Americans were found to be individualistic, whereas Canadians were more collectively oriented', more supportive of state provision of medical care or a guaranteed minimum income (Arnold and Barnes, 1979: 32).

The existence of an electorally viable social-democratic party, the New Democrats (NDP), in Canada, has been taken by various writers as an outgrowth of the greater influence of the Tory statist tradition and the stronger collectivity orientation north of the border. Conversely, the absence of a significant socialist movement to the south is explained in part by the vitality of the anti-statist and individualist values in the United States. There is, of course, good reason to believe, as Louis Hartz, Gad Horowitz, and I, among others, have argued, that social democratic movements are the other side of statist conservatism, that Tories and socialists are likely to be found in the same polity, while a dominant Lockean liberal tradition inhibits the emergence of socialism as a political force (see Hartz, 1955; 1964: 1–48; Horowitz, 1968: 3–57; Lipset, 1977: 79–83; 1983: 52–3). The emergence of a socialist movement advocating increased government intervention and ownership is much less disharmonious in conservative societies than it is in liberal ones.

The thesis that a Tory statist tradition is conducive to the emergence of socialist movements has been criticized on the grounds that socialist parties have been weakest in the most traditional parts of Canada, Quebec and the Maritimes (see Brym, 1984: 34–5). However, two Canadian political scientists, William Christian and Colin Campbell, see the recent rise to power in Quebec of a social democratic movement, the Parti Québécois, as reflecting the propensity for a leftist collectivism inherent in Canadian élitist values, that can appear only after the bulwarks of the traditional system break down. They conclude that the emergence of socialism

> in Quebec in reaction to the incursions of liberalism and capitalism is hardly surprising from a Hartzean viewpoint, for ... Quebec's stock of political ideas includes a strong collectivist element. This collectivism is deeply embedded in Quebec's institutions: from the earliest days of New France, the government actively intervened on a broad scale in economic affairs ... The church, by its nature a collectivist institution, has long encouraged community enterprise ... Quebec's collectivist past provided receptive and fruitful soil for socialist ideas once the invasion of liberal capitalism had broken the monopoly of the old conservative ideology ... (Christian and Campbell, 1983: 35–6)

However, there are other plausible explanations for the difference in the political party systems of Canada and the United States which suggest that the contrast in socialist strength should not be relied on as evidence of varying predispositions among the two populations. As I noted in an article on 'Radicalism in North America', one of the main factors differentiating the United States from Canada and most other democratic countries has been its system of direct election of the President. In America, the nation is effectively one constituency and the electorate is led to see votes for anyone other than the two major candidates as effectively wasted. Seemingly, the American constitutional system serves to inhibit, if not to prevent, electorally viable third parties, and has produced a concealed multi-party or multi-factional system, operating within the two major parties, while the Canadian focus on constituency contests is more conducive to viable third, and even fourth, parties (Lipset, 1976: 36–52).[19] And many, such as Michael Harrington, former national chairman of the Socialist Party of the U S, have argued that there is a social democratic faction in America that largely operates within the Democratic Party (Harrington, 1972: 250–69).[20]

Evidence, independent of the effect of diverse electoral systems, that the forces making for class consciousness and organization, linked to collectivity orientations, are more powerful in Canada than the United States may be found in trade union membership statistics. Canada not only has had much stronger socialist parties than America since the 1930s, but workers in the northern country are now much more heavily involved in unions than those in the south. By 1984, only 18 per cent of the non-agricultural labor force in the United States belonged to labor organizations compared to almost 40 per cent in Canada (Troy and Sheflin, 1985; Department of Labour, Canada, 1984: Table 1).[21] In the United States, the percentage organized in unions has fallen steadily from a high point of 32.5 in 1954, while in Canada the figure has moved up from 22. Organized labor in Canada surpassed that in the United States in 1973. In harmony with the opinion poll evidence that francophones are more collectivity oriented than anglophones, a larger proportion of workers in Quebec belong to unions than in the rest of the country.

To explain these changes and variations would go beyond the scope of this paper. It may be suggested, however, that the long post-war prosperity refurbished the anti-statist and individualistic values of the United States, undermined in the thirties and forties, while in Canada, which did not emphasize these values to the same degree, economic growth reinforced class and collectivity orientations (Lipset, 1986). Certainly, the successful campaign conducted by Brian Mulroney and the Progressive Conservatives in 1984 continued to emphasize the Tory welfare tradition, while anti-statist conservatism (Lockean liberalism) has been strengthened in Reaganite America.

Notes

1. My initial treatment of this subject was presented in Lipset (1963: ch. 7). The arguments presented there were elaborated in Lipset (1965: 21–64). This article was subsequently updated and incorporated as a chapter in Lipset (1970: 37–75). The page references to the article here are to the 1970 edition, which has the widest circulation of the three. The current article is both an extension on the theoretical level and a condensation of the empirical content of a recent analysis (Lipset, 1985: 109–60).

2. For a review of propositions in the literature see Arnold and Barnes (1979: esp. 3–6). See also Vallee and Whyte (1971: 556–75, esp. 559–64) and Archibald (1978: 231–41).

3. Northrop Frye notes that English Canada should be 'thought of . . . as a country that grew out of a Tory opposition to the Whig victory in the American Revolution . . . [Quebec reacted against] the French Revolution with its strongly anti-clerical bias. The clergy remained the ideologically dominant group in Quebec down to a generation ago, and the clergy wanted no part of the French Revolution or anything it stood for' (Frye, 1982: 66). For a discussion of Canada's three founding nationalities, the English, the French and the Scots (those who settled in Nova Scotia were Jacobites) as defeated peoples, see MacLennan (1977: 30).

4. Hartz, however, does note that English Canada is 'etched with a Tory streak coming out of the American Revolution' (Hartz, 1964: 34).

5. The so-called Laurentian thesis advanced by some economic historians suggests that without state intervention and economic links in Europe, Canada could not have survived as a separate country (see Innis, 1956).

6. For a comparable report by a historian of the 1930s in Canada see Neatby (1972: 10–14).

7. As Edmund Burke noted in his speech to Parliament trying to explain the motives and behavior of the American colonists at the time of the revolution, their religious beliefs made them the Protestants of Protestantism, the dissenters of dissent, the individualists *par excellence* (Burke, 1904: 180–81). Sociologists of religion have also noted that variations in theology (the fostering of individualism by the sects compared to an organic collectivity relationship nurtured by the churches) have affected the values and institutions of the two countries (see Lipset, 1979: 159–69).

8. See CARA (1983). The percentages for the United States are based on 1,729 respondents; for English-speaking Canadians, 913 respondents; and for French-speaking Canadians, 338 respondents.

9. These models are taken from the work of Packer (1964).

10. Data from the Roper Center, Storrs, Connecticut. A comparison of the attitudes of a sample of the public in Calgary in 1975 with those in Seattle in 1973 also indicate more positive attitudes towards police in Canada than in the United States (Klein, Webb, and DiSanto, 1978: 441–56).

11. The level of handgun ownership in Canada has been 'about one fifth that of the United States' (Thomas, 1983: 6).

12. Analysis of the 1975 Canadian data at the Roper Center revealed no difference in the attitudes of the two Canadian linguistic groups on this issue.

13. As economist Peter Karl Kresl puts it: 'Canadians have been described as a nation of ''satisficers''. By this it is meant that economic decision makers tend to be content with a pace

of economic activity and a degree of efficiency that is not the maximum possible but is rather one that is ''adequate'', or that suffices . . . Hand in hand with this is . . . the frequently observed lack of aggressiveness and competence on the part of much of Canadian industrial leadership' (Kresl, 1982: 240).

14. Canadian novelist Mordecai Richler has bemoaned Canada's lack of 'an indigenous buccaneering capitalist class', suggesting that Canadians have been 'timorous . . . circumspect investors in insurance and trust companies' (Richler, 1975: 32; see also Friedenberg, 1980: 142).

15. As summarized in Hiller (1976: 144). John Crispo also notes the 'propensity among Canadians to invest more abroad' (Crispo, 1979: 28; Kresl, 1982: 240–41).

16. Data computed at my request from Gallup studies in files at the Roper Center, Storrs, Connecticut.

17. The source is the Organization for Economic Cooperation and Development.

18. The CARA studies document that Americans are much more likely to belong to voluntary associations than Canadians. These results differ from those reported by James Curtis, who found little difference when he compared the data of two national surveys. See Curtis (1971: 874).

19. The argument that the difference in the voting strength of socialism is largely a function of the varying electoral systems has been challenged by Robert Kudrle and Theodore Marmor. They emphasize that the Canadian labor movement 'is more socialist than is the U.S. labor movement and always has been' and conclude that 'a real but unknown part' of the greater strength of the social democratic New Democratic Party, as compared to that received by American socialists, 'may be reflecting a different underlying distribution of values from the United States' (Kudrle and Marmor, 1981: 112; see also Rosenstone, Behr, and Lazarus, 1984).

20. Norman Thomas, the six-time candidate of the Socialist Party for President also came to believe that the electoral system negated efforts to create a third party, that socialists should work within the major parties (Harrington, 1972: 262).

21. In both countries, unions are much stronger in the public sector than in the private one. See also Rose and Chaison (1985: 97–111).

References

Aitken, H. G. J., 'Defensive expansionism: the state and economic growth in Canada', in H. G. J. Aitken (ed.), *The State and Economic Growth*, pp. 79–114, New York: Social Science Research Council, 1959.

Archibald, W. Peter, *Social Psychology as Political Economy*, Toronto: McGraw-Hill Ryerson, 1978.

Arnold, Stephen J. and James G. Barnes, 'Canadian and American national character as a basis for market segmentation', in J. Sheth (ed.), *Research in Marketing*, Vol. 2, pp. 1–35, Greenwich, Conn: JAI Press, 1979.

Arnold, Stephen J. and Douglas J. Tigert, 'Canadians and Americans: a comparative analysis', *International Journal of Comparative Sociology* 15 (March–June) 1974, 68–83.

Atwood, Margaret, *Survival: A Thematic Guide to Canadian Literature*, Toronto: Anansi Press, 1972.

— *Second Words: Selected Critical Prose*, Boston: Beacon Press, 1984.

Beer, Samuel, 'The modernization of American federalism', *Publius: The Journal of Federalism*, 3 (Fall) 1973, 49–95.

Bell, David and Lorne Tepperman, *The Roots of Disunity: A Look at Canadian Political Culture*, Toronto: McClelland and Stewart, Ltd, 1979.

Bercovitch, Sacvan, 'The rites of assent: rhetoric, ritual and the ideology of American consensus', in Sam B. Girgus (ed.), *The American Self: Myth, Ideology and Popular Culture*, pp. 5–42, Albuquerque: University of New Mexico Press, 1981.

Bissell, Claude, 'The place of learning and the arts in Canadian life', in Richard A. Preston (ed.), *Perspectives on Revolution and Evolution*, pp. 180–212, Durham, N.C.: Duke University Press, 1979.

Bourgault, Pierre L., *Innovation and the Structure of Canadian Industry*, Ottawa: Information Canada, Science Council of Canada, 1972.

Brown, J. J., *Ideas in Exile, a History of Canadian Invention*, Toronto: McClelland and Stewart, 1967.

Brown, Russell M., 'Telemachus and Oedipus: images of tradition and authority in Canadian and American fiction', Department of English, University of Toronto, n.d.

Bruckberger, R. L., 'The American Catholics as a minority', in Thomas T. McAvoy (ed.), *Roman Catholicism and the American Way of Life*, pp. 40–48, Notre Dame, Ind.: University of Notre Dame Press, 1960.

Bryce, James, *Modern Democracies*, Vol. 1, New York: Macmillan, 1921.

Brym, Robert J., 'Social movements and third parties', in S. D. Berkowitz (ed.), *Models and Myths in Canadian Sociology*, pp. 29–49, Toronto: Butterworth, 1984.

Burke, Edmund, *Selected Works*, Oxford: Clarendon Press, 1904.

Callwood, June, *Portrait of Canada*, Garden City, N.Y.: Doubleday and Co., 1981.

Campbell, Colin and George J. Szablowski, *The Superbureaucrats: Structure and Behaviour in Central Agencies*, Toronto: Macmillan of Canada, 1979.

Careless, J. M. S., *Canada: A Story of Challenge*, Cambridge: Cambridge University Press, 1963.

Center for Applied Research in the Apostolate, *Values Study of Canada*, code book, Washington, DC, May 1983.

Chandler, Marsha A., 'The politics of public enterprise', in J. Robert S. Prichard (ed.), *Crown Corporations in Canada*, pp. 185–218, Toronto: Butterworth, 1983.

Christian, William and Colin Campbell, *Political Parties and Ideologies in Canada*, 2nd edn, Toronto: McGraw-Hill Ryerson, 1983.

Clark, S. D., in H. F. Angus (ed.), *Canada and Her Great Neighbor: Sociological Surveys of Opinions and Attitudes in Canada Concerning the United States*, Toronto: The Ryerson Press, 1938.

— *Church and Sect in Canada*, Toronto: University of Toronto Press, 1948.

— 'The Canadian community', in George W. Brown (ed.), *Canada*, pp. 375–89, Berkeley: University of California Press, 1950.

— *The Developing Canadian Community*, Toronto: University of Toronto Press, 1962.

Clement, Wallace, *Continental Corporate Power*, Toronto: McClelland and Stewart, 1977.

Crispo, John, *Mandate for Canada*, Don Mills, Ontario: General Publishing Co., 1979.

Curtis, James, 'Voluntary association joining: a cross-national comparative note', *American Sociological Review* 36 (October) 1971, 872–80.

Davis, Arthur K., 'Canadian society and history as hinterland versus metropolis', in Richard J. Ossenberg (ed.), *Canadian Society: Pluralism, Change and Conflict*, pp. 6–32, Scarborough, Ontario: Prentice-Hall, 1971.

Department of Labour, *Information*, Ottawa, 26 June 1984.

Engels, Friedrich, 'Engels to Sorge', 8 February 1890, in Karl Marx and Friedrich Engels, *Selected Correspondence*, pp. 466–8, New York: International Publishers, 1942.

— 'Engels to Sorge', 10 September 1888, in Karl Marx and Friedrich Engels, *Letters to Americans*, pp. 203–4, New York: International Publishers, 1953.

Esman, Milton J., 'Federalism and modernization: Canada and the United States', *Publius: The Journal of Federalism* 14 (Winter) 1984, 21–38.

Friedenberg, Edgar Z., *Deference to Authority*, White Plains, N.Y.: M. E. Sharpe, Inc., 1980.

Frye, Northrop, 'Letters in Canada: 1952. Part I: publications in English', *The University of Toronto Quarterly*, 22 (April) 1953, 269–80.

— *Divisions on a Ground: Essays on Canadian Culture*, Toronto: Anansi, 1982.

Gibbins, Roger, *Regionalism: Territorial Politics in Canada and the United States*, Toronto: Butterworth, 1982.

Glazer, Nathan and Daniel P. Moynihan, 'Introduction', in Nathan Glazer and Daniel P. Moynihan (eds.), *Ethnicity: Theory and Experience*, pp. 1–26, Cambridge: Harvard University Press, 1975.

Glazier, Kenneth M., 'Canadian investment in the United States: ''Putting your money where your mouth is'' ', *Journal of Contemporary Business* 1 (Autumn) 1972, 61–6.

Grant, John Webster, ' ''At least you knew where you stood with them'': Reflections on religious pluralism in Canada and the United States', *Studies in Religion* 2 (Spring) 1973, 340–51.

Griffiths, Curt T., John F. Klein and Simon N. Verdun-Jones, *Criminal Justice in Canada*, Scarborough, Ontario: Butterworth, 1980.

Hagan, John and Jeffrey Leon, 'Philosophy and sociology of crime control', in Harry M. Johnson (ed.), *Social System and Legal Process*, pp. 181–208, San Francisco: Jossey-Bass, 1978.

Hardin, Herschel, *A Nation Unaware: The Canadian Economic Culture*, Vancouver: J. J. Douglas, 1974.

Harrington, Michael, *Socialism*, New York: Saturday Review Press, 1972.

Hartz, Louis, *The Liberal Tradition in America*, New York: Harcourt, Brace, 1955.

— *The Founding of New Societies*, New York: Harcourt, Brace, and World, 1964.

Hastings, Elizabeth H. and Philip K. Hastings (eds.), *Index to International Public Opinion, 1980–1981*, Westport, Conn.: Greenwood Press, 1982.

Hiller, Harry H., *Canadian Society: A Sociological Analysis*, Scarborough, Ontario: Prentice-Hall of Canada, Ltd, 1976.

Hofstede, Geert, *Culture's Consequences: International Differences in Work-Related Values*, Beverly Hills: Sage Publications, 1984.

Horowitz, Gad, *Canadian Labour in Politics*, Toronto: University of Toronto Press, 1968.

Horowitz, Irving Louis, 'The hemispheric connection: A critique and corrective to the entrepreneurial thesis of development with special emphasis on the Canadian case', *Queen's Quarterly* 80 (Autumn) 1973, 327–59.

Hueglin, Thomas O., 'The end of institutional tidiness? Trends of late federalism in the United States and Canada', Kingston, Ont.: Department of Political Science, Queen's University, 1984.

Innis, Harold A., *Essays in Canadian History*, Toronto: University of Toronto Press, 1956.

Kendall, John C., 'A Canadian construction of reality: northern images of the United States', *The American Review of Canadian Studies* 4 (Spring) 1974, 20–36.

Klein, John F., Jim R. Webb and J. E. DiSanto, 'Experience with police and attitudes towards the police', *Canadian Journal of Sociology* 3(4) 1978, 441–56.

Kresl, Peter Karl, 'An economics perspective: Canada in the international economy', in William Metcalf (ed.), *Understanding Canada*, pp. 227–95, New York: New York University Press, 1982.

Kudrle, Robert T. and Theodore R. Marmor, 'The development of welfare states in North America', in Peter Flora and Arnold J. Heidenheimer (eds.), *The Development of Welfare States in Europe and America*, pp. 81–121, New Brunswick, N.J.: Transaction Books, 1981.

Lipset, Seymour Martin, 'Democracy in Alberta', *The Canadian Forum* 34 (November, December) 1954, 175–7, 196–8.

— 'Revolution and counterrevolution: the United States and Canada', in Thomas R. Ford (ed.), *The Revolutionary Theme in Contemporary America*, pp. 21–64, Lexington: University of Kentucky Press, 1965.

— *Revolution and Counterrevolution*, revised paperback edition, Garden City, N.Y.: Anchor Books, 1970 [New York: Basic Books, 1968].

— 'Radicalism in North America: a comparative view of the party systems in Canada and the United States', *Transactions of the Royal Society of Canada* 14 (Fourth Series) 1976, 19–55.

— 'Why no socialism in the United States?', in S. Bialer and S. Sluzar (eds.), *Sources of Contemporary Radicalism*, Vol. 1, pp. 31–149, Boulder, Colorado: Westview Press, 1977.

— 'Value differences, absolute or relative: the English speaking democracies', in *The First New Nation: The United States in Historical and Comparative Perspective*, pp. 248–73, expanded paperback edition, New York: W. W. Norton, 1979 [New York: Basic Books, 1963].

— 'Socialism in America', in P. Kurtz (ed.), *Sidney Hook: Philosopher of Democracy and Humanism*, pp. 47–63, Buffalo, N.Y.: Prometheus Books, 1983.

— 'Canada and the United States: the cultural dimension', in Charles F. Doran and John H. Sigler (eds.), *Canada and the United States: Enduring Friendship, Persistent Stress*, pp. 109–60, Englewood Cliffs, N.J.: Prentice-Hall, Inc., 1985.

— 'North American labor movements: a comparative perspective', in Seymour Martin Lipset (ed.), *Unions in Transition: Entering the Second Century*, San Francisco: Institute for Contemporary Studies, 1986.

MacLennan, Hugh, 'A society in revolt', in Judith Webster (ed.), *Voices of Canada: An Introduction to Canadian Culture*, pp. 29–30, Burlington, Vt.: Association for Canadian Studies in the United States, 1977.

Manzer, R., *Canada: A Socio-Political Report*, Toronto: McGraw-Hill Ryerson, 1974.

Matthews, Ralph, 'Regional differences in Canada: social versus economic interpretations', in Dennis Forcese and Stephen Richer (eds.), *Social Issues: Sociological Views of Canada*, pp. 82–123, Scarborough, Ontario: Prentice-Hall, 1982.

McDougall, Robert L., 'The dodo and the cruising auk', *Canadian Literature* 18 (Autumn) 1963, 6–20.

McInnis, Edgar W., *The Unguarded Frontier*, Garden City, N.Y.: Doubleday, Doran & Co., 1942.

McKercher, William R., *The U.S. Bill of Rights and the Canadian Charter of Rights and Freedoms*, Toronto: Ontario Economic Council, 1983.

McLeod, J. T., 'The free enterprise dodo is no phoenix', *Canadian Forum* 56 (August) 1976, 6–13.

McMillan, Charles J., 'The changing competitive environment of Canadian business', *Journal of Canadian Studies* 13 (Spring) 1978, 38–48.

McNaught, Kenneth, 'Political trials and the Canadian political tradition', in Martin L. Friedland (ed.), *Courts and Trials: A Multidisciplinary Approach*, pp. 137–61, Toronto: University of Toronto Press, 1975.

— 'Approaches to the study of Canadian history', *The (Japanese) Annual Review of Canadian Studies* 5, 1984, 89–102.

McWhinney, Edward, *Canada and the Constitution, 1979–1982*, Toronto: University of Toronto Press, 1982.

Mercer, John and Michael Goldberg, 'Value differences and their meaning for urban development in the U.S.A.', Working Paper No. 12, UBC Research in Land Economics, Vancouver, B.C.: Faculty of Commerce, University of British Columbia, 1982.

Merton, Robert K., *Social Theory and Social Structure*, Glencoe, Ill.: The Free Press, 1957.

Michalos, Alex C., *North American Social Report: A Comparative Study of the Quality of Life in Canada and the USA from 1964 to 1974*, Vol. 2, Dordrecht, Holland: D. Reidel Publishing Co., 1980.

Neatby, H. Blair, *The Politics of Chaos: Canada in the Thirties*, Toronto: Macmillan of Canada, 1972.

Nelles, H. V., 'Defensive expansionism revisited: federalism, the state and economic nationalism in Canada, 1959–1979', *The (Japanese) Annual Review of Canadian Studies* 2, 1980, 127–45.

O'Toole, Roger, 'Some good purpose: Notes on religion and political culture in Canada', *Annual Review of the Social Sciences of Religion*, Vol. 6, pp. 177–217, The Hague: Mouton, 1982.

Packer, Herbert, 'Two models of the criminal process', *University of Pennsylvania Law Review* 113 (November) 1964, 1–68.

Porter, John, *The Measure of Canadian Society: Education, Equality and Opportunity*, Agincourt, Ontario: Gage Publishing, 1979.

Presthus, Robert, *Elite Accommodation in Canadian Politics*, Cambridge: Cambridge University Press, 1973.

— *Elites in the Policy Process*, Toronto: Macmillan of Canada, 1974.

— 'Aspects of political culture and legislative behavior: United States and Canada', in Robert Presthus (ed.), *Cross-National Perspectives: United States and Canada*, pp. 7–22, Leiden: E. J. Brill, 1977.

Presthus, Robert and William V. Monopoli, 'Bureaucracy in the United States and Canada: social, attitudinal and behavioral variables', in Robert Presthus (ed.), *Cross-National Perspectives: United States and Canada*, pp. 176–90, Leiden: E. J. Brill, 1977.

Pye, A. Kenneth, 'The rights of persons accused of crime under the Canadian Constitution: a comparative perspective', *Law and Contemporary Problems* 45 (Autumn) 1982, 221–48.

Richler, Mordecai, 'Letter from Ottawa: The sorry state of Canadian nationalism', *Harper's* 250 (June) 1975, 28–32.

Rose, Joseph B. and Gary N. Chaison, 'The state of the unions: United States and Canada', *Journal of Labor Research* 6 (Winter) 1985, 97–111.

Rosenstone, Steven J., Roy L. Behr and Edward H. Lazarus, *Third Parties in America: Citizen Response to Major Party Failure*, Princeton, N.J.: Princeton University Press, 1984.

Royal Commission on Bilingualism and Biculturalism, *Report*, Book 4, *The Cultural Contribution of the Other Ethnic Groups*, Ottawa: Queen's Printer, 1969.

Safarian, A. E., *The Performance of Foreign-Owned Firms in Canada*, Washington, D.C.: National Planning Association, 1969.

Schoenfeld, Stuart, 'The Jewish religion in North America: Canadian and American comparisons', *Canadian Journal of Sociology* 3(2) 1978, 209–31.

Schwartz, Mildred A., *Politics and Territory: The Sociology of Regional Persistence in Canada*, Montreal: McGill-Queen's University Press, 1974.

Science Council of Canada, 'Innovation in a cold climate: "impediments to innovation" ', in Abraham Rotstein and Gary Lax (eds.), *Independence: The Canadian Challenge*, pp. 120–31, Toronto: The Committee for an Independent Canada, 1972.

Smiley, Donald V., 'Public sector politics, modernization and federalism: the Canadian and American experiences', *Publius: The Journal of Federalism* 14 (Winter) 1984, 52–9.

Smith, A. J. M., 'Evolution and revolution as aspects of English-Canadian and American literature', in Richard A. Preston (ed.), *Perspectives on Evolution and Revolution*, Durham, N.C.: Duke University Press, 1979.

Smith, Denis, *Bleeding Hearts . . . Bleeding Country: Canada and the Quebec Crisis*, Edmonton: M. G. Hurtig, 1971.

Statistical Abstract of the U.S. 1982–83, 103rd edition.

Sutherland, Ronald, *The New Hero: Essays in Comparative Quebec/Canadian Literature*, Toronto: Macmillan of Canada, 1977.

— 'A literary perspective: the development of a national consciousness', in William Metcalfe (ed.), *Understanding Canada*, pp. 401–14, New York: New York University Press, 1982.

Swinton, Katherine, 'Judicial policy making: American and Canadian perspectives', *The Canadian Review of American Studies* 10 (Spring) 1979, 89–94.

Tarrow, Sidney, 'Introduction' in Sidney Tarrow, Peter J. Katzenstein and Luigi Graziano (eds.), *Territorial Politics in Industrial Nations*, New York: Praeger, 1978.

Taylor, Charles Lewis and David A. Jodice, *World Handbook of Political and Social Indicators*, Vol. 2, 3rd edn, New Haven: Yale University Press, 1983.

Tepperman, Lorne, *Crime Control: The Urge Toward Authority*, Toronto: McGraw-Hill Ryerson, 1977.

Thomas, Ted E., 'The gun control issue: a sociological analysis of United States and Canadian attitudes and policies', Oakland, California: Department of Sociology, Mills College, 1983.

Tocqueville, Alexis de, *Democracy in America*, Vol. 1, New York: Vintage Books, 1945.

Troy, Leo and Leo Sheflin, *Union Sourcebook*, West Orange, N.J.: IRDIS Publishers, 1985.

Underhill, Frank, *In Search of Canadian Liberalism*, Toronto: The Macmillan Company of Canada, 1960.

UNESCO, *Statistical Yearbook, 1982*, Paris: UNESCO, 1982.

United Nations, *World Economic Survey, 1983* (supplement), New York: United Nations, 1983.

US Arms Control and Disarmament Agency, *World Military Expenditures and Arms Transfers 1971–1980*, Washington, DC, 1982.

US News and World Report, 'How big is government's bite?', 27 August 1984, 65.

Vallee, Frank G. and Donald R. Whyte (eds.), *Canadian Society: Sociological Perspectives*, 3rd edn, Toronto: Macmillan of Canada, 1971.

Weaver, John Charles, 'Imperilled dreams: Canadian opposition to the American Empire, 1918–1930', Ph.D. dissertation, Department of History, Duke University, 1973.

Weber, Max, *The Methodology of the Social Sciences*, Glencoe, Ill.: The Free Press, 1949.

Weller, Geoffrey R., 'Common problems, alternative solutions: a comparison of the Canadian and American health systems', Thunder Bay, Ont.: Department of Political Science, Lakehead University, 1984.

Westhues, Kenneth, 'Stars and Stripes, the Maple Leaf, and the Papal Coat of Arms', *Canadian Journal of Sociology* 3(1) 1978, 245–61.

Westin, Alan F., 'The United States Bill of Rights and the Canadian Charter: A socio-political analysis', in William R. McKercher (ed.), *The U.S. Bill of Rights and the Canadian Charter of Rights and Freedoms*, pp. 27–44, Toronto: Ontario Economic Council, 1983.

Whyte, John D., 'Civil liberties and the courts', *Queen's Quarterly* 83 (Winter) 1976, 655–63.

World Bank, *World Development Report 1983*, New York: Oxford University Press, 1983.

3

The Latins: Southern Europe and South America

France

The Nature of Work Relations

Jean-Louis Barsoux and Peter Lawrence

Chapter 5, pp. 76 – 88 in Jean-Louis Barsoux and Peter Lawrence, *Management in France* (London: Cassell, 1990)

'C'est sûr qu'à l'égard des rapports de travail les Français sont plutôt constipés.' ('There's no doubt that in terms of work relations, the French are not particularly at ease.')

Conversation with Pierre Salbaing, Vice-President,
Conseil d'Administration, L'Air Liquide

This chapter takes its cue from the seminal work of Michel Crozier on work relations in a bureaucratic context in France. Crozier identified a number of themes which he believed characterized French organizational interaction, notably the isolation of the individual, the avoidance of face-to-face relationships, the compartmentalization of the organization, the struggle for privileges and the lack of constructive solidarity. The aim here is to put our view side by side with that documented so well by Crozier in the 1960s.

Impersonal

Our immediate impression of the ambience of the traditional French office is that it is less chummy and relaxed than the equivalent in Britain or the USA. An obvious manifestation is the relative absence of joking around (ribbing, running jokes, self-deprecation), probably because humour exposes one's personality. Or again, 'slouching' (sitting on or putting one's feet up on desks) is uncommon. Interestingly, the only French manager we saw who actually provided evidence to the contrary was a trainee store manager at Carrefour, who happened to be an English expatriate and readily rested his feet on the nearest available surface. This theme of non-verbal expression is explored in much detail by the American sociologist Lawrence Wylie, who maintains that the French are far more upright in their posture and controlled in their movements than the Americans:

> The French have a sense of vulnerability about their bodies that is greater than that of Americans who are less worried about their body boundaries. (Santoni, 1981, 38)

Social interaction in France makes a clear distinction between personal and professional relations. The role played in the office can easily be kept distinct from the person occupying the role through the use of a battery of props. [. . .] French *cadres* can exhibit astonishing awareness of their own 'split personality'. For instance, one production manager explained his actions to us by saying, '*qu'est-ce que vous voulez, je suis bête et discipliné – je fais ce qu'on me dit*' ('What do you expect? I'm well disciplined but unthinking – I do as I'm told'). In this assertion the *cadre* was demonstrating an ability to pull away from, and judge, his professional actions. An even more striking example of this distinction between the individual and his function was provided by Lawrence Wylie who quotes Montaigne's approach: '*Montaigne et le maire de Bordeaux sont deux*' ('Montaigne and the mayor of Bordeaux are separate') – which provided convenient justification for his leaving Bordeaux at the time of the plague (in Santoni, 1981, 61).

The notion of impersonality is developed by Desmond Graves, who suggests that the French tend to regard authority as residing in the role not the person. According to Graves, it is by the power of his position that a French manager gets things done (what Chester Barnard termed structural authority). This is in contrast to the Anglo-Saxon view that authority is vested in the person (personal, charismatic or moral authority). The distinction between the two cultures implies that a Frenchman will accept responsibility so long as it is attached to his role but will not actively seek responsibility, as a British manager might, for it adds nothing to his stature. As Graves puts it:

> He is '*le responsable*' – but not, as in our culture, 'the person responsible'. (1973, 293)

This counterposing helps to explain the paradox that the French are critical of orders but willing to accept big power differences.

The desire to keep function and personality separate has repercussions upon the nature of social contact. It is not possible to reconcile cordial relations and formal (as opposed to personal) authority. Consequently, office colleagues do not often try to meet each other socially, and there are few signs of fraternization between staff of differing grades. This is corroborated by Renaud Sainsaulieu who states:

> *En ce qui concerne les relations interpersonnelles d'amitié, elles sont assez faibles et fragiles, en ce sens qu'elles ne débordent pas les limites des catégories formelles des rangs et des statuts officiels.* (Interpersonal friendship ties are fairly weak in so far as they rarely transcend the formal boundaries of rank and status.) (1977, 245)

It is noteworthy that even in the more homely environment of a firm *à dimension humaine* (of human proportions) that we visited, the boss still insisted his staff call him *Monsieur*.

This low-level social openness finds spatial expression in the office layout where personal space seems to be a matter of some importance. Open-plan offices are scarce at *cadre* level and can cause quite a stir if they are imposed. Again the only exception encountered was an American subsidiary whose corporate culture is based on egalitarianism, an integral part of this being the total absence of personal offices. The French like to have a 'territory' to call their own – and the impregnability of the sanctuary tends to increase with organizational status. Three of the PDGs (CEOs) observed had soundproofed doors, great unwieldy things which were almost permanently closed and which simply encouraged people to seek access via the secretary's office. At lower levels glass partitions tended to be blocked out with posters and doors were generally closed – and one maintenance manager even had a spring-loaded door which shut automatically. Such clues tend to indicate low emphasis on dialogue, teamwork, confrontation of opinions as well as a negative view of conflict.

Formal

The pattern of interpersonal relations is formal. The French seem to adhere to a classical conception of management which favours work in isolation, punctuated by formal meetings. Such an approach restricts exchanges to a highly codified framework which precludes the need for personal involvement. This is in contrast, say, to the American approach, highlighted by Kotter (1982, 88) which is more interactive and unstructured.

A number of *cadres* in the sample commented on their preference for getting things done through formal meetings. One PDG (CEO) went as far as to say, '*c'est la seule façon de faire avancer les choses*' ('it's the only way to accomplish anything'). Meetings were seen as an opportunity to bring conflicts to a head ('déclencher l'orage' – 'to start the storm') or to obtain firm commitments from individuals thanks to peer group pressure. Meetings also constitute an economy of effort in that they allow information to be given quickly and clearly – particularly messages which are not transmissible in an office or casually.

There is therefore a case for suggesting that the French *cadre* is a meeting specialist, in much the same way as his Anglo-Saxon counterpart might be considered an adept troubleshooter. Certainly, meetings provide the *cadre* with a stage on which to display his oratory skill. The whole event is a sort of microcosm of organizational life where status can be enhanced by skilful advocacy and stylish expression or lost by poor eloquence. The agenda is known in advance as are the people attending and the proceedings are formalized – this reduces uncertainty and provides a perfect occasion for furthering personal aims or doing down opponents.

In some companies, there were complaints that the number of meetings was in fact becoming excessive – these companies were deemed to be suffering from *la réunionite* (meeting-itis). One PDG (CEO), whose American MBA gave him different terms of reference, posited that meetings were in fact status-lenders since they reduced access to the person in question. There were also hints that meetings were a means of self-justification – as one *cadre* explained, '*ça meuble une journée*' ('it fills up the day'). In this respect, meetings are comfortingly tangible and make what one has done at the end of the day easy to recall. This view of meetings as showy rather than functional was put more forcefully by a cynical production manager who revealed, '*parfois on parle pour le compte rendu*' ('sometimes we talk in order to have something to record in the minutes'). In such cases the importance of the meeting may lie elsewhere, for instance in terms of who has not been invited.

Another sign of the attachment to classical principles can be seen in the continued distinction between thinkers and executors. Corroboration of the lingering influence of Taylorism is perhaps seen in the way the French have embraced quality circles and discussion groups – working groups outside the normal hierarchical channels. The alleged intention of these new means of participation was to tap the resources of the entire personnel. Unfortunately, these groups have not provided the anticipated antidote – they have reinforced existing hierarchical relationships rather than opened up the way for wider involvement. Instead of using these informal work groups to designate their own spokesmen, many companies have imposed hierarchical heads – thus, underlining from the start a lack of faith in the personnel to elect sensible leaders and the fear that it would give rise to *une hiérarchie parallèle* which might undermine the so-called *hiérarchie naturelle* (chosen by the laws of nature?).

Furthermore, management still appears unconvinced by the capacity of those at the base to think for themselves. The entire management group at one company we visited attended an exposé on quality circles. The organizer started by detailing a handful of 'irrefutable' principles, along the lines 'we can improve productivity if we increase worker commitment'. When he reached the principle about each worker being an expert in his own work, the meeting hit a sticking point. A protracted discussion ensued about the validity of the statement, and the outcome was a redefinition which did away with the word 'expert'. What is more, this could not be dismissed as a one-off case of linguistic 'nit-picking'. It represented a serious lack of faith in worker aptitudes – something which was reiterated by the reaction to a subsequent statement: '*Il existe des reserves d'intelligence inemployées*' ('there are untapped intellectual seams'). Once again, the *cadres* felt they could not let the proposition pass unchallenged and suggested that '*intelligence*' be replaced by '*ressources*'.

Hierarchical

Thanks in part to the American scientific management practitioner, Frederick Taylor, the popular conception of an organization is that of a human pyramid, rather than, say, a well-oiled machine, a market or a beehive. This layered view of the organization can be seen in the nature of work contacts which are faithful reflectors of rank. For instance, one *cadre* explained that, as a rule, he would telephone a subordinate, but go and see a superior. Another manifestation of this desire to avoid contact with lesser mortals can be seen in the widespread use of secretaries to set up calls in other companies. In this way embarrassing rejections and lengthy explanations can be avoided. This practice is generally justified by the preciousness of the boss's time, though as one PDG (CEO) rightly pointed out, no sooner has he resumed work than his secretary will interrupt him. What is more, the use of an intervening filter to save time begins to look dubious when one considers the following exchange witnessed between a *cadre* and secretary:

'It's M. Dupont on the line.' – 'Not now, I'm busy.' – 'He says it's urgent – something to do with tomorrow's trip.' – 'What does he want to know?' – 'If M. Leroi will be coming along too.' – 'Tell him no!'

The duplication of effort together with the possible misinterpretation given the intervention of a third party makes the use of a secretarial barrier look less than necessary. But as one PDG (CEO) explained:

'*C'est pour les gens un peu péteux qui veulent se faire annoncer.*' ('It's for people who are a bit full of themselves.')

This keen sense of hierarchy militates against the mixing of various strata. For instance, the decision by a senior *cadre* we observed to take his son skiing on a works council holiday was greeted with much surprise by colleagues and subordinates alike. Such trips are theoretically for the benefit of all personnel but hitherto no senior managers had ever 'deigned' to mix with subordinates on such an intimate exercise.

Status consciousness was also visible at a company visited which refused to send senior and intermediary *cadres* on the same training courses. The logic behind that decision was that the benefits of training might be lost if the participants felt inhibited by the presence of superiors or subordinates – particularly in view of the potential loss of face which accompanies the learning situation.

In-house training can prove particularly disruptive with the trainers moving about between hierarchical levels and upsetting the established order. Computing is a notable example of an area which has thoroughly confused the neat 'intellectual/manual' boundary. Indeed, it has caused so much trouble that, as the head of a computing department explained to us, it was the subject of rare consensus among the departments:

'Ils peuvent tous se mettre d'accord pour dire du mal de l'informatique.' ('Slagging off computing is about the one thing they can all agree on.')

At a group level, status consciousness is made explicit by the collective designation of the management ensemble as *la hiérarchie*. It is a term which is borrowed from the bureaucratically organized hierarchy of the church. An example of its usage in business is:

'En France c'est l'appartenance à la hiérarchie qui légitime l'autorité de l'agent de maîtrise. Il commande parce qu'il a été choisi par la direction à cette fin, choix qui le distingue et l'éloigne des ouvriers.' (In France a first-line supervisor derives his authority by virtue of belonging to the management group. He gives the orders because he has been chosen to do so, a choice which sets him apart from the workers.) (*Revue Internationale du Travail,* January/February 1985, 1–16)

Segregation could also be seen in the existence at most companies of separate canteens for workers and management, common enough in Britain, of course, but unusual in Germany, Switzerland and Scandinavia. And even where there was a single dining-hall, it was not uncommon to see unofficial 'territories'. This 'intellectual apartheid' was sometimes cloaked in practical considerations – for instance, one company had a notice which designated one canteen for 'people in civilian clothes', the aim being to avoid mixing overalls and suits. Yet it transpired that production managers would change out of their overalls while secretaries would eat with the workers. Perhaps more striking was the fact that in the canteens people would generally eat in small groups rather than fill up tables with spare seats – again with very obvious layering by rank.

This awareness of hierarchy is reinforced by constant references to *la voie hiérarchique* (the formal chain of command). Individuals were discouraged from bypassing intermediary levels when communicating since it undermined the authority of intermediary levels and in some cases robbed them of their *raison d'être* (i.e. as information passers). Confirmation that French managers actually adhere to formal channels of communication is provided by Desmond Graves. He noted that the actual contacts of the French manager were very much in line with what one would expect after examining the organization chart. This, incidentally, was in stark contrast to British managers, who showed few qualms about breaching organizational protocol and whose 'patterns of communication bore no relation to the ''official'' organization chart' (1973, 296).

In France, circumventing is only permissible if the person who should have been informed does not hear – or else it constitutes a loss of face. This notion is confirmed by Boltanski (1987, 263 (Eng. trans.)), who maintains that one of the prime means of 'encouraging' a *cadre* to resign is to deprive him of information.

In effect, the hierarchy is as much supported from the base as it is maintained from the summit. Those on the bottom see emulation of those above as the only way up – so they mimic the attitudes of those at the top and unwittingly bolster the existing system. The notion of a professional pecking order permeates every stratum right down to the base. Even workers think in terms of more or less honourable professions. Skilled workers are referred to as *l'aristocratie ouvrière* (the manual aristocracy) in relation to unskilled workers. Thus, the workers are merely echoing the distinction higher up in the hierarchy between, say, graduate engineers in the noble speciality of electronics and graduate engineers in the 'common' field of mechanics.

Of course this stratification rests upon more than the historical distinction between what is 'noble' and what is not. The French researcher Marc Maurice drew particular attention to the qualification hierarchies and wage structure with the evocative '*grilles de classification*' ('classification matrices') which pit manual versus non-manual, skilled versus unskilled, supervisory versus non-supervisory and line versus staff *cadres* (Maurice *et al.*, 1986, 252).

Partitioned

Segregation within French firms is not merely vertical but also horizontal. This is perhaps a collective manifestation of the way individuals seek a personal 'territory'. There were numerous allusions to *le cloisonnement* (partitioning) at the firms visited. The clannish nature of interpersonal relations is partly due to the alumni of prestigious *grandes écoles* who tend to congregate in particular companies. But the practice is not restricted to the élite. Indeed, François de Closets names taxi drivers, bakers and pharmacists as three of the prime offenders in the perpetuation of *numerus clausus* (closed shops – 1982, 280). And Crozier supports this view when he says:

At all levels of society the French, once they gain entry into an influential group, instinctively try to keep others out. (1982, 26)

The French propensity for forming cliques was mentioned spontaneously by a number of interviewees. They alluded to *l'esprit de clan* (clannish mentality), *les chasses guardées* (preserves), *les petites bastilles* (small fortresses), *les querelles de chapelles* (warring factions), *les castes* (casts), *les fiefs* (feudal estates). The head of one small company in the survey explained how he was forced continually to reshuffle the personnel around the offices in order to break down cliques.

The essential function of the above-mentioned cliques is to protect and empower their members. It was noticeable, for instance, that once a right had been gained by a group, there was no way it could be abolished – it became *un droit acquis* (an acquired right). Two examples from our study involving bonus payments may serve to illustrate the point: one PDG (CEO) was trying to find a new appellation for a *prime de période de pointe* (a bonus for rush jobs) since the title no longer corresponded to reality. Another head was tackling a similar misnomer – *une prime qualitative* (a quality bonus) which had become institutionalized and had lost its exceptional nature. In both cases, suppressing the bonus was out of the question since it would be equated to a drop in salary. They had become acquired rights, and the only option was to rename them in order to show awareness of the situation.

So in spite of the much-vaunted egalitarianism associated with the French Revolution and the First French Republic, the French are deeply attached to the accumulation of privileges and distinctions which divide them. As René Reynaud put it:

L'attachement à l'égalité et la course auc privilèges. (A passion for equality and a race for distinction.) (Reynaud, 1982, 37)

Functional differentiation too is strong, as reflected by interdepartmental relations. The following complaints are culled from observation and interviews:

'*Le siège ne connaît pas nos problèmes.*' ('They don't understand our situation at head office.')

'La filiale cache tout et fait n'importe quoi.' ('They put up a smokescreen and do what they like at our subsidiary.')

'La production s'en fout.' ('Production doesn't give a damn.')

'Le personnel fait du social sans mesure.' ('The personnel department is obsessed with social considerations.')

'Les ventes ne pensent qu'à faire du volume.' ('The sales department only think about their sales figures.')

'Le marketing crée ses produits sans écouter l'avis du terrain.' ('Marketing doesn't pay a blind bit of notice to those in the field when it dreams up its products.')

These informal complaints are not all that different from what Keith Lockyer, for instance, identified in British industry (Lockyer and Jones, 1980). He established a sort of functional 'who hates whom' table which mapped out interdepartmental friction in British companies. What is surprising, then, is the apparent absence of corresponding French research into interfunctional conflict. The only real exception to this is probably the well-documented division between production and maintenance which Crozier first depicted in his classic study of a cigarette company (Crozier, 1964). More recently, Maurice *et al.* produced similar findings when comparing France and Germany. They quote a *cadre* who explains:

At informational meetings for all personnel you have to be very careful when you mention either maintenance or production, because you get the feeling that one false step can arouse two hostile armies. (1986, 264)

From the present research too, there were signs that the conflicting interests of the two departments have not yet been resolved – and with the gradual takeover by production of routine maintenance the situation was sometimes aggravated – '*chacun tire la couverture de son côté*' ('everyone's pulling the covers their side').

At one particular production plant in our sample efforts were being made to integrate the two functions in order to ease authority problems. These problems stemmed from the fact that maintenance men were geographically isolated from their boss, and unaccountable to the production supervisors – which meant they did very much as they pleased. As one neutral *cadre* explained, '*le médecin se fait attendre*' ('everyone awaits the doctor'). The production manager in that plant reiterated the point by referring to the maintenance department as '*l'état dans l'état*' ('a state within a state') – suggesting that little had changed since Crozier's classic study from the 1960s.

Political

Manifestations of political behaviour were less overt than in Britain or the USA, and French managers did not seem to derive the same sort of pride in divulging their political manoeuvrings as do their Anglo-Saxon counterparts. However, there were signs that political games were being played.

If we take written communications as an example, we can see that the coded nature of the interaction need not impair political thrust. To start with, opting for the written form, particularly in companies with a mainly oral culture, is in itself a powerful signal – it can be seen as *une agression* (an attack).

One administrative director in our study sent the purchasing manager a memo expressing his annoyance over some misdemeanour – this in spite of the close proximity of their offices and the fact that they saw each other regularly. The note was obviously motivated by the desire to register displeasure without overt confrontation. The administrative director knew he had made his point ('*marqué le coup*'), but by restricting the communication to the two parties (no other copies), the receiver knew there was no real malice.

In terms of contents, it would seem that almost anything is a good enough pretext for a memo, even if it is not adapted to the nature or the value of the information. We came across an interesting example at one of the large companies visited. The memo, which every single *cadre* had received, urged all personnel to cut down on the number of unnecessary photocopies (there's nothing like leading by example) – this in spite of the fact that the boss in question saw the entire management staff each morning for a meeting. Here the aim had been '*de laisser une trace*' ('to leave a trace') so that no one could claim they had not been informed. In view of such excesses, it is hardly surprising that one *cadre* complained of '*incontinence en matière scripturale*'. The resulting inflation of archives is tremendous because no one dares throw anything away – to wit, a manager who, on cleaning out his new office, found four drawers, each one packed with the archives of one of his four predecessors, like prehistoric strata.

Besides the contents, hidden messages can be transmitted in anodyne form in the list of recipients or date – details which the French manipulate with subtlety. One *cadre* explained that in certain cases, the importance of a memo lies in its timing rather than its content. The author may be trying to prove speedy reactions to events or a recent development.

As regards who the memo is dispatched to, there are a number of categories. First, there are the immediate recipients (*destinataires*) who are meant to act upon the information. Secondly, there are those who are not intended to take action but simply need to be informed, covered (*une note-parapluie*) or flattered. Finally, there are the unofficial recipients who receive an extra copy, sometimes termed a 'blind copy'. While these categories appear fairly clear-cut, one *cadre* explained that it may well be that the key recipient is in fact camouflaged in the category headed 'copies'. Another important point about the list of recipients is that it should reflect organizational status. Woe betide a *cadre* who places the PDG below a head of department, even his own, in the list of copies.

Further evidence of political behaviour in communications were the rumours which seemed to preoccupy several bosses. There were several references to *les bruits de couloirs* (rumours) or *le téléphone arabe* (the grapevine). Indeed a survey in *Le Nouvel Economiste* (12 May 1980) placed rumours ahead of one's immediate superior as a means of gaining information.

The importance of this form of information in the French context may be a reflection of the relative inefficiency or rigidity of normal channels of communication. It is only natural for rumours to flourish when there is an imbalance between the supply and demand of information. The rumour in France perhaps has a democratizing influence in an otherwise élitist system of communications – as one *cadre* put it, '*c'est le marché noir de l'information*' ('it's the information black market'). The speed of propagation easily outstrips official channels and responds to dual needs of the personnel: to be informed early and to make out one is privy to 'inside' information. It is from these needs that rumours derive their efficiency – they are sucked up by avid receivers and immediately re-emitted, though not always intact.

The managers we interviewed were aware of the possibilities of deliberately starting rumours but they showed wariness about indulging in a practice over which they had no control and which could easily backfire. The head of one production plant was particularly annoyed that every piece of unofficial information released, however positive, was somehow twisted to sound negative by the time it reached grass-roots level. He surmised that people heard what they wanted to hear, not what they were told – though he conceded that they (the *cadres*) did not always make things clear when they had something unpleasant to say. So any complaint that messages were not being received properly was partly '*une autocritique*'. What is more, the speed with which the message spreads depends on its content – as one *cadre* explained it is one thing intimating there may be a pay rise; it is quite another trying to get safety procedures respected.

The fact remains that beneath a formal exterior, French work relations make way for more supple practices – which probably serve to make the formal system workable and therefore contribute to its persistence.

Work Versus Social Relations

One might be tempted to say that the above description shows a relatively low carry-over in France from the social to the business setting – with individuals maintaining a permanent façade at work. This assumes that the professional persona is something which is donned before going to work in the morning. That is not necessarily the case. The relative impersonality and formalism found in organizational relations is echoed in French social life. If one looks at the traditional pattern of interpersonal relations inculcated in the basic associative life of a village, one can see the roots of the work relations described above.

The principles that indiscriminate friendship exposes one to manipulation, that property should be enclosed, that outsiders are not to be trusted – these defensive solidarities are all legacies of the village mentality which still has a strong hold over French social relations. As Wylie points out, the basic social arrangement in France is the circle – a person is responsible only to people in his own *cercle* and indifferent to people outside it. French dislike for people outside their own *cercle* is epitomized by Sartre's phrase, '*l'enfer c'est les autres*' ('Hell is other people' – *Huis clos*, scene V).

Overview

Whilst it would be foolish to suggest that the above description is universal, it certainly prevails in French companies. French work relations are, on the whole, more highly structured and more detached. From an Anglo-Saxon stance this may appear like a tremendous indictment of the French organizational model. However, in the French mind this lesser investment of the self is considered a means of preserving personal choice, independence and individual dignity.

It is noticeable in France that those companies which do try to impose a more informal style of work relations are often unpopular. There is a widespread belief that cordial relations merely serve as a means of motivating (and manipulating) *cadres*, of dismantling hierarchical and functional cleavages, and of encouraging a certain freedom of expression which facilitates decision-making – in other words, as an instrument which cleverly subordinates the interests of the individual to the interests of the firm.

This resentment towards informality as a manipulative device may explain the relative flop of Kenneth Blanchard's *One Minute Manager* in France. The transparency of his proposals was rather too much for French managers. Indeed, one *cadre* maintained: 'I would not take kindly to being patted on the shoulder

– not in the professional context at least' – which reinforces the idea put forward earlier in the chapter that the French do not like their body space violated.

Clearly, in the French context, the desire to avoid conflict and to be protected from arbitrary decisions and manipulation is more important than the immediate gratification provided by social contact. The idea is supported by Wylie, who studied a French village in the Vaucluse. He describes a boy who wasn't bright, never got into trouble and worked very hard. Why? '*Pour qu'on me laisse tranquille*' ('So I'll be left in peace' – in Santoni, 1981, 60). The desire for independence, even at the expense of not doing what you want, seems important in France.

This chapter basically concurs with Crozier's view of French work relations as impersonal, formal, compartmentalized . . . in short, predictable: consider here the much vaunted low tolerance for ambiguity in France. There is certainly an undercurrent of informal circles which help to 'oil the wheels', but that influence is better concealed than it is in Britain or America. Finally, it is posited that the dual roles played by French managers do not reflect a split between social and professional circles – but rather a broader distinction between public and private life.

References

Boltanski, L., *Les cadres: la formation d'un groupe sociale*, Paris: Editions de Minuit, 1982.

Crozier, M., *The Bureaucratic Phenomenon*, Chicago: University of Chicago Press, 1964.

— *On ne change pas la société par décret*, Paris: Grasset, 1979.

de Closets, F., *Toujours plus!* Paris: Grasset, 1982.

Graves, D. (ed.), *Management Research: A Cross-Cultural Perspective*, Amsterdam: Elsevier Scientific, 1973.

Kotter, J. P., *The General Managers*, New York: The Free Press, 1982.

Lockyer, K. G. and S. Jones, 'The function factor', *Management Today*, 1980, 53–64.

Maurice, M., F. Sellier, and J.-J. Silvestre, *Production de la hiérarchie dans l'entreprise: recherche d'un effet social Allemagne–France*, Laboratoire d'Economie et de Sociologie du Travail, Aix en Provence, 1977.

Le Nouvel Economiste, Cadres: la course aux pouvoirs, 12 May 1980, 42–7.

Revue Internationale du Travail (January/February 1985), 124 (1), 1–16.

Sainsaulieu, R., *L'identité au travail*, Paris: Presses de la Fondation Nationale des Sciences Politiques, 1977.

Santoni, G. (ed.), *Société et culture de la France contemporaine*, New York: State University of New York Press, 1981.

How to Do Business with a Frenchman

E. Russell Eggers

Chapter 5, pp. 136–9 in Theodore D. Weinshall (ed.), *Culture and Management: Selected Readings* (Harmondsworth: Penguin Books, 1977)

Condensed from *Harper's Magazine*, August 1965.

Obviously, there are problems in measuring Frenchmen by the standards of American industry. And vice versa. As one Frenchman put it, 'You Americans are well-trained executives of well-run corporations in the US. But abroad you are not clever enough, not flexible enough, not *débrouillard* (talented, resourceful, literally smart enough not only to pull strings but to disentangle them) enough to really get along in France. You are not French.'

For a more balanced look at the problem, consider the following laws, which pinpoint some basic differences between an American businessman and his opposite number in France:

1. *Whereas the American tries to think in a straight line, the Frenchman insists on thinking in a circle.* The American mistrusts complex things and tends to over-simplify. The Frenchman, by inclination and education, mistrusts simple things and tends to over-complicate. It is for this reason that no Frenchman, by American standards, can ask a simple, straightforward question when speaking in public. By French standards, no American speaker can give a full, sophisticated answer. A Frenchman tries to define the question; the American tries to answer it.

All this might be summed up in a hypothetical translation of Hamlet's soliloquy. In American business jargon, the soliloquy would probably come out: 'To be or not to be? Fine. Let's take a vote.' A Frenchman would say, '*Etre ou ne pas être. C'est là la question. Mais la question est mal posée*' – which freely translated means you cannot put the question that way.

2. *A French businessman mistrusts the very things in which an American*

businessman has the most confidence. Examples? The Frenchman is innately suspicious of the figures on a balance sheet, of the telephone, of his subordinates, of the law, of journalists and of what he reads in the press, of investment banks, and, above all else, of what an American tells him in confidence. The American, *au contraire*, has trust in all these things.

3. *An American executive tends to forget what he's said in a letter. A Frenchman never forgets what he's purposely left out.* This particular law of communication explains why negotiations often break down at a distance. After a meeting in Paris the American will write a letter so factual and so detailed that, in his own mind at least, it doesn't even require an answer. The Frenchman would consider any letter he addressed to a company in the US as the beginning of a long correspondence in which he would gradually elaborate on the nuance contained in the second line of paragraph three. The American will say about the French letter, 'It's very polite but what the heck is he trying to say?' The Frenchman will ponder the American letter. 'There are many details, *mais qu'est-ce que ça veut dire?*' What's he trying to tell me?

4. *An American will probably lose his typical enthusiasm for a project before a Frenchman gets over his typical reservations.* The business lunch in Paris is a case in point. The American executive rushing through on a two-day stop-over in France wants to talk business and then sit down to a quick snack. His potential French partner wants to eat his way graciously and cautiously to a few business remarks with the coffee. Sophisticated American negotiators know that no Frenchman can digest a new business proposition until dessert or, as the French put it, '*entre la poire et le fromage*'.

5. *A French company prepares its balance sheet and profit-and-loss statement not to show its stock-holders how much money it has made, but to show the tax authorities how little.* An American businessman considers his tax return a legal obligation to pay. But a Frenchman doesn't pay, he negotiates his taxes. The tax return is merely his opening offer.

6. *A Frenchman's thoughts are packaged in small and more specific sizes than an American's.* This is due partly to the metric system and partly to the fact that the French economy is only 13 per cent the size of the American economy. As a consequence, a Frenchman firmly believes that a small company is more efficient than a giant corporation, that custom-built products are of better quality than mass production, that the margin of profits is more important than volume of sales and profits, that details are more important than the big picture in

corporate planning. It is no accident that 'economy size' in French – for example, as seen printed on a box of soap flakes that is about the size of a transistor radio – generally means a small, not a large, package.

7. *To a Frenchman, economic prosperity is a series of non-durable pleasures of lasting value. To an American, prosperity is a tangible product with constant model changes.* Two items account for over 50 per cent of the average Frenchman's budget: food and vacations. Two items account for almost 50 per cent of the average American's budget: housing and the automobile. A Frenchman will not buy and does not really understand American refrigerators (particularly the un-refrigerated compartment for bananas) or automatic washing machines (with one of the special inside racks for the hand laundry). An American does not understand that the Frenchman's only do-it-yourself hobby is eating.

8. *A Frenchman feels as ill at ease with anything mechanical as an American does with a domestic servant.* It is surprising to what degree of suspicion and superstition a Frenchman will go to divorce himself as a person from strictly mechanical objects. To illustrate: in reply to a surprised comment from her American boss that she had been somewhat rude to a client on the telephone, an ordinarily charming French secretary said, 'But, Monsieur, I was not mad at him. I was mad at the telephone.'

9. *An American businessman treats his company like a wife: a Frenchman treats each of his companies like a mistress.* This is particularly true when a firm decides to set up a new subsidiary with a foreign partner. The American wants 100 per cent exclusivity and control over the long run. The Frenchman wants 100 per cent flexibility and freedom over the short.

10. *The word 'immoral' in English refers to what people do; in French it can apply to what companies do.* An American is shocked at the public love affair of a well-known businessman, at the fudging of tax returns, at taking back under the table what has been formally promised in an agreement. What shocks a Frenchman? A food firm that produces frozen chickens whose growth has been accelerated by hormone injections. A manufacturer in France who closes down his plant and lays off workers without warning to all concerned, especially the government.

11. *When a Frenchman is polite he is very, very polite and when he is rude, he is very, very French.* But a Frenchman is rude only in public places – waiting for a taxi, in a restaurant, behind the wheel of a car. He is supremely polite in

private places – in a letter, at a dinner, when he's being introduced. The typical Frenchman can make a prearranged telephone call to a good acquaintance and apologize three times during the conversation for calling. The same Frenchman could dial a wrong number at three in the morning and swear at the person whom he woke up. The two extremes of politeness give a Frenchman a sense of social equilibrium, and he is sure that it is more important to have discriminating manners rather than democratic ones..

12. *To the Frenchman a business career is usually a means to an end. To an American it is often an end in itself.* There are three sharp contrasts between a business career in France and the US. (a) The so-called 'poly-technician' – one of France's educated élite, the dominating class in French industry and government – considers his university career the toughest job he ever had; he'll never work that hard again. The American looks at his college days as the best time he'll ever have; he'd better start to work. (b) The ambitious young Frenchman will go to work for his government so that later in his career he can, to use the French expression, 'parachute' into a well-paying job in French industry. His counterpart in the US will go to work for a large corporation so that later in his career he can afford to work in Washington. (c) A Frenchman's idea of real success in industry is not to have a brilliant career within his company but make a fortune outside it.

Italy

Aspects of Italian Management

Pasquale Gagliardi and Barry A. Turner

Chapter 9, pp. 149–65 in David J. Hickson (ed.), *Management in Western Europe: Society, Culture and Organization in Twelve Nations* (Berlin and New York: Walter de Gruyter, 1993)

The Broad-Based Pyramid of Italian Industry

The economy of Italy has a distinctive and an idiosyncratic structure which strongly influences the options and opportunities open to Italian managers. Since the types of companies which make up this structure provide the environment within which Italian managers have to operate, we shall have to look at the features of these organizations and their interrelationships if we are to find out about the nature of Italian management. Italy has a primary sector made up of a handful of very large companies, many with very strong governmental involvement; these rest on the broad base of a secondary sector which contains a myriad of small and very small enterprises. Compared with other West European countries, Italy has a distinct lack of medium-sized companies between these two extremes (Istituto Centrale di Statistica, 1981). This slightly anomalous structure – sometimes referred to as the 'flattened pyramid' of the Italian industrial system (Fondazione Agnelli, 1974) – has been seen as an indication that Italian industry has a great deal of *imprenditorialità* or entrepreneurship amongst the multiplicity of small firms at the bottom, but a distinct lack of organizational skills (Fuà, 1980). This picture of the context of Italian management, however, is unduly oversimplified and in the following pages we will elaborate on it further.

Even as it stands, the picture shows contrasting qualities. A productive economic ferment has been generated by the multitude of small enterprises and, in the 1970s and 80s, they provided a new and characteristic industrial pattern. 'Flexible specialization' is seen as a distinctively Italian contribution to contemporary economic organization. This pattern also represents an Italian variant of the exploitative 'dual economy' with which we are more familiar in less developed countries. In the classic model of a dual economy, the primary sector of large, well-established organizations is typically a high status one, offering higher paid, more secure employment in positions which promise careers for life. By contrast, the secondary sector is more fragmented and more exploited. Its organizations are less permanent and they operate closer to the margins, drawing upon a different labour market, paying their employees significantly less and offering short-term, temporary or part-time employment with little or no security. Later on we shall look in a little more detail at the debate about this issue of *dualismo* or the dual economy in Italy.

Some Background

Italian industry has grown up against a backcloth of national diversity and major regional differences. Italy was established as a unitary state only in 1861. Before that time, the peninsula was made up of many small states, each with their own distinctive traditions which were endorsed and amplified by their various geographic and climatic contexts, their differing economic emphases and their different experiences of external domination by Austrian, French and Spanish invaders. These very strong cultural and linguistic traditions still persist in the deeply felt regional identities which are encountered across Italy. They are seen in their most extreme form in the *questione meridionale*, the economic and cultural split between the north and the south. This split is one which is always at the centre of Italian political debate, a division which persists in spite of the very large investments made by the government in attempts to eliminate it.

Superimposed upon such regional differences, we also find a rather different degree of diversity. This arises from the kind of differentiation of life-styles produced in all contemporary industrial societies by variations in social and demographic factors. Recent market research, for example, has identified 14 different types of Italian life-styles which depend upon age, census and class elements as well as having some cultural, geographic and historical variation (Eurisko, 1986). In trying to sketch a view of Italian management, then, we are looking at arrangements in a country which shows diversity arising from a strong pattern of regional identity, regional economies and regional government.

Italy is one of the most densely settled West European countries, with the second largest population in the European Community. Its per capita income is amongst the highest in the world and while both its production and occupational structures are those of an economically advanced country, its agricultural sector also continues to be very prominent. In the public sector, Italy runs a high budget deficit and its national debt has recently exceeded its Gross Domestic Product, although it has to be said that, at least up until the final removal of barriers to capital flows in 1992, much of the public debt was funded by Italy's traditionally high rate of domestic savings. Many public services are notoriously inefficient and also offer opportunities for corruption. Functionaries from all of the major political parties are involved, at every level, in issues which affect the management of public services, and this practice does little to improve efficiency or to reduce the possibilities for corruption. It is no secret that there is much organized crime in Italy, and difficulties and complications from this source are now spreading further into areas of public administration. This, then, is the Italian context: the variety of organizations which operate within this context provide the arena for Italian management.

The Family and the Enterprise

Italian life attaches high significance to the family, both as a basis for much social life and as a factor in Italian industrial development and Italian management (Haycraft, 1987: 116–78). The family is important in Italian life as reality, as structure and as metaphor. The *reality* of Italian family life is clearly evident in the patterns of housing, of social support and obligation, of inheritance and of socialization. The family provides an example for other *structures*, allowing the development of industrial patterns which either follow the ramifications of the family or which mimic them. The idea of the family is then available as a *metaphor* for the specification of obligations, for the setting of expectations about cohesion and loyalty and as a justification for regarding those who find themselves outside the boundaries of the family with a degree of wariness. The relevance of the familial pattern is often raised by Italian managers and consultants when they are interviewed about the organizations which they manage, study or confront. Aspects of family-related behaviour interpenetrate industrial enterprises at all levels, sometimes taking the form of *clientelismo*, a pattern of obligations and exchanges which uses linkages set by particularistic relationships and personal contacts.

The family enterprise is a fundamental of Italian capitalism, and it has a major contribution to make to its vitality, adaptability and competitiveness. The family enterprise develops when the family has the capacity to define economic objectives and to cooperate to mobilize human and financial resources to pursue those objectives (Boldizzoni, 1988). Of course, family companies are important in all major industrial countries, especially among the smaller enterprises, but in Italy, family and business links are much more widespread, most of the major private companies being family based. The family in Italy constitutes the main motivational basis for investment and for work and it also provides a way of handling the risks of economic activity, by offering protection and support in difficult situations. At the same time, of course, the need to use the members of an extended family network to handle complex industrial issues may inhibit decision-making, and often this limitation is not helped by the pressures on a paternalist system to favour family members systematically over outsiders, pushing the organization over the fine line which separates family cooperation from nepotism.

A particular difficulty which has been observed in family enterprises in many countries is the problem of the succession of leadership. This issue causes stress in both large and small family-owned Italian organizations. Succession is a problem for top companies outside the state sector which are family owned. The Gardini family in Ferruzzi Finanziaria, the Agnelli family of Fiat and the Pirelli family have all recently had to make hard decisions about the choice of family members to succeed to key executive positions. Other major Italian industrial families which may share similar problems are the de Benedetti, Benetton, and Pininfarina families. There is evidence, too, that some offspring who cannot be absorbed directly into such family firms are showing a preference for moving into senior positions in banking and finance, a development which shifts them into positions where they are likely to be able to continue to assist the family.

Boldizzoni (1988) suggests that whether succession proceeds smoothly or not depends upon the age and the life-cycle of the company, on the personal characteristics of the key executive to be replaced, on the availability of suitable candidates from amongst the family and their collaborators, and upon the nature and type of any succession plan they might have. The problem is most difficult with first-generation entrepreneurs who identify strongly with the company. Such men, for men they usually are, will often have exceptional personal qualities, but they may nonetheless be reluctant to prepare for their own replacement. There is a strong preference for keeping the company in the family, and a corresponding reluctance to bring in from the outside professional managers who might counter the lack of innovation which many small family companies display. Within this family setting it would be typical to find a reluctance to become involved in strongly expressed conflicts and a willing acceptance that power should be concentrated in the hands of the founder or his successor. Moreover, these family-influenced views of the way in which corporate power and conflict should be handled spill over into other, non-family and state-owned companies in Italy.

In the small family-run companies, there is no separation between ownership and control, and they tend to employ only a limited range of specialized professionals. The entrepreneur and the company tend to learn at the same time, usually reacting to problems rather than anticipating them. The particular types of enterprise-related behaviour within the company (cost reduction, diversification, exporting) and the policies of development are strongly determined by the size of the company (Gibbs and Scott, 1983).

The entrepreneurs in the family enterprises which Boldizzoni studied were strongly individualistic, strongly motivated and well educated, nearly half of them having attended university. A majority were influenced by the presence of other entrepreneurs within their family network. The companies had a strong sense of the reputation of the family and there was significant involvement of the family in management.

The Large Enterprises

The major Italian enterprises are either state owned or family owned. This means that, effectively, Italy has neither 'public' companies, nor the associated debate about the separation between ownership and control of such enterprises which has been heard in other regions of modern capitalism, particularly the Anglo-Saxon ones. The Italian state is also more deeply involved in the economy than is the case in any other capitalist country, the size of the public sector making the private sector the smallest of any Western European state.

The large state-owned, state-controlled or state-associated enterprises exert a major influence. Apart from their size and their dominance, they have also been important in the past in that they provided, at least at a more formal level, some models for Italian management. Their high level of influence has been traced both to the Italian totalitarian corporatism of the twenties and thirties (Heckscher, 1946: cited in Anheier and Seibel, 1990) and to a pattern which characterizes those civil law countries where the church played a dominant role in social reforms following the industrial revolution, and where absolutism was slowly or incompletely abolished. The power of these church and state-influenced models continued to be quite persuasive in the post-war period, and it still means that those organizations operating between the private, for-profit sector and the government (what is sometimes called the 'third sector') tend to look more like state agencies than for-profit firms (Anheier and Seibel, 1990). However, in the past twenty years, this influence has waned as the smaller companies started to make the running in the Italian economy.

After the major oil companies, IRI, the principal Italian state holding company, is the largest firm in Europe (Ward, 1990). Companies such as Fiat, ENI, Ferruzzi, Olivetti, Pirelli and Esso-Italia are included in the list of the top 500 non-American companies, but there are fewer of them than might be expected for a nation of Italy's size, the great majority of Italian companies having less than 100 workers. IRI itself, set up originally in 1933 by Mussolini as a measure to counter the effects of the Depression, has some 600 subsidiaries, including RAI – the national broadcasting corporation; the state tourism company, CIT; engineering companies and most of the steel industry; maritime insurance; the shipyards; telecommunications and four major banks. The state also has direct ownership of ENI, the State Agency for Hydrocarbons, and the two major financial agencies EFIM and GEPI, together with six other national banks, thirty-one lending banks and a group of regional savings banks, not to mention the Istituto Mobiliare Italiano (IMI) which funds the majority of Italy's public works. 'IRI, ENI, EFIM and GEPI together are responsible for almost 30 per cent of sales and almost 50 per cent of fixed investment in Italy' (Ward, 1990: 238).

Within the state-owned enterprises, the stability which one might expect from the continuity of state control under the direction of the *Ministero delle partecipazioni statali* is only partially evident, for, in practice, this form of direction means that with every change of government the stockholder changes. Even though the *Democrazia Cristiana*, or Christian Democrat, regime has provided long-term continuity of government since the Second World War, individual governments in Italy have been of very short duration. Moreover, while it is reasonable to assume that the board of a 'normal' company would be primarily interested in the profitability and development of the business, the state-owned enterprises are given additional, more political goals relating, for example, to employment, to the state presence in strategic, non-profitable sectors neglected by private entrepreneurs and to regional development. These goals, which may well at times be mutually contradictory, are very often expressions of the *lottizzazione* – the system by which there is an agreed attribution of particular areas of influence and managerial posts to each political party.

In addition, the state-owned enterprises have a multiplicity of stakeholders pushing each company in different directions: the unions, the employees, consumers, public opinion and the political parties all have a view, and the managers of the enterprise itself will add to the debate with their own interpretations of the 'social responsibilities' of the enterprise. These claims intrude not only into strategic decision-making, but are heard at all operational levels, so that state-owned enterprises exhibit a high degree of dependency upon many other groups, a condition which has been labelled 'allodependency' (Ferrario, 1978). Political goals and pressures of this kind cut across the patterns of management and organization which we might otherwise expect to be pursued by professional managers working largely according to criteria of economic rationality and efficiency.

The Small Enterprises

At the opposite end of the industrial scale, in contrast to the large, state-dominated enterprises which have been perceived over the past quarter of a century to be rather static and conservative, there has developed a distinctively new and lively form of industrial development, a form novel enough to have been called at times, 'post-industrial'. Many small Italian companies seem to have jumped, somehow, beyond the constraints of the mass-production technology and the management practices of F. W. Taylor and Henry Ford to create a new form of small-scale, craft-based family enterprise. These enterprises offer a high degree of responsiveness to customers and, because of their small size and their propensity to demonstrate a high degree of 'flexible specialization', are able to fit themselves into small adaptive niches. They also appear, from some points of view, to offer the benefits of a human-scale and a family-based pattern of relations in the workplace.

The small organizations of the secondary sector have been vigorously active since at least the 1960s. Already, at the start of this period, establishments with less than 100 employees produced 57 per cent of the value of manufactured goods in Italy, compared with around 40 per cent in Germany and France and 20 per cent in Great Britain and the United States (Barbetta, 1989: 157). There has, though, been little evidence of a consequent growth in size of the enterprises at the base of the system. This may well be because there are quite specific constraints upon the growth of small companies in Italy: legal, trade-union based, fiscal, economic and administrative (Barbetta, 1989: 184–9). As the Italian economy 'matured', we might have expected small companies to undergo a progressive process of industrial concentration but these restraining factors seem to have served to check such changes. In addition, there are other, specific constraints which relate to the nature of small, family-based companies which we shall look at in more detail below.

In the 1980s, however, a number of the pressures towards greater industrial concentration seem once more to have made their presence felt. After a decade of quite spectacular activity in the 1970s, the small enterprises are starting to cede some ground to larger corporations. The large enterprises in the primary sector turn out to have adopted strategies in this period which are very similar to those adopted by major companies elsewhere in Europe, and they have started to take on a similar look. The larger Italian enterprises during the 1980s have slimmed down workforces and increased both their turnover and their level of productivity. However, these strategies do also, in fact, contribute something to the growth of small enterprises in the secondary sector. As the larger companies move away from internal vertical integration and start to favour a decentralized form of production, the overall system accommodates its needs to adjust to variability of demand and increased costs of primary inputs by increasing the opportunities for small companies to join the system, but also to bear a significant proportion of the risks and the costs of possible downturns and reductions in business.

Over the past two decades, the development of the smaller enterprises has shown both continuity and a break with the past. Continuity from the sixties can be seen in the persistent growth of enterprises with between 10 and 100 employees, most of this growth occurring in the companies within the most 'advanced' industrial sectors – machine tool, transport, electrical and electronic – although it can be seen also, to a lesser extent, in basic industries and in traditional industries such as textiles, clothing and engineering. The rather surprising break with the past is visible in the growth which has taken place among companies with less than 10 employees, for, compared with the 1960s, these have increased both in number and in the aggregate number of people employed.

So far we have presented a sketch of some of the major features of contemporary Italian industry. However, this sketch must be taken with great caution. Quite apart from the high degree of regional variability, Italian industry has followed an intricate dynamic since the 1960s, with a series of complicated interchanges between the enterprises at the top and at the base of the industrial system. At some points, in the early sixties, for example, the bigger enterprises were placing emphasis upon larger and larger industrial units. The smaller enterprises grew by making use of opportunities which this policy overlooked. They were able to react more rapidly to market changes at times of high uncertainty, and this gave them benefits which carried them through the following decade. The search for advantage shifted from the large to the small enterprises and back again in a far from simple pattern, according to the period (Barbetta, 1989: 198). Since, however, the growth in the number of very small companies, and thus the degree of fragmentation at the base of the system, now seems to be increasing rather than decreasing (Lorenzoni, 1990), we do need to raise here the question of how such a fragmented system can compete effectively.

The Constellation and Flexible Specialization

Although it is impossible to offer a simple understanding of the processes of development during the last twenty years in Italian industry because of their great complexity, it is clear that the smaller enterprises have been responsible for many of the novel developments at the base of the structure. To gain a better understanding of these changes, it is useful to look at some attempts to analyse just how these companies related to other parts of the industrial sector.

Sabel (1982) characterizes the enterprises of Emilia Romagna, together with those of the Marches, Tuscany and Umbria, as small-scale, high-technology cottage industries which employ craft labour to supply diversified consumer tastes on a changing world market (see also Brusco, 1982; Brusco and Sabel, 1981). In what is perhaps a slightly Utopian view of the small- to medium-sized engineering, clothing and textiles artisan firms of these areas, he sees them as giving back to labour some of the creativity removed by Fordist mass production, since such small enterprises avoid both a minute fragmentation of work and a strict separation between conception and execution. The regional diversity and the Utopian appearance are both enhanced by the co-existence with industry of a mixture of both very rich and peasant subsistence agriculture. Sabel sees this rather complex texture of craft and agricultural enterprises as one which is being promoted positively by regional government, in collaboration with the PCI – the Italian Communist Party – and the trade unions. By offering support to innovative proprietors to strengthen their will to train apprentices for the future, regional government is encouraging the continuance of this novel industrial pattern. Thus, in this region of Italy at least, Sabel suggests that we find a system where the dominant Western mode of multinational mass production is being replaced by a new, forward-looking amalgam of work and politics on a more human scale.

A diametrically opposed interpretation has been offered by Murray (1987) who argues that Italy has been dominated, and continues to be dominated by large Fordist and neo-Fordist companies. He sees little evidence of the direction of development by regional administration, and points instead to the logic of international capital as the driving force of development. The small firms, which are themselves not free of conflicts between capital and labour, play their part in the system by making small batch, customized investment goods which are difficult to mass produce. Workers in these small firms are subdivided by race, gender and skill, and Murray suggests that Sabel neglects both the wide variety of working conditions to be found in the artisan sector, and the variation in the levels of wages paid. Because he concentrates upon the companies employing middle-aged, male, skilled, Emilian workers, he neglects those which employ predominantly women, or low-skilled Southern Italians and North Africans. For Murray, it is not only the small companies at the base of the pyramid which are splintering and fragmenting but also the working class, so that such solidarity as was developed in the seventies is now being considerably undermined.

Murray offers as an example the engineering industry in Bologna, which has several segments. Larger firms subcontract into the artisan sector to offset their own rigidity and to cope with market fluctuations. There is an extensive subcontracting network, which includes some firms with 'tragic' working conditions and very low unionization. The system provides an enormous degree of labour flexibility for the capital interests of the area. At the same time, the larger firms are investing heavily in information technology and new production technologies and developing their links with multinationals.

This stress upon the interlinkages of the system is echoed in a striking new analysis by Lorenzoni (1990) who has suggested that it is misleading to concentrate too much on trying to assess the capacity of individual small enterprises or wondering how it is possible for such weak units to survive in a rather tough economic climate. Rather than making reference to some unspecified qualities of entrepreneurship or to the benefits accruing from tax evasion or from the use of underpaid labour in order to explain the brilliant results which have been obtained, he suggests that we look at the enterprise system as a whole. A single enterprise, he says, is 'like a table without legs'. Instead of looking at a single component, we need to look at the properties of the complete pattern of linkages. Analysing a number of case studies which he has carried out, again in the Emilia region, he advances a theory which is valuable in understanding this pattern of organization which is so widely diffused in northern, eastern and central Italy.

His basic hypothesis is that rather than trying to explain the success of small Italian companies by reference to some single company or management factor we should look at the wider innovative pattern of inter-organizational relations which has been developing. Small companies in the Italian setting turn away from the possibility of developing through internal growth (*crescita interna*), either by increasing direct investment or by expanding the number of staff employed. Rather they develop by increasing their connections and links with other small companies through a pattern of networking and external growth (*crescita esterna*).

We have already noted that there are a number of factors – legal, fiscal and economic – which help to persuade many Italian companies to sustain operations on a small scale. These inclinations are reinforced by the family network which typically forms the base of the small Italian enterprise. The series of studies of both small companies and family-based companies by Boldizzoni (1985, 1988), which we have already referred to, has demonstrated that family companies grow by progressively co-opting members of the family into the enterprise, and that this means that the potential for the development of companies is proportional to the potential of the families involved. Even when the potential base of recruitment is enlarged by marriage links, using precisely the mechanisms by which mediaeval Venetian merchants secured the expansion of their enterprises, there is still a constraint upon the size of the enterprise if it is to be kept within family boundaries. In market terms, if we look at their competitive, structural and financial profiles, such small companies are weak in themselves, especially given the tendency to undercapitalization which they display (Boldizzoni, 1985). In aggregation, however, these companies can display strong competitive qualities.

Lorenzoni suggests that they achieve their strong competitive aggregate qualities by adopting a particular pattern of linkages based upon the development of complementary enterprise roles. One leading company becomes associated with a group of other small companies in an arrangement which Lorenzoni refers to as 'the constellation' – *la costellazione*. The leading company, the *impresa guida*, is typically managed by a creative and innovative entrepreneur, while the other companies, looked at individually, could be said to be managed by what Lorenzoni calls a style of *imprenditorialità limitata* or limited entrepreneurship. Those working in this style are far from the Schumpeterian archetype and are concerned to maintain their autonomy within a limited but stable sphere of activity defined by the existing enterprise and its family connections in a way which is already familiar to us from Boldizzoni's study of family firms. Such limited entrepreneurship focuses upon the efficiency of internal activity, mainly in production. It takes little or no interest in the wider business environment and has no desire for growth.

The typical constellation is held together by integration devices of extreme simplicity. It is not driven by a sophisticated project but by negotiation between the members to obtain a consensus on the 'facts' to be confronted and on the actions which then must follow the shared diagnosis of the situation. Business within the constellation is done with a degree of informality which presupposes a high degree of trust between members of the constellation. Like all such loosely connected networks (Gouldner, 1959), if the interests of the member units and those of the constellation as a whole are to be optimized, an appropriate balance has to be found between the autonomy of the member units and the benefits which they derive from their place in the constellation.

Although the pattern of networking which Lorenzoni describes may be one which has distinctively Italian features, in a more general sense, many of its traits can be found in a variety of other locations in the early stages of industrial take-off: in the metal-working firms of the English Black Country in the Industrial Revolution, for example, or in the nearby Birmingham jewellery quarter in the late nineteenth century. The physical proximity of a number of small, related and overlapping enterprises makes it both sensible and possible for them to tackle the division of labour needed for larger industrial projects by adopting a collaborative network in one form or another, while at the same time preserving the formal autonomy of their individual units. These conditions, Williamson (1975) would suggest, are ones in which the costs of the transactions to be carried out between the various participants are cheaper if small individual producers enter into the transactions than if all of the participants were merged into a single large organization. If a point is reached at which the formation of a single organization would lower transaction costs significantly, then on a strict economic calculus, the 'constellations' would disappear.

Against this economic view, however, we should set the quasi-familial pattern which is evident in the informal and consensus-based linkages of Lorenzoni's networks, an arrangement which is reminiscent of the clan pattern which Ouchi (1981) describes in his critique of Williamson's model. Japanese organizations, and some American ones which approximate to them, remain together rather than fragmenting in response to economic pressures, Ouchi suggests, because of the cultural commitment which their members share towards social cohesion. In an inversion of this relationship, the cultural commitment of Italian, family-based entrepreneurs to the autonomy of units of limited size within an informal, quasi-familial network of joint obligations may allow constellations to continue to operate even in situations where a pure transaction-cost analysis might suggest that there should be growth and aggregation into larger units. (For a complementary discussion of the ramifying symbolic benefits which may be gained when networks are specified, see Kreiner and Schultz's (1991) study of international networks in biotechnology.)

Management of the Organization

We can now finally turn to look at some of the features which characterize the way in which the complex and distinctive Italian industrial structure which we have so far been describing is managed. Although firmly based data is hard to come by, virtually everyone who has looked at the question has felt the need to try to relate Italian managerial characteristics to the patterns of Italian national culture. However, it is not easy to sketch in the characteristics of Italian culture, especially given the degree of diversity and difference which we have already noted. We can, though, make use of some survey evidence in attempting this task.

Very few studies have looked specifically at Italian managers. Instead we have to draw upon Latin and Italian characteristics identified in cross-national managerial studies. International surveys suggest that the Italian culture, and to some extent Latin cultures more generally, operate with a distinctive cluster of interrelated attitudes: specificity, familialism, a lack of trust in other people in general, combined with a general view that support and *favoritismo* rather than isolated individual effort are needed in order to succeed (Eurisko, 1991). The element of specificity reflects a preference for dealing with known individuals rather than with representatives of general categories or classes, a preference for the personal contact which can be regarded as an extension to the family. It then becomes more difficult to place trust in those who cannot be located socially in this fashion.

Laurent (1983), for example, characterized French and Italian managers as having a more personal and social concept of authority than American, Swiss or German managers; and as having a highly politicized rather than a structural view of their organizations. Italian managers in particular showed a preference for clarity and the control of uncertainty within their organizations, an arrangement which would minimize potential internal organizational conflicts. They were also suspicious of arrangements such as matrix organizations which blurred hierarchical relationships. These findings are echoed in other studies which suggest that Latin European managers prefer a strong hierarchy and that they display little autonomy, and gain little management satisfaction (Haire et al., 1966), or that they demonstrate individualism, autocracy, paternalism, a stress upon masculinity and a strong sense of hierarchy (Hofstede, 1976, 1977, 1980; Bollinger and Hofstede, 1987). These findings echo the preferences expressed among the members of family firms which we have already noted in the third section of this chapter.

In Italian family firms, Boldizzoni (1988) found that a characteristic pattern of management was a strong concentration by the chief executive or founding entrepreneur upon various key commercial, financial or productive activities. Those functions considered to be marginal or less important were delegated to members of the family or to collaborators. There was a strict relationship between the strong points of the company and the primary responsibilities of the entrepreneur. New managerial capacities were not well developed in such companies. They tended to improve and to consolidate the managerial competencies and strengths which they already possessed rather than developing additional ones. Planning tended to concentrate upon improving the quality of products and developing new ones rather than changing and improving other aspects of company activities.

Ciferri (1990) is preparing a comparative study of British and Italian management which will concentrate upon attitudes to actual management systems rather than the managerial preferences which Hofstede has examined in great detail. In spite of this difference in emphasis, however, he suggests that Hofstede's work offers an accurate compendium of findings to date, when he argues that, in Italy, subordinates at all levels of the hierarchy are heavily dependent on their superiors; that subordinates expect superiors to act autocratically; that the ideal superior to most managers is a benevolent autocrat or a paternalist; there is a wide expectation that superiors will enjoy privileges, laws and rules which are different from those of their subordinates; and that status symbols are very important in contributing to the authority of the superior manager. To these patterns can be added support for '*clientelismo*', that highly specific and person-based relationship which occurs between people with mutual interests or between those who need and those who can offer various forms of patronage.

As with the Arabic pattern of *wasta*, *clientelismo* recognizes the wider network of obligations beyond the organization in which the manager is located. Someone in a superior position not only has obligations and responsibilities within the company, but also responsibilities to and mutual obligations with family members and with other individuals who may be tied into a quasi-familial, personal network. Family-specific or family-like contacts and relationships make sense when there is an absence of reassurance about the reliability of those who cannot be located on such personal networks.

Some interesting insights into management in the *middle* layers of the industrial structure are offered by one study which has looked at a small group of 25 private companies. These are quite an élite group of mainly medium to large companies sophisticated enough to respond to quite an extensive and complicated questionnaire study. Rugiadini (1985) sought to try to determine the 'distance' which might exist between these Italian companies and a general 'universal model' of advanced European management which he had devised. The study distinguished four different areas of management practice: control, organization, planning and personnel appraisal, and defined an 'advanced' model for each of these. The criteria vary from one area to another, sometimes implying the adoption of increased levels of formalization or the use of specific methods, sometimes more substantial integration between levels and roles in management processes and sometimes the use of certain decision criteria.

He came up with the following findings. In general, in the first three areas of practice: control, organization and planning, the Italian companies studied were at or were close to the author's model. They diverged substantially from the model, however, in the fourth area, the field of personnel appraisal. In these companies, the managers did not organize or handle the merit-rating process systematically, and when they were carrying out appraisals, they did not attempt to refer to impersonal, objective criteria. The managers involved seemed either to resist or to refuse outright the acceptance of a clear definition of either individual responsibilities or objective appraisal criteria linked to company results. Instead they showed a response which is consistent with the general patterns of autocracy and paternalism which we have already noted.

To the general picture of the stance of Italian management which we have presented so far, we might add the common perception that there is a high degree of aesthetic sensibility in Italian culture and a concern for a widely construed notion of design which transmutes into the Italian flair for style, even if some writers see this flair constituted as adaptability to the tastes of others rather than a genuine design creativity (Ward, 1990: 251–7). There is, however, no doubt that the attribute most frequently associated with Italian organizations is a sense of *style*. The flair for design and visual appeal which grows out of the public concern with dress and the plastic and visual arts, is also associated with the special place of design and designers in Italian culture and in Italian managerial life. The absence of a clear dividing line between fashion, art, architecture and design, is accompanied by a high degree of public recognition for leading designers. This fits with the emphasis upon corporate image and styling in corporations such as Olivetti, Ferrari, Alfa-Romeo and Fiat. It also connects with the variety of design options available in the Italian marketplace, as part of the pattern of flexible specialization offered by the small, family-modelled organizations of the constellations. In seeking their own distinctive niches in the market, many of them are able to build upon or make use of the cachet of 'made in Italy', especially in the fields of textiles and fashion, motor car and electrical and domestic product design, circumventing to some degree the major standardizing demands of the process of mass production.

Concluding Comments

A first level of understanding of Italian management has to commence with a recognition of the diversity of the country and its enterprises, and of the skewed distribution of size shown by Italian enterprises, with much state involvement in the larger organizations. In addition to the formal factors which often make it sensible for small companies to remain small in Italy, the values, practices and structures associated with a strong emphasis upon the family also push towards the same end.

It does not make sense, however, to try to understand individual small enterprises without looking at the 'constellations' of collaborating companies of which they form a part. These constellations permit the continuance of traditional Italian views of interpersonal relationships and obligations and allow a concentration upon the quasi-domestic unit, even as the combination of such units form into novel industrial patterns. Their knack of flexible specialization has boosted the Italian economy considerably over the past two decades, but, while elements of the small-scale enterprises may have their Utopian appeal, it would be short-sighted not to recognize the ties which link all of these companies, admittedly sometimes very ineffectively, into an interplay with the larger private and state-owned companies which form the other major element of the Italian managerial scene. It is an open question how far these larger forces, especially those arising in the context of a unified European economy, are likely to exert pressures for industrial concentration which will remove many of the specifically Italian features noted above and how far the industrial diversification and cooperation provided by the existing industrial districts and constellations will resist such inroads.

In companies at both ends of the industrial scale, there is a distinctively Italian outlook on management which stresses dependence and paternalism or autocracy; personal relationships and *clientelismo*; and a clarity of hierarchical relations which makes it easier to avoid overt conflict. If the moves towards the Single European Market do bring about significant structural change in Italian industry, it could be expected that cultural lags associated with the strongly embedded Italian cultural patterns will make key values and beliefs rather more difficult to change, so that Italian management will be likely to retain its distinctive features well into the twenty-first century.

Note

The assistance of Marco Mariani is gratefully acknowledged in the preparation of this chapter.

References

Anheier, H. K. and W. Seibel, *The third sector: comparative studies of non-profit organizations*, Berlin: de Gruyter, 1990.

Barbetta, G. P., 'La evoluzione della struttura dimensionale dell'industria italiana' in G. P. Barbetta and F. Silva (eds.), *Trasformazioni strutturali delle impresse italiane*, pp. 155–205, Bologna: Il Mulino, 1989.

Boldizzoni, Daniele, *La Piccola Impresa: Gestione e sviluppo delle aziende minori*, Milano: Il Sole 24 ore, 1985.

— *L'Impresa Familiare: caratteristiche distintive e modelli di evoluzione*, Milano: Il Sole 24 ore, 1988.

Bollinger, D. and G. Hofstede, *Les differences culturelles dans le management*, Paris: Les Editions d'Organisation, 1987.

Brusco, S., 'The Emilian model: productive decentralisation and social integration', *Cambridge Journal of Economics* 6/3, 1982, 167–84.

Brusco, S. and C. Sabel, 'Artisan production and economic growth' in F. Wilkinson (ed.), *The Dynamics of Labour Market Segmentation*, pp. 99–113, London: Academic Press, 1981.

Ciferri, M., 'Managerial attitudes, values and perceptions: an Anglo-Italian study', unpublished research paper, May 1990.

Eurisko, *Sinottica: Indagine Psicografica*, unpublished market research report, 1986.

— Eurobarometro, *Social Trends* 54, 14, 1991.

Ferrario, M., 'Strategic management in state enterprises', unpublished doctoral dissertation, Graduate School of Business Administration, Harvard University, 1978.

Fondazione Agnelli, 'Il sistema imprenditoriale italiano', *Contributi di ricerca*, Vol. 3, 1974.

Fuà, G., *Problemi dello sviluppo tardivo in Europa*, Bologna: Il Mulino, 1980.

Gibbs, A. A. and M. Scott, *Strategic Awareness, Personal Commitment and the Process of Planning in Small Business*, Durham: Durham University Business School, 1983.

Gouldner, A. W., 'Reciprocity and autonomy in functional theory' in L. Gross (ed.), *Symposium on Sociological Theory*, pp. 241–70, New York: Harper and Row, 1959.

Haire, M., E. E. Ghiselli and L. W. Porter, *Managerial Thinking: an International Study*, New York: Wiley, 1966.

Haycraft, John, *Italian Labyrinth: Italy in the 1980s*, Harmondsworth: Penguin, 1987.

Hofstede, G., 'Nationality and espoused values of managers', *Journal of Applied Psychology* 61, 1976, 148–55.

— *Cultural Determinants of the Exercise of Power in a Hierarchy*, European Institute for Advanced Studies in Management, Working Paper 77–8, 1977.

— *Culture's Consequences*, Beverly Hills, CA: Sage, 1980.

Istituto Centrale di Statistica, *VI Censimento Generale dell'Industria, del Commercio, dei Servizi e dell'Artigiano* (industrial census), Roma: Istituto Centrale di Statistica, 1981.

Kreiner, Kristian and Majken Schultz, 'Soft cultures: the symbolism of international R&D projects', paper presented to the Eighth International SCOS Conference on Reconstructing Organizational Culture, Copenhagen, June 1991.

Laurent, André, 'Matrix organizations and Latin cultures', *International Studies of Management and Organization* 10/4, 1981, 15–41.

— 'The cultural diversity of Western conceptions of management', *International Studies of Management and Organization* 13/1–2, 1983, 75–96.

Lorenzoni, G., *L'architettura di sviluppo delle imprese minori*, Bologna: Il Mulino, 1990.

Murray, Winton, 'Flexible specialisation in the "Third Italy"', *Class and Capital* 33, 1987, 84–95.

Ouchi, William G., *Theory Z: How American Business Can Meet the Japanese Challenge*, Reading, MA: Addison-Wesley, 1981.

Rugiadini, A. (ed.), *La managerialità nelle imprese italiane*, Bologna: Il Mulino, 1985.

Sabel, C., *Work and Politics*, Cambridge: Cambridge University Press, 1982.

Ward, William, *Getting it Right in Italy: a Manual for the 1990s*, London: Bloomsbury, 1990.

Williamson, Oliver E., *Markets and Hierarchies: Analysis and Antitrust Implications*, New York: Free Press, 1975.

Organizational Behaviors and Cultural Context: the Brazilian '*Jeitinho*'

Gilles Amado and Haroldo Vinagre Brasil

From *International Studies of Management and Organization*, Vol. 21, No. 3, 1991, pp. 38–61

Introduction

To what extent is it possible to perceive specifically Brazilian organizational behaviors? What are they? Where do they originate?

This paper is within the scope of our previous works, which focused on cultural features, and tries to articulate the human 'reality' of organizations which takes root in a sociohistorical analysis that supports the observed and collected data. Concerning the Brazilian case, the data refer to the analysis of both training and development actions in a great number of organizations, as well as to the study of the organizations' images in the minds of managers and the attitudes demonstrated in negotiation processes.

The analysis of such data makes it possible to confirm the 'personalist' and 'social' dimension of the Latin organizations. Meanwhile, it brings to light typical Brazilian idiosyncracies. Thus, the importance and the original nature of the mediation systems among people are stressed, as well as those between the individual and the organization and between the person and the law.

These specific features are linked to the sociohistorical and anthropological interpretations of Brazil. The '*jeitinho*' category stands out as a hermeneutic key of the Brazilian culture, and is explored in its linkage with the gathered organizational data.

A great Brazilian intellectual, a half-blooded (African-Polish) man, who died recently, Paulo Leminsky, wrote a novel in the Joycean mode of expression, or in the Guimaraes Rosa mode of expression, that is a very significant piece of work on approaching the problems of cultural adaptation. Leminsky (1989) imagines that René Descartes came along on the Maurício de Nassau expedition, at the time of the Dutch occupation in part of the Brazilian Northeastern sites. By metaphorically placing Cartesius in the Brazilian tropical environment – a nonrecorded but very plausible fact, for the philosopher wandered, at that time, around the Netherlands – the novelist shows how the 'white' European logic collapses under the equatorial latitudes, melting in the heat and before a world that seems hideous and unclassifiable. 'How come,' asks Leminsky's Descartes, perplexed, 'not even nothing is what it seems back there!' 'It's a ''pro-return'' that goes neither backward nor forward,' the philosopher-physicist-mathematician-theologian concludes, in a neologism, a verbal attempt to root itself in reality. In order to live and to survive among so much fauna and flora blending with tropical exuberance, among a procession of Africans and Indians, his rationalism had to be broken up by strokes of nonsense, imagination, fantasy, and surrealism to be able to build up another logic that would be operational down here.

Such allegories are not born by chance. They are symptomatic and paradigmatic, and reflect an underlying reality. The problems of relationships among different cultures are synthesized here. Race, environment, customs, history, and the world viewpoint, in short, determine the personality of the human groups that facilitate or obstruct exchange.

Thus, the Brazilian way of being keeps a close relationship with its history as a colonial dependent and peripheral Third World country with its ethnic formation and geography. So it is a premise that Brazilian development in 'adequate' patterns will only happen if Brazilian people are able positively to recognize their 'cultural' personality.

One can scarcely find empirical works on the specific matter that might reveal, at the essence of the behaviors, what Celso Furtado calls 'the Brazilian cultural being' that has arisen out of the dependent modernization of the country.

Hence, our purpose is to follow a wake that, starting with the analysis of empirical data received from companies – particularly in the negotiation processes, managerial development interventions, and comparative studies with other cultures – should lead to a connection with the historical development and the Brazilians' sociopolitical formation, and help us understand current behaviors in Brazilian organizations better.

Organizational Behaviors in the Brazilian Company

In 1989, A. M. Hostalacio Costa, S. T. Diegues Fonseca, and M. L. Goulart Dourado, members of one of the most important consulting and action-research institutions in Brazil, the Fundaçao Dom Cabral, conceived a report based upon interventions dealing with management and the human relations training of managers in Brazilian companies. The work is based on data gathered from several questionnaires, from observations of role-playing exercises and case discussions in seminars, and also on studies based on interviews with managers from different hierarchical levels. The authors, specialists in the field of organization development, used the North American principles of Hersey and Blanchard, such as 'situational leadership', as well as Likert's principle of participative management, Maslow and Herzberg's motivational theories, and Latin and European approaches such as 'Institutional Analysis', which was mainly developed in France and Italy, as theoretical and methodological references.

In 1989, in a seminar on leadership, these authors presented their conclusions to a group of thirty executives of several client institutions with which they had worked previously. The conclusions about the way Brazilian organizations are managed were thus articulated as follows:

- Brazilian managerial performance is characterized by an immediatist view, directed toward short-term results with an emphasis on crisis solutions.
- There is a lack of strategic planning and/or a gap in planning between the tactical and the operational management levels.
- Decisions are centralized at superior hierarchical levels, with clear incompatibility between responsibility and authority.
- Organizational structure is excessively hierarchical, and the inner subsystems are excessively segmented, without integration.
- The system of control is partly marked as punitive, composed of follow-up mechanisms that are random and dissociated from a feedback process.
- Negotiations are carried out predominantly in an atmosphere in which winners lose and losers win and the main conflicts are not openly discussed. Attitudes tend to be imposed upon subordinates, and soothing behaviors are employed before superiors.
- Management has trouble occupying its own functional areas, for an inadequate distribution of authority associated with a punitive system of control leads to fear of assuming risks and consequently to a behavior of 'pushing the problem upwards' – that is, delegation to a superior.
- The authoritarian-benevolent system within the limits of interaction with the deliberative-consultative one (as in Likert's model) is predominant, even though the organizational discourse tends to be participative. This is when the gap between managerial discourse and practice becomes clearer. 'The discourse has to be made a practice'; 'Make practical the discourse in which people are the main resources of the company.'

Brazilian organizations are predominantly worried about immediate results, achievement, and short-term performance, which are particularly stressed by managers with an engineering background. Results are consequently restricted to a short- and medium-term strategic framework. Such actions impair the purposes and goals of productivity, cost reduction, and quality, as well as organizational efficiency.

When analyzing the organizational, managerial, and individual strengths and weaknesses, the groups have shown a great ease in determining weaknesses and a great difficulty in finding strengths. Primarily, they limit themselves to the professional's personal skill and technical competence, and to each person's commitment to the organization – 'we wear the company shirt' – and to one's best intentions of improving and developing.

Within the Brazilian organizational reality, there is a remarkable valorization of managerial positions, to the detriment of technical positions. Salary increases and promotions are closely bound to the executive positions, thus leading to a depreciation of technical duties. There is, however, a paradox in the promotion process, since managers are selected on the basis of their individual technical competence.

One of us, a Frenchman who took part in this seminar, was surprised by two phenomena: first, the findings were rather shocking because of their negative nature; and second, managers received the survey results, which were presented to them in an open and straightforward manner, with a surprising degree of ease. One might rather have expected them to feel crushed by the 'verdict'.

What to conclude? Was this survey clear and objective and were the Brazilian managers simply not sensitive and not in a defensive position? Or did they tend to submit themselves to the specialists' conclusions in an almost masochistic manner? We shall return to this question.

The above observations are none the less very consistent with the results gathered from several surveys conducted by other specialists with company managers. Thus, Cardoso (1964) noted an excessive direct control inside Brazilian organizations, where family control works as a tool to restrain the delegation of authority to subordinates, and to valorize and stress loyalty and trust as desirable characteristics of subordinates.

Prasad (1981), when researching in Brazilian companies and their foreign subsidiaries, concludes with a low opinion of the capacity of subordinates for leadership and initiative, as shown by Brazilian managers. But, surprisingly enough, while he found they were less democratic than the expatriates on leadership issues, they espoused a more democratic belief in internal-control issues.

Amado and Cathelineau (1987–8) presented a theoretical model and a methodological approach about the meaning of behavior in the context of

Table 1 Negotiation styles (concepts and behaviors). (From Amado and Cathelineau, 1987–8.)

Styles	*Concepts*	*Typical Behaviors*
Active		
PERSUADING	To have others take one's ideas in.	To propose and suggest. To argue, reason and justify.
ASSERTING	To impose and judge others.	To make requirements and rules known. To let one's point of view and wishes be known. To evaluate others and oneself. To punish, reward and yield.
Receptive		
LINKING	To understand the others' frame of reference.	To encourage participation of others. To search for agreement points. To listen and be empathetic.
SEDUCING	To open oneself while trying to involve the others.	To influence others through one's own behavior. To seduce, motivate others and raise their spirit. To share information. To admit one's own mistakes.
WITHDRAWAL	To keep a distance from immediate issues.	To stay apart, to jump out, to escape difficulties.

negotiations. Wey (1987), following this model and methodology, collected data for four years on Brazilian managers (900 from 75 private and state organizations) and different styles of behavior during negotiations. Her findings are summarized in Tables 1 and 2.

These tables show a very clear predominance of the 'receptive' style (linking and seducing – 63 per cent), rather than the so-called active style (persuading and asserting – 35 per cent), even if such differences are markedly more stressed in state organizations. Everything seems to happen in such a way that Brazilian managers try somehow to fix things up in order to avoid direct confrontation, which is experienced as dangerous (little capacity to withdraw), thus establishing

Table 2 Most characteristic negotiation styles (from Wey, 1987).

Styles	*State Organization per cent*	*Private Organization per cent*
Linking	52	46
Persuading	27	33
Seducing	17	15
Asserting	2	5
Withdrawing	2	1

Table 3 Negotiation styles (from Marcondes et al., 1989).

Negotiation styles among Brazilian managers – per cent		Outstanding negotiation styles among Brazilian managers according to their roles – per cent		
		Director/manager	*Superv.*	*Technicians*
Linking	46	49	43	46
Persuading	30	25	35	40
Seducing	18	18	15	10
Asserting	5	6	4	3
Withdrawing	1	2	3	1

Table 4 Negotiation styles (from Souza and Wey, 1989).

Styles	*State organization per cent*	*Private Organization per cent*
Linking	59	44
Persuading	18	26
Seducing	16	22
Asserting	6	8
Withdrawing	1	—

personal relationships and giving signs of an open mind and empathy.

Marcondes et al. confirmed these results in 1989 with the same methodology in a study involving 3,069 professionals. Their data are summarized in Table 3.

Regarding the submissive and the paternalistic attitudes that are evidently linked to the already mentioned authoritarian and hierarchical features, unpublished data collected in 1989 by Souza and Wey pointed out that the profile is consistent with the others' findings, with an emphasis on the tendencies listed in Table 4.

In Brazil in 1989, Amado and Cathelineau, in a yet unpublished study, used a case-study methodology based on a negotiation situation between two persons elaborated in France by Cathelineau with French managers in 1989. The 128 Brazilian managers have, overall, shown a very similar profile to that presented by the French investigators. If the latter researchers seem to be a bit more 'dialectic' than the Brazilian team (the Cartesian reasoning leads them to be more argumentative), the Brazilians appear more open-minded, more co-operative, more receptive, while their assertiveness and capacity to exert pressure remain weak (see Figure 1).

As Graham and Herberger (1983) point out, while the crux of the negotiation process for North American managers is persuasion, in Brazil it is neither information nor persuasion: 'Brazilians cannot depend on a legal system to iron out conflicts, so they depend on personal relationships' (p. 163). That is why they are victims of the 'wristwatch syndrome' – the fact that looking at your watch helps get things moving along. Say Graham and Herberger, 'impatience causes apprehension, thus necessitating even longer periods of non-task sounding' (p. 163).

Parallel to this study on negotiation, we carried out another study in 1989. Based on the work and methodology developed by Laurent in 1983, this study explored Brazilian managers' conceptions of organizations, compared with those of managers from other countries. Several statements on the management and the structuring of organizations were then proposed, and the degree of agreement found among managers was recorded, as indicated for each proposal in Figures 2–5.

Many of the results place Brazil in an outstanding position when compared to other nations. The Brazilian representatives seem to dream of eliminating conflicts inside organizations. To the first assertion, that 'Most organizations would be better off if conflict could be eliminated forever,' managers from various countries tend to answer differently (see Figure 2).

Brazilian managers worry about a precise definition of their roles. Responses to a second assertion, that 'Most managers would achieve better results if their roles were less precisely defined,' are indicated in Figure 3.

Figure 1 Average profile of Brazilian versus French attitudes in negotiation (from Amado and Cathelineau, 1989). This map is a synthesis of the results of research undertaken with 128 Brazilian managers, and 500 French ones, from a questionnaire presenting 28 situations of interpersonal negotiations with 4 possible solutions each. The results shown here reflect not direct observations but self-reports. When there is only one line on each scale, it means that Brazilian and French managers scored the same.

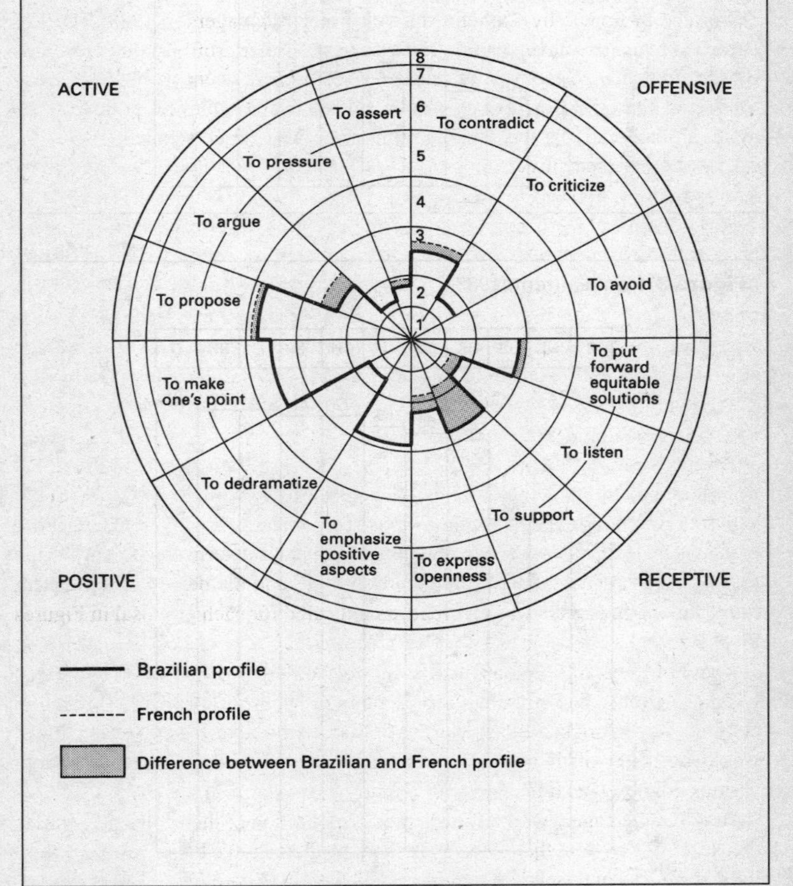

Figure 2 From Laurent, 1983. Abbreviations: US = United States; S = Sweden; GB = Great Britain; NL = The Netherlands; D = Germany; DK = Denmark; CH = Switzerland; B = Belgium; F = France; I = Italy; BR = Brazil

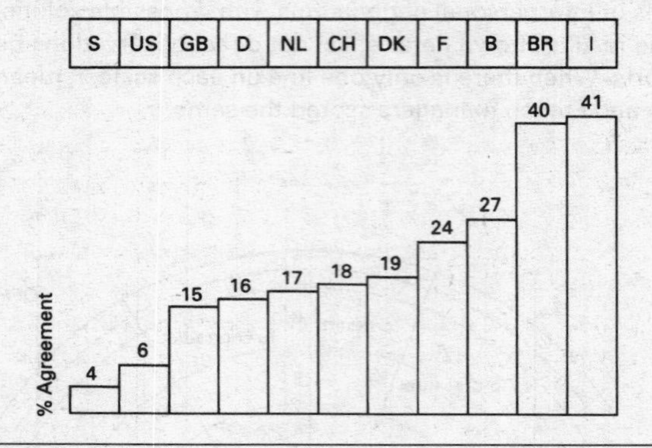

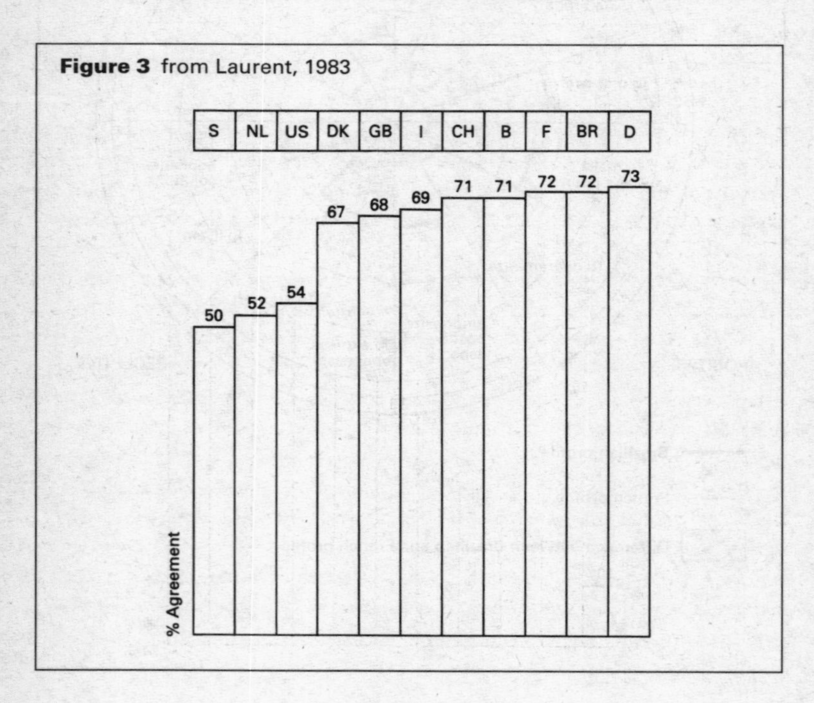

Figure 3 from Laurent, 1983

Figure 4 from Laurent, 1983

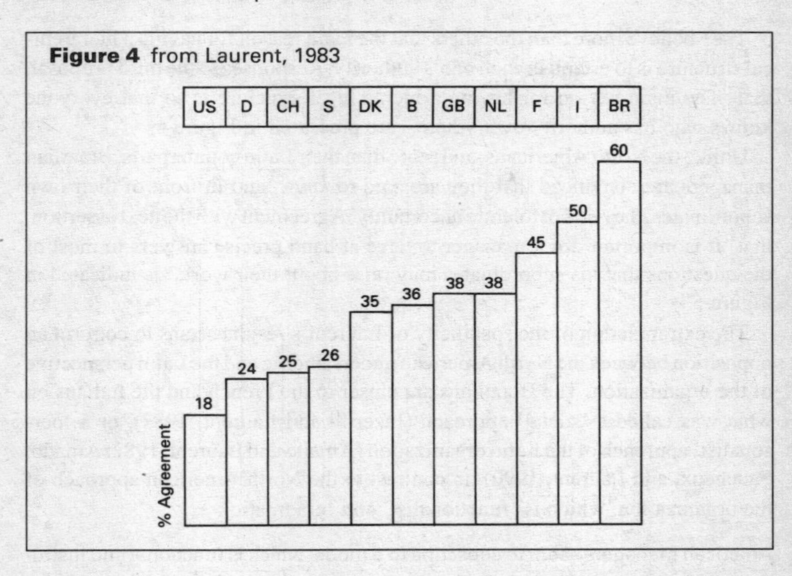

Figure 5 from Laurent, 1983

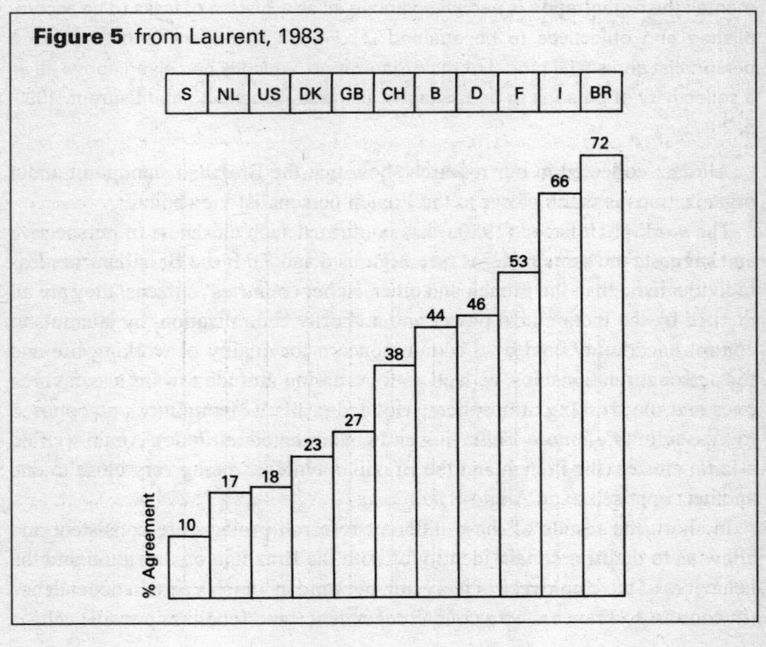

They believe more than the others that the main reason for having a hierarchical structure is to establish each one's authority. Responses to the third proposal, that 'The main reason for having a hierarchical structure is so that everyone knows who has authority over whom,' are presented in Figure 4.

Unlike the North Americans, and more than their Latin counterparts, Brazilian managers are convinced that they are paid to *know*, and in front of their own subordinates, they do not tolerate uncertainty. Agreement with the next assertion, that 'It is important for a manager to have at hand precise answers to most of the questions that his subordinates may raise about their work,' is indicated in Figure 5.

The extrapolation of the specificity of Laurent's results seems to confirm an opposition between the North American understanding and the Latin perspective of the organization. The Brazilians are closer to the French and the Italians on what was called a 'social' approach (Inzerilli and Laurent, 1983), or a 'personalist' approach of the Latin organization (Amado and Laurent, 1982; Amado, Faucheux, and Laurent, 1990), in contrast to the North American approach of the organization, which is 'functionalist' and 'pragmatic':

> American managers seem to subscribe to a model which is functional and instrumental: the organization is perceived above all as a system of tasks to be accomplished and objectives to be attained ... French managers tend to share a personalist and social model of the organization, which is perceived above all as a collectivity of persons to be managed. (Amado, Faucheux, and Laurent, 1990, p. 28)

All data collected in our research show that the Brazilian standpoint about organizations is much closer to the French personalist viewpoint.

The work of Hofstede (1980a) has confirmed such closeness of perspective and suggests the same patterns (see Figures 6 and 7). If the Brazilians are less individualistic than the French and other, richer countries' citizens, they are all marked by the hierarchical power and authority centralization, by attempts to control uncertainty, and by a certain concern for quality of working life and for personal relationships, as well as for a caring attitude toward less favored ones and the working atmosphere (Hofstede calls it 'femininity', as opposed to 'masculinity', a more 'achieving and goal oriented' attitude). Again we find a Latin cluster (the French and the Brazilian outlooks being very close to one another) opposed to an Anglo-Saxon one.

In short, the results of these different research projects are consistent and allow us to define a certain identity of both the Brazilian organization and the behaviors of the employees in it: a Latin pyramid in which a certain dependence (in contrast to France where counterdependence and rebellion prevail) echoes

Figure 6 The position of 40 countries on the power distance and uncertainty avoidance scales (from Hofstede, 1980a, p. 51)

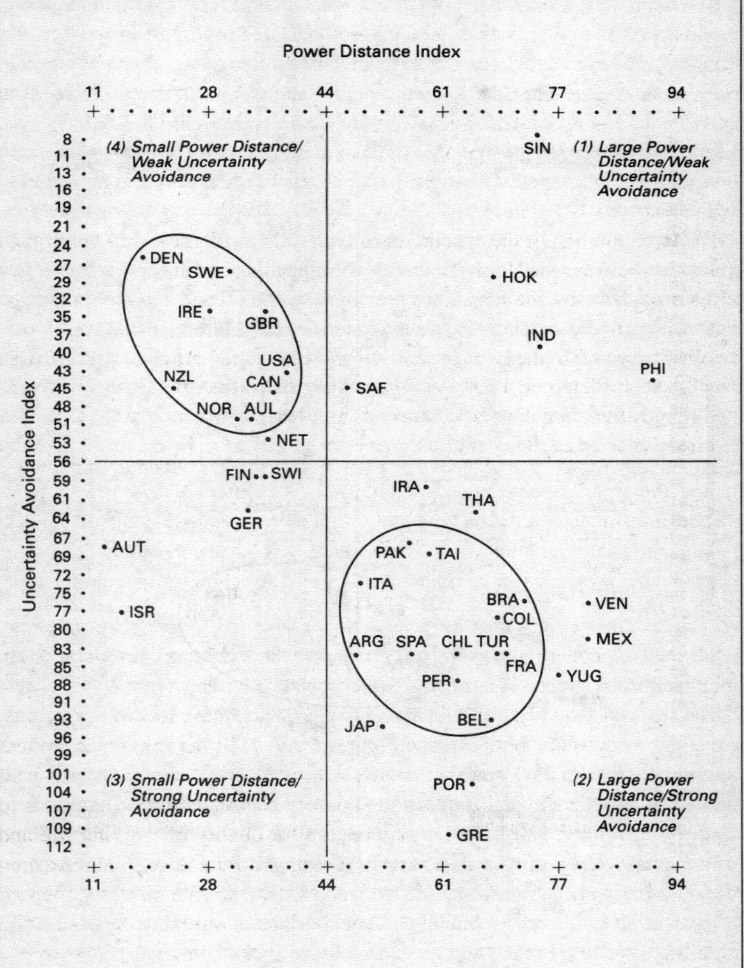

Figure 7 The position of 40 countries on the uncertainty avoidance and masculinity scales (from Hofstede, 1980a, p. 54)

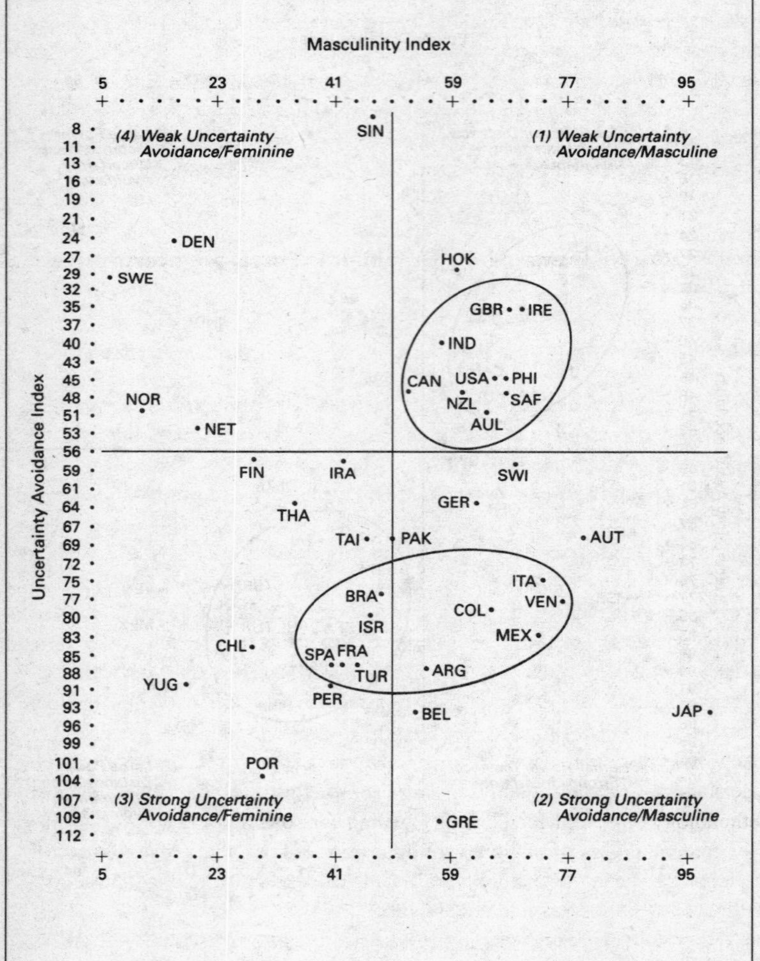

the centralization and control of a hierarchy concerned with asserting itself formally. Brazilian organizations seem to be comprised of members who are faced with the fear of unbearable conflicts, sensitive to the human dimension of work, and who are accustomed to avoiding difficulties thanks to personal interventions, which are the basis of the equilibrium.

This is where the most remarkable difference of the Brazilian man seems to lie. His history and his sociocultural roots are the basis for these intermediations, of which the Brazilian '*jeitinho*' – a special way of managing obstacles in order to find a way out of bureaucracy – makes a paradigmatic synthesis.

Sociohistorical Roots of the Brazilian Culture: an Interpretive Synthesis

Theoretical Background

This study requires as background Max Weber's epistemological principles, in which science does not validate value judgments, but yet it finds its basis in value premises when choosing references and leads to follow. This means that one must be aware that choices and theoretical orientations will be subject, from the beginning, to the researchers' world viewpoint. This fact pervades decisions and reflects cultural values. But this circularity does not invalidate conclusions if it has taken root in reality. Thus, keeping these principles in mind as a reference point makes it possible to reach reliable results, even if they always seem partial and temporary. Nevertheless, it is a mistake to think that these cultural features that are raised will stand together in a harmonic set, or even to think that they form a totally coherent structural model. The Brazilian culture, in particular, is marked by a high level of contradiction because it is young and its components are, just now, in a process of integration. To understand it more adequately, one has to use the similarity and difference methodology of Kant, which entails grasping concepts and categories dialectically in the darkness and lightness of opposition. But, in that process, it is still possible to achieve, at times, several levels of confluence and synthesis that shall come to reveal characteristic totalities.

We therefore see every attempt to search for uniform cultural patterns as stereotyping, and, at times, caricature. A culture itself is a game of transactions through which flow the worldview of people and societies, and even more restrictive groups with unconscious bearings.

When seeking out the origins of the current behavior of the Brazilian – that is, of his culture within this restricted sense – one should study what he says, writes, represents, and does. In this way, Schein (1980) outlines three 'windows' through which one may view a culture: the visible signs of its creations, patterns of behavior, and technologies; consciously incorporated values; and unconscious assumptions. The choice of the window (or windows) to which we will turn our eyes is methodologically very important.

It is our intention to find a way, starting with the Brazilian sociopolitical heritage, that will lead to a definition of the influence of the Brazilian culture in the management of organizations founded or based in Brazil. This endeavor will be only a glance through an opening in Schein's window.

In Brazil, the use of the 'Best Practices',[1] which originated in technologically more advanced cultures and in the context of capitalist economies, has proven that such transpositions are doomed to failure, or take much longer to become functional than is tolerable. And all, it seems, mainly because of cultural diversity. Recent studies carried out by several authors have pointed out that a blind, although well-meaning, use of managerial models might lead to failure and waste of time and money if the local culture is not taken into account. Such efforts are frustrating and usually lead to misgivings regarding the companies' modernization actions. Thus, in empirical terms, it is difficult to support the belief expressed by the so-called culture-free line of thought that, in large organizations that are very specialized and formalized, cultural differences are leveled, and this fact brings about a convergence of behaviors thanks to the common ideologies (Hickson et al., 1981). Such leveling is no longer possible, even in multinational companies operating in Third World countries. Therefore, we conclude that research on the influence of Brazilian culture over the management of national and international companies is both relevant and important. As a principle of regulation, every action in a social system (in this case, the company) is always influenced by the wider cultural system. Hofstede (1987), as mentioned before, was able to come to a kind of worldwide typology by exploiting international data reflecting differences among national cultures, defined within four reference parameters. But this mapping neglects the typical characteristics of each country, and is, thus, of little help to clear up those issues concerning the influence of a specific country's culture in the organization. Hofstede's contribution, however, reinforces our belief that cultural aspects cannot be neglected in transfers of technology, in the context of organizations.

Some may go even further. When comparing the strategies of negotiation of American and Japanese multinational enterprises, Hilb (1988) found that the methodology they use for social research on culture is itself pervaded by the cultural context in study. For instance, while quantitative approaches are more acceptable in the United States, the Japanese prefer a qualitative approach.

The Bureaucratic '*Estamento*' – a Social State of Being: the Base of the Brazilian Socioeconomical Organization (Faoro, 1958)

Brazil emerged, in early days, as a confluence of three human streams: the Portuguese, the African, and the Indian. Brazilians are a blend of races, but the leaders in the process are the Portuguese, who had political control and formed the élite. The racial fusion took place with the Metropolis as the catalytic agent and also as the sociopolitical reference. But the Portuguese people are themselves of mixed blood, with the Moors and even the Africans present in their ethnic background. Geographically, they are Europeans, even though their 'souls' are not as white as the souls of their continental neighbors, including Spain, their partner in the Iberian peninsula.

Such plasticity in the Portuguese ethnic background had deep influences in the colonization of Brazil. When the Portuguese came to Brazil, a long-standing and typical sociopolitical order, different from that in other European countries, had already been established in Portugal.

A centralized power, of military nature, replaced the yet incipient feudalism in Portugal. But such military aggregation had always revolved around the king's power, and the king chose his servants following a mercenary process. He rewarded them with goods and the promise of privileges, appealing simultaneously to the courtiers' greed and adventurous spirit. These servants of wealth did not have to pass through the sieve of the feudal barony which, for that reason, was slowly extinguished.

The state, as a personal enterprise of the prince, had a part in every private business, buying loyalty via the royal treasury, always eager for more contributions. The economy was at that time centralized on the state treasury, which collected revenues and taxes. It was the patriarchal entrepreneur and prince who controlled the kingdom as his own home. Everything was rather different from the rest of Europe, where business was held by private enterprise with a commercial and mercantilist angle.

Nevertheless, it must be stressed that the notion of 'state' was fundamental in the *anciens régimes*, and was based upon the old Indo-European distinction between the three states: the church, the army, and the peasants.

Portuguese capitalism flourished like an appendix to the royal house and as a dependent and minor partner. In that structure, traditionalism and centralization predominate and are almost synonymous.

The fundamental element in this machine was the bureaucratic '*estamento*', recruited by the king in order to accomplish his despotic will and goals, in the realm of a patrimonial state.

'*Estamento*', according to Faoro (1958), based on Max Weber, means a group characterized by an aspiration to privileges, which finds its accomplishment in differentiation through honor and the acceptance of individuals. It is different from class, which is the result and product of economic interests tied to the market. It is also different from bureaucracy, which is a simple apparatus of the establishment, its administrative staff performing on the borderlines of rational and professional behaviors. But, even so, *estamento* may sometimes appear as either a class or a bureaucracy, in some ways linked to the state. It cannot be seen as a dysfunction, but better yet as a distortion. It is also different from the political élite, since it is found in all strata.

The *estamento*, on behalf of the prince, is the nation's referee, and also its class's referee. It holds the economy materially as if it were the master of its sovereignty.

Within the limits of every definition, which always tends to be oversimplifying, these considerations describe this social category which the Portuguese transplanted to Brazil.

The country's colonization took place under an 'estamental' and patrimonial economic order. Later on, it became a state capitalism, highly supported by the bureaucratic *estamento*.

It was, thus, the country's trademark always to depend on the state, even after the Proclamation of the Republican Regime – theoretically considered as a reaction against monarchy, but which maintained the bureaucratic *estamento* unchanged. But the republic was imposed on the people, who were brought down to the rank of animals, as described by Carvalho (1987). In addition to this, 'it boycotted every single opportunity to consolidate citizenship'.

This economy, dependent on the state, started with the '*capitanias hereditarias*',[2] which were a king's donation to his 'protégés'; but they were inalienable and indivisible, to such an extent that they would eventually return to the donor's possession. The early explorers in Brazil themselves behaved as contractors and managers of the Power because they were used to being the king's commissioners, despite the fact that they were looking for riches and that they sometimes tried to break their commitments.

Thus, everything in colonial Brazil and in the kingdom of Brazil was delegated. After independence, the empire organized itself as a bureaucratic *estamento* that 'nestled into the Executive Power, in the lifelong senate and into the moderating power. This was the first symptom of the mechanism of intermediation and arbitrariness' (Faoro, 1958, p. 204).[3] Lifelong Senates, 'bionic senators'[4] are names to label the same reality. The king's 'moderating power' or the armed forces are identical categories that bear the purpose of maintaining the 'status quo'.

Joaquim Nabuco (1915, pp. 280–81) already predicted what is still true today when he wrote: 'Since the beginning, the heat, light and life for the larger organizations had come from the Treasury.' This fact implicitly includes a high grade of economic and legal regulatory power that the 'estamental' state holds, making private enterprise difficult. However, what is even more serious is that organizations found ways to get around such interventionism – that is, they avoided it by associating with the state, standing by its side, and by obtaining subsidies, protectionism, unofficial cartels, and exceptional financing. The government, by subjecting organizations to its will, provided for their needs.

In this way, the *estamento* has embodied the characteristics of a huge *advocacia administrativa* – a way of taking advantage of one's own individual and personal influence before the state in order to get privileges – which has become fundamental to the nation's functioning. Despite the fact that it is necessary to all modern societies, bureaucracy, in Weber's sense, is always conservative. Bureaucracy, in its 'estamental' distortion, obstructs the course of change processes because it is an end in itself, a power manipulator, a domination tool. In bureaucracy, formalism predominates in relationships, and it causes the displacement of objectives, a certain accommodation and a disharmony between the written rule and the behavior it induces. Even as a strategy to reduce conflicts, to hide the dualities found in the social structure, and to dissolve downtown-versus-suburb contrasts, such 'estamental' bureaucracy is the support of a culture that explains to a great extent the Brazilian people's characteristics and way of life. The popular answer to how to avoid or ignore this spurious usurpation is to create new behavior possibilities (Ramos, 1983) which become, in the course of time, deeply rooted in a culture or in the features of that culture.

The Brazilian '*Jeitinho*' as a Hermeneutic Key for the Brazilian Culture

It is in the conjunction of a society organized in the realm of a conservative, patrimonial, and 'estamental' state capitalism of a greatly differentiated ethnic background that the Brazilian man was formed, or is still in the process of being formed. The '*casa grande*' (owner's house on a plantation), in a certain phase of this social and economic evolution, where monoculture (sugar) was prevalent, provided the fusion of these traces to happen, as their components shared the same environment and means of living (Freire, 1954). The *casa grande* complemented by the '*senzala*' (the plantation's slave quarters), represented the whole economic, social, and political system – namely, labor and production, religion and sexual life, which have left marks in the Brazilian people's way of life and behavior. This monocultural system, with supports in slavery and large landed estates – in which the coffee farmer or the '*senhor de engenho*' (the owner and master of large sugarcane fields and sugar mills) was not only the landowner but also the master of men and women – reinforces the ongoing authoritarianism and centralization in the 'estamental' government, in colonial, imperial, or even in republican times.

The slavery regime – the base of the entire system – provided the blacks with economic support while they 'compounded' with the Portuguese *senhor de engenho*, exchanging culture and blood, and thus incorporating habits, behavior, food, sexuality, and life's rhythm. The '*capoeira*' (a dancelike wrestling practiced by the slaves in Brazil), the merrymaking, the music, most especially the '*samba*' (a popular Brazilian dance of African origin – the center of the yearly *Carnaval*), the '*feijoada*' (a popular Brazilian dish made of black beans boiled with bits of pork and sausage, seasoned with pepper sauce, and served with rice and manioc flour), the '*cocada*' (coconut candy), the seasonings, the '*vatapa*' (a Brazilian dish made of manioc meal, mixed with fish and shrimp), the celebrations, and the religious feasts are clear traces of this racial fusion. Moreover, the cultural syncretism found its way into the official religion of most of the population, Catholicism. The Catholic Church in Brazil has incorporated into its unofficial beliefs the rites and religious practices brought by the blacks from Africa. It is not at all by chance that the patron saint of Brazil, Lady Aparecida, is a black virgin miraculously found in a river (Da Matta, 1986).

All this makes the Brazilian. He is a citizen seeking for his soul in the dialectic profusion of his physical and spiritual components, who has had to develop a flexible, labile, plastic personality in order to survive, live, and build a country. In order to face an oligarchic social system, he developed a '*jogo de cintura*' – a flexibility of body and spirit to deviate from obstacles[5] – an aspect of what can be identified as a key to the Brazilian behavior, the *jeitinho*, a typical cultural feature. We are talking about plasticity and flexibility. The *jeitinho* is the common denominator, the hermeneutic basis from which an interpretation of the Brazilian culture becomes possible. It is not a question of making this one feature absolute, but rather is a matter of using this privileged front door so as to further deepen the exposition. In our analysis, the *jeitinho* provides us with the key for understanding what it means 'to be Brazilian', and for deriving some insights into Brazilian management. Of course, the deeper components of *jeitinho* remain to be explored in further research.

Two authors, as far as we know, have elaborated a sociological theory of the '*jeito*' – a way, manner, tact, appearance, adroitness, aptitude, dexterity . . . ('*dar un jeito*' is a very common expression meaning 'to find a way out to') – Guerreiro Ramos (1983) and Roberto Campos (1960).[6] They see *jeito* as the most genuine Brazilian process of problem managing, 'despite the contents of the rules, codes and laws', as the latter says, an efficient adaptive process for living in a closed, centralized, 'estamental', and formalistic society, with the advantage of avoiding deadlocks, extreme solutions, and paralyzing situations – all outbursts, in short. Because confrontation does not suit the Brazilian social training and way of life, this 'cordial'[7] facet of the Brazilian is a consequence of the way he interacts with the sociopolitical environment (Holanda, 1976). Such cordiality – which the European etymology cannot thoroughly translate – is the expression of a rich, overflowing, and sensitive world that rejects ritualism and seeks intimacy, in a different way from the almost religious reverence of the Japanese. Because Brazilians are fond of intimacy, they like to use the diminutive suffix '*inho*' – often used as a term of endearment – beginning with *jeitinho*, which does not mean only and strictly *jeito* (way, manner), but rather, a broadly fresh and intimate game. Thus, Brazilians relate on emotional terms and, even in business, they do not eliminate collective outbursts and nonconformity at the level of the people. Their social rebellions were nearly always cruel, if seen and studied in great depth (Rodrigues, 1982). The cordial man does not necessarily imply kindness, but only the predominance of apparently emotional behaviors; the epitomizing of these behaviors is not reflected on a collective level.

To return to the *jeitinho* as an adaptive answer and as the essence of the behavior the Brazilians have found to deal with this sociopolitical heritage, we notice that it is a highly functional and effective device. It bypasses a legal framework full of 'texts out of context – technical elaborations that were not born from customs but from a highly oligarchical power' (Campos, 1960).

This mannerism of the Brazilian personality has brought about typical characters in a society full of mediations: the '*despachante*', a kind of spokesman who represents someone's interests before the bureaucratic establishment (because of the nature of the reigning bureaucracy, Brazilians prefer to hire the services of such an agent, rather than waste their time standing in lines to resolve their issues); the *advocacia administrativa*, the several kinds of brokers and mediators present in business affairs. Each of these mediators takes care of someone else's interests in exchange for pecuniary benefits. As Campos (1960, p. 29) describes them: 'They patch up the gap between the law and the fact, making possible the impossible, legal the illegal, and fair the unfair. They grant flexibility to a formal and rigid law with excessive logical strictness.'

On the political level, the moderating power, which has acted ever since imperial times, is within this mediating line of behavior, as we have pointed out. At first the emperor strategically ruled conflicts from an upper standpoint, even above the constitution itself. Eventually his rule was assumed by the army.

But both always intervened in favor of the oligarchies and of the maintenance of the status quo, as it were.

Setting apart power aspects, these mediators are, in fact, institutionalized *jeitinho*. That is why there are in Brazil some laws that simply do not apply.

The simple fact that *jeitinho* exists allows for discrimination. There are laws for everything, a superabundance of them, in comparison with other countries (especially with Anglo-Saxon ones). Thus, it is easier to choose the one law that protects you or the one that punishes your opponents. '*Aos inimigos a lei, aos amigos as facilidades da lei*' (the law for your enemies, the advantages of the law for your friends), the proverb says.

Conflicts must be avoided at all costs. The Brazilian people appreciate euphemisms (Vinagre Brasil, 1989), which means escaping from the unpleasant, attenuating inconveniences or smoothing over reality. By postponing or watering down conflicts, Brazilians get *around* problems, and that, in a sense, means solving them – in the Brazilian way. Brazilians always escape from the radical standpoints of a confrontation in personal terms. That is why we find such aphorisms as '*deixa estar pra ver como é que fica*' (leave things as they are; wait and see what happens); '*O Brazil é um pais do futuro*' (Brazil is a country that belongs to the future); '*Deus é brasileiro*' (God is Brazilian); '*quem trabalha nao tem tempo de ganhar dinheiro*' (whoever works never finds time to make money); and in a paroxysmal extension, bordering on corruption, these lead to the '*Lei de Gerson*' – Gerson's law – which claims 'one must take advantage of every situation',[8] or that 'by giving one receives', which would be a '*lei do Sao Francisco as avessas*',[9] which was supported by some Brazilian physiologistic politicians (Vinagre Brasil, 1989).

Another very interesting category we may include in Brazil's *jeitinho* culture is that of '*gambiarra*', which is a kind of a nonprofessional, cheap, and quick repair or mending (Paulielo, 1984). *Gambiarra* as a rule 'breaks up' in very improper circumstances because the definitive arrangement is always postponed. In this way, a provisory solution becomes a permanent one, despite the risks involved in its adoption.

Brazilians use *gambiarras* to patch up cars, utilities, and even the federal constitution, because it is easier to make a quick repair than it is to give a matter some more thought. In a positive interpretation, *gambiarra* reflects flexibility.

Any analysis of cultural behavior cannot overlook aspects of time and space management. Thus, it is relevant to ask how a Brazilian manages time. We already received some information about this from a North American perspective about the negotiation process. But what do Brazilian anthropologists say? 'An hour in Brazil is not enjoyed as it is in the United States regarding rhythm and other living aspects,' Ramos (1983) confirms.

According to Da Matta, Brazilian people have differentiated and divergent temporalities: linear time in the outer world, cyclical time at home, and everlasting time in another world. In linear time we are in the realm of organized work, one thing after the other, where routine and repetition predominate; in cyclical time we are at home, all by ourselves, not worried with efficiency or cartesian logic, in a ludic state of mind. These are qualitative dimensions that are inseparable from quantitative ones, and they differentiate and complete each other in the outer world and home spaces. In this way, the Brazilian avoids experiencing a 'schizophrenic' time. It is not that other cultures do not incorporate such differences. But here they are much clearer and, paradoxically, more blended because of the importance of the sociopolitical organization, centralized within the state. Following a classification by Ramos (1983), we would say that the utilitarian Taylorian serial time, which makes time a merchandise (time is money), is counterbalanced by the social time one spends at home and during vacations and holidays. The Brazilian escapes from routine and repetition by keeping himself in transit between the two types of time.

Inside organizations, it is during the so-called transitional moments – coffee or conversation breaks – when people arrive or leave work, that one time is inserted into the other. Hence, people mark a wedge in the hierarchical and anonymous environments of organizations.

This expressive time management reflects how the Brazilian views work and the next day. Because, from the point of view of puritan capitalism transplanted to Brazil in its basic Anglo-Saxon ideology, work does not mean *today* but the *future*, such a viewpoint clashes with the Brazilian reality. The stubborn and oligarchic structure of the 'estamental' power makes people live life in a fatalistic manner, as destiny and not as construction. It is a little like the fable of the ant and the grasshopper. Brazilian people are the grasshoppers. That is why neither hurrying nor being punctual is worthwhile. Brazil is more than just a country. It is a continent. Its accomplishment is in the future. Its wealth, to the Brazilian, is inexhaustible and therefore one should not hurry, one should proceed slowly and constantly. Brazilian people believe in charismatic leaders and in magic solutions. It is not by chance that the '*jogo do bicho*', an illegal national lottery,[10] was created – a national institution that, despite its 'unofficial' status, is reliable and solidly established. The *estamento*, aware of its existence, creates dozens of lotteries – euphemistic ways of collecting taxes from everyone, including the poor. Then, the future is not history but a game. For the individual, it is not the work that pays off; rather, it is fate that decides if one will be rich or poor. After all, opposites meet . . . but space and time are interdependent. One cannot be managed without the other.

Public time and private time take place in public and in private spaces. Even the 'other world's' time is up there and down here in the family memories. In these spaces, intimacy and individuality exist in opposition with depersonalization and anonymity. Behaviors are functions of these spaces and they are inserted inside the logic of these oppositions or of these complementarities.

According to Da Matta (1986), Brazilian society is 'relational' because it is integrated through relations between spaces, where it builds transitional bridges. 'God is Brazilian', not because with him things will always work out, but, above all, because he is composed – as we are – of three persons or three distinct and absolutely complementary spaces. The father is the outer world, where the state is the relentless universe of impersonal laws, and the son is the home, with his warm relationship, his humanity, and the senses of a person made of flesh and bones. And the holy ghost is the relationship between the two, the other side of the mystery (Da Matta, 1987).

These spaces represented by the home, the outer world, and the other world have activities, specific objects, and time as well-defined and distinct ethics.

Some devices make the transit easier inside these spaces and times, bringing us to the proximity of our daily experiences. They are 'breaks' for witticisms and joke telling, to tell about real or imaginary sexual experiences, to have a cup of coffee, to tap someone on the back – in short, to be intimate.

In this three-dimensional world, the *jeitinho* prevails and works as a conflict reducer, smoothing the transit from one environment to another, and thus permitting a conviviality with the dysfunctions of work. The *jeitinho* replaces the law's mediation, which does not work among Brazilians, for the home and the outer world are then self-referential. The 'individual' and the 'person' at times are one, and at other times are opponents, and only the *jeitinho* can bring harmony to these indefinitions. That is why Brazilian people are obsessed with relationships and with personal bonds, so as always to be able to find the key to their own lives. This distinction between the individual (*o individuo*) and the person (*a pessoa*) is another key Da Matta (1987) offers to explain the 'Brazilian dilemma'. The individual is the impersonal subject of universal laws, while the person is the subject of social relationships, with their emotions and uniqueness. The tendency of Brazilians is therefore to reduce the power of the anonymous individual (or laws) to live and solve processes at a personal level. The outer world, which stands for work, is anonymous, full of surprises, temptations, and insecurity, and is compensated by the home, where Brazilians are personal, have their own bodies, and can keep up the moral dimension of honor, respect, honorability, and shame. This ambiguity is therefore a means of survival. It is also a way of life. 'The secret of a correct interpretation of Brazil lies in the possibility of studying what is "between" things,' Da Matta insists (1987, p. 26). The Brazilian *Carnaval* feast is a clear way of linking the home, the outer world, and the other world, or the intimate, the dangerous, and the magical, a typical way of promoting equality by a temporary denial of differences and frontiers.

Even in food, Brazilians care more for pasty dishes. These are 'relational' and intermediary, and neither purely solid nor liquid. '*Feijoada*', a stew, '*canjiquinha*', a traditional Brazilian dish of cornmeal and pieces of meat, with pork ribs and cabbage, '*munguza*', a dish made with milk, sugar, and cinnamon, corn and peanuts, '*vatapa*', in which shrimp float on top of the paste, oily with '*dendê*' (an African oilplant grown in Brazil) – these are all almost soups or even solid morsels dipped in something that is almost liquid, in short, pasty.

If the *jeitinho* is taken as a common denominator of oppositions, contrasts, and contradictions, it may not entirely define or explain the behavior of the Brazilians, even if it pictures them realistically. But are we dealing with a matter of definition? The demonstration of Brazilians' sociopolitical and cultural realities by means of the *jeitinho* allows us to find a common root for most of their behavior inside organizations.

These behaviors show a double facet, which makes them contradictory. By being flexible and labile, Brazilians have a chance to face their authoritarian and discriminatory environment, as well as to resist change. This explains why even the negative diagnoses discussed earlier in this paper are accepted, why a certain kind of conflict avoidance is displayed in negotiation, and why the new management technologies (Best Practices) are difficult to implement or do not work out at all.

This double facet of a mediation-type behavior is reflected, in Brazil, through the *jeitinho*. But we cannot ignore the analogies that may come to mind if we turn to other Latin countries. In France and Italy especially, the existence of similar mediation processes is striking. The 'system D' in France (where 'D' stands for '*débrouillardise*' – resourcefulness) and the '*combinazzione*' in Italy also have this double facet. Both of them are means used by individuals and groups to bypass centralization, an excessive rigidity or amount of laws and regulations, the power of the state, authoritarian modes of leadership. Although the 'D' system and the '*combinazzione*' help people to live in a satisfactory way with a real amount of flexibility and creativity, on the other hand they disqualify the power of social rules and lead to anarchy, parallel organizations, or mafias (either terrorist in Italy, or intellectual in France through the élitist castes).

Therefore, beyond its hermeneutic value for the understanding of the cultural

Brazilian reality, the *jeitinho* can become the living source of further research on the Latin modes of mediation used by people within organizations and society.

Notes

We would like to express our sincere thanks to the professors of Fundaçao Dom Cabral: Antônio Mauricio Hostalacio Costa and Sônia Teresa Diegues Fonseca, for having shared with us their vast experience in Brazilian companies gathered during so many years; Professor Roberto Da Matta (Notre Dame University, Kelley Institute), for his precious help in the understanding of the Brazilian culture; Professors Marco Aurélio Spyer Prates and Ulisses Ferreira Diniz e Betânia Tanure de Barros for the 'cross-fertilization' of ideas and opinions regarding the research project, 'Cultural Reality and Management Systems', being developed at Fundaçao Dom Cabral; Marc Cathelineau (Thomson and HEC Graduate School of Management) for giving us permission to use his questionnaire about negotiation behaviors and for analyzing the data collected; Professor André Laurent (INSEAD) for permission to use his questionnaire about 'organizational mental maps', and for his work, together with Cathy Petts, in the data analysis and editing of this paper; Professor Claude Faucheux (Erasmus University, Rotterdam School of Management, The Netherlands), for his comments and help in the editing of this contribution; HEC Graduate School of Management, its research direction and the 'Jouy-Enterprises' Association for their financial and administrative support in the research; Clarissa Rose and Maria Matta Machado for their assistance in the translation of this document; Sylvie Bonneau and Sylvie Metais for their secretarial help; Agnès Melot, director of the HEC library and her colleagues.

1. Best Practices are linked to administration models – management technologies conceived in developed countries and transferred to the Third World, generally without the necessary adaptation. Examples are: Management by Objectives, Total Quality Control, Just In Time, Zero Defect, among others.

2. In colonial Brazil, the *capitanias hereditarias* was a jurisdictional division corresponding to a province, allotted to a protégé of the prince.

3. The moderating power meant that the emperor and, after him, the army, had the role of a referee in the political game, deciding over parties and Congress if the 'estamental status quo' was in jeopardy.

4. The bionic senators were a class of senators nominated by the president during the military government in Brazil. They corresponded to a certain percentage of the Congress that had a greater representation.

5. This idiomatic expression was originally used to signify the way Brazilians play soccer as if they were dancing the *samba*. They used a swing of their hips to avoid their opponents – to deviate from the opponent's path. In life, it means the Brazilian has to avoid difficult situations.

6. See also Viera, Da Costa, and Barbosa (1982).

7. '*O homem cordial*' – the cordial man who reflects the myth of a mixed-blooded society.

8. Gerson was a world champion Brazilian soccer player who used this expression as a slogan in a cigarette advertisement. The fact that it took on a pejorative connotation at the time upset him.

9. Cardoso Alves, a member of the Brazilian Parlement, first used this expression in an interview in which he supported the '*fisiologismo*' of the politicians – that is, a supportive attitude adopted by some politicians toward the government in exchange for favors. '*As avessas*' means the other way around. San Francis is the author of a well-known prayer that says that by giving, one is already receiving. And Cardoso Alves was giving his support to the government, not taking into consideration the people's interest, but only his own.

10. The '*jogo do bicho*' was created by the Baron of Drummond in Rio de Janeiro to reward the visitors to his zoo. Today it is run by bookmakers. It is a highly reliable lottery network because it never fails to pay the prizes.

References

Amado, G. and Cathelineau, M., 'Estudo sobre os comportamentos na negociaçao', *Tendencias do trabalho*, December 1987, 12–16; January 1988, 23–7; February 1988, 15–18.

Amado, G., C. Faucheux and A. Laurent, 'Changement organisationnel et réalités culturelles, contrastes franco-américains', in J. F. Chanlat (ed.), *L'individu dans l'organisation: les dimensions oubliées*, Québec: Presses de l'Université Laval, 1990.

Amado, G. and A. Laurent, 'Organization Development and Change: A Comparison between USA and Latin Countries', IX Annual Conference of SIETAR, San Gimignano, Italy, May 1982.

Blanc, G., 'Culture et management: l'exemple du Brésil', *Cahier de recherche du Centre HEC*, No. 187, Jouy-en-Josas, France: HEC, 1981.

Campos, R., 'A Sociologia do "jeito" ', *Revista senhor*, 1960, 29.

Cardoso, P. H., *O empresario e o desenvolvimento industrial no Brasil*, São Paulo: Difusao Européia do Livro, 1964.

Carvalho, de, J. M., *Os bestializados*, São Paulo: Companhia das Letras, 1987.

Da Matta, R., *O que faz o Brasil Brasil*, Rio de Janeiro: Rocco, 1986.

— *A casa e a rua*, Rio de Janeiro: Guanabara, 1987.

Faoro, R., *Os donos do poder*, Porto Alegre: Globo, 1958.

Freire, G., *Casa grande e senzala*, 8th edn, Rio de Janeiro: José Olympio, 1954.

Graham, J. L. and R. Herberger, Jr., 'Negotiators abroad – don't shoot from the hip', *Harvard Business Review*, July–August 1983, 160–68.

Hersey, P. and K. Blanchard, *Management of Organizational Behavior*, Englewood Cliffs, NJ: Prentice-Hall, 1969.

Herzberg, F., *Work and the Nature of Man*, Cleveland: World, 1966.

Hickson, D. J., et al., *The Culture Free Context of Organization Structure*, The Aston Programme IV, Guilfort Biddles, 1981.

Hilb, M., *Japanese and American Multinational Companies: Business Strategies*, Gestion 2000, Université Catholique de Louvain, 1988.

Hofstede, G., 'Motivation, leadership and organisation: do American theories apply abroad?' *Organisational Dynamics*, Summer 1980, 42–63 (1980a).

— *Culture's Consequences: International Differences in Work-Related Values*, Beverly Hills, CA: Sage Publications, 1980 (1980b).

— 'Relativité culturelle des pratiques et théories de l'organisation', *Revue Française de gestion*, September–October 1987, 10–21.

Holanda, de, S. B., *Raizes do Brasil*, 9th edn, Rio de Janeiro: José Olympio, 1976.

Hostalacio Costa, A. M. and S. T. Diegues Fonseca, 'Sintese fenomenologica das açoes de desenvolvimento gerencial', Belo Horizonte, Fundaçao Dom Cabral, documento interno,1989.

Inzerilli, G. and A. Laurent, 'Managerial views of organizational structure in France and the USA', *International Studies of Management and Organization*, 8 (1/2) 1983, 97–118.

Lapierre, L., 'Imaginario, administraçao e liderança', in *Revista de administraçao de empresas*, São Paulo: Fundaçao Getulio Vargas, 1989.

Laurent, A., 'The cultural diversity of Western conceptions of management', *International Studies of Management and Organization*, 13 (1/2) 1983, 75–96.

Leminsky, P., *Catatau*, Porto Alegre: Sulina, 1989.

Likert, R., *New Patterns of Management*, New York: McGraw-Hill, 1961.

Maslow, A. H., *Motivation and Personality*, New York: Harper and Row, 1954.

Nabuco, J., *Um estadista do império*, Vol. 2, Rio de Janeiro: Garnier, 1915.

Paulielo, L., 'No pais das gambiarras', *Estado de minas*, Belo Horizonte, 27 June 1984.

Prasad, S. B., 'Managers' attitudes in Brazil: nationals versus expatriates', *Management International Review*, 21, 1981, 78–85.

Ramos, G., *Administraçao e contexto Brasileiro*, Rio de Janeiro: Fundaçao Getulio Vargas, 1983.

Rodrigues, J. H., *Conciliaçao e reforma no social*, Rio de Janeiro: Nova Fronteira, 1982.

Schein, E. H., 'Coming to a new awareness of organizational culture', *Sloan Management Review*, 25(2) 1980, 3–16.

Vieria, C. A., F. L. Da Costa and L. O. Barbosa, 'O ''jeitinho'' brasileiro como um recurso de poder', *Revista de administraçao publica* (Rio de Janeiro), 16 (2) 1982, 5–31.

Vinagre Brasil, H., 'Patologia da cultura brasileira', *Diario do comércio*, p. 2, Belo Horizonte, 1989.

Weber, M., *Essais sur le théorie de la science*, Paris: Plon, 1965.

Wey, V. L., 'Pesquisa revela quem é negociador brasileiro', *Tendências do trabalho*, pp. 9–11, July 1987.

4

The Northern Europeans and Israel

Germany

German Management

Malcolm Warner and Adrian Campbell

Chapter 6, pp. 89–108 in David J. Hickson (ed.), *Management in Western Europe: Society, Culture and Organization in Twelve Nations* (Berlin and New York: Walter de Gruyter, 1993)

Introduction

Germany occupies a central, if ambiguous role, in Europe. Although one of the largest states (covering 356,900 square kilometres with a population, in 1990, of 79,070,000) it is a relative newcomer to statehood (1870). Its history, and therefore its image of itself, diverges sharply from the longer-established nation states of Western Europe. In this respect, it more closely resembles the nation states of Eastern Europe (with the possible exception of Russia), its borders being drawn partly from ethnic and linguistic allegiance, and partly from the outcomes of complex military and diplomatic processes. As C. M. Bowra remarked of the ancient Greeks: 'A people lives by its geography' (1985: 3). Almost landlocked and with few natural frontiers, Germany increasingly dominates Europe (in practice, if not in recent years by intention) both East and West. Whilst the superpower *status quo* in Europe between 1945 and 1989/90 cancelled Germany's power in political and military terms, the economic advances of West Germany in the post-war period laid the basis for a strengthened role in the 1990s and beyond, following the collapse of the Soviet Union and the gradual diminution of direct US influence on the continent.

Germany has presented extremes of stability and instability as compared to other European States. From the perspective of the 1990s, it may be said that defeat in two world wars and the physical and psychological damage incurred by militarism, economic disasters in the 1920s and 30s and, of course, Nazism (1933–45), and the subsequent division of the country by the Iron Curtain (1945–89/90) have not altered the long-term momentum of German advance relative to the rest of Europe (see James, 1991).

Despite the fundamental uncertainties which underly German identity and destiny ('*die Deutsche frage*'), an uncertainty sometimes expressed by violent xenophobia in some quarters, Germany has also demonstrated a high degree of political stability over several decades. Prior to the end of the Cold War, the two German States presented particularly stable versions of their different economic systems. The Federal Republic has been characterized (largely) by consensus-oriented government based around corporatist 'social partnership' in the economic sphere, and a highly decentralized system of government – both of these foundations having been built up with the active participation of Allied occupying forces concerned with eliminating from the system any sources of dangerous instability (see Malzahn, 1991). The system's success drew on that side of German culture which values consensus and a joint, professional approach in all matters.

East Germany, meanwhile, provided the most stable and efficient of the Stalinist satellites of Eastern Europe. As late as 1989, the German Democratic Republic was being held up by hard-liners in Moscow as an example of how Communism could work if people were sufficiently disciplined. Although, with hindsight, the GDR's economic 'success' was largely a sham, and depended on Western subsidy, it none the less demonstrated another side of German culture – bureaucratic, disciplined and oriented towards control. The regimented orderliness of the GDR contrasted with the position of other Soviet-style economies, and drew on indigenous traditions which dated back to the military bureaucracy of Frederick the Great in eighteenth-century Prussia (of which the Soviet system was itself a direct descendant).

The Role of German Culture

How far do these historical and cultural factors influence the practice of German management? Does the national context determine variations of style in any coherent way? Although it is dangerous to generalize, Hofstede (1991) is surely right to recognize a degree of truth in the intuitive perception that nationality matters:

> In research on cultural differences, nationality – the passport one holds – should . . . be used with care. Yet it is often the only feasible criterion for classification. Rightly or wrongly, collective properties are ascribed to the citizens of certain countries: people refer to 'typically American', 'typically German', or 'typically Japanese' behavior. (1991: 12)

In industrial and economic terms, the traditions referred to above can still be perceived in Germany. On the one hand, there is the *Handwerk* tradition of the autonomous craft worker, which was successfully defended against US-imported Taylorism; on the other hand, there is the tradition of the stratified bureaucracy which found earlier expression in the military factories of Prussia and may still be perceived in the German public sector. What is remarkable is the way in which the Germans have achieved flexibility from the fusion of the two, particularly in the area of training. An emphasis on protracted training and education, and formal qualifications, has been used in such a way as to provide flexibility and autonomy on the shop-floor.

In later sections, we will be looking in more detail at the culture and principles of German management. However, perhaps the over-riding cultural characteristic of German society and management does not so much lie in the details of these beliefs, but in the strength with which they are held. Germans appear to want to belong to a tradition, to subscribe to a set of values. These values are likely to be explicit and non-negotiable. It may be said that, paradoxically, the success of German post-war consensus has been due to the strictness with which Germans have disciplined themselves not to follow divergent paths. Principles are stated and accepted. A system such as that of the traditional British mode of industrial relations, with its curious, pragmatic interplay of the formal and the informal, conflict and cooperation, would be quite alien to the German understanding of how things should be done.

This desire to be grounded in clear and unambiguous principles may be seen as a cultural response to the uncertainties which have characterized German history; the lack of that long-standing sense of security that characterizes Britain (or rather England) and France, a security which allows for irony, pragmatism and understatement. German philosophy has reflected this search for metaphysical certainty and for belonging. As Sir Isaiah Berlin has argued:

> Herder virtually invented the idea of belonging. He believed that just as people need to eat and drink, to have security and movement, so too they need to belong to a group. Deprived of this, they felt cut off, lonely, diminished, unhappy . . . To be human meant to be able to feel at home somewhere with your own kind. (cited in Gardels, 1991)

German culture is thus characterized by a striving for collectivism that clearly separates it from Anglo-Saxon culture, whatever the superficial resemblance between the two. As Canetti has argued, the difference may be expressed in terms of national symbols, the one individualistic, the other relatively collectivist:

> The Englishman likes to imagine himself at sea, the German in a forest. It is impossible to express the difference of their national feeling more succinctly. (Canetti, 1973: 203)

German Industrial Performance

Whatever the question marks that still surround Germany's future political role, its economic dominance in Europe is unquestionable. On the eve of unification, in July 1990, the then West Germany was producing 40 per cent of the European Community's manufactured output, with little more than a sixth of its population. One third of this output was exported annually, and Germany maintained positive trade balances with ten out of its eleven EC partners. In cars, mechanical engineering, chemicals, textiles, and electronics, it maintains a powerful competitive industrial base.

It is too early to say how this solid performance will be affected by reunification with the former GDR (whose industries have been devastated as a result) or by the revolutions that have occurred in Eastern Europe and the Soviet Union. These developments may either consolidate or overstretch Germany's role as the engine-room of the European economy. In this chapter, we will not attempt to answer this question, but rather to look back at the management traditions which shaped the success of West Germany up until the end of the 1980s.

Here, another note of caution is required. German management has acquired something of a symbolic status as the antithesis of Anglo-Saxon management, the *laissez-faire* traditions of the United Kingdom and the United States, which Germans themselves have been known to disparage as '*Manchesterismus*', the capitalism of the nineteenth century. In setting up such a contrast, it becomes easy to forget that Germany's post-war growth has not been substantially different from that of most West European nations. France, Sweden, Austria, Italy and Spain and the rest could all claim to have experienced economic miracles – it is the British case rather than the German that has been puzzling (Pollard, 1981).

However, the scale of the German economy has meant that its management approach has attracted outside interest to a degree only surpassed by Japan. Just as the United States' economic success fuelled interest in what is now termed 'Fordism' and the approach to management embodied in the Master of Business Administration or MBA degree, so the German post-war economic miracle or *Wirtschaftswunder* has led to a search for a German 'model', at least as far as manufacturing industry is concerned.

This interest, however, has usually focused around the German vocational training system, since German management itself has proved less amenable than Japanese management to broad stereotyping and characterization (whatever the accuracy of the latter in Japan's case). Despite a number of thorough analyses, including landmark studies such as that of Lawrence (1980), and the comparative work by Granick (1962), Maurice *et al.* (1980) and Sorge and Warner (1986), German management presents a picture that is difficult to categorize. Whilst it may be said that, in general terms, German companies have tended to be more product-led than market-led, bank-funded rather than stock-financed, managerial rather than entrepreneurial (Randlesome *et al.*, 1990: 1), the reality is somewhat more contradictory, as will become clear below.

A German Model of Management?

Any view of German management must be coloured by the post-war recovery, which was assisted by the 'Marshall plan'. Here, we find the first paradox. American 'Marshall aid', so often vaunted as the single most important reason for Germany's subsequent prosperity, is ranked by commentators such as Lawrence (1980) as merely one of a number of factors, and very likely less important than the mixing of population (the ten million refugees from the East), the experience of starting from starvation-point ('*Die Stunde Null*'), the diversion of national self-expression away from diplomatic and military symbols towards business, and the associated clarity with which exporting was seen from the start of reconstruction as the *sine qua non* of growth rather than as a means of balancing the books. Divided from its hinterland in East Germany and the former Prussian lands (re-)ceded to Poland, and cut off from traditional markets by the then Iron Curtain, West German industry turned its attention westwards, taking an early lead in the growing market of the EC.

Henceforth:- 'High value-added products, high technology and technical innovation' (Randlesome *et al.*, op. cit.: 8) became the order of the day for manufacturing managers. These imperatives led to Research and Development expenditure rising to as high as 10 per cent in some companies. The share of exports in output rose from 22 per cent in the mid-1960s to over 32 per cent by the late 1980s. With manufactured goods accounting for more than three quarters of exports, there were few doubts as to the central role of the sector in guaranteeing national survival.

There was a clear emphasis on quality and product design, although criticisms regarding 'over-engineering' remained. The strength of the Deutschmark did not deter sales, and the demand for German goods tended to be price-inelastic. German firms made reliability and after-sales service (*Kundedienst*) into decisive sources of competitive advantage well before the Japanese. Opinions may differ over the extent to which the punctuality and punctiliousness of such managerial practices reflected national cultural attributes, but it seems likely that the training of managers and workers, and the principles by which they were organized, played a large part (as we shall see below).

Economics and Regulation

Although the social market philosophy of West Germany consistently emphasized the need for free markets and competition, the way in which this market has been designed and regulated differs from any standard neoclassical approach. The German emphasis on economic regulation tends to be practical and based around what will support industrial success, rather than ideological, which might damage competitiveness (although this was allowed to take a heavy toll in East Germany after reunification).

In particular, German industry has tended to be highly resistant to the idea of hostile takeovers on the Anglo-Saxon model, and its stand is broadly in line with the rest of Western Europe, excluding the UK. However, rather than a strong regulatory approach, such as that which characterizes France and Italy, Germany typically operates on a basis of cultural values backed up by a regulatory framework – hostile takeovers do not occur (although some slight movement has occurred in this direction over the last two years) because German managers basically do not think they add much to the efficiency of firms or to the economy as a whole. As Woolcock *et al.* (1991: 14) put it:

> the whole environment is one that tends to foster commitment to the company rather than provide incentives to sell up. All major stakeholders – including the major banks and insurance companies, which hold about 20% of all shares in the large joint-stock companies – and their employees, through their participation on the supervisory board, are directly involved in the future of the company.

The structure, itself, of board-level management in large German companies (AG) works against short-term restructuring. The supervisory board or *Aufsichtsrat*, which supervises the performance of the executive board or *Vorstand*, is elected for five years and can only be changed if there is support for such a move from 75 per cent of the voting shares. Takeover activity is low and is regulated by the Federal Cartel Office (*Bundeskartellamt*), set up in 1973 in order to separate merger policy from politics – although ministerial intervention in favour of the MBB–Daimler–Benz merger belied this arm's length arrangement (Woolcock *et al.*, op. cit.: 12).

Though German companies such as Siemens have been expanding by cross-national acquisition in recent years, the general tendency has been very much in favour of organic growth, from which takeovers are seen by many as a distraction.

In 1988, Britain accounted for 73 per cent of all takeovers in Europe, Germany for only 4 per cent (of which 40 per cent were cross-national). This approach limits *de facto*, although not explicitly, the degree to which German industry is likely to fall into foreign hands.

Some divergence has begun to occur between the strategies of service companies, such as banks, and manufacturing in this regard. The service companies are increasingly building up their presence through acquisition elsewhere in the EC, whereas in manufacturing, the market position of the big companies has tended to confirm them in their preference for organic growth, the assumption being that market deregulation will consolidate their leading role in Europe, rather than fragment it (op. cit.: 106).

While in favour of competition in general, German management tends to oppose deregulation, particularly if carried out for ideological rather than practical reasons. German management, after all, emphasizes continuity, with change occurring only insofar as it is necessary and will add to efficiency. The partnership with the trade unions *via* the works council system, and the system of worker directorships, has tended to reinforce this. The long view taken with regard to product development and manufacture is matched by an unwillingness to risk long-term relationships and carefully negotiated consensus for the sake of short-term gains.

Technology and Management

Technology in Germany is assimilated by the industrial and managerial logics that have characterized its management over the long term. The 'conception and practice of technical work and training, organisation and industrial relations' (Sorge *et al.*, 1983: 40) follows a distinctly German path. Companies train skilled workers for production, as well as for maintenance work, for example. Apprenticeships are pervasive, with examination and certification of skills at all levels. The line management hierarchy is more technical than in many other countries, with closer liaison between line managers and technical experts (Maurice *et al.*, 1980; Sorge and Warner, 1986; Campbell and Warner, 1992). The German organization is distinguished by its tightly-knit technical staff superstructure, closely linked to supervisory and managerial tasks, which, when combined with a highly trained workforce, produce high levels of performance. Compared with French or British industry, German enterprises have 'a lower centre of gravity', that is they have less proliferation of administrative and technical staff support functions – skills are rooted to the shop-floor or around line management as far as possible (Sorge and Warner, 1986: 125). Whereas in some other countries, the trend has been for manufacturing to look more and more like service industry – to the extent that production becomes a poor relation from which those employees with ability will try to escape – in Germany manufacturing follows an unmistakably manufacturing logic, with production centre stage rather than falling behind areas such as marketing and R & D.

The technical emphasis of German management is not a new creation. The mid-nineteenth century saw the development of a specifically German industrial–technical capitalist tradition, which emphasized long-term aims rather than short-term profit maximization (Landes, 1960). This concern with the product rather than the bottom line combined with bank-led financing to provide German management with its characteristic long-term perspective.

Product Focus or Marketing Focus?

This inclination to see profit as a secondary objective appears to have left a strong imprint. Up to one fifth of smaller independent German firms (according to one study) have been found not to measure the profitability of their business or its component units on any routine or continuous basis (Reid and Schlegelmilch, 1988: 17). Indeed, the same study found that, contrary to received views of the punctilious, analytical German manager, it was in fact British firms who exercised more comprehensive control over finance and marketing than the Germans, rather than *vice-versa*.

To this must be added the qualification that Germans, while largely unconcerned with the type of detailed management accounting information required by Anglo-Saxon firms, do tend to know their costs in detail, even if profitability as such often remains a matter of trust as a result. The authors implied that success in marketing on the part of German firms might be linked to the primacy of production – improving the cost, quality and reliability of the product, and then allowing price flexibility in marketing, in which they were less interested, as a focus of managerial policy and control.

Somehow or other, the Germans appear to have avoided the negative aspects of being producer-driven. Granick (1962: 160) cites German senior managers complaining about the 'short-sightedness of "technicians" who measure the company's success by its tonnage'. Of course, sales and marketing have been given considerable emphasis, since this was required to boost the export-drive on which the country's continuing growth depended. However, this was merely relative to a pre-war past in which exporting had been much less of a priority, and had in any case been coordinated through State institutions rather than through specific functions at the enterprise level.

Post-war up-grading of the sales and marketing functions should not therefore be taken as achieving the thoroughgoing 'Americanization' it was purported to mean. The product-oriented approach to management was adapted, but not fundamentally altered. The emphasis on marketing was in any case focused towards quasi-technical areas such as after-sales service and the meeting of deadlines. Granick's account also refers to senior management concern over high wages, and the danger that the latter might lose Germany's cost advantage and therefore its open access to export markets (Granick, op. cit.: 161). In practice, as is well known, German industry was able to position itself as competitive on quality rather than price (although the industrial partnership with the unions allowed productivity to rise along with wages).

The Manager as Specialist

Many of the characteristics of German management and organizations may be traced back to national training patterns. In Germany, a person's occupation (*Beruf*) is especially important as the basis of social identity, reflecting the strength of craft and technical training traditions.

The tendency not to separate technical expertise and management should not be seen as applying only to the preserve of the professional, hired manager. On the contrary, it is well established in small family firms as well as in giant concerns (still in some cases family-owned). Product engineering is not unusually the special responsibility of the owner in such small firms.

Larger firms are more formally structured, but organization charts and similar outward symbols of status differences tend to be applied less than in US or UK companies. Hierarchies are flat, with technical expertise as close to the shop-floor, and as close to the production/line hierarchy, as possible.

The longer time-horizon of German management referred to above applies not only to capital investment decisions, but also to human resources management. There is a high degree of educational attainment in engineering at all levels of the hierarchy, and career paths tend to remain within the internal labour market in the larger firms. These factors, together with the industrial union system, reinforce the stability of manufacturing and the close links between industrial and financial capital (Lane, 1990: 250–51).

Most German managers are trained as engineers, and more than a few have passed through craft apprenticeship training as well. Where engineering training is concerned, there is little formal detachment of academic from practical aspects of training, nor is engineering practice regarded as intrinsically separate from 'pure' scientific work. This fact may help account for the high rate of

R & D spending, 2.9 per cent of GDP in the late 1980s, compared to 2.3 per cent in the UK.

Education of Senior Managers

Many directors of the larger German companies have doctorates (Handy *et al.*, 1988: 136). In the case of Siemens, no less than 14 out of 20 main board members have such titles, although lawyers are increasingly taking top positions from scientists (*Financial Times*, 15 April 1991). The larger the company the more likely are board members to have doctorates. The highest density of technically qualified managers is in the chemical industry. Over 1,370 managers in this sector have doctorates, mostly in scientific areas. Regarding first degrees, two in three German managers have such qualifications, a similar level as in France, twice as high as in the UK, but far lower than the 90 per cent recorded in Japan and the USA (see Handy *et al.*, 1988: 3).

Two further points are worth noting: first, that in Germany first degrees in subjects such as engineering contain management education as an integral part of the course, part of a more general tendency for technical courses to be broader-based than in many competitor countries. The broad-based nature of training occurs at all levels – chemical industry workers above a certain level will know both chemical and mechanical engineering disciplines almost as a matter of course. Second, German degrees take longer than in Britain, usually between three and six years. If we then take into account study for the second or third degrees which so many managers in Germany have, not to mention the fact that many will have preceded university with vocational training qualifications as craft workers (not seen to be irrelevant to a career in management), then it becomes clear that German managers enter employment at a much later age than their counterparts in Anglo-Saxon business culture, where there is an implicit trade-off between education and the 'real world'.

This late entry into the managerial job market limits the extent to which 'fast track' careers for young graduates can be the staple of human resource planners that they are in some other European companies. Indeed, German management tends overall to be less concerned with advancement for its own sake – there is less pressure to 'get into management' in order to be taken seriously, and, accordingly, less pressure to leave one's professional discipline behind. In this connection, we may also note the broad bands of discretion that divide one level in the hierarchy from another. Fewer levels is widely seen to have improved job satisfaction among skilled workers, and to have provided sufficiently broad roles for managers that advancement is less of an imperative than in more centralized, multi-level organizations elsewhere. In general, qualifications and status attributes vary much less between levels in Germany than in comparable US or UK firms.

Remuneration

Where salaries are concerned, if we apply the 'buying power' measures of salary developed by the ECA (Employment Conditions Abroad) consultancy (see *Financial Times*, 22 November 1991) we find that in Germany and France, junior management pay represents 38–9 per cent of senior management pay, whereas the comparable figure for the UK and US is 44 per cent – so that despite status differentials, 'Anglo-Saxon' pay, within management, is slightly less differentiated between levels. In terms of absolute pay levels, if we take US pay as 100, German managers receive 82–94 per cent, French managers 73–8 per cent, and UK managers 65–9 per cent, these differences being broadly in line with productivity variations between the countries concerned.

We may note that since 1985, there has been a much closer alignment of relative pay with relative output between the UK, France, Italy and Germany, so that unit labour costs in the three countries were virtually level in 1990. The main changes were a relative decrease in French and British labour costs, and an increase in German labour costs, partly due to the increased strength of the Deutschmark. Further devaluation of the other currencies would have undermined German price competitiveness, although the Exchange Rate Mechanism was designed to prevent this (*Financial Times*, 11 November 1991).

Expert Knowledge and Managerial Authority

Professional status is thus more important than purely organizational or managerial status. As Lawrence (1980) describes it, German industry provides an example of what Chester Barnard termed the 'sapiental' as opposed to the 'structural' basis of authority. Thus from the first-line supervisor or *Meister* upwards, supervisors and managers are respected for what they know rather than who they are. The *Meister*'s formal training reflects this emphasis. In West Germany, 52,000 first-line supervisors are formally qualified every year, compared to 15,000 in the UK (*Financial Times* letters, 16 November 1991).

This professionalization of all levels reflects a culture that involves a considerable degree of self-discipline and self-programming. German managers, at least in the major manufacturing sectors, are not as likely as their US counterparts to play the 'macho' role of leader. Instead, it is assumed that workers and supervisors will meet deadlines, guarantee quality and service, and since these matters are not negotiable, they do not need to be followed up and enforced so regularly. Independence within agreed parameters characterizes the preferred mode of working or managing. The idea of manager as administrator seems relatively weak in Germany, holders of such posts frequently preferring the more entrepreneurial connotations of '*Unternehmer*'. Although less inclined than Anglo-Saxon counterparts to improvise, German managers are more likely to idealize the independent family firm (Granick, 1962; Lawrence, 1980).

However, working reliably to rules and instructions is not the same as decentralization of the significant decisions. Child and Kieser (1979) found that more decisions were made higher up the hierarchy in Germany than in the UK (although some key decisions were taken at higher levels in the latter). This is supported by Heller *et al.* (1976), who found that older German managers centralized more than older British managers.

Hofstede (1980: 158) has argued that setting and abiding by clear rules is a way of avoiding uncertainty in a culture which is inclined to seek to do so. Similarly, Horowitz (1978), comparing French, German and British managers, found that the French and Germans relied more on short-term feedback than the British, and were more prone to 'uncertainty avoidance'. In general, roles and rules are more defined in German organizations either in formal documentation or personally. The search for rules and unambiguous directions leads to greater emphasis on planning. If in Britain it may be said that 'the more difficult it is to plan, the less you need full-time professional planners', the opposite may be true in Germany (Hofstede, op. cit.: 161). The flat hierarchy in German firms is qualified by management's technical orientation and associated love of detail. Horowitz (op. cit.) found that whereas UK top managers tended to engage more exclusively on strategy, German (as well as French) managers tended to concern themselves with details as well, which, as Hofstede (op. cit.: 188) points out, is another sign of 'uncertainty avoidance'.

The paradox of German management lies in the fact that Germans (according to Burnett, 1977) score high on anxiety and assertiveness but (according to Hofstede, op. cit.: 232) low on individualism. Like the Japanese, Germans project the image of purposive, collective effort towards agreed goals.

German Management and 'Post-Fordism'

Despite a leaning towards the pedantic, and the application of formal rules, German management none the less emerges as quite distinct from the Taylorist/Fordist model, with its sharp separation of concept and execution, of strategy from operations, and ruthless division of labour. It is therefore not surprising that Germany (in particular Baden–Württemburg) should, along with the 'third Italy', become the focus of attention in the debate over 'flexible specialization' (Piore and Sabel, 1984), which sees the survival of non-Fordist approaches to products and markets as the key to future prosperity. This debate was given a specific German focus with the work of Kern and Schumann (1987) on 'new production concepts'. Kern and Schumann's research in the car, machine tools and chemical industries in Germany led them to the view that a major change had occurred in terms of management of labour. The trends included greater integration of tasks, re-skilling and professionalization of production work, and management perception of skilled labour as a 'positive planning concept rather than a necessary evil' (op. cit.: 161). Whilst these changes did not uniquely occur in Germany, they found fertile ground there in that these views were implicit in the management approach of many German firms, even when such thinking ran counter to the conventional wisdom.

'Organizational Shamelessness'

As Lawrence (1980: 92) has noted, German management is self-sufficient, pragmatic (regarding theory as opposed to principles) and less open to external influence. Lawrence describes the episode of the (1973) Booz Allen Hamilton Report on German Management, which castigated the Germans for their lack of business-school training, their ignorance of techniques such as PERT and financial planning, and conservatism about moving between sectors (see Lawrence, 1980: 89–92). The lack of concern that German management has shown faced with these and similar criticisms testifies to a down-to-earth distrust of 'secondary' disciplines, those which may distract from the matter in hand, or the product itself. Lawrence terms this attitude 'organizational shamelessness', an unwillingness to conform with conventional wisdom on economics or business administration just for the sake of doing so. German conformism is expressed quite differently, through the wish to maintain specific operational standards, and the relationships involved in meeting those standards.

'Technik'

Behind these educational and organizational patterns stands a particular notion of technical competence. Lawrence (1989: 154) uses the phrase '*Technik über alles*' to stress the three-fold distinction made by Germans between:

Wissenschaft – formal knowledge (arts or sciences),

Kunst – art, but specifically artistic output or practice,
and
Technik – knowledge and skills related to work.

This division diverges from the Anglo-Saxon dichotomies between arts and science, and between 'pure' and 'applied' sciences. As Randlesome *et al.* (op. cit.: 51) put it:

> The concept of *Technik*, the art and science of manufacturing useful artefacts, is so widespread in the country, that West Germany can be regarded as a manufacturing-friendly society.

Over 40 per cent of Gross Domestic Product is derived from manufacturing and construction. Not only was West Germany in 1990 responsible for half the exports within the EC, but it exported more per head than any other country.

The persistence of *Technik* as a strength in German management might have been thought by some to be a potential Achilles' heel. Critics might point to the post-industrial service-oriented society as the wave of the present and future. Could it be that the continuing German emphasis on the traditional industries of vehicles and machine-tools, the massive *Maschinenbau* sector, is a potential time-bomb, a 'sunset' or 'smokestack' industrial strategy?

This view would be in line with the 'information society' or 'post-industrial' theory which gained ground in the United States and the UK, in particular during the 1979–83 recession. This theory assumes that old industries can be expected to disappear as a result of an evolutionary process. Whilst it is undoubtedly true that employment is steadily being transferred away from manufacturing, this does not mean that an absolute cut in production levels in that traditional sector represents progress. The maintenance of production levels, and even of employment levels, in many 'traditional' sectors in Germany and Japan, let alone in the Newly Industrializing Countries, calls the simplified logic of this theory into question.

However, the increase in manufacturing efficiency has now reached a point where some might rightly call into question the German strategy of mass craft training for industry, although this approach would still seem to be erring on the right side. Critics such as Spies (1985) highlight mismatches between supply and demand which result from the mass training of the dual system, and argues that the British tripartite system was less employer-dominated and more flexible. There was a view, during the early 1980s, that German vocational training for sixteen- to nineteen-year-olds merely camouflaged unemployment, and led to the 'best-trained dole queue in the world' (Spies, op. cit.: 24). Recession and rising labour costs are now major concerns (*Financial Times*, 3 March 1993).

Innovation in Traditional Sectors

Whereas mechanical engineering has been allowed to waste away as 'cash cow' or 'dog' in some competitor countries, in Germany it has been kept in the mainstream and provided with leading-edge technology. Thus, we find that the German mechanical engineering sector has distinguished itself by its rapid adoption of microelectronics into both products and processes. Furthermore, German mechanical engineering companies have not simply replaced electro-mechanical components with microelectronics, but have proved adept at integrating the design and assembly of microelectronic components into their own enterprises, in contrast to similar companies investigated in the UK (Campbell *et al.*, 1989).

This achievement is an example of the German preoccupation with the product as a whole (and the need to maintain control of the whole product) serving as the impetus to rapid innovation and adaptation, even in the most traditional sectors. Rather than promote a distinct 'sunrise' sector, at the expense of older sectors, German industry has redefined and updated these sectors to accommodate new technical developments. Its ability to do this has been closely linked to the maintenance of a particularly strong base of intermediate skills, with workers being trained well beyond the demands of any one job (Campbell, 1991). This success in traditional areas has not yet been matched by expansion into new sectors such as biotechnology, lasers, IT systems and optamatronics. Here, there have been attempts to fill the gaps through federally funded R & D institutes. The direct benefits to industry have thus far been disappointing and funding has been cut back in order to encourage firms to carry out their own R & D in these newer areas (*Financial Times*, 24 September 1991). Although such sectors have not seen aggressive or even effective competition from the Germans, the experience of microelectronics product applications suggests that product design and assembly can be integrated relatively quickly, once firms have become sufficiently aware of how to apply the technology.

The flexibility of German industry as a whole in achieving such shifts lies not only in the depth and breadth of non-graduate training, but also in the use of graduate science and engineering recruits. These have not been concentrated into semi-protected areas such as defence. Instead they have been spread wider across the range of middle-of-the-market sectors in which practical application of science holds sway, rather than the 'back-room' isolation of R & D common elsewhere.

Simplicity and Narrowness of Focus

It would be wrong, however, to see German management as sentimentally tied to traditional holistic methods of manufacturing. A recent study of the German machinery manufacturing sector (Rommel, 1991) found that successful German manufacturers followed a set of rigorous, commercially driven principles, several of which call into question attempts to explain German success in terms of 'flexible specialization'.

It was found that the more successful companies in Germany were those which narrowed their product range, concentrated R & D on that narrower product range and produced the product at a dedicated factory, thus avoiding the complexity of mixed production sites. This narrowness of focus simplified manufacturing so as to enable a more genuine and far-reaching decentralization of authority to middle and junior management. It also allowed successful companies to economize through more effective targeting of R & D, and enabled new products to be launched more rapidly. Products were modularized so as to postpone customization to as late a point in the manufacturing process as possible.

Shop-Floor Training

Not only are German managers well-educated; the human capital of German industry is supported by what may be regarded as the best vocational training system in Europe. The training tradition, combined with the model industrial relations practice, facilitates efficient production of goods and services – this despite periodic speculation that both training and industrial relations systems are too inflexible and expensive to adapt. Although the European Single Market may place a question mark over long-term competitiveness of the German labour market, the strength and quality of labour market and industry did seem likely to postpone the day of reckoning. Germany was able to absorb more than 2.5 million migrant workers in less than two years without any significant impact on unemployment – the difficulties of absorbing labour from abroad appeared to be mainly political not economic (*Financial Times*, 28 October 1991). By 1993, however, unemployment in the western *Länder* reached 8 per cent (and 15 per cent in the east).

German industry is also noteworthy in that the gap between large firms and small and medium-sized firms (*Mittelstand*) is not so wide as might be expected. The 'dual system' of financing training ensures that all firms pay for training, and therefore share the benefits without the problems of 'free-riders' and 'poaching' that beset the training systems of certain other countries. In addition, the bank-led finance system for industry provides significant backing for smaller firms, who are therefore not the 'poor relations' that they are elsewhere when recession occurs.

The dual system implies a degree of interested cooperation between large and small firms. The large firms over-train and then choose the people they want, whilst the smaller firms who do not have the facilities for training (although they pay for it) then hire the others. There is some evidence that the dual system is under strain, particularly following reunification – it is seen as too inflexible and too centred around qualifications. However unwieldy its output, it is nevertheless impressive – 120,000 workers gained engineering qualifications in 1990 (*Financial Times*, 3 June 1991). However, training too has been hit by the post-unification squeeze. In early 1993, the Federal Office of Labour ran out of money altogether (*Financial Times*, 23 February 1993).

Conclusion

To sum up, the image of 'German management' appears as less of an abstract force, divorced from production, than its Anglo-Saxon counterparts. It is specialist rather than generalist, and product-led rather than market-led – although it could be argued that the German style of management avoids the need for such clear-cut choices.

Most senior managers are trained as engineers with practically oriented *Technik* rather than academic science as their starting point. Thus, German managers do not manage as a general activity, they manage *something*. Management is linked to objects rather than concepts, to specialist knowledge rather than status. It is no coincidence that business schools in the North American sense scarcely exist in Germany, and appear not to be missed.

The management system is characterized by tightly knit technical staff superstructures, backed up by a highly trained workforce. High levels of competence allow management to operate through flat structures and large spans of control, with discretion pushed down the hierarchy. Initiatives of the 'total quality management' type, aimed at re-activating craft-type pride in performance in bureaucratic structures, would appear less than necessary in the average German manufacturing company.

Although promoting self-supervision of skilled workers, German managers are not averse to getting involved in the details of the tasks concerned. The distinctions that have characterized traditional Western hierarchical management thinking – strategy/operations, or conception/execution – would appear not to operate in such a clear-cut fashion in German industry. Although German management is averse to uncertainty, this potential weakness is compensated for by the thoroughness and consistency of its training and co-determination arrangements, which allow flexibility to be built into the system.

However, German managers may, because of the very specific cultural context of their country's success, be less geared to operating as multinational executives, indeed too few of their top managers have worked or studied abroad. The very strengths of *Technik*-based training may paradoxically lead to a certain 'parochialism' (Randlesome, 1988: 160). Managers' skills are based on function- or area-linked specialisms, and their development is often company-specific. The challenge, therefore, as in the Japanese case (although much less so), is to develop a truly international set of repertoires and outlook.

All in all, managers in Germany benefit from (and help to maintain) a high level of investment, due to a very positive savings ratio and consistently low inflation. This boon results in highly developed human capital at all levels, which in turn facilitates enterprise efficiency and effectiveness. The upshot is likely to be that just as the Deutschmark has come to dominate European finance, so too will the West German (and perhaps soon the all-German) business culture influence managerial practice within the European Single Market. It seems that German 'parochialism' will know fewer and fewer boundaries. This at least is the theory.

References

Bowra, C. M., *The Greek Experience*, London: Weidenfeld and Nicolson, 1985.

Burnett, L., *Die Bundesdeutschen*, Frankfurt a-M: Leo Burnett Werbeagentur, 1977.

Campbell, A., 'Issues of training strategy in British manufacturing' in J. Stevens and R. Mackay (eds.), *Training and Competitiveness*, pp. 25–35, London: Kogan Page/ National Economic Development Office, 1991.

Campbell, A., A. Sorge and M. Warner, *Microelectronic Product Applications in Britain and West Germany*, Aldershot: Gower, 1989.

Campbell, A. and M. Warner, *New Technology, Skills and Management*, London: Routledge, 1992.

Canetti, E., *Crowds and Power*, Harmondsworth: Penguin, 1973.

Child, J. and A. Kieser, 'Organization and managerial roles in British and West German companies: an examination of a culture-free thesis' in C. J. Lammers and D. J. Hickson (eds.), *Organizations Alike and Unlike*, pp. 251–71, London: Routledge, 1979.

Gardels, N., 'Two concepts of nationalism: an interview with Sir Isaiah Berlin', *New York Review of Books* 32, 1991, 19.

Granick, D., *The European Executive*, London: Weidenfeld and Nicolson, 1962.

Handy, C., F. Gordon, I. Gow and C. Randlesome, *The Making of Managers: A Report on Management Education, Training and Development in the USA, West Germany, France, Japan and the UK*, London: Manpower Services Commission, National Economic Development Office, British Institute of Management, 1988.

Heller, F., R. Mays and B. Wilpert, 'Methodology for multi-national study of managerial behaviour. The use of Contingency Theory', paper presented at the Third Congress of Cross-Cultural Psychology, Tilburg, Netherlands, July 1976.

Hofstede, G., *Culture's Consequences*, Beverly Hills, CA: Sage, 1980.

— *Cultures and Organizations: Software of the Mind*, London: McGraw-Hill, 1991.

Horowitz, J., 'Management control in France, Great Britain and Germany', *Columbia Journal of World Business* 13/2, 1978, 16–22.

James, H., *A German Identity, 1770–1990*, London: Routledge, 1991.

Kern, H. and M. Schumann, 'Limits of the division of labour: new production and employment concepts in West German industry', *Economic and Industrial Democracy* 8, 1987, 151–70.

Landes, D., 'The structure of enterprise in the nineteenth century; the cases of Britain and Germany', Berkeley California Institute of Industrial Relations, Reprint No. 152, 1960.

Lane, C., 'Vocational training and new production concepts in Germany: some lessons for Britain', *Industrial Relations Journal* 21, 1990, 247–259.

Lawrence, P., *Managers and Management in West Germany*, London: Croom Helm, 1980.

— 'Management education in West Germany', in W. Byrt (ed.), *Management Education: An International Survey*, pp. 151–71, London: Routledge, 1989.

Malzahn, M., *Germany 1945–1949: A sourcebook*, London: Routledge, 1991.

Maurice, M., A. Sorge and M. Warner, 'Societal differences in organizing manufacturing units: a comparison of France, West Germany and Great Britain', *Organization Studies* 1/1, 1980, 59–86.

Piore, M. and C. Sabel, *The Second Industrial Divide: Possibilities for Prosperity*, New York: Basic Books, 1984.

Pollard, S., *The Wasting of the British Economy*, London: Croom Helm, 1981.

Randlesome, C., 'West Germany', in C. Handy, F. Gordon, I. Gow and C. Randlesome, *The Making of Managers*, pp. 125–62, London: Pitman, 1988.

Randlesome, C., W. Brierley, K. Bruton, C. Gordon and P. King, *Business Cultures in Europe*, London: Heinemann, 1990.

Reid, D. and B. Schlegelmilch, 'Planning and control in the U.K. and West Germany: a cross-cultural comparison within the mechanical engineering industry', University of Edinburgh Department of Business Studies Working Paper 88/20, 1988.

Rommel, G., *The Secret of German Competitiveness*, London: McKinsey, 1991.

Sorge, A., G. Hartmann, M. Warner and I. Nicholas, *Microelectronics and Manpower in Manufacturing: Applications of Computer Numerical Control in Great Britain and West Germany*, Aldershot: Gower, 1983.

Sorge, A. and M. Warner, *Comparative Factory Organisation*, Aldershot: Gower, 1986.

Spies, B., 'Does myth blur the facts of West German training?', *BACI Journal*, September 1985, 22–4.

Woolcock, S., M. Hodges and K. Schreiber, *Britain, Germany and 1992: the Limits of Deregulation*, London: Pinter/Royal Institute of International Affairs, 1991.

Management and Society

Peter Lawrence and Tony Spybey

Chapter 4, pp. 54–68 in Peter Lawrence and Tony Spybey, *Management and Society in Sweden* (London: Routledge & Kegan Paul, 1986)

The overall purpose of this chapter is to look at the connections between management and society in Sweden. To begin with it may therefore be helpful to 'block in' some pictures of Swedish society and the business context. At various points in this book tribute is paid to the high-minded internationalism of Sweden, and rightly so. But for the moment we will look at the other and neglected side of the coin – nationalism.

Nationalism in Sweden

There is a tendency for some small (by population) rich countries to be cultural client states, to be dominated or characterized by larger neighbours. In this vein we have an Anglicized Australia, an Americanized Canada, Belgium as a Franco-Dutch hybrid, and Switzerland as a scenic extension of Bavaria. But Sweden is itself; it is the biggest and most influential of the Scandinavian states, and the dominant member of the Nordic Union. Although Norway, thanks to its oil, is coming to rival Sweden in the GNP-per-capita stakes ('baby brother is trying to become big brother', as one Swede put it to us), Sweden still has the largest population and land area, and certainly better internal communications (it is one of Scandinavia's transport ironies that from Narvik in northern Norway there is a direct train service to Stockholm, but no train connection at all to Oslo). Swedes are also conscious that Norway was once ruled by them (1815–1905) and are resentful of Norway's throwing off of Swedish rule; to make matters worse 'national day' in Norway is 17 May, the anniversary of independence from Sweden. Finland was a Swedish possession for centuries before its conquest by Russia during the Napoleonic Wars, and Swedes still speak approvingly of Finland as being 'like us in many ways'; they clearly regard it as a proper place for Swedes to go to (and feel mildly superior to). Swedes also think of themselves as superior to the Danes, whom they regard as a bit flash and pushy, and Swedes actually speak of 'going to the Continent', which means going to Denmark (in the first instance).

If we emphasize Sweden's nationalism here, it is because it is not generally recognized at all. Sweden's long-standing neutrality and high-minded internationalist stance in foreign affairs do not prepare the visitor to Sweden for manifestations of homely nationalism. To give a simple example of this phenomenon, there are an awful lot of flags in Sweden; boats are festooned with them, and no *residence secondaire* is complete without one. The Swedish flag colours, a very attractive yellow cross on a blue background, also figure endlessly in design and decoration, on everything from T-shirts to hold-alls. To offer another small example, in the fruit and vegetable market in the Hogtorget in Stockholm most produce is labelled as Swedish and the province of origin is also given (the reverse convention prevails among British greengrocers, who only label produce if it is foreign). This symbolizes the fairly widespread conviction that if it's Swedish it must be good and the responsible citizen will want to steer clear of foreign rubbish.

Swedish economic life is both internationalist and insular at the same time. On the one hand there is the tremendous commitment to exporting; the typical Swedish company has works in other countries, and these will be real production facilities, not just sales outlets. English-speaking ability is near universal among Swedish managers. It is much more common for Swedish managers to have worked abroad, as opposed to having made foreign business trips, than, say, their British or West German colleagues. It is also clear that Swedes benefit from their socialist-neutral image in business dealings in some other parts of the world; it is regarded as an advantage in eastern Europe and a distinct advantage in the Third World. On the other hand, in Sweden itself a foreigner is struck by the relative absence of non-Swedish elements; for example, there are no foreign banks in Sweden by law, though one is assured that they may trade there using a Swedish bank as an intermediary. There are relatively few foreign companies by British or German standards; there are, for instance, no Ford or General Motors car factories in Sweden – indeed the only cars made there are Volvo and Saab. Nestlé is a minor presence, trading under the name of Findus; ITT is represented by Standard Radio and Telefon, but is dwarfed by the indigenous telecommunications concern of L. M. Ericsson; there are no British or American cigarette factories (cf. West Germany); and most Swedes need to have a good think before they can name any Japanese company operating in Sweden.

Swedishness and Homeliness

Another feature of Swedish business life is its indigenous homeliness. Since it is not a big country in population terms, everyone knows everyone else at the top.

This small happy family ethos finds expression in the composition of boards of directors. The board of a Swedish company is predominantly non-executive in composition; apart from the managing director and mandatory trade union representatives, the members are outsiders, not senior executives of the firm concerned. However, these non-executive directors tend not to be mere status-lending amateurs but senior executives in other major firms, with one of the major banks as a common denominator. So, as one Swedish interviewee jocularly expressed it, 'when you meet the board of a Swedish company you will find the fellow from SKF, the one from ASEA, the chap from Electrolux, and so on'. In other words, via the mechanism of non-executive directors, there is a high level of interlock among the major Swedish companies, certainly among those in the same 'bank blocks'.

On the subject of these bank blocks there are some differences of opinion. If one asks Swedes which groups of companies are associated with which banks, i.e. which companies form the different blocks, the answers are usually slightly different – it is like asking Germans to describe the *Abitur* ('A' level) system. However, the gist of it is that a substantial group of companies, including Saab-Scania, L. M. Ericsson and Electrolux, is associated with the Skandinaviska Enskilda Bank; others, of which the most eminent is Volvo, are associated with the Handelsbank; and a third, if lesser, block is associated with the P. K. Bank. The second difference of opinion among Swedes relates to the rigidity of the block system. One senior manager suggested that the blocks give companies an unusual degree of financial security and effectively remove the possibility of takeover as the ultimate sanction for inefficiency. In contrast, another interlocutor suggested that this state of affairs is a thing of the past, that takeovers do now occur across bank lines and that 'our stock market is quite like yours'.

Nationalism and the Status of Industry

So far we have tried to outline the stereotype of Sweden: it is a small country, but it is big in Scandinavia – and conscious of this fact; it is somewhat on the edge of Europe yet it has a distinctive culture; it is both neutral and internationalist but at the same time shows a robust and homely nationalism. Furthermore, Swedish business life is marked by elements of national exclusiveness.

It is possible to go further and link Swedish nationalism to the Swedish view of industrialization. If one inquires as to the status of industry in Sweden, again this may elicit contradictory answers. In the narrow sense, this question relates to career choices among able and well-qualified people. Where the status of industry is high, management will be the first career choice of the able and ambitious, as in the USA, West Germany or Japan; where it is low, national talent will be drawn rather to the state service or the free professions – the traditional case in Britain. In this narrow sense Swedes disagree as to whether industry or the civil service carry more esteem. However, this formulation misses the main point!

There is no doubt about the standing of industry in Sweden; it is simply the case that civil service employment carries high prestige too, though obviously for different reasons. Thus the broader consideration which surrounds the notion of the status of industry is that of the place of industry and industrialization in the popular mind. Critics of Britain have claimed that both industry and industrialization have been near 'dirty words' in the British folk memory. Both Correlli Barnet (1972), and Martin Wiener (1981) have argued that in Britain the rejection of industrialism, with a corresponding attachment to notions of rural bliss and aristocratic values, has played a central role in Britain's decline. The important thing is that there is no echo of this in Sweden; indeed the reverse is the case.

In Swedish folk memory the story is something like this. Once upon a time there was a poor and isolated country in northern Europe; then along came industrialization and everything started to get better; then barely a hundred years later they found themselves just about the richest country in the world. There are few countries which have been so completely transformed by industrialization. For Sweden the starting date was late, but the finishing point was high, and Swedish national pride is inextricably linked with this achievement.

Differentiation

Low differentiation – between individuals, groups, classes and sexes – is a feature of Swedish society. It is possible to go further and argue that a number of things follow from this low differentiation, or can be cited as manifestations thereof.

Firstly, Sweden has achieved a high degree of sexual equality. This equality exists as a legal, social and behavioural phenomenon. For a foreigner it is most observable in the deportment of women; they defer less, compromise less, marry later (free legal abortion removes one cause of early marriage), are more likely to work, and have greater claims to an independent (of their husband's) career.

Secondly, although it is possible to designate social classes or status groups by occupation or educational level, class is a weak behavioural construct; that is, it is not easy to identify or classify people by social class – there does not seem to be the range of class-related behavioural and stylistic differences with which one is so familiar in England. Swedish society is not quite a monochrome – something that Swedes themselves claim – but one does have to work harder to 'spot the differences'.

Thirdly, in Sweden there is relatively low differentiation as to net earned income. To say that 'differentials' are lower in Sweden would be true, but this English usage of the word is too narrow. It is not just that wage differences between various skill grades of blue-collar workers, or between production workers and first line supervisors, are narrower; the wage span for the whole occupational structure falls between closer limits than is the case in Britain. Thus the differences between managerial and worker salaries, between the salaries of various managerial grades, between graduate and non-graduate salaries, are all rather less than one is used to in other western European countries.

In his connection it should be remembered that Sweden is not just a rich industrial country, 'like all the others'. It has had a social democratic regime for the majority of the last fifty years, and all the triumphs of modern Sweden sustain its image and standing. This combination of high GNP per capita plus long-standing socialist government gives the country a different profile in regard to actual observable wealth. Its most obvious manifestation is a steeply progressive personal income tax, such that marginal taxation rates of 70 to 85 per cent are common among middle-class salary earners. The wider phenomenon is that Swedish national wealth shows up in the absence of poverty, in the high minimum incomes, in the statutory care of the unfortunate and disadvantaged, and in the level of welfare benefits. It does not show up in conspicuous consumption among the rich, which is generally frowned upon. Nor does it show up in terms of greater (than in Britain) affluence among the middle class.

Fourthly, there is a strong commitment to egalitarianism. Not only is Swedish society undifferentiated, as suggested here; there is also a widespread feeling that this lack of differentiation is right, that this is the way things should be.

Swedish vernacular is replete with expressions of the *en man är lika god som en an* (a man is as good as anyone else) kind. It is bad to act 'uppity', to set yourself apart from others; displays of wealth are frowned upon, and styles tend to be national rather than segmented or stratified. Associated with the egalitarian norm is the norm of accessibility, bureaucrats, politicians and public office holders are expected to be accessible. If you recognize the minister of transport in the airport lounge you can complain to him about the delay. To give an actual example, alcoholic drink is a state monopoly in Sweden, all purchases being made at a chain of government off-licences called a *systembalo-get*. When the government decided not to open the *systembolaget* shops on Saturday mornings, it proved a wildly unpopular move. Several people told us that at the time of the controversy they had rung up the relevant cabinet minister to voice their views. In Sweden you have to have a good reason for not seeing someone, and putative status differences are not enough. The present study has undoubtedly benefited from this phenomenon; if you want to interview managing directors in Sweden you just call them up and ask them!

Fifthly, it is conceded by many people that Sweden's tradition of neutrality in world affairs is paralleled by a certain avoidance of conflict, a non-aggressive peaceableness at home. Patience, restraint, moderation, emotional control are Swedish virtues. Swedes do not like conflict, confrontation and inter-personal challenge. Problems should be solved by discussions leading to compromise, not by *force majeure*. Stockholm is probably the only European capital in which one can drive across the downtown area in the rush hour without hearing a car horn 'sounded in anger'.

Sixthly, there is a corporate dimension to Swedish society. Individuals join groups, associations and federations; it is a way that one expresses one's adult citizenship and claims one's civic rights. And, of course, the biggest corporation of all is the government in the widest sense, including the civil service and associated bodies. Employment in this government bureaucracy is extensive, and increased throughout the 1970s (Telesis Inc., 1980). Right-wing politicians seeking to strike a Thatcherite pose threaten merely to reduce the *rate of increase* of the bureaucracy.

It is possible to argue that Sweden's blossoming bureaucracy and plethora of corporate organizations is not simply a reflection of the social welfare responsibilities assumed by the state (the common assumption). It can also be argued that it is a reflection of the lack of differentiation which has been the *leitmotiv* of the present chapter. Sweden prefers group values to individual values, and group values naturally find corporate expression.

Some of these themes have a characterizing effect on Swedish management. The issue of corporatism is a case in point, as exemplified by the SAF, the Swedish Employers' Federation. Although most countries have such an organization, the SAF (Svenska Arbetsgivareföreningen) is unusually well-established. It has a central place in the Swedish industrial relations pay bargaining arena and is the focus of considerable loyalty from member companies.

SAF gained its strength after 1944, when the massive demand for Swedish manufactured goods, accompanied by a labour shortage, increased the need for employer discipline on pay settlements and poaching. What, however, makes SAF distinctive is that it has a central role in Sweden and evokes a high level of member loyalty. There is a famous and recent case in which Volvo made a pay deal with employees in excess of that ordained by the SAF–LO agreement (about 4 per cent in excess). SAF responded by fining Volvo; Volvo paid the fine, and came back into line. This kind of occurrence is absolutely inconceivable in Britain, where the corresponding organization, the Confederation of British Industry (CBI), is no more than a loosely structured interest group.

This expression of neutrality, this avoidance of conflict in Swedish society, is also relevant as a characterization of industrial management. Again the point may be expressed in a personal way; in interviewing Swedish managers one is struck repeatedly by their reasonableness, and in some cases by a quality almost of gentleness. Swedish managers are less aggressive, less individualistic and less wilful than their colleagues in Britain and Germany. To this impression should be added a consistent finding from the interviews. Swedish managers, when asked open-ended questions about problems and difficulties, mention conflicts, misunderstandings and aggravation with other functions and departments much less than is the case with their British colleagues. And this applied particularly to production managers. Production managers are a good test case because the production function is central; it has dealings and dependencies with many other functions and is often in conflict with them (Hutton and Lawrence, 1978). It was noticeable that these Swedish production managers were very sparing in their criticisms of other departments – of engineering, design, quality control, sales, maintenance, purchasing and so on. And where criticisms were expressed they tended to be more restrained, often denoting attempts to see the other person's point of view, so that one encountered remarks like 'Purchasing do find it difficult sometimes' rather than 'purchasing has let us down again', or 'Of course quality control has to have a different set of priorities' rather than 'Quality control are buggering us around as usual.'

In one of the later interviews we discussed this impression with a senior Swedish manager. He expressed the view that Swedes, more than most nationalities, would be reluctant to admit to internal rivalries and conflicts. This may well be so, yet the present interpretation was supported by a Swedish lecturer at a management training establishment who listed for us the things managers attending a series of courses complained of – and this enumeration did not include conflict or difficulties with other departments. Again, during our time in Sweden we also had the good fortune to meet several British expatriates, some with considerable experience in business and management. This lack of aggression cum disposition to reasonableness was a common theme among this group as well. One, a manager with some twenty years experience in Sweden, argued that there is, relatively speaking, a lack of 'politicking' in Swedish companies. There is less inter-personal rivalry, less bucking for promotion at all costs, and less in the way of manoeuvres to advance one's own interests at the expense of someone else. A particular example proferred in this connection was the British trick of setting up a superior so that he discredits himself, in the hope of being promoted to replace him; this, it was said, was pretty well unknown in Sweden.

This aspect of Swedish management has so far been expressed very much in negative terms – avoidance of conflict, relative absence of inter-departmental strife and personal rivalries. However it would also be fair to draw attention to the positive aspect – what might be called the cult of competence. There is in Sweden no amateur point of view; if you don't know, you shut up and let those who do know tell you. In so far as initial contacts in Sweden have a hidden agenda, it is to establish the competence of the various parties, not their relative status.

This cult of competence is one dimension of Swedish egalitarianism. Competence is, at least in theory, something which all can acquire; as such it is a more acceptable discriminator than some kind of acquired status. Competence is also very Swedish in another sense. In the Swedish view, for any challenge, task or problem, there will, on the whole, be one best way of making it, doing it, solving it or arranging it. To reach this desirable end point, competence is what one needs, plus patience and a readiness to compromise where necessary.

The behavioural manifestations of Swedish egalitarianism are quite striking. One aspect of this is linguistic. The Swedish language has two words for you, *ni* and *du*. They are respectively the formal and the intimate forms of address, corresponding to *vous* and *tu* in French, or more closely to *Sie* and *Du* in German. This said, the *du* form in Swedish is used almost universally, from juniors to seniors, from workmates to total strangers at bus stops. The use of the *ni* form, one Swede avowed, would suggest that the speaker was a high government official. An expatriate Englishman claimed the *ni* form was now used only at SAS (Scandinavian Airlines System) check-in counters.

This egalitarianism of manners is also held to be of relatively recent origin. As late as the 1950s the Swedes were still being described as excessively formal and off-puttingly reserved. Furthermore, this egalitarianism is a quality of which Swedes are now militantly proud, and it has clear implications for management. For example, egalitarianism should reduce the gulf between 'the two sides of industry', or, more modestly, between management and workers. It should facilitate communication inside factories and favour communication upwards from the shop floor. It should reduce inter-personal friction between ranks, and be a value to which all may appeal. And, in fact, Swedes tend to claim that all these things are true. Egalitarianism and ease of communication between manager and worker was the most frequent response to an open-ended question about the distinctiveness of Swedish management, and it was also made a point of comparison in Sweden's favour between Sweden and other countries, with Britain stigmatized as a hot-bed of stiff-necked privilege, the USA (occasionally) as pseudo-democratic, and Germany as hierarchical and authoritarian. As a small aside on the last point, Swedes seem to hold ferociously hostile stereotypes of the Germans, somewhat worse than those prevalent among elderly Englishmen. Perhaps the Swedes need some *alter ego* for differentiation purposes – some other nation as a backdrop to their own shining egalitarianism.

Mobility and Motivation

Some of the features mentioned here – high sex equality, low class-based behavioural differences, and a relatively narrow income distribution reinforced by a highly progressive income tax – are together relevant to a discussion of manager mobility and motivation.

The Mobility of Managers

Let us take mobility first. Swedish managers are not very keen to be moved (geographically), and are similarly not very keen on promotion which involves moving. It may be helpful here to do a burlesque Anglo-Swedish comparison. When an English manager is moved, the move is typically in the form of promotion; in a rank-and-status-crazy society, that promotion is worth something – more so than in Sweden. The move–promotion will generally be accompanied by a salary increase, and this is worth having too, even after tax. The move may also be accompanied by a new (bigger and better) company car. Furthermore, the mobile manager's progress around Britain will be smoothed by the panoply of company-paid estate agent's and solicitor's fees, bridging loans where necessary, and a relocation allowance. Wives may grumble a bit, but not too much, and even if it is a bit of a bore having to make new friends, there will be material compensations, including spending the relocation allowance – an orgy of soft-furnishings and fitted kitchens.

In Sweden, on the other hand, the manager's wife will probably be a working graduate with a career she will be reluctant to jeopardize or interrupt. And in many cases this will be the end of the matter. Furthermore, the promotion itself will count for less in egalitarian Sweden than in Britain: the accompanying pay rise will be less than it would be in Britain, and will be further reduced in value by a steeper income-tax progression; company cars are few and far between in Sweden, and are heavily taxed (fringe benefits in general are scarce by British, let alone American, standards, and are taxed to near worthlessness); and Swedish kitchens are all magnificently fitted anyway (and have so many electric gadgets that it is a wonder the floors in some of these multi-storey flats can support them).

Going to work abroad is a special instance of the problem for Swedish managers. The question of what is owed to the wife is then even more acute since she is very unlikely to be able to work in the foreign country; her career is thus in suspense for the duration of the foreign posting, and may suffer permanent damage. On the other hand there are material benefits in the case of an overseas posting. The pay rise is likely to be more substantial; it will conform to local or international norms, not Swedish ones. It is an established part of Swedish management folklore that the expatriate head of a foreign subsidiary will earn more than the overall chief executive back home in Stockholm or Gothenburg. The expatriate manager will also pay tax at local rather than Swedish rates. And there are further 'corrupting inducements' associated with working abroad, of which the most frequently mentioned is having servants (unthinkable in Sweden, for obvious reasons).

It is also the case that an overseas posting is more common for Swedish managers anyway than for their British counterparts, partly because of the strong export orientation of Swedish industry and partly because so many Swedish companies maintain manufacturing establishments outside Sweden. In fact, only a small minority of all the managers we interviewed had not worked abroad. Thus the possibility of such a posting is something with which the individual must come to terms. One management consultant suggested that although starting salary should not be the subject of too much hard bargaining in the appointment interview, it is quite in order to take a hard line on foreign postings. You should actually say 'I don't expect to have my life turned upside down and be sent to Brazil in a couple of years.' Alternatively, in the unlikely event that you would welcome such a posting, you should certainly say so, because it would be a great selling point. A Swedish MD summed up the ambiguity surrounding foreign postings with the remark 'You've got two problems; the first is getting managers to go abroad, and the second is getting them to come home.'

Motivation and Rewards

There is, of course, a wider issue than the Swedish manager's reluctance to move – the more central question of motivation and rewards.

The three key facts relating to this issue have all been mentioned already, but it is probably helpful to restate them together. First, Swedish managers are poorly paid by international standards. They know it, and are frequently voluble on the subject. Second, an income-tax system which is more sharply progressive than that in most west European countries reduces further the net income of the Swedish manager. Third, fringe benefits are few, and are invariably taxed. Thus the 'material rewards package' enjoyed by Swedish managers compares unfavourably with that in many western countries.

If one deduces anything from this it must be that there is some lessening of motivation and involvement; this would certainly be the American orthodoxy. It is also fair to say that plenty of Swedish managers, and others such as consultants passing an informed opinion, say that this is indeed the case. However it is possible to go even further and point to particular alleged manifestations of this impoverished motivation.

The first is diminished concern with promotion. It has to be said that not every young Swedish manager wants to get to the top, or at least get as far as he can, but in speaking of their objectives Swedish managers are more likely to express themselves in terms of an equation of work and family satisfactions, without the implication that the former should dominate the latter. Now it may be objected that managers in other countries are not really so overwhelmingly committed to work and advancement, or at least that not many of them are. However, even if this counter-argument is conceded, it is still true that there are other countries which pay lip service to the ambition-drive-achievement syndrome. Sweden does not do this; instead Swedes typically take, according to your prejudices, a more balanced or less involved view of the relationship between a manager and his employing organization. Certainly several senior managers in Swedish companies referred to the difficulty of getting people to accept promotion.

Second, there is an alleged, and obviously related, tendency to avoid exposed line jobs in management. By line jobs we mean posts where the manager is manifestly accountable for performance, where he often has large numbers of subordinates and where he is generally 'in the thick of things'. Such positions are typically in sales, production and general management. The implicit contrast is with more advisory, more 'sheltered', staff jobs. Indeed, it is noticeable that such line jobs are often staffed by people who appear younger than their opposite numbers in other countries. Popular wisdom is that only the young are ready to accept the challenge (and aggravation) of such positions, in default of adequate financial rewards.

Third, a corresponding tendency is both alleged and, in our view, observable, this being the sideways slide into relatively protected staff jobs. Several times such instances were pointed out and it was clear that individuals were sometimes prepared, in the relative absence of a financial deterrent, to give up increments of power for the prospects of a quieter life. Managerial 'decolonization' is at least as common as empire building.

There are some further manifestations of impoverished motivation, relating not just to low pay but to wider family values. These are, briefly, a reluctance to work long hours, a disinclination to engage in business travel (especially trips which violate the weekend) and the view that holidays are sacrosanct. It is a standing joke in Sweden that the country closes down in July, when it is impossible to get anything done in the business world (and August is not a great deal better). Another point sometimes mentioned in this context is a lack of enthusiasm for business entertaining, felt to be either an unreasonable demand on the manager's (working) wife or an intrusion on family leisure time. Finally, there is the previously discussed phenomenon of reluctance to move.

In so far as these latter charges are true, it is not necessarily, or only, a reflection of the relatively impoverished material rewards package. Sex equality, the importance attached to family life in general, the Swedes' characteristic enthusiasm for nature, scenery and second houses in the country, are all relevant. All one can say is that the Swedish manager is less likely to be deflected from these alternative leisure-family-equality values by crude financial incentives than are his opposite numbers in other countries.

However, even if we accept American orthodoxy on the importance of a high level of financial reward in order to sustain a high level of motivation, and therefore assume that there is some loss in the Swedish case, it cannot be said that it is all loss. In short, there are some corresponding gains.

First, there may be a gain in what one might call 'purity of motive'. Swedish managers who do move, who accept promotions and who fill exposed line posts are rather less likely to be 'doing it for the money' than their colleagues in other countries. Those who get to the top must want to be there for intrinsic rather than extrinsic reasons. Second, the lower financial incentives defuse somewhat the struggle for promotion; if there is a loss of thrusting dynamism there is the corresponding gain which has already been referred to – less politicking, fewer power struggles, more cooperation between functions and hierarchical levels. Third, there is a certain ritual element, in both Britain and the USA, in moving managers around geographically – it is a habit, a *rite de passage*, a test of the manager's loyalty and a celebration of Anglo-Saxon generalism. However, this nonsense element is likely to figure less in Sweden; if it is difficult to get people to move anyway it is therefore more likely that they will only be asked to do so for serious reasons. Fourth, not only are Swedish managers poorly paid by international standards; so are Swedish engineers – and of course the two categories overlap substantially. This is another way of saying that Swedish engineers are cheap – the second cheapest in Europe (after British engineers). In turn, this should be significant for an advanced industrial economy with a lot of highly engineered up-market products. After all, it is commonly said that high blue-collar wages in Sweden push up the cost of Swedish manufactures and tend to make them uncompetitive; but if this argument is accepted, then so should the countervailing argument about the cheapness of Swedish engineers.

Standing Back

It is always a good move to examine the links between management and society in any country as this often provides clues to interesting differences. Looking at this relationship is an integral part of the characterization exercise.

This general argument is given a particular thrust in the case of Sweden because there is, in Sweden, a tension between socialism and capitalism.

The socialism–capitalism tension has one very tangible manifestation which has been indicated here, this being the gap between the reward-and-allocation system developed by a welfare socialist state on the one hand, and the near-universal norms relating to the reward and remuneration of managers on the other. This tension has implications for the geographical mobility of managers, for self-selection for management posts, for attitudes to overseas assignments, for promotion and for the readiness to be promoted. Furthermore it is felt to contribute to the reasonable and cooperative ethos of the typical Swedish company.

Side by side with this tension – between the objectives and achievements of a socialist society and the values and operating mode of free-enterprise capitalism – is another odd contradiction, the fascinating mixture of internationalism and nationalism in Sweden. It is unusual for countries to have a commitment to internationalism as strong as that of Sweden's, and the fact that this 'cohabits' with simple folksy nationalism is really remarkable.

A further point of interest is the way that Swedish industry benefits from both these characteristics. Sweden's internationalist stance does offer Swedish companies an *entrée* to eastern European and Third World markets, while 'nationalism at home' tends to protect domestic consumer markets. As we have agreed earlier, it is also the case that national pride is fuelled by a sense of industrial achievement, and in turn constructively supports that achievement.

References

Barnet, C., *The Collapse of British Power*, New York: William Morrow, 1972.

Hutton, S. P. and P. A. Lawrence, *Production Managers in Britain and Germany*, Report to the Department of Industry, 1978.

Telesis Inc., *The Engineering Industry and Swedish Industrial Policy*, Report to the Sveriges Mekanförbund, October 1980.

Wiener, M. J., *English Culture and the Decline of the Industrial Spirit 1850–1980*, Cambridge: Cambridge University Press, 1981.

If Not Now, When?

Peter Lawrence

Chapter 5, pp. 65–76 in Peter Lawrence, *Management in the Land of Israel* (Cheltenham: Stanley Thornes Ltd, 1990)

This phrase has attained a certain currency since Primo Levi's novel about a group of Jewish partisans in the Second World War appeared in English.[1] Indeed the Song of the Partisans, according to Levi, runs:

> If I am not for myself, who will be for me?
> If not this way, how? If not now, when?

It expresses engagement, conviction, existential responsibility, and of course, a propensity for action. It is relevant to the present undertaking in two ways. First, it has merit as an emblematic characterization of Israeli management. Second, there comes a point in such an exposé where enough has been said about context and background, and one should confront the question: What is Israeli management like?

Action

Israeli management is active, interventionist, and energetic. The Israeli manager is always happier doing something than thinking about what might be done. The Israeli manager is at his best in situations where something has to be done quickly, to save the day. In the redolent phrase of Peters and Waterman, Israeli management has 'a bias for action'.[2]

This key feature of Israeli management may be restated in terms of the conventional body metaphors. Israelis believe in 'hands-on' not 'arm's-length' management. There is a view of management which presupposes the manager's task to be about direction, planning and control. This implies that managers will need to distance themselves a little from their subordinates, the day-to-day events, operational crises, and the plethora of ongoing detail. This is not the Israeli way. Israeli managers want to be down there among it, up to their armpits in operational exigencies, savouring every action-packed moment. The Israeli manager does not want olympian detachment, he wants to know what is going on – all of it, the big and the small, the short term and the long term, his own business and everyone else's.

Again the idea may be recast in terms of twentieth-century thinking about management work. The classical management school that dominated the first half of the century propounded a formalistic view of management as a somewhat impersonal exercise in organization and control, depending heavily on a species of administrative rectitude focusing on such issues as clear lines of communication, unambiguous reporting lines, clearly defined responsibilities, and matching increments of authority. Indeed a lot of these prescriptions were codified by Henri Fayol, French mining engineer become chief executive, in a book which became the charter of the classical management school.[3]

The resulting view that management was restrained, rational, and rectitudinous, or at least that it ought to be this way, was largely unchallenged until the Swedish economist Sune Carlson made a study of what a group of chief executives actually 'did all day'.[4] Lo and behold it emerged that these top managers spent all day talking to people – in meetings and informally. Their olympian detachment was much less in evidence than had been supposed; these managers worked long hours and felt themselves to be under pressure; their involvement in operating and problem-solving decisions was much greater than had been expected. By their own admission they neglected planning, strategy, and the longer-term view.

But Sune Carlson's reaction to these findings is interesting. His view was largely censorious: his chief executives were departing from the detached and rational view of top management, violating classical management prescriptions, and caught up in an awareness that they were doing the wrong things without being able to get back on course, a phenomenon that Carlson labelled 'administrative pathology'.

It was left to a later researcher, the Canadian Henry Mintzberg, to argue on the basis of a new American study that produced the same findings as those of Carlson that this indeed was the way management should be.[5] That management was bound to be about handling exceptions, about operational involvement, about informal and human sources of information and understanding.[6]

This development is relevant to an appraisal of Israeli management in two ways. First, accepted thinking about the nature of management work has changed, to some extent coming into line with Israeli practice. This means that the *global critique* that Sune Carlson, never mind Henri Fayol, would have levelled at management practice in Israel, would be inappropriate today (though there are criticisms to be made).

Second, building on research of the Carlson–Mintzberg kind it is now appreciated that there is a continuum running from olympian detachment to compulsive involvement and that managers as groups or individuals may be 'plotted' on that continuum. In other words detachment/involvement are not absolute characteristics of management work but variable features.[7] In particular they can be seen to vary with:

- the level of management that is examined
- the department or function of management (function in the sense of sales, personnel, production, R&D, or whatever)
- the national context.

Thus it is relevant and meaningful to characterize Israeli management as 'hands-on' and action oriented. It is an important contribution to showing what is distinctive about management in Israel, and one which needs to be developed here.

Immediacy

Israeli management style is also marked by a penchant for immediacy. Not only do Israeli managers want to know everything, they want to know it now. They have a predilection for face-to-face encounters, for 'hot' information, for being 'on the ball'. They want to be battlefield commanders, not armchair strategists. This predilection has further implications.

It means, for instance, that Israeli managers are not over-enamoured of the written word. They will not write what can be said. They are not by nature memo writers; they do not 'put it on paper' just to 'have it on file'. Israeli companies are not strong on mission statements, policy directives, job descriptions, the written-evaluative side of personnel management; even correspondence may get short shrift. This is not a truism, or a universal disposition of managers. Managers in France, for example, are well-known for their liking for the written word, for giving priority and their best endeavours to that which may be recorded in writing.[8]

It also means that Israelis are not office bound. Israelis like Management by Walking About (MBWA). It is more proactive, more immediate, gives one a faster access to current developments (and is better for one's image). Furthermore there is an international dimension to Israeli MBWA; Israeli managers like to meet their agents, distributors, suppliers, customers, partners, and bankers – wherever they may be. And they like to take an international aura with them. The Israeli manager *en mission* somehow seems to communicate to his interlocutors abroad the idea that he is really part of an international organization, that just happens to be located in Israel!

Interaction

Interaction, of course, goes with action; Israeli managers gives a high priority to interaction. They see management work in interactive terms, prize their social skills and communicative abilities, know that this is something they do well.

Again this is not a truism. Although all management work is interactive to some extent, there are differences of degree, preferred mode and pattern of interaction. What, then, is distinctive about Israeli practice?

First the point already made that it is strongly inclined to verbal, face-to-face interaction, with a relative under-utilization of written forms of communication. Second that there is an emphasis on horizontal communication, an interaction between hierarchical equals, not (just) communication up and down a chain of command. Third, there is an even greater emphasis on diagonal communication, between 'un-equals' in different departments or areas of management's work, whereby all partners satisfy their craving to know everything about everything. Finally in this connection, while there is no slighting of traditional vertical, up and down, communication, these 'vertical channels' are subject to Israeli norms of immediacy and may be modified in practice. Thus the chief executive who knows there is something that the gatehouse porter should know, may go and tell him personally. When the production director arrives in the morning he may well find a worker outside his door waiting to complain that someone has moved his machine.

The Israeli penchant for verbal interaction has a further ramification. It means that decision-taking in Israeli companies is a verbal-processual, talked through affair, with an emphasis on real-time persuading and bargaining. One cannot imagine the Japanese ringi system taking root in Israel. Ringi is the system where the proposer confides his initiative to paper, circulates it widely in both hierarchical and functional terms, so that the proposal attracts assent, comments, qualifications, measured responses, and so on, such that at the end of the exercise the senior management knows what is desirable and viable, and can implement it expeditiously. Of course, it takes time.

An Israeli manager, however, who has a brilliant idea does not want to 'ringify it'. He wants to tell people, face-to-face, straight away. And if they do not like it/see its instant brilliance, then they are wrong-headed fools, and he can start to work on them without more ado.

So the Israeli penchant for direct interaction is not only about a preferred mode, but about processes as well. And it is an important clue to esteemed qualities among Israeli managers. The Anglo-Saxon idea of 'being able to communicate' is too tame for the Israeli context. Israelis put a premium on persuasiveness, argumentativeness, being able to take criticisms – and then confound them.

Busy Line

The Israeli manager's drive to communicate underlies, of course, the passion with which the telephone is embraced. While the telephone is a universal management tool, studies of managers in Britain and Germany show both individual and national differences in the pattern and frequency of use.[9] The Israeli manager's commitment to the telephone is qualitatively different: *il s'agit d'amour*.

For the Israeli manager the telephone has the great advantage of eliminating time and space barriers to verbal communication: as such it is neither tool nor toy, but executive fulfilment in hard plastic. Israeli managers suffer easily from telephone deprivation. On arrival at airports they stampede to the phone booths; on arrival in other people's organizations they always need a phone more urgently than a parking space, cup of coffee, or visit to the WC.

Most Israeli managers do not have their secretaries monitor incoming phone calls; they respond with apparent relish to each and every ring. To say that 'they do not mind the interruption' is true but too tame a way of putting it. Israeli managers appear to enjoy the stimulus of switching attention between calls and other tasks. Indeed the Israeli's ability to re-focus on a conversation without needing a cue or prompt after an 'interrupting' telephone discussion of something quite different is truly remarkable. Israelis also show in the same context an ability to switch languages without 'interference' – the running into one language of odd words and expressions from another language currently or recently used. Israelis do this much more than say Scandinavians, although the latter are much more accomplished speakers of English as a foreign language.

Israeli managers are engagingly aware of their love affair with the telephone. Stories circulate of the visitor to a senior executive who, irritated by the intermittent loss of his host's attention due to incoming phone calls, went into a neighbouring office to phone him to be sure to engage him without fear of interruption.

A Universal Agenda?

When people speak a foreign language well, the occasional words or phrases from their mother language which they intrude when speaking the foreign language are often culturally significant. The Dutch, the world's leading speakers of English as a foreign language, frequently use the word *agenda* when speaking English. For the Dutch the *agenda* is not a list of items tabled for discussion at a meeting, or some metaphorical variation on this theme. *Agenda* is diary; not the type to which one confides an account of one's feelings and doings (not what Anne Frank wrote), but a book in which one schedules one's commitments, meetings, appointments, deadlines, and so on. Even Dutch schoolchildren will speak of having an *agenda*, which will list things like the birthdays of their school friends, as well as whether they should be doing physics or geography at 11.00 a.m. on a Tuesday.[10]

The Dutch falter at the rendering of *agenda* in English because taking the agenda seriously is an integral part of being Dutch. The Dutch are inclined to be humble, to recognize the punyness of man before some of the great forces which confront him. In particular the Dutchman feels humble before the objective majesty of time. Israelis are not afflicted in the same way.

This is not a fanciful way of saying that Israelis are unpunctual and a bit unreliable. The issue here is rather that Israeli managers have a different view of time. Time does not confront the Israeli manager as an objective constraint. Time is not an absolute, but a circumstantial variable. The way to handle time is to get out there and do things to it, before it does them to you. The Israeli manager sees time as something on which he can impose himself; time can be squeezed, stretched, or overloaded as needs may dictate.

This Israeli view of time is only implicit, yet it is quite distinctive. It is also consistent with the broad Israeli management style being depicted here. A commitment to action-intervention-interaction-immediacy cannot be diluted by unmanly clock-watching – and it is not.

This disposition is unrealistic, and Israeli managers get caught out by it. At the same time it is a strength. It is a strength in the sense that ignoring limitations sometimes is a way to overcome them. There have been so many instances in the short history of Israel where a sober and rational estimation of the task would be quite paralysing. So perhaps it is not surprising that Israeli managers often treat the constraints of time like a speed limit; something to be violated, and with a bit of luck you won't be caught out and will chalk up another success.

Style and Structure

The stylistic propensity of Israeli managers has a number of implications for organizational structure. Israeli managers like structures which are open, flexible, and unconstraining.

Or to put this in the language of organization theory the Israeli managerial preference is for what Burns and Stalker have called organic structures not mechanistic ones.[11] The mechanistic structure is, broadly speaking, a bureaucratic one, marked by precision and clarity as to areas of responsibility, degrees of authority, reporting lines and communication channels. The organic structure is by comparison both flexible and vague. No one is quite sure who is responsible for what, cleverness and specialist knowledge are esteemed, everyone has a licence to talk to everyone else, and it is understood that (scientifically) creative achievement will legitimate organizational chaos. Israelis love it.

There are some more particular points. Israeli managers often have large spans of control (i.e., large numbers of people reporting directly to them). Israeli managers often accept a large span of control because they value more the stimulus and input of people communicating than the relatively greater control over periods of disposal time that would accrue from narrower spans of control (i.e. fewer people reporting).

A variation on this theme is that Israeli managers often accept a situation where people who do not in theory directly report to them do so in fact. Again there is a gain in immediacy, knowing what is going on in an unmediated fashion, having the stimulus of direct inputs, that for the Israeli manager weighs more heavily than freedom from interruption or an over-burdening of upward communication channels.

A wider version of the same phenomenon is the situation where the organization chart is little more than readily acknowledged fiction. In most cultures the state of formal authorities and relationships depicted in company organization charts is seen as capable of modification in practice, but Israeli companies go further in treating the organization chart, if they have one, as purely for the sake of appearances – as something like 'bosses bottles' in the British catering industry, or a 'clean' set of accounts for the tax man in an Italian family firm.

There are gains in this practice: gains of freedom, flexibility, and an investment of personal resources that follows the discarding of status labels.

There is another way of expressing this phenomenon. We have suggested at several points that Israel has more entrepreneurs (rather than professional managers) running companies – a result of the youth of the Israeli state, the relative smallness of manufacturing companies, the premium on the exploitation of opportunities in the years after 1948. It is meaningful to take a step further and say that a lot of Israeli management is metaphorically entrepreneurial, whatever the details of actual corporate ownership. That a lot of Israeli managers, that is, comport themselves as though they were entrepreneurs in the classic sense, whether or not they are. This in turn means a certain kind of wilfulness, personalized leadership, and exuberant running of risks, rather than a *petit bourgeois* respect for the small-print of organizational propriety.

Informality and Bureaucracy

Visitors to Israel see a centralized, omnicompetent, and generally interfering government. There are more rules and regulations in Israel than in many states, more things in which the government has an interest and seeks to control. The Israeli manager sees this, but sees other things as well.

Where the (square) outsider sees regulations, requirements, and prescriptions, the Israeli sees groups to whom he can appeal, people who owe him favours, contacts that can be turned to account, reasons that can be adduced for doing it in a different way. As one Israeli manager put it:

> Between the official requirements there is a vast ocean of informality.

Israeli managers, for the most part, know what to do with this ocean of informality. They know what kind of craft will float, and where to launch them; they have an instinctive feel for the quicksands and the safe harbours. This aptitude is not obvious to outsiders, but it is there, and it is important to recognize that it is part of the energetic, proactive Israeli style.

Israeli and American Styles

There is some resemblance between American and Israeli styles in management – but it is superficial. The case for the putative similarity is that Israelis like Americans (and certainly depend on America) and indeed like them a lot more than they like the British. They see resemblances between the USA and the

State of Israel, albeit ones that discount geographic size. Both, in their day, were new societies, the expression of aspirations and ideologies, both a reaction to constraints, even persecutions, in 'the old world'. Both sought to tame and convert the territories they inherited, the Americans with McCormick's reaper-binder and the Colt peacemaker, the Israelis with drip feed irrigation systems.

In organizational settings, and in inter-personal relationships, (apparent) similarities persist. Both societies reject inherited status, formal titles, and the stuffiness of formal rank. Both preach openness, drive, and achievement, and an equality of manners.

There are two differences. First the American abnegation of hierarchy and formal authority, the parade of relaxed equality, may be only skin deep. As Athos and Pascale have argued in comparing American with Japanese management, beneath an egalitarian surface in American companies a structure of macho authority relations survives intact.[12]

Second, it is only fair to say that the informal quality of relationships in American companies is real. It is not contrived, not there to deceive, not a trap for the unwary. But it is predicated. It is based on effective management systems – of control, information, and target-setting. These systems represent the real authority in American companies. With these systems in place, a certain informality, even casualness, certainly a 'laid-back' stance is acceptable. Middle managers will be deemed 'out of line' when the control systems show them to be so, not when they offend status conscious superiors: and until that happens, they can call the boss Chuck and put their feet on his desk.

We have developed the point in order to position Israeli management, to show how it differs from American. In the Israeli case the informality is not skin deep, it is not predicated on a set of management systems, and for the most part such systems of information and control are not there. Israeli management is not system-driven, but aspiration-driven. And much of what facilitates achievement within companies is not a controlled and rational allocation of resources matched to tasks but a genius for improvisation.

Improvisation, Ingenuity and the Modification of Rules

Israelis are very much aware of their flair for improvisation. One can scarcely claim citizenship without it. As one managing director observed:

> If you cannot improvise, you're dead. And if all you can do is improvise, you're dead anyway.

We will leave aside the counter-criticism contained in this epigram. For the moment the purpose is to ask: what is this improvisation, how and where does it show, what ends does it serve?

One aspect is that Israelis see a link between improvisation and creativity. This understanding focuses on the flair for improvisation as a cerebral quality, associated with phenomena including higher enrolment in university education, the scientific achievements of Israeli society, the high level of technical inventiveness. It is the view captured by one top manager with the remark:

Creativity shows itself in improvisation as well as in technical invention.

This view shades into that which sees improvisation primarily in terms of technical resourcefulness, but of an unplanned, stop-gap kind. One company, for example, was pioneering an electronic aid to quality control. It took in some 'finished products' from several potential customers to demonstrate for them the efficacy of this inspection aid. Unfortunately the potential customers sent the products but not the software that went with them. Not liking to ask, and not wanting to wait, the company concerned improvised and cannibalized the software and proceeded with its test-demonstration. It may have been a ruse to get out of a tight spot, but it remains a ruse that is only available to the clever and sophisticated.

This view in turn shades into an understanding of improvisation as operational resourcefulness. One plant manager who brought up the theme of improvisation spoke of the measures resorted to when customers required an order to be processed fast and only a limited supply of the basic raw material is available: these measures included cannibalization from other less pressing customer orders, opening temporarily a new production line to process orders in parallel, and selecting high-output workers for the rush job. Another plant manager referred to delivering and installing systems with bits missing and hoping to patch them up before anyone noticed. There was a jocular reference here to the company's sales drive in one particular (export) territory being constrained 'by the lack of a resident fixer'.

It should be added that this kind of resourcefulness is not peculiar to Israel. Stories of this kind may be extracted from plant and production managers the world over. On the other hand, there seems to be a difference of degree in the case of Israel, and it is noticeable that these instances are typically cited with zestful satisfaction.

Another dimension in Israel's improvisation is the manager's instant plausibility. Things may not be going well, the manager may not even know how they are going at all, but this will not impede the display of understanding and confidence. A personnel director, generalizing about managers in Israel, observed:

> They can give an answer to any question even if not prepared.

Another interlocutor, a member of an accountancy practice, remarked:

> Improvisation! You should see my boss perform, especially in front of clients.

There is widespread agreement in management circles that this instant plausibility is an Israeli specialism; it is also something on which recent immigrants frequently comment.

Another view is that improvisation is the necessary concomitant of bureaucracy. That the centralism-formalism-proceduralism of the Israeli state sets off both a reaction in the form of rule-dodging resourcefulness as well as generating a need for informal lubrication. This idea is caught by one interviewee who remarked:

> Improvisation. Part of our pride and culture that we are great at it. Organisations are so sluggish and bureaucratic that you have to improvise to get things done. Probably comes from founding a state in a void.

Several managers we talked to volunteered this idea of improvisation as rule-dodging, system-negating, procedure-modifying. We can do the non-routine, we can handle exceptions, we can find ways round the rules, was a common cry. In one case a manager explained how performance-monitoring budgets were based on non-valid data, so that while appearances were being maintained no one need worry too much about violating the budget if it proved inconveniently rigorous. Plan modification was another *leitmotiv*. One has a plan, but may modify it to fit the realities of later performance so that sales plans, for instance, may be revised upwards or downwards to fit the subsequent achievements of the sales force. Consistency is the hobgoblin of small minds.

Again a qualification is needed. A lot of management is about constructive rule-breaking. Getting things done will always seem more important than preserving the integrity of systems and controls. Or to put it another way, if the whole operation is 'going according to the book' then it probably does not need managers to run it – clerks will do fine. It is the incidence of non-routine and discretionary exigencies that signals a need for management rather than administration. On the other hand Israelis often display a particular élan for this aspect of management work.

Improvisation: Identity and Pride

Running through much of the above is a thread of national pride. The idea that Israelis have a greater need to engage in improvisation, and are better at this. This idea was quite explicit in some of the discussions. One general manager, for example, on the subject of improvisation remarked that:

> It is nature and culture. We are living in the Middle East, not in a crystalized culture, but reacting to events, impatient.

In other words Israeli managers often see the need and flair for improvisation not just as a characteristic but as a distinguishing feature.

It is interesting that while Israelis like the USA and are well-disposed towards it, they do not see themselves as being remotely like Americans. And they see this formal versus informal, play-it-by-the-book versus creative deviousness as an important line of cleavage. One manager with work experience in the USA commented:

> If Europe invented the wheel, America must have invented the square. (I.e. is given to playing it straight.)

Another manager with postings in Latin America and the USA behind him asserted:

> I don't think the USA is dynamic. They're just building on mass. They cannot improvise at all!

Israelis see Americans as more conforming, more willing to merge their individuality in, for instance, a corporate identity, and of course more willing to take on the constraints of a professional (management) discipline. One Israeli manager with experience in his company's US subsidiary felt that American managers had stronger planning as well as profit and loss orientations, and saw them as more corporately indoctrinated. In contradistinction he saw Israeli managers as more oriented to training on the job (greater scope and need for improvisation), and, as he put it, less 'prepared' by their companies, the implication being not so much under-trained, as unmoulded. Israeli managers are conscious of not being 'organization men', which would require too much willing suspension of disbelief, and are in this sense different from their American colleagues.

The Israeli manager whose views on contrasted orientations were cited above also saw discretion operating at a lower level in Israeli companies than in British or American ones. People lower in the hierarchy in Israel, that is, were exercising discretion/making decisions. Some of this discretionary behaviour is no doubt in the form of improvisation.

Where Does it Come From?

We have tried in this brief discussion of the Israeli penchant for improvisation to show what it consists of and what ends it serves. This leaves open the question, how did Israeli managers get this way? True to the spirit of improvisation, Israelis have an answer to this as well, or rather a set of layered answers.

It all starts, they say, with the Jewish settling of an inhospitable area, with its challenges and hardships. A pioneer spirit developed, and became a national trait. Again this pioneer spirit – resource, adaptation, making do – found its high point in the kibbutzim (one small legacy today is that the kibbutzim and moshavim supply most of the members of the IDF's élite military units).

This resourceful element in the Israeli character was fostered even more in the 1940s; outwitting the British (this is the period of the White Paper and Aliya Bet), clandestine military training and arms smuggling in the run up to Independence, and then attacking on several fronts. The post-independence period brought another challenge in the form of Operation Magic Carpet as it was called, the ingathering of the exiles (Jews from other lands). It was in the Zionist logic of events, yet the fledgeling state was not equipped or resourced to handle it; another national experience putting a premium on adaptation and improvisation.

So, runs the argument, it would be surprising if Israeli managers, like the citizenry in general, did not exhibit some flair for improvisation.

These arguments are much rehearsed in Israel for the benefit of inquiring visitors. They are also instantly comprehensible and plausible. Yet they are advanced so often that there may be the shadow of an alibi here. That Israeli managers engage in improvisation because they like it and are good at it, rather than because it has been circumstantially ordained. It is temperamentally consistent behaviour. It is the outlet *par excellence* for that dynamic cross between intelligence and nervous energy.

It is a strength, an accomplishment, indeed a skill that managers need. But it also reflects a weakness, that must be probed elsewhere.

Notes

1. Primo Levi, *If Not Now, When?* (London: Sphere Books Ltd, 1987).

2. Thomas J. Peters and Robert H. Waterman Jr, *In Search of Excellence* (New York: Harper & Row, 1982).

3. Henri Fayol, *Industrial and General Administration* (London: Pitman & Sons, 1930).

4. Sune Carlson, *Executive Behaviour* (Stockholm: Strömberg, 1951). Carlson's book is difficult to obtain; a summary is offered in Peter Lawrence, *Invitation to Management* (Oxford: Basil Blackwell, 1986).

5. Henry Mintzberg, *The Nature of Managerial Work* (New York: Harper & Row, 1972).

6. Ibid.

7. The debate is summarized in Joanna Buckingham and Peter Lawrence, 'The real work of managers' in Peter Lawrence and Ken Elliott (eds.), *Introducing Management* (Harmondsworth: Penguin, 1985).

8. Jean-Louis Barsoux and Peter Lawrence, *Management in France* (London: Cassell, 1990).

9. Peter Lawrence, *Management in Action* (London: Routledge & Kegan Paul, 1984).

10. Peter Lawrence, 'Management in the Netherlands: a study in internationalism?', Report to the Technische Hogeschool Twente, Enschede, The Netherlands, 1986.

11. T. Burns and G. M. Stalker, *The Manager of Innovation* (London: Tavistock, 1961).

12. Richard Tanner Pascale and Anthony G. Athos, *The Art of Japanese Management* (New York: Simon & Schuster, 1981).

5

The East-Central Europeans

Socialist Legacy

The Soviet Prototype *and* Research on Cultural Sources of Differences between Socialist Countries

Witold Kieżun

Part I, pp. 1–6 and Chapter 11, pp. 299–316 in Witold Kieżun, *Management in Socialist Countries: USSR and Central Europe* (Berlin and New York: Walter de Gruyter, 1991)

The Soviet Prototype

Sooner will a perpetual motion machine be discovered and the immortality elixir found than the West understand the spirit of Russia and its character.

Fyodor Dostoyevsky

Introduction – the Structure of Goals in the Prototype

The goals of the communist system have been unambiguously defined both theoretically, in terms of the ideological principles formulated by Marxism-Leninism, and pragmatically, in terms of official documents issued by the Soviet Union, the former Constitution of the USSR, signed in 1977, being of primary importance here.

The structure of theoretical-ideological goals is subordinated to one ultimate goal which is a complete development of the individual's personality within the framework of a new, classless society operating in a 'planned economy' system, with no exploitation of man by man.

According to Karl Marx:

in a higher phase of a Communist society after the enslaving subordination of individuals under division of labour, the antithesis between mental and physical labour will have vanished; after labour has become not only a means of life but

> life's prime want; after the productive forces have also increased with the all-round development of the individual, and all the springs of co-operative wealth flow more abundantly – only then can the narrow horizon of the bourgeois right be crossed out in its entirety and the society will inscribe on its banners: 'From everyone according to his ability, to everyone according to his needs.' (Marx, Engels, 1958)

Friedrich Engels, the co-founder of the Communist model, emphasized that a united proletariat would create a system which:

> through the planned organization of all production will multiply the social productive forces to the degree which will provide everybody with all his rational needs on an increasing scale. (Marx, Engels, 1972)

The planned production organization will, according to Engels, satisfy even the needs of luxury:

> human production provides a certain degree of development at that level, which can satisfy not only the basic needs, but also the needs of luxury. (Marx, Engels, 1976)

This well-defined structure of goals is clearly related to a Marxist system of values and to the dialectical theory of social development. The 'socialist man' is somebody who accepts dialectical materialism as the ideology which explains social development and which creates a new system of values, in which the collective interest prevails over the individual one.

The complex structure of goals requires a general political strategy to destroy the enemies – all bourgeois forces which are against these ideas.

These ideological goals were to be realized in the model of the Soviet 'new state', which would serve as a means to realize the expansionist idea of a new, universally established, communist, dialectic-materialist civilization.

In the preamble of the Constitution (Fundamental Law) of the Union of Soviet Socialist Republics (1984), we read: 'The Great October Socialist Revolution . . . created the Soviet State, a new type of state, the basic instrument for defending the gains of the revolution and for building socialism and communism.'

In the next statement the goals of the Soviet State are presented in greater detail: 'The supreme goal of the Soviet State is the building of a classless communist society in which there will be a public, communist self-government. The main aims of the people's socialist state are: to lay the material and technical foundation of communism, to perfect socialist relations and transform them into communist relations, to mould the citizen of a communist society, to raise the people's living and cultural standards, to safeguard the country's security and to further the consolidation of peace and development of international co-operation.'

These main statements well define the instrumental role of the 'new state' realizing the ideological aims of building communism in the Soviet Union.

The role of the new state in the building of the world socialist system is clearly presented in the following statement: 'Humanity, thereby, began the epoch-making turn from capitalism to socialism' or 'taking into account the international position of the USSR as part of the world system of socialism, and conscious of their internationalist responsibility'.

The Soviet Union is now a state 'of the whole nation', because: 'the socio-political and ideological unity of the Soviet society, in which the working class is the leading force, has been achieved. The aims of the dictatorship of the proletariat having been fulfilled . . . The leading role of the Communist Party, the vanguard of all the people, has grown.' This recent document from 1977 is a logical continuation of former fundamental laws, which, it is spelled out explicitly, are concerned with: 'preserving the continuity of ideas and principles of the first Soviet Constitution of 1918, as well as the 1924 Constitution of the USSR and the 1936 Constitution of the USSR'.

It is also necessary to mention that this structure is logically linked with the Marxist theory of historical materialism and Marxist determinism in social development. This fact is discussed by the Russian academician Professor Afanasyev in his *Marxist Philosophy* (1980):

> The current bitter struggle between communism and bourgeois ideologies will be won by communist ideology. Behind it is the truth of life, and the truth is invincible. This great truth lies in the ideals of communism which are winning the minds and hearts of all honest people in the world. As regards bourgeois ideology, it has not passed the test of history. Its downfall is just as inevitable as the demise of the social system it represents. Mankind has discerned the real image of capitalism and does not want and will not tolerate its further existence. Moribund capitalism will be replaced by a new, and most just society – communism. Such is the objective law of social development, such are the objective dialectics of history.

In accordance with the determinist Marxist theory of social development, the Soviet Union today is already in the phase of 'building communism', having completed the period of 'building socialism'. Since all other countries are still in the socialism-building phase (this description refers to the so-called 'people's democracies') or in the stage of 'the struggle to enter the path of socialism', the Soviet management system has the value of being a prototype model, the only socialism in operation (since no other real socialism exists).

Table 1 The Structure of Objectives of the Soviet Union as a New Type of State, and of the Soviet Communist Party

Phase	*Role*	*Main objectives*
Building of communism in the USSR. The 'capitalism to socialism epoch' in the international arena.	The Soviet state, a new type of state, instrumental in: a) Construction of communism in the USSR b) Consolidating the position of world socialism c) Supporting the struggle of peoples (outside of the USSR) for national liberation and social progress.	1. to defend the gains of the Revolution 2. to lay the material and technical foundation of communism 3. to perfect socialist social relations and transform them into communist relations 4. to mould the citizens of a communist society 5. to raise the living and cultural standards 6. to safeguard the country's security 7. to ensure international conditions favourable to building communism in the USSR 8. to support any struggle for national liberation and social progress 9. to consistently implement the principle of the peaceful coexistence of states with different social systems 10. to strive for victory and consolidation of socialism in the international arena 11. withering away of any of the state after the building of the communist society and the victory of socialism in international arena

Sources:
Constitution of the USSR, 1977, Moscow, Novosti Press Agency Publishing House, pp. 9–12, 23.
Programme of the Communist Party of the Soviet Union, 1961, Moscow, Novosti Press Agency Publishing House.

Therefore, the USSR is instrumental in the construction of communism in the USSR and a consolidating force for socialism in the world.[1] A formalized structure of goals of the USSR and of the Soviet Communist Party is presented in Table 1.

The most essential objectives of the USSR are to defend the gains of the Revolution, which means retaining power, to make the society communist in the ideological sense, and to help in the process of the transformation of capitalism into communism all over the world by supporting the struggle of people for 'national liberation and social progress'.[2] This last objective remains in a dialectical relationship with the accepted principle of peaceful coexistence of states with different social systems. In reality this refers to a situation where, for example, a revolutionary communist movement in a foreign country is supported, morally and financially, while peaceful coexistence with the bourgeois government of this country is maintained.

The final goal which assumes the liquidation of the institution of the state after the victory of socialism all over the world is a reflection of a Marxist vision of a communist world and therefore can be treated as an objective that has not been formulated precisely. It is important, however, that even this imprecise formulation echoes the deterministic vision of materialism and dialectic worldwide civilization.

Motivation for the world-aimed Soviet expansionism has intrigued many journalists and politicians. Kisielewski, an outstanding representative of the opposition writing in Poland, maintains that the Soviet Union is forced to participate in the struggle for the world which is taking place today and that the Soviets do so not for ideological reasons but because of:

a) the inefficiency of their own system reinforced by the apprehension that their society will eventually realize it;
b) the stupidity and naïvety, lenience and aimless unfocused generosity of the capitalist West;
c) the existence of China. (Kisielewski, 1980)

Professor Brzezinski (1986), former Security Adviser to President Carter, also assumes that competition exists between the two imperialistic systems of the US and the USSR, and he points out that 'Moscow's empire is the product of a sustained and unrelenting historical drive by the Great Russian component of the USSR' and that 'Russia's imperial consciousness has, in the modern era, helped to generate and sustain a world outlook, in which the drive to global predominance has become the central energizing impulse.'

The view that the sources of Soviet expansionism should be searched for in the backward-looking tradition of tsarist imperialism, a sort of inherited atavism, is shared by many Russian thinkers (Heller, 1988). In her memoirs from the Soviet gulag, Wiktoria Kraśniewska (1985) quotes a statement of a prisoner, a Russian intellectual, who says that 'a Russian can be starved, can be put in prison or be persecuted by the Soviet Administration yet he will always experience the feeling of enormous pride when he sees the red colour spreading on the map marking a newly acquired territory'.

I encountered a similar attitude in 1945, during my stay in the Krasnovodsk gulag, in a prisoner of that camp, Prince Balutin, who had been an aide-de-camp to the last tsar, Nikolai II. Prince Balutin would confide to me his feeling of pride that Communist Russia did become the second power in the world, and that it has a chance to realize the tsarist idea of building the Third Rome thanks to the attraction communism enjoyed in the countries of the Third World.

Independently of its origins, Soviet expansionism was part of the structure of goals of the Soviet system and as such must be considered here.

Special attention must also be paid to the goal which is defined by the words 'to mould the citizen of a communist society'. What we have in mind here is the process of social engineering aimed at forming a new man, 'homo sovieticus'. A precise definition of 'homo sovieticus' can be found in many Soviet publications. The definition given in the introduction of the USSR-published book entitled *The Soviet People* which itself bears the title *Homo Sovieticus* (Heller, 1988) is as follows:

> The most important characteristic of a Soviet man is his communist idealism and Party consciousness. Whether he is a member of the Communist Party or not, his Party consciousness manifests itself in his whole philosophy, in his clear vision of the ideal and in his fervent zeal to make it come true. Homo sovieticus, however, is first of all, 'a man of labour'. Work is the most important thing in his life. He is also 'a man of the collective', a man wholly and without reservations devoted to his socialist, multinational homeland. He is a man aware of his responsibilities, a man involved in all phenomena, both of the worldwide nature and those concerning the life of his next-door neighbour. He is a man of high ideals . . . actively integrating the principles of Great October into life. He is a man who develops harmoniously, who is taken care of by the state. He can see the state's protection everywhere, he can feel it at every single step of his life.

The realization of this clearly specified structure of goals in the USSR facilitates a better understanding of the development tendencies in the Soviet theory of management and organization as well as of the full dialectical conflict and operational pragmatism in management practice.

There are two objectives of unvarying priority:

a) maintenance of power that has been gained, and
b) military and ideological expansion.

Efficient realization of these goals is made possible by centralization of the ownership of the means of production, together with administrative and ideological power, and a parallel multiplication of the reserve management lines and the growth of the control and supervision matrix structure.

Research on Cultural Sources of Differences between Socialist Countries

Differences in Style of Living

The historical development of (socialist) countries in Central Europe has led to four types of cultural characteristics, each defined in terms of its own set of features. They can be summarized as follows:

Type I: Bulgaria, Romania
- Orthodox church;
- Autocratic rule tradition;
- Severe discipline;
- Rural culture;
- Lack of freedom and democratic traditions.

Type II: East Germany
- Protestant;
- Military discipline;
- Obedience;
- Urban-industrial culture;
- Lack of democratic traditions;
- Aggressive dynamism.

Type III: Czech (only the Bohemian part of Czechoslovakia, Slovakia's background is more rural and more non-conformist).
- Roman Catholic;
- Lack of religious tolerance;
- Discipline;
- Obedience;
- Urban-industrial subculture;
- Conformism.

Type IV: Poland (also Hungary, to some extent, which is additionally characterized by elements of urban-industrial culture developed in the nineteenth century)

- Roman Catholic;
- Religious tolerance;
- Noblemen and rural culture;
- Non-conformist;
- Strong individualism;
- Low level of discipline;
- Tradition of noblemen's democracy.

While cultural traditions have been shown to be varied, there are also some basic differences in the style of living, its standard and degree of liberalization.

It is not without reason that Freedom House, an American organization which estimates citizen's freedom in every country in the world (Atlaseco, 1984) on a three-step scale of:

1. full citizen's freedom,
2. partial freedom,
3. lack of citizen's freedom,

in 1982 evaluated Poland and Yugoslavia as countries with partial citizen's freedom while all other socialist countries were placed at number 3 – lack of citizen's freedom. Yugoslavia is not included in the present discussion but Polish liberalism is well known in the contiguous countries.

It is interesting to note that in the pre-Gorbachev period the Polish press was very popular in the Soviet Union. Many of the Soviet professors I know subscribed to Polish papers in order to have access to more extensive and varied information than was available in the very schematic and indeed one-sided Soviet press. In the Gorbachev epoch the situation changed significantly. The Soviet press has become more interesting, and some periodicals such as *Ogoniok* and *Novyie Vremia* discuss many questions that were taboo until recently.

Another difference in the style of living is the real buying power of the population. In 1976 I made a comparative study of the contents of a shopping basket containing 20 products, and of some services, in relation to the average pay reported in official statistics of the six socialist countries, in order to define the buying potential of an average employee. A rough estimate of the results is as follows. If the buying power of an average Polish employee is defined as 100, the buying power of an employee in East Germany equals about 250, in Czechoslovakia 200, in Hungary 90, in Bulgaria 80, in Romania 60 and in the Soviet Union 50. These results are obviously not representative of the real proportions since the official average earnings in the Soviet Union, Poland, Romania, Bulgaria and Hungary are, as a rule, supplemented by additional income. Only an employee in the GDR and Czechoslovakia remains, more or less, within the structure of their official earnings.

In the remaining countries additional sources of income include natural products from private vegetable gardens and orchards (the so-called '*działki*', agricultural shares of land), additional private work executed without registration (repairing of appliances, electrical work and so on), non-registered evening work in private workshops (Poland, Hungary), illegal transactions involving currency and goods exchange, coaching, private teaching (e.g. music lessons, foreign-language lessons), smaller and larger gifts (national health service, schools, trade, services, administration). The form of these 'occasional gifts' is currently very popular in all these countries where goods supplies are in greatest disproportion to needs, i.e. in the USSR, Romania, Poland. Meney (1982) gives a whole tariff of 'corruption in the USSR' starting with a bottle of vodka as a traditional present for an administrative service or for selling an inaccessible product which is in great demand.

These differences in the standard of living in particular socialist countries, clearly illustrated in my pilot study, agree with popular opinion. Thus, the standard of living in the GDR is shown to be twice as high as in Poland (in the 1970s), which, subsequently, is twice as high as the standard of living in the Soviet Union.

This evaluation was confirmed by my meetings with Russians who visited Poland in the 1970s, on business or privately. I remember the words of a Russian intellectual, head of the University library, who subsequently defined her estimate of the difference stating: '*Vy uzhe zhiviote w komunizmie*' ('you already live in communism'). Such statements, recognizing the superiority of the standard of living in other European socialist countries, particularly in relation to housing, numbers of cars and store supplies, is usually accompanied by the explanation that the Soviet Union constantly helps its allies and this is the cause of such economic differences. I have heard this argument frequently in discussions with Russian intellectuals who mention the high cost of Russian support of Cuba and Vietnam, economic help sent to the developing countries and aid given to the countries 'fighting for freedom'. These facts were usually quoted with a feeling of satisfaction because of the mission being accomplished by their country. It is hard to say what percentage of the Soviet population shares this satisfaction. In the intellectual milieu of university professors and scientists this attitude was not uncommon.

Differences in the supplies of goods in socialist countries have given rise to a 'private, tourist trade'. It is well-known which articles can be sold in a given country and what can be bought with the cash received from the sale. In the second half of the 1970s Polish tourists in the USSR were selling jeans, ladies' wigs, ladies' umbrellas, shirts, Western T-shirts, ties and pop-music records. Numerous tourists from Poland heading for Romania via the Soviet Union (Lvov, Tarnopol) were pestered by locals wanting to buy these products. The first question at hotel reception desks or at camp sites was: '*chto vy prodaiotie?*' (what are you selling?). On the other hand, however, it was a good bargain for a Polish tourist to buy a Russian iron and electrical appliances, but the best bargain of all was anything made in gold, which was much cheaper in the Soviet Union.

Similar types of trade flourish in all other socialist countries, even rich ones, like East Germany and Czechoslovakia. For none of these markets has enough goods to meet consumer demand. Also the structures of prices, different in each country, allow profits to be made by trading articles with different prices in different countries. The same refers to the hard currency black market. In 1978, for example, the price of 1 $ US in Bulgaria was 3 leva which enabled Polish tourists to buy American dollars at 50–60 per cent of the price they would have to pay for this currency on the Polish black market. Other currency speculations involved bringing Hungarian forints to Austria where this currency was officially exchangeable into hard Western money in the banks.

The structure of prices on the free, unofficial market, which was highly developed in countries like the USSR, Poland and Romania, frequently indicated the exceptionally high values of some articles in relation to average pay. In the USSR in 1978 for example, a pair of jeans cost about 100–150 roubles, a Western pop-music record 50–200 roubles, a Western T-shirt about 50 roubles. Considering that the average Russian salary at this time was about 140–160 roubles a month the prices of these attractive goods appear very high.

The supply of everyday commodities was the poorest in Romania, then in the Soviet Union and in Poland.

The Polish market was well supplied in the early seventies but from 1975 it began to worsen, reaching the bottom in 1981 when acute shortages of practically all food and industrial articles were experienced. The situation has visibly improved since 1982.

From the beginning of its existence, the Soviet Union has always suffered from shortages. The day when basic food and industrial products can be bought without queuing has yet to arrive. In many places food is still rationed and the degree of difficulty in acquiring everyday articles can be measured in the average number of hours devoted to shopping for food and other basic products. The 5th October 1984 issue of the Soviet newspaper *Izvyestia* published an article by Professor Patrushev who stated that the Soviet citizens 'lose 65 billion hours of their time to do their shopping', which equals 'the number of hours worked in a year by 35 million employees in the socialist economy system'. In another *Izvyestia* article from 2nd February 1988, a Soviet economist Dr Lacis concluded that the number of people waiting in queues in the Soviet Union equals the number of people employed in Soviet industry, i.e. 37.6 million.

I am sorry to say that, at the grassroots level, the first years of perestroika did not yield positive results. On the contrary, queues multiplied and became longer and food rationing was introduced in many cities. In Moscow, sugar rationing was introduced in 1989 (every Muscovite had the right to 1 kilogram of sugar a month).

I now turn to an analysis of the range of individual rights and freedoms: free access to impartial information, freedom of speech (the right to criticize), reduced censorship of the press, openness of debate in the country's representative bodies and freedom of scientific expression. In this area, in accordance with the estimate of Freedom House mentioned before, Poland (next to Yugoslavia) was clearly different from other socialist countries. Poland was the only socialist country where the law concerning censorship of publications and public shows (passed on 31st July 1981) gave editors the right to mark deletions of parts or whole articles with a brief note: 'Law of 31st July, 1981'. This is why articles in the Catholic press, for instance, were sometimes interrupted with the statement 'Law of 31st July 1981, on control of publication' and gave a number which relates to the reason for withholding publication.

In my research on the role of cultural traditions in establishing management methods, Hungary is distinguished, after Poland, by the fact that its censorship laws have been slightly more lenient.

The degree of freedom, liberalization and censorship changed radically in the Gorbachev period. Previously, according to my own observations and the opinions of Polish scientists and academics who have visited the socialist countries under consideration, the degree of freedom, in descending order, was as follows: Poland, Hungary, Bulgaria, Czechoslovakia, German Democratic Republic, USSR, Romania. After the few years of Gorbachev's administration, the USSR moved to third position in this hierarchy, after Poland and Hungary. In 1989, a new situation was created in which Czechoslovakia, the German Democratic Republic and Romania clearly drifted apart from the remaining socialist countries.

However, in the area of visas, the USSR maintains its rigorous regulations, as did the German Democratic Republic and Romania. In these countries visitors were severely restricted in their movements (only selected routes could be taken by car and border controls were very rigid and thorough). In the USSR all foreigners must possess both entrance and visitor's visas (this regulation applies to the citizens of socialist countries as well) which grant permission to visit the city of destination and exclude all other places (e.g. permission to stay only in Moscow including the surrounding area up to 40 kilometres from the city).

With the exception of Poland and Hungary, all socialist countries strictly limited their citizens' visits to capitalist countries (till 1989). In popular opinion, Romania was thought to have the strictest internal policy. However, Romania's foreign policy presented an interesting contrast, being relatively independent. This policy has created a belief in the West that Romania has a certain political 'non-conformity'. The internal situation of Romania has been relatively little known in the world, whereas in the common opinion of the Polish society, for example, Romania was placed on a par with the Stalinist regime.

Comparative Research

Research on cultural sources of differences among European socialist countries was undertaken by me in 1976. The hypothesis which I wanted to verify was that there is a distinct correlation between cultural traditions of different nationalities and the system of management introduced in large enterprises. This hypothesis is, of course, based on another hypothesis, namely that managers try to introduce a system which allows them to obtain maximum efficiency.

This research was organized in the following way: we invited university professors, whom we knew personally and who were recognized authorities in management and administration in five socialist countries (Bulgaria, Czechoslovakia, the German Democratic Republic, Hungary and Romania) to take part in this investigation. Each was to conduct an individual research inquiry in one large state establishment in their country, employing 2,000 to a maximum of 3,000 workers specialized in some type of machine production (machine tools, various types of technical equipment and machinery). In Poland similar research was carried out by Mreła in one machine tool factory. Having defined the character of productive activity and the size of the establishment according to the number of workers employed, we left the choice of the factory or company itself to the interested professor. A questionnaire was used which included the following factors, each assessed on a scale of 1 to 3:

- Style of management (autocratic, democratic, laissez-faire);
- Level of bureaucracy (number of regulations, instructions, forms);
- Level of criticism by employees;

- Level of efficiency in production (quantity, quality and costs);
- Level of centralization;
- Level of social self-discipline in factories.

In order to make the evaluation of the degree of bureaucratization as precise as we could we prepared a detailed description of possible types of regulations and all written documentation distinguishing the following five types:

a) regulations addressed to supervisors;
b) regulations addressed to all employees;
c) work instructions (regulations concerning sequence, instructions as to the process of work);
d) documentation concerning employees' personal dossiers (personal questionnaires, leave applications, evaluation sheets concerning amount and quality of work);
e) minutes of work discussion meetings.

Depending on the amount of documentation in a given year (with respect to items a, b, c, d) and on the degree of detail (with respect to all types of documents) we distinguished three levels of bureaucratization: very high, high, lower.

The level of employee criticism was measured by the number of claims and organizational improvement proposals presented at internal staff meetings.

From the minutes of work discussion sessions in a single year researchers were requested to find out the number of registered complaints and proposals. To compare the data received from the several professors we classified three levels of criticism: low, higher, highest.

The level of centralization is indicated by the proportion of the decisions made by enterprise directors (general and deputies) and by their representatives at subordinate levels. Depending on the proportion (defined in percentages) of strategic, tactical and operational decisions made personally by the head director and his substitutes (vice-directors) in relation to the total of all decisions made in a single month (which we picked at random and turned out to be November) we defined three levels of centralization: very high, high with exceptions, high with elements of decentralization. The category 'high with exceptions' applied to situations where the board of directors temporarily delegated their authority to a lower level. 'High with elements of decentralization' was applied to cases where some decisions were permanently delegated to a lower level.

The level of social self-discipline in a factory was measured by absenteeism, the number of deliberate delays (or strikes) and the number of conflicts between superiors and subordinates, and classified as high, more than average, average.

Efficiency was measured by the average output (of the same product) per employed worker.

To evaluate the style of management we utilized the model proposed by Brown (1962) with his distinctions between autocratic, democratic and laissez-faire types, and the detailed characteristics he provided.

Where it was impossible to carry out a direct inquiry, we asked the co-operating university professors for an answer on the basis of previous surveys completed, or at minimum expressing their own judgement on the subject on the basis of their personal experience and knowledge of the situation. So we assumed the application of the Delphi-method as well. In most cases, assumptions underlying the research as well as a comparative analysis of the results were discussed with the participating professors.

Independently of the opinions expressed by the professors, I myself applied a method of participant observation to analyse the degree of intensity of visual political propaganda in the given countries. I also included one general question to estimate the strictness of political control of publications (censorship) in each of these countries by asking the selected professors to evaluate 10 statements on the reaction of the censors if these statements were to be published, rating the censorship as follows:

a) the censor will accept the statement for publication;
b) will accept it after some alterations;
c) will not accept it at all.

The statements contained fictional information concerning:

a) negative evaluation of the development of some branch of industry (e.g. 'The results of the inspection carried out show that the quality of the machine tools produced by the State Company for Machine Tool Construction is not satisfactory. About 15% produced last month were defective. The inspectors demanded that disciplinary consequences and penalties be imposed on the company's management');
b) positive evaluation of economic activity in capitalist countries (e.g. 'According to a recent estimate of the American Statistics Office further improvement of the US economic situation has been noted. Inflation diminished, and this fact is connected with an increase in production which is higher than foreseen');
c) negative evaluation of development in the USSR (e.g. 'Following a further decrease in corn production the USSR was forced to make additional purchases from the USA, Canada and the Argentine. These purchases were financed from the increased production of gold in Eastern Siberia').

On the basis of the professors' answers to these questions, I estimated the severity of censorship. I used official statistics for the data concerning the degree of tolerance with regard to the private sector, the national growth level and GNP (1975).

Field research was conducted in Poland, Hungary and the German Democratic Republic. As to the remaining three countries, Bulgaria, Czechoslovakia, Romania, we had to use the answers received from the participating professors only. They responded to all items of the questionnaire and their answers were based on their personal knowledge and experience accumulated during their own separate research on which they had been engaged. Direct comparative enquiry was not permissible.

All my respondents asked to remain anonymous, explaining this request as a precaution to avoid long and painstaking administrative procedures which would be needed in order to obtain official permission to carry out international comparative research. One of the professors said that internal regulations forbad passing information of this kind to neighbouring countries (even the countries of the same socialist bloc) without appropriate permission. In this way, my attempted inquiry, which was intended to be the starting point of a large comparative research project, ended up as a very tentative study. Even so, it yielded the results shown in Table 2.

Differences in Management Methods

It can be seen from Table 2 that East Germany and Czechoslovakia have the highest level of productivity. This is also connected with a high degree of bureaucracy and an autocratic style in management, although this is based on a well-developed tradition of self-discipline. The military–industrial traditions gained during the harsh discipline of 'scientific management' ingrained the attitude of subordination, acceptance of hierarchy and obedience, making it easier to adjust to the socialist collectivism philosophy. In spite of this, the management system remains rigid, with tough censorship and extensive propaganda. In both these countries, but more so in Czechoslovakia, at the time of the research in question, highways and important motorways were covered with banners with propaganda slogans such as 'long live eternal friendship with the Soviet Union', as well as with the big portraits of the native Party leaders and the leaders of the USSR. Both these countries, with their well developed industrial traditions, are also the richest socialist countries, with the highest GNP per capita.

Bulgaria and Romania are also characterized by a traditional attitude of

Table 2 Interpretation of Management Methods in Socialist Countries (1976)

Criteria of		*I Type*	*II Type*	*III Type*	*IV Type*	
Organization	*Bulgaria*	*Romania*	*East Germany*	*Czechoslovakia*	*Poland*	*Hungary*
Style of management in factories	Autocratic	Autocratic	Autocratic with self-discipline	Autocratic with self-discipline	Less autocratic, workers' councils	Less autocratic
Bureaucracy level	Very high	Very high	High	High	Lower, informal structures	Lower
Criticism in organizations	Low	Low	Low	Low	Higher, sometimes high	Higher
Productivity	Average	Average	High	High	Average and more than average	More than average
Centralization level	Very high	Very high	High but with exceptions	High but with exceptions	High with elements of decentralization	High with elements of decentralization
Level of social self-discipline in factories	Average	Average	High	High	Average	More than average

Character of visual political propaganda	Banners with slogans, pictures of leaders on roads	Signs with slogans, leader's cult everywhere	Signs with slogans, pictures of leaders	Many signs with slogans on the roads	Very poor visual propaganda (except in Silesia)	Very poor visual propaganda
Censorship	Very harsh	Very harsh	Very harsh	Very harsh	Relatively liberal	Not so harsh
Rate of economic growth (1971–1975)	4.6	7.1	2.4	1.9	5.7	1.2
Private sector in economy	Marginal	Marginal	Gives 5% of employment	Marginal	Produces 17% of national income	Marginal
GNP per capita 1976 (in $US)	2,646	2,402	4,162	3,821	2,642	2,642

Source: from research – Warsaw 1976.
Atlaseco, Les Editions SGB Paris – 1987.

subordination, but with a lower level of productivity. This seems to be connected to the lack of industrial tradition and the habits shaped during the centuries under foreign domination, where no possibilities of career were open to individuals and their natural tendency to increase productivity was suppressed. In Bulgaria, though, up to 1989, a highly dynamic rate of development has been observed, which to a large degree can be explained by exceptionally good relations with the Soviet Union. Bulgaria is the only socialist country in Europe whose friendship with the USSR has a truly national character, resulting from emotional pro-Russian traditions, extremely strong since the time when Russia liberated Bulgaria from the Turks after centuries of Turkish domination.

Hungary and Poland, countries of similar cultural background with a strong notion of individualism and a long struggle for independence, have a similar conception of management at the time of this research – more democratic, less autocratic, little formalized, with a high degree of criticism. Of the two, Poland accepted the private economic sector more readily and developed extensive informal structures (working illegally, corruption). With further development in the period following the research, Hungary has managed to stay within the strict regulations of collective discipline. Some slight deviations have not diminished the productivity of the country.

On the other hand, Hungary and Poland are different from the remaining socialist nations in Europe, and this is reflected in the different methods of management and style of living in these countries.

Summary and Conclusion

The results of this tentative study have confirmed some conclusions derived from the analysis of the economic and political development after the Second World War and the analysis of cultural traditions.

The methods of taking power employed by communists, who constituted an unquestionable minority in all the countries of Central Europe, followed Leninist strategy: coalition with all forces of the Left, supervision of the security apparatus within the coalition, gradual elimination of particular partners accomplished with other partners' approval, uniting with the social-democratic Left to form one party, finally taking over of all power.

The German Democratic Republic, which as an occupied country was put under Soviet military administration, is an exception to this pattern. It was created as a completely new formation, with no pre-war predecessor. In Poland too, the communist take-over acquired a specific character. Military struggle with guerrillas,[3] which mainly consisted of ex-soldiers from the former underground Polish Army that had fought against the Nazi occupiers during the war and did not accept the occupation of Poland by the Red Army, continued for the first two years after the war. This military struggle ended in the defeat of guerrilla forces and the 1947 amnesty for the soldiers of the underground, who were guaranteed freedom if they revealed themselves and returned their arms. In conformity with the strategy based on the principle of unity between morality and politics, however, the most important individuals were arrested later, as a rule under false accusations. Some of them survived till the amnesty in 1956 when they were fully rehabilitated but many died in prison, receiving only posthumous recognition.

The attitude of resistance against uncompromising forms of communist dictatorship has been continually present in Polish society. Thanks to numerous violent protests from workers, students or intelligentsia (1956, 1968, 1970, 1976, 1980) Polish citizens have acquired the highest range of citizen's freedoms among the countries of RWPG (Council for Mutual Economic Assistance). This exceptional attitude of Polish society can be explained in the light of their tradition of individualism, independence and freedom in making personal decisions.[4] These typical features even characterize Polish noblemen who, representing a much higher percentage of the general population (*c.* 12 per cent) than was the case in Western countries, have influenced the country's land-owners and farmers and the working class which has its roots in the country.

Here lies the source of the psychological maladjustment to the system which assumes the discipline of collective cooperation in a state that is the only employer and where the whole population (not excluding the farmers) is supposed to play the part of clerks in bureaucratic hierarchical structures.

Poland is also the only socialist country in Central Europe where farmers' collectivization did not work. About 10,000 kolkhozes organized in the Stalinist period broke up automatically in 1956, and in 1989 76.7 per cent of cultivated land was owned by private farmers.

Cultural maladjustment does, of course, affect work efficiency in state-owned enterprises. Our investigations have shown that efficiency is lower than in similar enterprises in the German Democratic Republic and Czechoslovakia. A Polish worker uses the minimum of his potential at work, just enough to keep his professional position. He would rather save his energy for professional activity in the informal 'second economy'.

The culture-based conflict has brought about a second trend in the Polish economic, cultural and scientific life. The enormous number of illegal publications which saw light beyond the reach of censorship, often edited in a rich graphic form (such as leather-binding, for example), private theatre performances, concerts, lectures, discussions, and numerous unregistered organizations have outgrown the capacity of the security apparatus to locate them and eliminate them. A truly paradoxical situation was created, in which Professor Krawczuk, the Minister of Culture (1987), officially announced that the other illegal literary scene does exist, his worry being the fact that even here, in the samizdat literature, no outstanding literary works could be found.

The independence gained in the constant struggle with communist dictatorship is also reflected in a courage to vote in accordance with one's opinion. Poland was the first to break the socialist tradition of elections where 97 or 98 per cent (or even 99.9 per cent as is the case in Albania) of the votes were for candidates designated by the Party. In the referendum organized by the Party in November 1987 only 42.4 per cent of those eligible to vote gave the 'yes' answer to the first question asked, and 46.3 per cent answered 'yes' to the second question.

In the 1989 Senate election, 99 per cent of seats were won by the 'Solidarity' opposition and the new chairman of the Senate was the former adviser of 'Solidarity', Professor Stelmachowski.

So in 1989 we thus witnessed a paradoxical situation where another type of life, governed by its own laws, does exist in Poland. What explanation of this paradox can be furnished other than that the cultural traditions have created attitudes which run counter to those assumed by the bureaucratized socialism? Stalin was indeed prophetic when he foresaw the impossibility of harnessing Poles to Communism. Poles have shown their gratitude to him by an exceptional demonstration of independence. Poland is the only socialist country where a monument to Stalin has never been erected.

In some respects a similar attitude can be observed in Hungary, which belongs to a similar culture model. The violent outbreak in 1956 was a reflection of the non-conformist tradition, with its origin in the old chivalric tradition of Hungarian noblemen which was, in a way similar to that in Poland, accepted by the society as a whole. But Hungarian cultural maladjustment has found its expression in a manner less controversial than in Poland. Another life has not been created but the 'goulash communism' model that has been introduced was meant to release individualistic tendencies and reduce frustrations resulting from the realization that one is nothing but a cog in bureaucratic machinery. Our investigations have shown that work efficiency and the level of social discipline at work in state-owned enterprises in Hungary are higher than in Poland, which can be attributed to certain traditions that have been formed in this country.

Since 1867 Hungary was an equal partner in the Austro-Hungarian Empire which enabled it to develop independent capitalist industrial production as well as modern forms of services which helped to create efficient work habits. At the same time Hungarians have managed to save their life-style which is reflected in an intensive social life, high level of gastronomic traditions and the culture of entertainment.

This economic liberalism has not, however, led to the relative political liberalism observed in Poland, nor did it lead to the creation of a separate informal economic, cultural and scientific structure.

The Hungarian official press has always been more orthodox than the press in Poland. The illegal literature and press circulation system has been relatively poor. Occasional samizdat publications do appear from time to time, and élite centres of dissident intelligentsia are in existence. The importance of the Catholic Church in Hungary cannot be compared to the role this Church has in Poland. The Church is tolerated but unlike in Poland, it has not become an advocate of culture and science or the second significant political force in the country. In spite of these differences, it can be stated that similarities in the culture of Poland and Hungary clearly lead to a similarity in attitude towards the communist model and a search for original ways of development.

Interesting in its diversity from the model of culture represented by Poland and to some extent Hungary, is Czechoslovakia, or to be more exact its Western part: Czech and Moravia, which can be briefly defined as a country of bourgeois-industrial traditions. The essential features of this tradition are: caution, rational calculation and conformism, orientation on gain, and finally, social discipline. These cultural traditions enabled Czechs to survive Nazi Occupation with relatively low human loss and no material loss. Also towards the communist regime Czechs applied the same, rationally conformist policy, joining the Communist Party en masse and stressing their loyalty towards the USSR in a number of external symbols.

During my own official visit to the State National Bank in Prague in 1956 I had a frank talk with one of the Bank's directors, who tried to explain that the mass membership of his employees in the Party is an expression of a rational and realistic attitude: 'If we, professionals, do not join the Party it will accept incompetent people, whereas we ourselves will be able to build socialism the way we want it, without repeating the Soviet errors. We are an industrial country and socialism as a system is better suited to our conditions than those in Russia.' It transpired, however, that it fell to them to propose a system of reforms that might bridge the distance between work efficiency and theoretical dogma. The 'Prague Spring' was not a spontaneous mutiny of the working class like the rebellion in Poland in 1956. It was an initiative proposed by the leadership of the Party, a reform project very similar to the 'perestroika and glasnost' reforms of Gorbachev proposed in the Soviet Union nearly twenty years afterwards. It was the Central Committee of the Communist Party that wanted to introduce a new 'Czech' model of management expanding the idea of glasnost to the suggestion that censorship should be abolished. The error of this conception lay in a poor understanding of the fundamental structure of goals of the USSR, where external expansion and maintaining power are priority goals. The Prague Spring was an occasion to formulate what was called 'Brezhnev's doctrine', which restricted sovereignty in socialist countries. This doctrine is in clear opposition to the Constitution of the USSR, which foresees the possibility of even Soviet republics leaving the Union.[5]

Traditions of conformism explain the low level of criticism expressed by employees of enterprises examined in our research; they are also manifest in the severe and rigorous censorship of publications. The bourgeois industrial traditions, however, are responsible for the highly developed self-discipline in the work-process and relatively high productivity.

Czechoslovakia is (after East Germany) the second-richest socialist country and, in spite of some clear symptoms of economic crisis, invariably maintains a relatively good level of market supply.

The most efficient socialist country of Central Europe, however, was East Germany. The '*Ordnung muß sein*' slogan is still valid and obeyed. On the other hand one must not forget that the first rebellion of workers against a communist regime in Central Europe took place in Germany when in June 1953 Berlin workers demonstrated against an arbitrary decision of the authorities to raise the obligatory work norm by 10 per cent. A general strike in Berlin was followed by riots all over East Germany, which were finally put down on 19 June 1953 after the Red Army had intervened. 21 people were killed, and 187 wounded (Chronique, 1987). Since that time, after millions of Germans had emigrated to West Germany, the German Democratic Republic reached a high degree of political and economic stabilization. It still maintains its first place in the comparative table describing national income per capita in socialist countries. Work efficiency indicators and the country's national debt are also good by comparison.

The following table showing national income per capita, country's national debt, and the relation of this debt to the value of yearly exports (i.e. an estimate of possibilities to pay off the debt) illustrates the position of the German Democratic Republic.

East Germany was an extremely bureaucratized country, with strong centralization and a well-developed reporting system. Conformity of political attitudes was strongly emphasized with its overt manifestations in a dogmatic press and external symbolism. One could postulate that all these elements relate to the military-industrial tradition. Considering the number of similarities in social attitude and economic situation in East Germany and Czechoslovakia one could state a hypothesis that the planned economy with its high degree of centralization, demanding subordination and high-level work-discipline, operates most efficiently in societies which have experienced the capitalist training of merciless discipline, optionally strengthened by military discipline of the Prussian type.

Table 3 Economic Indicators in Socialist Countries

Country	*National income per capita, position among 203 countries*	*National income per capita*	*Country's debt per capita in US$ in 1986*	*National debt relation to yearly exports in % in 1986*
East Germany	15	10.958	449	30
Czechoslovakia	35	7.643	583	17
Soviet Union	45	6.299	111	35
Bulgaria	49	5.905	398	26
Poland	53	5.120	781	255***
Romania	94	1.708	292	51**
Hungary	89	1.843*	906	88***

Source: Maly Roctnik Statystyczny – 1987 GUS Warsaw, Atlaseco 1987 Paris.
*See page 17 Atlaseco 1987, where it is suggested that these data are distorted by a low interest international credit. Real income per capita is estimated as 2500–3000$.
**In 1989 was 0 – Romania reimbursed all foreign credits.
***In 1989 the situation was worse – in Poland this relation was *c.* 320
in Hungary this relation was *c.* 160.

Minimized individualism, impersonalization, conformism, control, discipline and order become factors associated with high productivity. What is more, these are the typical features traditional capitalism furnished a bureaucratic system with, as Max Weber described it. It is quite possible that Marx was right when he said that communism requires a prerequisite stage of capitalism, in the nineteenth-century form with which Marx was familiar.

Bulgaria and Romania have similar cultural origins and they represent similar attitudes today. What strikes one in Bulgaria, however, is the phenomenon of irrational, literal adherence to regulations by administration officers who do not engage in any kind of individual thinking activity on their own. This attitude is typical of first-generation civil servants who come from the milieu of peasants and farmers, shaped by the tradition of obedience to the old-time Turkish administrator occupiers and, later, to the Bulgarian tsarist regime. A clerk blindly follows regulations which give him the satisfaction of wielding power over the client, while at the same time fulfilling his need for subordination and belonging to a definite place in a hierarchical system.

Another interesting characteristic of Bulgaria is the total absence of any dissident activity opposing the system in power till 1989. In the entire period over 40 years of the communist regime in Bulgaria there has been no anti-government demonstration and no independent political centre which opposes the official line has been formed.[6]

Considering the fact that communists were a minority here and that they first came to power by operating in a coalition, the existence of a culture of obedience seems to have been an important factor.

Both in Bulgaria and in Romania collectivization of private farms was efficient, having been accepted with no resistance. This attitude, so different from the attitude of the Polish peasant, can be explained by the tradition of collective exploitation of water-springs. Water economy in the southern part of the Balkans required a collective effort to secure access to the source of water: a common well had to be built for a community and people were used to collective work and collective ownership of water sources. There is also a strong tradition of neighbourly help, especially when one wants to build a house. Even today we can observe cases where on Sunday a whole village helps one of the members of their community build a house.

In Poland, which is a country with rich and easily accessible water reserves, a farmer would build his own well in his own territory, strengthening his independence in this way.

The degree of resistance against the communist regime in particular socialist countries corresponds to the culture model these countries represent. Opposition activity in Romania developed mostly in centres where there was a Hungarian minority. Riots in Brasov in 1987, which were the most significant expression of protest against the government and the depressing living conditions in Romania, can be treated as the beginning of a growing wave of protest against the regime.

To conclude, we can state that an analysis of political-economic developments and my own pilot studies both support the thesis that there is a link between the observed differences in management methods and specific cultural traditions. This hypothesis has been confirmed by the different methods these countries have used to pass from the totalitarian Communist system to democracy. Poland and Hungary went through a long-lasting, extremely exhausting period of social opposition, Czechoslovakia and East Germany applied a short, well-organized and peaceful protest action, after the results of the Polish experience had already proved positive, Bulgaria opted for peaceful changes within the Party, while

Romania chose the method of coup d'état, steered by the opposition within the Party who employed Stalinist methods (the 'trial' and the 'execution' of Ceauşescu) after the substantial experience of all other countries.

The socialist countries of Central Europe constitute a specific cultural mosaic, and today they still exhibit essential differences, not only in the life-style of their inhabitants, but also in the methods of management they use.

Here was the source of error in the conception of American conservatives who proposed to treat countries of the 'socialist bloc' as one uniform organism and suggested the same USA policy for each. This follows from ignorance of the existing situation and has already caused problems in US politics towards Central Europe.

A more general conclusion which can be drawn from the contrasting analysis presented here is that adjustment to the central bureaucratic socialist system was easier in countries which have gone through the experience of nineteenth-century capitalism or the two-centuries-old autocratic system which also neglects human rights.

Notes

1. At the present moment (1990) these statements are merely historical in character. Brzezinski (1989) is right when he says that 'in the eyes of Communists anywhere in the world the Soviet experience, which is not the subject of cult any more, should now not be imitated but avoided. Thus, at the present moment, Communism does not have a practical model for others to follow.'

2. In the new Gorbachev version of the Programme of the Communist Party of the Soviet Union passed at the 27th Congress in March 1986 we read: 'The CPSU actively promotes the cooperation and cohesion of the fraternal Socialist countries, the world system of socialism, the international communist and working class movement . . . The CPSU expresses solidarity with the nations waging a struggle for national and social liberation against imperialism and for the preservation of peace.'

3. Typically for a communist system syndrome, these formations were called 'bands'.

4. Poland was the first noblesse democracy in Europe, with free elections of the King by the nobility since 1572 and a 'liberum veto' system of voting in Parliament (a law could be passed only with a 100 per cent vote).

5. Stalin, questioned about the possibility of leaving the Union of Soviet Socialist Republics, is said to have answered: 'But what could they leave the Union for? Where could they go?'

6. This statement was true until the 1989 'Autumn of Nations' when peaceful demonstrations were organized in Bulgaria. But in 1990 the Communist Party transformed into the Bulgarian Socialist Party constantly is taking power.

Russia *and* Poland

Chapters 10, pp. 195–206 and 6, pp. 117–32 in Keith Sword (ed.), *The Times Guide to Eastern Europe: Inside the Other Europe* (London, Times Books, 1991)

Russia

Official name	Russian Soviet Federal Socialist Republic (RSFSR)
Area	17,078,005 sq. km (6,592,100 sq. miles)
Population	147,386,000 (1989)
Capital	Moscow (Moskva)
Languages	Russian, many minority languages
Religion	Russian Orthodox
Currency	rouble

The Russian Soviet Federal Socialist Republic (RSFSR) is the largest of the fifteen Union republics that make up the Soviet Union. Its population in January 1989 stood at 147.4 million. For such a large territory it is remarkably ethnically homogeneous. The RSFSR stretches from Vladivostok on the Pacific Ocean in the east (nearly 10,000 kilometres and eleven time zones) to the border of Byelorussia in the west. Even further to the west is the Baltic enclave of Kaliningrad, which is cut off from the rest of the RSFSR by Lithuania. This territory was originally part of German East Prussia, annexed to the Soviet Union after World War II, and is now settled by Russians. Then, the RSFSR extends from Murmansk on the Arctic Ocean in the north (2,800 kilometres) to Pyatigorsk in the Caucasus mountains in the south.

The republic's eponymous ethnic group makes up the overwhelming majority of its population (82.6 per cent in 1979). There are many minority peoples, sometimes grouped in their own autonomous republics or national areas. The largest of these minorities are the 6 million Tartars, who have an autonomous republic on the Volga with Kazan as its capital. Nearby are the closely related 1.5 million Bashkirs. Apart from the other small Volga peoples such as the Mordvinians and the Chuvashes, there is also a patchwork of autonomous republics in the north Caucasus: Dagestan, North Ossetia, Chechen-Ingushia and others. There are two other minorities who do not have a national area: the Jews and Germans. (The Jewish national area of Birobijan in the far east was an artificial creation, and few Jews actually live there.)

The European Russian heartland was not well endowed by nature. The rigours of the Russian climate are proverbial. It is continental in pattern with harsh winters (Moscow's average winter temperature is −8°C) and relatively warm summers (July temperatures of 20°C are typical). The growing season is short and, for the most part, the soils are poor except for the fertile black earth region in south-central Russia and the steppe that extends eastwards. Despite the unpropitious environment in some parts of north European Russia, dairying is successfully practised. For most of central Russia mixed farming is the norm, with potatoes and hardy grains the typical crops. Further south, however, are rich grain belts with sugar beet and maize also grown on a wide scale.

European Russia lacks natural resources. There are no major coal fields or oil deposits and few minerals except in the Urals mountains, where there is copper, iron, nickel, zinc, aluminium and magnesium. The climate compounds with distance to make communications difficult. So although Russia does have extensive timber reserves, they have proved difficult to exploit. Russia is also constricted by a lack of ice-free outlets to the sea, thus hampering foreign trade. Murmansk, although it is in the far north, is navigable throughout the year, but its distance from the main population centres limits its importance. Leningrad, which is further south and the centre of a major industrial region, is closed for three months of the year. In contrast, Siberia is rich in minerals. It has extremely large oil deposits in west Siberia around the city of Tyumen, and coal reserves for several thousand years in the Kuzbass and east Siberia, at the present rate of extraction. There are extensive deposits of all kinds of ferrous and non-ferrous metals, including gold, aluminium, molybdenum, manganese and iron. There are also large diamond workings. West Siberia has considerable reserves of natural gas and east Siberia a large surplus of hydro-electric power.

Russia's economic strength has stemmed from its agriculture and the creativeness and hard work of its people. It is a potentially rich country, but realizing that potential requires an immense input of human effort, and for most of its history it is the peasants who have made the country productive. In the pre-revolutionary period the productivity of Russian agriculture was low compared with West European countries, but the gradual penetration of the market into the countryside began to transform subsistence agriculture. In the south large estates were producing grain for export and the Siberian dairy herds did the same with butter. One of tsarist Russia's last prime ministers, Pyotr Stolypin, introduced measures to encourage the development of individual peasant farms out of the old semi-feudal structures based on the peasant commune, the *mir*. Fast industrial growth was also achieved.

The introduction of the market into the countryside and the inequalities that went with it caused social tensions. During the Revolution the peasants seized the large estates and divided them up. Individual peasant farmers were forced back into the *mir*, which was a major setback in the development of Russian agriculture. In 1917 the Bolsheviks had been able to secure the passive support of the peasants by calling for the division of the landlords' land, but then gradually alienated them during the Civil War, until they rose in rebellion. The Bolsheviks abandoned their policy of grain requisitioning and their plans to introduce collective farms, and in early 1921 introduced the New Economic Policy (NEP). Under the NEP the problem of grain production was approached by offering peasants incentives, and recovery from the famine of 1921–2 was remarkably quick. The peasants showed that they were able to respond to these incentives, despite the restrictions placed on them by both the *mir* and the Soviet state. Under NEP, grain deliveries to the cities were dependent on the market, and if prices were not good enough the peasants would not and frequently did not sell. At the end of the 1920s, under pressure to get grain into the cities to support the industrialization programme, requisitioning was reintroduced and systemized under the collective farms. In its collectivization campaign the Communist Party tried to exploit the resentment that the more successful peasants, the *kulaks*, aroused.

Russia's lack of natural resources and poor communications have encouraged the state to play an important role in the development of the country's economy. Both under Peter the Great at the beginning of the eighteenth century, when industry was built up with serf labour, and the much more grandiose project of Stalin in the 1930s the state was used to pull the country up by its bootstraps. It is the negative consequences of this last 'revolution from above' which are now being tackled by Soviet economic reformers.

From the beginning of the 1930s a rapid process of industrialization was carried out in Russia, as elsewhere in the Soviet Union, and, as elsewhere, it transformed the traditional life-style and economy of the bulk of the population. In less than ten years Russia's traditional peasant agriculture was replaced by collective farms. This was a disaster. Many peasants regarded collectivization as a return to serfdom, with the forced labour for noble serf-owners (*barshchina*) being replaced with forced labour for the state. Production of most agricultural commodities fell, but the number of peasants needed to produce them fell faster. Although there was thus an apparent rise in productivity, Russian agriculture was now permanently depressed. This was partly due to the centre's persistent neglect, compounded by its failure to take account of local conditions and also because of the lack of incentives given to individual peasants. Some Russian intellectuals now argue that collectivization permanently destroyed the peasants' interest in the soil, but this is belied by the success of their private plots, which make a contribution to Russian food production out of all proportion to the size of their area.

Russia's rapid urbanization and the development of heavy industry gave the impression of modernization. The population of old-established cities grew rapidly and new ones were built from scratch. From being an overwhelmingly peasant country in 1928, by 1941 Russia was becoming a nation of city dwellers. During the 1930s the output figures for iron, electricity, coal and machinery shot up, and by 1941 a massive industrial potential had been created which was the basis of the Soviet war effort. The structural bias towards heavy industry was established in the early five-year plans, and Russia's economic geography was transformed by the establishment of large new metallurgical combines at Magnitogorsk in the Urals and Kuznetsk in west Siberia.

Soviet economic development has been particularly profligate with the country's two most precious assets, its natural resources and its people. Cheap natural materials have been made to substitute for capital and technology and waste has been compounded by the lack of proper controls on costs. As a result, it now takes three times as much energy to produce a tonne of copper in the Soviet Union as in Germany. Industrialization was wasteful in people not only because of the physical destruction of millions as *kulaks* and in famine. Low productivity is structural to the Soviet economic system. Western social scientists have described a sort of 'social contract', whereby the regime bought political quiescence with gradually rising living standards to be enjoyed roughly by all citizens, no matter what contribution they made to society. Wage differentials were small, job security almost total and pressure to increase productivity minimal. Russian workers called this the system of 'we pretend to work and they pretend to pay us'. The Soviet system has created a highly educated but greatly under-utilized workforce. Typically, across the Soviet Union today there are thousands of research institutes where highly educated graduates 'pretend to work'.

What is Russia?

Formally at least, it would be no exaggeration to say that 70 years of Soviet rule reduced Russia to the status of an administrative concept. Indeed, for many foreigners Russia is synonymous with the Soviet Union. In recent years, however, the fundamental questions that are being asked about the future of the Soviet Union are encouraging Russians to think about their own national identity. Russia's history, in many ways, separates it from the other nations that make up the Soviet Union and from those of Eastern Europe. In the past, both Russians and foreigners have tried to define Russia in terms of either its European or its Asiatic heritage. In practice, Russian culture has been European for over two centuries, although the Russian state and its relationship to society makes this a nation *sui generis*.

Modern Russian history began in the fifteenth and sixteenth centuries, with the campaigns of Ivan III and Ivan IV, the Terrible, to free Russians from Mongol and Tartar rule. To stave off its enemies in the east and later in the west (at first, Poland and Sweden, and later, France, Britain, Austria and Germany), the need for a powerful state to mobilize all available resources developed. However, the Russian autocracy was not merely a strong state: it was a very personal form of absolutism in which there were no intermediate institutions, such as an independent church, an aristocracy (as opposed to a service nobility) and rule of law. There were attempts to replace the 'bootstrap-pulling' convulsions to catch up with rivals who were always ahead and create a self-sustaining process of development by releasing the creative forces in society. Catherine II, the Great, tried to raise the prestige of the nobility, for example. In 1861 Alexander II abolished serfdom, and subsequently set up a judiciary and a representative form of local government, the *zemstva*. After the 1905 Revolution Nicholas II granted a limited representative assembly, the *Duma*. However, the Bolshevik determination to industrialize the country through state planning represented a resumption of the state tradition.

The Communists have exploited aspects of Russia's political culture to maintain their rule, in particular peasant egalitarianism, and this is one reason for the ambivalence with which Russians have sometimes regarded the Soviet regime. However, Communist rule has destroyed a great deal more than it borrowed from Russia's traditions, and not just those of the Europeanized élite. Collectivization did not entail just the destruction of an economy, it also meant the elimination of a way of life. The *mir*, for example, restricted individual freedom in some respects but it did provide a basic form of mutual aid and even collective decision-making. The highly developed village handicrafts industry (*kustar*), which provided the bulk of the peasants' consumer goods and work tools, was destroyed during industrialization. The *artel* was a peasant-based form of cooperative work that had great social and economic potential, and it persists in various forms to this day, both sanctioned by the state (*brigady*) and unofficially (*shabashniki*).

The Soviet Union is, at least, the territorial heir to the Russian Empire, and for many in the non-Russian republics they merge into one. While many Russians feel a sense of patriotism about the Soviet Union, it is usually not without reservations. Professor Geoffrey Hosking, the 1988 Reith Lecturer, put it very well:

> One nation in the Soviet confraternity is in a very singular position, and that is the Russians. They are to all appearances the imperial nation, the 'elder brother', in Stalin's words. They have no worries about their territory, or language, or alien immigration: in fact other nations feel threatened by *them*. Yet, curiously enough, in some respects the Russians feel like a national minority discriminated against in their own country. They know that the non-Russians are often more prosperous. And they can see that since 1917 their church has been undermined, their rural way of life mortally enfeebled, their finest writers, artists and thinkers banned, driven into the underground and emigration.

This discontent manifested itself in a search for roots among Russians that began long before perestroika. The best recent Russian prose writers, such as Valentin Rasputin and Viktor Astafev, eulogized the disappearing village way of life. Among many Russians there was a growing interest in and respect for religion. The Soviet regime reduced the Russian Orthodox Church to a state of complete subservience, and it was in no position to play a role similar to that of the Roman Catholic Church in Communist Poland. None the less, in recent years Russians have increasingly turned to the Church both to express their rejection of Communist ideology and to affirm their national identity. Gorbachev attempted to capitalize on this when the marking of the millennium of the Russian Orthodox Church in 1988 was made the occasion for unprecedented official celebrations.

At a time when politics could not be openly articulated, Russian national feeling also was expressed in opposition to the Siberian rivers project, whereby water from the north-flowing Siberian rivers would be diverted to irrigate the arid lands of Central Asia with potentially serious ecological consequences, and occasional complaints that, alone of the Union republics, the RSFSR did not have its own capital (Moscow was better known as the capital of the Soviet Union) and did not have its own Academy of Sciences or even Party organization. When glasnost revealed the extent of national feelings in the non-Russian republics,

Russians were forced to examine even further their own national identity.

As the tightly centralized Soviet state gives way to a much looser federation or even breaks up entirely, Russia will be forced to review its relationship with its Slav neighbours and the many minorities within the RSFSR. In September 1990 Aleksandr Solzhenitsyn, who still lives in the USA after being exiled from the Soviet Union in 1974, published a programme for the future development of Russia in Soviet newspapers. He advocated that Russia should separate itself from the three Baltic republics, Moldavia, the three Transcaucasian republics and the five Central Asian republics. On the other hand, the long political and cultural ties between the three Slav republics, Russia, Byelorussia and the Ukraine, meant that they should remain united along with a large part of Kazakhstan, populated by Russians.

Solzhenitsyn is a key figure in contemporary Russian political thought, and the fact that his proposals attracted wide interest shows that for many Russians the Empire is no longer regarded as worth holding on to. However, despite the historical ties alluded to by Solzhenitsyn, many Ukrainians and Byelorussians look to the West rather than Russia. Furthermore, since the incorporation of Siberia into the Empire in the sixteenth century Russia has been geographically an Asian as well as a European power. The great majority of Siberia's population is ethnically Russian, the native peoples such as the Yakuts and the Buryat Mongols have their own autonomous areas, and it will remain closely tied to European Russia, but regionalist tendencies are bound to grow. Russians will also have to decide on their attitude to other minorities, Tartars, Jews and Germans. In particular, the increasing assertiveness of the 16 autonomous republics in the RSFSR poses serious problems. Most of them have declared sovereignty and several, including Tartarstan, Bashkirstan, North Ossetia and Chechen-Ingushia, refused to participate in the referendum about the establishment of an executive president in the RSFSR. Indeed Tartarstan deleted the paragraph in its constitution which said it was part of the RSFSR.

The rise of nationalism in the Soviet Union has made the way that Russians regard the Soviet Union, either as a genuine expression of their own statehood or as a system alien to their traditions, one of the crucial factors affecting the outcome of the present period of rapid change in the Soviet Union.

The Prospects for Economic Reform

At various times the Communist regime has attempted to mobilize popular Russian hostility to social inequality. The campaign against the *kulaks* is a prime example, and has reinforced negative attitudes towards private enterprise.

The problems encountered by the present reforms which call for greater incentives and a larger role for the market indicate that such attitudes are indeed commonly held by Russians. Mostly impressionistic evidence suggests that they are less common among the Baltic and Transcaucasian peoples. If perestroika is to avoid the fate of NEP it will be important to investigate the real extent of such attitudes. Opinion polling in the Soviet Union is not very sophisticated, but some polls have given interesting results.

During the present reforms the question of reducing the massive Soviet budget deficit, which stood at 36 billion roubles at the beginning of 1989, by closing unprofitable state enterprises has frequently been raised, but the government has always failed to take action in the face of the spectre of mass unemployment. Another way of reducing the deficit would be to cut subsidies on basic foodstuffs and utilities, such as electricity and rents, and to introduce market prices. At the end of May 1990 a decision by the Presidential Council to double the prices for staple goods such as meat, fish and milk and triple that for bread led to panic buying in major Russian cities, forcing the measure to be suspended. Food supply in Russian cities continued to deteriorate, and at the beginning of December the new popularly elected city councils in Moscow and Leningrad introduced rationing schemes.

The co-operatives have been a particular butt for popular hostility to private enterprise. A poll carried out in Moscow, one of the most liberal parts of Russia, at the beginning of 1989 found that 23 per cent of men and 8 per cent of women thought that people who worked in co-operatives 'were businesslike people full of initiative' and that they merited respect and support. Almost half of the men and about a third of the women had reservations about the co-operative movement and about a quarter of the men and 38 per cent of the women thought that people who worked in co-operatives were 'swindlers and businessmen who make a lot of money at the expense of honest working people'. At the end of September 1989 an attempt by a group of deputies in the Supreme Soviet to ban all commercial co-operatives as opposed to production co-operatives was narrowly defeated, but in the middle of October the Soviet bowed to popular pressure and gave local authorities the right to set 'maximum price levels' on 'essential public goods' for sale in co-operatives. Such popular hostility and the activity of protection rackets run by organized crime, the so-called 'mafia', make the position of Soviet co-operatives unenviable.

There are more optimistic signs for reformers, though. A poll conducted in Moscow at the end of 1989 found that 57 per cent of those asked agreed that the private ownership of the means of production should be allowed. Positive responses were much more common among the young. Many people seem to be prepared to give the co-operatives a chance. When asked whether the development of co-operatives would help to ease shortages, 39.4 per cent of those questioned agreed, 37.9 per cent disagreed and 22.7 per cent did not know. A particularly bad sign for the co-operative movement was the demand of many of the strikers in the summer of 1989 for their closure, but by the end of the year a degree of understanding between the two sides seems to have been established when the co-operative union agreed to provide financial and material help to the strike committees.

In general, the old 'social contract' has broken down, and there does seem to be widespread acceptance of the need for greater incentives or, as it is put sometimes more hesitantly, payment by results. Many Russians feel that the present economic system does not give them the opportunity to realize their potential. The Russian government, formed as a result of the March 1990 elections, has consistently pursued more radical economic reform than the All-Union government. The failure of Gorbachev to come up with a radical reform programme prompted the Russian government to commission the economist Stanislav Shatalin to draw up an alternative. When the All-Union Supreme Soviet rejected his proposals for massive privatization and economic decentralization within '500 days' at the end of October the Russian Supreme Soviet agreed to it in any case. Meanwhile, Russia had been signing bilateral trade agreements with the other republics, which was an implicit challenge to the Union. At the beginning of December the Russian Supreme Soviet voted to allow, with some restrictions, full private ownership of land.

Political Choices

Perestroika is presenting the Soviet citizen, for the first time, with political choices. This is so no less for Russia than elsewhere in the Soviet Union. As Marxist–Leninist ideology dissolves and the Communist Party fractures, groupings within the apparat are seeking new bases of support among the many informal organizations that are springing up. On the face of it, the Communist Party in Russia, untainted by deference to a foreign power, might expect to receive considerable support. At the end of June 1990 a Russian Communist Party was formally established but it was dominated by 'conservative' elements, some connected with the OFT (see below), symbolized by its leader, Ivan Polozkov, and as long as Russians continue to support further radical reform its appeal will be limited. By the middle of 1990 the Russian political spectrum looked something like this.

On the extreme nationalist right are organizations like *Pamyat* (Memory). *Pamyat*'s roots go back to officially sponsored organizations set up in the 1960s and 1970s to channel popular demands for action to preserve Russia's national monuments, especially its devastated churches. When the organization, as such, surfaced in 1986 its ideology had clearly been formed under the influence of anti-semitic *samizdat* literature, such as that hoary old fake *The Protocols of the Elders of Zion*, which had been circulating in the 1970s. Gauging the support *Pamyat* really enjoys is very difficult, not least because the organization (if it was ever a single organization) has split into up to a dozen little *Pamyats*, the largest led by Dmitrii Vassiliev. *Pamyat* does not enjoy mass support, but it does have determined groups of activists in many Russian cities. More seriously, certain figures in the cultural intelligentsia give it their tacit support, and there is some evidence that elements in the KGB and the militia are sympathetic or even use it for their own ends.

The United Front of Workers (OFT) also has Russian nationalist tendencies, especially through its links with the Interfronts in the Baltic republics, but the OFT is more properly a child of 'conservative' elements in the apparat. In the search for a new base, some Communist politicians, most notably the Leningrad First Secretary, Boris Gidaspov, are trying to make capital out of the concerns of workers that the introduction of market mechanisms will lead to a fall in their living standards. The OFT undoubtedly has a resonance with popular anxieties, and has organized branches in different parts of the country. However, it has not been able to overcome workers' suspicions of the Communist Party and attract a mass following. Gidaspov's refusal to stand as a candidate in the elections to the RSFSR Supreme Soviet speaks volumes in this respect.

There are other radical political groupings which do not take part in electoral politics. Perhaps the most prominent is the Democratic Union (DS). With strong dissident roots a political party in opposition to totalitarianism was formed in Moscow in August 1988. Since then, they have been active in street demonstrations, with a radical programme for dismantling Soviet power. The DS is a small grouping. It has about 1000 members over the Soviet Union and does not have mass support – its attempts to link up with striking miners were rebuffed. On the other hand, it is well organized, with a strictly defined form of membership, in contrast to other informal organizations, and it produces a large number of publications. Anarchists have also made themselves visible but also (not surprisingly) do not participate in elections.

The strongest political force at present is represented by a coalition of radical Communists with liberal Russian nationalists, social democrats, Christian democrats and non-party radicals, particularly in the Russian popular fronts, which came together in January 1990 to form an electoral bloc, Democratic Russia, for the RSFSR Supreme Soviet elections in March. Democratic Russia draws its inspiration from the moral authority of the late Andrei Sakharov, includes members of the Inter-Regional Group of deputies, whose most well-known member is Boris Yeltsin, and has the grassroots support of some of the most active informal political associations. The elections marked an historic turning-point in Russian history. Approximately 35 per cent of the deputies elected to the Russian Supreme Soviet were supporters of Democratic Russia. Although Gorbachev threw his personal authority against him, Yeltsin's authority was such that he was elected president of the republic. In Moscow and Leningrad the radicals' victory was total. In the capital the radical economist, Gavrill Popov, was elected leader of the council and in Leningrad the equivalent position was taken by Anatolii Sobchak, who had made his name as a leading radical member of the All-Union Supreme Soviet.

On 12 June the new RSFSR Supreme Soviet declared republican sovereignty, that is, the supremacy of its laws over All-Union laws and that all the resources of the republic come under its jurisdiction. Inevitably, the Russian Supreme Soviet quickly came into conflict with the All-Union government. Conflict over the Shatalin plan was only one aspect of this. At the practical level, in August, the Russian government moved to block an agreement between the All-Union government and De Beers over diamond sales. At the end of 1990 the All-Union government was unable to present a budget because the Russian government was determined to drastically reduce its contributions. At the same time, the failure of Yeltsin to come to an agreement with Gorbachev cast doubts over reform in Russia. By the beginning of 1991 there were signs that the Russian government was in danger of losing its way. In mid-October 1990 Grigorii Yavlinskii, a co-author of the Shatalin plan and a deputy prime minister, resigned from the Russian government in frustration, as did Boris Fedorov, the Russian Finance Minister, in December. Similarly, some radicals criticized the introduction of rationing in Moscow and Leningrad as a step back from market reform. However, the election, by a large majority, of Boris Yeltsin as executive president in popular elections at the beginning of June 1991 holds out the prospect of a new impetus being given to reform.

Many observers argue that Russia is, at last, experiencing the emergence of a 'civil society'. By this they mean that institutions and a political culture are being created which will allow forces in society to advance their aspirations, even against the state, in a coherent way. While great progress has been made in terms of political education, however, it is not clear that such institutions have really established themselves, and the Russian political scene continues to be dominated by a process of fragmentation. The contours of the new Russia are still obscure.

Conclusions

Russia is now going through a very painful transition process, a transition that has been made more difficult by 70 years of Communist rule. There is a risk of a backlash against political and economic liberalization: the treatment of minorities such as the Jews and Tartars will be a touchstone for this. In the nineteenth century intellectuals divided into those who saw Russia as having its own particular path of development (the Slavophiles) and those who saw its future in representative democracy and in the development of a Western-style economy (the Westernizers). The isolation that Slavophilism implied and that the Bolsheviks imposed is not an option for Russia at the end of the twentieth century. The overwhelming majority of Russians appreciate the opening of links with the outside world. Polls have shown consistently that the most popular way of improving incentives is increasing the imports of foreign consumer goods.

The Slavophile/Westernizer controversy hinged not only on the relationship of Russia to the rest of the world but also on attitudes to private property. The sort of hostility to private property that the Slavophiles showed is not as strong a force now as it was at the beginning of the century. This is so first, for good or ill, because of the disappearance of the peasantry and second, because of the discrediting of Marxist–Leninist ideology. The experience of 70 years of authoritarian rule has also raised popular consciousness of the need for civil rights to be guaranteed. Despite these Westernizing tendencies, the political system of a sovereign Russia would probably differ in many ways from those prevailing in West Europe. Popular ecological concerns, which border on anti-industrialism, and decentralizing tendencies will be prominent. The main question facing Russians now (with the rise of nationalism in the Soviet republics) is the attitude they take towards the empire. If they refuse to accept demands for greater autonomy they will be forced to return to authoritarian styles of government. The indications at present are that as long as the process of liberalization is not discredited, Russians will become reconciled to this.

Poland

Official name	The Republic of Poland
Area	312,685 sq. km (120,695 sq. miles)
Population	38,210,000 (annual growth rate 0.9 per cent)
Capital	Warsaw (Warszawa)
Language	Polish
Religion	95 per cent Roman Catholic
Currency	złoty

The political transformation which occurred in Poland during 1989 has been called a 'step-by-step revolution'. Although Poland produced the first non-Communist prime minister in the Soviet bloc, and the first government not controlled by Communists, the changes which occurred were not so much an overthrow of Communist power as a negotiated withdrawal by the Party. In order to understand the historic compromise which occurred in Poland, we must know what went before.

Prewar Poland

Modern Poland is the descendant of a powerful and prosperous kingdom which once stretched from the Baltic to the Black Sea. Its decline in the seventeenth and eighteenth centuries ended in partition at the hands of three powerful, imperial neighbours – Russia, Austria and Prussia. Released after over a century of captivity, when the three empires collapsed during World War I, Poland was reborn in 1918.

Poland's short-lived period of independence between the wars was plagued by political, economic and social problems. Rapid attempts were made to unite the three partition zones – their economies, administration and transport systems. The early years, however, were marked by political instability, and in 1926 a *coup d'état* was carried out by Marshal Józef Piłsudski. Subsequently government, although more stable, became increasingly less democratic and tolerant. Poland's economic plight grew worse in the wake of the Depression, and the position of her large minority populations also deteriorated.

In 1939 Poland became the first nation to resist Hitler's territorial demands. The Nazi–Soviet Pact paved the way for the invasion of Poland and the outbreak of World War II followed. Partitioned again by two powerful neighbours, Poland succumbed to a long and bloody occupation. Some six million of Poland's inhabitants died, including virtually the whole of its Jewish population. Material damage and cultural losses were also severe. Polish resistance was stout and heroic – but was treated with savagery. The Warsaw Rising in August 1944 resulted in a quarter of a million people killed and the capital being razed to the ground by the Germans. The Polish government took up residence first in Paris and later in London. Throughout the war its soldiers, sailors and airmen fought alongside the Allies, under British operational command.

At the end of the war Poland faced once again the consequences of its geographical position. Strategically located on the Soviets' route to Berlin, the country found itself under Red Army occupation. At the 'Big Three' wartime conferences of Teheran and Yalta it had been agreed that Poland would come under Soviet influence. The Polish government, although a wartime ally, was not consulted. In a sense one could say that Poland was the price the West paid Stalin for the Red Army's successes, and sacrifices, on the eastern front.

Postwar

The postwar Polish state was a very different structure from that of 1939. First, it was moved bodily to the west, losing half of its territory to the Soviet Union and being compensated at the expense of Germany with territory in the north and west. The transfer of territory was accompanied by massive exchanges of population – 3½ million Germans were expelled from the 'recovered' territories in the west, while almost 4½ million Poles 'returning' from Soviet-acquired territory took their place. Second, Poland was now a remarkably homogeneous state, with relatively small numbers of non-Poles and overwhelmingly Roman Catholic.

The Western leaders hoped that Stalin would be content with this settlement (he gained virtually the same area of Poland that he had been allotted under the 1939 Nazi–Soviet Pact), would consider that Soviet security interests had been satisfied and would not feel it necessary to communize Poland. Their hopes were misplaced. Stalin was unsure of whether Communist rule could be imposed on Poland or whether it would be wise to try (he once likened it to 'putting a saddle on a cow'). There was a long legacy of hostility in Polish–Russian and Polish–Soviet relations, which had not been assuaged by Stalin's cynical and brutal policies from 1939 onwards. Indeed, if it is true that Poland suffered more than any other nation during World War II, then much of that suffering was due to Soviet actions: the mass deportations to the USSR, the murder of Polish officers at Katyn and failure to help the Warsaw insurgents during the 1944 Rising.

In addition, there were few native Communists Stalin could count on, since he had liquidated the leadership of the Polish Communist Party in 1938. The few Party members who had survived the purge were those who had been in Polish jails or else who had refused the summons to Moscow and gone to ground. The pro-Soviet Poles who had gathered in Poland towards the end of the war and formed the Lublin Committee (a provisional government under Soviet auspices) were a poor bunch of nonentities, who had little following. Indeed, they were regarded as traitors by many of their own people. Their great virtue from Moscow's viewpoint, though, was that they would do Stalin's bidding. The word 'Communist' was intentionally dropped.

The Communist Party was re-created in 1942 as the Polish Workers' Party – later (in 1948) to become transformed into the Polish United Workers' Party (PUWP). It did not start from any significant base of support, although from an estimated 8000 members at the beginning of 1943 the Party had built up its membership to some 20,000 in mid 1944 and 30,000 by January of the following year. As people saw which way the wind was blowing, more and more decided to join the Party as the road to political or vocational advancement. In the summer of 1947, some six months after the elections, there were one million members (out of a population of some 24 million).

In July 1945 the USA and Britain recognized a 'Provisional Government of National Unity', in which both 'Moscow' Poles and members of the Polish exile government in London took part. Stanisław Mikołajczyk, leader of the Peasant Party, was the most prominent of the 'London' group, and his return to Poland was something of a test of Soviet intentions and good faith. The distribution of Cabinet posts was significant: some two-thirds of the portfolios, including the key posts of Internal Security and Defence, went to Moscow nominees.

The Yalta formula provided for 'free and unfettered elections' in Poland, but not for any mechanism for international monitoring of these elections (as in Greece). It was to be a year and a half before elections took place (in January 1947). They were preceded by a campaign of terror and intimidation against opposition parties, including the murder of many supporters of Mikołajczyk and the splitting of his party. Even so, the election results when they appeared were grossly falsified, the Communists and their allies receiving 80 per cent in official figures. Western protests that the conditions set out in the Yalta agreement had not been met were rejected by Moscow. A few months after the elections, Mikołajczyk fled to the West, fearing for his life.

Poland's period of Stalinism lasted until 1956 and was relatively bloodless, by comparison with neighbouring Czechoslovakia. In 1948 a campaign was mounted on Moscow's orders against Władysław Gomułka for advocating a 'Polish road to socialism'. Gomułka had objected in particular to the demand that agriculture be collectivized. In the flurry which followed Tito's heresy in rejecting the Stalinist line, Gomułka became a victim of Moscow's clampdown on all forms of national deviationism. He was denounced publicly and in the following year removed from his position as deputy premier and from his seat on the Party's Central Committee.

In 1956 the first Polish protests against deteriorating economic conditions took place. Following Khrushchev's intervention, Gomułka was rehabilitated and assumed the mantle of Party leader, but despite his popularity the reforms he introduced were ineffective. The economy became increasingly inefficient and declining living standards resulted in further outbreaks of popular unrest, notably in 1970, when Gomułka himself was removed from office and replaced by Edward Gierek.

Gierek's period of office was notable for three factors, all of which were setbacks to Communist rule and were to stimulate the Polish drive for freedom and democracy. First, Gierek's policy of a massive, investment-led drive for growth – funded by Western banks and governments – failed miserably due to the structural inadequacies of the Polish economy. Debts accumulated and the huge interest repayments required to service this debt handicapped later attempts to improve investment and trade performance. Gierek stated at the XVI Party Plenum in October 1979 that the 1980s would be 'the decade of the greatest progress (economic and social) in the history of People's Poland. We have created a fine basis on which to build the future of our country.' The future was anything but sure or rosy, and within a year Gierek himself was forced out of office, the victim, once again, of popular protest.

The second major event was the formation in September 1976 of KOR, the Workers' Defence Committee, following the arrest of striking workers at Radom. It was the first organized body to oppose the Communist authorities and to defy them in the name of the workers. Although its members were harassed by the authorities (one of them, a young student named Stanisław Pyjas, was killed in Kraków in May 1977), the movement, nevertheless, gathering confidence from the Helsinki accords, extended its activities to include defence against all infringements of human rights. It provided a training ground for many of the dissidents (such as Adam Michnik and Jacek Kuroń) who were later to advise the Solidarity trade union.

The third event was an act of God – the election in October 1978 of Kraków's Cardinal Wojtyła as Pope. Not only was Wojtyła (or John Paul II as he chose to become) the first Pole to ascend the Throne of St Peter, he was a living contradiction – the head of a universal church numbering hundreds of millions of adherents who came from a formally atheist, Communist-bloc state. It is difficult to overstate the emotional effect that Wojtyła's election had on the people of Poland. It was a matter of national pride that a son of Poland had been elected to such an illustrious position, but it was also a reaffirmation of Poland's place in Christian and Western civilization – to which Poles had always felt they belonged. What is more, henceforth ordinary Poles were to feel the confidence that they had a stout and powerful defender on their side. The Pope's first return visit to his homeland in June 1979 inspired scenes of mass enthusiasm, and seasoned observers of the Polish scene were not slow to contrast them with the dour demeanour of marchers on the Party-orchestrated May Day parades.

The Rise of Solidarity

In the summer of 1980, instigated by sudden food price rises, a wave of strikes swept across Poland, from Lublin in the south-east, to Silesia and the Baltic Coast. The mood of protest reached the Lenin Shipyard in Gdańsk, where a Strike Committee was set up on 16 August under the leadership of a shipyard electrician named Lech Wałęsa. The Committee drew up a list of 21 demands which included the 'acceptance of free trade unions independent of the Party and the employers'. Following much-publicized negotiations with the government, agreement was reached, although at a political cost. Prime Minister Babiuch was removed and at the beginning of September, Gierek himself stood down as Party First Secretary. The official reason given for his departure was 'health grounds'. A caretaker leader, Stanisław Kania, was brought in.

Moves towards the creation of independent unions did not go smoothly. The authorities dragged their feet over registration and were clearly unhappy about licensing unions to act on a national, as opposed to a local, basis. Nevertheless, the success of the union in forcing the government to talk and then to recognize it officially was considerable, and a landmark in the history of postwar east-central Europe. At last the Party, self-professed champion of proletarian interests, was forced to admit that it did not command the loyalty or support of the working masses. The momentum which had been created by the historical agreement in Gdańsk did not slacken. The 'Solidarity' union increased its following across the country until it had an estimated 10 million members.

As Solidarity attracted the hopes and the loyalty of millions of Polish citizens, so the morale of the Party membership, ashamed and disenchanted by the incompetence of their own leaders, plummeted. Many Party members flocked to join the ranks of Solidarity. A movement within the Party for reform and renewal scarcely got off the ground. In the course of 1981 it became clear that events in Poland had moved too fast for the Soviet leadership. A powerful vacuum had formed in Poland, as those holding the reins of power proved impotent to control events and those who enjoyed popular confidence and support were blocked from the positions of true authority.

A state of martial law was declared on 13 December 1981 and was accompanied by the arrest and internment of several hundred Solidarity activists. The move came as a complete surprise, although it had clearly been planned well in advance. The operation was put into effect by General Wojciech Jaruzelski, Kania's replacement as Party leader. It was essentially a move by the military wing of the Party to bolster the sagging morale of the civilian Party's leadership and to restore order and discipline, on both the political and the economic fronts.

It now seems clear that Jaruzelski and his colleagues acted to forestall possible Soviet intervention, along the lines of Budapest in 1956. At the time, however, the repressive measures which came into force were greeted with a chorus of protest both inside and outside the country. The protest demonstrations and strikes which broke out were put down harshly and a number of deaths resulted. In the international arena, the Jaruzelski leadership became a diplomatic leper – shunned by all except its extremely relieved socialist bloc allies. Most damagingly, the USA imposed economic sanctions on Poland, thereby considerably hindering the task of economic recovery.

Indeed, although martial law ended a period of extreme uncertainty, it is arguable whether its introduction facilitated the task of governing Poland. The formation of a Military Council of National Salvation (Polish acronym, WRON) was designed to override the established structures of political – and Party – rule. Jaruzelski added the chairmanship of WRON to his Party first secretaryship and several other posts, concentrating power in his own hands. He faced though a sullen and uncooperative people whose history had taught them that, if it was unwise to engage in any dramatic and fruitless gestures of resistance against such overwhelming military force, they could not be compelled to do any more than the bare minimum by way of cooperation. The spirit of wartime occupation was revived among a younger generation as a flourishing underground press sought to evade the censor's blockade.

Indeed, the Communist regime, having proceeded to outlaw the Solidarity opposition, found that it had no one to talk to. Wałęsa, as the Polish media and Party spokesmen insisted, was merely a private citizen. (For a while, he had been detained by the authorities, but never subjected to long-term imprisonment or internment, like other Solidarity figures.) The desire of the Communists to relegate him to obscurity proved unsuccessful. He had already achieved too great a status, having become famous far beyond Polish borders. When eventually foreign leaders began to make their way to Warsaw they made a point of visiting Wałęsa during their stay. This meeting with the unofficial opposition leader was always made during the private section of their visit. (In 1983 he was awarded the Nobel Peace Prize.)

Although Solidarity was outlawed in October 1982, martial law itself was lifted some nine months later. The Communist leadership made strenuous efforts to achieve 'respectability' and to convince world opinion that the situation in Poland had returned to normal. Unfortunately, the leadership's hopes that a mood of reconciliation and unity would result from the Pope's second visit to Poland during June 1983 were disappointed. In October 1984 news of the brutal seizure and killing of the pro-Solidarity priest, Father Jerzy Popiełuszko, shocked the world. The fact that the murder was carried out by agents of the Interior Ministry drew attention to the murky role of the Polish security forces in establishing 'order' in the country. In the course of the decade scores of deaths were to occur in mysterious circumstances.

Economic Reform

Gradually, following successive amnesties of interned Solidarity activists, there was a slight thawing of the diplomatic atmosphere which resulted in the lifting of US trade sanctions in 1983. The sanctions certainly damaged the Polish economy, and helped exacerbate the most serious underlying economic problem – foreign debt repayment, the legacy of Gierek's profligacy. Although the economy had picked up from its low point of 1981–2, shortages and queues remained. Attempts undertaken during 1983–5 to decentralize economic decision-making had no noticeable effect and the poor foreign trade performance indicated that more radical measures were called for. At the beginning of 1988 the Polish authorities launched a new initiative – the 'second stage' of economic reform – having first appealed to the population in a referendum. This was received by a weary community with scepticism. Party organs also began to voice the opinion that there was no way out of the morass if the traditional forms of one-party rule were not relaxed.

Throughout the 1980s thousands of Poles left the country, seeing no future for themselves. They went abroad as tourists and remained as refugees. Special camps were created in Austria, a favourite destination, to house them. From there they sought to move on to Canada, South Africa and Australia. They included large numbers of trained and qualified personnel – engineers, for example – which Poland could ill afford to lose.

In mid-January 1988 the Party weekly *Polityka* published an open letter to both Jaruzelski and Wałęsa from the Warsaw historian, Professor Jerzy Holzer. Holzer's message was apocalyptic. He pointed out that the crisis which had engulfed Poland was rapidly reducing it from membership of the mid-developed group of countries to that of a backward state in terms of civilization. A feeling of helplessness and apathy hung over the country. The authorities had not managed to enlist the support of the majority of the population since the introduction of martial law. Their struggle with Solidarity had undermined the authority of both sides and left a gulf. It was important, continued Holzer, that those who were able to influence the future of Poland should meet and – if only temporarily – overcome their animosities. Otherwise, he warned, Poland stood before a threat equal to that which faced the country in the eighteenth century (i.e. extinction). History would not forgive those who had a chance to save Poland and failed to act.

Other analysts pointed to the cyclical nature of Polish upheavals, and the pattern that these confrontations demonstrated. While there was no doubt that each crisis had left some permanent change to the system of government, Poles could perhaps hope for a more evolutionary, less painful and damaging means of bringing about change. Even political commentators from the Party ranks admitted that the era of ideological confrontation was in the past. The vocabulary of socialism was bankrupt; no one now wanted to talk about 'improving socialism' or 'introducing real socialism'. The need for greater cooperation with the opposition had dampened polemics.

The 'second stage' of economic reform, the attempt to rally support for one more 'push' on the economic front, was undermined by ill-conceived price rises in the early part of 1988. A further wave of strikes in the spring and summer of 1988 forced Jaruzelski and his advisers to the conclusion that Poland could no longer be governed by force. Some kind of compromise had to be found with the opposition.

The Consultations Begin

The breakthrough came in August 1988 on the eve of the Party's VIII Plenum, when Interior Minister General Czesław Kiszczak offered to convene a series of meetings with 'representatives of various social and workers' organizations' to take the form of round-table talks. This face-saving formula – stressing 'various' groups, including 'workers' groups, but omitting the name of Solidarity – was intended as an olive branch to the opposition, which, nevertheless, would not unduly alarm hardline Party elements (or Moscow). The Plenum agreed to base the system of government in Poland on a wider national understanding.

Kiszczak's offer of talks was quickly taken up. The Interior Minister had a series of meetings with Wałęsa and opposition leaders (including Church representatives) during the late summer. At the same time, Wałęsa invited groups of expert advisers to consult with him in Gdańsk about the way in which negotiations with the authorities should be conducted. Meetings had begun in 1987, and the fifth such conference took place on 18 December (of 135 people invited, 119 attended). These advisers represented more than purely political and economic expertise; they included Church representatives, and figures from the world of culture. In Western terms, the consultations amounted to the drawing up of a political manifesto by a party's policy-making committee. This loose assembly of experts was eventually transformed into a 'Citizens' Committee' linked to the Solidarity leadership. It developed fifteen sub-commissions dealing with specific topics such as political reform, trade union pluralism and the national minorities.

When, on 19 September 1988, the Sejm passed a vote of no confidence in the government of Zbigniew Messner, Poland's eighth prime minister in the postwar period, he was replaced by Mieczysław Rakowski. Rakowski, formerly editor of the Party weekly *Polityka*, took the unusual step of consulting with Cardinal Glemp before appointing his Cabinet. In another departure from orthodoxy, he appointed a millionaire private businessman, Mieczysław Wilczek, his Minister for Industry.

The year 1988 proved a crucial one for the ending of one-party rule in Poland. (The decision to enter into round-table talks was, as one political commentator wrote, like 'giving the opposition the ball and inviting them to play . . .'.) Communists themselves voiced their perplexity at times that there should be a crisis of confidence in the government at precisely the moment when it had attempted to introduce new policies of openness and consultation, when radical economic reforms were being attempted, and when people could say and write almost what they wanted. This was naïve, though, and if genuine, indicated how little they understood the strength of the distrust and resentment that lay beneath the surface. The desire to get the Communists out after years of mismanagement, of official lies and of subservience to Moscow was overpowering.

Although formal round-table talks had been planned for November 1988 they did not take place until February of the following year. The talks lasted for nine weeks and the legislative proposals which resulted were far-reaching. They involved significant changes to the Constitution and to political structures. First, they recommended the creation of a second, upper chamber (Senate), which meant a return to the bicameral system of government abandoned by the Communists in 1946. Second, they foresaw the restoration of the presidency, the candidate to be elected by a National Assembly (i.e. a joint session of the Sejm and Senate). Most importantly, they recommended multi-party, competitive elections – the first in Poland since 1947, and a departure from the 'plebiscites' by which the Communists had formerly called on the populace to support a closed list of Party nominees. There were also far-reaching economic proposals. The Sejm approved the measures in April 1989.

The Elections

The elections were held in two stages in June 1989. All seats to the Senate were fought competitively, but in the Sejm only 35 per cent of seats were 'open'; the other 65 per cent remained reserved for the Communists (PUWP) and their allies (ZSL and SD). While this meant that the Communists were guaranteed a continued presence in government, it was conceived as an interim measure – a period of coalition or 'guided democracy', leading to completely free and competitive elections planned for 1993. All parties were to be free to conduct their own election campaigns. In May 1989 a new independent daily newspaper, *Gazeta Wyborcza* (*Election Gazette*), came into being with official approval. Its chief editor was Adam Michnik, historian and long-term dissident who had been imprisoned under martial law. The *Gazeta Wyborcza* was founded to report the election campaign and especially the point of view of the opposition candidates.

The course of the two-stage June elections and the subsequent manoeuvring to form a government was unprecedented for a state in the Soviet bloc. As expected, Solidarity candidates virtually whitewashed the Communists, securing 99 out of 100 seats in the Senate and all the 35 seats which they were able to run for in the Sejm. However, this still left them in a minority in the lower chamber, and most onlookers expected that Solidarity would be content to continue its opposition role, except this time in a more formal setting. Statements from Wałęsa and other Solidarity leaders confirmed that they would bide their time, and not participate in any Communist-led administrations.

In the aftermath of the elections the office of presidency had to be filled. General Jaruzelski, the architect of martial law, made an early announcement of his decision not to stand, fearing that his record would count against him and would result in a humiliating defeat. When it became clear, though, that Wałęsa was not standing for office, the general reversed his decision. On 19 July he was elected president after an eight-hour televised debate, having received 270 votes against 233 votes opposed to his candidature (34 deputies abstained). The majority of Solidarity deputies voted against him.

Jaruzelski's subsequent decision to ask former Interior Minister, Kiszczak, to form a government was greeted with hostility. It was a blow to Solidarity, since Kiszczak was the person responsible for interning so many people during martial law. With the prospect that they would capture both the presidency and the premiership, many felt that the Communists were merely taking over where they had left off. Wałęsa issued a statement opposing the choice, which deepened the crisis. Faced with such firm opposition, Kiszczak found it impossible to form a government. Solidarity persuaded the Communists' formerly loyal allies, the Democrats (SD) and the Peasant Party (ZSL), to turn against them. Kiszczak was forced to admit defeat.

The way now became clear for adoption of the formula proposed by Adam Michnik in the columns of *Gazeta Wyborcza* – 'Your President, Our Premier'. On 24 August 1989 Tadeusz Mazowiecki, a Catholic journalist and one of Wałęsa's advisers since the early days of confrontation in the Gdańsk shipyard, was appointed prime minister. He immediately set about constructing a Cabinet. By 12 September he was able to submit 23 names to the Sejm. While eleven of the Cabinet posts were allocated to Solidarity deputies, and only four to the PUWP (Communists), the latter were granted the key ministries of the Interior and Defence. (Since control of the military and security forces had been the springboard from which the Communists had taken power in the period 1945–7, this raised some eyebrows, but it was a necessary part of the compromise.) Other Cabinet posts were allocated to the Democrats (3) and to the Peasants' Party (4), with one portfolio going to an independent.

The assumption by Mazowiecki of the premiership, the first non-Communist prime minister in the Soviet bloc, was received with justified acclamation and even incredulity in the West. Within the Communist world reactions varied, from the guardedly welcoming to the openly hostile. It was the Romanian leader Ceauşescu whose hostility went furthest. While Ceauşescu had not supported the Warsaw Pact invasion of Czechoslovakia in 1968 and had broken with Moscow over it, he now tried to persuade the Soviet leader Gorbachev that intervention in Poland by friendly socialist states was necessary. Such entreaties were futile, of course. The Soviet leader had been hinting for some time that he was not in sympathy with the Brezhnev Doctrine and had made his rejection public in a number of speeches during the summer. The Poles immediately made soothing noises, by stressing their intention to honour existing agreements, and specifically to remain members of Comecon and the Warsaw Pact.

'The First Comprehensive Market-Oriented Reforms in Eastern Europe'

The new government rapidly set about rolling back the frontiers of Communism. This process began with changes to the Constitution, including the deletion of Article 3, concerning the leading role of the Communist Party. A team was charged with drafting a new Constitution, which, it was hoped, would be ready by May 1991 – the 200th anniversary of Poland's, and Europe's, first. Poland's official name reverted to the prewar 'Rzeczpospolita Polska' (that is, Polish Republic, rather than People's Republic). The country's symbol, the white eagle, had its royal crown – a legacy of the Polish monarchy – restored. Across the country, the symbols of Communist rule were stripped or torn down. Busts and statues of Lenin were toppled, and there was great satisfaction when the statue of Feliks Dzierzyński, the Pole who created Lenin's secret police, was taken down in the Warsaw square that had borne his name.

The most difficult task facing the incoming administration was that of tackling the economy. In addition to the crippling burden of overseas debt which approached $40 billion by the end of 1989, inflation had accelerated dramatically and was estimated at 1000 per cent. Part of the boost to prices had been caused by the Rakowski government's attempts during August to 'marketize the food economy'. While the measures had given producers free rein to raise their prices, they had not been able to ensure an adequate supply of goods to satisfy market demand.

The young Finance Minister and Deputy Premier, Leszek Balcerowicz, had to consider with his colleagues how to control the rampant inflation, and at the same time put the Polish economy on the road to recovery. Negotiations began with the International Monetary Fund (many loans from Western governments were dependent upon IMF approval of the restructuring arrangements). The package eventually agreed was the most radical break with socialist policies ever attempted, and in the words of *The Economist*, 'the first comprehensive market-oriented reforms in Eastern Europe'. There was to be an end to price controls and remaining subsidies. Prices would be determined by the market, but wages would be held down to avoid a wage–price spiral that would accelerate inflation. The private sector would be freed from government restrictions, while the state sector would be slimmed down by privatizations, and subjected to the discipline of the marketplace. The government undertook to adopt responsible monetary and fiscal policies (e.g. balanced budgets), and stressed its eventual aim to bring about convertibility of the złoty.

The measures were introduced on 1 January 1990. The first twelve months of the Balcerowicz programme produced notable achievements and a number of surprises. Inflation was forced down from the stratospheric levels of late 1989 and in August 1990 – the best month – prices rose by only 2 per cent. The złoty also held firm against the dollar, following its 30 per cent devaluation at the beginning of the year. Queues and empty shelves in the shops – so much a feature of life under Communist rule – largely disappeared. There was evidence of greater work discipline: strikes were fewer and the number of days lost through sickness or absenteeism dropped appreciably.

These achievements, though, were gained at a high cost. The drop in output was far greater than the 5 per cent the government had expected. Furthermore, many sections of the population began to experience great hardship. Unemployment, as expected, rose steadily through the year. It reached 443,000 by May 1990 and in October passed the million mark – 7 per cent of the working population outside of the agricultural sector.

Added to this misery was the fact that public-sector pay levels have been prevented from rising with inflation. As a result, disposable incomes have dropped by between 30 per cent and 40 per cent since the beginning of 1990 – this from a figure which was already low at the end of 1989. An average monthly wage, in the summer of 1990, of just under a million złoties, sounds a lot, but at a rate of 18,000 zł to the pound this amounted to only £55. By April the Poles were spending 60 per cent of their incomes on food.

A major surprise was the improvement in the balance of trade. As declining incomes led to a dampening of demand, import levels fell while domestic producers had to seek overseas markets more vigorously. Therefore although the government had expected the trade balance to deteriorate, in fact 1990 produced a series of monthly trade surpluses. But the surplus on overseas trade, even if it could be sustained, would not be enough to solve Poland's debt problem. In February 1990 the 17-member 'Paris Club' of international debtors agreed to defer interest payments on the massive Polish debt for twelve months to allow the Polish reforms time to take effect. The interest was not being written off; it was being added to the debt already outstanding and this had reached $46 billion by the end of 1990. During a visit to Washington in May 1990, Finance Minister Balcerowicz made an early attempt to have the country's official debt reduced to manageable proportions – say, by 80 per cent. His efforts brought success. In March 1991 the USA had agreed to write off some 70 per cent of the (admittedly relatively small) debt owed them, and encouraged their Western allies to follow suit. The 'Paris Club' members agreed to a 50 per cent reduction in the existing value of the official debt. (Poland has been more fortunate than the South American debtor countries in that a large proportion of its overseas debt was owed to governments, rather than to commercial banks.)

The Polish privatization programme was slower in getting off the ground than expected. Indeed, the government's original aim to privatize half of state enterprises in the course of the first five years began to look extremely ambitious. The privatization bill was passed by the Sejm in July 1990 and a fully fledged Ministry of Ownership Transformation created under the leadership of economist Waldemar Kuczyński. The first group of firms were sold off to the public during November.

The Polish government's bold measures have excited admiration and interest, not least among Soviet economic advisers. But what are the chances of success for the Balcerowicz programme? The 'turn-around' in the Polish economy (initially forecast for 1991) now looks even further off. There is concern over whether the reform programme has been effective in changing underlying structural weaknesses in the economy. Is it in fact the most efficient of the industrial enterprises that have been going out of business? Furthermore, like other states in the region, Poland had been hit heavily by the collapse in Comecon trade and the effects of the Gulf crisis. Finally, it remains to be seen whether social pressures force the government to 'soften' or slow down the reform programme.

Politics

The political landscape altered radically during the course of 1990. So much so that Poland ended the year with a new President, a new Prime Minister and the Solidarity movement in tatters.

In January the Polish United Workers' Party disbanded and became the Social Democratic Party of the Polish Republic. A breakaway faction named itself the Social Democratic Union. The efforts of these successor parties to inherit the massive estate of the defunct PUWP were largely foiled. A government commission discovered that the Communists and their allies had occupied some 5,000 buildings, only 86 of which, however, were legally in their possession; the remainder had been appropriated from the state. In early April, the great majority of these were returned to the people.

As in the other post-Communist states of the region, a multitude of political parties came into being. In the June elections to some 2,383 local councils many of the smaller parties were still campaigning under the Solidarity banner. The election itself, an important further step in the gradual removal of the Party *nomenklatura* and the first completely free election in Poland for more than half a century, resulted in a disappointing turnout (42 per cent). Solidarity-backed candidates, as expected, did well in the traditional centres of opposition support (e.g. Gdańsk, Kraków), but the much-reduced support for the movement shown elsewhere was an indication of disenchantment with the government's performance and with squabbles in the Solidarity leadership.

In the spring of 1990 Lech Wałęsa began to demand that General Jaruzelski should step down as president, making it clear that he saw himself as the natural successor. But he also attacked the performance of the Mazowiecki government – composed for the most part of former Solidarity colleagues and advisers he himself had nominated for office.

What caused this change of tack? Certainly, Wałęsa sensed the frustration felt by many Poles that they had been left behind in the region's transition to democratic rule. Apart from the presidency, two-thirds of the seats in the lower house were still occupied by former Communists and their allies. This legacy of the 1989 'round-table' agreement had become an anachronism. But Wałęsa was also aware that public anger was growing at the hardship caused by the government's economic policies. Resentment was fuelled by a belief that the Mazowiecki government had not done enough to root out the old Communist *nomenklatura* and to prevent the former Party apparatchiks from setting themselves up comfortably in consultancies and enterprises created with funds appropriated from the state.

Wałęsa later played on latent anti-semitism and paranoia in the community to suggest that the transition to full democracy had been hijacked. He demanded that the reform programme be accelerated (especially the privatization programme), that the *nomenklatura* be removed and be held accountable for past excesses, and that more urgent moves be made to remove Soviet troops from Polish soil. A rift with former colleagues rapidly developed as criticism of government policies turned into personal attacks. Wałęsa chided the government intellectuals for their remoteness from the people. In calling for a 'permanent political war' and talking of 'spontaneous democracy and mass social activity' he framed an unashamedly populist appeal. But opponents were alarmed by the authoritarian tones in Wałęsa's statements (e.g. that when elected President, he would rule by decree if necessary).

On 22 September 1990 the Sejm voted its approval for a presidential election to take place on 25 November. By the beginning of September two political groupings had already been formed. One, the Centre Alliance (*Porozumienie Centrum*), was to support Wałęsa's candidacy for the presidency; the other, Citizens' Movement–Democratic Action (known by its Polish acronym ROAD), was formed to oppose Wałęsa's bid for power. While Wałęsa declared his candidacy early, and stated publicly his confidence that he would receive

60 per cent of the votes, Mazowiecki's late decision betrayed perhaps some reluctance to stand, and even a lack of confidence.

The hesitation was, perhaps, justified. For Mazowiecki the election was a disaster and a humiliation. He received just 18 per cent of the first-round vote and was relegated to third place. But Wałęsa too suffered from the electorate's disillusionment. His 40 per cent of the votes was enough to gain him first place, but insufficient to avoid a second round of voting. His opponent in the second round would be an unknown émigré businessman, Stanisław Tymiński, who claimed to have made millions from business interests in Peru and Canada. The 42-year-old Tymiński, who won almost a quarter of the votes cast (23.1 per cent), profited from the electorate's disillusionment with the squabbles in the Solidarity camp.

The second round of voting on 9 December was preceded by a strong campaign against Tymiński. His mental health was questioned, and accusations made that his campaign was directed by former Communists (there were former security service personnel in his team of advisers). This did not, however, seem to greatly harm the 'Peruvian Pole', and in the second round – although soundly beaten by Wałęsa – he still received one in four of the votes cast. Wałęsa was sworn in as President on 22 December. The ceremony was marked by the return to Poland, after 50 years in London, of the historic insignia of office, handed over by the President-in-Exile, Ryszard Kaczorowski.

Mazowiecki, following his first-round defeat, had immediately offered his resignation and that of the government, while remaining in a caretaker capacity until a successor could be found. He also requested his electoral support team to continue its work, signalling his intention to serve in opposition to Wałęsa and the new government. Wałęsa's initial attempts to nominate a new Prime Minister ran into difficulties. However, some three weeks after Wałęsa's election a little-known 39-year-old economist, Jan Krzysztof Bielecki, was able to form a government. Key figures from the Mazowiecki Cabinet, such as Finance Minister Balcerowicz and Foreign Minister Skubiszewski, have been retained, thus ensuring continuity of policy in two key areas.

Bielecki was expected to be a stop-gap figure, since new elections were expected in the spring. However, in April the Sejm voted to postpone a general election until the autumn, thus prolonging the life of the Bielecki government. The vote defied a presidential proposal for early elections, and disappointed members of Wałęsa's entourage suggested that former Communists (and others with no political mandate) were desperately clinging to power. (The existing Sejm is still that formed from the 'controlled' elections held under the 1989 'round-table' agreement.) In fact, the reality was more complex: opposition to an early election also came from former Solidarity members now ranged in opposition to Wałęsa. It remains true, however, as presidential supporters pointed out, that Poland will not gain membership of the Council of Europe until free elections are held.

The 1990 presidential campaign signalled an end to the Solidarity consensus and paved the way for the development of a true party political system. Apart from the pro-Wałęsa Centre Alliance and the opposition ROAD (Citizens' Movement) group, a number of other parties will be in contention when elections arrive. These include the Democratic Union formed by former premier Mazowiecki, various ZSL (Peasant Party) groupings, the Social Democrats (successor to the Communists), the right-wing Catholic National Christian Union (ZChN), and Party X. The last is the creation of the defeated presidential candidate, Tymiński, and, after his exploitation of the 'disaffected vote' during the presidential campaign, it would be unwise to dismiss his chances completely.

Economic Change

The Politics of Economic Transformation

Judy Batt

Chapter 4, pp. 72–83 in Judy Batt, *East Central Europe from Reform to Transformation* (Chatham House Papers, London: Pinter Publishers, 1991)

All past attempts at economic reform in East Central Europe failed primarily because of the political obstacles posed by the communist parties' monopoly of political power. The ideology of the regimes placed severe constraints on the elaboration of models of economic reform by insisting that central control over economic processes be retained to an extent that undermined the effectiveness of the operation of markets. Even where, as in Hungary and Poland, party leaders were prepared to sacrifice important elements of the ideology for the sake of coherence in the economic reform, they found it impossible to put the reform into practice because of the resistance of bureaucratic interests entrenched in the power structures upon which their own positions ultimately depended. Moreover, the regimes lacked basic popular legitimacy, and thus faced an unacceptable risk of mass revolt in reaction to the inevitable impact of economic reform on the standard of living, particularly that of workers in hitherto high-priority traditional industrial sectors.

The events of 1989 have fundamentally changed these political conditions by sweeping away the power of the communist parties and their ideology: the economic task is thus no longer 'reform' but 'transformation', or, as Miklos Nemeth (the last Hungarian communist Prime Minister) put it, the creation of 'a market economy without any qualifying adjectives'. The stated aim of the new regimes is to 'separate economics from politics': that is, to bring about an economic system that can function primarily according to the laws of the market rather than according to bureaucratic political preferences imposed, often against all economic logic, through directive central planning. Government intervention in the economy thus should undergo a qualitative change, to become guided by, rather than overriding, these laws; it will, moreover, be subjected to free public criticism and checked by democratic parliamentary control.

Nevertheless, economics will remain profoundly political, not only because this is the case in every politico-economic system, but because in the specific context of East Central Europe the task of economic transformation presents unprecedented political challenges. Democracy may be a necessary political condition, but it is by no means sufficient to guarantee a trouble-free and popularly supported passage to a market economy, especially given the profoundly disturbed state of the economies of East Central Europe; and their democracies are still based on fragile foundations. There are apparently convincing political arguments for gradualism in the economic transition; democracy itself would suffer if untested and over-hasty radical economic measures provoked mass popular rejection of the new governments. But there are also convincing arguments for 'shock therapy' – rapid and simultaneous introduction of the basic requisites of a market economy – on both political and economic grounds. It is not clear that economic gradualism under democratic rule would be more successful than it was under reform communist rule, or that gradualism can realistically promise to soften the economic blow. 'Shock therapy' could shorten the painful period of transition, but at the risk of intensifying its social and political impact. But the fact that the task of economic transformation is quite unprecedented means that both lines of argument rest on unproven assumptions, and therefore that it will inevitably remain a subject of intense debate among economic experts, which in turn will breed doubt and scepticism in society and generate conflict among politicians. But doubts must be overcome, and conflicts managed and resolved, if anything is to be achieved. What is required is clearly 'strong' government, but in a form that is also compatible with the preservation and development of democracy – a tall order indeed.

Ralf Dahrendorf, reflecting on the relevance of the experience of West Germany in the immediate postwar period for East Central Europe today, has pointed to the 'incompatible time-scales of political and economic reform'.[1] Whereas political change can be effected in a matter of months, economic recovery takes several years; in the intervening period, the passage through the 'valley of tears' of economic upheaval and social dislocation makes extraordinary demands on political leadership. A major ingredient of the West German success, according to Dahrendorf, was the particular constellation of personalities of that time: on the one hand, there was an economic team led by Ludwig Erhard, with a clear-headed and determined commitment to economic liberalism, presented in a package labelled the 'social market economy'; on the other, there was the Chancellor, Konrad Adenauer, whose personal authority provided the 'political cover' for the programme; and, finally, there was a group of politicians, notably Thomas Blank, first Federal Minister of Social Affairs, Hans Katzer, chairman of the CDU 'Employees' Committee', and the trade-union leader Hans Bockler, whose contribution was to make the social guarantees effective:

The conclusion is that it takes more than one political leader to achieve this feat. Somebody has to provide the protection of political power, somebody has to have the practical courage to take an economy from central planning to more open pastures, and somebody has to insist on certain social policies which are appropriate in their own right and also make the harsher side effects of the new-found market bearable.[2]

In this chapter, we begin with a general outline of the dimensions of economic transformation, in order to clarify the nature of the political challenge it poses. In the second section, we will examine the new governments' preparedness to meet this challenge in terms of their internal cohesiveness, their parliamentary support-base, and the extent of their popular legitimacy. We will also focus on particular political 'flashpoints' in the early stages of economic transformation in order to illustrate the emerging new patterns of interaction between politics and economics.

From Economic Reform to Economic Transformation

The attempts at economic reform under communist rule in East Central Europe until the 1980s were based on a model of what has been called 'the regulated market' system, and assumed the continuation of state ownership of the major part of land and productive assets.[3] The failure of this approach to generate any significant improvement in economic performance led to its complete rejection by economists in East Central Europe, and its more or less explicit abandonment by the communist regimes in Poland and Hungary in the 1980s. The aim of this model was to improve efficiency, not by abandoning planning altogether, but by changing its focus significantly, in order to allow substantial enterprise autonomy and the revival of the role of the market at the microeconomic level. The central planners and industrial branch ministries would no longer be concerned with drawing up detailed annual plan-targets for enterprises, but would concentrate on the medium- and longer-range perspectives of development of the economy as a whole, of geographical regions and selected priority branches. Enterprises would draw up their own production and development plans on the basis of market stimuli, and would have the right to choose their suppliers, set their own prices, and offer performance-related incentives and bonuses to their employees. But planners would continue to exert considerable control over enterprises *indirectly* in order to ensure that the basic economic trends developed in conformity with central objectives, or, as the model's proponents put it, in conformity with 'the social interest'. The central authorities retained control over the use of enterprise assets and the distribution of their income by means of 'regulators': i.e. rules governing deductions to the state budget, wage-setting and bonuses, the retention of funds for decentralized investment, and so on. The major part of resources for investment remained under the control of the central authorities, and far-reaching price and wage policies were also employed.

Even in theory, it was clear that the market and enterprise autonomy were going to be very much more circumscribed than in the case of even the most developed corporatist, welfare-state variant of Western capitalism; in practice, the model turned out to be little more than a modified version of central planning. Even where the model prescribed scope for autonomous enterprise decision-making, managers usually found it easier, if not essential, to rely on informal contacts with the central authorities, and because the ministries still controlled the appointment and promotion of enterprise managers, the latter had strong reasons to comply with informal central demands, even where these might conflict with the economic interests of the enterprise. Access to centralized investment, subsidies to continue import-substituting production, negotiations around wage regulations and price-setting all still required constant close interaction between planners, ministerial bureaucrats and managers. Moreover, no satisfactory provision for bankruptcy of economically unviable enterprises was made in the reform. The 'plan bargaining' that had characterized the traditional system was therefore merely replaced by bargaining over the regulators;[4] enterprises thus achieved not autonomy but at best 'dual dependence', vertically on the bureaucracy and horizontally on their customers and suppliers.[5] The system in Hungary was described by one of its foremost critics as one of 'neither plan nor market',[6] pointing up not only the internal contradictions of the model but also the state of imminent paralysis to which it was leading in practice.

But what also became clear in the course of the reforms was the crucial role played by political obstacles to radical change in the economy: the interlocking interests of managers and state bureaucrats in minimizing the operation of the market and undermining enterprise autonomy and managerial responsibility. This came to be seen as the central problem of the economic reform model itself. These interlocking bureaucratic interests were closely tied into the structure of communist party power itself. A solution to the economic problem thus required the end to the communist party's monopoly of power; but it also required the establishment of firmer economic foundations for enterprise autonomy. Even before the disintegration of communist power, the regimes of Poland and Hungary took some steps in this direction by, for example, abolishing the meddlesome industrial branch ministries, breaking up the giant monopolistic enterprises, introducing forms of enterprise self-management councils with responsibility for managerial appointment, and expanding the scope for certain types of small-scale private enterprise. But, by the 1980s, East Central Europe's economists were convinced that the crucial ingredient of the transformation of decaying state corporatist economies into dynamic, flexible market economies was missing. That ingredient was the wholesale privatization of the bulk of productive assets, an objective that came on to the public agenda only after the removal of the communist parties from power.

Privatization as a general objective appears to have won majority support not only among economic experts but also among the new political élites and the populations as a whole. Although there may still be some room for academic debate about the necessity of private ownership for the effective operation of a market economy,[7] practical experience has convinced East-Central Europeans that the two cannot be separated. As a result, there is now deep reluctance to entertain any further experiments in search of alternative 'third roads' between capitalism and socialism, and a preference for policies and programmes that have been tried and found to work at least reasonably well in West European countries. Thus privatization is accepted as a component of the broad political programme of the 'return to Europe'.

However, the initial sympathetic reception of the idea of privatization in general has rapidly given way to acute controversy and conflict within the new governments, parliaments and public opinion about how to proceed. The establishment of new firms on the basis of private capital from domestic or foreign sources is generally welcomed, but the question of transferring existing state enterprises to private ownership poses much greater economic and political problems. For one thing, there is the technical complexity of the task in itself, and the lack of precedents for privatization on such a scale. For another, as concrete plans for privatization of specific enterprises are drawn up, so the initial socio-political consensus gives way to sharp differentiation, if not polarization, of attitudes. Privatization raises not just technical economic questions, but political questions (narrowly defined) of winners and losers, and (broadly defined) of social justice.

Thus, although a broad consensus can be reached on the desirability of privatization *per se*, serious economic and political dilemmas begin to develop when the question of implementation comes to be considered.[8] Three possible courses have been identified in the East-Central European debates: restitution to former owners, sale to new private owners, or free distribution of shares to the population as a whole. The reasoning behind the restitution argument is mainly ethical: confiscated property ought to be returned to its rightful owners. It is thus connected with the political legitimation of the new regimes, which are expected by the people to rectify the wrongs committed under communist rule, and generally to show respect for property rights. However, in practice, restitution will be a far from straightforward matter: there is the problem of identifying the original owners, whose legal title to property may be hard to establish, who may have emigrated or died in the meanwhile. The legal owners or their heirs either may not know of their rights to regain their property, or may no longer be interested in it. Moreover, in many cases, the property will have undergone change in the course of time, either degenerating through neglect, or being transformed and extended by investment in the past decades under state control. The property in these cases cannot simply be returned to former owners; but the impoverished and indebted states cannot offer to provide satisfactory financial compensation for losses or to buy out the shares of former private owners. What they can offer in the form of shares or bonds may not be seen as adequate by the former owners. Legislation on restitution must therefore allow a reasonable time for people to submit their claims, and for these to be authenticated and adjudicated fairly. This necessarily prolongs the period of uncertainty about the status of all property, delaying the process of privatization in general and creating considerable uncertainty, which discourages urgently needed new investment, particularly of foreign capital. In Hungary, where the restitution of agricultural land to former private owners has been a subject of bitter controversy, this uncertainty is threatening to disrupt agricultural production, and thus not only domestic food supplies but export earnings. Restitution is likely to have a further undesirable effect, in addition to delaying economic transformation, in that it perpetuates the tendency of people to direct their energies into claiming resources from the state rather than to work hard to earn such resources.

As for the second option – the transfer of state property into new private hands – the most straightforward approach would appear to be outright sale to the highest bidder at auctions. The advantage of this is clearly that it would provide revenue to overstretched state budgets. Moreover, property would presumably end up in the hands of those most interested in using it to best economic effect. But how to establish a fair price, in the absence of functioning capital markets? And to whom to sell? A major problem is the inadequacy of domestic sources of capital, but it is politically unacceptable to allow free rein to foreign capital, which would undermine the government's legitimacy as defender of the national interest, especially where there are no means of determining an objectively fair price, thus exposing it to charges of simply 'selling out' national assets at knock-down prices to foreigners. Moreover, there is the question of enterprise debts: will the new owners also take these over, or can the state afford simply to write them off?

Selling state property to the highest bidder unavoidably favours the rich, which would be controversial anywhere, but even more so in the East European context, where the rich tend to be members of the former *nomenklatura*, who turn out again to be the winners even in the new post-communist conditions, transforming their political power into economic power – to the understandable rage of the rest of society. Banks might be able to offer credits to broaden access to ownership, but such credits would have to be tightly controlled in order to prevent their feeding additional inflationary pressures into the economy, and they would present high risks, since banks would have no way of assessing the entrepreneurial record of the new owners.

Moreover, the earlier reforms introducing enterprise self-management councils have also created ambiguities about property rights: does the state still 'own' self-managed firms, or have property rights been transferred to employees? In Hungary and Czechoslovakia, the new governments have had to 'renationalize' enterprises, while in Poland a powerful 'self-management' lobby in parliament has created considerable obstacles to the passage of privatization law. If the workers are to be bought out, how much compensation for the loss of their property rights should they be offered, and will they accept this in principle? Should workers be permitted priority rights in the purchase of shares at special, reduced prices? Workers in profitable and viable enterprises would do much better than workers in neglected and underinvested enterprises, and their relative positions could hardly be related to their respective merits as workers. But why should enterprise workers be so privileged at all? What about the interests of non-workers or the retired? After all, as Kornai points out: 'The wealth embodied by the firm at the moment of ownership transfer has not been created exclusively by that firm's workers; every citizen has contributed through the state investments and the state subsidies the firm has received.'[9]

Finally, of course, we must not lose sight of the fundamental *economic* purpose of privatization. In Kornai's view, 'the prime consideration is not legal entitlement to acquire property but the ability to run it well'.[10] It is not clear, to say the least, that full self-management will bring such efficiency with it.

A further major drawback of privatization through direct sales is the time it would take to make real inroads into the massive state sector. In Britain, the privatization of a few state firms has taken ten years; at the equivalent pace in Hungary, it would take a century to reduce state ownership to proportions comparable with those found in Western economies. For Kornai, the conclusion is that an extended period of 'dual economy' must be reckoned with, since in his view 'it is impossible to institute private property by cavalry attack'.[11] But if, as other East European economists are convinced, private property is a necessary concomitant of the establishment of the market, a quicker solution must be found.

This concern lies behind the third scheme for privatization: the free distribution of shares to the population at large. This would be done by providing all adults with vouchers, which they could then exchange for shares in companies of their choice. Competitive bidding by prospective share purchasers would thus help generate market 'prices' for shares, which could then be used as a basis for direct sales to foreign and domestic purchasers. This scheme appears to have the further merit of social justice, since it is in accord with the assumption that all citizens have an equal interest in state property. But it is an untried, and therefore highly risky, approach. It is likely to prove very costly to administer, and will not generate revenue for the state budget. Moreover, in the case of heavily indebted states, there could be argued to be prior claims on the part of foreign creditors to some share in the state's assets. It could also be argued that it would be a dereliction of duty on the part of the state simply to give away national assets to all and sundry: 'Its apparatus is obliged to handle the wealth it was entrusted with carefully until a new owner appears who can guarantee a safer and more efficient guardianship.'[12]

The free distribution of shares would create a wide dispersal of ownership among inexperienced and possibly indifferent shareholders, and would thus be unlikely to produce the effective check on managerial performance that is supposed to be the main result of privatization. To some extent this problem could be expected to diminish over time as shareholding became concentrated in fewer hands. From the public's point of view, even disregarding its lack of experience, the difficulty of assessing the relative merits of companies would be enormous, given the lack of objective market information to start with.

It is thus not surprising that privatization legislation has taken longer to materialize than originally expected. In Hungary and Poland, some backtracking occurred in 1990, as the state sought to regain control over the process after some highly unpopular and politically damaging scandals that arose as a result of 'wild' privatizations in which state assets were acquired by enterprise managers and former *nomenklatura* officials without proper valuation or outside control. Corruption seems to be an endemic risk in the process. Nevertheless, by the end of 1990, all three countries in our study had prepared more or less detailed privatization plans.

In Hungary, both restitution and the voucher scheme have been rejected in favour of direct sales, and accordingly the government at first seemed committed to a rather slower pace than in Poland and Czechoslovakia. In terms of preparation, however, Hungary is further advanced than its neighbours, having begun to implement the necessary legislation to transform state enterprises into joint-stock companies from the beginning of 1989.[13] A series of state enterprises were put up for sale in the last months of 1990, after some hesitation and delay, but the State Property Agency (SPA), which has been set up to oversee the process, also turned down a number of proposals.[14] A major stumbling-block in Hungary has proved to be the question of reprivatization of agricultural land, which has divided the government coalition and been rejected by the High Court as unconstitutional. The question has diverted attention from the overall strategy of privatization, into which it must be integrated consistently. Following government changes at the end of 1990, a more accelerated pace seems likely. In January 1991, new regulations were introduced permitting interested investors to initiate privatization by making an offer to the SPA. A wider range of employee and management buy-out schemes is also in preparation. Over three to five years, the government expects to privatize 50–60 per cent of state assets.

In Poland, more than a dozen drafts of privatization legislation were considered by the Sejm between autumn 1989 and July 1990, when a compromise was reached. A major point of conflict emerged between, on the one hand, representatives of workers in the large state enterprises (Solidarity's traditional bedrock of support), and allied proponents of self-management, who argued forcefully for transfer of ownership to enterprise employees, and, on the other, the government, backed by the majority of Solidarity deputies, whose proposals aimed at unrestricted sales and distribution by vouchers. Considerable popular hostility emerged to the sale of state property to foreigners. The Act on Privatization that resulted from these cross-pressures has been described as 'eclectic', and to some extent has merely postponed final decisions about actual privatization.[15] But it provides a flexible framework, allowing for a wide variety of methods of privatization, including the sale of shares, the use of vouchers, and some preferential allocations of up to 20 per cent of enterprise shares to employees. Foreign investors can buy up to 10 per cent of any enterprise's shares, but beyond that, approval must be won from the president of the Foreign Investment Agency. This restriction was greeted with dismay by potential Western investors, but the government has attempted to reassure them that such approval was likely to be granted readily. The current expectation is that about 50 per cent of state enterprises should be privatized within three years.

In Czechoslovakia, a Restitution Law has been a matter of lengthy debate. The original draft, published in autumn 1990, covered property confiscated between 1955 and 1961, but in early 1991 the Federal Assembly decided to extend this back to 1948. About 70,000 properties are now in the process of being restored to their original owners. This issue has delayed the passage of the law on privatization of large enterprises. The draft law, still under consideration as of March 1991, is also more eclectic than originally envisaged: the enthusiasm of the Minister of Finance for the voucher method of privatization has been tempered by political pressures and expert economic advice, and the draft also envisages the use of direct sales. Between 40 and 80 per cent of an enterprise's shares, according to various criteria, can be disposed of in exchange for vouchers. But implementation of the scheme will await the conversion of state enterprises to joint-stock companies, which will not begin before spring 1991. The Law on Small Privatization, covering about 100,000 shops, restaurants and small businesses, was passed in October 1990. These were offered directly for sale to Czechoslovak citizens at auctions, the first of which – in January 1991 – were judged to have been very successful.[16]

'Strong Government'?

Despite the differences in their economic starting-points, the most obvious of which is the rather more favourable position of Czechoslovakia in terms of its internal economic balance and external indebtedness in comparison with Poland and Hungary, the basic tasks confronting the new governments are similar, and they face many common political challenges. All three countries have introduced stabilization programmes to tackle budget deficits and bring about long-delayed structural adjustments. Price liberalization and the introduction of internal convertibility of the currency have been introduced with the aim of opening up the economies to the world market and generating real prices that should force enterprises to use resources more efficiently. Demonopolization of the industrial structure, measures to stimulate competition and the formation of new private firms, and the reorganization or liquidation of chronically unprofitable enterprises are in preparation or beginning to be implemented. The collapse of the CMEA, the transition to hard-currency trade with former socialist trading partners, the crisis in the Soviet economy, and the economic fall-out of the Gulf war have all generated enormous pressures for acceleration of the transition, while at the same time intensifying the problems involved and the social counter-pressures.

The political challenges confronting the new governments come from the as yet only partially dismantled structure of corporatist interests and from popular expectations shaped by past experience. While there may be a general acceptance of the need for structural adjustment, there is an equally widespread expectation that such transformation should not be allowed to encroach on the interests of any major social group. As one Polish commentator observed, 'For a considerable part of the society the understanding and accepting of the rules of market economy finishes at the level of expectations of quick success and reaching a Western standard of consumption.'[17] The problem is, of course, that these expectations are unrealistic, and the fears of the significant sections of the workforce of unemployment and the rising cost of living are wholly justified. These have only been reinforced by observation of the impact of 'shock' tactics on East Germany since economic unification in July 1990. The new East-Central European governments have as yet only rudimentary social security nets in place, and are unable to finance them adequately without external aid, which must be a priority in Western aid packages.

The governments must seek to mobilize political support from new economic groups with an interest in change, who expect to benefit from the transition to a market economy. In the short term, such groups (especially new businessmen) are limited in numbers, scattered and politically fragmented, while the organized interests of traditional state industries are still highly influential. Because privatization is only at a most preliminary stage, the bulk of the economy is, and will continue to be for some years to come, state-owned, as a result of which governments find it extremely difficult to avoid being drawn back into patterns of corporatist interaction with major economic interest groups, particularly in threatened traditional industries. Moreover, there are strong expectations on the part of the population that the new 'democratic' governments will be even more responsive to all their various demands than the former communist regimes. Thus the pattern of making direct demands on the government as 'employer', as if it had both the resources and the responsibility to respond, remains far stronger than the pattern of active searching by individuals and enterprises for ways of adapting to and seizing new opportunities offered by new economic conditions. Moreover, where change in the pattern of interest articulation is taking place, this seems only to complicate the government's task: pluralization has brought competition between new unions and interest-based parties to win support by making ever sharper attacks on the government and ever higher demands on the state's overstretched resources. Where governments give in to demands in order to avert social revolt, they merely delay the necessary changes, confirm population expectations, and provoke further demands from other aggrieved groups.

Notes

1. R. Dahrendorf, *Reflections on the Revolution in Europe* (London: Chatto and Windus, 1990), p. 85.

2. Ibid., p. 92.

3. The classic elaboration of this model was that of the Polish economist Włodzimierz Brus: see his *Economics and Politics of Socialism* (London: Routledge and Kegan Paul, 1972) and *Socialist Ownership and Political Systems* (London: Routledge and Kegan Paul, 1976).

4. See L. Antal, 'Development – with some digression', *Acta Oeconomica*, Vol. XXIII, nos 3–4, 1979.

5. J. Kornai, 'The Hungarian reform process: visions, hopes and reality', *Journal of Economic Literature*, Vol. XXIV, December 1986.

6. T. Bauer, 'The Hungarian alternative to Soviet-type planning', *Journal of Comparative Economics*, Vol. 7, 1983, 304–16.

7. See, for an unfashionably sceptical view, M. Nuti, 'Privatization of Socialist economies: general issues and the Polish case', paper presented to the OECD Conference on the Transformation of Planned Economies, Paris, 20–22 June 1990.

8. A very useful paper clarifying the issues is B. Milanovic, 'Privatization in post-communist societies', mimeo, Washington DC, World Bank, 12 September 1990. I have also relied heavily on Janos Kornai, *The Road to a Free Economy* (New York and London: W. W. Norton, 1990).

9. *The Road to a Free Economy*, p. 90.

10. Ibid., p. 91.

11. Ibid., p. 54.

12. Ibid., p. 82.

13. See Act VI of 1988 on Business Organization, reproduced in T. Sarkozy (ed.), *Foreign Investments in Hungary: Law and Practice* (Budapest: Lang Kiado, 1989).

14. See M. Jackson, 'The privatization scorecard for Eastern Europe', *Radio Free Europe Report on Eastern Europe*, Vol. 1, No. 50, 14 December 1990; also N. Denton, 'Privatization programme under pressure', survey of Hungary in *The Financial Times*, 17 September 1990.

15. See I. Grosfeld and P. Hare, 'Privatization in Hungary, Poland and Czechoslovakia', *European Economy*, 1991.

16. For a more detailed account of Czechoslovak developments, see P. Martin, 'Privatization: a balance sheet', *Radio Free Europe Report on Eastern Europe*, Vol. 2, No. 5, 1 February 1991.

17. J. Hausner, 'The new interests structure', in *Polish Economy in Transition* (Warsaw and Cracow: Zycie Gospodarcze, 1991), p. 41.

6

The Asians

Alternative Concepts of Management: Insights from Asia and Africa

Magoroh Maruyama

From *Asia Pacific Journal of Management*, Vol. 1, No. 2, 1984, 100–111

Large-scale, complex business planning and management existed in the ancient civilizations of Egypt, Mesopotamia, India, China and several other parts of the world. In our age there has been a misconception that theories of business and management are something new, or that the *ancient* theories and methods would be useless in *modern* business. In the 1950s and 1960s Japan was regarded as an economically retarded country, and the Japanese practices of management such as job security and groupism were considered as the cause of the 'Japanese' inefficiency. The 'Japaneseness' was looked down upon in business.

However, the recent success of Japanese business has elevated these presumably 'obsolete' practices to the status of the cause of superefficiency and high productivity. This change stimulated two trends. On the one hand, many business firms in both rich and poor countries began to imitate the Japanese management practices. On the other hand, some presumably 'backward' countries have begun to study ways to apply their traditional management principles and methods to improve productivity and efficiency. In this *Zeitgeist*, endogenous concepts and theories have begun to emerge in some countries (Kimura, 1972; Camara, 1975; Iwata, 1977; Hamaguchi, 1977; Marbun, 1980; Maruyama, 1982; and Ting, 1983).

Within Asia and Africa there are many different cultures, and within some countries there is great cultural diversity, for example in Indonesia and India. There ought to be many different endogenous theories, not only for improvement of management within each culture or subculture, but also for smooth cross-cultural and multicultural management.

Not only are there differences in theories, but also there are metatheoretical differences. For example, the difference between a theory which says some variable H is the cause of another variable J and another theory which says K is the cause of J, is a difference within the same causal model 'X causes Y'. On the other hand, the differences between theories which allow for causal *loops* and those which do not is a metatheoretical difference (Maruyama, 1961, 1963, 1977, 1978a, 1979, and 1980). Likewise, the difference between theories based on value-ranking and those based on a non-ranking universe is at a metatheoretical level.

A move from European and North American (ENA) theories to Asian, African or Arabic theories, and in some cases a move from one culture or subculture to another within Asia, Africa and Arabia, is to cross a theoretical difference at a very different level compared to a move from one theory to another within ENA. The difference is at the epistemological level, i.e. in the structure of perceiving, thinking and reasoning.

Heterogenistic Logic

Take, for example, the conceptualization of heterogeneity. In the ENA cultures, heterogeneity is often considered to be a source of conflict while homogeneity supposedly fosters peace. On the other hand, among the Mandenka of West Africa (Camara, 1975), heterogeneity is the source of mutually beneficial, positive-sum, 'win-win' cooperation, while homogeneity is regarded as a source of competition and conflict. This view is more scientific and ecologically correct. Animals convert oxygen into carbon dioxide, and plants do the opposite. In so doing, animals and plants help each other. The richness of life on the coral reef or in the tropical rain forest is due to the heterogeneity of species. Tall trees, short trees and algae absorb solar energy in different ways. If all animals ate the same food, there would be a food shortage. And if there were some animals whom no other organisms ate, there would be an intolerable accumulation of corpses. But the advantage of the heterogeneity goes beyond resource diversification and disaster risk dispersion: it generates positive-sum relations. For example, some birds eat the food debris from between the teeth of alligators. The alligators get their teeth cleaned, and the birds get not only food but protection from potential predators who are scared away by the alligators.

In ENA management, it is often considered efficient, economical, fair and democratic to regard all workers in the same category in a homogeneous, 'equal' manner, though there are exceptions such as Hewlett-Packard and IBM, who have the policy of allowing individuals to develop their own ways. But note that even in these organizations the emphasis tends to be on the maximization of *individuals'* potentials rather than on mutually beneficial *combinations* of individual differences. We will return later to the topic of a new type of efficiency as well as to fairness by destandardization and heterogenization.

It is a common fallacy among ENA theorists (and sometimes even among Japanese theorists) to regard Japanese workers' groups as homogeneous. A Japanese workers' group is like the traditional Japanese garden design, which avoids repetition of similar elements and composes a harmony of dissimilar elements. The members of each group know one another well enough to appreciate each individual's characteristics and spontaneously combine the diversity in a mutually beneficial way. This heterogenistic mutualism is facilitated by several interrelated tendencies: (1) situational adaptability (instead of adherence to pre-set instructions or principles); (2) Non-Aristotelean individual identity and *aidaschaft* (Kimura, 1972). Already 50 years ago, Watsuji (1935) had characterized the Japanese person as '*kiwamete henka ni tom shitsuteki tayoosei ni oite onore o miidashite iru nipponjin*' (The Japanese discovers himself through the qualitative heterogeneity which is rich in extreme changes).

Polyocular Vision in Africa and in Asia

Another aspect of the epistemology regarding heterogeneity deals with the concepts of objectivity, agreement and 'consensus'. Among the Mandenka as well as among the Japanese, the notion of 'objective' truth is usually neither important nor useful. Different individuals have different points of view, and the *differences* constitute indispensable information which enriches every person's understanding. This is the principle of polyocular vision (Maruyama, 1978b). Binocular vision works, *not* because the two images are additive, *but* because the differences between the images enable the brain to compute a dimension invisible to both eyes. In the ENA, there tends to be a belief in the existence of 'objective' truth. Differences are often considered to be due to errors. 'Let us stick to where we agree and discard what we disagree on' is a statement often heard. But if you discard the parts of the object on which the two images differ, what is left is only a flat surface (if the object has any) perpendicular to the line of sight. The result is much less realistic than the polyocular vision. When the Japanese translated the foreign word 'objectivity', it became *kyakkanteki* which means 'the guest's point of view', while 'subjectivity' was translated as *shukanteki*, which means 'the host's point of view'.

In Japanese culture the polyocular vision is cultivated implicitly in the process of growing up. On the other hand in the Mandenka culture, there are several systematic, explicit ways. One of them is the social function rotation. In his/her lifetime, a Mandenka is made to go through several jobs and functions: carefree childhood; several phases of initiation rituals into various social roles; early adulthood with great administrative responsibilities; late adulthood with advisory functions. Each person heterogenizes himself/herself through these different activities, and learns to see the same situation from different points of view. Older persons are admired for their having developed more of this ability. The Mandenka are afraid of westernization which locks a person into one job and makes him/her incapable of seeing a situation from other persons' points of view. Another method is the practice of joking relations. Joking relations serve two purposes: (1) feedback channels; (2) polyocular vision. Formally the Mandenka society has a hierarchical structure. However, there are many effective feedback channels in the form of specified joking relations. For example, a man must obey his father who, in turn, must obey the former's grandfather. But the man is in a joking relationship with his grandfather and this gives him an effective feedback channel over his father's head. There are many other channels. A man's other joking relations are his older brothers' wives, his maternal uncles. A woman also has several sets of joking relations. And in the entire social structure, there are official clowns who can criticize and ridicule anyone in the society with impunity, including the kings. Obviously the joking relations are important as feedback channels. However, a less visible but more crucial function of joking relations is that they help achieve polyocular vision. Persons in joking relations can criticize each other and must take the criticisms without getting angry. One is forced to see himself/herself from others' points of view. Psychologically, during one of the initiation phases, a person takes the role of a clown, enjoys the role, and later identifies himself/herself with his/her critics, and can therefore 'internalize' the others' criticisms.

It is a fallacy to say that the Japanese mode of decision making is by 'consensus' if 'consensus' is meant to be 'reaching the same opinion'. In order to appreciate its fallaciousness, let us look at the Navajo way of decision making, which has a similarity with the Japanese mode but is more explicit. Suppose that a community must decide whether to build a bridge. Regardless of which way the decision is taken, the Navajos realize that some individuals will be inconvenienced while others will benefit. The main focus of the decision process is on how to compensate the inconvenience of those who might be a minority, or even a single individual. In the Japanese mode, the compensation may be made later at another opportunity, but each individual's benefits or inconveniences are recorded in everyone's mind for future adjustments. This philosophy is quite different from the 'consensus' in the ENA sense, in which it is assumed that the unanimous decision satisfies every person and no adjustment is needed.

Job Rotation for Mental Togetherness and Self-Heterogenization

As in the above example, similar-looking behaviour may have very different dynamics and assumptions beneath the surface. Another example, very important in management, is the practice of job rotation. Job rotation is practised in many cultures, but often for different reasons. For example, in Sweden there are three main reasons for job rotation: (1) to prepare human spare parts – if a worker learns to perform several tasks, he/she can replace a sick worker; (2) to relieve muscle fatigue – for this purpose in many Swedish factories the workers are rotated every two hours or so within a small range of tasks; (3) to reduce psychological monotony for the individual. In contrast, in Japan (1) the most important function the job rotation serves is that the workers become able to think 'in one another's head' and consequently feel *mentally connected* (see the discussion on *aidaschaft* below); (2) the second is convertibility and self-heterogenization of each individual, in which the individual becomes able to see the same situation from different points of view. In Japan a worker may be rotated through as many as 40 jobs (Koike, 1978).

Aidaschaft

One concept, which is most difficult to explain to ENA theorists but inherent in the Japanese and some other Asian and African cultures, is *aidaschaft*. This word combines the Japanese *aida* and German *schaft*. *Aida* has no equivalent in English. The closest English word is 'between', but it is *misleading* to equate 'between' with *aida*. The full meaning of *aidaschaft* will be explained from several angles since no simple explanation suffices. The difficulty arises from the epistemological difference between the Aristotelean logic underlying the ENA concepts and the non-Aristotelean logic represented by the Japanese and Mandenka concepts. ENA theorists tend to insist that they understand *aidaschaft* when they have reduced it to the dimensions available in their mental universe (Maruyama, 1979) in such a way as to attain an internal logical consistency in their dimension reduction. The consistency gives them the illusion of correctness of their interpretation. Kimura and Maruyama report their frustration in trying to help ENA theorists overcome the dimension reduction. It is like attempting to explain some colors to color-blind persons. We shall, nevertheless, make another attempt from several angles. For the time being let us say that in some Asian and African countries the individual feels mentally connected to others in the group, works with others without rigid division of labor and with flexible unwritten adaptability to changing situations, and feels responsible for the success or failure of the entire group (Kimura, 1972; Iwata, 1977; Hamaguchi, 1977).

Different Philosophies Behind Groupism

Many of the ENA theorists misinterpret the Japanese groupism as the submission of the individual to the group, in which the individual is sacrificed. This misinterpretation is based on ENA theorists' own concept of the individual and of the hierarchy. In Japan the group is *not* a supra-individual entity but a network of interpersonal relations (Hamaguchi, 1977). The individual makes use of the group to his/her own advantage (Iwata, 1980), and the group members can use one another for mutual benefit in positive-sum relations. Hazama (1971) has stated that 'A person who acts for the sake of his company in a manner that seems (to foreigners) to involve self-sacrifice perceives his action as ultimately for his own benefit rather than a sacrifice of his own interest to others'. In Japan, the concept of the individual is of a being who thinks and acts in the interpersonal context (Maruyama, 1970). ENA theorists tend to misinterpret this as a sort of homogenization. This fallacy was pointed out earlier in this article. But some perceptive ENA researchers have correctly understood this. For example, Pascale and Athos (1981) state '(in Matsushita Company) a manager should learn each subordinate's potential from many directions and match the individual to the right job', though the authors do not discuss the mutual self-matching and self-adaptation among workers.

Differences within Asia

Added to the Asian endogenous theories are some emerging theories on the cultural and subcultural differences within Asia. For example, Ting (1983) postulates that Hong Kong management is based primarily on individualistic (I), and secondarily on hierarchical (H) and morphogenetic (G) (interactive pattern-generating) principles (abbreviated as I-H-G); Singapore management is mainly H-I-S (where S means: interactive pattern-stabilizing); Taiwan management is mainly H-S-I and South Korean management is mainly H-S-I and

S-H-I. Earlier Maruyama found that Japanese management tends to be of the types H-S-G and S-H-G (1980) while American management is often of the type H-I-G (1983). In a very limited preliminary set of interviews, Cho (1983) found higher hierarchical tendencies (obedience and regimentation) and individualistic trends (job hopping) in Taiwan and South Korean management practices than in Japan. Iwata (1980) quotes Koreans saying that 'one Korean is stronger than one Japanese, but three Japanese are stronger than three Koreans', indicating that groupism is weaker and individualism stronger in South Korea than in Japan.

Aidaschaft and its Origins

Aidaschaft may appear to resemble *Gemeinschaft* in Tönnies' sense, but it is at an epistemologically different level. Both in *Gesellschaften* and *Gemeinschaften*, the concept of the individual is based on the Aristotelean logic of substance, identity, boundary and specialization and the interpersonal relations are logically conceptualized in terms of separation, distinctiveness, juxtaposition, opposition, tension and extension. In other words, there ontologically is first the individual; then individuals who are distinct from one another; and something must be done to establish relations between the individuals. This is based on the ontology and logic of substance and identity.

In contrast, *aidaschaft* is based on a non-Aristotelean logic of continuity, convertibility, self-heterogenization, boundarilessness, absorption, permeation, and symbiotization of diverse individuals who *remain heterogeneous*. There are first relations before the individual is born. The baby is *born into the aidaschaft* of relatives (*Geburt in die Aidaschaft*). The baby has his/her *unique personality* which is added to the *harmony of aidaschaft* without losing his/her uniqueness, just as in the traditional Japanese garden design in which every element is different from others, and *contributes to the design through his/her uniqueness*. But just as each rock's location is generated *in terms of its shape in the context of other rocks* and acquires its meaning in terms of the relations, the baby acquires his/her 'identity' through the social context. That is, there is first the pre-existing context, which the baby enters at birth to generate new relations which include him/her. Similarly, when a new employee enters a firm, he/she steps into the *aidaschaft* of fellow workers, which bestows on him/her a relational identity (in contrast to the ENA individual identity), while he/she strives to contribute to the growth of the *aidaschaft* among fellow workers.

In order to go a step further in the understanding of the difference between

Japanese concepts and contrasting ENA concepts, it is necessary and helpful to trace the historical development of a number of basic concepts in Japan and in Europe.

Historical Development of Japanese Concepts

Let us first examine how the concepts such as the heterogenistic logic, polyocular vision, mental connectedness, self-heterogenization and *aidaschaft* developed in Japan.

In contrast to the ENA theorists who have developed, refined and elaborated their concepts and principles through written forms since the ancient Greek philosophers, the Japanese have preferred *nonverbal* means such as garden design, flower arrangement and architecture for the same purpose. To discover the highly developed and elaborated non-Aristotelean principles of connectedness, convertibility, self-heterogenization, boundarilessness, absorption, permeation and harmony of heterogeneity, we must examine such aesthetic design principles (Maruyama, 1981).

In the traditional Japanese house, a room can be a dining-room at meal times, a bedroom at night and a living room for the rest of the day. Furniture is stored away and brought out for specific functions. Partitions between rooms can be removed. Moreover, the entire house is often designed to be connected to the outdoors. The outer shells of the house can be removed. When the partitions between rooms are opened, one can sit in the innermost room of the house and see and smell the garden. Thus the space is continuous, convertible, self-heterogenizing and boundariless. Exactly the same applies to the concept of the individual. Individuals are mentally connected and feel together. They are convertible to one another's jobs, perform varied jobs as needs arise, respond to changing contexts rather than adhering to pre-set instructions, can be moved easily from department to department, comprehend the operation of the entire factory and improve each specific job accordingly.

On the other hand in the ENA conceptualization, each room has a permanently specialized function and most of its space is taken up by specialized furniture. It is enclosed by walls. The house itself is designed to separate humans from the outdoors. In the European conceptualization, space is defined as something between masses, for example, between walls or between buildings. Space itself is a transparent mass and has boundary, shape, volume, identity, specialized function and immutability. There is the principle of opposition between mass and space as well as between spaces. Tension between points and extension of a line or a surface of a mass generate 'shafts of space' and 'axes of mass'. Again, we find a parallel in the ENA concept of the individual, who has an identity, boundary and specialized function.

In order to deepen our appreciation of the difference between the Aristotelean epistemology and the non-Aristotelean epistemology, we must look into their historic and prehistoric developments.

Japan had at least three cultural origins: Jomon which began 9,000 years ago and was of the G-type; the lyrical Yayoi which began 2,300 years ago and was of the S-type; and the hierarchical Yamato of the H-type which arrived via Korea 1,500 years ago. The prehistoric Jomon culture was full of vitality, with considerable emphasis on the concepts of birth, life, change and death, often mixed with fear and awe. The concept of Mononoke must have had its origin in the late Jomon period.

Each locality had a *Mononoke*. Mononoke was the quality or the feeling which filled the locality. Gradually, through the early Yayoi period, Mononoke was considered to condense into rocks, rather small in size (often less than thirty centimeters). Here the word 'condense' is not quite adequate. Our American colleagues tend to interpret it to mean 'become', i.e. to cease to fill the entire space of the locality. But in the Japanese way of thinking, the Mononoke continued to fill the space even though it manifested itself in rocks and other phenomena (*shinrabanshoo*). Thus rocks came to *represent* the *quality* of the space. If there were many rocks, their interrelations represented the quality of the space. Therefore objects were not masses, and objects neither opposed space nor one another. The European notion of opposition did not develop in Japan.

During the Yayoi period, agriculture advanced and life became easier. Thanksgiving festivals were held, and nature was considered to be kind to humans. Instead of the fierce and vigorous clay figures of Jomon, the Yayoi people made lyrical and passive ones. Appreciation of the nature and preservation of harmony became important. With the cultivation of rice, the concept of land as property occurred. Land was marked with stakes or ropes, but not with walls. Ceremonial grounds were often marked with white pebbles spread like a carpet. Such space still had continuity with the outside.

The transmission of Yamato culture from Korea, which occurred 1,500 years ago, brought to Japan the concepts of hierarchy and enclosure. The Ise Shrine, which was built soon after the arrival of Yamato culture, had four layers of fences around its main sanctuary as well as crossbars on the roof to indicate the ranks of the deities.

But the three cultures did not form a succession of dominance. Instead they co-existed in Japan, mixed in different proportions in different social classes and geographic regions. The ruling class tended to be of the H-type with many shades of the S-type. The farmers tended to preserve the Jomon spirit of the G-type. The middle class, which expanded since the Meiji Reform in the nineteenth century, had a propensity towards S and H types. Today the three types co-exist, mixed in different proportions in different individuals. Most of the Japanese are of SHG and GSH types. (See note at the end of this article.)

Watsuji's Theory

Another important consideration was proposed by Watsuji (1935). People who developed their cultures in monsoon regions where climatic events such as rain and storms brought both abundance of harvest and disaster, were dependent on weather which had both regularity and unpredictability. They developed an attitude of receptivity and high adaptability to changing conditions. This had a great influence on their social interaction patterns, philosophy, aesthetics and religion. In human relations they tended to be interactive and mutually accommodating. They saw animals and plants as partners of humans.

It is no coincidence that Japan, which is in the monsoon region, developed a heterogenistic and harmonistic logic which was reflected in garden designs and flower arrangements. The big question, however, is whether other cultures in the monsoon regions developed a similar logic and similar design principles. Watsuji's opinion is that Japan is somewhat unique among the countries in the monsoon regions, because it also combines cold weather in winter resulting from the Siberian and Manchurian influences, which increase the range of heterogeneity and variability compared to other countries in the monsoon regions. We need to study the countries in monsoon regions which also combine cold weather for reasons such as high altitude or continental climatic patterns.

Watsuji also observed that Europe had a much more benign, docile climate compared to the monsoon regions. Storms, hurricanes and floods were much milder in degree and much less frequent compared to those in the monsoon regions. Added to this was the fact that weeds and crop-damaging insects were rarer in Europe than in monsoon regions. Japanese farmers had to spend 80–90 per cent of their labor fighting weeds and insects during the crop-growing seasons. But the European farmers had no comparable problems: plants grew more or less automatically until harvest time. The tempo of harvesting was also much easier for European farmers. In Japan the harvesting had to be accomplished within a very narrow span of time between the end of the growing season in August and the typhoon season which began in September. A short delay could mean destruction of the crops by typhoons. Therefore harvesting required very intensive work and a high degree of coordination and cooperation among the farmers. On the other hand European farmers could accomplish their harvesting at a much less hectic pace. The Japanese climatic environment required the farmers' efforts to be more intensively coupled with the changing conditions in the environment.

In Europe, nature not only was benign but also had a high degree of predictability. In fact, the European sewage and river systems would be unable to handle a fraction of the precipitation volume discharged frequently on the lands in monsoon regions. Animals and plants were also more easily under human control: less efforts were needed to keep them under control. Trees have regular forms due to the lack of strong storms in most parts of Europe. Even where there are strong winds, such as the Normandy Coast in France, all trees are bent in the same direction, resulting in another type of regularity. In contrast, trees in Japan tend to have irregular forms due to stress and damage by storms and avalanches.

In Europe, humans were masters over animals and plants, not interactive partners. Together with the regularity in nature, this fostered a hierarchical, rational view of the universe. Regular forms were considered beautiful. European designs are often based on principles of geometric regularity and repetition.

Historical Development of ENA Concepts

To this observation by Watsuji, we can add the following analysis (Maruyama, 1967). The European hierarchical logic required that there should be something which was the highest. This 'something', a product of the European logic, became the European concept of god. In the European theology, god was often defined as 'that to which there is nothing superior'. And the rationality and regularity of the universe were attributed to this god since the time of early Greek philosophers. In the sixth century BC, the scientist Anaximandros conceived the notion of infinity as the inexhaustible protosubstance of the universe. As no materials knowable by human senses fulfilled his requirements for the infinity-substance, he thought that the substance must be beyond all human experience. Xenophanes applied this concept to religion. Proud of his 'discovery' and scornful of the human-like gods of Greek mythology, Xenophanes declared that his infinite god was incomparable to humans and was eternal. In the fifth century BC Anexagoras invented the notion of a power-substance which penetrated things and caused them to move. He thought that this substance must be a soul and must have order and purpose. He ascribed rationality to the power-substance. In aesthetics the Greek philosophers' notion of beauty often consisted in regularity and arithmetic proportions. Much of European art, especially architecture and music, still retains the same concept.

A little later, the Sophists taught the principle of identity and the law of contradiction, and originated the tendency toward the formation of the ontological logic of mutual exclusion, negation, opposition, separation and categorization. Plato gave higher reality to abstract ideas than to concrete things, and advocated that true reality had no materiality. Here was the beginning of the dichotomy between the mind and the body. The fallacious notion that art is an 'escape' from the material world, which is held by some European intellectuals, had its origins here. However, in many of the Asian and African cultures, art is the expression of and a means of articulation, transmission and education of the human interaction principles, social organization and ethics. Japanese garden design and flower arrangements and African folklore are examples of this.

The European image of god was actually an idealized human. Europeans created their god in the image of man. This was logical because Europeans considered humans to be the highest category of living creatures. Exploitation of animals, plants and the environment by humans was sanctioned by this god. The monotheistic religion also contributed to the ENA homogenism. But in most of Asia, Africa and among original (non-white) Americans, heterogenistic harmonism prevailed.

Epistemological Bases of ENA: Misinterpretation of Some of the Asian and African Concepts

ENA theorists are often convinced that they 'correctly' understand Asian and African concepts such as heterogenistic logic, polyocular vision, mental connectedness, self-heterogenization and *aidaschaft*. But what they have done, in many instances, is to perform a dimension reduction (Maruyama, 1962 and 1979) in which an internally consistent but dimensionally reduced interpretation is obtained, in the sense that a three-dimensional object is reduced to a two-dimensional shadow. The internal consistency, and what the mathematical logicians and set theorists call 'completeness' – in that no additional new elements can be generated by the operations available within the system – of the dimensionally reduced interpretation give the ENA theorists the illusion that they have attained the correct interpretation. The same can happen to their interpretation of our preceding discussion using nonverbal design principles. It seems to depend on the epistemological predispositions of the readers.

There are at least two aspects to the difficulty of overcoming the dimension reduction. The first is the ENA epistemology based on substance, identity, boundary, separation and distinctness. In this epistemology an individual is a thing; many individuals are many distinct things; and there must be things before there are relations. On the other hand, in many of the Asian and African cultures, there are also individuals but they derive their meaning from interrelations. To take an imperfect analogy, the concept *mother* is meaningless without *child*. The analogy is imperfect because in the ENA epistemology the mother is first an individual, and *motherhood* is more or less an incidental or auxiliary attribute of the individual. Prior to all social relations, there is supposed to be first the individual personality and identity. On the other hand in the Asian and African traditions there is no such pre-relational identity; the identity *is* the relations, not the individual in isolation.

The second aspect is more crucial in the dimension reduction. The ENA epistemology is basically built on a one-dimensional continuum (in the sense of geometry) between homogenistic hierarchy and random, independent individualism. Everything is supposed to fit somewhere in this continuum. The 'mainstream' ENA philosophy, from Xenophanes, Plato and Aristotle to Descartes, Kant, Darwin and Einstein, has been of the H-type. The rebellions which occurred within ENA cultures, from the mediaeval Nominalists to the recent hippies, have been mainly of the I-type, though there have been important exceptions (Maruyama, 1980) including Kierkegaard (I-H), Heidegger (I-S), Sartre (I-G), Durkheim (H-G), Mannheim (S-G), Prigogine (I-H-G) and others. Even many of the ENA music composers and architects, in their attempt at doing something new, are confined in the mixture of H and I (Maruyama, 1981). ENA theorists tend to think that S and G are found somewhere between H and I. This is a misinterpretation and dimension reduction. The crucial point is that S and G *mindscapes* are based on causal *loop* epistemology (Maruyama, 1963 and 1980) which is shared neither by H nor by I. S and G therefore lie outside the H-I continuum.

Likewise, the ENA theorists tend to misinterpret *aidaschaft* and groupism in terms of the submission of the individual to the whole as well as in terms of homogenization. But as I have discussed, *aidaschaft* is non-hierarchical and interactive, and in *aidaschaft* the individuals utilize their diverse individualities for positive-sum mutual benefit.

Our next question is to what extent *aidaschaft* exists in cultures other than Japan. We have no solid comparative data. However, Ting's observations (1983) indicate that *aidaschaft*, if it exists at all, is much weaker in Hong Kong, Singapore, Taiwan and South Korea than in Japan. On the other hand, judging from the scores obtained by Laurent (1983) which are much more recent than Hofstede's (1980), it is possible that something similar to or even stronger than *aidaschaft* may exist in Indonesia.

In addition to the concepts discussed above, which are difficult to explain to ENA theorists because they are outside the latter's epistemological dimensions, there are concepts which become easily distorted in translation even though appropriate dimensions are available in the ENA epistemology. This occurs because of differences in the classification of categories, and can happen even when the translator is Japanese. Here are two examples:

In the English edition of *Japanese Style Management*, Iwata (1982) uses the word 'conformity' to indicate 'sharp perception of the situation, unique sense of adaptation with reality, quick orientation and reaction to cope with various situations, responding to the needs of the overall situation'. This Japanese sense of 'conformity' corresponds to the English word 'flexibility', while the American sense of conformity implies rigidity and inability to change. This difference is due to the fact that in the ENA epistemology, permanence is basic and normal, while change is something more unusual. On the other hand, in the Japanese epistemology, change is taken for granted. Hofstede (1980) seems to have misinterpreted his 'uncertainty avoidance' scores of the Japanese in a way related to this epistemological difference. Iwata (1982) points out that in Japan the workers automatically respond to changing situations and therefore the managers do not need to give detailed instructions. But in the USA the manager must provide very specific and detailed instructions; instructions which come from the manager rather than from the changing situations.

Another example is what Iwata has called 'diffused responsibility' or 'shared responsibility' at one time or another. Several of my ENA colleagues have misinterpreted this concept. For example, they thought that, if there are five persons in a group, 'shared responsibility' means that each person takes 20 per cent of the total group responsibility, while 'diffused responsibility' would mean that each takes less than 20 per cent of it. But what Iwata meant was exactly the opposite: each person takes 100 per cent responsibility, with the result that the group as a whole takes 500 per cent responsibility. This misinterpretation comes from the fact that in English, 'to share' means to divide without overlapping (the classificational H-I mindscapes), and 'to diffuse' means to weaken. In contrast, in Iwata's sense, 'to share' is 'to duplicate' (the principle of continuity and non-division of the S and G mindscapes), while 'to diffuse' means 'to multiply'.

Another frequent misinterpretation involves the term 'generalist'. In American practice a 'generalist' is often an abstract theorist who proceeds deductively and axiomatically, and tends to look for similarities and often uses (and misuses) analogies, while being uninterested in specifics and differences. In contrast, in Japan a generalist is a person who has been job-rotated and has experienced and worked in all different parts of the factory or firm, knows the differences between them, and can work in any of the specific parts with his/her knowledge of the context of all other parts.

Note

The different types may be summarized as follows. For details, see the article 'Mindscapes and Science Theories' (Maruyama, 1980):

H-type: It considers standardization of workers as well as products to be efficient, scientific and desirable. It is also hierarchical and classificational. It assumes adversarial (zero-sum) relations between labor and management as well as between the ecosystem and industry. It favors centralization.

I-type: Individual separation and insulation are believed to lead to efficiency and high productivity (negative-sum assumption). It favors decentralization and individualization.

S-type: It regards heterogeneity as basic, indispensable and desirable. Diversity is the source of *mutually* beneficial (positive-sum) cooperation in which all sides gain. It favors computerized customerization of products which eliminates inventory-carrying costs and reduces pre-production market research costs, post-production advertising costs and stock-out costs. In labor relations, it encourages a mutually beneficial combination of individual differences instead of standardization of workers.

G-type is similar to S-type. The difference between the two types is that the S-type seeks mutually maintained stability, while the G-type seeks and generates new patterns by interaction.

References

Camara, Sory, 'The concept of heterogeneity and change among the Mandenka', *Technological Forecasting and Social Change*, Vol. 7, 1975, 273–84.

Cho, Wangha, 'Comparison of the Chinese, Japanese and Korean management: preliminary interviews', unpublished report, 1983.

Hamaguchi, Esyun, *Nippon Rashisa no Saihakken*, Tokyo: Nihon Keizai Shinbunsha, 1977.

Hazama, Hitoshi, *Nihonteki Keiei*, Tokyo: Nihon Keizai Shinbunsha, 1971.

Hofstede, Geert, *Culture's Consequences*, Los Angeles: Sage Publications, 1980.

Iwata, Ryushi, *Nihonteki Keiei no Hensei Genri*, Tokyo: Bunshindoo, 1977.

— *Nihonteki Sensu no Keieigaku*, Tokyo: Tooyoo Keizai, 1980.

— *Japanese Style Management*, Tokyo: Asia Productivity Organization, 1982.

Kimura, Bin, *Hito to Hito to no Aida*, Tokyo: Koobundoo, 1972.

Koike, Kazuo, 'Japanese workers in large firms', *Keizai Kagaku*, Vol. 26, 1978, 1–37.

Laurent, André, excerpted by Hofstede, *Euro-Asia Business Review*, Vol. 2, No. 1, 1983.

Marbun, B. N., *Konsep Manajemen Indonesia*, Jakarta: Lembaga Pendidikan dan Pembinaan Manajemen, 1980.

Maruyama, Magoroh, 'Morphogenesis and morphostasis', *Methodos*, Vol. 12, 1961, 251–96.

— 'Awareness and unawareness of misunderstandings', *Methodos*, Vol. 13, 1962, 255–75.

— 'The second cybernetics: deviation-amplifying mutual casual processes', *American Scientist*, Vol. 51, 1963, 164–79; 250–56.

— 'The Navajo philosophy: an esthetic ethic of mutuality', *Mental Hygiene*, Vol. 51, 1967, 242–9.

— 'Toward human futuristics', paper presented at the American Anthropological Association Meeting, 1970, reprinted in *Cultures of the Future*, ed. Maruyama, The Hague: Mouton Publishers, 1978.

— 'Heterogenistics: an epistemological restructuring of biological and social sciences', *Acta Biotheoretica*, Vol. 26, 1977, 120–36.

— 'Heterogenistics and morphogenetics: toward a new concept of the scientific', *Theory and Society*, Vol. 5, 1978a, 75–96.

— 'Endogenous research and polyocular anthropology', in *Perspectives on Ethnicity*, ed. Regina Holloman and Sergei Arutiunov, The Hague: Mouton Publishers, 1978b.

— 'Trans-epistemological understanding: wisdom beyond theories', in *Currents in Anthropology* (Sol Tax Festschrift), ed. Robert Hinshaw, The Hague: Mouton Publishers, 1979.

— 'Mindscapes and science theories', *Current Anthropology*, Vol. 21, 1980, 589–99.

— 'Denkmuster: Meta-prinzipien der Umweltgestaltung', *Garten und Landschaft*, October 1981, 806–15.

— 'Mindscapes, management and workers', in *Japanese Management*, ed. Sang M. Lee, New York: Praeger, 1982.

— Paper presented at the Second Japan/USA Business Conference held in Tokyo, April 1983.

Pascale, R. T. and A. G. Athos, *The Art of Japanese Management*, New York: Warner Books, 1981.

Ting, Wenlee, 'Management models and business cultures in the NICs: new perspectives', paper presented at the International Congress of Anthropological and Ethnological Sciences, August 1983.

Watsuji, Tetsuroo, *Fuudo*, Tokyo: Iwanami Shoten, 1935.

China

Management in China: Economy and System

John Child

Chapter 2, pp. 11–34 in John Child, *Management in China during the Age of Reform* (Cambridge: Cambridge University Press, 1994)

This chapter looks at three key features of the context for managing enterprises in China. These are the country's status as an industrializing and modernizing economy, its system of industrial governance, and its culture. Each is first described so as to set the scene and then its implications for Chinese management and organization are discussed. In this way, the chapter lays a foundation for understanding Chinese management in terms of its main contextual fundamentals.

An Industrializing and Modernizing Economy

Economic Overview

Although China is still a developing country, with a per capita national income in 1992 of US$367, it has already become a major economic power. It is the world's largest agricultural producer and among the eight largest industrial producers. It is the world's third largest economy, calculated on a purchasing power parity basis. China's industrial development was led historically by the textile industry which remains a significant force, but other industries have developed rapidly, often with the help of foreign capital and know-how. China has, for example, become the world's third-largest shipbuilder and fourth-largest steel producer. It is also the third-largest producer of beer in the world, put under the table only by the United States and Germany.

This significant industrial presence stems from the combination of a huge population, a relatively high share of national income attributable to industry,

Figure 1 China: provinces, population and per capita income, 1990.
Source: 'A Survey of China: When China Wakes', *Economist*, 28 Nov. 1992

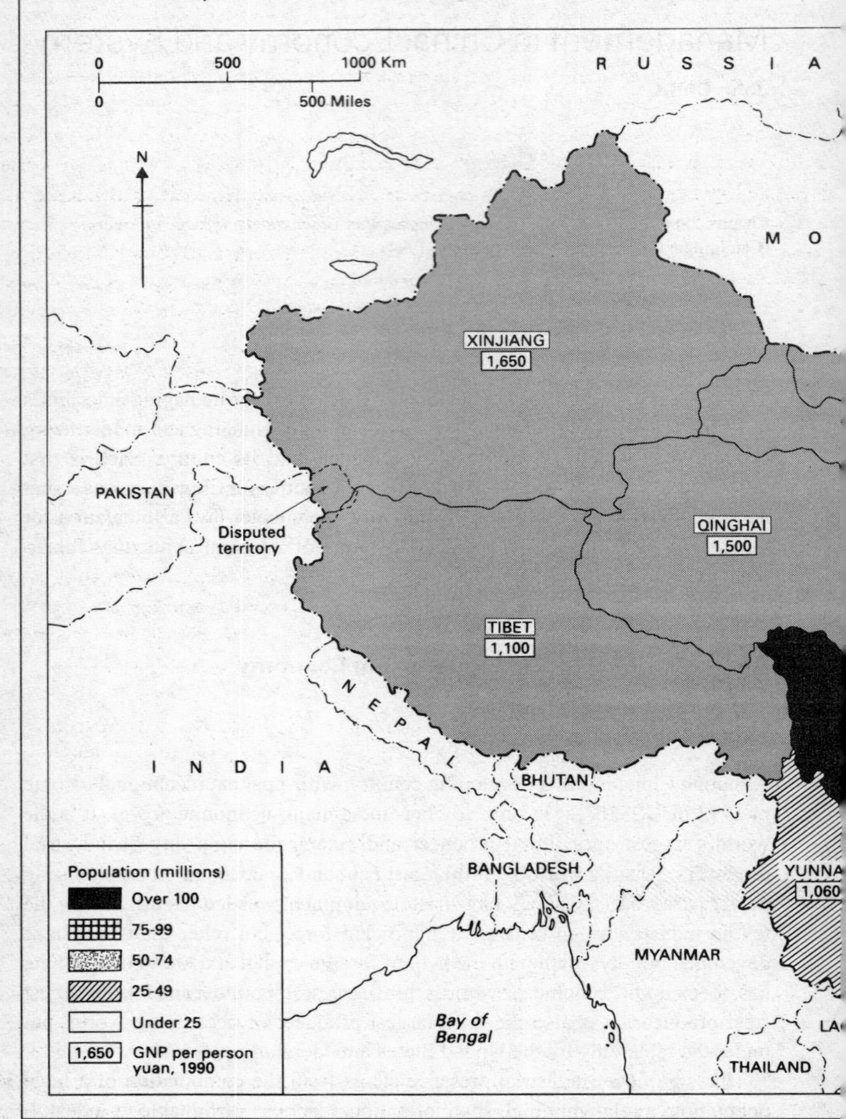

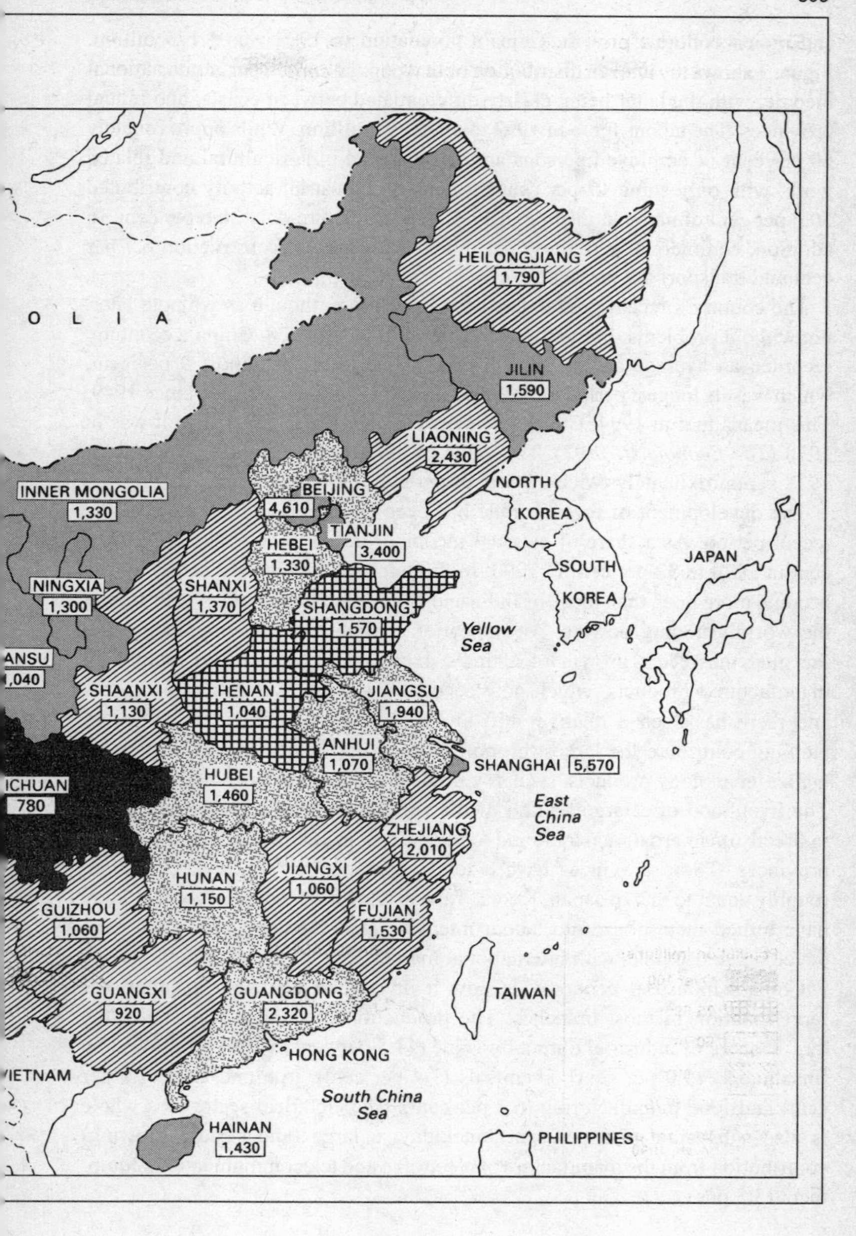

HEILONGJIANG
1,790
JILIN
1,590
LIAONING
2,430
O L I A
INNER MONGOLIA
1,330
BEIJING
4,610
TIANJIN
3,400
HEBEI
1,330
NORTH
KOREA
SOUTH
KOREA
JAPAN
NINGXIA
1,300
SHANXI
1,370
SHANGDONG
1,570
Yellow
Sea
ANSU
,040
SHAANXI
1,130
HENAN
1,040
JIANGSU
1,940
ANHUI
1,070
SHANGHAI
5,570
ICHUAN
780
HUBEI
1,460
East
China
Sea
ZHEJIANG
2,010
HUNAN
1,150
JIANGXI
1,060
GUIZHOU
1,060
FUJIAN
1,530
GUANGXI
920
GUANGDONG
2,320
TAIWAN
HONG KONG
IETNAM
South China
Sea
HAINAN
1,430
PHILIPPINES

and rapid economic growth. China's population in 1992 was 1.175 billion. Figure 1 shows the uneven distribution of that population and per capita national income, with the latter being clearly differentiated between coastal and inland provinces. The labour force in 1992 totalled 594 million. While approximately 60 per cent of employed persons are still engaged in agricultural and related work, with only some 17 per cent in industry, industrial activity contributed 50.6 per cent of national income in 1992 and agriculture only 28.6 per cent. In addition, commercial activities contributed 9.2 per cent, construction 6.7 per cent and transport 4.9 per cent.

The country's recent growth has been impressive, though as we note later, not without problems. In the fourteen years following 1978, China's economy recorded an average annual growth rate in real terms of almost 9 per cent, which was its longest period of high and relatively stable expansion since 1949. This means that in 1994, China's economy is four times larger than it was in 1978 (*The Economist*, 1992). The value of industrial output has grown since 1978 at approximately twice the rate of agricultural output value.

The development of foreign trade has been another marked feature of the recent period. As a share of national income, foreign trade rose from 10 per cent in 1978 to 32 per cent in 1990. In these terms, the Chinese economy has become more open than those of India and Brazil, and it now ranks 11th among the world's trading powers. An indication of industrial development is the fact that the recent growth of China's exports has been driven mainly by manufactured products, which now account for some two-thirds of exports, and there has been a relative shift away from raw materials. Textiles and clothing contribute the largest proportion of export value, though exports of higher technology products, such as electrical goods, have been rising rapidly. The livelihood of a large section of the population now depends directly or indirectly on international trade and foreign investment, especially in the coastal provinces. These provinces have a total population of almost 200 million, roughly equal to that of Japan, Korea, Taiwan and Hong Kong combined. They have turned themselves into labour-intensive manufacturing bases and have developed close links with international markets.

China's industrial economy is now a diversified one with a significant representation in most branches. The production of textiles contributes the largest share of industrial output by value (11.5 per cent in 1991), followed by 'machinery' (9.0 per cent), chemicals (7.4 per cent), iron and steel (7.0 per cent) and food manufacturing (6.7 per cent). The electrical sector as a whole is also substantial (7.6 per cent), including a large (and rapidly growing) contribution from the manufacture of electronic and telecommunications equipment (3.5 per cent).

In 1991, China had approximately 808,000 industrial enterprises. Of these, 419,000 had the status of 'independent accounting units' and they contributed 78.2 per cent of total gross industrial output. According to the Chinese classification of enterprise size based on asset value, the industrial population divides into relatively few large and medium-size enterprises (1 per cent and 2.3 per cent of the total respectively), and an overwhelming number of small firms. If one includes village and household units as well, then small enterprises in China account for over 50 per cent of total industrial output. As Hussain (1990: 5) comments, this weight of small firms distinguishes China's industrial structure both from those in the former planned economies of Eastern Europe and the Soviet Union and from those of market economies.

This size distribution of firms is important because in China the size of firms has been connected with their ownership and the extent of their integration into the planning system. Larger firms are generally state owned. In formal terms they are owned by the whole people though, as we note later in this chapter, the property rights attaching to them are complex and far from clear cut. Those enterprises which continue to have to produce part of their output according to the state plan are normally in the largest size bracket. Small enterprises were never effectively incorporated into the planning system and now coincide with the non-planned sector which today also includes many medium-size and some large firms. Therefore the scope of output planning in China depends not only on government reform policy but also on the relative growth rates of small enterprises *vis-à-vis* large ones.

The ownership of enterprises has become more diverse during the period of economic reform. In terms of output, the pre-1978 economy was dominated by state-owned enterprises. Since then the collective sector, comprising enterprises owned by communities or their own employees, has grown dramatically and a new dynamic sector of individual and private enterprises has also prospered (albeit temporarily set back by ideologically inspired policies following the Tiananmen Square incident of 4 June 1989). Foreign ownership has also been permitted, primarily in the form of equity joint ventures though since 1988 the number of wholly owned subsidiaries has increased rapidly.

Between 1978 and 1992 the proportion of industrial output contributed by state-owned enterprises dropped from 80 per cent to 48 per cent. The collective sector grew according to the same measure from 19.8 per cent to 38 per cent (including township and village collectives: 13.0 per cent) and the individual/private sector grew from 0.2 per cent to 6.7 per cent. Companies with foreign investment accounted for over 5 per cent of industrial output in 1992. The growth of the non-state sector within the economy as a whole has in effect amounted to a process of de-nationalization without privatization (Qian and Xu, 1993).

The state-owned sector remains the largest by some margin in spite of its relative decline. State-owned enterprises are heavily represented in the extractive and heavy industries, and also in areas of strategic importance such as energy and defence-related production. Much of the rapid growth in other sectors has been concentrated in consumer industries such as textiles and in services such as hotels and restaurants.

As well as being generally larger in scale than those under other forms of ownership, state-owned enterprises also harbour a relatively large part of the underemployment that exists within Chinese industry. Estimates are that at least one-fifth of the workers in state industrial enterprises, which is some 20 million, are unproductively employed. It is not surprising therefore that the share of industrial employment accounted for by these firms is considerably higher than their relative contribution to output value. At the end of 1990, employees in state-owned urban industrial enterprises made up 68.3 per cent of total urban industrial enterprise employment, with collective enterprises taking up only 29.0 per cent of the same total. State-owned enterprises have tended to be the dinosaurs of Chinese industry and the main thrust of the economic reform towards industry has been directed primarily towards their revitalization.

Another point to note is that ownership status, size of enterprise, branch of industry and regional location are not independent of each other in China. The heavier sectors of industry producing energy supplies, basic materials and mechanically-engineered products are generally comprised of large state-owned enterprises, some of which have now entered joint ventures with foreign partners (as is the case with most state automobile producers). Areas of strategic importance such as aircraft, defence and transportation equipment are also under state ownership. The larger, more capital-intensive state enterprises tend to be concentrated in the North of China. Many of these were developed with Soviet assistance during the 1950s and adopted the Soviet system of concentrating authority into the hands of factory directors.

Smaller, lighter industry tends to be concentrated in the coastal areas south of the Yangtze River. China's textile industry for instance grew up in and around Shanghai and adopted a more collective mode of work organization. Southern China is predominantly characterized by labour-intensive production which in the beginning was often based on traditional craft products such as toys, but which today has a strength in more advanced products such as light electronics. Some heavy industry is also to be found in inland provinces such as Sichuan, where it was often established for reasons of national security rather than economics.

Collective and private enterprises are spread over a wide area of China and these include so-called township and village enterprises which have grown in small towns and villages as rural reform has released large numbers of agricultural workers. These patterns of differentiation within the Chinese industrial economy have to be borne in mind when reading this chapter, which draws heavily on investigations in one location – Beijing – and only into state enterprises. Its data on foreign joint ventures are rather more widely based, though even then the writer's research is intensive rather than extensive in coverage.

Detailed information on the total population of foreign-funded enterprises in China is not readily available, but there is no doubt about their significance in recent years as a vehicle for importing both investment and know-how. The inflow of foreign direct investment from capitalist countries has increased from virtually zero in 1978 to US$221 billion in terms of negotiated funds and US$60 billion in utilized direct investment by the end of 1993. Over 50,000 foreign-funded enterprises had gone into operation, employing more than 5 million Chinese workers. The majority of these were equity joint ventures, which accounted for 39.6 per cent of all foreign investment in China at the end of 1991.

In short, state-owned enterprises are still the dominant ownership type, and also constitute the sector widely recognized to be in most need of improvement. Enterprises with foreign management, especially ventures with Chinese state firms, possess a special potential for accelerating China's development.

Implications of Industrialization

Economists and sociologists have long debated the implications of industrialization for the organization of economy and society (Kumar, 1978). Industrialization signifies here the mechanization and the rational organization of productive activity, not just in manufacturing but in any or all of the sectors of the economy (Moore, 1962). The debate remains inconclusive over the large question of whether industrial societies have eventually to adopt similar economic, social and even political systems in order to be competitive and effective, an issue revived by recent developments in Eastern Europe. On the one side is the argument that industrialism has a 'logic' which stems largely from its use of science and technology (cf. Aron, 1967) and which requires the 'modernization' of a society's competences and institutional practices for its successful realization (cf. Harbison and Myers, 1959; Kerr et al., 1960). This implies a convergence between industrial societies in these characteristics. Critical of this view are those who point out that different countries, including those of East Asia, have successfully adopted contrasting models of organizing an industrial society (cf. Whitley, 1994) and who could therefore argue that the logic of industrialism has limited rather than overwhelming social and organizational implications.

Clark Kerr, a long-time exponent of the thesis that the logic of industrialism will lead to convergence between economic and social systems, subsequently modified his position to allow for a tension between opposing forces bearing on this issue. In so doing, he nevertheless held to the view that the process of modernizing economies and opening them to international competition creates a drive towards a convergence between countries around the most effective way of organizing such economies:

> The forces most strongly at work [for convergence] are the drive for modernization, the intensity of competition among nations, the existence of common human needs and expectations, and the advent of common practical problems with common solutions. The main barriers to convergence are inertia, inefficiencies, resource constraints, and the holding power of any antagonistic preindustrial beliefs. (Kerr, 1983: 86)

China is now striving to achieve modernization, and is encouraging a degree of competition both internally and through opening up to foreign trade. It shares human needs and practical problems with other nations. The implication of Kerr's argument is that it will therefore be obliged to adopt forms of economic management and organization comparable to those which have assisted the successful modernization of other nations. Indeed, this is part of the rationale expressed by Chinese leaders for inviting foreign companies to participate in the modernization process, although they do also talk about adapting these to suit China's situation. The thesis that industrialization is a compelling social force therefore draws attention to certain features which, it claims, are liable to accompany the process of modernization on which China is now engaged.

Although there are differences of emphasis among exponents of the industrialization thesis, there is wide agreement on the core features of the process. These are an increasingly complex division of labour and skills, the development of the factory system of production and subsequently of large formal organizations, the extensive commercialization of goods and services and their exchange through the market, a growing scope and density of communications, and an educational and training system capable of filling positions within the evolving occupational structure. The sophistication required to manage these more complex organizations and transactional arrangements will clearly grow in step with them. Professional management is therefore also identified as a requisite for industrialization. Additionally, to provide the engine of growth and hence the wherewithal to invest in further modernization, the dynamic force of entrepreneurship and a striving for achievement and betterment among the population at large need to be encouraged (cf. Burns, 1969; Feldman and Moore, 1969).

Central to this thesis is the view that successful industrialization requires resources to be allocated and managed on the basis of rational decision criteria. This means that the character of economic management should differ from that in traditional or non-industrial society. Weber (1964) believed that management based upon and operating through legal-rational authority was of this rational type and enjoyed a superiority in basing its actions upon technical knowledge and modern methods without the sources of inefficiency, such as nepotism, corruption or narrow ideologies, which accompanied traditional or charismatic authority systems.

In the case of China, the argument from a logic of industrialization implies the need for policy initiatives in several key areas which are listed below. Policy makers have indeed paid considerable attention to these factors since the initiation of the economic reform. The reform itself is officially linked to the goal of modernization, though a major point of discussion concerns how far this modernization can be achieved through institutions and practices which retain 'Chinese characteristics'. The notion of Chinese characteristics in this context can signify the recognition of the society's strong link with its past; it can also signify the political intention to pursue modernization within a framework of socialist objectives and institutions. This recalls the fact that industrialization has now been attained in ways that diverge from the earliest 'Western' examples, most notably involving a more directive and interventionist role of the state.

The conclusions for China from applying the logic of industrialism are that it needs to:

1. introduce rational systematic methods of managing complex organizations;
2. train people in the necessary technical and managerial competences;
3. grant sufficient autonomy to those in charge of enterprises for them to exercise entrepreneurship at least to the extent of formulating and pursuing their own business plans;
4. encourage the development of systems to motivate people at work;
5. create efficient means for the exchange of goods, services, information and other communications, so that markets can function efficiently.

This list implies that China as a developing country will have to overcome a set of opposite characteristics, namely a lack of management systems, limited levels of technical and managerial competence, restricted enterprise autonomy, underdeveloped motivation systems and limited and/or inefficient market transactions. It is arguable that some of these characteristics are also underpinned in China by the system of state socialist industrial governance and the continuing strength of traditional culture. The economic reform tacitly accepts that both the system of industrial governance and traditional culture present obstacles to effective modernization. Their implications for management are now reviewed in turn.

The System of Industrial Governance

Ownership and Property Rights under Chinese Socialism

China remains officially a political and economic system based on socialist ownership. Following 'the socialist road' is one of the regime's four Cardinal Principles and the country's Constitution declares that all the means of production are publicly owned. Jiang Xiaoming (1992) points out, however, there is a substantial difference between the Western concept of ownership, together with the property rights attaching to it, and that conventionally followed in China. The Chinese concept of ownership (*suoyouzhi*) is appreciably more ambiguous and is a political and ideological consideration rather than an economic and legal one. The term *suoyouzhi*, when used in China, implies an overall system of governance based on the ideological principles of socialism, such that all the means of production are ultimately a public asset and that the state acts as the custodian of this public ownership.

A fundamental problem with public ownership is that of identifying any specific owners to whom the managers of industrial assets should be accountable. Who actually owns Chinese 'state-owned' enterprises is a particularly vexed question which has not been resolved, but which is extremely germane to proposals now being discussed for issuing shares in these enterprises to members of the public and/or to employees, or even privatizing them entirely. While the owners of collective enterprises are defined more precisely as all the people who belong to them, the situation remains confused since there is a wide range of *de facto* positions in regard to their property rights. For some collectives these approximate to the position of a state enterprise, while at the other extreme some can more or less function as private firms. Many state-owned enterprises and most collectives are heavily dependent upon the goodwill and sanction of local governments, which in this way are significant holders of industrial property rights (Granick, 1990).

A key element in the Chinese economic reform has been the aspiration to separate the functions and officials of government from those of enterprise management. Government, indeed 'the state', in China includes both administrative and political (party) wings. So while confusion remains over the question of industrial ownership, the reform has in important ways proceeded to modify the property rights attaching to the management of industrial assets. These changes under the reform provide some parallel to the so-called 'divorce of ownership from control' in Western economies (cf. Berle and Means, 1932). The distinction between property rights and ownership is a critical one to make with regard to the Chinese system of industrial governance and changes occurring in it under the reform.

Property rights refer to the right to determine the use of assets, to dispose of them, and to decide on the distribution of the income stream they produce including its re-investment. In Western societies the sanctity of private property is deeply rooted; property rights normally attach to private ownership and they are safeguarded by law. This contrasts markedly with the Chinese notion of *suoyouzhi* which implies that in the final resort property is held only on the sanction of the ruling authority. However, since this principle is extremely general and vague, it has not interfered with the pragmatic ground-level redistribution of industrial property rights under the economic reform. The long-standing decoupling of property rights from ownership in China has, in fact, permitted the reform of industrial governance through amending property rights to take place under a socialist regime in which ownership remains nominally unchanged.

Before considering the reform itself and its main provisions, a description of the main features of the Chinese industrial governance system is required, together with the general implications these have for the management of enterprises (particularly state-owned ones).

The Structure of Industrial Governance

Although policies of overall economic management have altered considerably in China over the past forty years, there has been rather less change in the structure of urban industrial governance. As with all systems of state socialism, the government and the party are inextricably linked – both constitute 'the state'. State socialist societies are above all political economies. The structure of China's industrial governance therefore contains two parallel hierarchies, that of administration and that of the party.

The essentials of the administrative structure were laid down in the early 1950s on the pattern of the centralized Soviet model. It locates the enterprise within a matrix comprising two administrative lines leading down to two categories of bureau which relate with state-owned enterprises. Party organs are parallel and are embedded in each unit of the structure, which is outlined in Figure 2.

Figure 2 The higher administrative structure of state companies.

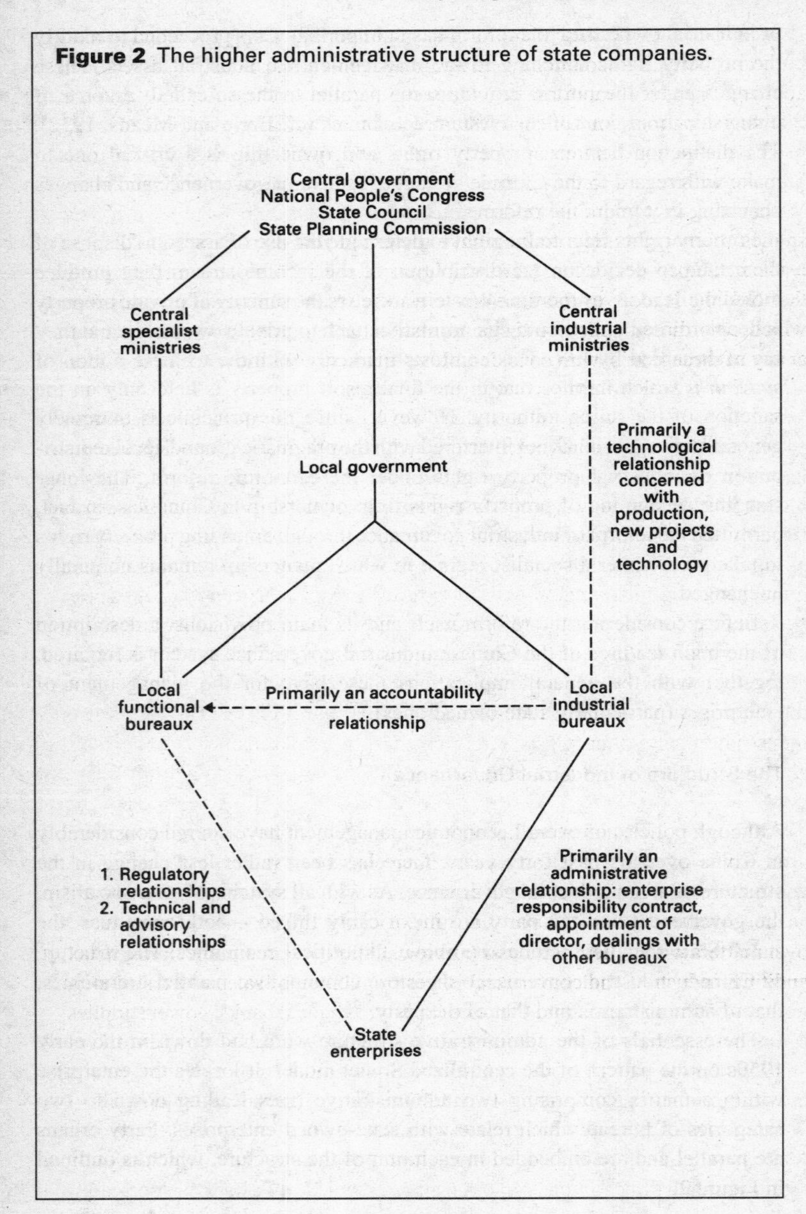
Central government
National People's Congress
State Council
State Planning Commission
Central specialist ministries
Central industrial ministries
Primarily a technological relationship concerned with production, new projects and technology
Local government
Local functional bureaux
Primarily an accountability relationship
Local industrial bureaux
1. Regulatory relationships
2. Technical and advisory relationships
Primarily an administrative relationship: enterprise responsibility contract, appointment of director, dealings with other bureaux
State enterprises

At the apex of the matrix are the National People's Congress which makes laws and issues the country's principal regulations, the State Council which approves the more important regulations governing enterprises, and the State Planning Commission which formulates such industrial regulations and can itself issue the more minor or specific ones. There are also national ministries, both for industrial categories and for specialized functions such as taxation. Within this set of national bodies, Lieberthal and Oksenberg (1988) in their studies of energy policy making have discerned four tiers: 'the top 25 to 35 leaders; the personal staffs, leadership groups, research centers, and institutes that link the leaders to the bureaucracies; the supra-ministerial commissions which co-ordinate policy; and line ministries. Energy decisions can be made at any of these levels, with considerable consequence for the range of considerations that are taken into account.' (pp. 27–8)

Below the central government there are local government administrations at the municipal and provincial level. Cities not enjoying provincial status have their own administrative bureaux of lesser rank. At this level, the local industrial bureau (today often renamed an industrial 'corporation') has a particularly close relationship with the enterprise. Its involvement can extend to any aspect of the latter's work and operation and includes the significant powers to appoint directors and to approve contracts specifying enterprise performance targets. Such a relationship approximates more to that of a holding company than of a multidivisional corporate group. This is because the bureau generally fails to develop any strategic rationale itself, which is usually left to the enterprise. Local industrial bureaux have a reporting line to the relevant industrial ministry, but (unlike the former USSR) their main line of accountability is to the local government. This is the first hierarchical administrative line.

The second administrative line is a functional one and divides at the local authority level into two types of bureau: one regulatory and the other technical-cum-advisory. Local regulatory bureaux, colloquially known by the Chinese as 'the Mothers-in-Law', have the right of direct intervention in enterprises over matters within their particular purview. Different bureaux specialize in tax, auditing, industrial and commercial issues (regulation of sales and distribution channels), pricing, investment finance (through the local bank), power supplies, personnel matters (personnel regulations and keeping cadres' files) and workers' employment. While these bureaux have their own lines to equivalent specialist national ministries, such as the central treasury, their strongest channel of accountability has, under the devolution of administrative powers, become that to the local government. The technical-cum-advisory bureaux do not have the right to initiate direct interaction or negotiation with enterprises. They perform support functions concerning, *inter alia*, technology development (the research institutes) and system reform.

In parallel with this system of administrative governance is one of political governance through the hierarchical structures of the Communist Party of China (CPC). The powers and direct managerial involvement of the CPC have waxed and waned at different times since the 1949 Revolution.

The party continues to have a formal role within the enterprise to promote ideological awareness and to 'guarantee and supervise' the implementation of government and party policies. This role embraces the organization of party activities inside the enterprise, the communication of information on policies and the approved 'line', and the monitoring of employees – especially managers. A key issue in China has been how best the party can fulfil this role, and this remains a live question so far as the relationship between enterprise party officials and management is concerned. Most managers are members of the party, and political loyalty is an important factor in the promotion of personnel.

Chinese trade unions are ideologically regarded as 'mass organizations of the working class led by the party'. There are fifteen industry unions, which at the end of 1987 had over 93 million members accounting for 89.7 per cent of the country's total workers in urban state enterprises. The top council of these unions, the All-China Federation of Trade Unions (ACFTU), has departments dealing with the economy, finance and accounts, international issues, organization, propaganda, safety, wages, and women's needs. Below it are federations or councils which duplicate these functions at regional, provincial and municipal levels; there are also industry unions organized in a similar form at these levels and down to that of the enterprise (Ng, 1984; O'Leary, 1992). Trade unions are not mandatory in firms with foreign involvement, such as joint ventures. However, 92 per cent of foreign or foreign-participating firms in the Shenzhen Special Economic Zone were said in 1987 to have trade unions operating (Nyaw, 1991) and it is likely that they are present in the majority of such firms.

Within the enterprise, as well as providing the executive arm and secretariat for workers' congresses (Workers' and Staff Representative Congresses), the union's other formal roles are to assist management make a success of running the enterprise and expanding its productive forces, to defend the legitimate rights and interests of staff and workers, and to assist management in carrying out government decrees concerning workers' interests and welfare. In practice, the union movement has continued to be subordinate to the authority of the party, which has regarded it as a potentially rival political force, which it clearly became during the protest movement of Spring 1989. In the words of one commentator union activities have 'been constrained by party authority into forms of practice which have severely compromised its ability to represent the industrial concerns of workers' (O'Leary, 1992: 371).

At the local level there are other institutionalized interests which bear upon the activities of management. The responsibilities of managers in the PRC extend beyond economic effectiveness into the area of social provision for employees, in terms of a wide range of welfare and other benefits and payments. Within the enterprise, the workers' congress enjoys rights to comment on managerial policy from the standpoint of its members' interests and to be consulted on matters such as the proposed dismissal of an employee. The enterprise is also obliged by local government bureaux and agencies to support the local community, in ways ranging from the funding of community projects to the provision of street cleaning.

The hierarchical lines from administration and party create vertical dependencies for enterprise management, although (as we note later) these are to a significant extent counterbalanced by the dependencies of external organs on the success of the enterprise for tax revenues, incomes, contributions to the community and so forth. Under the former planning system, managers were obligated to their higher administrative authorities for the fulfilment of quotas and targets, while they relied upon them to arrange the supply of necessary scarce resources. These authorities also continue to control senior managerial appointments and they can significantly influence the allocation of managers' personal rewards.

Under the current responsibility system, managers are responsible to the authorities for meeting agreed profit and investment targets, and for contributing tax revenues from profits. On the political side, managers are accountable to party officials and committees for ideologically acceptable conduct. Enterprise managers also depend on cooperation from workers for the fulfilment of economic goals. Most workers enjoy job security as well as a privileged ideological legitimacy as members of the proletariat. They are therefore in a strong position to withhold such cooperation. Moreover, they can readily voice their dissatisfaction through the workers' council or its officials in the trade union (both of which come under the leadership of the party) and in this way bring further pressure to bear upon management. The way that enterprise management is lodged within this system of dependencies is portrayed in Figure 3.

Walder (1986) has analysed the extension of these relationships into the factory itself by reference to the concept of 'communist neo-traditionalism'. In using this term he does not intend to imply that the features in question are not 'modern' and betray a continuing influence of traditional culture, but rather to point out their affinity with the characteristics associated in Western social

Figure 3 Location of Chinese enterprise management within a system of dependencies

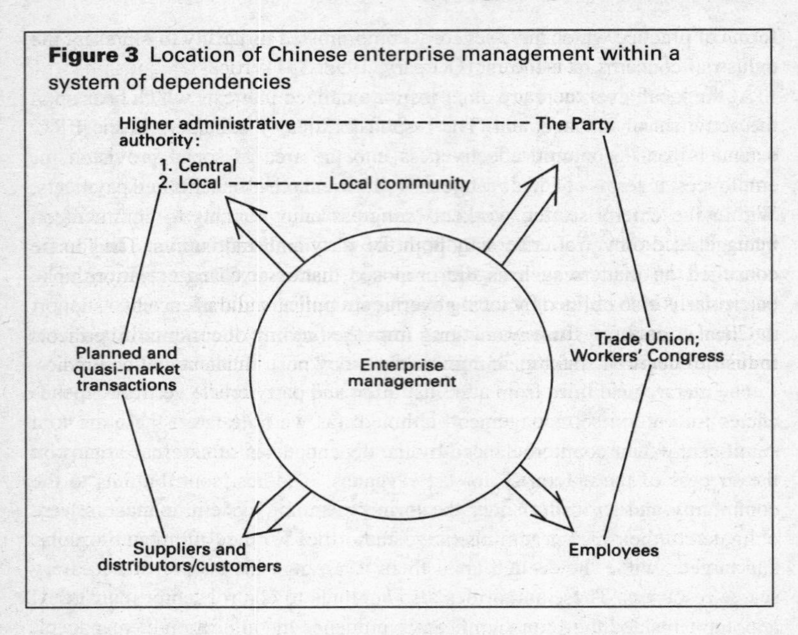

science with traditionalism, namely dependence, deference and particularism (p. 10). In fact, Walder concludes that such features are primarily the product of the way state socialism is organized rather than of specifically national traditions:

After my field experience, when I read about other institutions in China and other communist societies, I frequently detected the same underlying themes of dependence and vertical loyalties, even though the authors often did not draw attention to them. I gradually came to view the patterns of authority I had studied in state-owned Chinese factories as sharing certain generic features with other communist institutions, and I came to understand these generic features as the outcome, albeit unintended, of basic features of the organization of established Leninist parties and of central planning. (pp. xiv–xv)

Implications of the Industrial Governance System

The management of Chinese enterprises is located within a network of interlocking relationships (Henley and Nyaw, 1986). Walder (1989) points to the constraining nature of these relationships in describing four 'facts of life' in the world of the Chinese managers of state enterprises and many larger collective firms as well. The first is the continued importance of vertical relationships with the government bureaucracy, the cooperation of which can still considerably influence management's ability to secure prosperity for its enterprise. The second is that 'the enterprise is a political coalition' in which managers continue to require the support of other enterprise officers, particularly the party secretary. The third is that 'the enterprise is a socio-political community' with managers being judged on social criteria by both the party and trade union. The fourth concerns the continuing importance of non-market exchange relationships, particularly in the area of securing shortage supplies and trade credit.

Clearly, each of these conditions impinges on the locus and criteria of industrial decision making. In combination they pose fundamental contradictions for enterprise directors who are expected to reconcile economic with ideological criteria and to embody the interests both of the state (through their contractual responsibility to the administrative hierarchy) and of the enterprise as a corporate social group (Yang, 1989).

The institutional context of the management process in China must in large degree be understood as a dynamic system of interdependency relationships, especially between levels in the governance structure. It is a system of power, but one in which there is the potential for actors and their agencies (including managers and their enterprises) to intervene in decisions from different levels and points in the system. The dominant dependency is that of the enterprise upon higher authorities, but it is not a one-way relationship. As Montias (1988) points out, centrally planned economies that have evolved from the original Stalinist model are all characterized by bargaining between system levels.

Clegg's (1989) work on power captures some important essentials of the Chinese situation. He argues for an extension of the analysis of power beyond a concentration on its causality to a consideration of its use in the light of strategy, necessity and the organizational framework within which the parties are located. This leads him to a representation of the 'circuits of power' in which what he terms 'agencies' are the source of rules and obligatory procedures for social relations. In the PRC, the term would apply to governmental regulatory bodies. The rules and procedures establish rights of access to resources and to their disposition. Agencies are potentially in tension with the operational units which they are endeavouring to control but upon which they at the same time depend. Through developing their own rationales of production and discipline, the operational units deploy what Clegg calls 'facilitative' power which itself empowers and modifies the social relations upon which agencies are constituted. Clegg's analysis thus depicts mutual dependencies and dynamic processes of action within recursive circuits of power. Within these circuits there are 'obligatory passage points' at which the parties concerned attempt to fix expectations and rights in stable representations of necessity and normality.

The responsibility systems introduced under the economic reform programme have been intended to shift the balance of power and initiative from higher administrative agencies to operational units and within such units from the party towards management. As with any realignment of powers, considerable resistance could be expected, particularly regarding the system's obligatory passage points. The structures of central planning and hierarchical administrative control have been solidly laid down, or 'sedimented' in Clegg and Dunkerley's terms (1980), and are not easily removed. These structures constitute accretions of power over enterprise management with respect to both operational and personal resources. Operational resources include finance, information, access to markets through control over approved product lists, and assistance in the supply of materials, power and local services. Personal resources include senior managerial appointments and salaries. The functionaries running the sub-hierarchies within the system will be unwilling to forgo benefits that accrue from these powers of patronage, and which include opportunities to benefit from corruption. The bodies which previously enjoyed institutionalized powers over enterprises, namely the governmental administrative hierarchy and enterprise party committees, may be expected to strive to retain those powers, compensating for formalized changes through reliance on non-formalized strategic personal connections through which the enterprise can be either assisted or sanctioned.

Opposition to the reform might also be expected from the workforce and local community insofar as its implementation through labour rationalization and the introduction of differential performance-based payment schemes threatens respectively job security and the terms of reward previously struck with management (the 'effort-bargain' as Behrend (1957) called it). Moreover, many enterprise managers will be reluctant to acquire the new perspectives and learn the new behaviours and techniques required to put their greater autonomy to fruitful use under more competitive conditions which pose a greater risk of failure and fewer possibilities of being rescued from it.

Further problems arise because the infrastructure of macro-economic regulation is not yet sufficiently developed in China to support the decentralization of responsibility for economic performance to enterprises. For example, until prices are freed from subsidies and administrative control, it is extremely difficult to assess enterprise performance objectively, and decentralization through arm's-length accountability depends upon the availability of reliable performance measures. The absence of valid price indicators creates a problem for the economic evaluation of investment which is likely to permit the intrusion of other criteria such as the personal influence of bidders with funding agencies. Because of the underdevelopment of mechanisms for indirect regulation of the economy, the autonomy formally extended to enterprises is liable to be retracted by the central authorities in responding to economic or political crises, as happened in the latter part of 1985 and to a much greater extent after September 1988.

Chinese Culture

Main Characteristics of Chinese Culture

Although the history of China has been marked by periodic political upheavals of a violent kind, its majority Han people have experienced the longest span of homogeneous cultural development of any society in the world. Chinese culture and tradition is therefore particularly deep-rooted and before the present century it was largely undisturbed by foreign influence. It is a strong attribute of Chinese society, of which the members remain very self-conscious. As Fairbank has put it (1987: 367), 'the influence of China's long past is ever-present in the environment, the language, the folklore, and the practices of government, business and interpersonal relations'. Other writers have also emphasized the influence of China's culture on the way that its organizations are managed (e.g. Pye, 1985; ECAM, 1986; Lockett, 1988; Redding, 1990).

There are in practice many difficulties in defining 'culture' and also in assuming that it is equally shared by all the members of a nation-state. Kroeber and Kluckhohn (1952) cited 164 definitions of culture which taken together encompass a whole range of components: knowledge, values, preferences, habits and customs, traditional practices and behaviour, implements and artifacts. Keesing (1974) made a useful distinction within this range between 'ideational systems' and 'adaptive systems'. The former are those sets of ideas, shared symbols and meanings which are transmitted intergenerationally and which can be expected to mould work attitudes, expectations and behaviours through the process of socialization. The latter are the institutional arrangements which express a society's values in relation to the needs of its members to cope with the environment.

In the PRC since 1949, many of the society's institutions, such as its educational system and its system of industrial governance, have been given a strong political character both to reflect the new political ideology and with the intention of using institutions as instruments for bringing their members' values into line with the ideology. If political ideology becomes established in people's minds and is handed on by them to the succeeding generation, then one could consider that it has become part of the culture. This has probably not happened to a great extent in China. Redding (1990) contrasts the persistence of traditional Chinese culture with 'the communist veneer of the People's Republic' (p. 41), and quotes the confidential comment of an elderly professor in Guangzhou that 'the thing you must remember about China is that for the past thirty years we have all been acting'. Assuming this to be correct, we prefer to treat Chinese political ideology as an aspect of the institutions of political economy rather than as an indigenous part of the culture. The following discussion will therefore concentrate on the ideational aspects of Chinese culture which may be expected to have some bearing upon managerial behaviour and practice.

Fairbank has commented that in China 'regional differences are too great to be homogenized under a unitary state' (1987: 363). In so large and diverse a country as China, a further complication arises in the use of the term 'culture' since, while the population may generally share the core elements of a common culture, they will also exhibit contrasts in attitudes and behaviours. Such contrasts are often remarked between northern and southern China, which at certain times have been divided politically and which have not even had a common spoken language. Northerners, for example, are said to be more formalistic and less entrepreneurial and to reflect the ethos of the bureaucratic Bei Jing ('northern capital').

Various authorities on Chinese culture put forward somewhat different lists of key elements which are likely to have a particular bearing on management. There is, however, wide agreement on the following, which derive primarily from Confucianism. As Shenkar and Ronen (1987) state:

> The culture of traditional China encompasses diverse and competing philosophies, including Taoism, Buddhism, Legalism and a host of local 'little traditions'. Nevertheless, Confucianism is most clearly defined as the foundation of China's great cultural tradition, and Confucian values still provide the basis for the norms of Chinese interpersonal behavior. (p. 266)

The Confucian tradition has a concern for the correct and well-mannered conduct of one's duties, based on a sound respect for the social conventions of a patrimonial system. It stresses order, hierarchy, quality of relationships and obligation to social collectivities, especially the family (Smith, 1974; Waley, 1938). Age is respected, particularly in the case of male heads of family, while education is also valued as the means to achieving a better social status which reflects well on the family.

Lockett (1988) identifies four cultural values which he argues have particular relevance for management in China:

1. respect for age and hierarchy;
2. orientation towards groups;
3. the preservation of 'face';
4. the importance of relationships.

Principles such as harmony (Shenkar and Ronen, 1987) and the superiority of moral over legalistic control of behaviour (Boisot and Child, 1988) are also culturally significant in China and relate closely to the features in Lockett's list.

It is widely agreed that the Chinese respect age, authority and hierarchy. This stems from the Confucian concept of *li* (rite, propriety) which plays an important role in maintaining a person's position in the social hierarchy. As Needham (1980: 284) has argued, this ancient concept proved more suitable than any other for the traditional bureaucratic system in Chinese society. The tradition it embodies favours organizational hierarchy and centralized decision making.

In Chinese tradition, the extended family is the basic social unit, which encourages the development of a strong collective and group orientation. Within the bounds of the family or clan, its members are expected to maintain harmonious relationships. The family's moral judgement, especially as expressed by the father, provides the standard for approved behaviour. These same features also characterize in a somewhat diluted form the individual's attachment to other groups. They direct people's loyalties towards their family and work groups, and to the specific standards these apply, rather than to broader social entities.

'Face' is essentially the recognition by others of a person's social standing and position. There are two Chinese concepts of face, *lien* and *mianzi*. Whereas *mianzi* stands for prestige and personal success, *lien* stands for the confidence which others have in one's moral character. Losing *lien* can incapacitate a Chinese person as a member of his or her community (Bond and Hwang, 1986). The Chinese attach importance to the views others hold of them far more than most other cultures. Any form of idiosyncratic behaviour carries the risk of losing face and is culturally inhibited in China. The preservation of face connects with group identity since there is a strong expectation that any conflicts within the group will remain private; if publicized, the group as a whole is demeaned.

The fourth particularly significant concept in Chinese culture is *guanxi*, which refers to the quality of a personal relationship outside an individual's immediate family. Thus, when a petitioner asks a resource allocator to disburse a social benefit under his control, the latter will first consider the *guanxi* between them and then adopt appropriate rules of social exchange. Persons who have *guanxi* usually have at least one fundamental characteristic in common such as birthplace, lineage or surname, or they share a significant experience such as attending the same school, working together or belonging to the same organization (Jacobs, 1979).

Implications of Chinese Culture

To date, there have been fewer studies into the effects of traditional Chinese cultural attributes on management in the PRC than on their relevance for non-mainland business and management (e.g. Redding, 1990). It is nevertheless reasonable to assume that these cultural characteristics will reinforce the hierarchical and conformist attributes of the top-down command structure that China's economy has acquired under socialism. For they lead to a high value being placed on social control, virtually as an end in itself.

The specific attributes of traditional culture can cause problems for the improvement and reform of Chinese management. Respect for age can inhibit an acceptance of the younger, qualified managers whom the exponents of economic reform wish to see appointed to lead the re-invigoration and modernization of Chinese industry (cf. CPC, 1984: 32–3). Despite a major investment in training, there remains a shortage of professional and technical skills among managers, many of whom have stayed in their positions for a long time. The cultural respect for age and hierarchical position makes it difficult to resolve the problem, since it inhibits any challenge to older managers (Lockett, 1988).

Chinese organizations face major problems of collaboration and communication of a horizontal kind between different departments. Identities and loyalties are vertical in direction, and reflect the high respect that Chinese people have for their own hierarchies. The problem is further exacerbated by group orientation. This tends to be most strongly directed towards the immediate working group and its leadership, which is the workplace equivalent of the family. Here is a clear case where the vertical loyalties built into the command system are likely to be reinforced by the culture.

A strong orientation towards the group can have further consequences. It may undermine attempts to separate party from managerial functions which were previously undertaken by one senior group within the enterprise. It tends to unite with the preference for egalitarianism and present difficulties for the development of individual responsibility and for rewarding performance on an individual basis. A belief in egalitarianism has been encouraged in China both by tradition (especially in peasant society) and by the leftist strand of socialist ideology. Unwillingness among Chinese managers to assume personal responsibility is a frequently expressed concern of foreign partners in joint ventures. It is the product of a centralized hierarchical system, evident in former command economies such as Hungary (Markoczy, 1990), and one which the Chinese cultural environment is likely to reinforce.

Individual initiative and the evaluation of personal performance can be severely discouraged by the significance attached to face, as are frank contributions to discussions or problem solving. The preservation of face will be reinforced by the value attached to preserving harmony; conflict usually ends with a loss of face for one party, and sometimes both.

A preference for an implicit and moral basis for business dealings rather than a formal legal footing means that the viability of dealings rests upon trust between the parties. Within business relations, the norm of reciprocity applies with the expectation that one favour will eventually be repaid with another. Mutual favours are performed and 'strings pulled' on the basis of the *guanxi* between people, both within and across organizations. As Lockett has stated:

> In Chinese organizations continuing relationships are of great importance, in part based on family and other ties, such as clan, shared surname, home village, region, education or other shared experience . . . In business, relationships are important as contracts are often not strictly specified in legal terms but rely on trust between the parties. (Lockett, 1988: 489)

When there are shortages of supplies, the cultivation and use of *guanxi* by enterprise managers can make the difference between continuity and disruption of production. On the other hand, the use of relationships to 'go through the back door', as the Chinese put it, can undermine the credibility of formal systems and distort the allocation of resources according to economic or strategic criteria.

There is a wider implication of the fact that Chinese tradition favours the implicit structuring rather than precise formalization of social relations (ECAM, 1986). For if a preference for ambiguity is carried into the rules and regulations governing the implementation of economic reforms, then the latitude for re-negotiating and even negating them will be enhanced. Weber (1968) concluded from Western experience that the codification and routinization of laws and economic rules are two necessary conditions for firms to be able to exercise autonomy. In other words, the rules of the game applied to relations between enterprises and external parties, especially government, have to be codified with respect to matters of law and financial obligation. Secondly, government must apply the rules in a routine manner – in other words consistently and predictably – so that the managers of enterprises can use their autonomy to plan ahead.

When laws and regulations are poorly codified, as is often the case in China, *ad hoc* obligations are liable to be imposed upon enterprise managements by local, essentially patriarchal, agencies which may inhibit them from concentrating on economic objectives and also from entering into wider market transactions (Blecher, 1989). Here, then, is another example of how behaviour encouraged by the structure of industrial governance is likely to be reinforced by its cultural milieu.

Conclusion

The main characteristics of the Chinese economy and system posited by the three perspectives of industrialization, system of industrial governance (state socialism) and culture, are summarized in Table 1 which is adapted from Lu (1991). It is evident from this tabulation that the characteristics of Chinese culture and tradition are more compatible with the system of state socialism than either of them are with the attributes claimed for successful industrialization. Boisot (1990) argues, in a rather similar vein, that the Chinese are not yet attuned to a 'Schumpeterian' kind of learning process based on disequilibrium models of innovation and opportunity; both their culture and governance system are more attuned to an equilibrium model.

This observation leads to the proposition that, inheriting a culture with strong feudalistic origins, China provides a favourable context for the social acceptance of the paternalistic public bureaucracy system that has characterized state socialism. Both the culture and the system emphasize unified leadership and authority, collectivism, mutual dependence, moral incentive and conformity of thought. These characteristics sharply contrast with the pluralism of ownership, competition, individualistic entrepreneurship, economic incentive and innovation, which have generally been associated with successful Western industrialization. Although Walder (1986) does not attach much weight to the impact of traditional Chinese culture, except to admit that the recent system of industrial authority 'represents the integration of patrimonial rule with modern bureaucratic form' (p. 251), our suggestion that this culture provides fertile ground for the acceptance of patrimonial bureaucracy is not inconsistent with his empirical observations.

Some further implications arise from this comment. First, if in China both the culture and the system lead to similar managerial characteristics, it is important to discover whether one of these contextual factors is the more potent influence. Potency here refers to both the strength and the embeddedness of the influence. The combination of two comparisons would throw useful light on this issue: (1) between countries with similar systems but contrasting cultures,

Table 1 A comparative summary of characteristics posited by the perspectives of industrialization, industrial governance system and culture applied to China

	Perspective		
Type of characteristic	*Industrialization*	*Industrial governance (state socialism)*	*Culture*
1. Economic and socio-political governance	separated	unified political and economic governance	unified authority of leadership and senior kinship roles
2. Dominant mode of authority	rational bureaucracy	one-party leadership	traditional (official and family) status position
3. Economic management	market economy	central planning	local networks but with official intervention (especially in crises)
4. Ownership	diverse ownership	state monopoly of ownership	imperial/feudal ownership dominant
5. Control over enterprise management	ownership separate from management	state control	family control
6. Economic elites	professional managerial elites	political appointees	government officials and major property owners
7. Decision mode	entrepreneurial	collective	family/collective
8. Dominant ethos	innovation	conformity	conservatism
9. Socially approved motivation	economic	political	pursuit of traditional values (especially regarding relationships)

Source: adapted from Lu (1991).

and (2) between countries with the same cultures but different systems. These comparisons should indicate whether management, and indeed particular features of management, are moulded primarily by culture or system. A lead into this kind of investigation was provided by Shenkar and Ronen's (1989) comparative study of the 'work goals' expressed by Chinese managers in the

PRC and other Chinese communities, which pointed to differences of priority in those areas where one could expect system contrasts to have a direct bearing.

Secondly, although it is conceivable that a socio-political ideology such as Marxism–Leninism can in time become an internalized culture for successive generations of people, the evidently limited appeal of such ideologies in socialist and formerly socialist countries makes it more plausible to suggest that traditional cultures have helped the acceptance of communist neo-traditionalism rather than that communism/state socialism has itself had a significant cultural impact. This means that the historical process has been one in which culture led to system. Once the system with its authoritarian grip was in place, it could then contribute itself towards shaping observable patterns of organizational behaviour.

Thirdly, whether it is culture or system that is the more powerful force shaping Chinese organizational behaviour, both tend to work against the success of an economic reform. Within a centralized system, reforms that are introduced on a top-down basis will, of course, carry some weight, but their implementation relies on the instrumentality of intermediate institutions and their acceptability at those levels. The successful implementation of changes at the enterprise level in turn depends on sympathetic developments in external institutions, such as the introduction of more liberal rules of the economic game. The attempt to modernize Chinese management and the factors which frustrate this persist in Chinese management today.

References

Aron, R., *The Industrial Society*, London: Weidenfeld and Nicolson, 1967.

Behrend, H., 'The effort-bargain', *Industrial and Labor Relations Review*, 10, 1957, 503–15.

Berle, A. A. and G. C. Means, *The Modern Corporation and Private Property*, New York: Macmillan, 1932.

Blecher, M., 'State administration and economic reform', in D. S. G. Goodman and G. Segal (eds.), *China at Forty*, Oxford: Clarendon Press, 1989.

Boisot, M. H., 'Schumpeterian learning', unpublished paper, 1990.

Boisot, M. H. and J. Child, 'The iron law of fiefs: bureaucratic failure and the problem of governance in the Chinese economic reforms', *Administrative Science Quarterly*, 33, 1988, 507–27.

Bond, M. H. and Hwang Kwang-kuo, 'The social psychology of Chinese people', in M. H. Bond (ed.), *The Psychology of the Chinese People*, Hong Kong: Oxford University Press, 1986.

Burns, T. (ed.), *Industrial Man*, Harmondsworth: Penguin, 1969.

Clegg, S. R., *Frameworks of Power*, London: Sage, 1989.

Clegg, S. R. and D. Dunkerley, *Organization, Class and Control*, London: Routledge, 1980.

CPC [Communist Party of China], *China's Economic Structure Reform: Decision of the CPC Central Committee*, Beijing: Foreign Languages Press, 1984.

ECAM [Euro-China Association for Management Development], *Chinese Culture and Management*, Brussels: European Foundation for Management Development, 1986.

Economist, 'A survey of China: when China wakes', 28 November 1992.

Fairbank, J. K., *The Great Chinese Revolution 1800–1985*, London: Chatto and Windus, 1987.

Feldman, A. S. and W. E. Moore, 'Industrialization and industrialism: convergence and differentiation', in W. A. Faunce and W. H. Form (eds.), *Comparative Perspectives on Industrial Society*, Boston: Little, Brown, 1969.

Granick, D., *Chinese State Enterprises: A Regional Property Rights Analysis*, Chicago: University of Chicago Press, 1990.

Harbison, F. and C. A. Myers, *Management in the Industrial World*, New York: McGraw-Hill, 1959.

Henley, J. S. and M.-K. Nyaw, 'Introducing market forces into managerial decision making in Chinese industrial enterprises', *Journal of Management Studies*, 23, 1986, 635–56.

Hussain, A., 'The Chinese enterprise reforms', research programme on the Chinese economy, paper no. 5, June 1990, London School of Economics.

Jacobs, J. B., 'A preliminary model of particularistic ties in Chinese political alliances: *Kan-ch'ing* and *Kuan-hsi* in a rural Taiwanese township', *The China Quarterly*, no. 78, 1979, 232–73.

Jiang Xiaoming, 'The evolution of property rights in China: a long-run analysis with special reference to Hefeng textile mill', unpublished PhD thesis, University of Cambridge, 1992.

Keesing, R. M., 'Theories of culture', *Annual Review of Anthropology*, 3, 1974, 73–97.

Kerr, C., *The Future of Industrial Societies: Convergence or Continued Diversity?*, Cambridge, MA: Harvard University Press, 1983.

Kerr, C., J. T. Dunlop, F. Harbison and C. A. Myers, *Industrialism and Industrial Man*, Cambridge, MA: Harvard University Press, 1960.

Kroeber, A. L. and C. Kluckhohn, 'Culture – a critical review of concepts and definitions', papers of the Peabody Museum of American Archaeology and Ethnology, Harvard University, 1952.

Kumar, K., *Prophecy and Progress*, Harmondsworth: Penguin, 1978.

Lieberthal, K. and M. Oksenberg, *Policy Making in China. Leaders, Structures and Processes*, Princeton, N.J.: Princeton University Press, 1988.

Lockett, M., 'Culture and the problems of Chinese management', *Organization Studies*, 9, 1988, 475–96.

Lu Yuan, 'A longitudinal study of Chinese managerial behaviour: an inside view of decision-making under the economic reform', unpublished PhD thesis, Aston University, May 1991.

Markoczy, L., 'Case study of the Inter-Europa Bank', unpublished paper, Budapest University of Economics, 1990.

Montias, J. M., 'On hierarchies and economic reforms', *Journal of Institutional and Theoretical Economics*, no. 144, 1988, 832–8.

Moore, W. E., 'The attributes of an industrial order', in S. Nosow and W. H. Form (eds.), *Man, Work and Society*, New York: Atherton, 1962.

Needham, J., *The Shorter Science and Civilization in China*, volume 1, Cambridge: Cambridge University Press, 1980 (paperback edition abridged by C. A. Ronan).

Ng Sek-Hong, 'One brand of workplace democracy: the Workers' Congress in the Chinese enterprise', *Journal of Industrial Relations*, 26, 1984, 56–75.

Nyaw, M.-K., 'The significance and managerial roles of trade unions in joint ventures with China', in O. Shenkar (ed.), *Organization and Management in China 1979–1990*, Armonk, NY: M. E. Sharpe, 1991.

O'Leary, G., 'Chinese trade unions and economic reform', in E. K. Y. Chen, R. Lansbury, Ng Sek-Hong and S. Stewart (eds.), *Labour-Management Relations in the Asia-Pacific Region*, Hong Kong: Centre of Asian Studies, University of Hong Kong, 1992.

Pye, L. W., *Asian Power and Politics*, Cambridge, MA: Harvard University Press, 1985.

Qian Yingyi and Xu Chenggang, 'Why China's economic reforms differ: the M-form hierarchy and entry/expansion of the non-state sector', research programme on the Chinese economy, paper no. 25, July 1993, London School of Economics.

Redding, S. G., *The Spirit of Chinese Capitalism*, Berlin and New York: De Gruyter, 1990.

Shenkar, O. and S. Ronen, 'The cultural context of negotiations: the implications of Chinese interpersonal norms', *The Journal of Applied Behavioral Science*, 23, 1987, 263–75.

— 'Culture, ideology or economy: a comparative exploration of work goal importance among managers in Chinese societies', in *Managing the Global Economy III*, Proceedings of the Third International Conference of the Easton Academy of Management, Hong Kong, June 1989.

Smith, D. H., *Confucius and Confucianism*, London: Paladin, 1974.

Walder, A. G., *Communist Neo-Traditionalism: Work and Authority in Chinese Industry*, Berkeley, CA: University of California Press, 1986.

Waley, A. (trans.), *The Analects of Confucius*, London: Allen and Unwin, 1938.

Weber, M., *The Theory of Social and Economic Organization* (trans. A. M. Henderson and T. Parsons), New York: Free Press, 1964.

— *Economy and Society: An Outline of Interpretative Sociology*, New York: Oxford University Press, 1968.

Whitley, R. D., 'Varieties of effective forms of economic organisation: firms and markets in comparative perspective', *Organization Studies*, 15, 1994.

Yang, M. M. H., 'Between state and society: the construction of corporateness in a Chinese socialist factory', *The Australian Journal of Chinese Affairs*, no. 22, 1989, 31–60.

Hong Kong and the 'Overseas Chinese'

The Chinese Family Business *and* The Significance of the Overseas Chinese

S. Gordon Redding

Chapters 7, pp. 153–69 and 10, pp. 227–36 in S. Gordon Redding, *The Spirit of Chinese Capitalism* (Berlin and New York: Walter de Gruyter, 1990)

The Chinese Family Business

The Firm's Internal Structure

The basis for this account is a parallel study to that analyzing the beliefs of managers. It is part of the Aston series of organization studies, and as the account of it presented here is written for the non-specialist in organization theory, some introduction to its aims and methods will be justified. A note should perhaps also be injected here that this chapter is principally about the spirit which moves these organizations rather than about their detailed mechanisms. Even so, that spirit cannot be seen in context unless some basic understanding is also available of the economic instrument which such a spirit gives rise to. Chinese capitalism has a special way of coordinating and controlling economic action. It can best be understood by reference to the ways adopted in other economic cultures. The Aston research method facilitates this comparison. A total of 94 companies were studied in Hong Kong, Taiwan, the Philippines, and Indonesia, each with an interview schedule of 114 pages.

The language for describing organizations, as it has been refined through the Aston studies, sees them as varying along five major dimensions.

1. *Centralization*, which conveys a sense of where hierarchically in the organization the majority of decisions are taken.
2. *Specialization*, which reflects the extent to which labor is divided. It includes

dividing an organization into specialized units, and also allocating tightly defined roles to people.

3. *Standardization*, or the extent to which rules and definitions are used to regularize procedures and roles.
4. *Formalization*, or the extent to which activities are formalized through paperwork systems.
5. *Configuration*, which conveys the balance of line vs. staff personnel.

There are fairly obvious connections between specialization, standardization, and formalization, in that they all reflect the degree to which a company is 'organized'. If they are clearly evident in an organization, it suggests that somebody has designed the system to allow people to focus on specialist activities, somebody has laid down a set of guidelines, and somebody has designed a paperwork system to keep track of what is happening. These managerial activities commonly go together as they are all parts of the same momentum to get things under tidy control. It is possible thus to combine these three, calling the result 'structuring of activities' and allowing it to represent the degree to which the behavior of employees is overtly defined.

In contrast with this tendency to have work systematically designed, there is another organizing principle which, put at its simplest, is telling people what to do. If people can get on with their work without being told what to do, it is another way of saying that authority has been decentralized. For this to happen, the authority figures at the top usually want some assurance that the authority delegated will be exercised within certain understood boundaries, and with some defined discretion. For this reason, a higher degree of structuring of activities usually goes with more delegation. If, on the other hand, a boss wants to retain the complete say-so in everything, he does not need elaborate structures to control subordinates' discretion because they don't have so much. High centralization of decisions usually means low structure. Delegation requires structure.

It is also intuitively obvious that as an organization grows larger and more complex, there will need to be a process of delegation if the top is not to become overloaded with decision making. Research findings demonstrate this clearly, so that larger size means (a) more structuring of activities, and (b) less centralization of decisions.

The way in which the structuring of activities proceeds to grow as the organization expands divides into two alternative paths. Some organizations bureaucratize everything relating to employment, and they tend to have central recruiting, selection, discipline and dismissal procedures, formally constituted committees, appeal procedures, and the like. The way they organize concentrates more on the employment contract than the daily work activity itself. Such an organization is called a *personnel bureaucracy*, and they are typically found in government structures or in smaller branches of large corporations.

An alternative route is found in much of manufacturing industry and in big business generally. This is based on the idea of structuring activities around the flow of work and is based on the use of such control devices as production schedules, quality inspection procedures, output records, etc. This combination produces a *workflow bureaucracy*.

It is also possible for both of these forms of organizing to be combined into what is termed a *full bureaucracy*, and this is normally found in organizations which are at the same time large, complex, and decentralized.

The data will lead us to the conclusion that the typical Chinese family business remains small and relatively unstructured. Because of cultural restraints on the sharing of trust, it does not develop decentralized decision making, and this acts as an inhibitor to successful growth. It therefore forms a type of its own, with low structure following the universal tendencies of the size/structure relationship, but with the reason for staying that way having much to do with a particular social psychology. Where it does exhibit higher structure, it does so selectively and usually in the field of control of basic workflow operations.

In order to connect the social psychology and the organizational outcomes, we may now bring into the account the views of the chief executives, and use them as a framework to organize the comparative data.

The overwhelmingly consistent theme in discussions about their organizations by Chinese executives is patrimonialism. That word as such is not used by them, but it is the only word which captures adequately the themes of paternalism, hierarchy, responsibility, mutual obligation, family atmosphere, personalism, and protection. Out of it flow three related themes which are in some sense expressions of it, namely: the idea that power cannot really exist unless it is connected to ownership; a distinct style of benevolently autocratic leadership; and personalistic as opposed to neutral relations. Given the working of these three influences and of the paternalist climate, a number of organizational outcomes are discernible: problems over high-level skills; small scale and product/market concentration; the repression of organizational talent.

Paternalism

Let us begin by considering the paternalism *per se* in the sense in which it is discussed by Chinese executives. We shall then proceed to analyze the three consequent topics which flow from it.

To be able to say, as did *Shek*, 'My staff is my family' requires not just a knowledge of how to turn such a view into an economically efficient system of relations, but also a set of inner convictions to sustain the chief executive in making often hard decisions which affect such an organizational culture. Firing or not firing someone, determining rewards, dealing with discipline and control are all tests of an executive's inner morality as well as his economic pragmatism. The sustaining of familistic organizations on the scale that is evident in the Overseas Chinese case suggests that these inner convictions are strong.

Perhaps because Chinese morality is based in relationships rather than in more abstract ideals, one might anticipate the enhancing of a sense of responsibility towards workers. *Hoi* in discussing whether there was a moral base for authority, observed that ' ''Moral'' is perhaps a misnomer. It does not represent the quality of being always on the straight and narrow. It is more a matter of respect in treating workers and the company.'

Or, as others put it,

Hsien:
The Chinese mentality is to have the tax rate low and let the owner be benevolent to his surroundings.

Teng:
In a smaller business, affection and relationships between boss and staff is important for good working. The human factor is very important, even though the sole purpose of management should be growth. I pay a great deal of attention to such interpersonal relationships with staff, and every year I will hold a party for all my staff and their families first to feel close with them like one family.

Hu:
I believe I was doing the staff a good deal [growing the company]. All the staff that are under me, they served me well and I look after them. That is a very well-known Chinese way. I believe in it so much that I feel if I have more people – I haven't got that many, only sixty or seventy [note professionals] – it's not that many, but I've built up from ten people, so my success is more or less based on the people, so I provide happy employment. That may seem a little bit philosophical.

It is of course inappropriate to isolate such a component from the culture in which it is embedded, and necessary, in consequence, to acknowledge that this view, as it were, from the top, tends to be balanced by and in tune with the view from below:

Huan:

The best factory of all I know was the one my mother worked for. The reason is that the boss had managed to extract a lot of people from the same village. He helped a lot of people and their livelihood, and he used a lot of his earnings, his money, and distributed it to his relatives – buying houses, flats for them. I admire him a lot. The thing that has a shaping influence on me is that kind of caring. It's not exploitation as such.

Hioe:

Generally the Chinese employees normally respect managers. They are mostly rather obedient type of people. It's from the traditions and from the educational system. The first thing you have to do you have to listen to the leaders – to do what the leader tells you to do – until you have experience and know-how and try to do what you want to do – but not until then. I see many young graduates and they are very respectful, very obedient in the first place. But psychologically you have another burden – that means that you have to take care of these guys. They keep holding your hand.

Responsibility comes thus to be exercised partly from moral purpose in the Confucian humanist tradition, and partly in response to a somewhat deferential and dependent mentality on the part of many workers. The responsibility spreads over both task and welfare aspects of employment. Managers expressed regularly a view that they were responsible for fitting people into the right slots, for stewardship of resources, for helping the inefficient, providing security for the older ones, for being understanding.

Hap:

In any incident which might involve firing, my advice to supervisors is to assess the blame. If you assess 10 per cent to the company and the worker 90 per cent – I call it even – you don't fire . . . I walk around my factory – my symbol is a bottle of beer in my hand, no glass – my workers drink Blue Riband, I order San Mig, the cheaper price. I think I'm very paternalistic. I think I have an obligation to look after my men. But I know that if I look after them eventually I look after myself. That is my philosophy.

Our normal staff bonus has averaged nine months per year over the last three years, paid twice yearly. If we paid it monthly they would spend it . . . At the time of a recession, the first bonuses cut are the directors' and senior managers'.

Reporting very similar approaches in Indonesia, *Ip* noted that the function of the family atmosphere was to foster cooperation, a matter discussed from inside a very large financial corporation by *Han*, who described the chairman knowing about the staff's families, giving out the red packets at Chinese New Year, joining the singing at Christmas.

> There is something which goes beyond a staff and superior's relationship, and they like this working environment. And, erm – dictatorship – is seldom needed in the company. A lot of people would tend to think if the boss wants it done this way, he must have some reason for it, it must be good for the company. Not many people will think about whether this is right or wrong. Chinese are less inclined to face an issue direct. It's more related to family training.

In a consideration of the contrast between relationships based on contract and those based on personal obligation, *Hsien* expressed the opinion that 'More medium-sized firms – even very large firms – in Hong Kong – if you are looking at the contractual at one end of the scale and the extended family at the other end – I would think probably it tilts toward the extended family. It still is, I think, in Hong Kong.'

The cooperation which results in these structures, although clearly a major contributor to organizational efficiency, is bought, as are most organizational features, at the cost of something else, and there are inevitable weaknesses in paternalism acknowledged by several observers. The most obvious target of criticism of the familial approach was nepotism, a problem illuminated by a number of dramatic corporate collapses in Hong Kong, Singapore, and Taiwan. But very little was said about the need for a more neutral and professional approach. In fact, only one respondent said, 'You should run a company like a company and not a family' (*Sit*), an exception which may be left to prove the rule.

The cultural legacy of Overseas Chinese business has caused to emerge a distinct view of power and legitimacy. Power derives from ownership which is in turn vested in the family rather than an individual. While this does create the kind of unquestioning obedience just noted, it also introduces one very distinct, and particularly Chinese, organizational defect. This is that nobody outside the owning group can generate for himself truly legitimate authority. This becomes a very significant handicap to the grafting on of a middle and senior management group made up of competent professionals, and it becomes an important component of the explanation of why Chinese family businesses are unable to escape from the formula of family domination. Although there are occasional exceptions, and although change is possible and occurs in many fields, the overwhelming impression is that the status quo as regards authority being legitimated only through ownership is proving remarkably resilient and resistant to the forces of modernization. What is happening fits the culture, and some of its most deeply embedded features change at a rate which can only be described as glacial.

The matter is put clearly in a conversation about the nature of authority, which went as follows:

Hsien:
The staff would naturally look towards the highest source of authority, who is the boss, the real owner of the company. He will take commands from that level. Even though a manager tells him to do this and that and he knows that is probably the right track – the boss can come around and overrule the manager, and the lower level would listen to the boss instead of the manager – because he knows where the paycheck is coming from. Even though the boss may not be right.

Hwa:
I think most people would say it's the ownership that gives the authority. In the old days, the emperor said that he owns the entire country. In many Chinese organizations, deep inside I think the boss thinks he owns everything – you are my people, my subjects.

Question:
If the natural form of legitimacy is ownership, that must make it almost impossible to create an alternative form of intermediate authority, correct?

Hwa:
That makes the life of a manager very difficult. That's right.

Hsien:
That is the case.

Hwa:
I think for many managers the criterion for making a decision is to ask how would the boss react to it. Would he overrule it? You have to avoid loss of face.

This very revealing conversation, with all its overtones of a somewhat stifling atmosphere for a really talented middle manager who does not belong to the family, provides a further reason for the obsession to control which fuels the constant upsurge of entrepreneurial talent. The reason is that anybody really good is just as much pushed out as tempted out.

The idea of the *eminence grise* standing behind all decision making is noted in Chinese as well as French. As *Hsu* noted, 'If you're talking about the Chinese family business, definitely ownership and managerial responsibility overlap – and the owner carries far more status than ever – he is the real boss (*Lau bak*).' This 'realness' is explained by a number of respondents, often with the brutal simplicity of *Huen*: 'Maybe they are aware that I sign the checks,' or of *Hsia*, 'We own the company, so we have the authority.'

The big boss also may have his surrogates, and the line between responsible involvement and meddling may become blurred.

Tin:

In a family business, the family and especially the older generation can't help interfering in decision making in the business.

There are no really viable alternatives in normal use. As *Heung* says, 'I don't think we have the concept of a public company.' 'Being a son of the founder is a logical mandate in Chinese society' (*Siu*), and will always bring compliance even if not always respect.

There are also protective devices which help to preserve such authority from being undermined, one of the most insidious being reminiscent of the old Chinese tradition of some other unfortunate taking your punishment for you.

Har:

My father taught me that in a situation where, say, the owner of the company is at loggerheads with the staff, then someone in management is to take the blame. It's not going to be him. There has to be a scapegoat, because the Chinese believe in a very untarnished reputation . . . It is important that he remains the god. In fact, his nickname was Jesus in Chinese, because he preaches a lot. He would take them out to a restaurant, or a cooked food stall, to take the air, to take food and also preach at them.

Such an Olympian perspective does not, however, prevent realism, and it is not unusual now for companies to offer shares to really crucial non-family executives, in partial acknowledgement of questions of legitimacy, and also questions of commitment. The hoped-for outcome is the kind of influence able to be exerted by, for instance.

Hap:

We had a big order and needed three floors of the factory to work from the third day of Chinese New Year instead of the seventh. The factory manager asked and 65 per cent agreed. It was not enough. So I wrote to everyone and the response was 98 per cent. And the three workers who could not, came to me in person to explain why.

The retention of power in this way, at the top of the organization, is of course only conducive to overall effectiveness in certain kinds of organization, and perhaps at certain stages of their development. The cost of autocracy, whether or not it is benevolent and responsible, is that fewer people are doing the organization's thinking for it. As *Ho* puts it:

As an owner, no one will challenge what you say. They accept. They do what you want. But in a way I don't find it very healthy, because they don't become responsible people. They just let you make the decisions.

Evidence for these forces at work is available from the Aston data about organization structuring given in Table 1.

Table 1 Main elements of organization structure described statistically using the Aston measures comparing Hong Kong Chinese companies and UK companies

		mean	*SD*	*range*
Role specialization	UK (n = 34)	26.2	13.8	0–62
	HK (n = 53)	18.5	14.4	0–69
Standardization	UK	74.4	20.4	30–117
	HK	59.8	23.0	11–111
Formalization	UK	19.8	9.9	4–41
	HK	19.7	10.0	1–41
Centralization	UK	80.9	13.9	57–116
	HK	109.9	15.2	70–139
Configuration	UK	29.7	17.2	6–72
(percentage nonworkflow)	HK	13.5	12.5	0–75
Size	UK	727	435	241–1,749
(no. of employees)	HK	512	494	50–2,600

Note: For details of Aston methodology, see Pugh and Hickson (1976)

The main elements of structure are described statistically in Table 1, using a comparison of Hong Kong and UK companies within the same size range. From this, it is clear that the degree of organizing which takes place in the Chinese case is less than in the British case.

Role specialization indicates the extent to which an organization has taken the trouble to specify precisely what people are to do. It is evident in such practical manifestations as organization charts, titles on people's office doors, job descriptions given to people to make clear what they do, whom they report to, whom they are responsible for. It is particularly an indication of the organization's wish to organize a concentration of skill on some aspect of its work, and to leave that concentration more or less undisturbed. In this regard, the UK score is 30 per cent higher than that of the Hong Kong companies, and is compelling support for an earlier description of Overseas Chinese organizational behavior by Silin (1976) in which he describes the allocation of managerial responsibilities as diffuse and shifting, with responsibilities kept deliberately open to change and reinterpretation by the chief executive.

In a sense, giving people clearly defined roles is a way of decentralizing authority. It makes it more difficult to impose new or alternative requirements on them and thus reduces the discretion of bosses to impose their will differently later. There appears to be resistance to placing such a limit on managerial discretion. Instead, the paternalist ethos, with its non-negotiable definition of authority residing in ownership, means that the boss can still intervene. The subordinate needs still to adjust. To exaggerate the point, there is no job definition to hide behind, or at least less of one. As *Tsai* succinctly put it, 'There is too much stupid loyalty to the boss.'

Standardization displays a similar pattern. The UK score is 20 per cent higher than the Hong Kong score and again indicates a lower level of 'organizing' for the Chinese. Here the question is one of the regularizing of procedures and again indicates the difference in the balance achieved in each case between the pull to use a neutral bureaucratic system and the pull to rely on a more personalistic over-ride. The latter with its capacity to fit with expectations about specific bonds of reciprocity, and also with the urge for centralized control, would appear to be preferred.

Formalization is the only dimension where scores are the same, but a closer examination of the detailed scales reveals that this is because the Chinese organizations are particularly strong on the use of paperwork to control the workflow process of the organization, stronger than the Western counterpart. This sense of urgent control of things such as production scheduling, and the keeping of detailed records related to the work process, are indicators of the intensity with which attention is brought to bear on the managing of the lifeblood of the organization – productive efficiency. Here is a glimpse of the hard-nosed pragmatism of the owner-manager, standing guard over the efficient use of his personal capital, concerned to a special degree with the real fundamentals of the business. Reflected here also is the problem of trust outside the inner circle, and the very basic tools needed to motivate a workforce whose loyalties inevitably lie with their own families to a degree unusual in many cultures (Redding and Wong, 1986).

The Chinese score for centralization is 27 per cent higher than for the UK, indicating that there are more decisions made at the top in the Chinese case. This accords well with expectations of a paternalist system, and with the fact that virtually all Chinese family businesses are headed by a dominant paterfamilias who becomes deeply immersed in the minutiae of daily operations.

The configuration score is an intriguing index of pragmatism. It measures the percentage of people in the organization who are not directly concerned with producing the output, what used to be called 'staff' as opposed to 'line'. In the UK case, the figure is 30 per cent, whereas in Hong Kong only 13.5 per cent. Some acknowledgement has to be made that the complexity of the UK environment, and the imposition of government regulations, etc., will demand the employment of more specialists to handle such matters, certainly compared to the non-interventionist, unregulated atmosphere of Hong Kong. Even so, the difference cannot all be accounted for thus, and it remains striking. One is tempted to see it as a sign that Overseas Chinese organizations contain no frills and carry no fat. If you are not helping directly to produce profit, there is little room for you.

Another influence reflected here is the suspicion of professionals. To have a personnel department, for instance, or a financial analyst, or work-study function, is to bring into the organization a possible challenge to managerial authority. Expert power can undermine the power of relationship or patronage, and this may also account for the apparent reluctance to build up the 'staff' side as opposed to the 'line'. There may thus be several reasons for this feature: an unwillingness to spend money on organizational 'frills', a suspicion about the threat of being undermined, a simple lack of examples to follow, or organizations being too small for such finesse. In reality, no doubt all features are present.

What has been said so far about paternalism will have imparted some of the flavor of Chinese leadership style, a style summarized in Silin's monograph on the topic as 'didactic' – retaining power by rationing information and assuming the superiority of the teacher. As this appears to be a core component of leadership behavior, it will bear some scrutiny before looking at other related aspects of style. In all this, it is inevitably necessary to acknowledge that individuals will interpret such norms via their interpersonal behavior in ways which display wide variation, and that not all will fit into this pattern. There is, however, a chorus of comment about it which suggests that across the respondents the interpretation of how power is best exercised does take on a certain coherence, and that this is not understandable unless the socio-cultural surroundings are taken into account.

It does not come as a surprise that decision making is not an open affair. If it were, many more people would feel the right to become involved and that, in turn, would threaten the hierarchy. In any case, there appears to be a consensus among subordinates that their duties do not include taking on the responsibility normally resting with owners. It is not the subordinate's job to make decisions, and his reaction would be a conflation of (a) he has no right to, without ownership, and (b) he is not paid to, so why should he?

The mixture of power with ownership, nobody else being responsible, and accustomed deference, allow the leader, in the Chinese tradition of the paterfamilias keeping his own council, to quietly ruminate over the issues until he arrives at a strategy by a process most conveniently, but not necessarily accurately, labelled 'intuition'. Such a label does insufficient justice to the accumulation of information and experience in the chief executive's head, and the clarity with which he normally perceives his goals.

But whether he commits himself openly to a public declaration of his intent, is another matter entirely. In fact, he is very unlikely to, for open communication is a taken for granted side effect of a democratic style, and these are not democratic organizations.

Hsu:

I think communication is a Western concept. It's never been a Chinese concept. We never talk about the skill of communicating. If you're smart, you learn to feel it. You learn to be very observant. You look at the face of your boss – the little actions that he does – and you pick up the hints, you know. You would be very bloody stupid if – until the boss told you, to do certain things. Although you know how to do it.

Question:

What's the function of that?

Hsu:

It's the art of ruling that I put you in a situation where you have to keep guessing what I'm thinking. So I put you in a role where you are always trying to please me . . . In the older Chinese style, quite often what is not said is more important than what is said – and they just deliberately leave little hints without being explicit – to test you. And this is said to be the highest art of leadership and management.

As the superior–subordinate relationship is a crucial building block of organization, it will bear further scrutiny:

Hwa:

In a Western system, people can argue and disagree – openly. If the decision is made by someone higher up, then you follow but you can make him know that you disagree. But with the Chinese then, it's different. You try to think what the top man is thinking and then you tend to agree. You say something that he would agree –

Hai:

Otherwise you lose your job –

Hsien:

Well, that's part of the Chinese culture as such – trying to avoid confrontation.

Hwa:

The culture itself is the submissiveness. The Chinese are so used to it generation after generation.

Given a style of decision making as introverted as this, and given the parallel willingness by subordinates to accept it, it is not surprising that a senior person would allow himself the indulgences of (a) unaccounted-for changes of direction, and (b) interference. Changing direction may, of course, be a strength in that it provides the organization with a sometimes remarkable level of flexibility – a feature which in many industries can be crucial to survival. It can also, however, lead to wasted resources and much lower-level frustration. The astute executive would not wish to be judged erratic and would control that impulse, but there is much evidence that such astuteness is not universal.

Interference, a version of the same possessiveness over strategy, and an index of the inhibitions over delegation which are equally a part of the leadership style, is also commonly reported. As *Hu* confesses,

I have a lot of trust in my own staff. I believe they will not do anything bad which brings harm to the company. But I do not trust them well enough to just let go, and let them run the business, or run departments in the business. I still want to interfere in most of the decision making.

This is not to say that a more democratic style is not seen as an ideal. It undoubtedly is at the level of 'I would *like* to be able to do it that way.' There are also rising subordinate expectations about participation, as better educational standards and exposure to alternative societal norms make such notions seductive. But old habits die hard and if the majority of subordinates are unwilling to accept the responsibility which goes with full participation, there will be an automatic brake applied to the process of transformation. That they are so unwilling is a consistent and long-standing lament in multinational corporations operating in Asia where this particular clash of expectations is a permanent battleground.

Further down in the Chinese family organization, at the level of middle management and first-line supervision, leadership style tends to reflect the combination of personalism and hierarchy which typifies the whole. Although this was not a central concern in a study of chief executives' beliefs, a number of reflections on it came to the surface when discussing Chinese leadership behavior.

It has been noted a number of times that avoidance of confrontation is a normal part of the Chinese make-up, as indeed it is for most collectivist cultures. It has also been noted that leadership style would tend to be more autocratic than participative, although such autocracy may be benevolently exercised. The style of decision making would lead to a distancing between the ranks, and this would be exacerbated by Confucian deference to superiors and emotional aloofness with those outside the personalistic circles of family or clique. Power, moreover, only really derives from ownership.

These features would predispose the supervisory system to certain weaknesses, and may explain further why 'interference' is felt to be necessary by chief executives. The weaknesses are likely to surround the combined difficulties that (a) ownership of the company's problems cannot easily be transferred outside family membership, as information about problems is likely to be closely guarded and real trust limited and (b) supervisors are likely to replicate on a smaller scale the paternalism and personalism in which they are embedded. This latter feature may well result in priority being given to keeping relations smooth rather than to disciplined pursuit of company goals, a softening of emphasis which will be reinforced by the wish to avoid disciplinary confrontations. Such inhibitions were a focus of occasional chagrin, as in *Hsieh*'s outburst about the comparison of supervisory quality between the Western-managed Star Ferry Co. and the Chinese-managed Hong Kong and Yau Ma Tei Ferry Co., the latter being regularly complained about for a lack of cleanliness, and inefficiency, and the former the opposite.

The special feature of Chinese 'face' also introduces barriers which occasionally inhibit supervisory involvement, as association with certain tasks is a matter for finely tuned demarcations. The idea of rolling up your sleeves and pitching in with the boys on the shop floor is not looked upon favorably, and perhaps understandably so when authority beyond the family itself is only delicately maintained and easily undermined. It is protected by a certain hauteur and aloofness which can become dysfunctional.

Im:

We had recent production problems because the supervisors did not check directly on site where problems arose. They felt embarrassed to work with their subordinates on the site. They see themselves too highly.

Constantly referred to as 'old style', this form of organization is clearly understood for its weaknesses. Chinese owner-managers know that their organizations are inhibited. They see examples of major successes by, for instance, Mr Li Ka Shing, Mr Fung King Hey, Mr Liem Sioe Liong, Mr William Suryadjaya, and they know that one of the elements in those successes is coming to terms with the delegation of trust. In such discussions, however, the exceptional nature of that capacity to trust is always acknowledged. They know their weakness but are seemingly unable in most cases to surmount it. Centralized decision making is easier to manage, and democracy very trying for those in power. As long as the workforce is both dependent and conformist, there is little incentive in most industries to change, and companies are likely to continue with a style which, while being culturally adapted, also eventually chokes the organization's long-term growth. Deference to 'modern' management methods and espousing of the notion of delegation may remain matters for lip service in the majority of cases.

The feature of Overseas Chinese organizations identified as 'personalism' makes up a third element in the set of subsidiary features within the overall paternalistic corporate culture. It means that personal relationships and feelings about other people are likely to come before more objectively defined concerns such as organizational efficiency, or neutral assessment of abilities. It turns the organization into a world where who you know is more important than, or at least as important as, what you know.

Personalism lies on a continuum with extremes of favoritism at one end and cold rationality at the other. Clearly at each end, there are dangers for any organization. Favoritism will destroy it in time, and cold rationality will equally drive away most people in normal circumstances. The kind of personalism in question is not of the extreme kind, but it certainly veers towards that end of the continuum rather than the other.

It has been argued earlier that the Chinese person carries his relationships round as part of his persona. Social needs are comparatively more significant than in the Western case. Friendship is an especially important item of currency. Also authority is based largely in the exchange of balancing obligations, and these are transacted through subtle processes which are at once interpersonal and highly personal.

It is almost impossible to find any chief executive anywhere in the world who would not make some statement equivalent to, 'What this company is really all about is people.' The experienced boss will inevitably acknowledge that he can do nothing without others. Where this human universal is taken to a more extreme point by the Chinese is in allowing it to displace more neutral means of coordinating effort, such as formal control systems. In saying this, however, it should be noted that more formal control systems may be redundant (and therefore an unjustifiable cost) in a society where strong hierarchical discipline is imported into the organization in the heads of its members. People will tend to do as they are told, they will not answer back, they do not need to be controlled to the same extent as in many other cultures. Qualities of diligence and what Kahn (1979) called 'seriousness about tasks and responsibilities' are inbred, and are available as a feature of the majority of personnel. Given this feature, the managerial job is to create an atmosphere in which work may be directed towards organizational purposes. In the intensely social world of Chinese people, this is largely done by social means.

This is patently not how the textbooks say it should be done, and there is therefore a degree of reluctance in acknowledging it, but it occasionally comes to the surface in statements which appear like the tip of an iceberg.

Hwa:

People are more loyal to people than to an organization. I like people to be loyal to me. People down below should be loyal to the superior rather than to the firm itself.

Hon:

A Westernized company will be run with a very organized manner, will move people as in chess – it doesn't matter who is the man.

For many chief executives, as *Hap* observes, 'I'm people-oriented. Making money is not enough for me.' Or,

Har:

I don't know why I've got a love for it and a lot of loyalty whenever I work. This firm I've already worked for, for fifteen years. I have seen it grow from small and become a big company and now growing bigger and took over a lot of subsidiaries. I don't know but I think if I work for myself, I can earn maybe four times more than my salary. But I've got the love of the company and also the joy of our colleagues with me.

Such people orientation, while not being universal in the world of the entrepreneur in any country, is perhaps unusual in the Chinese case for the inhibitions it may bring with it, especially over matters of discipline. In this the Chinese abhorrence of confrontation, with all its overtones of incivility or being uncivilized, comes to the fore:

Huen:

In my organization, we have many different performances, but I would still be reluctant to fire the one who is ineffective. I would try to keep him and maybe try to help him improve. I just cannot bear to fire people. I don't think we have ever fired anyone in the company, except one accountant who was cheating.

Huan:

We decided to fire a production manager in the San Po Kong factory and my partner was trembling. He simply could not do it because he was so bound up with this man.

Some of the atmosphere of the organization run in this way is captured in *Hu*'s description of his father's way of working as an owner:

He owned the largest Chinese-operated facility in Hong Kong. He would report to work at about seven, and he would talk to all the workers; the painters, the mechanics; he would stand next to the panel beaters and talk and offer cigarettes to them. He did not worry about finance. Human relationship was important.

Question:
When you say he wouldn't worry about the finance, he would still presumably be fairly good at finance?

Hu:
He left it to a trusted accountant. He had some very simple form of monitoring. All the rest of his time was spent on building up the relationships.

When personalism radiates to and from the chief executive in this way, it may well be a positive force, in that it is likely to extend his influence into the body of the organization and stamp it with his vision. If, on the other hand, one examines personalism at lower levels in the hierarchy, one begins to see in it potentially divisive features. These arise because of the taking of positions on personal grounds, and the forming of factions and cliques, something for which Chinese social life is notorious.

Cliques can form on a number of bases, and examples would be, say, a Chiu Chow or other regional group within an organization, or a group doing the same work such as the drivers, or the messengers. Cliques can also develop between organizations, for instance that of secretaries coming from one foreign city, or members of one family playing the stockmarket jointly but operating from individual bases in large company corporate planning departments. The point about such hidden networks is that they are capable of placing their own interests above those of their organization, and this can become damaging if undetected or unchecked.

Hui:
I joined a firm of professionals but was not satisfied with the structure of this firm because it was so loose. It was very Chinese style. The interpreters had a firm grip.

When there is competition between cliques, then dissension begins to destroy the cooperative framework on which day-to-day operations depend. The chief executive finds himself lobbied by one group against the others.

Har:
And another thing is the camps . . . They've got different camps. Things are fed back to the boss, and he can learn who's been doing this. And things like that. I think this kind of situation even makes it worse. Maybe their whole philosophy [i.e. bosses guilty of encouraging this] is they think, you know, people come to see you and talking about 'This thing, he's not doing it right.' He can appreciate this, it's right, that's why you create the camps. Modern bosses, Chinese bosses, they've got the foreign education. They can see things better.

If cliques of this nature are tolerated on the grounds that 'divide and rule' will loosen up the channels of information flow to the boss as one group watches

Figure 1 Degrees of formal organization in different managerial functions

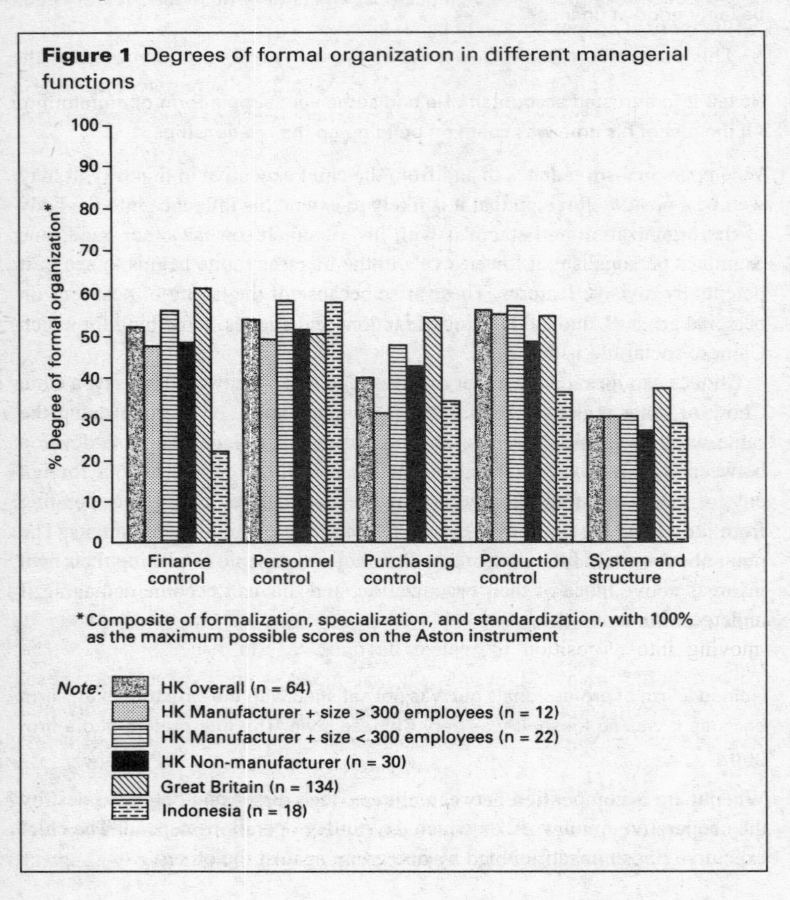

*Composite of formalization, specialization, and standardization, with 100% as the maximum possible scores on the Aston instrument

another, there is one other clique which has formal approval and which should be noted. This is the in-plant subcontracting group. Common in the Chinese manufacturing context is the 'gang leader' who brings in his own people and takes responsibility for a part of the manufacturing process. His group may be ten or twelve people and, when observed on the factory floor, they look just like other workers. They do not, however, have a direct authority relationship with the factory owner. This is an indication of the common preference in Overseas Chinese organizations to generate predictable behavior by trusting people (i.e. the gang leader), rather than adding systematic control procedures. Again this goes back to the endemic problem of limited trust, both a cause and a consequence of the reliance on personal bonds of obligation, without which willingness to cooperate cannot be assumed.

This discussion of the Chinese family business has been conducted at the level of the general principles likely to permeate the corporate culture of a typical company of this type. In simple terms, it has examined what patrimonialism means in a present-day organization.

The Significance of the Overseas Chinese

The central purpose of this section is to put the Overseas Chinese on the map. They have for too long been acknowledged as intriguing, seen as possibly powerful, but never really been understood outside their own sphere. Even inside their own sphere, remarkably little scholarship has addressed the question of their economic life. And yet they are clearly significant. As actors on the world scene they cannot be ignored.

In a sense, they are also moving inexorably towards center-stage. At first, this drift towards the spotlight was because of their dominant influence in the little dragons of East Asia, only Korea in that set being non-Chinese. More recently, their significance has taken on a new aspect and that has emerged because the possibility has dawned that China might finally be moving into a position to realize its quite awe-inspiring potential. That capacity to inspire awe, however, when applied to something so hypothetical, must be seen in context. It may well have been a false dawn. China's potential may always be just that. The performance may never be delivered. If it ever is, it is more than likely that the Overseas Chinese will have had a great deal to do with it. Their role may be only grudgingly acknowledged, but China has no more significant set of catalysts waiting to be added to its mixture of material and human resources, land, ideologies, and ambitions.

To consider more carefully the significance of the Overseas Chinese, requires some breakdown of the interests for which such significance finds meaning. The world of Western business could be argued to be one of these, as it has a powerful and little understood competitor invading its traditional preserves at a time when it is still bewildered by, and licking its wounds from, the onslaughts of Japan. China is clearly another, as it would appear to have much to learn from its adventurous and experienced compatriots. In a quite different sense, the world of those thinking about the nature of organizations, the teachers of management theory, and the practitioners of consultancy might also be expected to ponder carefully the importance of a powerful form of organization playing by rules not found in the textbooks and not found either in the literature on that other compelling Asian phenomenon, Japanese management; something in fact a very long way removed from Japanese management in the way it works.

Finally, and also at the level of concepts prior to practice, the study of economic development, already now so concerned with re-adjusting to the unarguable realities of the last thirty years in East Asia, needs to come to terms with the particularly Chinese cultural component of the miracle of the little dragons.

There are then four constituencies where implications may be held to be important: the world of Western business, China, the world of organization and management theory, and the world of those trying to understand the economic development and modernization of societies.

The Overseas Chinese and Western Business

Western businessmen who might have on their agendas questions relating to Overseas Chinese are those who might be doing business against them as competitors, such as an American shirt manufacturer, or those who might be working in collaboration with them, such as an international distributor of brand-name toys. Viewing them as competitors or collaborators naturally provides very different perspectives, as fundamental organizational characteristics come into the account as weaknesses to be exploited or strengths to be built on.

The Overseas Chinese as competitors bring to the arena a number of specific advantages, all of which are related to production efficiency, and one major disadvantage which is related to marketing.

When observing the range of manufactured goods now extensively available in Western markets, and originating in areas of Overseas Chinese dominance, their common denominator is price advantage. For price to be an effective advantage, certain minimum quality standards must also be adhered to, and in consequence it is normal for the items to be able to 'perform', to have the same functions as their competitors. They may lack the glamor, the brand identity of the functionally equivalent Western-derived item, but Overseas Chinese strategy has normally been to say, in effect, to the customers, 'we do the same basic job without the frills at less cost'. Leaving aside, for the moment, the question of the Overseas Chinese manufacturing of Western brand-name goods (such as the Christian Dior shirt made in Hong Kong which I wear as I write), and concentrating on items sold in Western stores carrying a little-known brand name, their market penetration is based on perceived value for money. This in turn rests on a low landed price, and that in turn on a low factory production cost, and efficient long-range transport.

The sources of the productive efficiency lie only partly in the kinds of technology used. They lie in the workforce's quality of diligence, in the intensity of managerial effort devoted to the firm in the eventual pursuit of the family fortune, in the financial shrewdness and the efficient use of money, in the flexibilities possible within a network of companies allied by ties of mutual obligation and shifting easily to match market needs. There is much borrowing, and there is careful selection of areas of focus. Research and development is borrowed; design is borrowed; in a sense, the process of marketing is borrowed, or at least linked to in ways which reduce the Chinese need for deep involvement. Concentration is on the core operations of producing the goods, areas where the balance of risk against value added can be made very favorable, given long production runs and the safety of making to order.

Production ability, then, is a strength. Marketing, as already hinted, is a weakness. That is, if one sees the firm through Western eyes. The most noticeable characteristic of Overseas Chinese companies is their apparent reticence to enter the world of mass marketing of brand-name goods. In reality, this may be less a reticence than a result of the size limitations of the family business form and the consequent restriction of the range of activities which can be managed inside its boundaries. Once there are executives in other continents, analysing consumer needs and concerned to influence policy, once an international brand name is created which requires large-scale coordination of research, production, quality control, distribution, marketing techniques, public relations, then the strains on a core group, which insists on centralized decision making, are immense. The Chinese appear to sense these hazards and avoid them. They appear to know that they cannot thrive in such endeavors like the Japanese do.

Marketing, of course, takes place, but it is collaborative and it is in this field that possibilities exist for fruitful cooperation with Western firms. Given the Chinese sense of wishing to work within their own restricted organizational boundaries, this brings to a cooperative venture two benefits: firstly, a Chinese partner does actually need the marketing or design services which a Western company can offer as a bridge to Western markets; secondly, the Chinese partner is not likely to be harboring ambitions about extending its activities forward or backward into the areas which the Western firm sees as its own preserve. Partnerships of this kind can be genuinely beneficial to both sides and can become long lasting and stable. In the Japanese case, by contrast, the Western firm is often dealing with a monolithic corporation well able and anxious to take over the full set of operations in the Westerner's traditional preserve; collaboration in those circumstances is inevitably more circumspect.

Creating successful collaborations between Western firms and Overseas Chinese firms requires the acknowledgement of one important caveat. This is that a mismatch may easily occur if the Western firm is highly bureaucratized, a normal feature of any large organization. This introduces requirements for systematic behavior and neutral rationality which the Chinese firm is commonly unable to deliver. Such collaborations are rarely stable unless the relations between the firms are genuinely hands-off, a feature only attainable in certain industries. What appears to be more effective is the connection between firms where the Western half of the link is a firm with an understanding of, acceptance of, or sympathy for, the kind of personalism and informal structure used quite appropriately and normally efficiently by the Chinese firm. Such Western firms tend to be small and may also be family dominated, or have a personalistic, informal culture.

Thus the Overseas Chinese can and do link their economic activities efficiently and effectively into the Western economic system. They carry out the manufacturing component of a longer and more elaborate total system linking ideas to customers. This is also extendable into service fields such as typesetting, programming, transport, and communications. They can also deliver directly into Western markets goods which can satisfy the needs of customers emerging in the base layer of the mass consumption markets of prospering economies.

Western firms looking at Asia must also come to terms with the fact that on their own 'home' territory of East and Southeast Asia, the Overseas Chinese in business are a force to be reckoned with. Doing business in that region, particularly if it means marketing into the region, but very often also if it means manufacturing or commodity extraction, is a matter of doing business with the traditional Chinese 'middlemen' whose grip has grown increasingly strong. Finding a local distributor, an after-sales service agency, a transport company, an intermediate processor, an insurance agent, an accounting firm, an advertising agency, a warehousing company; all these searches will lead regularly to the Overseas Chinese sector. Similarly, the filling of executive or professional positions, and the hiring of professional services, will lead an outside company again to the diligent Chinese who have managed their education with the zeal necessary to place them in large numbers in such categories.

Such East–West linkages are normally fruitful, mutually respectful, and stable, but there is one over-riding issue which comes to affect the otherwise apparently placid scene, and that is the deep-seated desire of most competent Chinese to own their own company. This will regularly cause the employment bond to be broken, as a person leaves to set up on his own, and may introduce rivalry as the Westerner sees, in his terms, a cuckoo leaving the nest. This does not, of course, affect all cases, but it is sufficiently prevalent to cause a degree of wariness to enter into the Westerner's calculations as his or his firm's experience accumulates.

If a large Western corporation employs Chinese executives in the region, some other trade-offs may be anticipated in addition to the risk of being an entrepreneur's training ground. These stem largely from contrasts in behavioral norms and expectations, and it is not difficult to sustain the view that the contrasts have cultural origins. The point commonly at issue is the taking of responsibility on behalf of the organization, a perceived Chinese weakness which is a source of regular lament by senior executives of Western companies. There are, of course, many exceptions, but the comments, and presumably the reasons for them, remain widespread.

To understand this contrast in perceptions, it is necessary to enter into the mental world of the aspiring executive brought up in Overseas Chinese culture but now working in a non-Chinese multinational, typically the child or grandchild of immigrants, educated towards a career, brought up in an atmosphere of Confucian order, deference, and vertical authority, disciplined, hard working, and dedicated to upward mobility. He or she enters the multinational, sometimes after experience in a Chinese company, or if not, then with expectations, especially about the nature of authority, which have created a predisposition to understand paternalism as the normal mode of handling power.

Such a person looks upwards for guidelines and is prepared to accept and follow them. There are understandings that more senior people in the hierarchy will hold responsibility and will expect an exchange of obedience upwards for a degree of protection downwards. It is a context in which initiative from below is something of a deviation. Expectations are high about the boss doing his job by giving orders.

With this set of ideas about how the core process of organizing should be conducted, the Overseas Chinese individual enters a non-Chinese organization which is publicly owned, and where managers are professional administrators on behalf of a system which, while it may have developed a corporate culture and an organizational soul, does not normally have in it the kind of symbols around which the Chinese organizational soul is constructed, namely its owners. Nor does it have a counter-attraction to the Chinese person's family as a source of psychological belonging. Unlike many Chinese companies, the multinational is rarely familistic despite attempts often to be so; its countervailing pull is inadequate to win the battle of divided loyalties going on in the heads of many of its local members. In the end, their own families, and whatever best serves the fortunes of those families, will determine their behavior. This opposing pull against the organization's attractions has a dampening effect on loyalty, and the creation of the 'organization man', so much a part of the Western and even more so the Japanese tradition of creating cooperative systems, is very much more difficult when an alternative organization of family dominates consciousness.

The Overseas Chinese and China

Perhaps the most significant thing to be understood about China today is that it still displays most of the elements of a pre-modern form of society. It is still in essence patrimonial. This is somewhat similar to saying, of a Western society, that it is still feudal. It does not contain the feudal structures typical of past European societies in which ties of allegiance to a local land-owning aristocracy were the basis for stabilizing order and providing security. Landowners in traditional China were normally not motivated by ideals of *noblesse oblige*, nor were they permanently ennobled by family to perpetuate their ascendancy. Instead, authority resided in the state via the mandarinate which became the focus of an alternative and unusual form of what could still be argued today to be state patrimonialism. Dependence on aristocratic protection and favor of the kind found in Europe was instead represented in China by dependence on the favor of personified officialdom, and this is still the key to fostering any important activity in China today. Without using the networks of *guanxi*, nothing significant can happen. The communist party has replaced the mandarinate and replicates its functioning, in that (a) it represents central authority, (b) it extends its influence into all areas of Chinese life, (c) its power derives from an ideology which although enshrined in a literature can nevertheless only be legitimate when interpreted by the power holders, (d) it has state military backing, (e) its source of influence at the center is a specific person with an emperor-like role, a change of person bringing a potentially massive change in ideology.

Stemming from such a structure, in which official favor is a requirement for most significant activities, from giving birth to trying to get a pay rise, from buying a van to locating a factory, it is not surprising that the principal dilemma in the background of any attempt to improve economic activities in China is the problem of fostering decentralized decision making. Given the switches of ideology possible when central authority is so personalized, and given the ravages of the red guards in the cultural revolution, or the PLA in Tiananmen Square, it is not surprising either that the problem of decentralizing authority is compounded by a large element of fear, or at least anxiety. In a society which can kill, maim, or exile to an equivalent of the saltmines, millions of its *own* people, people learn to watch their backs. Risks are not taken. Being responsible for something has, in the past, not done many of their friends and relatives any good at all, and they may be next in some uncertain future.

To break down this barrier is proving very difficult. It requires some move away from the historical Chinese pattern of central control towards something never before experienced in the state of China, namely real decentralization of authority. Given the massive complexity and sheer size of China, the danger of things getting out of control is severe, and always has been. Attempts in this direction have consequently only been tentative and partial.

Two further and related requisites exist which will have the effect of barriers if they are not available. They are developed property rights, and bureaucratic order.

When a system of property rights has become elaborated and stable, it has commonly been given much of the credit for a society's capacity to mobilize motivation to perform in the economic sphere. The psychology is simple. A person who can secure his prosperity, and can keep the fruits of his labors, will try harder. The development of property rights in China is still at a very rudimentary stage, and although movement to improve is discernible, the lack of the second element, bureaucratic order, is acting as a brake on progress.

To say that China lacks bureaucratic order when a claim could be made that China invented the classic government bureaucracy is a reflection both on the decline of government quality in the last two centuries, and also the highly limited sphere within which the mandarin bureaucracy operated. What is meant here by bureaucratic order is a set of organizing principles and their resulting institutions which provide the average individual with certain predictable frameworks. In a crude sense, a person knows where he or she stands, and can make decisions accordingly. The ability of people to operate within areas of discretion such as choosing where to live, what work to do, what prices are appropriate, can only take place on a large scale if other areas of life come under some form of accepted order: where a deal is a deal to be relied upon; where what is legal or illegal is clearly understood and respected by all; where the allocation of scarce resources is handled openly according to agreed principles; where seniority in terms of power is accorded to those judged worthy of exercising it; where systems of redress are open. For most societies which have achieved this condition, the major institution on which the structure rests is law, and the most effective source of its maintenance and protection is an incorrupt civil administration, preferably dedicated to the public good.

In the case of China, the traditional and still prevalent means of attempting to establish order is to rely upon a plethora of authority figures imbued with an ideology, each of whom has the power to resolve a dispute. Its resolution becomes a matter for that individual's judgement, and the framework within which such judgements are arrived at, although well intentioned, is still nebulous. There is no parallel authority enshrined in codified or precedent-based definitions. There is little redress. Dependence on the superior individual is still very high indeed, for most crucial issues. Hence the patrimonial state. Hence also the extreme dependence of the average individual on authority figures, and hence also the obsession with cultivating connections, the national pastime of *guanxi*.

It is in this context that the position of the potential entrepreneur may be viewed, and it is a position of extreme disadvantage compared to that of his cousins in Hong Kong, Taiwan, Singapore, or most of ASEAN. The surrounding order in which he attempts to make decisions is still highly contingent on 'currying favor'. The identity he can have with ensuing rewards is still much looser than it could be. Risks are higher than they might be, rewards are lower.

Seeing the two centuries old question of comparatively slow development in China in this light, in other words from the perspective of power relations and social order, reaches down to the fundamentals of the problem but takes no account of more tangible aspects lying nearer the surface. These must be considered briefly.

The Overseas Chinese make up one of the world's most effective economic cultures. Always seemingly capable of being successful middlemen, they have blossomed in the last thirty years, within certain political and economic circumstances, to transcend dramatically the restrictions of that earlier role. The organizational combinations made possible in the conducive climates where they flourish allow them to create economic systems of world significance. It is necessary to note how this is done and to point out the contrasts in China. In saying this, acknowledgement must at the same time be given to the essence of China's difficulties which is that, compared to most states, and certainly compared to all those inhabited by the Nanyang Chinese, the sheer scale of China, and the consequent difficulties of managing and controlling its life, makes its governance more challenging than for any other political body. One should never forget the weight of a fifth of the world's population.

Many of the key components of the state superstructures in East Asia imply a political philosophy supportive of capitalism and thus present a substantial ideological challenge to China but they are nevertheless considered here for what they are worth as key determinants of progress and leaving aside their political implications. Their common denominators are *laissez-faire*, export-oriented capitalism, based on stable, absolutist but decentralized government, using systems in tune with the specific cultural tendencies towards vertical order, contingent cooperation, and pragmatic motivation.

Laissez-faire capitalism is the precise opposite to the communism which so permeates Chinese economic life. Despite a clear move towards a softer version of the creed, and despite the replacement of references to communism by the somewhat more flexible socialism, still the demands of a totalitarian state conspire to undermine the three components of this general category, namely (a) a free enterprise environment, (b) developed property rights, and (c) efficient transaction costs.

An environment for free enterprise has been recently visible in China in family-based agriculture and in small-scale trading. The reforms of the 1980s have indicated both the ease with which this tendency comes to the surface, and more pointedly the completeness with which it may be blocked out by a regime obsessed with control. It can only be said at present, however, to be in a very fragile condition, and much else will be needed in the way of support and reassurance if a robust environment for enterprise is ever to emerge.

Property rights are a function of law, and particularly in the field of commercial law, China's condition can only be judged as primitive. Again the drift towards more predictable frameworks is visible, but it is tentative and slow.

The efficiency of transaction costs achieved by the Overseas Chinese is largely based on the use of interpersonal trust bonds as replacements for more formal contracts. These bonds, however, only work well between people who can genuinely control events under their discretion, in other words, people who have the power to keep promises. In the totalitarian state by contrast, the layers of overlapping authority are such as to reduce the average person's discretion substantially. He has to consult more people, and his commitments are far less reliable. Transaction costs are thus swollen by the need to negotiate a labyrinth of entanglements and clear a morass of official channels.

Entirely predictably it may thus be seen that China is not fertile ground for *laissez-faire* capitalism, and that despite the occasional surfacing of a will to change, the obstacles are deep-rooted, ideological, and require many years of consistent adjustment in one direction.

Export orientation is a clear feature of China's present industrial strategy, and most outsiders going into joint ventures are encouraged to produce for export. There is, however, a wide gap between wanting to export and knowing how to do so effectively. The latter requires a willingness and capacity to understand the foreign customer, something which the isolation of China, the disparity in living standards between it and its markets, and the persistence of a tribute mentality, have done nothing to foster.

The availability of capital, although often helped by inputs from foreign sources, must, in a healthy economy, eventually rest on internally generated surplus. Assuming the eventual growth of such a surplus, this in turn will only work for development if there are mechanisms for channelling it. Assuming property rights, such mechanisms are typified by the highly developed Japanese and American linkages between the citizen's savings and the stockmarket. Without such channels, the surplus will continue to flow into the traditional Chinese *culs-de-sac* of owning gold or property.

The question of the intensive use of labor as it applies to China evokes the old dilemma of the high-level equilibrium trap: the intensive use of labor is inhibited by the sheer volume of labor available, and compounded by the poverty of capital investment in labor-efficient productive systems. Moreover, progression towards a highly paid and productive labor force must rest on a free labor market, free that is from the viewpoint of both employee and employer, a feature only emerging recently, partially, and experimentally in China.

When considering the institutions of government, under the overall requirement that administration be stable and (at least in Asia) can apparently also be 'absolutist', certain subtle differences emerge between the case of China and those of its prosperous neighbors. There is a deceptive stability to the government of China which conceals the fact that it is fundamentally inconstant. Dependence on highly personalized political strategies, such as Maoism, Dengism, anti 'gang of four'-ism, bourgeois liberalization, anti-bourgeois liberalization, leave the country to swing, occasionally literally violently, from one side to the other, each strategy emerging as an unpredictable outcome of the play of individual power politics from which the leaders emerge. Stability is thus an illusion, and although absolutism abounds, of itself it is inadequate to make the kind of business-like government, lean, disciplined, flexible, strong but fundamentally benevolent, under which the Chinese flourish overseas.

The inability to decentralize decisions has been remarked upon earlier as possibly China's most crucial weakness, representing as it does so much else in the way of mistrust and potential disorder.

The subtle influence of the 'need to strive', noted by so many as a contributor to the success of the little dragons, finds little in the way of an echo in China. Very few people there are aware of how relatively backward the country is, even fewer have personal knowledge of conditions elsewhere, and even if they did, mobilization of the will to improve which is feasible in a small country, such as Taiwan, Singapore, South Korea, is immensely difficult over the huge scale of China. Moreover, the all-embracing support of the communist state, reducing all to more or less equal poverty and removing most incentives to strive, is the least appropriate context in which to try and replicate the competitive spirit of the overseas compatriots, honed as it has been on the twin challenges of deprivation and opportunity.

It has been observed that the cultural elements were more deep-rooted than the rest and by nature largely immutable. If that be the case, then the communist state might be argued to have produced a temporary distortion in their manifestation but not to have altered them radically. The unit of cooperation, the most natural collectivity, remains the family, and it would appear to be returning to its traditional centripetal role, as communes are dismantled, as the success of family-based agriculture provides vindication, and as small production and trading units proliferate again.

Cooperation through personalistic networking appears not to have changed at all in structure or process, but simply in the identifying of appropriate members. *Guanxi* is as essential as it ever was.

Vertical order is still visible in the patrimonialism of China, and the old Confucian order uniting relatives lies not far below the manifest surface.

Deep-seated cultural features remain, and are available as contributors to the overall mixture. Their potency remains, however, dependent on what they are mixed with, and this is nowhere more evident than in the cases of the work ethic and entrepreneurship. Both of these crucial ingredients lie dormant until incentives emerge to bring them to active life. Such incentives lie in the economic and political domains, in such features as property rights, free markets, and decentralized decisions. For these combinations to begin working, China has still a very long road to travel.

References

Kahn, Herman, *World Economic Development: 1979 and Beyond*, London: Croom Helm, 1979.

Pugh, D. S. and D. J. Hickson, *Organizational Structure in its Context*, Farnborough: Saxon House, 1976.

Redding, S. G. and G. Y. Y. Wong, *The Psychology of Chinese Organizational Behaviour*, in M. H. Bond (ed.), *The Psychology of the Chinese People*, Oxford: Oxford University Press, 1986.

Silin, R. H., *Leadership and Values: The Organization of Large-Scale Taiwanese Enterprises*, Cambridge, MA: Harvard University Press, 1976.

Japan

Japanese Management – a Sun Rising in the West?

Peter B. Smith and Jyuji Misumi

Chapter 4, pp. 117–57 in Cary L. Cooper and Ivan T. Robertson (eds.), *Key Reviews in Managerial Psychology: Concepts and Research for Practice* (Chichester: John Wiley & Sons, 1994)

Japanese management methods have evoked steadily increasing interest in the West over the past few decades. The changing quality of that interest is reflected in the contrast between Abegglen's (1958) classic observations of Japanese factories, and the same author's more recent discussion of the evolving *kaisha* or Japanese corporation (Abegglen and Stalk, 1984). During this period Western commentators have moved from an interest in a phenomenon seen as strange and unusual, to a realization that the consequences of Japanese management are, and increasingly will be, felt throughout the world. There has also been a wide divergence of views as to whether the essence of Japanese management lies in its structures or within the processes or styles with which those structures are operated. In this chapter we shall take the view that structure and process are yin and yang – that we shall understand little about organizational behaviour if we do not take account of both structures and processes. Nonaka and Johansson (1985) lament the lack of emphasis upon 'hard' as well as 'soft' aspects of management in earlier reviews, and we aim to heed their advice. With passing time, increasing numbers of Japanese researchers are publishing their work in English as well as in Japanese, and a further aim is to ensure that their work is as fully represented here as is that authored by non-Japanese. Finally, we aim to highlight and consider more fully, in the concluding section, areas where the research findings do not support the conventionally accepted view as to the nature of Japanese management.

Research methods have also evolved over time with the early preponderance of case studies giving way to more systematic surveys and studies using comparative measures collected in several countries. The literature has grown to the point where this review cannot hope to be comprehensive within the space available. Emphasis will be given to studies focusing upon human resource management, while studies of methods of production, marketing, and research will only be considered where their implications for human resource management are evident.

Our review will first consider the various characterizations of Japanese management which have been advanced and how well founded they may be. Later sections will consider the evidence as to whether Japanese management is changing over time and what happens when Japanese plants open in other parts of the world. Finally, we shall consider whether the current successes of Japanese management hold lessons for us all or whether we must be content with some form of cultural relativism.

The Classical Descriptions of Japanese Management

Keys and Miller (1984) propose that the distinctive qualities of Japanese management may be summarized under three heads: long-term planning, lifetime employment, and collective responsibility. Hatvany and Pucik (1981) distinguish the development of an internal labour market, definition of a unique company philosophy and identity, and intensive socialization of organizational participants. We prefer to use four, although the boundaries between the elements in such classifications are diffuse. These will be termed *time perspective*, *collective orientation*, *seniority system*, and *influence processes*. In each of these areas one may discern organizational structures, policies, and procedures which are said to be distinctive.

Time Perspective

Abegglen and Stalk (1984) propose that the strategy of the Japanese *kaisha* is to assure its long-term survival through the preservation of market share and growth in size, rather than the goals more strongly favoured by Western firms such as short-term profitability and high share values. A recently completed large-scale survey comparing Japanese, US, and European firms supports this view (Nonaka and Okumura, 1984; Kagono, Nonaka, Sakakibara, and Okumura, 1985). Responses were received from a general sample of firms in manufacturing and mining. The highest priority stated by the 277 US and 50 European firms responding was return on investment, whereas the 291 Japanese firms ranked increased market share more highly. Abegglen and Stalk suggest that the ability of the *kaisha* to take a longer-term view has been partly due to the absence of a substantial threat of takeover bids. However, they make clear that this absence should be considered as much a symptom as a cause of Japanese industry's long-term perspective. If the preoccupation of Japanese management is with planning a long-term strategy which ensures the survival of the firm's organization, issues such as disposal of resources which are underutilized or the acquisition of ailing organizations are a low priority. More important is the recruitment of a loyal and skilled workforce, investment in long-term research, and the identification of distinctive markets. The data of Kagono *et al.* (1985) again support these assertions. The Japanese firms in their sample reported spending proportionately more on research into new technologies and development of new products, whereas American firms put more into improving and updating existing products. Nonaka and Johansson (1985) see extensive information search more generally as a key attribute of Japanese organizational behaviour. By continual scanning of the environment a capacity is developed to anticipate long-term developments. Information search is not simply greater, but also involves the seeking out of different types of information. For instance, Johansson and Nonaka (1987) describe Japanese scepticism of Western market research and preference for talking to retailers and observing customers instead.

An emphasis upon long-term planning is also evident within the production technologies first popularized within Japan. Examples are the *kanban* and other just-in-time procedures which have accomplished such enormous cost savings within the automobile and electronics industries (Schonberger, 1982; McMillan, 1985). These instances, like many other recent advances in production management, have benefited from the development of increasingly sophisticated computers. As such techniques have become widely known, they have proved increasingly attractive to managements of Western firms. It remains to be seen in what way Western firms will implement just-in-time procedures. The time may come when they will not be thought of as distinctive to Japanese management.

Another aspect of time perspective which has been widely commented upon is the system of lifetime employment. By assuring employees that once they have joined the organization they are guaranteed continuing employment, it is argued that Japanese firms ensure the loyalty and security of their workforce. Research studies suggest, however, that this is by no means so widespread as was once believed. Oh (1976) estimated that no more than 30 per cent of the Japanese labour force work for the same firm throughout their career, while Cole (1979) showed that rather more Americans than Japanese continue to work for their first employer. There are a number of reasons why this may be so. Most large Japanese firms utilize numerous subcontractors, and these do not enjoy security in time of cutbacks. Indeed, Oh makes it clear that lifetime employment can be effective only because of the existence of such a dual labour market, whereby the risks of recession are borne by the subcontractors – 70 per cent of the goods and services required for the manufacture of a Nissan car are represented by orders to subcontractors. In textile machinery the figure rises to 90 per cent (Clark, 1979). However, it is an oversimplification to represent the labour market as a dual one. There is no definite boundary between the large first-rank companies and the others, but rather a series of hierarchical gradations (Nakane, 1970), which we shall explore in a later section.

Several other factors also restrict the extensiveness of lifetime employment. Many of the women recruited by the major firms work for only a few years before marriage. In addition, the age of retirement in Japan was most usually 55, although there is currently some tendency for it to increase. Hazama (1978) showed that within three years of first employment, 73 per cent had left small firms, many of whom would be subcontractors, while only 38 per cent had left the larger firms. Lifetime employment should therefore be thought of as a process affecting predominantly male workers within the larger corporations. We should also note that the oft-cited low figures for unemployment in Japan are computed in a different manner to those from other countries. Taira (1983) has estimated that if the U S system were used, rates of unemployment in Japan would be more than doubled.

A further point of contrast is that those who stay with one firm for long periods in the West may well have exercised some choice to do so. For a Japanese within the lifetime employment system this choice is effectively absent. Lifetime employment is sometimes written about as though it were simply a guarantee of a permanent job. In understanding the system it is important to bear in mind that in exchange the employee may be expected to accept loss of the very substantial pay bonuses which Japanese firms pay when they are profitable, to work extra unpaid hours or forgo holiday entitlements, to accept an actual salary cut, to transfer to an entirely new type of work or to be assigned to another company within a related 'family' of companies. Hazama gives data from a comparative survey of workers in Japan and Britain. Asked why they took their present job, the most frequent Japanese responses were firstly the stability of the company, and secondly that there was no other suitable job. In Britain, workers cited the lack of other suitable jobs, wages, working conditions, and other reasons pertaining to the company. For British workers the stability of the company ranked ninth. The bases upon which employees are committed to a Japanese organization are thus different from those which are most frequent in the West. This has implications for the valid study of job satisfaction, and we shall return to this theme in the next section. For the present we should note that for the Japanese employee as for his employer a longer time perspective than that found in the West predominates.

Although few observational studies of Japanese managers have yet been reported, it appears that this difference in time perspective is evident even in the structuring of daily activities. Doktor (1983) found that in his observation sample, 41 per cent of Japanese managers undertook tasks which took more than one hour to carry through, compared to only 10 per cent of American managers. Conversely, 49 per cent of Americans but only 18 per cent of Japanese undertook tasks of less than nine minutes. Given that most Western observational studies of managers have shown the average transaction to last no more than three or four minutes, Doktor's data show a remarkable contrast.

Collective Orientation

The collective nature of Japanese society has been frequently discussed (Nakane, 1972). Individualistic behaviour has traditionally been seen as selfish, and within family and school it is discouraged. The work organization provides the principal locus of adult male Japanese identity, and identification with one's immediate work group of peers and superior is frequently very intense (Dore, 1973; Clark, 1979). Comparative studies reveal that Japanese employees see work as more central in their lives than do employees in ten other countries (Meaning of Working International Research Team, 1987). This study showed that it is not simply the case that Japanese employees identify more with their work, but that they draw the boundaries between what is considered to be work related and what is not in different ways. Thus, many Japanese would expect to spend substantial periods of time eating or drinking with their workmates after work and before going home. Atsumi (1979) found in his survey that 62 per cent of white-collar workers did this on two or more evenings per week. Among those from smaller firms only 26 per cent went out with their workmates that often. Employees are likely also to participate in company-organized sports, holidays, and outings. All of these activities would be undertaken in the absence of one's spouse or children. The bond between the employee and his organization and most especially his work group may thus take on some of the qualities of village life in traditional Japanese life. However, Atsumi cautions against the assumption that employees necessarily participate in all these activities simply for their own pleasure. The Japanese concept of *tsukiai* specifies one's obligation to develop and maintain harmonious relations with one's work colleagues. As Atsumi points out, the fact that employees in large firms engage in much more after-hours socializing than do those in small firms means that one cannot simply attribute the phenomenon to Japanese culture. Its meaning must lie in the culture of the large firms, the commitment they require, and the individual needs which are met by such informal contact. Further support for this view comes from the findings of the Meaning of Working International Research Team's (1987) findings. Asked to define the nature of work, Japanese were more likely than those from other countries to refer to concepts related to duty, which appeared in the Japanese version of the questionnaire as *gimu*.

Many large Japanese firms devote substantial resources to encouraging the collective commitment of their workforce. Matsushita, for instance, expects that all employees will participate each morning in singing the company song and reciting the employees' creed and seven spiritual values (Pascale and Athos, 1981). The values in question are: national service through industry, fairness, harmony and cooperation, struggle for betterment, courtesy and humility, adjustment and assimilation, and gratitude. Many other companies emphasize similar values, with most frequent emphasis upon the importance of *wa* or harmony. Commitment to the company is also fostered by extensive training programmes for new recruits, and by the fact that employees are not recruited to do a specific task but to share overall responsibility for the work of their team. Over time, those destined for senior positions are assigned to teams in each of the various functions within the organization, thus ensuring a generalist rather than a specialist view of the work to be done.

Loyalty to the firm is also fostered by a distinctive set of personnel policies. Pascale and Maguire (1980) compared policies in operation at ten Japanese plants with a matched sample of US plants. As one might expect, expenditure on social and recreational facilities per employee was more than twice as high in the Japanese companies. Pascale and Maguire also attempted to compare job rotation by comparing numbers of jobs per year of employee tenure. They found no difference, but this is most probably due to the tendency of Japanese firms not to label distinctive jobs as separate positions. Other widespread practices which encourage identification with the firm include the wearing of company uniforms and the provision of communal eating facilities. The existence of company unions rather than trade unions also aligns the interests of union and management more closely, and it is not infrequent for union officials to achieve management positions later in their career.

The concept of 'groupism' in Japanese management has been the subject of a number of Japanese-language books, some giving it a central role (Iwata, 1978), while others see it as one element among several (Tsuda, 1977; Urabe, 1978). In evaluating the function of groupism within Japanese organizations it is important to acknowledge a further Japanese distinction, that between *tatemae* and *honne*: *tatemae* refers to what might be considered ideal or correct concerning relations between two persons or groups. *Tatemae* will frequently derive from long-past events which have defined the state of relationships between the two groups in question; *honne* is what happens in practice. It is clear that the ideal values espoused by many Japanese organizations favour harmony and collective action within the organization. Detailed case studies by, for instance, Dore (1973) in an electrical plant, Rohlen (1974) in a bank, and Clark (1979) in a corrugated board manufacturing company indicate that the *honne* or what actually occurs is more complex. Clark suggests that: 'perhaps one could say that in the West decision making is presented as individualistic until adversity proves it collective. In Japan it is presented as collective until it is worth someone's while to claim a decision as his own' (p. 130). In other words the basic assumption within a Western organization would be individualistic, until such time as it was desirable to share the blame around for some setback, whereas in a Japanese organization the basic assumption would be collective, unless there was some specific incentive for claiming a success as one's own. Hazama (1978) also compares the relation of the individual and the group in Japanese and Western work teams. He suggests that the difference parallels that between certain types of team sports. In baseball, for instance, the group's task is differentiated between a series of individually defined roles. Each individual's separate performance may be recorded and evaluated. A collective enterprise is carried through by a series of individualized performances, just as is the work of organizations in Western countries. In the tug-of-war, by contrast, a collective sport is undertaken which has no clear demarcation of individual roles. The team either wins or loses and no one knows which individuals contributed more or less to the result. Hazama points to the parallel between the way in which Japanese work groups do not have clearly differentiated work roles. All members are equally responsible for the success of the team's efforts.

There is substantial debate as to whether the collective orientation of Japanese primary work groups arises from the personal preferences of those who join them, or whether it is more true to say that what occurs is a matter of conformity to existing norms of harmony and solidarity. The existence of the concept of *tsukiai* provides an indication that, at the least, personal preference is enhanced by social obligation. Wagatsuma (1982) argues that commentators have certainly overstated the occurrence of harmony in Japanese society. There is clear evidence of conflict both within and between organizations. For instance Clark (1979), as part of his case study, scrutinized questionnaires which the company required employees to complete annually. He found no lack of criticisms and complaints, particularly from those who had subsequently resigned from the company. Thus the harmony of the work group may to some degree be sustained by a sense of obligation rather than by inherent pleasure in harmony. There are times at which it is acceptable for such obligations to be relaxed, such as after having a few drinks together, and criticisms made on such an occasion are treated as off the record. Leaving such occasions to one side, it is much more likely that conflict within an organization will be between teams rather than within them.

Considerations as to how far Japanese work team behaviour is a matter of choice or of obligation provide a vantage point from which to examine studies of the job satisfaction of Japanese employees. Western writers have usually expected that the joint impact of lifetime employment and involvement in the work group would ensure that Japanese workers were more satisfied than those in Western organizations. There are now a sufficient number of published findings reporting that, on the contrary, Japanese workers are *less* satisfied than Western workers that some explanation is required. The reported studies cover two decades of research and a variety of industries. During the 1960s, Odaka (1975) completed five studies in Japanese organizations varying from manufacturing to department stores and electricity companies. In all of these, less than half the respondents declared themselves satisfied with their work, which compares with substantially higher figures from most Western countries. Only in West Germany were lower figures reported. Around 1970, Cole (1979) compared work satisfaction of workers in Detroit and Yokohama. The Japanese were again substantially less satisfied. The more recent studies are based on large heterogeneous samples and have all repeated the same finding (Azumi and McMillan, 1976; Pascale and Maguire, 1980; Naoi and Schooler, 1985; Lincoln and Kalleberg, 1985). In the most extensive and recent of these studies, Lincoln and Kalleberg compared the job satisfaction of 4567 US employees drawn from 52 plants in Indiana with 3735 Japanese employees at 46 plants in Kanagawa prefecture. Four work satisfaction items were used and the Japanese scored lower on all items, in excess of one standard deviation on three of them. The largest difference was on the question 'Does this job measure up to your expectations?'

Several explanations are possible of lower Japanese job satisfaction. The most obvious possibility is that many Japanese work extremely long hours and do not find their pay adequate. A recent survey by Sohyo (the Japanese General Council of Trade Unions) reported that of a sample of 26 800 respondents, 76 per cent stated that they worked too hard. Asked what would be necessary for an improved lifestyle, 70 per cent cited wage increases and 62 per cent cited shorter working hours (*Japan Times*, 1988). Although no more than one worker in four belongs to a trade union in Japan, these figures are likely to be representative of frequent sources of discontent among non-unionized workers also. Kamata's (1982) descriptive account of shopfloor work at Toyota is consistent with this explanation. Lincoln and Kalleberg's data showed age to be much more strongly related to dissatisfaction in Japan than in America. This accords with the view that a major source of dissatisfaction in Japan is low wages among younger workers.

Cole (1971) proposes that Japanese workers are dissatisfied because they have higher aspirations for their job. High involvement and commitment lead to expectations which the organization cannot satisfy and which workers in the West would not look to their employer to satisfy. Support for this view comes from the fact that in the Lincoln and Kalleberg study the largest difference found was on the item referring to expectations.

There are difficulties in concluding that the difference in satisfaction is due to different levels of organizational commitment. Additional data in the Lincoln and Kalleberg (1985) study indicate that the Japanese sample also scored lower than the Americans on the six-item Porter Scale of Organizational Commitment. A further study by Luthans, McCaul, and Dodd (1985), using the same measure, showed that broad samples of Japanese and Korean employees both scored lower than Americans on the scale. Since both Lincoln and Kalleberg and Luthans *et al.* sampled a very wide range of organizations, their respondents will have included both those having lifetime employment with first-rank companies and those without job security – 41 per cent of respondents in the Sohyo survey reported that their jobs were 'precarious'. The surprising findings obtained by these two studies may be accounted for by their confounding together those with lifetime employment and those without. An alternative possibility is that those who feel low commitment to U S organizations feel freer to leave than do those in Japanese organizations. These two factors could also account for the lower Japanese job satisfaction found in the various other studies.

There is a third possible explanation of the reported differences which has to do with the difficulty of comparing mean scores on questionnaires which have been translated into different languages. While at least some of the studies under discussion used back-translation procedures to assure equivalence of meaning, one cannot control for differences in cultural norms. Japanese norms favour a modest presentation of self, while those in the United States encourage a more assertive presentation. It is quite possible that Japanese respondents would show lower mean scores than Americans on *any* self-descriptive questionnaire to which they were asked to respond. Buckley and Mirza (1985) cite a European Productivity Agency survey which showed that in 1980 only 50 per cent of Japanese described themselves as satisfied with life, compared to 89 per cent of Americans and 91 per cent of British. Lincoln, Hanada, and Olson (1981) studied Japanese-owned plants in the United States and found that Japanese-Americans employed there were less satisfied than Americans *in the same plants*. Of the explanations discussed here only the response bias explanation can account for this last finding, since presumably the conditions of employment were similar for all workers in these plants. The study by Pascale and Maguire (1980) asked respondents to compare their satisfaction with that of others similar to themselves. This way of phrasing might be expected to reduce the response bias problem to some degree, but we have no way of knowing by how much.

It is probable that all three explanations of lower Japanese job satisfaction contribute to the findings which have been obtained. For this reason it is unlikely that a definitive conclusion can be reached as to whether or not the Japanese are more dissatisfied with their jobs. In any event what is of more interest in our discussion of Japanese management is not so much the absolute level of satisfaction, but what types of structures or processes cause it to increase or decrease. We shall return to this issue when we discuss influence processes.

Seniority System

Japanese society is not only collective, but is also based upon a hierarchical status system. This is difficult for many Westerners to envisage, since in the West hierarchy is often thought of as opposite to collective activities such as participation. The Japanese language incorporates a wide variety of 'respect language', whereby it is impossible to speak to someone without making it clear whether that person is regarded as superior or inferior to oneself. The distinctions to be made are far more complex than the *tu/vous* distinction, for example, in French. Modes of address are formal and frequently refer to a person by rank rather than by name. A first-line supervisor is likely to be addressed as Mr Foreman (*handcho-san*) or Foreman Tanaka, even after long periods of working together.

The bases upon which such hierarchy is determined are numerous, including education, age, gender, and the firm one works for. The position of institutions in society, such as the firms in a particular industry or the universities in Japan, is also ordered in terms of an agreed hierarchy. One's own status is determined by the institutions one is or has been associated with combined with personal attributes such as age and gender. Wives take on their husband's status among other women. All of the above contribute to the *tatemae* of one's position relative to others, but in addition there will be factors relating not to one's own lifetime experiences but to one's family of origin.

Such processes are clearly operative also among Western business organizations, but in much more covert ways. In a business meeting or in office layout in Japan, status positions are likely to be physically represented, with high status persons furthest from the door. Behavioural differences such as amount of speaking and depth of bowing will also reflect hierarchical rank.

The management of hierarchy is exemplified by promotion procedures used within the large firms. Employee recruitment typically occurs only from school-leavers and college graduates and is followed by a substantial period of in-company training. This serves to strengthen commitment to the firm and inculcate the firm's favoured values. For about the next fifteen years, salary increases are paid regularly to all employees, with only relatively minor differentiation between high performers and low performers. This is the *nenko* system. Payment of a salary increase does not necessarily entail a change in work, but those who are destined for further promotion may be given the more interesting assignments. Thus throughout this period status differences are minimized between the members of a particular intake. Promotion beyond this point is more related to accomplishment. At the point when it becomes clear which members of a cohort are to be appointed to very senior positions, their peers may be encouraged to move to a job with one of the organization's subcontractors. By these devices, a situation is accomplished where it is rare for someone's boss to be younger than himself. It is thus possible to maintain a hierarchy of deference without confusing incongruities of age or gender. One's prospects for promotion are strongly dependent upon links with a more senior 'mentor' within the company. Assignment to a particularly senior mentor will depend upon the strength of one's prospects on entry. Wakabayashi and Graen (1984) have shown just how predictable this system makes ultimate promotion. They showed that the evaluation of the mentor–recruit relationship on entry to one of Japan's largest department store chains was a strong predictor of promotions achieved within the subsequent seven years.

In considering studies of Japanese organizational structure, it is important to bear in mind the description given above. Japanese organizations have two types of hierarchy – a seniority system for individuals, and a hierarchy of organizational ranks. The two systems do not necessarily overlap, since an organizational rank may quite frequently be left vacant. At the same time more than one person may be promoted to a particular seniority level, if their age, expertise or *tatemae* requires it. For instance in Clark's (1979) case study, 43 out of 109 ranked management positions were vacant at the time of the research. Dore's (1973) study at Hitachi gave a similar finding.

Researchers into organizational structure have mostly made use of Western measures, even though it is doubtful how far some of these may capture the aspects of organization just described. Lincoln, Hanada, and McBride (1986) drew upon the same comparative sample of organizations in Indiana and Kanagawa as has been discussed above. As they had predicted, they found that Japanese organizations had less functional specialization, that is to say fewer duties which are assigned exclusively to one individual within the organization.

They also had a significantly greater number of seniority levels and a higher proportion of clerical staff. The most interesting aspect of this study was its findings concerning decision making. Respondents were asked at what level in the organization did authority rest formally for the taking of each of 37 types of decisions. They were then asked at what level these decisions were actually taken in practice. It was found that formal authority was located at significantly *higher* levels in Japanese firms than American ones, but that in practice decisions were taken at significantly *lower* levels in the Japanese firms than in the American ones. In the US firms the formal and informal locus of decisions was thus not that far apart; but in the Japanese firms the mean difference was greater than one level in the seniority system. The data thus reflect the distinction between *tatemae* and *honne* and shed light on the manner whereby a Japanese organization might appear to Western eyes to be both autocratic and participative.

The survey by Kagono *et al.* (1985) also included questions about organization structure. Within Japanese organizations, job descriptions were shown to be more general and less concrete. Power was said to be more widely shared and less systematized, particularly in respect of horizontal relationships. This survey did not distinguish between formal and informal procedures, but its findings are more in accord with Lincoln *et al.*'s description of decision making in practice. In these two surveys there is probably less reason to worry about response bias as a source of erroneous findings, since respondents were required to describe not themselves but their organizations.

Most researchers with interests in organization structures are interested not so much in absolute differences between Japan and the West as in whether the relationships between different aspects of formal organizational structure are the same within Japan as has been found elsewhere. Horvath, McMillan, Azumi, and Hickson (1979) examined the degree of formalization, specialization, and centralization within twelve matched trios of firms in Britain, Japan, and Sweden. Size and the degree of an organization's 'internal dependence', that is its links to parent organizations, were found to be the strongest predictors within Japan. Azumi and McMillan (1979) compared a larger sample of 50 Japanese firms with a databank of 128 British organizations. The Japanese sample scored much higher on centralization and on number of vertical levels, and somewhat higher on formalization, a measure which reflects the number of written documents used. These authors found no relationship between scores on centralization, formalization, and specialization, a finding which differs markedly from studies in Western countries. The most likely explanation for this is that the measures used in this and the preceding study, which are those developed by researchers at the University of Aston in England, fail to detect crucial aspects of Japanese organizational behaviour. As the later study by Lincoln *et al*. shows, there is an important distinction to be made between formal and informal decision procedures. Furthermore, the measure of specialization is defined in terms of assignment of specialist duties to *individuals*, where such specialization is much more likely to be carried through by teams in Japan.

Marsh and Mannari (1981) also made use of the Aston measures among others, but their prime goal was to compare the relative impact of size and technology as determinants of organizational structure and processes within 50 Japanese factories. They found that the type of technology employed was a somewhat stronger predictor than was size, whereas the reverse had been found earlier in Britain. In a similar study, Tracy and Azumi (1976) found that plant size and task variability were predictors of the level of automation and formalization. Lincoln *et al*. (1986) also studied the effect of type of technology. They concluded that the effects of technology were not, on the whole, detectably different from those in their US sample. However, on certain variables, particularly the centralization of decision making, the effects do differ. The US data show strong effects of technology type on both the formal and informal decision measures, while the Japanese data do not. Lincoln *et al*. conclude that variables other than technology are more crucial in Japan in this area. However, they do point out that newly emerging technologies such as highly automated process industries are precisely those in which Japan is at the forefront, and these types of plant may be ones in which it is less crucial to link supervision to technological processes. Although this may well be true, the sample used by Lincoln *et al*. spanned a wide range of technologies, and the implication of their finding is that it is not technology but something intrinsic to Japan which determines the type of decision making used. The most plausible candidate for such a cultural explanation would be the deeply rooted seniority system.

Seror (1982) attempts to specify a firmer basis upon which comparisons may be made of Japanese organizational structures and those in other countries. She proposes that before conclusions may be reached which favour universal theories of organizational structure, studies must be made that span several clearly defined cultures and show how the structures studied affect organizational effectiveness. The only study which approaches these requirements is that by Lincoln and Kalleberg (1985). In addition to the analyses within their paper that have already been discussed, these authors examine the effects of different organizational parameters upon satisfaction and commitment of employees. These are clearly not unambiguous measures of organizational effectiveness, but a study of them is none the less a step forward. Commitment in Japanese firms was found to be lower in small firms and in firms with tall hierarchies. A large span of control and low formalization was linked to positive commitment and satisfaction in the United States, but not in Japan. The implication would be that in the United States close contact with the supervisor is aversive, while in Japan it is not. A number of other differences which the authors had anticipated did not emerge. For instance there was no linkage between tenure and commitment. However, it is not clear why there should be such an effect. An employee who enters the lifetime employment system already knows the nature of the commitment he has made: there is no reason why commitment should increase with the passage of time. Lincoln and Kalleberg conclude that the differences they found in the effects of organizational structure in the two countries were rather modest. A possible reason for this may be that the effects of structures are not inherent in those structures, but in how they are interpreted and utilized in a particular cultural setting. This is a theme which we take up in the next section.

Influence Processes

The attributes of Japanese management outlined thus far delineate a system with clear positive qualities, but what may appear also to be substantial disadvantages. Japanese employers are also agreed upon the nature of these disadvantages. Hazama (1978) reports a survey made in 1967 by the Japan Federation of Employers' Associations. Among those who responded, 92 per cent agreed that lifetime employment caused employers to retain workers with inferior ability and those who were not needed, thus causing a large loss due to labour costs. Similarly, 84 per cent agreed that the seniority system led to a loss in vitality within the establishment, and 72 per cent said that the system adversely affected the morale of able workers. Whether such disadvantages are outweighed by the benefits must depend upon the manner in which the structures so far described are operated in practice. Such evidence is crucial, since when one reads descriptions of, for example, the seniority system, it is inevitable that one's reactions to it are coloured by the way in which such a system would be evaluated within one's own national culture.

Most discussions of Japanese management gave substantial emphasis to the occurrence of upward influence, particularly through the *ringi* system of decision making and through the widespread use of quality control circles. While these are certainly important and we shall discuss them shortly, it is necessary first to consider the nature of superior–subordinate relations in Japanese society. *Ringi* and quality control circles may then be seen as particular instances of a more fundamental attribute. Within Western societies a rigidly hierarchical system would most likely be one in which influence flowed down the hierarchy rather than up it. Those in high power positions would at times need to protect themselves from threats to their status from more able persons below. In Japan the position of a senior person is relatively invulnerable to such attack, due both to lifetime employment and to the fact that status derives principally from attributes which cannot be changed by others. Thus the senior manager in Japan has less reason to be threatened by suggestions from below. The traditional pattern of superior–subordinate relations in Japanese society depends upon the *oyabun–kobun* system, which derives from the parent–child relationship and now means patron–client relationship. Within modern organizations this is represented by the *sempai–kohai* or senior–junior system. This is an intense relationship of mutual obligation. The superior is expected to protect the subordinate's interests, develop his skills through training and feedback, and advance his position. The subordinate is expected to show deference and loyalty, as expressed through commitment and hard work, as well as the making of suggestions and the giving of gifts on occasions such as the New Year. The subordinate's commitment may be expressed through working extra unpaid hours, or through not taking up holiday entitlements, although as Lincoln and Kalleberg's (1985) data suggest, this may be due not so much to commitment as to an unwillingness to fall out of favour with one's superior. The superior's obligations may well extend to such matters as helping the subordinate to find someone to marry, where this is desired. The superior will be given credit for the achievements of the work team, but this will be due to the need for deference, rather than as a distinction to be made between the supervisor and his team of subordinates. It also motivates the superior to look out for valuable suggestions from subordinates. This pattern of superior–subordinate relations derives from the traditional obligations of Japanese village life, which are known as *ie* (Nakane, 1970).

The survey by Kagono *et al*. (1985) also included a series of questions about leadership styles. Japanese leaders were reported by respondents to be significantly higher than those in America and Europe on the following behaviours: strictness in applying rewards and punishments; clarifying and gathering information; adherence to the values of the current chief executive officer (CEO) or founder; conflict resolution through the use of authority; exchange of information prior to meetings; sharing of information down the line; use of a control system based upon employee self-discipline and commitment to work; long-term performance evaluation; consensus decision making; frequent informal and social exchange; commitment to change; and promotion policies from within. Few of the differences reported are surprising in view of the preceding discussion, but since the respondents were asked to describe practices within their company as a whole, their responses probably reflect *tatemae* rather more than *honne*.

The principal organizationally structured mode of upward influence within the Japanese organization is that of *ringi*. This is a procedure whereby proposals for new policies, procedures or expenditures are circulated through the firm for comment. An initial proposal is written by a junior member of the organization. The paper is then sent to all those who might be affected if it were implemented, each of whom writes comments or indicates approval with his personal seal. The document is circulated in ascending order of seniority. The above description outlines what occurs in theory. In practice, with increasing size of modern Japanese organizations, such procedures become exceedingly time consuming and a number of modifications may be noted (Misumi, 1984). For instance, the organization may use *ringi* only for important decisions, and may authorize managers at particular seniority levels to commit expenditures up to a given level without such broad consultation. Less important decisions may be handled by *ringi* among middle managers and never submitted to the highest level. It will be noted that the success of *ringi* requires a high degree of consensus among those affected. Consultation documents circulated within Western organizations are frequently criticized, negotiated over, and amended. The preferred procedure within Japanese organizations is to engage in such consultations *before* the *ringi* proposal is circulated. This informal procedure is referred to as *nemawashi*, whose literal meaning is the trimming of a tree's roots prior to its being transplanted. Only when it is clear from *nemawashi* that a proposal is likely to succeed will a written *ringi* proposal be put forward. The nearest Western equivalents, grapevine or bush telegraph, have a different connotation, since they refer to dissemination of information rather than preparation for decision. Through *nemawashi*, harmony in the organization will be preserved, but rather than being a method of decision making, *ringi* has become more a method of recording and reporting decisions already reached (Misumi, 1984).

A *ringi* decision may be thought of as the nearest which a Japanese organization will come to issuing job descriptions. The decision which is recorded will specify that certain tasks will be carried out by a particular group or groups, but it differs from a formal system of job descriptions in two senses. Firstly, it will relate to a particular task and hence will lapse when that task is complete. Secondly, it will specify the task to be done by one or more teams rather than by individuals. In practice, differential abilities and influence processes within the team may mean that one member does much more of the work than others, but *tatemae* says that all are equally responsible. The individual who does more than his 'share' will know that such industry may in the end lead to slightly more rapid promotion, but in the meantime all are equally accountable for what is done.

A further issue concerning *ringi* is the question of where the initiative comes from for the formulation of a new policy. It is often implied that the new idea derives solely from the junior member of the organization, and no doubt many ideas do so. But it must also be remembered that within the seniority system, subordinates are obligated to take note of the wishes of their superiors. Thus a superior who favours a particular initiative may drop hints to subordinates, who will then formulate a proposal in that direction. Clark (1979) reports instances where this occurred – *ringi* is thus not something apart from the rest of organizational processes. It is the product of *nemawashi*, and the fostering of both *ringi* and *nemawashi* is an integral part of the leadership processes occurring within Japanese organizations. Just as *ringi* exemplifies upward influence within the ranks of management, so does the extensive use of quality control circles and allied procedures at shopfloor level. However, QC circles will not be extensively discussed here, since they are the subject of a separate review (Van Fleet and Griffin, 1989).

Detailed studies have been undertaken of the processes of leadership within Japanese organizations (Misumi, 1985). These have shown that leaders whose effectiveness is rated most highly are those whose behaviour is perceived as high on two functions termed P and M. These initials stand for performance and maintenance, and they parallel distinctions made by US leadership researchers between, for instance, task and socio-emotional behaviours. However, while US researchers have found that environmental contingencies require different leader styles, Misumi's studies have shown that effective leaders score high on P and M in a very wide range of organizational settings. Misumi emphasizes that although measures of P and M are factorially independent, they cannot be thought of in isolation. Within the actions of an effective manager, the exercise of the P and M functions interacts, so that the effect of each augments the other. Over a period of more than 30 years his studies have included laboratory studies, field surveys, and field experiments. Within the Nagasaki shipyards, for instance, leadership training emphasizing the need for a PM style led to very large decreases in the rate of accidents (Misumi, 1975). On the face of it, effective Japanese leader style is less environmentally contingent than are US styles, just as we reported earlier that Japanese organizational structures appear to be less driven by technology. However, in the case of leader styles, comparative studies are not yet complete which would test for alternative explanations, such as the use of different measures of leader style in different countries.

Comparative data are available from three studies which do test the linkage between various organizational processes and ratings of work satisfaction or performance. Pascale (1978a) compared matched samples of US and Japanese companies. He found that in the Japanese companies written communications were used more frequently, that there were more superior–subordinate interactions initiated from below, and that implementation of decisions was rated more highly. These last two variables were positively correlated, so that where there was more upward influence, decision implementation was better. Using the same sample, Pascale and Maguire (1980) report correlations between their one-item measures of leader style and work satisfaction which are generally low. The highest correlations with work satisfaction within the Japanese sample were for 'supervisor pitches in' (+0.23) and mean number of supervisor–worker interactions (+0.30). The equivalent correlations for the US sample were −0.15 and +0.05, but the significance of these differences is not tested. Strongly significant correlations between supervisor style and absenteeism were found in the US sample, but these were absent from the Japanese sample probably because absenteeism was very much lower there. Another relevant finding from the Lincoln and Kalleberg (1985) study was that participation in quality circles in the United States was positively linked to organizational commitment. In Japan this was less true but participation in *ringi* showed a stronger effect.

More direct tests will be required before a firm conclusion is possible, but there are certainly some grounds for the belief that the effects of leadership and of group processes more generally may differ within Japanese organizations from those found in the West.

This concludes our survey of the classical model of Japanese management. The different attributes which we have outlined are summarized in Table 1.

Change and Stability in Japanese Management

In his earliest analysis of Japanese factory organization, Abegglen (1958) argued that the structures he described were derived from traditional Japanese society. It is now widely agreed that this was incorrect, not least by Abegglen himself (Abegglen, 1973). A more tenable view is that many of the distinctive qualities of Japanese management have in fact evolved over the past few decades (Dore, 1973; Odaka, 1975; Cole, 1979; Urabe, 1984). In the first section of this review Japanese management was discussed as though it were a fixed and static entity. In this section we shall consider evidence as to its diversity and rate of change. Such a type of analysis is replete with irony, since as we shall see, many of the aspects of Japanese management which have been 'discovered' by Western writers in recent years, have their roots in the West as much as they do in the East.

The principal difficulty in the way of analysing what is stable and what is in process of change lies in the Japanese genius for searching out new approaches,

Table 1 The classical model of Japanese management

Attribute	*Effect*	*Source of vitality*	*Difficulties*
Lifetime employment	Stable tenure Job rotation Simultaneous recruitment Future abilities unknown Internal promotion	All in the same boat Can devote self to work Whole person contributes Sense of belonging	Low job mobility Small incentives to develop self Small incentives to perform well No right of dismissal
Collective orientation	Put company first Multilateral flow of information	Wish to contribute to group Sense of belonging Interchangeability of jobs Power of the group	Stress from suppression of ego needs Group process problems Unclear powers and duties
Seniority system	Gradual promotion Equitable system of promotion Job rotation	Long-term incentive Boosts collective morale Sense of belonging	'Tepid' management Promotion of low ability persons to management Elite morale low
Influence processes	Responsibilities delegated Many views sought Participative management	Flexible structure Young employee vitality Free resources utilized Shared strategy formulation	No unified control No hard-line policy Diffusion of responsibilities Time consuming

wherever they may be found and adapting them to their own purposes. It is doubtful whether there is another country in the world which has devised a system of notation for the sole purpose of incorporating into its own language words and concepts from other countries. Such a practice may in itself be no more than symbolic of Japanese enthusiasm for the importation and adaptation of technologies and procedures. None the less, the cumulative impact of such openness may have profound implications for the future of Japanese organizations, as for many other aspects of Japanese society.

Cole (1979) summarizes three views of the development of Japanese organizations. The first of these proposes, in line with Abegglen's (1958) thesis, that Japanese organizations are a unique product of Japanese cultural history. The second proposes that there are inexorable consequences of the use of specific technologies and that the structures of the modern industrial organizations of all societies are therefore destined to converge. The third alternative, which Cole himself supports, is that there may in fact be several ways in which organizations can successfully cope with the problems of production and marketing which they face. Organizational structures may therefore be expected to show some convergence, but also some diversity which is explicable in cultural terms.

The first or culturalist view has something of the status of the null hypothesis. That is to say, if studies show no evidence of change in Japanese organizations over time, its merits are enhanced, but if change is found, it is weakened. A judgement as to whether or not the changes found would require dismissal of the culturalist view, would also entail an evaluation of whether the changes found were explicable simply as a developmental stage within a unique culture, or whether they showed convergence towards the culture of other advanced industrial countries. Such judgements are by no means easy to make.

Despite such difficulties, certain facts are now well established. For instance, the system of lifetime employment for those working in first-rank companies arose after the Second World War (Cole, 1979). Between the wars there was little security of tenure, and considerable industrial conflict, sometimes violent (Urabe, 1986). The system of lifetime employment evolved out of these conflicts. Cole points out that the system is not a legally formalized one, and that in a period of expansion such as Japan has experienced since the Second World War, it may be difficult to distinguish between those who are entitled to lifetime employment and those who have merely experienced continuous employment. In the current situation, where there are already, or soon will be, substantial cutbacks in employment opportunities in such industries as coal mining, shipbuilding and car manufacture, the distinction is likely to become more explicit. Cole's (1971) survey of workers in Yokohama certainly revealed some confusion among his respondents as to the nature of their conditions of service.

There is an equal degree of uncertainty about the *nenko* system. In Cole's study at Toyota Auto Body, he found that no more than 40 per cent of a worker's pay was based upon the seniority principle, while the remainder was based upon abilities and work content. He comments that the criteria for abilities and work content were sufficiently vague that, in practice, they might well prove to be correlated with seniority. Nevertheless, since the 1960s, this and many other firms sought to include a job-based wage system (*shokumukyu*) within their criteria for determining pay. The impetus for this came from study of the personnel practices of American firms and Japanese protagonists of such changes sought to justify them by emphasizing that they are more modern (Cole, 1979, p. 130). *Shokumukyu* was found to require precise job descriptions and most firms have replaced it by an element of *shokunokyu* or payment by ability within their payment system. No evidence is available as to whether such payments do in practice conflict with the seniority system.

The *ringi* procedure has also been frequently attacked as insufficiently modern, and as we have seen its function has been changing. Takamiya (1981) reports that in 1961, 82 per cent of corporations surveyed used *ringi* for making decisions, whereas by 1969 many of these regarded *ringi* as a method for recording decisions. The other side of this picture is given by the survey conducted by Takahashi and Takayanagi (1985). They asked 299 firms by what method they took their most recent decision on a location plan for a factory, branch or office. They found that 63 per cent of the decisions were taken through *nemawashi*, 30 per cent through decision by the superior, and the remainder by conference. The firms using group-based decision methods (*nemawashi* and conference) were more likely to employ what the authors call a 'fixed size' procedure, in other words the simultaneous evaluation of a range of options. These firms tended to be those who are listed on the Tokyo Stock Exchange, and particularly those whose share performance is high. Thus this study indicates that *nemawashi* is currently most widespread among the successful first-rank companies.

The picture presented above is certainly one of change, but there is little indication that the changes which have occurred simply represent the adoption of the practices of the United States or of other industrialized countries. Cole (1979) cites several further examples of the manner in which innovations derived from the United States have been substantially amended as they are incorporated within Japanese practice. A widely known example is the manner in which the ideas of Deming on statistical quality control by staff experts were transmuted into the group-based procedure known as quality control circles. A less familiar one is the rapid adoption in the early years of this century of F. W. Taylor's prescriptions for scientific management (McMillan, 1985). The notion of work study and of production management was enthusiastically adopted, while the associated idea of performance-related pay was completely ignored. Japanese writers point out that Taylor himself was an advocate, not simply of work study but equally of 'hearty brotherly cooperation' (Mito, 1983).

The view that convergence of Japanese and Western organizations is inevitable is advanced by Marsh and Mannari (1976). Their study examined three firms manufacturing ships, electrical appliances, and *sake*. Their analyses were based both upon detailed case studies and also upon questionnaire surveys completed by the workforce of the three plants. Data collection occurred between 1967 and 1970. They found that variables such as organizational rank and work satisfaction were actually more strongly associated with 'universal' factors than with variables which might be derived from distinctively Japanese practices. For instance it was found that extra-organizational variables such as age, gender, and number of dependants had more effect upon reward system variables such as pay than did intra-organizational variables, such as education, seniority, and rank. Work satisfaction was related to rank, age, gender, promotion chances, and the cohesiveness of the work group. Marsh and Mannari argue that since the variables which proved the strongest predictors are not distinctive to Japan, the convergence or 'modernization' theory is more strongly supported than the cultural theory. Such a reading of cultural theories exaggerates their claims. None of the proponents of cultural theories (e.g. Abegglen, 1958; Rohlen, 1974) put forward the view that Japanese organizations have *nothing* in common with Western organizations, only the more moderate view that there are unique processes within them that have substantial importance. Furthermore, as Cole (1979) points out, it is difficult to arrive at a valid reason for classifying some predictors as 'modern' and others as 'traditional'. Marsh and Mannari think of payment by ability as modern, in contrast to the *nenko* system. However, among their respondents 48 per cent who favoured *nenko* also considered that ability should be the prime determinant of pay. Thus their respondents appear to see no contradiction between what Marsh and Mannari consider to be traditional and modern. One possible resolution of such a puzzle is that advanced above in discussing Cole's (1979) study at Toyota Auto Body. It may be that ability payments are in practice correlated with seniority ranks. In the Marsh and Mannari data, job classification certainly correlated highly with seniority (+0.77 and +0.51 for the two companies in which it was computed).

Marsh and Mannari take their argument further by suggesting that those firms with traditional Japanese emphasis will experience increasing difficulty in surviving. They support this argument by devising an index of worker performance and showing that high performance is again linked more strongly to factors such as rank, gender, and work satisfaction. However, their measure of performance was based not on actual productivity records, but upon answers to five questions, three of which had to do with the submission of suggestions for improvements. The conclusions drawn from this study are thus rather more general than the data might justify. It is difficult to draw valid conclusions about cultural differences in the absence of comparative data from different cultures. Conclusions about changes over time ideally also require data collection over some extended time period. However, the study does provide an illustration of the way in which there were substantial differences between the three firms studied, and thus contributes to the reduction of the belief that there is a single unified system of Japanese management. It does also validly demonstrate that among the sample studied the various elements postulated to make up the Japanese management system were not correlated with one another in a linear fashion. There was no particular tendency for instance for those who scored high on their measure of paternalism to express more company concerns, to have had no other previous jobs with other firms, to live in company housing, to score high on group cohesiveness or to be committed to lifetime employment. Marsh and Mannari suggest that this means that these aspects of Japanese organizations do not comprise a unified whole, but that employees participate in each one of them where they see it to be advantageous to them. This seems highly plausible.

An alternative version of the modernization hypothesis is that put forward by Dore (1973). Basing his thesis upon comparative case studies of electrical plants in Japan and Britain, he proposes that far from being backward or traditional, Japanese company organization may illustrate a form of welfare corporatism towards which other countries will converge. He reasons that since Japanese industrialization has occurred more recently than in Western countries there have been opportunities for Japan to learn from Western errors and thereby to create more advanced organizational structures. We should therefore expect more future changes in Western organizations than in Japanese ones. Cole (1979) is sceptical that Japan qualifies for 'late-developer' status, given the openness to Western ideas from the beginning of the Meiji era onwards, but acknowledges a wide range of ways in which Japanese organizations have observed and learned from Western organizations during the past century. We have noted some of these above. What are required, but have not yet been fully described, are accounts of the degree to which such innovations have been rendered into distinctively Japanese forms.

Comparative case studies of sixteen matched pairs of companies in Japan and the United States are presented by Kagono *et al.* (1985). They conclude that the strategies of these firms differ in five ways. The Japanese companies compared to the US ones were found to define their domain more broadly; to emphasize continuous in-house resource accumulation and development; to emphasize human resource development; to distribute risk through organizational networks; and to use inductive methods of problem solving, particularly focused upon improvement in production strategy. They conclude that both US and Japanese strategies are well adapted to certain types of market, but that each will need to change in response to continuing market change.

The most authoritative account of how such gradual transformations in

Japanese firms are being accomplished is provided by Urabe (1984, 1986), the doyen of Japanese management writers. He stresses the manner in which the human and the technological innovations accomplished have been interrelated. Lifetime employment has enhanced the growth of company-specific skills. The *tatemae* of seniority has been preserved, while in practice pay differentials between senior and junior members of the organization have declined, and non-working directors have become a rarity. These changes and the payment of substantial bonuses have facilitated the convergence of management and union interests. The shift to process production increases the power of workers to disrupt production, and the trust accorded to workers by allowing them to halt a production line when necessary enhances the responsibility of their actions.

Urabe considers the potential of Japanese and Western organizations for the creation of change. He concludes that Japanese firms are well adapted to a continuous process of small incremental changes. Such changes are more likely to be the focus of resistance and negotiation in the West. Western organizations, on the other hand, may be better at making radical changes, and Urabe concludes that in this area lies a major problem for the Japanese organizations of the future. Urabe's reasoning is neatly complemented by the recent research of Yoshihara (1986), who made case studies of five Japanese firms which did accomplish successful innovations. The innovations were mostly changes into radically different markets, of which the best known is Canon. Yoshihara reports that in contrast to the popular view of Japanese firms having a 'bottom-up' system of influence, each of these firms had a strong and visible leader at the top who actively directed the innovations made. Numerous examples of the developing business strategy of specific Japanese corporations are also discussed by Itami (1987).

A major source of innovation and change in Japan as elsewhere lies in the management of research and development, and some studies of this process are now available. Kono (1986) surveyed the research facilities of 244 Japanese firms. He found that three sources of new product ideas were more frequent in the more successful firms: top management, central research groups, and divisional development teams. Westney and Sakakibara (1985) compared research and development within three Japanese and three American firms in the computer industry. Japanese researchers identified more strongly with the research administrators of their group and with the manufacturing function within their firm. US researchers gave more weight to professional colleagues and family. Promotion in Japanese labs was based upon seniority and track record, while in the United States it was based upon technical expertise and track record. Japanese researchers worked longer hours. US researchers had more choice of assignment to their next project. Kanai (1987) surveyed 49 research teams within a Japanese firm. Strong correlations were found between the leader's personal style, his network of links with other parts of the organization, and the team's performance. These studies suggest Japanese research labs share the characteristics identified in earlier sections, but also indicate that within this function as elsewhere, influence flows down the hierarchy as well as up it.

The work of Urabe and of Yoshihara confirms that substantial changes continue to occur in Japanese management practices, even though they are not necessarily convergent with Western practices. Dunphy (1987) also favours the view that these changes are the product of thought-out strategy choices by Japanese managements, rather than the inevitable consequence of culture or of technology. The work of Okubayashi (1986a, 1986b, 1987) gives some pointers as to how this process will continue in the face of further automation. He showed that the introduction of robots had not led to job losses within the firms installing them, and that unions are generally favourable to their use. His survey of 167 companies showed that automation has accentuated the division between highly skilled workers and unskilled ones. It has also led to shorter hierarchies and more decentralized decision making on production, but greater centralization of financial and personnel functions. These changes are likely to threaten wage systems based upon seniority and to pose particular difficulties for women and for older workers.

Further studies of workers have been reported which also suggest that evidence for convergence between Japanese and Western organizations is much less than might be expected, given the increasing rate of intercultural contact. The most striking evidence is that provided by Whitehill and Takezawa (1968) and Takezawa and Whitehill (1981). In this unique pair of studies, the same set of questions was posed to comparable samples of 2000 Japanese and US workers employed by eight large companies, at an interval of thirteen years. The survey included 30 questions, and significantly different patterns of response were found on every single question. The differences detected were consistent with the portrayal of Japanese management presented earlier in this chapter. The repeat survey found remarkably little evidence of convergence. Indeed on the majority of questions the gap between the United States and Japan had widened. Japanese responses showed more change than did US ones, but the strongest effect was that the attitudes of younger workers were now more similar to those of older workers.

Opinion surveys of the Japanese population have been undertaken every five years since 1953. Hayashi (1987) reports that over this period there has been remarkably little change in expressed preference for a work supervisor who 'looks after you personally', rather than one who never does anything for you that is unconnected with work. In the most recent survey, 89 per cent preferred the first of these two types of supervisor.

One other source of evidence for lack of change over time lies in the series of studies of leadership by Misumi (1985). There has been no change in support for PM theory from the earliest studies conducted in coal mines in 1963 (Misumi, 1985, pp. 22–7) to the present day.

The studies reviewed in this section provide substantial evidence of change over time in the specific practices employed by Japanese organizations. At the same time, the evidence that these changes necessarily entail the decline of those aspects of Japanese organizations which are distinctive is scant. Completed academic studies necessarily lag somewhat behind the day-to-day life of organizations, so that one might propose that such change is present and increasing. The most substantial study indicating lack of change (Takezawa and Whitehill, 1981) was completed almost a decade ago. More recent commentators (Taylor, 1983) suggest that some at least of the younger generation show rather different attitudes to work. Taylor notes the recent appearance in the Japanese language of 'myhomeism', a phrase used to criticize those Japanese who choose to go home after work rather than work extra hours or participate in *tsukiai*. It is also indisputable that the proportion of young to old in the population is changing rapidly, and that disrespect for one's elders, as measured by such indices as reports of assaults on schoolteachers, is on the increase. These changes, in addition to the effects of automation, are likely to place the seniority system under increasing strain during the next two decades.

However, experience to date suggests that such changes will find a mode of expression which assimilates them to Japanese culture, as has happened with some regularity over the past century. Hayashi's survey data (1987, 1988) provide the best clues as to how this will occur. He notes a decline in both those whose views are compulsively traditionalist and those who are compulsively 'modern'. The increasing trend is for respondents to state that their response to a situation would depend on the circumstances. This change in attitude mirrors the increasing pragmatism of Japanese organizations which we have already noted.

The Japanese Abroad

In recent years, a variety of economic and political pressures have led many Japanese firms to establish both manufacturing plants and sales facilities abroad. Although this process has been quite rapid, the title of Trevor's (1983) book,

Japan's Reluctant Multinationals, conveys the impression of many observers that recent developments have been more a matter of necessity than of preference. The reasons for it have been fully explored by Ozawa (1979). He distinguishes the move into neighbouring Asian countries, primarily in search of lower labour costs, from the more recent worldwide expansion. The move towards multinational operation has been possible even for Japanese firms which are quite small, due to the existence of the giant *sogo shosha* or trading companies.

Generalizations about the performance of Japanese firms abroad need to be made with considerable caution, since not only do the reasons for setting up operations in various parts of the world vary, but so also does the manner in which firms are then staffed. Ozawa cites figures issued by the Japanese Ministry of Trade and Industry in 1971, indicating that the *average* number of Japanese nationals working within each overseas venture varied between 20 in the United States and 1 in Asia. While such differences no doubt represent an amalgam of the needs of each type of venture, and the preferences of Japanese to be stationed in particular parts of the world, they are likely to very strongly affect the degree of 'Japaneseness' of each venture.

Some studies are available of Japanese plants within Asia, but their focus is mostly general rather than specific. Ozawa indicates that the dual labour market within Japan is increasingly being replaced by a pattern where Japanese firms in other Asian countries pay very low wage rates, while more skilled work is retained within Japan. This has been encouraged by governments in Asian countries who are keen to foster foreign investment.

The loyalties of the Japanese to their in-group pose considerable problems for the Japanese abroad. They find it difficult to make contact with non-Japanese, particularly in Asian countries (Nakane, 1972). Those Japanese who do enter local networks or marry local women are thought of as having ceased to be Japanese. A wish to hire those who do understand the ways in which Japanese do business has led to preferential hiring of Japanese who already live there, especially in Hawaii and southern California. Japanese speakers are also preferred in countries where these are available, such as Korea and Taiwan. The difficulties which Japanese firms in Asia face have also included the fact they have allied themselves with the élites in some countries where those élites are unpopular, particularly in Indonesia (Ozawa, 1979). Everett, Krishnan, and Stening (1984) studied the mutual perceptions of Japanese managers and local managers working in plants in six South-East Asian countries. Factor analyses of ratings yielded three dimensions, which were termed managerial, entrepreneurial, and congenial. Japanese managers were generally rated high on the managerial factor, which included adjectives such as industrious, cautious, and honest. On the entrepreneurial factor they were rated high by Thais, Indonesians, and Hong Kong Chinese, but low by Filipinos, Malays, and Singaporeans. This factor was centred on the adjectives assertive, extroverted, and ambitious. On the congenial factor, all but the Thais rated Japanese managers low. This factor was based upon the adjectives tolerant, flexible, and cooperative. This study thus supports the more qualitative account provided by Ozawa.

Yoshino (1976) studied 25 Japanese firms operating in Thailand, and conducted some interviews also in Malaysia and Taiwan. Contrary to the figures cited by Ozawa, he found many more Japanese expatriates in post than there were in European or American firms in this area. He found this to be a consequence of Japanese mistrust in the abilities of locals to follow Japanese methods of decision making. In some plants, management was Japanese right down to the level of first-line supervisor. This pattern of staffing has one of two effects upon locally recruited management trainees. Either the locals observe that only minimal promotion is going to be available, and they therefore put in the minimum possible level of work. Alternatively, they eagerly seek out opportunities for training, including extended periods in Japan. When this is accomplished, they then leave the firm, since their level of training makes them attractive to other local firms. In both of these patterns, Japanese mistrust of the possibility of promoting local managers is enhanced. They see little prospect that locals will develop the company loyalty which a Japanese firm would expect of its employees. Negandhi, Eshghi, and Yuen (1985) discuss similar problems faced by Japanese firms in Taiwan.

Negandhi and Baliga (1979) summarize an extensive survey of 124 multinationals operating in developing countries, including 27 which are Japanese. While agreeing with Yoshino's view that Japanese firms face some difficulties in internal decision making, they found that Japanese firms had less conflict with governments and official bodies than did American firms.

Published comparative studies, with more detail of actual procedures used, focus almost entirely upon Japanese multinationals operating within advanced industrial countries. In considering these studies we need to bear in mind that not all Japanese multinationals are necessarily successful ones, despite the massive media coverage suggesting that they are. McMillan (1985) cites the case of Come-by-Change oil refinery in Newfoundland, which resulted in the bankrupting of one of the big ten *sogo shosha* companies, and of Mitsubishi Rayon, which withdrew from Canada after a thirteen-month strike. Other Japanese firms in Britain have experienced strikes, while in the United States there have been court cases alleging discriminatory hiring practices (Sethi, Namiki, and Swanson, 1984). None the less, these instances are more than balanced out by documented examples where plants have accomplished productivity levels equivalent to that of comparable plants in Japan (McMillan, 1985; Sethi *et al.*, 1984).

Fruin (1983) analyses the development since the Second World War of the Kikkoman Corporation, manufacturers of soy sauce, including their establishment of a plant in Wisconsin in 1972. He concludes that throughout this period management paid much more attention to what would work in a particular circumstance than to principle as to how things should be. Such pragmatism has proved to be a frequent attribute of Japanese multinationals, and has spawned a flood of articles in which authors enquire whether Japanese management is really distinctive at all. Kobayashi (1980) has pursued this direction by surveying 80 Japanese multinationals in comparison with 23 European and American multinationals. Respondents were asked to describe their present overseas structure and to predict how it might change in the future. Most envisaged a movement towards some type of matrix organization within a multidivisional structure. Asked which aspects of the classical Japanese approach would survive, the most frequently endorsed were (in order): joint ventures with host country firms; emphasis on market share rather than profits; joint ventures with *sogo shosha*; location close to raw materials; paternalism; lifetime employment and *ringi*. In a similar type of survey, Negandhi (1985) compared 120 US, German, and Japanese multinationals. The Japanese firms reported considerably more autonomy from headquarters. In comparison with the other multinationals they indicated that the problems they faced most frequently concerned personnel, marketing, and sales. This may not mean that they had more problems in these areas, but that they gave them greater priority.

A series of studies by Pascale and colleagues tests how substantial are current differences between American and Japanese firms operating in both Japan and the United States (Pascale, 1978a, 1978b; Pascale and Maguire, 1980; Maguire and Pascale, 1978). Fourteen American-owned units were compared with thirteen Japanese-owned units within the United States. There was a predominance of manufacturing and assembly but retailing and banking were also represented. Surprisingly few significant differences emerged. Comparing ten measures, Pascale and Maguire (1980) found only two that differed. The Japanese-owned firms spent more than twice as much per head on social and recreational facilities and they did more than twice as much job rotation. Furthermore, a larger number of differences were found between the Japanese-owned units and the comparable units owned by the same firms back in Japan. The Japanese subsidiaries in the United States were found to do more job rotation, to have supervisors who were rated more likely to listen to subordinates, and workers who were more satisfied, but also a much higher rate of absenteeism.

Some differences were also noted between the firms in the United States at managerial levels (Maguire and Pascale, 1978). Managers in the American-owned firms held larger meetings and spent more time in them, saw themselves as initiating more downward communication and receiving more upward communication. Their method of decision making more frequently involved obtaining the facts from subordinates and then deciding the matter themselves. The managers of the Japanese-owned firms more often used written communication to confirm the outcome of meetings and to request time off. They interacted more with their boss and less with their subordinates. They were more oriented towards consensus decision making, both with their subordinates and through being involved with their own boss. The personnel practices of these managers were also surveyed (Pascale, 1978b). The Japanese-owned firms had a smaller span of control at supervisor level and were more willing to allow workers to talk to one another on the job. Workers in the Japanese units reported significantly less of each of eighteen counterproductive behaviours, such as taking tools home from work. They were also stated to be more satisfied, although this is contradicted by Maguire and Pascale's (1980) report of the same data.

In summary, Pascale's project did succeed in finding a number of attributes on which Japanese-owned firms in the United States differed from locally owned firms. Most of these differences are consistent with the portrayal of Japanese management as practised in Japan. The majority of differences noted were at shopfloor level, but this may simply be because these are easier to detect. However, an equally important outcome of the project was the detection of an equally large number of differences between Japanese firms at home and abroad. This should encourage us further in the view that Japanese management abroad does not simply consist in the transposition of Japanese practices to other settings. A more active process appears to be involved, as Fruin (1983) reported, in which managements seek out what does and what does not work in a particular location.

This process of search is likely to include both the selection of worksites which appear more congenial, and the hiring of employees who will feel familiar with Japanese procedures. Lincoln, Olson, and Hanada (1978) predicted that Japanese managers and workers would prefer organizational structures with a tall hierarchy and less horizontal differentiation into specialized groups. They found that among a sample of 54 Japanese-owned firms in America, the larger the proportion of Japanese or Japanese-American employees, the more the organization took on this form. In a subsequent paper (Lincoln, Hanada, and Olson, 1981), they showed that Japanese and Japanese-Americans were also more satisfied in organizations which had this type of structure.

A further series of detailed studies has examined some of the Japanese firms in Britain. White and Trevor (1983) studied three manufacturing firms and three banks. They report that there were marked differences in the degree to which these organizations had become noticeably 'Japanese'. The plant which had gone furthest along this path had employees who were no more satisfied than employees of other British and American-owned firms in the locality, although they did feel more secure in their jobs. Their managers were not seen as particularly oriented towards human relations. However, management was more strongly concerned with timekeeping, quality control, and efficiency generally. More meetings were held. The workforce worked hard but was willing to accept management's standards. White and Trevor propose that this was because management worked the same hours. Managers were keen to impart their expertise and wore the same clothing. Further aspects of a related study which compared the personnel practices of four manufacturers of colour televisions are reported by Takamiya and Thurley (1985). The authors propose that generalizations about Japanese management are hazardous in the light of substantial differences they found between the culture of the different companies studied. Of the two Japanese firms in the study, one was markedly more 'people oriented' than the other. None the less, both firms had considerably better productivity than the matched non-Japanese firms. Other attributes shared by both Japanese firms included dealing with only a single union and a less differentiated personnel function. The conclusion drawn from this study, as from the one by White and Trevor (1983), is that what best accounts for the superior performance of the Japanese firms is their meticulous attention to production management, their superior coordination of different organizational functions, and the management of their relations with trade unions.

The evidence discussed above derives most directly from the shopfloor level of manufacturing plants. In other types of organization and at more senior levels, it appears that it may be less easy to create a distinctively Japanese organizational climate within Western countries. White and Trevor's (1983) study indicated that although the encouragement of collective responsibility was popular among assembly-line workers, there was more reservation among the white-collar employees of Japanese banks located in London. A similar contrast is evident in a detailed case study of the operations of the subsidiaries of the YKK manufacturer of zip-fasteners in Britain and France (Davis, 1979). Although good relations with the workforce are described, an instance of conflict with secretarial staff is included. It is likely that white-collar staff would wish to retain a stronger sense of their individual skills and possible career mobility.

Yoshino (1975) suggests that one of the principal difficulties to be faced by Japanese multinationals lies in the area of decision making. There are two principal sources of difficulty. Firstly, remoteness from head office is likely to make participation in *nemawashi* particularly difficult. Yoshino argues that the creation of autonomous international divisions at least reduces this problem. This position is consistent with the data collected by Kobayashi (1980) which we cited earlier. In a more recent work, Yoshino and Lifson (1986) propose that the strength of the *sogo shosha* lies precisely in their capacity to practice a worldwide network of *nemawashi*. The second problem of multinationals concerns unfamiliarity of non-Japanese managers with *nemawashi* and *ringi*. Studies in Britain by Kidd and Teramoto (1981) and Trevor (1983) confirm that some Japanese firms in Britain do use *ringi*. Instances were found, however, where this was restricted to Japanese employees and the British managers within the plant were unaware even that the system was in use. Similar barriers between Japanese and non-Japanese are said also to exist in some firms in relation to promotion, as Yoshino (1975) found in Asia. Above a certain level, only Japanese are appointed. This means that local managers with ambition for further promotion are likely to seek posts elsewhere. The same problems will occur in more acute form within joint ventures.

Such problems will only be overcome when Japanese management is able to trust local managers to the same degree that managers trust one another. Given the strength of organizational socialization processes within Japanese organizations in Japan, this is likely to be a continuing problem. Studies by Sullivan, Peterson, Kameda, and Shimada (1981) and Sullivan and Peterson (1982) have addressed the issue. In both these studies, managers were asked to complete a questionnaire concerning a hypothetical joint venture. Japanese managers expressed greater trust in the future of the enterprise when a Japanese was in charge, and where decision making was initiated by a Japanese. This held true whether the sample was in Japan or in the United States. Where an American was in charge, Japanese managers felt that disputes should be resolved through the use of binding arbitration, but when a Japanese was in charge mutual consultation was thought preferable. American respondents showed none of these differences in preference. Sullivan and his co-workers conclude that Japanese see themselves as expert in avoiding uncertainty and conflict, but that where they are not in charge they have no confidence that similar outcomes can be achieved. Such issues become particularly important within negotiations. Miyazawa (1986) analyses the multiple pressures surrounding the establishment of legal departments within Japanese firms in the United States, on the basis of a survey of 233 firms. Crucial issues are whether the department shall include U S nationals and whether it may be headed by one, particularly when seniority indicates that this should be done. Tung (1984) surveyed 113 U S firms which had experienced negotiations in Japan. The parties to negotiation were reported as frequently using different negotiation styles. Failures were most frequently attributed to these differences, while successes were strongly associated with adequate prior preparation by US negotiators as to Japanese methods. A study which also addresses differences in perceived styles is that by Miyajima (1986) who asked Japanese managers in Britain to complete a test of managerial orientation and to predict how their British colleagues might complete it. The Japanese managers saw themselves as focused upon task issues, while they saw the British as more concerned with power.

A final issue concerning the experience of Japanese multinationals has to do with the processes whereby managers are prepared for overseas assignments. Tung (1987) reports a survey of European, American, and Japanese multinationals. The Europeans and the Japanese were found to have much lower failure rates, whereby managers returned home before their term was complete. Japanese multinationals were shown to be particularly thorough in their preparation of those sent abroad, both in terms of language training and of provision of prior information and of resources on arrival. Such preparation shows the same meticulous attention to detail as does Japanese production management. For instance, YKK's managers in Europe are instructed not to drive Japanese cars (Davis, 1979), as a sign of willingness to integrate with the local community. The study by Negandhi and Baliga (1979) also found Europeans and Japanese better prepared for overseas assignments, partly because they thought in terms of longer postings.

This section has shown that the experiences of Japanese corporations abroad are many and various. Only the rhetoric of popular writing could have led us to expect a uniform Japanese style to emerge everywhere, when there are substantial divergences of organizational culture even within Japan. None the less we do have evidence that Japanese-owned organizations in many parts of the world appear to function differently from those with other types of ownership. In the final section we shall discuss further how sure we can be as to why this might be so.

Culture and Managerial Effectiveness

The first three sections of this review have surveyed the studies which have been made at home and abroad. A number of discussion points have been made in passing, but in this section we shall consider more thoroughly what types of conclusion the research studies permit. The issues at stake are basically three. We need to evaluate the widely held view that Japanese management is both distinctive and effective. Assuming a positive answer to this question for the moment, we need to know why this is so. Finally, we need to consider what implications our conclusions might have for managements, both Japanese and non-Japanese.

Within Japan there exists a flourishing literature known as *nihonjinron*, which seeks to distil exactly what it is about the Japanese which makes them unique. It is a truism that all ethnic groups are unique, but many Japanese believe that they are more unique than other cultural groups. In evaluating studies of Japanese management we need to be sure whether what we are considering is a particular instance of the Japanese fascination with, and perhaps even exaggeration of, their differentness, or whether there are indeed categorical differences between Japanese management and all other types of management. The studies we have reviewed make it plain that it will become increasingly difficult to argue that Japanese management is distinctive and unique. We have noted its evolution over time within Japan, and the manner in which Japanese corporations have been adept at modifying procedures and structures to align with the local needs of subsidiaries in varying parts of the world. On a broader front also, *nihonjinron* has received substantial critique (Mannari and Befu, 1982; Dale, 1986).

However, a number of more recent commentators have gone further and suggest that what characterizes Japanese management is no different from the policies which are pursued by the more progressive American corporations (Pascale and Athos, 1981). A more moderate position is that of Abegglen and Stalk (1984) and Buckley and Mirza (1985), who assert that there is no reason why Western firms cannot adopt policies and practices similar to the Japanese, even if they have mostly not done so yet.

Buckley and Mirza (1985) point out that whether or not Westerners should be in awe of Japanese management skills depends very much upon the manner in which one chooses to make comparisons with the West. While some sectors of the Japanese economy are extremely efficient, others such as agriculture and retailing are not. Still other sectors, while they may be efficient, are none the less in decline, just as they are in the West. These are industries focused upon the extraction and processing of raw materials, such as coal mining and the processing of aluminium and steel. Thus we do better to enquire not why the Japanese are such skilled managers, but why they are skilled at the management of certain types of enterprises.

Abegglen and Stalk (1984) indicate their position rather concisely in the sub-title of their book: 'How marketing, money and manpower strategy, not management style, make the Japanese world pacesetters'. Abegglen and Stalk analyse the basis upon which Japanese firms have been able to create competitive advantage within particular markets. They show that the ratio of labour costs in American and Japanese firms is directly related to *the number of separate operations required during manufacture of a product*. Where the number of operations is as high as 1500, as in car assembly, Japanese labour costs are half those of American car manufacturers. Where the number of operations is no more than ten to twenty, as in steel or paper manufacture, there is little difference in labour costs. The implication of such statistics is that Japanese firms are superior in the coordination of complex tasks. They also secure competitive advantage by restricting product variety and using large-scale facilities, both of which render coordination easier.

Although Abegglen and Stalk's lengthy sub-title dismisses management style as a source of Japanese success, this appears largely addressed towards those who suggest that analysis of management style is by itself sufficient to account for Japanese successes. Abegglen and Stalk do in fact discuss traditional Japanese management practices and assign them considerable importance. A better summary of their position might therefore be that Japanese management style is a necessary but not a sufficient explanation of the successes of the *kaisha*. While it is undeniable that Japanese firms are good at devising systems for coordinating production such as *kanban*, just-in-time and the like, it may well be that the collective orientation of the workforce assists in the devising and implementation of these systems. The same point could be argued with regard to the collaborative arrangements which Japanese firms sustain with banks and with trading companies.

Those who favour technologically oriented explanations of Japanese success (McMillan, 1985; Takamiya and Thurley, 1985) point to the way in which Japanese firms in Western countries can achieve equally impressive productivity, even where the workforce is almost entirely non-Japanese. There are two weak points in such arguments. The first is that most Japanese plants in the West have been open for a few years at most. One might anticipate a 'honeymoon' period for any new organization, particularly where the workforce has been newly recruited, and the production system is already tried and tested elsewhere. The YKK plant in Britain which was opened in 1967, and has frequently been written about as a success story, recently experienced an extended strike. Only passing time can show how well other plants in the West can sustain their initial successes. The second point is that most Japanese plants in the West utilize production systems which have already been designed in minute detail by Japanese in Japan. Many of the large number of assembly plants opened in Europe during the past several years in response to Common Market protectionism have been referred to as 'screwdriver' plants, that is to say that their task is only to assemble and package materials which have been designed and manufactured in Japan. While many such plants intend to make greater use of locally manufactured components, the processes of research, production design, and control remain firmly located in Japan.

It may be that rather than debating the 'hardware' versus 'software' explanations of Japanese successes, we should see them as the two faces of the same coin. It could be that the cultural context of Japan makes possible and encourages certain patterns of government, financing, research, production control and marketing and that these patterns have advantage in contemporary conditions. The firmest position from which to discuss the value of such a 'culturalist' explanation is the work of Hofstede (1980). Hofstede compared the values of managers working within a single (non-Japanese) firm located in 40 countries around the world. His analysis of the Japanese responses in his sample showed them to be particularly distinctive on two of the four dimensions used. The Japanese ranked fourth out of 40 on 'Uncertainty Avoidance', and top out of 40 on 'Masculinity'. The remaining two dimensions, 'Power Distance' and 'Individualism–Collectivism' were not wholly separable, and the Japanese scored an average ranking upon them. Hofstede's findings have been criticized for possible unrepresentative sampling, but they are none the less of great value. The classical attributes of Japanese culture are frequently portrayed as collectivism and the seniority system. Yet on Hofstede's dimensions of Power Distance and Collectivism, Japan was no more than average. The study suggests that there are numerous other countries with a more strongly collective orientation and a more hierarchical structure. On the other hand, Hofstede's data imply that Japanese are very strongly oriented towards Uncertainty Avoidance. Many attributes of Japanese management are indeed readily interpretable as attempts to reduce uncertainty, including their management of time perspective, investment in research, production and quality control systems and extensive use of *nemawashi*. However, Japanese avoidance of uncertainty is a selective process. We have seen that job descriptions are deliberately left open, and the practice of negotiation and of conflict management is enhanced by preserving areas of ambiguity (Pascale and Athos, 1981). The labelling of Hofstede's final dimension of Masculinity has been criticized. High-scoring questionnaire items loading upon this factor emphasize the centrality of work goals in the life of the respondent. If we assume that the Japanese respondents were male, it need be no surprise that they scored high here also.

In evaluating this type of culturalist explanation, we need to take account of the 'ecological fallacy', which cross-cultural psychologists have noted. That is to say, we should avoid the assumption that because a mean score on one of Hofstede's dimensions is higher for Japan, all Japanese individuals or all Japanese organizations are high on that scale. What we are discussing are population *means*. No doubt, there are many Japanese who enjoy the challenge of uncertainty or who hate work, just as there are those in Western countries who seek identity collectively or favour hierarchical authority. We also need to bear in mind that Hofstede's data derive from the late 1960s, and that many commentators see evidence of increasing individualism in Japan since that time.

Further evidence relevant to the culturalist model is provided by the rapid development of the Pacific rim economies, triggered by Japanese investment. While there is substantial cultural diversity in the area, there are some common elements not shared by Western cultures. Abegglen and Stalk point out that those nations in which growth has been particularly strong have more uniform ethnic groupings and low birth rates, while those with diverse populations and high birth rates have prospered less. The high growth nations – Korea, Taiwan, Hong Kong and Singapore – share a Confucian value system, with many elements in common with Japanese modal values. As Buckley and Mirza (1985) point out, Confucian values have a long history, and cannot plausibly be used to account for recent events on their own. However, they may provide a necessary though not sufficient basis for the optimal utilization of the types of production systems which the Japanese have pioneered. Low wage levels no doubt contribute also, but these are present equally in the low-growth South-East Asian nations.

Adler, Doktor and Redding (1986) propose that the modes of thought which predominate in Pacific Basin nations and Western nations differ in quite fundamental ways. If we are to understand the operations of firms within these countries we need to investigate not simply what is done, but how it is done and why. Such a proposition may at first sound close to the *nihonjinron* type of argument, except that it is generalized to the Confucian nations of the Pacific rim. However, it is based upon a detailed review of comparative studies of management, and may be helpful in summarizing what our review has found. Their suggestion is that while Western thought tends to focus upon the study of causal relations between abstractly conceptualized entities, Eastern thought focuses more upon the achievement of harmony between practical, concrete performance criteria such as quality control or sales targets. The value of this distinction between the abstract and the concrete can be illustrated through reference to Misumi's (1985) theory of leadership.

The theory proposes a distinction between the general functions of groups and organizations and the specific behaviours by which those functions are accomplished. Such a distinction has not been advanced by Western theorists. Our review has covered a number of areas in which such a distinction may prove valuable. For instance, studies of the intercorrelations of dimensions of organizational structure have shown some differences between Japan and the West. It may be that aspects of organizational structure such as centralization or formalization are indeed universal attributes of organizations, but that these attributes serve different specific functions in each cultural setting according to the meanings which attach to them. Similarly, dimensions of leadership behaviour such as task structuring and maintenance of good working relations may be universals, but the specific behaviours required to implement them in varying cultures may be entirely different (Smith and Tayeb, 1988). Thus it may be that while organizations in all parts of the world are faced with the same general problems, culture patterns in East and West encourage different patterns of specific problem solving. Growing internationalization may then reveal to us that some of these specific problem solutions have value not just within their culture of origin but much more widely.

Our argument thus leads to the view that Japanese management may indeed have lessons for Western nations, but that those lessons will need to be translated into the specific idiom of Western cultures if they are to prove applicable there. The findings to date suggest that this may prove easier in blue-collar occupational groups, and in market sectors where it is possible to retain functions key to organizational success within Japan. More substantial efforts to transplant entire Japanese organizations to Western settings are likely to encounter substantial difficulties, particularly in the areas of management decision making and promotion.

Consideration of the success of Japanese firms in the West leads us to our final discussion point: the impact of Japanese methods upon the practices of Western firms. This is most readily apparent in firms that supply components to Japanese firms in the car and electronics industries. In order to win contracts, they have been required to satisfy quality standards and delivery schedules specified by the Japanese. There has been some movement towards the development of long-term contracts between manufacturers and suppliers, with consequent reduction in the numbers of suppliers. Just-in-time systems have been widely implemented in the United States and British car industries (e.g. Turnbull, 1986). The joint venture between Honda and Rover has led to enhanced emphasis on quality within Rover (Smith, in press). Quality circles have been introduced within a wide variety of firms. On the whole the magnitude of these changes is not large, so that substantial differences most probably remain between the practices of local firms and their Japanese neighbours in Western countries, as the studies by Pascale and his colleagues showed a decade ago.

Dispassionate analysis of Japanese management is hard to come by. Japanese writers have tended either to stress its uniqueness or to foresee convergence with American practice. Western authors, on the other hand, have preferred either the view that its essentials are readily applicable in the West, or the view that it is a coercive system which would never work in the West. We have sought a middle path between these views, but it is time which will show to what degree the varying industrial cultures of the world will converge upon one another.

Note

Thanks are due to the Japanese Ministry of Education, Science and Culture, the British Council and the Unit for Comparative Research in Industrial Relations at the University of Sussex for grants to Peter B. Smith which made possible the writing of this review, and to Toshio Sugiman, Toshihiro Kanai, and Tadao Kagono for comments and assistance.

References

Abegglen, J. C., *The Japanese Factory: Aspects of its Social Organization*, Glencoe, IL: Free Press, 1958.

— *Management and Worker: The Japanese Solution*, Tokyo: Sophia University Press, 1973.

Abegglen, J. C., and G. Stalk, *Kaisha, The Japanese Corporation*, New York: Basic Books, 1984.

Adler, N. J., R. Doktor and S. G. Redding, 'From the Atlantic to the Pacific century: cross-cultural management reviewed', *Journal of Management*, 12, 1986, 295–318.

Atsumi, R., 'Tsukiai – obligatory personal relationships of Japanese white-collar employees, *Human Organization*, 38, 1979, 63–70.

Azumi, K., and C. J. McMillan, 'Worker sentiment in the Japanese factory: its organizational determinants', in L. Austin (ed.), *Japan: The Paradox of Progress*, pp. 215–30, New Haven, CT: Yale University Press, 1976.

— 'Management strategy and organization structure: a Japanese comparative study', in D. J. Hickson and C. J. McMillan (eds.), *Organization and Nation: The Aston Programme IV*, pp. 155–72, Farnborough, UK: Gower, 1979.

Buckley, P. J., and H. Mirza, 'The wit and wisdom of Japanese management', *Management International Review*, 25, 1985, 16–32.

Clark, R. C., *The Japanese Company*, New Haven, CT: Yale University Press, 1979.

Cole, R. E., *Japanese Blue Collar: The Changing Tradition*, Berkeley: University of California Press, 1971.

— *Work, Mobility and Participation: A comparative study of Japanese and American industry*, Los Angeles, CA: University of California Press, 1979.

Dale, P. N., *The Myth of Japanese Uniqueness*, London: Croom Helm, 1986.

Davis, S. M., *Managing and Organizing Multinational Corporations*, New York: Pergamon, 1979.

Doktor, R., 'Culture and the management of time: a comparison of Japanese and American top management practice', *Asia Pacific Journal of Management*, 1, 1983, 65–71.

Dore, R. P., *British Factory, Japanese Factory*, London: Allen and Unwin, 1973.

Dunphy, D., 'Convergence/divergence: a temporal review of the Japanese enterprise and its management', *Academy of Management Review*, 12, 1987, 445–59.

Everett, J. E., A. R. Krishnan, and B. W. Stening, *Through a Glass Darkly – South East Asian Managers: Mutual Perceptions of Japanese and Local Counterparts*, Singapore: Eastern Universities Press, 1984.

Fruin, W. M., *Kikkoman: Company, Clan and Community*, Cambridge, MA: Harvard University Press, 1983.

Hatvany, N., and V. Pucik, 'An integrated management system: lessons from the Japanese experience', *Academy of Management Review*, 6, 1981, 469–80.

Hayashi, C., 'Statistical study on Japanese national character', *Journal of the Japan Statistical Society*, special issue, 1987, 71–95.

— 'The national character in transition', *Japan Echo*, 25, 1988, 7–11.

Hazama, H., 'Characteristics of Japanese-style management', *Japanese Economic Studies*, 6, 1978, 110–73.

Hofstede, G., *Culture's Consequences: International Differences in Work-Related Values*, Beverly Hills, CA: Sage, 1980.

Horvath, D., C. J. McMillan, K. Azumi and D. J. Hickson, 'The cultural context of organizational control: an international comparison', in D. J. Hickson and C. J. McMillan (eds.), *Organization and Nation: The Aston Programme IV*, pp. 173–86, Farnborough, UK: Gower, 1979.

Itami, H., *Mobilizing Invisible Assets*, Cambridge, MA: Harvard University Press, 1987.

Iwata, R., *The Environment of Management in Modern Japan* (in Japanese), Tokyo: Nihon Keizai Shimbun, 1978.

Japan Times, 'Sohyo members complain about long hours, low pay', 17 January 1988.

Johansson, J. K., and I. Nonaka, 'Market research the Japanese way', *Harvard Business Review*, 65, 1987, 16–22.

Kagono, T., I. Nonaka, K. Sakakibara, and A. Okumura, *Strategic vs Evolutionary Management: A US–Japan Comparison of Strategy and Organisation*, Amsterdam: North-Holland, 1985.

Kamata, S., *Japan in the Passing Lane: An Insider's Account of Life in a Japanese Auto Factory*, New York: Pantheon, 1982.

Kanai, T., 'Differentiation of contrasting cosmologies among R and D personnel: subtlety in Japanese R and D management', *Annals of the School of Business Administration, Kobe University*, 31, 1987, 109–41.

Keys, J. B., and T. R. Miller, 'The Japanese management theory jungle', *Academy of Management Review*, 9, 1984, 342–53.

Kidd, J. B., and Y. Teramoto, 'Japanese production subsidiaries in the United Kingdom: a study of managerial "decision-making" ', working paper no. 203, University of Aston Management Centre, UK, 1981.

Kobayashi, T., *Japan's Multinational Corporations* (in Japanese), Tokyo: Chuo Keizai, 1980.

Kono, T., 'Factors affecting the creativity of organization: an approach from the analysis of the new product development', First International Symposium on Management, Japan

Society for the Study of Business Administration, Kobe University, 1986, 271–326.

Lincoln, J. R., M. Hanada, and K. McBride, 'Organizational structures in Japanese and US manufacturing', *Administrative Science Quarterly*, 31, 1986, 338–64.

Lincoln, J. R., M. Hanada, and J. Olson, 'Cultural orientations and individual reactions to organizations: a study of employees of Japanese-owned firms', *Administrative Science Quarterly*, 26, 1981, 93–115.

Lincoln, J. R., and A. L. Kalleberg, 'Work organization and workforce commitment: a study of plants and employees in the US and Japan', *American Sociological Review*, 50, 1985, 738–60.

Lincoln, J. R., J. Olson, and M. Hanada, 'Cultural effects on organizational structure: the case of Japanese firms in the United States', *American Sociological Review*, 43, 1978, 829–47.

Luthans, F., H. S. McCaul, and N. G. Dodd, 'Organizational commitment: a comparison of American, Japanese and Korean employees', *Academy of Management Journal*, 28, 1985, 213–19.

McMillan, C. J., *The Japanese Industrial System*, Berlin: de Gruyter, 1985.

Maguire, M. A., and R. T. Pascale, 'Communication, decision-making and implementation among managers in Japanese and American managed companies', *Sociology and Social Research*, 63, 1978, 1–22.

Mannari, H. and H. Befu (eds.), *The Challenge of Japan's Internationalization: Organization and Culture*, Tokyo: Kodansha, 1982.

Marsh, R. M., and H. Mannari, *Modernization and the Japanese Factory*, Princeton, NJ: Princeton University Press, 1976.

— 'Technology and size as determinants of the organizational structure of Japanese factories', *Administrative Science Quarterly*, 26, 1981, 33–57.

Meaning of Working International Research Team, *The Meaning of Working*, London: Academic Press, 1987.

Misumi, J., 'Action research on the development of leadership, decision-making processes and organizational performance in a Japanese shipyard', *Psychologia*, 18, 1975, 187–93.

— 'Decision-making in Japanese groups and organizations', in B. Wilpert and A. Sorge (eds.), *International Perspectives on Organizational Democracy*, pp. 525–39, Chichester, UK: Wiley, 1984.

— *The Behavioral Science of Leadership*, Ann Arbor, MI: University of Michigan Press, 1985.

Mito, T., 'Japanese management principles and seniority systems', *The Wheel Extended*, pp. 4–8, special supplement 12, 1983.

Miyajima, R., 'Organization ideology of Japanese managers', *Management International Review*, 26, 1986, 73–6.

Miyazawa, S., 'Legal departments of Japanese corporations in the United States: a study on organizational adaptation to multiple environments', *Kobe University Law Review*, 20, 1986, 97–162.

Nakane, C., *Japanese Society*, London: Weidenfeld and Nicolson, 1970.

— 'Social background of Japanese in southeast Asia', *Developing Economies*, 10, 1972, 115–25.

Naoi, A., and C. Schooler, 'Occupational conditions and psychological functioning in Japan', *American Journal of Sociology*, 90, 1985, 729–52.

Negandhi, A. R., 'Management strategies and policies of American, German and Japanese multinational corporations', *Management Japan*, 18, 1985, 12–20.

Negandhi, A. R., and B. R. Baliga, *Quest for Survival and Growth: A Comparative Study of Japanese, European and American Multinationals*, New York: Praeger, 1979.

Negandhi, A. R., G. S. Eshghi, and E. C. Yuen, 'The management practices of Japanese subsidiaries overseas', *California Management Review*, 27, 1985, 93–105.

Nonaka, I., and J. K. Johansson, 'Japanese management: what about the "hard" skills?', *Academy of Management Review*, 10, 1985, 181–91.

Nonaka, I., and A. Okumura, 'A comparison of management in American, Japanese and European firms', *Management Japan*, 17(1), 23–29; 17(2), 20–27, 1984.

Odaka, K., *Toward Industrial Democracy: Management and Workers in Modern Japan*, Cambridge, MA: Harvard University Press, 1975.

Oh, T. K., 'Japanese management: a critical review', *Academy of Management Review*, 1, 1976, 14–25.

Okubayashi, K., 'The impacts of industrial robots on working life in Japan', *Journal of General Management*, 11, 1986a, 22–34.

— 'Recent problems of Japanese personnel management', *Labour and Society*, 11, 1986b, 18–37.

— 'Work content and organizational structure of Japanese enterprises under microelectronic innovation', *Annals of the School of Business Administration*, Kobe University, 31, 1987, 34–52.

Ozawa, T., *Multinationalism Japanese Style: The Political Economy of Outward Dependency*, Princeton, NJ: Princeton University Press, 1979.

Pascale, R. T., 'Communication and decision-making across cultures: Japanese and American comparisons', *Administrative Science Quarterly*, 23, 1978a, 91–109.

— 'Personnel practices and employee attitudes: a study of Japanese and American managed firms in the United States', *Human Relations*, 31, 1978b, 597–615.

Pascale, R. T., and A. G. Athos, *The Art of Japanese Management: Applications for American Executives*, New York: Simon and Schuster, 1981.

Pascale, R. T., and M. A. Maguire, 'Comparison of selected work factors in Japan and the United States', *Human Relations*, 33, 1980, 433–55.

Rohlen, T. P., *For Harmony and Strength: Japanese White-Collar Organization in Anthropological Perspective*, Berkeley, CA: University of California Press, 1974.

Schonberger, R. J., *Japanese Manufacturing Techniques*, New York: Free Press, 1982.

Seror, A. C., 'A cultural contingency framework for the comparative analysis of Japanese and US organizations', in S. M. Lee and G. Schwendiman (eds.), *Management by Japanese Systems*, pp. 239–55, New York: Praeger, 1982.

Sethi, S. P., N. Namiki, and C. L. Swanson, *The False Promise of the Japanese Economic Miracle*, Marshfield, MA: Pitman, 1984.

Smith, P. B., and M. H. Tayeb, 'Organizational structure and processes', in M. H. Bond (ed.), *The Cross-Cultural Challenge to Social Psychology*, Newbury Park, CA: Sage, 1988.

Sullivan, J., and R. B. Peterson, 'Factors associated with trust in Japanese–American joint ventures', *Management International Review*, 22, 1982, 30–40.

Sullivan, J., R. B. Peterson, N. Kameda, and J. Shimada, 'The relationship between conflict resolution approaches and trust: a cross-cultural study', *Academy of Management Journal*, 24, 1981, 803–15.

Taira, K., 'Japan's low unemployment: an economic miracle or statistical artefact?', *Monthly Labour Review*, 106, 1983.

Takahashi, N., and S. Takayanagi, 'Decision procedure models and empirical research: the Japanese experience', *Human Relations*, 38, 1985, 767–80.

Takamiya, S., 'The characteristics of Japanese management', *Management Japan*, 14(2), 1981, 6–9.

Takamiya, S., and K. E. Thurley (eds.), *Japan's Emerging Multinationals: An International Comparison of Policies and Practices*, Tokyo: Tokyo University Press, 1985.

Takezawa, S. I., and A. M. Whitehill, *Workways: Japan and America*, Tokyo: Japan Institute of Labour, 1981.

Taylor, S. J., *Shadows of the Rising Sun: A Critical View of the 'Japanese Miracle'*, Tokyo: Tuttle, 1983.

Tracy, P., and K. Azumi, 'Determinants of administrative control: a test of a theory with Japanese factories', *American Sociological Review*, 41, 1976, 80–93.

Trevor, M., *Japan's Reluctant Multinationals*, London: Pinter, 1983.

Tsuda, M., *Theory of Japanese Style Management* (in Japanese), Tokyo: Chuo-Keizai, 1977.

Tung, R. L., 'How to negotiate with the Japanese', *Californian Management Review*, 26, 1984, 62–77.

— 'Expatriate assignments: enhancing success and minimizing failure', *Academy of Management Executive*, 1, 1987, 117–26.

Turnbull, P. J., 'The Japanization of production at Lucas Electrical', *Industrial Relations Journal*, 17, 1986, 193–206.

Urabe, K., *Japanese Management* (in Japanese), Tokyo: Chuo-Keizai, 1978.

— *Japanese Management Does Evolve* (in Japanese), Tokyo: Chuo-Keizai, 1984.

— 'Innovation and the Japanese Management System', Keynote address, First International Symposium on Management, Japan Society for the Study of Business Administration, Kobe University, 1986, 11–49.

Van Fleet, D. D., and R. W. Griffin, 'Quality circles: a review and suggested future directions', *International Review of Industrial and Organizational Psychology 1989* [*Volume 4*], Ch. 7, pp. 213–33, Chichester: Wiley, 1989.

Wagatsuma, H., 'Internationalization of the Japanese: group model reconsidered', in H. Mannari and H. Befu (eds.), *The Challenge of Japan's Internationalization: Organization and Culture*, pp. 298–308, Tokyo: Kodansha, 1982.

Wakabayashi, M., and G. B. Graen, 'The Japanese career progress study: a 7 year follow-up', *Journal of Applied Psychology*, 69, 1984, 603–14.

Westney, D. E., and K. Sakakibara, 'The role of Japan based in global technology strategy', *Technology in Society*, 7, 1985, 315–30.

White, M., and M. Trevor, *Under Japanese Management*, London: Heinemann, 1983.

Whitehill, A. M., and S. I. Takezawa, *The Other Worker: A Comparative Study of Industrial Relations in the United States and Japan*, Honolulu: East-West Center Press, 1968.

Yoshihara, H., 'Dynamic synergy and top management leadership: strategic innovation in Japanese corporations', First International Symposium on Management, Japan Society for the Study of Business Administration, Kobe University, 1986, pp. 353–376.

Yoshino, M. Y., 'Emerging Japanese multinational enterprises', in E. F. Vogel (ed.), *Modern Japanese Organization and Decision-Making*, pp. 146–166, Berkeley, CA: University of California Press, 1975.

— *Japan's Multinational Enterprises*, Cambridge, MA: Harvard University Press, 1976.

Yoshino, M. Y., and T. B. Lifson, *The Invisible Link: Japan's sogo shosha and the organization of trade*, Cambridge, MA: MIT Press, 1986.

Japan: Myths and Realities

Kenichi Ohmae

Chapter 15, pp. 215–41 in Kenichi Ohmae, *The Mind of the Strategist* (Harmondsworth: Penguin Books, 1982)

I have repeatedly cited Japanese products and Japanese companies to illustrate general points about strategic thinking and strategy. It should go without saying that I have not chosen these illustrations because I think Japanese business practices hold any special fascination for Western readers. The reason is simply that although I have served as a consultant to many leading companies in Europe and North America, my experience and knowledge of Japanese business and business strategy is still probably my principal qualification for writing. And perhaps it was partly that background which led you to begin reading. In view of Japan's business successes around the world, what a Japanese business consultant has to say about business strategy might, after all, be worth looking into.

However that may be, it is certainly true that Western businessmen have been hearing a lot about Japan, and a lot of what they have heard is both mystifying and misleading. Accordingly, I want to talk here directly about Japan, expose some of the myths about Japan that have confused Western businessmen, and outline – for whatever they are worth – the realities behind some of the strategic successes achieved by Japanese businesses on the world competitive scene. Keep in mind that we will be looking at comparatively large corporations; smaller companies can seldom compete successfully on the international scene.

The real differences between the Japanese and Western business systems can probably best be considered under four headings, which we will take up in turn. Let me put them as simple assertions:

- The concept of the corporation is fundamentally different in Japan.
- To the Japanese businessman, organization *really* means people.

- In Japan, the government acts as the coach, not the captain.
- The central notion of Japanese business strategy is to change the battleground.

Concept of the Corporation

Before World War II, Japan copied its corporate system from the West. There were capitalists and laborers, haves and have-nots. The big capitalists had come into being in the late nineteenth century as a direct result of the Meiji government's determination to catch up with the strong Western nations. Most of them, including the five famous *zaibatsu* (Mitsubishi, Mitsui, Sumitomo, Furukawa, and Yasuda), took over in one way or another, at very low cost, government-initiated textile mills, copper mines, shipping companies, steel mills, and the like. Japanese companies were run much like most Western companies after the Industrial Revolution; in other words, the rich got richer, and the poor stayed poor. The laborers, exploited and lacking any job security, engaged in the usual organizing rituals. Communists were active, and companies everywhere were under pressure from strikes and demands for improved working conditions.

Most Japan watchers in the West regard the nation's current industrial system – with its characteristic features such as lifetime employment and docile labor unions – as uniquely Japanese. In reality, it was forced by necessity in the turmoil of the post-World War II days. Nearly everyone was jobless. Virtually all factories had been burned to ashes. Money had become nearly worthless, with inflation exceeding 100 per cent per annum. The capitalists – the Big Five as well as many smaller companies – were broken up by *zaibatsu kaitai* because General MacArthur was convinced that some sort of military-industrial complex had pushed Japan into war.

There was virtually nothing there with which to start a corporation. Fortunately, the technology that had been devoted to the creation of tanks, airplanes, and ships was preserved in the heads of trained engineers, and some of these got together with a handful of managers from the prewar *zaibatsu* companies to start small factories producing rice cookers, clothing, and other necessities. These enterprises welcomed skilled labor but lacked money to pay wages, and so most of them paid in food, which in those days was more important than money.

In a way, these embryonic companies were more like communes than corporations. People shared their lives, hardships, and toil. If anyone tried – and some did – to organize and run a company in the old way, seeking to exploit the hungry laborers, strikes would break out. Not surprisingly, at this time the Japanese chose – though not for long – to live under a socialist government. In fact, people would have welcomed any regime that promised food.

Presently, some of these communes began to achieve a measure of success in producing commodities for consumers and hardware for the occupation forces. But their future looked uncertain until the Korean War, when all at once they were under pressure to produce goods at more than their full capacity. They reaped handsome profits and promptly reinvested them in productive capacity as well as paying wages to the commune residents, who thereafter became monthly salaried workers.

From that point on the story is well known. The Japanese enthusiastically deposited their savings in the banks, which in turn lent quite liberally to corporations that wanted to invest for growth. Even during the growth spurt, most of these corporations kept the original commune inhabitants as their founding fathers, and indeed the sort of villager mentality that prevailed in the early days has pretty well been preserved to date.

Before any political parties, let along national unions, were really able to organize, these commune residents had organized modest company unions in order to ensure good communications with the management and a fair share of the profits. Even today, being the leader of such a company union is regarded as a prestigious stepping-stone for an ambitious young worker on the way up the corporate ladder.

All these circumstances have been vital to the success of the Japanese corporate sector, and contemporary Japan watchers often point to them as the reasons for Japan's success. Some have even tried to copy features of the system. But the Japanese concept of a corporation, based on this commune or village concept, is fundamentally different from the Western model, which sees the stockholders as the owners of the corporation and the work force as employed labor.

In Japanese eyes a corporation is nothing but an assembly of people, each known as a *sha-in*, or member (*not* an employee), of the corporation. The stockholders are a group of wealthy and interested moneylenders. Like banks, they are simply another source of capital, willing to invest in the collective viability and wisdom of the corporation.

Many Japanese chief executives, when asked what they consider their main responsibility, will say that they work for the well-being of their people. Stockholders do not rank much higher than bankers in their list of concerns. Most Japanese chief executive officers (CEOs) are in fact employed in much the same way as factory workers, having climbed the corporate ladder starting in their early twenties and having been members of the company union before becoming *kacho* (section chiefs) in their mid-thirties.

Japan's high institutional stockholdings and relatively underdeveloped stock market can be understood only in this historical perspective. The important point is that the well-known Japanese 'system', with its lifetime employment, promotion by age, and rather compliant company unions, is a consequence of the postwar communal growth, not of any preprogrammed strategy. It is a matter not of an ancient cultural heritage but of a pragmatic institutional arrangement that has now endured for more than thirty-five years.

Today the earliest of these villagers are approaching retirement age. How long the social values of the large Japanese enterprise will be able to survive their departure depends on the art of individual management. In my opinion, the ad hoc creativity of the Japanese will enable most corporations to preserve their current attitudes and customs for quite a while.

The social climate I have described, however, is peculiar to the older, larger, and more prestigious companies; it is not found in smaller enterprises. During 1979 alone, Japan saw over 17,000 companies fail, and of course there was no job security for their members. Smaller companies, which are seldom unionized, tend to hire and fire as their overall workload fluctuates. This gives the system a built-in dynamism, encouraging the relocation of labor from less to more competitive enterprises. Letting the weak companies die instead of sending in a government rescue team is yet another unpremeditated advantage of the Japanese approach.

Organization Means People

Once the historical roots of the Japanese industrial system are understood, it should be clear in what sense 'organization' means 'people' in Japan. But let us go one step beyond history.

Most Japanese corporations lack even a reasonable approximation of an organization chart. Honda, with $5 billion in annual turnover, is obviously quite a flexible, strategy-oriented company, capable of making prompt and far-reaching decisions. Yet nobody knows how it is organized, except that it employs project teams very frequently. In most large corporations the managing directors (*jomu*), enjoying a very great influence on operations, are not even shown in line organization charts; they are simply footnoted as 'in charge of . . .' Many 'deputies' (a title frequently given to the number two executive in a section or department) do have line responsibilities, but these are not shown on the charts. From the Western corporate point of view, such an arrangement would be confusing and unworkable. Yet most Japanese corporations can react to a changing environment much more readily than their Western counterparts.

The Western organization concept, one must remember, is copied from the military. It is an organization without redundancy, designed to eliminate all confusion in lines of command and to respond infallibly in times of emergency. It separates thinkers from doers, and information collectors from strategists. Strangely enough, the Japanese have copied this concept from Western corporations. Typically, however, they copied only the form; the substance remained Japanese, or communal.

Grossly oversimplifying, one could say that in Japan every member of the village is equal and a generalist. As far as division of labor is concerned, by mutual understanding one worker may do the accounting and another the engineering work. But managers are frequently switched around so that in theory everyone has an equal chance at the presidency. In fact, this theory verges on fantasy as far as large, established corporations are concerned today, but it does suggest the underlying spirit of the organization.

Because of this same spirit, an employee who has been handed a certain responsibility does not limit himself to this responsibility alone but rather interprets his duty as somehow more encompassing. Because he feels married to the company for life and believes their fortunes will rise or fall together, he has, in a way, a top management perspective. He knows that his colleagues are lifetime colleagues and that they all need to get along well together. Thus, lifetime employment inhibits these expansive generalists from indulging in destructive power struggles and generally guides them to seek a more sensible consensus, which is the long-term well-being of the corporation.

The Western military-type organization, on the other hand, defines jobs a priori by means of functional descriptions and tries to fit the worker to the job. The worker who best meets the job description may not quite fill all the specifications. As a rule, he will always leave something to be desired. If he is a superb performer and bigger than the job description, he will either leave the company for a better position or be promoted to a higher one. In this way, a Western corporation is never staffed with overqualified managers; in fact, it is normally staffed with below-quality managers who have yet to make the grade or, having made it, never achieve much better than mediocre performance (the well-known Peter Principle).

This is one reason why so many Western companies fail to react to environmental change as successfully as Japanese corporations, which adjust so quickly to energy crises, currency fluctuations, microelectronic revolutions, extraordinary advances in production technologies, and other major discontinuities. Such causes of competitive obsolescence typically happen at functional interfaces, further complicating the problem for most Western organizations. Consider, for example, such issues as these:

- At the interface between engineering and marketing and possibly between other functions as well: Should Company A install computer-aided design (CAD) to free up and reassign some engineers into marketing so as to develop product concepts closer to the actual needs of the end users?
- At the interfaces between R&D, engineering, and purchasing: Should Company B manufacture large-scale integrated (LSI) circuits internally to protect the confidentiality of the circuit design, or should it purchase them from outside to take advantage of other manufacturers' economies of scale?
- At the interfaces between international, personnel, legal, production, and possibly others: Should Company C consolidate its overseas production plants and invest in a modern production facility at a single location?
- At all interdepartmental interfaces: Should Company D allow each operating division to establish its own international operations, or should it provide a corporate presence to host divisional growth in each country entered?

As any experienced manager knows, there is seldom a single decisive answer to all these questions. Neither is it possible to satisfy everyone concerned. These are issues over which some managers (mainly those worried about protecting their traditional functional or operational authority) will be hurt when a final choice is reached.

Separate functional units are normally incapable of addressing such complex issues, and a company organized along functional lines will be unable to resolve them without an overall central entity to coordinate problem solving. Japanese organizations, in which each function is loosely defined and each manager's area of responsibility slightly overlaps others, are typically much better placed to identify interface issues and act accordingly without major reorganization or rewriting of job descriptions.

But this tendency is by no means unique to Japan. Similar characteristics can be seen in some US and European corporations, typically those headquartered in small towns, in which key managers tend to grow with the company, rather like the Japanese lifetime employment system. According to a recent McKinsey & Company study, excellent US companies display many of the characteristics of the much-praised Japanese system. The key element seems to be that each corporation, regardless of its ownership, is run in a truly democratic and humane way, as an organization 'of, by, and for' the people.

Another striking characteristic of many US corporations is their heavy emphasis on long-range strategic planning. For Japan, which like West Germany has no business schools, it is a matter for envy that American managers seem so adept at developing rigorous and objective strategies. A Japanese planner who had just been introduced to the comprehensive computer-assisted strategic planning process of a large US company, exclaimed: 'My goodness, it looks as complicated as building a chemical plant!' In effect, most large US corporations are run like the Soviet economy. Many are centrally planned for three to five years, with their managers' actions spelled out in impressive detail for both normal and contingency conditions. During the on-going implementation process, each manager is 'monitored' on how accurately he has been adhering to the agreed objectives.

Long study of communist and socialist regimes has convinced many observers that detailed long-range planning coupled with tight control from the center is a remarkably effective way of killing creativity and entrepreneurship at the extremities of the organization, the individuals who make it up. The experience of large Japanese corporations, on the other hand, confirms the wisdom of relying heavily on individual or group contributions and initiatives for improvement, innovation, and creative energy. In Japan, the individual employee is utilized to the fullest extent of his or her creative and productive capacity through such participative methods as suggestion boxes, quality circles, and value analysis-value engineering contests. The whole organization looks organic and entrepreneurial, as opposed to mechanistic and bureaucratic. It is less planned, less rigid, but more vision- or mission-driven than the Western organization. The basic difference is that the Japanese company starts with people, or individual constituents, trusting their capabilities and potential.

Japanese companies have many built-in devices to develop individual capabilities, ranging from language and skill-training sessions to extended sojourns in the *Jieitai* (Self-Defense Force) and in Zen temples for mental and attitudinal development. Lifetime commitment to a company and to one's colleagues acts as a very positive and sustained driving force in self-development.

Another key factor in a well-run Japanese organization is the typical career path, especially for the élite. Even the highest-ranking graduates of the best universities and graduate schools start as beginners, not experts. If they are employed in a bank, for example, they will sit behind a teller's counter or go about collecting money from private householders and 'mama-papa' stores. In a manufacturing company, such graduates may start as production rescheduling clerks, working between the machinists and the line supervisors. In short, each newcomer starts where the action is and seldom where his brainpower would seem to direct him.

This emphasis on actual experience underlies the pragmatism and provides the basis for the seemingly long-term orientation of Japanese executives, in contrast to the short-term, analytical mentality of the West. Their strength lies in understanding what is really happening in the outside world among customers and competitors as well as on their own production floors.

Actually, in my opinion, many Western corporations already suffer from too much strategic planning. In the West, and particularly in the United States, there has been a tremendous emphasis on brainpower. One might call it a 'McNamara syndrome' or a 'von Braun complex'. The assumption seems to be prevalent that because some people are more intelligent than others, it is up to the smart people to tell the less gifted – through such devices as planning processes and job descriptions – exactly what to do. The 'smart' people, typically coming from law schools or business schools, enter corporate life at a pay level well above the top of the range for many middle managers. Compare, for example, the current compensation of today's typical top business school graduate with the pay of a retiring blue-collar worker or even a line supervisor.

In Japan, where tenure-based compensation is accepted as normal, a worker fresh out of college or graduate school earns – regardless of 'brains' – no more than a high-school-educated machinist. Western society has somehow managed to embrace equal employment opportunities (EEO) regardless of sex and race, but it seems to me that more EEO in training and promotion, regardless of people's educational and intellectual backgrounds, would be at least as important and pertinent to business performance.

In my observation, many of the problems of Western corporations are related to execution rather than strategy. Separation of muscle from brain may well be a root cause of the vicious cycle of the decline in productivity and loss of international competitiveness in which US industry seems to be caught. One 'blue-chip' executive I know, brought in from the recruiting market like many others, looks quite cheerful when he is talking about pricing decisions and competitive cost analysis, but his enthusiasm fades noticeably whenever I bring up his company's poor production technology and procurement practices, the real reasons why the business is unprofitable. Moreover, he seems at a loss for language to use in communicating with the work force. His élitist terminology – DCF, ROI, EPS, PPIC, price elasticity, and the like – means nothing to the straightforward people on the shop floor. They show every sign of having decided that they are indeed inferior to the élite and had better just follow orders or, when orders are not forthcoming, stick as closely as possible to whatever was laid down long ago in their job descriptions.

In striking contrast, Japanese top managers, having started out 'where the rubber meets the road', never tire of reminding the employees that they, the workers, know the business best and that innovation and improvement *must* come from the *genba* (where the action is).

Not surprisingly, in such well-run companies as Toyota, Matsushita, and Hitachi, that is precisely where many of the best new ideas have in fact originated. When the Japanese say that organization is people, they really mean it. They know that a great many contemporary corporate problems fall outside the scope of organization or planning in the paperwork sense. Only active and alert organization members, working as an integrated team, can properly address and resolve them.

Government as Coach, Not Captain

Few observers have understood the critical importance of primary school education in Japan. From age 6 to age 12, one theme was drilled into me: how Japan could survive. Our nation – so my teachers kept telling me – has no resources, but it still has to feed over 100 million people living on a mountainous piece of land, only 10 per cent of it arable, that is smaller than the state of California. The only solution to this problem, pupils were and still are told, is to import raw materials, add value to them, and export, thus earning the wealth needed to buy food from outside. We must do this or perish.

This cultural upbringing is the mainspring of the 'workaholic' nature of the Japanese. People fear not to work, because if they stopped working, the country would cease to function. If they stopped exporting, they would starve. In a sense, it is almost like a robot mentality, a posthypnotic suggestion permanently implanted in the Japanese mind. People argue that because Japan is now rich, it ought to begin behaving like a big country. But this century-long psychological conditioning cannot be altered overnight. The Japanese still believe that if the work ethic should deteriorate, the country would collapse.

A population of 100 million people really dedicated to work represents a monumental victory for any nation's educational system. Although it is not explicitly stated as policy, Japan's government is indeed dedicated at the highest level to creating a people with a unified value system. That value system is shared by all ministries, from the Ministry of Education (MOE) to the famous Ministry of International Trade and Industry (MITI). My 6-year-old son, for example, is now in the last year of the three-year kindergarten program. I would have liked him to be taught arithmetic and reading, but the school's overriding emphasis has been on getting him to learn to work and play with others. This is not very different from my own upbringing thirty years earlier. Whenever I wanted to do my own thing, I was constantly reminded that the nail that sticks up gets hammered down.

Because the Japanese education system emphasizes group harmony, it discourages heroes and superperformers. No genius is permitted to skip grades or advance faster than the others. Gifted children are taught to use their extra margin of intelligence to smooth out interpersonal relationships and help their slow-moving classmates. And that, of course, is just the sort of talent required of a successful Japanese corporate executive today. Without this kind of educational upbringing, the successful features of what is known as the Japanese management approach – QC circles, suggestion boxes, and promotion by tenure, to name just a few – could not possibly work as they have done.

Western upbringing, in contrast, lays a much heavier emphasis on individualism. In the West, people are taught to state their views and defend their individual rights uncompromisingly. Few people worry very much about the effect of these values on social harmony and cooperation in a congested urban industrial society. Is it any wonder that such individualists employed by large corporations occasionally show a distressing lack of concern for the well-being of the organization as management sees it? At any rate, for Western corporations that may be tempted to copy Japanese management approaches, this fundamental cultural difference in upbringing is worth keeping in mind.

Did the Japanese government deliberately formulate this educational policy in order to support a shrewd industrial strategy? Probably not; it came about as the result of historical consequences. Before World War II, the same realization – that Japan is a small country without resources – led to a totally different conclusion: 'Therefore, the nation must expand.' Now that history has demonstrated that such a solution doesn't work, the conclusion has become: 'Therefore, we must work harder than any other nation.'

Doubtless this is far more constructive than the expansionist doctrine of the 1930s. Yet today, faced with pressures from a West perturbed by their economic successes, the Japanese are beginning to talk in terms of a trade war. They think they feel pressures from the West similar to those which emerged from the naval conferences held in London during the 1930s, when the United States joined Britain in insisting on a 6 to 10 ratio of heavy cruisers against Japan. Take, for example, two recent headlines picked at random from the popular Japanese weekly magazine *Shukan Gendai*: 'American Retaliation Against Japan Is Inevitable' and 'Occupation Plan of Japan by Reagan and His California Defense Industry Mafia.'

The situation is by no means surprising. While trade is only one of several options that Western nations can pursue, it has been Japan's only postwar option. Thanks mainly to a constitution that bans the possession of military force, all the aggressive energies of a hyperdynamic nation have been funneled into economic and trade recovery. Sensing that its hard-won trade is at stake, Japan feels a sense of tension almost akin to that preceding a military showdown.

This is probably difficult for non-Japanese to comprehend, but it becomes more understandable after closer examination of the education system. Again, it is not a question of the nature of the Japanese per se. Japanese children of preschool age are probably among the most privileged and coddled in the world. Later, they are *taught* to behave in ways that advance the public good, *taught* to harmonize with others, and *taught* to work lest they starve. Education begins so early, and these implicit values are implanted so pervasively, that it is easy to miss the point that the work ethic is the direct result of education.

Many developing nations suffer from the lack of a work ethic and are consequently plagued by the problems of frequent job-hopping by skilled workers. It is no wonder their behavior appears more Western than Japanese. The educational systems of most of these countries were strongly influenced by their colonial masters. Education is probably the biggest reason why the Japanese are so dissimilar in social and industrial behavior to other Asian nationalities.

At any rate, it is no coincidence that this supreme value system should be shared by MOE and MITI, two seemingly unrelated ministries. Since World War II it has been an implicit national consensus that Japan's lifeblood is trade based on value added. This is why the Japanese government, although the smallest in any OECD nation relative to GNP, has so cleverly served as coach and cheerleader in support of the nation's long-term objective: achieving economic success without a military buildup.

This shrewd coaching role played by the government has been evident from the start. In the early 1950s, for example, MITI encouraged aggressive investment in steelmaking with the slogan 'Steel is the nation.' What it did in terms of subsidies was negligibly small, but by openly endorsing a company (Kawasaki) that was committing itself to a rather bold growth strategy, MITI fired up the whole industry to join in a 'me too' investment game. As a result, Japan as a nation has been able to produce high-quality steel at the lowest cost in the world. This competitive steel has been the underlying force behind Japan's current position in shipbuilding (50 per cent of global tonnage construction), automobiles (30 per cent of global units produced in 1980), and many other export-oriented industries, such as home appliances, machine tools, steel structure, and plants.

Today, MITI feels that the days of steel's dominance are about to end and is looking to very large scale integrated (VLSI) circuits to power the next industrial era. It has begun referring to VLSI as the 'rice of industry', meaning that it feeds into all industries, much as rice is the basic daily food of all Japanese. That kind of open endorsement is credible enough to motivate all companies in information-based businesses to join in a massive race to develop VLSI. Many foreigners, critical of the Japanese government's 'subsidies' to VLSI, mutter about Japan, Inc., or unfair competition. The truth is that the government chipped in a mere $130 million of the $320 million required by a four-year-long project. The governments of other nations might spend 10 times as much simply to subsidize microelectronics research and development in defense- and space-related industries.

Apart from rare investments of this kind, MITI has confined itself to openly endorsing vital R&D programs, mainly to develop alternative technologies for VLSI production. With this objective, five companies – Hitachi, Fujitsu, Mitsubishi, NEC, and Toshiba – formed an ad hoc cooperative in 1976, which dissolved itself in 1980 after four years of joint R&D efforts. Because they live in such a tough competitive environment, participating companies will keep investing heavily in VLSI; last year, for example, NEC alone invested close to $150 million in LSI production. None of the five can afford not to take advantage of the fruits of those four years of joint effort.

Already, products that fully reflect Japan's prowess in microelectronics – electronic cash registers, hand-held calculators, digital and analog quartz watches, cars equipped with microprocessor devices, microwave ovens, and the like – have become Japan's new export aces, and Japanese producers of VLSI itself, in the form of computer memories and microprocessors, are scoring further spectacular market successes abroad.

Once again, MITI's role with respect to VLSI is similar to its role with respect to steel twenty-five years ago: to encourage an industry critical to the survival of a nation obliged to live on value-added trade. Its financial contribution in this multi-billion-dollar undertaking, however, was a mere drop in the bucket. What is interesting, and in American eyes perhaps even a bit bizarre, is the government's immense credibility with industry. When MITI publishes a long-range plan, white paper, or the like, companies will study the document very seriously and – given the highly competitive nature of Japan's free economy – will immediately make a dash to get ahead of the competition.

Not long ago, in conversation with a high-ranking official at the Ministry of Industry in a European capital, I suggested that MITI's white papers might be worth studying as a model for providing industry with implicit guidance on the reallocation of resources. The official replied gloomily: 'It wouldn't work. We don't have the credibility; the industry would laugh at us. What's more, the Ministry of Trade will counter our proposal.' It was only then that I recognized how lucky the Japanese had been in combining under a single ministry both international trade and industry. Here again we see reflected the supreme conviction of the Japanese that international trade must be a national way of life.

Changing the Battleground

The consciousness of the nation's poverty of natural resources and of its late arrival on the industrial scene has had a significant influence on Japanese corporate strategies. Technology, marketing skills, and capital funds have all been handled very differently from the way they would have been handled in the West. Let us look more closely at each of these resources and see what perspective they yield on corporate strategy, Japanese style.

Technology

Before World War II, the Japanese government took a fairly liberal attitude toward equity participation by foreign companies in Japanese industry. For example, Siemens had a 30 per cent position in Fuji Electric through 1945, General Electric 50 per cent in Shibaura (Toshiba) in 1910, Westinghouse 10 per cent in Mitsubishi Electric in 1923, B. F. Goodrich 45 per cent in Yokohama Rubber in 1917, and Western Electric 54 per cent in Nippon Electric (NEC) in 1899. After the War, when most of these companies had been totally destroyed, very strict controls were imposed on foreign capital stakes in critical Japanese companies. This situation lasted until the mid-1970s, when the rules governing foreign capital participation in Japanese corporations were liberalized. During the intervening thirty years, Japanese companies aggressively borrowed Western technology through licensing arrangements so that technology would not become a critical bottleneck to their growth. It was during those days that the Japanese were called 'copyists'.

That is one side of the story. The other is that the Japanese are so resource-conscious that they do not themselves engage in all the activities necessary to bring products to market. For instance, while they were borrowing basic technology or design, many Japanese companies were working on other functions such as production technology, quality assurance, and yield improvement in order to generate the margins necessary to pay for the imported technology and to fund expansion of capacity. In the end, they caught up with the licensers technologically. Some of these companies, in industries such as microelectronics, steelmaking, and audiovisual home entertainment systems, are now innovating to advance the state of the art. Recently, some Japanese companies have been furnishing technical assistance to their opposite numbers in the West, reversing the traditional flow of technology.

Clearly, the habit of resource saving has served the Japanese well. Japanese industry would certainly not be where it is today if companies had tried to develop their marketing, technological, and financial capabilities all at once. They would have been weak on all fronts compared with the Western giants and unable to break out of the vicious cycle of underinvestment, lack of competitiveness, low profitability, and capital scarcity. Nor would they ever have become competitive in high-technology industries where cheap labor is no longer a decisive factor. It is therefore not surprising to see some prestigious Japanese companies contracting, as so-called original equipment manufacturers (OEMs), to supply components or even whole products to be sold under the trademark of Western competitors. These companies simply put long-term success ahead of the short-term pride and ego satisfaction of selling under their own brand names.

Many Western companies, especially the automotive giants, made the mistake of taking for granted the superiority of their own resources, especially their technological competence and engineering and marketing know-how. The automakers were exhausting their engineering competence in the effort to develop gas-turbine and solar-battery-driven cars at a time when the far more immediate challenges were to improve the emission efficiency of the traditional internal combustion engine and to reduce exhaust pollutants. Almost overnight, they found themselves forced to contend on a different battleground. By changing the design concept, relatively small, strategy-minded Japanese companies such as Honda, Toyo Kogyo (Mazda), and Mitsubishi had proved that a clean engine was possible.

This strategy of changing the battleground is a very basic habit of Japanese companies. They see it as the one effective way to compete against Western companies, with their larger markets and greater cumulative experience in technology, production, and marketing.

Today, some Japanese companies have emerged as global leaders, innovative not only in production technology but also in basic engineering and design. Moreover, recent technological advances have tended to emerge from the combination of several advanced technologies, and it is not surprising that the Japanese, with their talent for maximizing their strengths by combining available resources, should be pushing the state of the art.

Recent breakthroughs in VLSI technology, for example, have come from a combination of know-how about single crystal growth and about the electron microscope – both being areas in which the Japanese excel. Again, the home videotape recorder (VTR) became commercially viable as a result of advances in the recording density of magnetic tape and in ultraprecision machining techniques, again two areas of Japanese excellence.

Industrial robots, destined to become another big success in world markets, are likewise based on technologies – three-dimensional image sensors, microprocessors, and actuators – that are all highly advanced in Japan. Antibiotics, a large and growing field in the pharmaceutical industry, is becoming another Japanese specialty area; the basic technology consists of fermentation (soya sauce and MSG technology!) and knowledge of fungus production.

As a result of all these developments, Japan seems certain to make an increasing contribution to innovations in global technology. At long last, a handful of advanced Japanese companies can now afford the luxury of funding even quantum-jump innovation, from basic research through to commercialization. Since such innovation typically occurs at the interfaces, the flexible Japanese organization concept has therefore become an asset, especially when catalyzed by a generalist-oriented staff.

Marketing

In marketing too, the Japanese have avoided going global all at once. When they have an exportable product, they test it out in Southeast Asia and a few US cities (notably Los Angeles) in order to learn how to market it abroad. When the situation looks risky, they ask trading companies to do the overseas marketing on their behalf, again to prevent their lack of a critical resource (in this case, marketing know-how) from becoming a bottleneck to international growth.

Such caution does not reflect a lack of interest in overseas trade. On the contrary, the company will typically dispatch a high-caliber liaison officer, usually on the CEO's orders, to such places as New York, Chicago, and Los Angeles with a specific mission to develop plans for eventual direct marketing. Many of today's top corporate executives have been on such missions at some time in their careers. The fact that the company may ask trading companies to handle their initial overseas marketing or may accept OEM deals under well-known American or European brands is likely to reflect a methodical, one-step-at-a-time approach to the long-term goal of becoming a global brand.

It is clear in hindsight that such Japanese companies as Canon, Ricoh, Panasonic, and Pentax all had an ambition to become world leaders, but each started with a trading-company, dealer, and/or OEM arrangement. Once confident of their product quality and cost-competitiveness, however, they began to address their marketing inefficiencies, gradually bypassing first the trading companies and eventually the distributor and OEM partners. Some of them still accept OEM relationships, but they will soon begin to insist on own-brand marketing as well. Dual-brand strategies have in any case been hard to administer in the United States as a result of antitrust legislation, internal administrative complexities, and conflicts over allocation of engineering resources. It was because of such difficulties that Pentax left Honeywell and Ricoh left Savin. Both aspire eventually to become global marketers in their own right.

Sequencing their marketing resources is the wisdom of these companies, whose natural human and capital resources are so scarce. But the ability to achieve and sustain consensus on a single overriding corporate goal is a major factor enabling Japanese companies to take a sequenced approach. If they were organized like their Western counterparts and staffed with managers with challenging job descriptions and associated reward systems, taking a step-by-step approach would be extremely difficult, because some managers might look embarrassingly like underperformers.

Capital

Another instance of Japanese companies trying not to allow a weakness to block the achievement of their objectives is their high financial leverage.

In the immediate postwar era, capital was very short. The Japanese people were and are assiduous savers, but the future of most corporations was then so uncertain that they lacked the confidence to invest their savings in private enterprise. Instead, they put it into the banks, which enjoyed infallible credibility. It was through the banks that corporations with dynamic growth plans borrowed money. Freed from the need to justify complex growth plans to individual stockholders or prospective investors and from the need to worry about keeping the stock price high, corporate executives could devote all their energies to business: people, production, and products. They were convinced that by doing a superb job on these three P's they would earn the fourth P – profit – needed to repay the debt. And they were right. Had they been obliged to worry about making their financial performance look better in order to get the financing, they would have fallen into the vicious cycle of cosmetic financial management, opting for short-term profit maximization and neglecting long-term investment.

Again, sequencing was critical. Thanks to the integrative Japanese management style and governmental system, these corporations were not forced to perform before they were ready.

Another big helping hand in corporate finance came from the Japanese government's foreign capital phobia. The Ministry of Finance (MOF) and MITI, for example, in their determination to keep foreign capital from acquiring massive chunks of Japanese corporate stocks on the Tokyo Stock Exchange, did their best to encourage institutional stockholding. Although this stance is now gradually being relaxed, nearly 70 per cent of Japanese corporate shares are still institutionally held. This helped Japanese companies tremendously, not only because stock prices were less affected by the transactions of individual stockholders but also because these institutional owners were, like the banks, much more understanding of the long-term strategies of the companies in which they invested. And mutual holdings within a group of companies made it impossible to exercise short-term buying and selling options.

A Success Recipe

These examples amply demonstrate the way in which Japanese companies approach corporate strategy. Their long-term goal or ambition is to become global marketers, because that is what an island nation must do if it wishes to grow. But their realistic appreciation of resource bottlenecks has caused them to follow a sequential approach, taking, despite their ambition, one rather modest and humble step at a time. Their approach is designed to prevent any shortcoming from becoming a bottleneck to growth. Hence they have been led to seek a much wider range of strategic alternatives in production, engineering, and marketing.

Obviously, this approach is not without its pitfalls; many companies have disappeared from the scene in the aftermath of wrong strategic choices. Indeed, the number of Japanese corporate casualties has averaged between 13,000 and 15,000 annually. It is this tough, live-or-die domestic competition that helps Japan's free economy remain healthy.

A key aspect of Japanese corporate strategy, again prompted by the awareness of resource limitations, is the tendency to look for a different battleground on which to compete with the Western giants. For example, it was to capitalize on emission-control regulations that Honda entered four-wheel-vehicle manufacturing in the early 1970s, designing plant and car (the Civic) simultaneously so that they would be competitive in productivity with such experienced automakers as Toyota and Nissan. This approach, known as value design and zero-based production, has been one of the biggest single factors contributing to the success of assembly-oriented Japanese manufacturers.

Choosing the battleground so that they would not have to fight head-on against large Western enterprises has been the key to their success. They have sought out markets, functions, and product ranges where they could initially avoid head-to-head competition. As a result, Japanese production styles, design and engineering approaches, and personnel management philosophies are so different today that Western companies find it extremely difficult to fight back or catch up with their Japanese competitors.

Doing as the Japanese do, even if it were possible, would not be the answer. But Japanese strategic approaches, properly understood, can be a valuable source of insight for any thoughtful corporate strategist.

7

The Arabs of the Middle East

Organizational Behavior in Islamic Firms

P. Wright

From *Management International Review*, Vol. 21, 1981/2, 86–94

Introduction

Increasingly, American and Western European multinational corporations are viewing Islamic countries (particularly those with significant oil revenues) as profitable markets for their products and services[1]. As in other parts of the world, subsidiaries and joint ventures – employing, at least initially, cadres of managers and staff specialists from the home office – are important vehicles for developing these markets. Since few Westerners comprehend the 'Moslem mentality', these expatriate personnel typically receive little forewarning of the organizational behavior problems they are likely to encounter. As a consequence, their dealings with their Moslem subordinates, co-workers, and superiors tend to be frustrating, at best, and frequently are highly unproductive.

Below, several important areas in which individual attitudes and behavior in Islamic organizations tend to differ from their Western counterparts are discussed. Obviously, in such discussions, generalities are stated that do not apply in all cases. Nevertheless, an understanding of these fundamental differences will be helpful to Westerners who hope to succeed in Islamic firms.

Perception and Decision Perspectives

Perhaps initially it would help to delineate the 'mentality' of the typical Moslem vs. the Westerner through a discussion of their perception and decision perspectives. The enlightened Western businessperson tends to perceive organizations as being subsystems of the broader environment. Ordinarily, such a person also knows the enterprises are systems with their own subsystems of human and non-human resources. One of the challenges facing the knowledgeable corporate individual is to be aware of the relevant interrelationships that exist between the subsystems of the organization as well as the relationships between the organization and the society (Haire *et al.*, 1966).

Analyses of 'systems' by Western businesspeople primarily take into account worldly factors and their interrelationships on the bases of 'facts', 'issues', 'problems', among others. That is, the parameters of systems thinking for the Western businessperson are set by observable and/or worldly events.

Systems thinking for the Islamic executive takes on broader perspectives. The Moslem manager believes decisions should be made while perceiving interrelationships between worldly incidents as well as metaphysical events. Hence, while a US superior may be hesitant to terminate the services of an elder employee because it may be bad for organizational morale and because it would be a 'shame' (to discharge a person with long years of excellent service), the Moslem manager would share the feelings of hesitancy but because it would be a 'sin'! The Lord would not be pleased with ungentle treatment of a senior citizen.

As a case in point, several years ago, an Egyptian employee told her American boss who had just fired her: 'Look, what you have done to me will bring a curse on you. Don't you think you will be staying here for much longer!' Soon afterwards, the manager became very sick with intestinal disorders. The company flew him back to the US for treatment. When he became well, he was sent back to Egypt. However, the same disease struck again and the American manager finally had to be transferred out of Egypt.

The Egyptian marketing manager's reaction to the events was, 'Well, it is possible that the curse had its effect.' Conversely, the American financial manager in the same firm argued: 'Baloney! What's all this about a curse? We all know Egypt has hygiene problems and so our general manager was a victim of the poor hygiene in this country.'

Here, it is evident that the Egyptian manager has perceived an interrelation between worldly and deital phenomena while the US executive has viewed the same situation from the perspective of worldly interrelationships. These perspectives are, of course, very divergent and may result in serious misunderstandings when individuals from the two different cultures have to work together.

The basic reason for the Moslems' unique perception and decision perspectives lies in their monolithic view of the world through Islam. They approach their religion as an all-embracing, total system containing its own political-legal, economic-technological, and socio-cultural subsystems. Virtually nothing is imagined outside of this Islamic super-system. The depth and breadth of this 'system' is determined by the Koran (Moslem holy book).

Organization and Personnel

The Western and Islamic superior-subordinate relationships are significantly different from each other. Let us examine some of the main differences by focusing on personnel evaluation and promotion of the Moslems vs. the Europeans and Americans.

Personnel Evaluation

Westerners look at their employees categorically. Typically, a Western manager may evaluate the personnel by assessing their strengths vs. their weaknesses. To the North American and the European manager, such evaluation would have a net result (Allport, 1958). It may be that the employee is a net asset or a net liability to the organization, in the opinion of the manager.

The evaluation of the job performance of the Western employee by the boss would tend to affect the likelihood of success or failure of the subordinate in the corporate structure. It is also true that if an employee is very talented, but rates low with the immediate superior in personal aspects, the Western superior may promote that subordinate anyway (Katona, 1951). The emphasis is primarily on job performance, not the personality of the subordinate.

For the Islamic managers, the first consideration is the employee as a total person with related personal characteristics. And the person is more the concern of an Islamic executive than the job which is to be done (Pezeshkpur, 1978). All considerations, of course, take place within a religious parameter. The following case may clarify the way the Westerners approach their personnel vs. their Moslem counterparts.

A subsidiary of a European multinational corporation, located in a Middle Eastern country, witnessed the transfer of its American marketing manager to another nation. The outstanding salesperson in that firm, who was a European, was passed over for the manager's job partly because of his arrogance and partly because of his shortcomings in administrative skills. An African national was given the manager's job. The previous American sales manager had found the European salesman to be offensive, but had kept him on because of his outstanding performance on the job.

Soon after the African manager took over the management of the marketing department, he transferred the European salesman from his department to the personnel department. Not liking his transfer, the European salesman resigned from the firm. The verbal elaboration of these events by the new African manager of marketing is revealing:

> Sure, Patrick (the European) is a capable salesman. But he consistently got on my nerves as much as I tried to play ball with him. He was consistently impolite to me and uncivil to the others. He had no loyalties to me or to his peers. How could he have any loyalties to the firm if he did not have any toward its personnel? I would have fired him. But then he has a wife and three children. Firing him would not have pleased God. So I transferred him to another department. It was the good will of the Lord that Patrick resigned and saved us all a lot of trouble.

Promotion

The Western subordinate expects his/her promotion and future with the organization to depend substantially on initiative and performance on the job (Charles, 1971). The Western employee also knows that display of loyalty toward the boss and the firm may be helpful. The cultural environment of the West, of course, tends to encourage such expectations.

The overall climate of the Islamic firm, as influenced by its environment, seems to indicate that performance on the job has little to do with who moves up to become a higher and higher superior. The reason is that the person as well as personal factors are considered supreme and divine – not aspects of the individual such as specific areas of expertise or initiative on the job.

In the West, the quest is to fit the right person into the right job. In Islamic regions, the emphasis is to fit the good person in any job opening that may come up.

This is partly why Westerners are surprised to find that in Islamic private and public organizations official titles may have little relation to job functions. In Great Britain, Harry, the accountant, is in the financial department of his company. More than likely, his job involves accounting and financial matters. In Indonesia, Hatta is also in the financial section of a company. But, in actuality, his main function is to be the troubleshooter for his firm with the government sector. Financial matters are taken care of by others in that firm, not Hatta.

If it is not expertise or job performance, then what does affect promotion in Islamic organizations? Most likely it is a system of interpersonal relationships extending from the lowest to the highest levels of the corporate structure which influences upward mobility (Bass, 1971).

The Moslem employee seems to know that, in addition to being religious, it is necessary to cultivate the 'right' people, particularly his immediate superior, to have a successful career. And the subordinate tends to be aware that the typical Islamic executive values personal loyalty and goodwill (over and above competence). The principal function of the loyal employee, within this context, is to serve as a buffer for the immediate superior. If anything goes wrong, the loyal subordinate will do anything to blame other variables for the problem at hand, not the boss, even if the problem is obviously caused by the boss (Pezeshkpur, 1978).

So, whereas both the Islamic and the Western employee believe loyalty does help one's career, it is the concept of loyalty held by each individual which distinguishes the behavior of the Western subordinate from that of the Islamic subordinate. In Islamic societies loyalty can only be felt toward people and religious matters. In the West, the concept of loyalty can also apply to non-human and non-spiritual entities like the organization.

The Western employee, relative to the Moslem employee, would be more prone to uphold organizational interests when those interests cross the personal interests of the boss or the very person of the employee. This would be a display of loyalty and goodwill toward the organization. Contrarily, the Moslem subordinate is somehow convinced that what is good for the boss and the self would also be good for the organization.

The ambitious subordinate in the Moslem organization usually seeks to be chosen by a higher and higher-level superior who, in exchange for personal services, will promote the interests of that subordinate. But the shrewd Moslem must always leave a gap between himself and the immediate superior. The relationship may backfire if one's immediate superior goes out of power because the superior's boss becomes displeased with the subject superior's 'performance'.

Organization and the Basic Needs of the Employee

In order to eat, have shelter, and safety, the Westerner often looks to the organization as the means for obtaining physiological necessities. A German worker's statement seems to support this contention: 'I would like my job in this manufacturing plant to be steady and make compensations for rises in living costs so that I can provide security for myself and my family.'

In the Islamic markets, if the individuals are not able to guarantee for themselves and their offspring basic necessities, then it is not the organization to which they turn, but the Lord. There is a saying in some Moslem communities which is telling: 'Whoever provides teeth, will also provide the bread,' referring to ultimate security provided by divine power. This is why, for instance, many international managers are puzzled by the relatively low concern of Moslem employees with the possibility of losing their jobs.

Organizational Work and Social Esteem

It is not uncommon to find the reply of a Westerner to the question 'What do you do?' to be 'I'm associated with Hoechst', or 'I'm with Harvard University.' This type of reply associates the person with the organization.

Because most Western organizations of wide repute command prestige in their societies, the individual employee is thereby claiming social esteem by identifying the self with the prestigious organization (Scott, 1965). In such cases, necessarily the Western person would consider himself/herself subordinate to the organization.

The Moslems, however, because of their emphasis on the person, consider the organization of secondary importance. In response to the question, 'What do you do?', a Libyan professor recently answered, 'Through the grace of God, I do an excellent job of teaching business courses. My department and university have witnessed a substantial improvement ever since I began my teaching career in this college.' Here, the organization appears subordinate to the self.

Authority vs. Accountability in the Organization

The motivation of organizational personnel has received attention across Western and Eastern societies. The Western organization, relative to its Islamic counterpart, allows upper-middle-level and top managers much authority and in return expects accountability. This is perhaps why the Western organization has little concern with the motivation of its higher-level executive. Most motivational programs in the Occident are aimed at the middle managers, supervisors, and their personnel.

But in the Islamic organization, accountability is demanded by superiors from subordinates, although authority is rarely delegated (Pezeshkpur, 1978). The ramification is that with the exception of the very top managers, all other executives are left with little authority. As a result, even insignificant matters are often pushed up the organization by the personnel for top-level decisions. Rarely would the Moslem employees initiate any activities. This remains the case until and unless jobs are specifically assigned to particular employees by the top management. The exception to this kind of predisposition is strictly routine work which the employee has done throughout the years.

Contrarily, the Western employee is much more prone to display initiative and action in facing and solving problems. European and American employees and managers tend to be comparatively more action-oriented because they seem to know the parameters of their levels of authority better (Webber, 1969). They are also more likely to sense the degree of power associated with their position and their personal attributes.

Exercise of Power in the Organization

The Western executives may desire power in the organization as may the Islamic managers. But here again, the approaches to power take enormously different forms. The American or European manager may want power, but would consider it socially unacceptable to hunger for it (French and Raven, 1960). Those executives who have power, deny having it. And the exercise of power by the Westerner is usually done discreetly.

Seeking power and using it is done openly in the Moslem organization. Since the middle and lower-level Islamic personnel know that their chance of possessing and exercising organizational power is limited, they capitalize on what little power they may have whenever possible. This is manifested by the authoritarian behavior of lower level personnel towards their underlings. And the higher-level Moslem managers, being aware of their positions, not only desire power openly but flaunt it.

The Islamic managers generally believe that corporate entities need strong leaders who are willing to force their wills on their organizations. Consequently, contrary to Western organizations which tend to have comparatively stable goals, organizational goals in Moslem markets seem to shift with the changeover of organization heads.

Even the Islamic bosses of very large and public organizations are quite willing to superimpose their desires on their establishments. A while back, for instance, an African nation's public administration's benefit program shifted its emphasis from helping farmers in the agricultural sector to building national infrastructures, reflecting the different wills of two successive program directors.

As another example, when a larger Kuwaiti trading firm had a changeover of the top manager (from father to son), the bulk of business soon veered away from consumer imports and toward trading of industrial products within several Middle Eastern countries. Noteworthy is that the Islamic top executives are, in fact, expected by their cultural environments to make their enterprises what they will regardless of successful past or existing corporate purposes. The Western managers, in contrast, are culturally expected to follow an evolutionary course. Generally, winning past corporate purposes are to be built upon, not revamped.

Groups in the Organization

People across societies join organizational groups in order to establish quid pro quos, materially and psychologically (Smith, 1973). That is, certain personal disutilities are borne by individuals in order to acquire certain utilities through the work group and organization.

At least theoretically, unless the net effect of this disutility/utility spectrum is at a break-even point, the individual would be predisposed to separate the self from the group. While initially most people would join a work organization for economic rewards, within such organizations they tend to combine with other groups for professional and psychological reasons.

One way to visualize the group in an organization is through the notion of synergy. This notion suggests that an amalgam of people in a group may display characteristics, behavior, and productivity significantly different from the individual persons composing it.

Positive synergy means that the summation of individual efforts within a group yields more than the addition of each individual's efforts in isolation from the group. Negative synergy holds the opposite meaning.

In the Occident, the work group is believed to be able to accomplish goals not attainable through individual efforts. In fact, much of Western advancement is attributed to effective group efforts.

Positive synergy appears to hold validity for many European and American groups since their individuals believe in the cooperative spirit. Cooperation denotes modifying one's own behavior to allow for the viability of a group.

But in Islamic markets, most groups can only exist for as long as the individuality of each member is not threatened. Moslem people are reluctant to alter their behaviors in order to belong to certain groups – including work groups. Furthermore, Moslems are hesitant to submerge their individual goals in order to meet group goals.

That is why voluntary team work, in or out of the work place, has never taken root in the Islamic culture. Only authoritarian formal groups may be expected to function with any potency. But even authoritarian formal work groups are predisposed to negative synergism because of their inherent lack of cooperative spirit.

Departmentalization and Specialization vs. Personalization

Given the purposes of a corporate entity, the attempt in the Western organization is to identify and structure unit tasks, to group these tasks into individual jobs, to group the jobs into administrative units, and to amalgamate these units into larger departments in order to achieve the corporate purposes. Because the Western organization has evolved in response to modern science and technology, the trend toward departmentalization has received a strong impetus from the tremendous advancements in scientific and technological breakthroughs.

The Western organization is also characterized by having specialists. It is the specialists and their abilities to interact with various corporate 'hardwares' and 'softwares' which provide the Western enterprise with its competitive edge. With growth, more specialists have been recruited and with more specialists, again refinements in departmentalization have occurred. The American and European firm has incorporated departmentalization and specialization in order to improve productivity (and hence profitability) within an ever-accelerating scientific and technological corporate environment.

But the Islamic corporate entity has essentially remained a charismatic organization. Although with national development plans select Moslem organizations have, to a limited degree, responded to science and technology, these organizations are not likely to be administered efficiently. The reason for this is that, unlike the emphasis of the Western enterprises on productivity, the Islamic firms stress various factors, one of which may be productivity.

The corporate entity in Islamic markets is prized mainly as a vehicle for promotion of the interests of the individual as well as the interests of the family members and friends. Needless to say, such an approach to organizations would not significantly contribute to productivity. Even Moslem entrepreneurs and small businesspeople hardly ever display an overriding concern with productivity per se.

The approach to the management of large Islamic organizations is also through personalization – not departmentalization or specialization. That is, often the organization is molded and remolded around the individual personalities of the top executives.

When specialists are required and the members of the family and friends simply do not have capabilities of accomplishing specialized tasks, one of two alternatives is generally chosen. Either outside consultants are hired (often from abroad) or specialists are brought into the organization. In the latter case, rarely would the specialists acquire organizational authority and power beyond the sphere of their expertise.

Organizational Perspective and Corporate Planning

One of the most glaring differences between Western and Islamic executives is their time orientation. The very concept of organization in America and Europe is futuristic – the organization has eternal life. Western managers generally dwell on the route from the present to the future.

For generations, the Western society has been programmed to anticipate evolutionary changes. Even upshots in science and technology have produced complementary changes to the past and existing Western ways of life. Therefore, it makes sense to be future oriented in the Western organization.

The Islamic mentality primarily dwells on the past, with some emphasis on the present and practically no concern with the future (Moore, 1976). Nearly all Moslems believe in predestination. That is, they believe that the affairs of the world, nations, organizations, individuals and all else have been worked out by the Heavens. Nothing can be done to alter fate.

Backgrounds of most Moslems seem to give credence to believing in elements of predestination. The people of Islam as well as the developing world mainly can look back to hectic, random, revolutionary changes in their nations as well as in their organizations (Pye, 1962). Thus, the Moslems almost find it futile to be concerned with the future. For what is the use of thinking ahead when predicting the future and one's control of it appears all but impossible? Given this scenario, corporate planning, which in Europe and North America has been resorted to by increasing numbers of well-managed firms, has rarely been applied in Moslem markets.

Top Managers

The chief executive officer and other top executives in the Western firm tend to conduct tasks which are different from those middle-level managers and lower-level supervisors. Given the opportunities and constraints in the environment, the American and European top managers are architects of their organizational purposes. The general managers preside over enterprises which contain many technical specialties.

It is not uncommon to find that in the Occident, managers delegate decision-making authority of specialized areas to their various management teams. The role of the top managers often is to define corporate objectives, to plan, to organize, to motivate, to control, to mediate, and to coordinate.

In Moslem regions, the top managers, in fact, play the role of assistants to the heads of their corporate departments as well as the middle- and lower-level executives. As was mentioned earlier, because authority is seldom delegated down the corporate structure, even trivial matters are pushed up the organization for top-level decision-making. A typical day for the Islamic manager entails having to attend to multitudes of organizational problems – some of them surprisingly insignificant. As an example, a Moslem Malaysian top executive recently had to settle a dispute between two production workers on who should work the morning shift and who the afternoon shift.

Conclusion

The successful conduct of business in Moslem regions of the world requires attitudes and skills significantly different from those needed to operate in Europe and North America. Western expatriate managers should realize that compromise and an open mind would be prerequisites for triumphant corporate management in the Islamic countries. Awareness of the 'Islamic way' does not automatically assure US business of great results in the Islamic markets. But such awareness may allow for the development of more imaginative and effective approaches to management in the Islamic world.

Notes

1. A recent study by R. A. Ajami suggests that Arab élites or opinion leaders generally hold favorable and receptive views of foreign multinationals. See 'The multinational firm and host Arab society: areas of conflict and convergence', *Management International Review*, Vol. 20, 1980/1, 16–27.

References

Ajami, R. A., 'The multinational firm and host Arab society: areas of conflict and convergence', *Management International Review*, Vol. 20, 1980/1, 16–27.

Allport, Gordon W., 'What units shall we employ?', in *Assessment of Human Motives*, ed. Gardner Lindzey, New York: Holt, Rinehart and Winston, 1958.

Bass, B. M., 'The American advisor abroad', *The Journal of Applied Behavioral Science*, No. 3, 1971.

Charles, A. W., 'The self concept in management', *S.A.M. Advanced Management Journal*, April 1971, 32–8.

French, J. R. and B. Raven, 'The bases of social power', *Group Dynamics: Research and*

Theory, pp. 607–23, eds. D. Cartwright and A. Zander, New York: Harper & Row, 1960.

Haire, M., E. E. Ghiselli and L. W. Porter, *Managerial Thinking: An International Study*, New York: John Wiley & Sons, 1966.

Katona, George, *Psychological Analysis of Economic Behavior*, New York: McGraw-Hill, 1951.

Moore, James, 'The Islamic bequest', *New Scientist*, 1 April 1976, p. 34.

Pezeshkpur, Changiz, 'Challenges to management in the Arab world', *Business Horizons*, Vol. 21, No. 4, August 1978, pp. 47–55.

Pye, Lucian W., *Politics, Personality, and Nation Building: Burma's Search for Identity*, New Haven: Yale University Press, 1962, pp. 54–5.

Scott, W. A., *Values and Organizations*, Chicago: Rand McNally, 1965.

Smith, Peter, *Groups within Organizations*, New York: Harper & Row, 1973.

Webber, Ross, *Culture and Management*, Homewood, Illinois: Richard D. Irwin, 1969.

Social Pressures and the Executive Role *and* Conflict Management

Farid A. Muna

Chapters 3, pp. 26–43 and 5, pp. 63–70 in Farid A. Muna, *The Arab Executive* (London: Macmillan, 1980)

Social Pressures and the Executive Role

All the world's a stage,
And all the men and women merely players;
They have their exits and their entrances,
And one man in his time plays many parts

Shakespeare (1564–1616),
As You Like It, II, vii, 140–43

Social pressures impinge on the Arab executive's attitudes and behaviour. These pressures impose on his time, energy, and performance. In the first part of this chapter we examine the nature and extent of these pressures. In the second part we 'zoom in' and focus more closely on the Arab executive at the micro-level by examining his role in his community as well as in his organization.

Social Pressures

The Arab executive is viewed as a person who is at the helm of an organization which, in turn, is perceived as a business-oriented social system embedded in the larger systems of community and society. Viewed from this perspective, we may regard the executive as both a *target* and an *agent* of social influence and change.

Figure 1 The executive and his environment

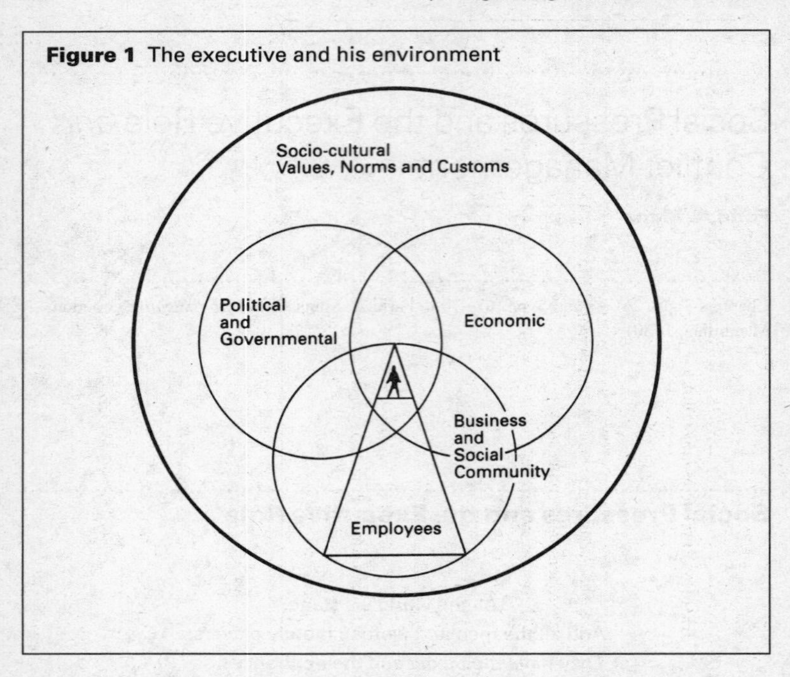

One helpful way of conceptualizing the executive's environment is depicted in Figure 1. In this section our focus is on the social pressures stemming from the wider systems of community and society. Of course, one must bear in mind that the conceptual separation shown in Figure 1 is only meant to simplify social reality and aid in its analysis.

The term social pressure refers here to the expectations, demands, or constraints which society places on its members. These pressures can be seen as the price of membership which individuals must pay to belong to a social system. In turn, these expectations, demands, and constraints originate from, and are shaped by, the socio-cultural values, norms, and customs. As in all societies, these values, norms, and customs (often summed up by the term culture) have their roots in a long history of traditions, in religion, and past and present philosophical, political, or economic ideologies.

A large number of social pressures were mentioned by 52 Arab executives from six Arab countries in my research. However, only those mentioned by three or more executives are summarized in Table 1. Although closely

Table 1 Social pressures as reported by Arab executives ($N = 52$)

Socio-cultural		Business and social community	
Type	*Frequency of mention**	*Type*	*Frequency of mention**
1. Low value of time	19	1. Fusion of business, social, and personal life	18
2. Lack of industrial mentality	10	2. Reputation in community	17
3. Restrictions on women	9	3. Top-man syndrome	11
4. Individualistic approach to work	6	4. Social visits at the office	10
5. Dislike of manual work	4	5. High expectations for success	5
6. Marketing constraints	3	6. Nepotism	3
7. The week-end problem	3		

*It must be pointed out that the frequency of mention shown in this table is a conservative estimate of social pressures as felt by Arab executives. This is because open-ended questions were utilized and therefore the above responses were *volunteered* by the executives. Now that these pressures have been identified, future research on this subject will do well to use more structured questions.

interrelated, these pressures are categorized into those that stem from the wider society (socio-cultural) and those pressures from the executives' immediate business and social communities. We discuss very briefly each of these pressures, leaving until later an explanation of how they influence the executives' managerial and interpersonal styles.

Socio-Cultural Pressures

Low value of time Nineteen Arab executives voiced concern over the low value which their fellow countrymen place on time. The examples given by the executives range from lack of punctuality in time schedules and appointments; procrastination and 'tomorrow' (*buqra*) attitude; to a general lack of respect for time. Moreover, this seems to apply to many people, from employees and clients to government officials. Interestingly, these nineteen executives were nationals of all six Arab countries, and were almost equally distributed among these countries.

Lack of industrial mentality Closely related to the above, this attribute was seen by ten executives as a constraint on their performance. This attribute is exemplified by the lack of industrial discipline in such things as aversion to systems and procedures, lack of organization (especially delegation), and a non-professional attitude toward business. Again, the ten executives were nationals of all six Arab countries.

Restrictions on women Nine executives considered the societal restrictions on women – especially their exclusion from the work arena – as a constraint on their organizational performance. Five out of the nine executives were from Saudi Arabia; two were Lebanese executives who were referring to their extensive business operations in Saudi Arabia; and two were Jordanian executives who had women on their payroll but complained that it was difficult to include them in the social activities of their companies. Although women in the other four Arab countries are, comparatively speaking, far from being liberated, none of the executives from these other countries considered the present level of women's involvement in business as a serious problem.

Individualistic approach to work Six executives (from five countries) felt that Arab employees are individualistic as exemplified by a preference to work alone rather than in a team; and by the tendency to take sole credit for good deeds and to pass the blame to others, or to circumstances, when things go wrong.

Dislike of manual work Three Saudi Arab executives and one UAE executive expressed displeasure regarding the dislike of manual work by the nationals of their respective countries. These executives felt that 'it is a shame that our young men demand only clerical and administrative work'.

Marketing constraints Three executives felt that societal values and norms restrict certain types of advertising or marketing. For example, one executive in the consumer industry complained that he cannot advertise certain women's garments and articles in many parts of the Arab world. Another executive felt that it may take years for door-to-door selling and mail advertising to become acceptable. The third executive pointed out that the Arab consumer (including the industrial buyer) often bases his buying decision on the personality of the salesman rather than the quality of the product being sold, and/or after-sales service offered.

The weekend problem For those executives whose business is highly interrelated with Western companies, there exists the problem of the 'two weekends' in which communications are difficult for 3½ to 4 days out of each week. The weekend for Arab companies is usually Thursday afternoon and Friday, meanwhile the Western firms observe Saturday and Sunday as their weekend. Only three Arab executives mentioned this as a practical problem which they face, but if the volume of business with foreign companies increases it is likely that this problem will be felt by more Arab executives, as well as the foreign businessman.

Pressures from the Business and Social Community

Fusion of business, social and personal life This heading refers to the inability of executives to separate business affairs from social or personal life. As one executive put it: 'In the West one may be able to compartmentalize his business life, his social life, and his personal life, but it is not easy in the Arab world . . . they are often one and the same.' This was a problem for eighteen Arab executives from all six countries. Both employees and outsiders (clients, suppliers and government officials) would call on them at home and on weekends to handle business problems. Also, many of their social affairs are meant to enhance the business. These executives felt *compelled* to accept this sort of pressure in order to remain successful.[1] Only a minority of four executives indicated that they have been able to escape this pressure by making it well known to employees and outsiders that evenings and weekends 'belong to me and my family'. The remainder of the executives did not seem to see this pressure as a problem – for, either they encourage this practice, or they willingly accept it as part of their work even though it taxes their time, energy, and family life.

Reputation in community The executives were asked to name those people whom they take into consideration when making personal decisions; in short, people whose opinion and approval matter. Twenty-eight executives said that what mattered was the opinion of family members, close friends and/or employees. This was an expected response since the reference groups and 'significant others' to most persons usually are a small circle of family, friends and work groups: those people whom one knows personally and is affiliated with.

What is interesting, however, is that as many as seventeen executives mentioned the 'larger' community as their reference group, or those whose judgement and approval matter. This community includes those people whom one knows personally as well as those people one does not know. Here, these executives repeatedly mentioned the word reputation – often family reputation. They felt that this reputation is at stake if one did not conform to the community's norms and expectations. Indeed, three of these executives said that when travelling (within Europe) they are able to relax and 'let their hair down'. One executive said: 'I don't care what people think or say when I am in London, for example.' In short, these seventeen executives (from five Arab countries) felt that the community is exerting a pressure on them to which they must *conform*. Perhaps some are conforming to the social pressure because they consider it correct and right (that is they have internalized the community's values and norms); others may be conforming because they feel that the cost of membership in the community is not too high. It is not our purpose here to determine the reasons for conformity, but it is interesting, nevertheless, that several executives voluntarily stated that they do lead a different lifestyle when they are in an alien country.

Of the remaining executives, four said they 'did not care what people would think or say'. Three others preferred not to express their views on that question.

Top-man syndrome The top-man syndrome refers to the insistence by clients, suppliers, and government officials on dealing only with the head of the organization. Eleven executives (from five countries) considered this an unnecessary burden on their time and energy.

There are two aspects to this problem. First, there is the feeling among outsiders (clients, suppliers, and so on) that only the top man of an organization can get things done: their trust and confidence is often in the person rather than in the organization. As one president of a large company (over 10,000 employees) put it: 'They [clients] insist on my presence during the negotiations . . . They are offended if I am not personally involved . . . I am unable to delegate these things to my specialized subordinates.' Another executive complained: 'People with a problem come here and demand to see me; they start from the top instead of starting from where the problem eventually gets solved.'

The second aspect concerns the executive's inability to escape from his many ceremonial duties such as invitations to social events, conventions, and various other ceremonies. Although these executives accept their role as formal representatives of their organization,[2] it is the *excessive* pressure on their time which troubled them.

Social visits at the office Ten Arab executives (from four countries) were annoyed by the custom of close friends who would drop in to the office for non-business chats over coffee or tea. This phenomenon is closely related to some of the items discussed above such as value of time and the fusion of business, social and personal life. It is difficult for the busy and over-burdened executive to discourage such a custom since it stems from the strong societal norm of hospitality.[3] There were a few executives who actively discouraged this custom, but as one executive said: 'It takes time before we can change these deeply rooted habits.' Another executive from the Gulf area – who incidentally considered himself a maverick not only in breaking this custom but also with his management style – admitted to having two offices in the same city, mostly to escape from such visitations by friends and colleagues. In some respects, those executives who slowly and carefully discourage these customs can be considered as agents of change in their respective countries. More will be said about this role shortly.

High expectations for success Five executives, three from Kuwait and two from Saudi Arabia, felt that they were under great pressure from friends, colleagues, and government officials who expect them to succeed in any new venture they undertake. One Kuwaiti executive said: 'After receiving our university education we came back with no work experience . . . we had no models to follow . . . we were the pioneers and the older generation could not advise us and yet their expectations were always high.' A Saudi executive stated that government officials often approve industrial projects and the formation of new companies in which he is involved, expecting – or rather taking for granted – a successful outcome. This type of pressure was well described by a Lebanese executive who works closely with executives from the Gulf area: 'These men took charge of large companies when they were still young and with little, if any, on-the-job training . . . The pressure on them is high . . . it is really unfair to them.'

Nepotism The struggle against nepotism was reported by only three executives – two Lebanese and one Jordanian. One executive indicated that many of his relatives are 'angry at him', because of the self-imposed regulation prohibiting nepotism in his organization. But he quickly added that his help to his close-knit extended family takes the form of financial assistance and educational grants. The rest of the executives seemed willing to accept this strong socio-cultural pressure to hire relatives, although four of them considered it a potential burden since they had ultimately to accept the final responsibility if the relatives' performances were poor.

Two main observations are possible when we analyse the social pressures enumerated above. First, there are both similarities and differences among the six Arab countries in terms of the social pressures felt by the executives of these countries. Thus, for instance, executives from all countries complained about the low value of time; lack of industrial mentality and the fusion of business, social and personal life; while, on the other hand, restrictions on women, dislike of manual work, and the high expectations for success were more keenly felt by executives from the Gulf area.

A brief word on women's status in the Arab world. Although restrictions on women differ vastly from one country to another, the trend towards female emancipation has accelerated in most Arab countries, possibly at a relatively faster rate than was the case for Western women some fifty years ago. In Kuwait, for example, one finds women employed in business organizations and government agencies. Indeed, one of the largest Kuwaiti contracting companies is headed by a Kuwaiti woman.[4]

Second, the Arab executives facing these social pressures can be viewed both as targets and agents of social influence. We have seen that some of them are actively discouraging those socio-cultural values and norms which they regard as an unnecessary burden on their time, energy, and performance. Examples were provided in which a few executives attempted to minimize the following social pressures: fusion of business, social and personal life; social visitations at the office; and nepotism. The majority of executives, however, seemed either willing to accept these pressures as a price of membership in society, or did not consider these pressures as burdensome.

The Executive Role

The examination of social pressures in the preceding section leads us to the important question of what specific behaviour is expected by those people around the Arab executive, by virtue of his position in the community and in his organization. In short, what role is the Arab executive expected to play in his immediate community and in his organization? Let us first examine his role in the community.

Role in Community

For the Arab executive, the community consists mainly of his extended family, friends, business associates, and government officials. From each of these groups the executive is aware of a set of expected activities; a role which he feels obligated to carry out. And with each role there is usually a pattern of reciprocal obligations and claims.

The essence of reciprocity is the give-and-take characteristic in which people are often mutually dependent on one another. In this section, we shall emphasize the executive's obligations, the 'giving' aspect. First, we will consider the executive's role with his extended family.

The extended family plays an important part in the rural and urban communities of the Arab world. Recent studies indicate that the extended family has maintained its importance in spite of the economic development and modernization process now taking place in the region.[5] Prothro and Diab (1974) conclude that 'even though the extended family is not living in one household, it is nevertheless a strong social psychological reality'.[6]

In view of these findings, the executives were asked to describe their relations with their extended family. Based on these descriptions, their answers were coded into three categories: extremely strong, strong to moderate, and weak.[7] Not surprising for the Arab world, relations with the extended family were extremely strong for 67 per cent of the executives, 27 per cent described them as strong to moderate, and only 6 per cent said that they were weak. It must be re-emphasized that although the extended family is often physically scattered, family ties and relations are still strong. Thus, a few executives mentioned that although their relatives are living in many parts of the world, yet they maintain strong family ties (correspondence, visitations, financial assistance, and so on). Modern living and working conditions have, as expected, physically separated the extended family; but it seems, at least so far, that the psychological bonds remain strong.

The patriarchal family system is still the basis of Arab society.[8] Research studies on group affiliation of Arab students at the American University of Beirut showed, in 1958, that the family had a clear preference over other loyalties such as the nation, political party, or religion. When the study was repeated in 1971 there was a slight decline in religious affiliations but the family still came first.[9]

It is interesting, for instance, that when Arabs meet their countrymen for the first time, they usually attempt to establish each other's family identity. In the West, on the other hand, it appears that the initial conversation revolves around a person's occupation or profession. In Japan, introductions are made with reference to one's organization or company rather than profession.

The importance of the family becomes more apparent when we investigate the responses of the 52 Arab executives to the open-ended question about the expectations of their extended family. Thirty-nine executives (75 per cent) mentioned that their extended family demand and receive from them all sorts of help and assistance. Some of the more frequently mentioned examples include:

1. consultation on personal problems or family decisions;
2. employment in his organization or other organizations with which he is associated;
3. contacts or pressure on government agencies or other institutions (that is, to act as the intermediary);
4. family visitations and/or maintaining family contacts and ties;
5. financial assistance and loans.

Some executives, when asked to give additional examples, replied: 'All kinds of help is expected . . . all kinds that the mind can imagine.' In fact, four of the 39 executives described their role as the 'leader of the family', or the 'head of the family', and one even described himself as the 'godfather' of his extended family. Needless to say, these demanding roles add to the executive's existing responsibilities and burdens, and are especially taxing on his time.

Of the remaining executives, 6 viewed their role as limited to maintaining contact through visits, correspondence, and the telephone; or as one executive put it 'a need to maintain roots'. Finally, 7 executives felt that there were very few or no expectations from their extended family.

The executive's role toward his friends, business associates, and government officials is also distinguished by the prevalence of reciprocal obligations and claims. Let us briefly examine the nature of these obligations. When asked to enumerate the expectations which the community held towards them and to describe their role in their community, 49 executives were able to describe a variety of expectations. Only 3 executives felt that they had no role to play in the community, and that the community had no expectations of them by virtue of their positions. The replies given by the 49 executives were wide-ranging but described quite similar patterns. The most frequently mentioned examples were:

1. *Social responsibility.* Under this general title the following expectations were mentioned: efficient management of one's organization; development of the industry in which the executive is engaged (innovation and being kept up-to-date); and the recruitment and training of local and national employees. The executive is also expected to give opinion and guidance to friends, associates, and government officials. In short, the executive is expected to be an active member and a responsible leader in his community.
2. *Contribution to the national interest.* This heading refers to the expectations (especially by government officials) of contributions to the national economic plans of the country. Many executives felt a commitment to achieve, in the national interest, such aims as economic progress, modernization and industrialization.
3. *Financial assistance to community.* Executives were expected to extend financial help to those friends and associates who are in trouble, and also to support financially social activities in the community, including charitable groups.
4. *Intermediary role.* The intermediary role refers to the executive's use of family and friendship ties (and of course his position) to expedite, advance, or influence the course of events in favour of other relatives and friends. In the Arab world, one speaks of having 'connections' or 'contacts' in order to get things done faster or as desired.[10] Here, the executive is usually at both the giving and receiving ends of this reciprocal activity.
5. *Link between organization and community.* Executives saw themselves as the crucial link between their organization and its community. This role includes public relations activities such as enhancement of company reputation and standing, and official representation of the organization in the community. This role is akin to Mintzberg's (1973, p. 56) 'spokesman', 'liaison', and 'figurehead' roles. Of course, these are the roles which provide unique opportunities to the effective executive who turns these obligations to his advantage.

It is quite likely that most of the above activities are performed by chief executives from all parts of the world. However, the significance lies in the important nuances such activities have in various societies. Note, for example, that for the Arab executive there is the lack of political affiliation or activities;

the lack of organized pressure from labour unions or consumer groups; and the heavy emphasis on the executive's intermediary role.

So far we have perhaps overstressed one aspect of the executive's role in his community; namely the concomitant obligations of that role. Let us briefly examine the other side of the coin. The top executive of an organization, while discharging some of the above-mentioned obligations, is in a unique position to act as his organization's *radar*, scanning the environment for vital information, pertinent events and trends, business opportunities, and so on. The ability to do this is similar to what has been called the 'helicopter view', or the ability 'to see the forest from the trees'. It was referred to by some as the *conceptual* ability of top management as contrasted with the interpersonal and technical skills of middle and lower managerial levels.[11] Similarly, Katz and Kahn advocate that organizational leaders must adopt the external perspective (or system perspective) in order to avoid stagnation or failure:

> External perspective is in part a *sensitivity* to environmental demands, to the requirements that an organization must meet in order to maintain a state of equilibrium with its environment. In part external perspective involves a *sensitivity* to environmental opportunities, to the possibilities of achieving a more advantageous relationship with the environment. Finally external perspective requires *sensitivity* to trends and changes in the environment, which is characteristically in a state of movement both with respect to the demands it makes on organizations and the opportunities it affords to them. [Emphasis added.][12]

This 'sensitivity' to processes in the environment, along with the ability to foresee how the organization fits within that environment, are executive-level skills. These skills can be learned and achieved by the executive if he is willing to cultivate the obligations and the opportunities provided by his role in the community.

Role in Organization

It was mentioned earlier that the family is one of the dominating social institutions in Arab society. We also referred to the strength of the extended family. The question that comes to mind is whether executives and their employees bring with them to the work organization any of these strong values and norms? In order to explore this topic we asked the Arab executives how they viewed their role in the organization? And what they perceived as the main expectations which their employees held towards them? Responding to these open-ended questions, the executives gave the following answers. Twenty-three executives (44 per cent) described themselves as the *chief execut-*

ive of their respective organizations. These executives used a variety of terms to describe this chief executive role. Here are some examples: the leader; the 'motor' of the company; the decision maker; the person who is responsible for the profitability and growth of the company; and various other functions and duties relating to the 'good management' of the organization. In most cases these 23 executives also mentioned that their employees expect good wages, good working conditions, promotion, training, and help in personal and family matters. For convenience, this role will be referred to as the *chief executive role*.

Table 2(a) Executive role and organizational size*

	Family	*Chief executive*	*Total*
Small (180–499)	10	8	18
Medium (500–999)	7	7	14
Large (over 1000)	12	8	20
Total	29	23	52

$\chi^2 = 0.4$; not significant.
*Size = number of employees.

Table 2(b) Executive role and organizational ownership

	Family	*Chief executive*	*Total*
Family-owned	12	8	20
Partnership	9	11	20
Government-owned	8	4	12
Total	29	23	52

$\chi^2 = 1.68$; not significant

What is interesting, however, are the responses of the other 29 executives (56 per cent). These executives perceived their organization as a *family*, and they described their roles using familial terms. Thus, of the 29 executives, 11 saw their role as the 'head of a family'; 11 more described their role as a 'father'; 6 used the term 'elder brother'; and one saw himself as the 'godfather' of his organization. In contrast to the *chief executive role* let us refer to this role as the *family role*.

Immediately, one would suspect that the executives who saw themselves in the family role are in charge of smaller organizations, or they are possibly the heads of family-owned organizations. In short, is the *family role* related to size or type of ownership of the organization? Looking at the findings, as shown in Table 2 (a and b), the answers to these questions are unmistakably in the negative.

Using the chi-squared (χ^2) test, we can ascertain that there are no statistically significant relationships between executive role and organizational size or type of ownership. Similar tests were used to see whether or not family role is related to the executive's age, or his education. Again, no significant relationships were found. It is interesting to note, however, that the younger executives were more likely to describe their role as the 'elder brother', while the older executives would use the terms 'father' or 'head of family'.

An explanation of the phenomenon of *family role* can be found, in part, when we examine how the Arab executives perceive their employees' expectations. Other than the usual demands for increased wages, better working conditions, promotions, and so on, the executives felt obligated to help employees with their personal and family problems (both financial and emotional). Employees' expectations, as seen by the executives, included 'kind and humane treatment', 'care', 'respect', 'control', and 'guidance'. These were some of the terms used by the executives; the examples of help to employees ranged from assistance with governmental agencies (getting a passport, a visa, or even cancelling a traffic violation); advice about housing problems or a divorce; to providing guidance regarding the children's education or future.

A classical self-fulfilling prophecy seems to be at work here: employees' expectations (and behaviour) towards the executive reinforce his perception of his role as a 'father'. Alternatively, the executive's behaviour towards his employees is paternal and this reinforces the employees' perceived role as members of a family. Either way, it seems that both parties' expectations of one another coincide. Let us briefly look at the employees' attitudes on this matter. Although employees were not included in this study, there are some research findings which supplement and support the present study. Research studies by MEIRC, S.A. were carried out in three oil companies operating in three Gulf countries.[13] The main results of these studies indicate that the Arab employees interviewed ($N = 205$) had three expectations of what they considered as a 'good' manager. First, employees expected to be 'treated well' by their manager and their organization. For the employees, a good manager would treat his employees in a considerate and humane manner. He would be interested and willing to provide good services and facilities as well as 'care and guidance' to their personal problems, on and off the job. This is closely related to the expectations as seen by the executive, which is to play the father role. Second, employees expected to be 'paid well' in terms of higher salary levels and improved employee benefits. Third, the employees expected their skills to be 'used well' in their present jobs, and they expected to be trained (in and out of the company) in new skills in order to enhance their future careers.

Unfortunately, the MEIRC studies are the only ones available which shed some light on the expectations of Arab employees. Although these studies covered employees in a specific industry (oil) and region (Gulf area), their findings are relevant and lend support to our investigation of the Arab executive's role in his organization.

In this chapter we began by examining the nature of the social pressures as felt by Arab executives. We discovered that these pressures act as constraints on the executives' behaviour, attitudes, and time. However, we found that these pressures vary from one country to another, and that the reaction of the executives to the social pressures also varied. Thus, while most of the executives accepted many of the socio-cultural values, norms, and customs (thus, being targets of social influence), a small number of executives were attempting to change those values, norms, and customs which they considered as burdensome (thus, acting as agents of social change).

In the second part of the chapter, we investigated the roles of the Arab executive in his community and in his organization. We drew attention to the strength and importance of the executive's relations with his extended family. An attempt was made to differentiate between the obligations and opportunities afforded to the executive, especially by his role in the community. Finally, when examining the executive's role within his organization, it was found that the majority of Arab executives viewed their organization as a family unit. They described their role in familial terms such as father or elder brother. It seems that the executives' expectations coincide with those of the employees in the form of a self-fulfilling prophecy.

Conflict Management

I apply not my sword where my lash suffices, nor my lash where my tongue is enough. And even if there be one hair binding me to my fellowmen, I do not let it break: when they pull I loosen, and if they loosen I pull.

Caliph Mu'āwiyah, AD 661–680

The main interest in this chapter is on conflict between the Arab executive and his immediate subordinate during or after the decision-making process.

Specifically, we are interested in the extent of such conflict, and how the Arab executive uses his power to manage it. In general, the Arab executive experiences relatively low opposition from his immediate subordinates. The executive reduces the frequency of conflict either by 'authoritarian' behaviour and/or by frequent consultation with his subordinates. Furthermore, the Arab executive prefers to avoid open confrontation whenever conflict occurs. This is done either through the mediation efforts of a third party or by complete avoidance of the issue in conflict.

There is a wealth of literature on conflict by scholars from a wide variety of disciplines. It covers many types of conflict at many levels, from the international, social, organizational, departmental, to conflict between individuals.[14] There is, however, little available literature on how Arab executives handle conflict in organizational contexts. One would expect that Arab executives would be influenced by societal values and norms in managing conflicts within their organizations. This is what we set out to explore in this chapter.

It is important to note that our concern here is deliberately limited to dyadic conflict along the vertical dimension of a hierarchy (executive and his subordinate) and our interest is on one of the parties to the conflict only – the executive. Lastly, the conflict is over an episode involving a business decision.

Dyadic conflict (conflict between two persons or two social units) is defined as a process in which the actions of one person tend to prevent or force some outcome against the resistance of another person.[15] Thus, an executive may impose a decision against the resistance of his subordinate, or he may intentionally block a decision favoured by the subordinate.

We have examined the extent to which Arab executives retain or share their decision-making power. It was found that, on average, the Arab executive chose to limit his subordinate's influence on decision outcomes. Indeed, the executives chose Style 1 (own decision) and Style 2 (consultation) an overwhelming 77 per cent of the time; both styles tend to limit subordinate's influence. A few questions immediately come to mind: what about opposition or resistance from subordinates, if any, when they do not agree with the decision? How is it handled? And what are the executive's reactions to proposals submitted by his subordinate if he does not favour these proposals?

To answer these questions, the executives were presented with hypothetical incidents in which two types of conflict situations were present. Conflict situation Type 1 is when the hypothetical issues are favoured by the executive, but opposed by the subordinate. Type 2 is the reverse: the issues are opposed by the executive, but favoured by the subordinate. Each executive was given two incidents and was asked to describe how he would handle the conflict situations Type 1 and Type 2. One of the incidents involved a personnel-related conflict:

a disagreement between the executive and his immediate subordinate about the promotion of a key employee working for the latter; while the other incident was at the organizational level: a disagreement between the executive and his immediate subordinate about an expansion plan (or a new product/project) which involves the department/division of the subordinate. The executives were familiar with the incidents since both were an extension of the decision-making section of the interview to which they had just responded.

Furthermore, each executive was asked to provide a proverb or a saying which guided or influenced his thinking when facing the sort of conflict described above. This approach was designed to add depth to our understanding of the executive's conflict management techniques.

Let us now turn to the results of the interviews. We shall first present a brief summary of the overall findings. Later, we shall discuss the implications of these findings for conflict management. There were five major findings:

1. *Insufficient opposition from subordinates.* Five Arab executives complained that, in general, there was insufficient resistance or opposition from their immediate subordinate(s). They felt that the frequency and magnitude of resistance and opposition were undesirably low. In short, they wished more of their subordinates would act as genuine devil's advocates from time to time. This, of course, would be beneficial as long as the devil's advocate role is not institutionalized or systematized, in which case it may become useless.[16]
2. *Open confrontation is taboo.* When irreconcilable positions were reached, neither executive nor subordinate allowed it to develop into direct or open confrontation. Values and norms dictate the use of a third party to convey the message of rejection. The role of a third person (a mediator) in Arab society is crucial in conflict management.[17] Open confrontation is also avoided by the use of other indirect methods to communicate one's position, such as non-verbal behaviour, deliberate procrastination, or even a complete avoidance of the issue.
3. *Consultation reduces conflict.* Seven executives believed that the frequency of conflict was substantially reduced because the immediate subordinate was often consulted, and his opinion taken into account. If the subordinate's advice and opinions are occasionally incorporated into the decision, then to that extent consultation will tend to reduce conflict. If, on the other hand, consultation turns into a ritual where the executive is repeatedly asking for opinions and advice, but then always making decisions contrary to such advice, then conflict might be exacerbated and long-term relationships will suffer.

4. *Reliance on position power.*[18] With the above comments in mind, it was found that for Type 1 situations (executive favours, subordinate opposes) the power tactic most favoured by fifteen executives was 'pulling rank' or going ahead with a decision in spite of subordinate's opposition.

   For Type 2 situations (executive opposes, subordinate favours) the power tactic most often used was non-decision making. Twelve executives used such phrases as 'freeze it', 'keep it pending', and 'give it time to die', to describe their non-decision-making tactics.

   Finally, many of the executives preferred not to differentiate between Type 1 and 2 conflicts and stated that they would initially attempt to convince the subordinate of their viewpoint by reasoning with him, using knowledge or information only they possess, or will attempt to persuade the subordinate using their 'diplomacy' and 'personal touch'. Failing all that, the executives will resort to their formal authority and power, as described above.

5. *Importance of issues does not change tactics.* The importance of the issues (personnel *vs.* organizational) was related to the likelihood of conflict occurrence. For example, many executives indicated that it is unlikely that conflict will occur over the personnel issue, but may occur over the organizational one.

   However, when asked to assume that conflict did happen on the hypothetical personnel issue, an interesting reaction took place. The executives would use the same firm tactics they used for the organizational conflict. This indicates that the importance of the issues at stake is not as relevant as the fact that opposition did occur (albeit, hypothetically). One would expect milder tactics (such as persuasion, bargaining and the like) to be employed; instead, the same tactics as reported above were most commonly used. One is reminded of the several research studies showing that conflicting action (opposition from subordinates) evokes similar reactions (pulling rank or non-decision by executives).[19] Role expectations (such as boss has the final word) clearly influenced the executive's behaviour.

The above five findings, if taken separately, are clear and do not need further elaboration. However, if we examine the first finding (insufficient opposition from subordinates) in relation to the other four, then a contradiction becomes apparent.

One way of explaining the phenomenon would be to take an increasingly popular view which states that, in general, certain kinds of conflicts are not only inevitable but also desirable (functional) to the conflicting parties if effectively managed.[20] This broad statement invites further questions, such as: what level or magnitude of conflict?; how do we effectively manage it?; and so on. These questions are appropriate and necessary, but are beyond the scope of this chapter. However, using this perspective and keeping these questions in mind provides us with a frame of reference, a context, to discuss the findings. Viewed in this context, the five findings can be translated into two observations: (a) the frequency and magnitude of opposition leading to conflict is low – as reported by a number of executives and as observed by the interviewer; (b) Arab executives tend to handle these conflicts in such a manner as to discourage future opposition. What we have here is a classic dilemma – or even ambivalence. A desire for some opposition from subordinates, and a concomitant fear of losing control and influence (power) if the executive yields to the opposition.

Let us look at the first element of this ambivalence: insufficient opposition. The reasons given by some executives for the low occurrence of conflict support the notion that power is often wielded in the following manner:

Executive's preferences

↓

Subordinate's anticipation of executive's future reactions

↓

Subordinate's response (in our case, compliance)

(With feedback loops, of course)

Here is how one executive described it: 'The subordinate gets to know his boss so well he can "read his mind" – he is so eager to please his boss that he is unlikely to think of or engage in activities which may displease the boss. The result . . . no opposition.'

This type of executive power is creating subordinate compliance[21] which probably is at an unhealthy level. If a reasonable amount of conflict and opposition does lead to creativity and positive stimulation[22] then subordinate's over-compliance could indeed be unhealthy. (Bearing in mind that we are discussing subordinates at a high managerial level reporting directly to top executives.)

The question, then, becomes: what is a reasonable amount of conflict? Again, it is beyond our present scope: it must be noted, however, that future research on this question must include the norms, expectations, and attitudes towards authority and conflict prevalent in the countries being studied.[23] Nevertheless, the fact remains that a few executives did express their desire for more opposition (devil's advocate role, as some put it).

The other side of the ambivalence equation is the fear of losing power if conflict is encouraged. One Egyptian executive summarized it well: 'If a leader, whether on the national or organizational level, does not suppress opposition, then people (including my employees) would think he is weak, thereby losing respect.'

The solution to this dilemma, *if a solution is desired*, is entirely in the hands of the executive. Two of the several choices he has are: (a) to change the attitudes and predisposition of his employees towards authority, conflict, and power. This is a difficult and a very slow process, but not impossible; and (b) to modify role expectations and/or organizational structure with the aim of creating manageable conflict. This would be done through the creation of devil's advocate roles, suggestion boxes, and other devices to encourage opposition – designed to fit the needs and the climate of the organization at that stage of its growth and development.

The above findings were based on responses from executives who were asked to describe their hypothetical behaviour.[24] However, as mentioned earlier, another approach was used which assessed the executive's values and beliefs about dyadic conflict. This was accomplished by asking each executive to provide a proverb or a saying (in either Arabic or English) which guides or influences his thinking when facing this type of conflict. The proverbs/sayings told by the executives added further support to the earlier findings.

Twenty-four of the 52 executives gave a total of 18 proverbs/sayings (all in Arabic). Here is a translation of three proverbs (mentioned by more than one executive):

1. Four executives mentioned this proverb: 'Time is a problem-solver', or 'Time solves problems'.
2. Three executives recited this Quranic verse: 'Consult them in affairs of the moment, then, when thou hast taken a decision, put thy trust in God' (III, 159).[25]
3. Two executives referred to the famous words in Arab history attributed to the founder of the Umayyad Caliphate, Mu'āwiyah (AD 661–80). The Caliph Mu'āwiyah, known for his political finesse, was reported to have declared: 'I apply not my sword where my lash suffices, nor my lash where my tongue is enough. And even if there be one hair binding me to my fellowmen, I do not let it break: when they pull I loosen, and if they loosen I pull'.[26]

The other 15 proverbs conveyed various messages, most of which can be summarized in a few advisory sentences: be reasonable; avoid extremes; avoid confrontation; be cooperative; and finally, there are many things that an executive ('apex of pyramid') sees, or hears, that cannot and should not be seen, or heard, by the subordinates.

A moment of reflection will show that the values reflected by these proverbs do not contradict the executives' responses as summarized earlier. In fact, they add support to them. Thus, we have the proverb, 'Time is a problem-solver', relating directly to non-decision-making tactics; the Quranic verse associated with the use of consultation to reduce potential conflict; and finally Mu'āwiyah's political finesse of being 'diplomatic but firm', and avoiding head-on confrontation or the risk of 'breaking the hair' which binds the executive to his subordinates.

In this chapter, we have seen that Arab executives, in general, experience relatively low opposition and resistance (low in frequency and magnitude) from their immediate subordinates. This could be partly attributable to their consultative style; but it can also be attributed to the societal values and norms which shun open confrontation and encourage rather authoritarian behaviour on the executive's part. We have also examined the dilemma facing those executives who would like to see increased 'constructive' resistance from their immediate subordinates – bearing in mind that these subordinates are top-level managers. Finally, we were able to look at some of the power tactics, as well as the thoughts behind these tactics, which Arab executives use in managing conflict.

Notes

1. This group included both the owner/partner and the non-owner executive.

2. This role of a formal representative is termed by Mintzberg the 'figurehead' role. As he points out, it is very likely that executives utilize this role to maintain strong links (informational and friendship) with other businessmen and government officials; Mintzberg (1973), *The Nature of Managerial Work*, pp. 58–60, 126–7.

3. On hospitality of Middle Eastern people, see Antoun (1965), 'Conservatism and Change in the Village Community', p. 7; Gulick (1976), *The Middle East: An Anthropological Perspective*, p. 46.

4. This executive was the subject of the cover article in a business magazine, *Alam Attijarat*, February 1978, pp. 26–7. For further articles on this executive and on women's status in Kuwait, see *The Times* (London, 12 June 1978), p. 4.

5. Tomeh (1970), 'Reference-Group Supports Among Middle Eastern College Students', pp. 156–65; Prothro and Diab (1974), *Changing Family Patterns in the Arab East*, pp. 70–3; Farsoun (1970), 'Family Structure and Society in Modern Lebanon', pp. 257–307.

6. Prothro and Diab (1974), p. 70.

7. The three categories were based upon the intensity of contact and commitment to extended family. It includes, for example, visitation to and time spent with relatives; emotional and financial support; and other miscellaneous help and support.

8. It is interesting to note in this respect that the middle name for most Arabs consists of their father's name, see Gulick (1976), pp. 39–42, 215–21.

9. Melikian and Diab (1959), 'Group Affiliations of University Students in the Arab Middle

East', pp. 145–59; Melikian and Diab (1974), 'Stability and Change in Group Affiliations of University Students in the Arab Middle East', pp. 13–21; and Melikian (1977), 'The Modal Personality of Saudi College Students', pp. 166–209.

10. Farsoun (1970), pp. 269–70. Farsoun describes the intermediary role as follows: 'The term *wastah* is colloquial Arabic for an "intermediary", a go-between, or the process of employing an intermediary or go-between, "a process of mediation" in almost any and all types of activity' (p. 269).

11. Mann (1964), 'Toward an Understanding of the Leadership Role in Formal Organizations'.

12. Katz and Kahn (1978), *Social Psychology of Organizations*, p. 504.

13. MEIRC, S.A. (1975), 'Job Attitude Survey of Saudi and Kuwaiti Employees'; MEIRC, S.A. (1976a), 'Job Attitude Survey of Omani National Staff'; and MEIRC, S.A. (1976b). 'Das Island Attitude and Motivation Survey'.

14. For reviews and analyses of recent literature on conflict see Thomas (1976), 'Conflict and Conflict Management', pp. 889–935; Nightingale (1976), 'Conflict and Conflict Resolution', pp. 141–64; and Katz and Kahn (1978), *Social Psychology of Organizations*, pp. 612–51.

15. From Katz and Kahn (1978), p. 613.

16. See Thomas and Bennis (eds.) (1972), *Management of Change and Conflict*, pp. 17–19.

17. Ayoub (1965), 'Conflict Resolution and Social Reorganization in a Lebanese Village', pp. 11–17. Also see Farsoun (1970), 'Family Structure and Society in Modern Lebanon', pp. 257–307.

18. As opposed to other bases of power; reward, coercive, referent, and expert power, to use French and Raven's (1959) typology. A sixth base of power, information power, is usually added by many others.

19. Katz and Kahn (1978); Thomas (1976); Thomas and Walton (1971) 'Conflict-handling Behaviour in Interdepartmental Relations'.

20. Coser (1956), *The Functions of Social Conflict*; Hall (1971), 'Decisions, Decisions, Decisions'; and Katz and Kahn (1978).

21. Even if we wish to use one of Kelman's (1958) other categorizations (compliance, identification, or internalization), the end result for our purposes is the same – minimum opposition from subordinates.

22. Katz and Kahn (1978), p. 641.

23. For example, Melikian found that there is 'a general willingness among Saudi college students to accept the authority of a "boss" and to esteem it . . . this acceptance and esteem of authority are accompanied by a willingness to be in that position themselves'. See Melikian (1977), 'The Modal Personality of Saudi College Students', p. 180.

24. Aided by quasi-participant observation by the author during the periods of waiting for and conducting the interviews.

25. Ali, *The Holy Qur'ān: Text, Translation and Commentary* (1975).

26. As quoted in Hitti (1970), *History of the Arabs*, p. 197.

Saudi Arabia

Bureaucracy and Development in Saudi Arabia: A Behavioural Analysis

Saud al Nimir and Monte Palmer

From *Public Administration and Development*, Vol. 2, 1982, 93–104

Bureaucracies in the developing areas, as in all societies, are responsible for executing the decisions of the political leadership and for maintaining the day-to-day regulatory and service functions of the state. Unlike their counterparts in the world's more industrialized societies, however, bureaucracies in the developing areas are being asked to transform their respective societies into modern entities. Once the political leaders of the state have decided upon the course of economic and social development, it is the bureaucracy that must (1) generate development projects, (2) coordinate those projects within the confines of a comprehensive development plan, (3) supervise the execution of those projects and (4) both operate and maintain those projects once they have reached fruition (Heady, 1979; Caiden and Wildavsky, 1975). Given the problems that have beset most bureaucracies in the developing areas, this is a tall order, indeed.

If the bureaucracies of the various developing areas are unable to perform the above functions, the social and economic development of the states involved will more than likely stagnate. In most instances, there is no other agency, public or private, capable of such a pervasive undertaking. In this regard it should be noted that the private sectors of most developing economies are beset by fears of socialism and political instability. Their primary emphasis tends to be on short-term profits and on investments in the safe money markets of the West. Bureaucracies in the developing areas are thus deprived of an ally that played such a vital role in the development of the United States and Western Europe.

The centrality of the bureaucracy to the economic and social development of the Third World suggests that the development potential of any state might well be gauged by the developmental potential of its bureaucracy (Montgomery and Siffin, 1966). This is particularly true if one defines development in terms of the productive capacity of the state as opposed to its capacity to purchase goods and services from the world's more economically developed societies. The oil-producing states of the Middle East, for example, rank at the top of most development scales in terms of per capita income and similar consumer indicators. Their capacity to produce industrial products, however, is virtually nil. Unless the members of such societies become psychologically involved in the development process, the use of oil revenues to purchase products and services merely results in the transformation of their population into a leisure class of sophisticated consumers increasingly dependent upon foreign labour. The client or rentier state is thus deprived of the substance of development in terms of building a cadre of achievement-oriented, innovative, and technically skilled public servants both willing and able to absorb the technology purchased through the expenditure of their oil wealth (Meyer, 1959; Mahdavy, 1970).

The capacity of a bureaucracy to perform the developmental functions outlined above appears to rest largely upon two components: the structure of the bureaucracy and the behaviour and attitudes of the individuals managing the bureaucratic apparatus.

Early bureaucratic analyses were motivated by the hope that structural or organizational realignments could somehow transform lethargic bureaucracies into a vital force in the development process (Waldo, 1976). Such optimism faded as repeated organizational reforms, while of some benefit, failed to produce the desired miracles. While some bureaucratic structures clearly possess a higher efficiency potential than others, it is doubtful that any organizational structure can be more effective or more dynamic than the individuals responsible for its operation. Bureaucratic organizations, as all inanimate structures, remain at the mercy of human beings.

In the light of the above comments, the object of the present paper is to evaluate the developmental potential of the Saudi bureaucracy in terms of the innovative or developmental attitudes of its members. The paper is divided into four sections: (1) a brief discussion of the research procedures used in the study, (2) an analysis of group perceptions of innovative values within the Saudi bureaucracy, (3) an analysis of the innovative attitudes of Saudi bureaucrats and (4) an analysis of the factors inhibiting the development of innovative behaviour among Saudi bureaucrats.

Methodology

During the autumn of 1980 a questionnaire containing a variety of items relating to administrative behaviour was administered to a quota sample of 500 middle-range bureaucrats in the Ministries of agriculture, education, finance, petroleum, social welfare, information, health and municipal affairs. Middle-range bureaucrats, ranges 6 to 10, were selected for the study inasmuch as middle-range bureaucrats bear primary responsibility for the actual execution and supervision of development projects.

Of the 500 questionnaires distributed, 300 valid questionnaires were returned. The respondents were not interviewed directly, as this would have been considered a breach of privacy and would have placed inordinate pressure upon the respondents to search for answers they believed the interviewers would find pleasing. To promote spontaneous answers and to overcome resistance to the questionnaire, every effort was also made to assure the respondents that the questionnaires would remain confidential and that the respondents would remain anonymous.

It should also be noted that the administrative items used in the questionnaire had been pre-tested among a sample of thirty-seven bureaucrats during the spring of 1979. Objectionable questions or questions that tended to induce unreliable answers were either deleted or restructured.

The reliability of the survey was ascertained by examining responses to questionnaire items of similar content. Response-bias problems were checked by examining items of similar content presented in reverse order. Both reliability tests suggested a high level of reliability for the questionnaires received. Those respondents likely to provide less than reliable responses chose instead not to answer any or all of the questions. This group, as noted above, constituted two-fifths of the sample.

Self Perceptions of Innovative Values within the Saudi Bureaucracy: A Study in Group Dynamics

Change and development are group phenomena. Single individuals, regardless of how creative or how motivated they might be, are likely to find it difficult if not impossible to give expression to their innovative tendencies in a stultifying group environment (Cartwright and Zander, 1968). To ascertain our respondents' perceptions of the innovative climate in which they functioned, the questionnaire contained a variety of items requesting respondents to evaluate the innovative behaviour of their peers (but not themselves). The text and percentage distributions for these items appear in Table 1.

This procedure involved the disadvantage of requesting individuals to express essentially negative attitudes toward their peers and their organization, a process they were somewhat reluctant to do. Criticizing one's organization also runs the risk, by implication, of criticizing one's self as well. For these reasons, approximately 10 per cent of the sample either did not respond to the self-evaluation item or chose to check positive responses for each item systematically. These respondents were necessarily eliminated from the analysis.

Having adjusted for the response-bias problem, the results of the self-analysis portray a work environment in which the value of innovation is clearly minimized. Few individuals, for example, were perceived as looking for new ideas, and an even smaller number were perceived as willing to take risks. The prevailing concerns appeared to be the avoidance of conflict and the maintenance of job security. The latter tendency is particularly revealing, for few bureaucrats in the world would appear to be as secure as Saudi bureaucrats.

The fact that an overwhelming majority of the respondents found their work environment to minimize the value of innovation can, in all probability, be extended to mean that individuals possessing a high innovation potential find that their enthusiasm for innovation threatens the position of those individuals – some 80 per cent without adjusting for response bias – who appear to be primarily concerned with conflict avoidance and job security. This may be particularly true because Saudi Arabia is a conservative society in which almost any form of innovation runs the risk of conflict. The more a group opposes innovation – and group theory is very clear on this point – the more innovative individuals tend to moderate their innovative tendencies for the sake of gaining acceptance within the organization (Cartwright and Zander, 1968).

From a group dynamic perspective, then, the Saudi bureaucracy appears to be poorly suited to play the development role envisaged by recent Saudi development plans.

Bureaucratic Behaviour and Development in Saudi Arabia

Having gained at least a general picture of the innovative climate within the Saudi bureaucracy, the next step in the analysis involved examining the development-oriented behaviour of Saudi bureaucrats. Three categories of bureaucratic behaviour were considered: (1) achievement values, (2) attitudes towards change-related policies and (3) routinization behaviour.

Table 1 Innovation as a group dynamic

Items and scale	*Frequency*	*Percentage*
Item 1:		
Most Saudi bureaucrats are receptive to new ideas.		
(1) all of them	12	4.3
(2) most of them	70	25.1
(3) few of them	181	64.9
(4) none of them	16	5.7
Non-response 21	279	100.0
Item 2:		
Most Saudi bureaucrats are primarily concerned with job security.		
(1) all of them	90	32.2
(2) most of them	82	29.4
(3) few of them	87	31.2
(4) none of them	20	7.2
Non-response 21	279	100.0
Item 3:		
Most Saudi bureaucrats attempt to avoid conflict.		
(1) all of them	108	38.8
(2) most of them	107	38.5
(3) few of them	58	20.9
(4) none of them	5	1.8
Non-response 22	278	100.0
Item 4:		
Most Saudi bureaucrats are unwilling to take risks.		
(1) all of them	124	45.0
(2) most of them	78	28.4
(3) few of them	59	21.5
(4) none of them	14	5.1
Non-response 25	275	100.0

Achievement Values

If a bureaucracy is to play the vigorous developmental role outlined in our introductory remarks, it would appear to be essential that its members be aggressive in their desire to achieve their professional goals. In this regard one would expect that their desire for achievement would involve a willingness to take risks, a willingness to relocate in geographic areas favourable for advancement, and a willingness to tolerate a less-than-ideal work environment. It is clearly difficult to imagine how a bureaucracy could play a vital role in the development process if its members were not willing to take risks, were not willing to move to the areas where their skills were most needed and were not willing to work at least temporarily in rural or uncomfortable environments.

To tap these dimensions of bureaucratic behaviour the questionnaire contained some 7 items, the text and marginal distributions for which appear in Table 2.

If the group dynamics section of our paper painted a general picture of a less-than-innovative bureaucracy, the results of the achievement behaviour section give substance to that picture by describing a bureaucracy that is almost totally lacking achievement motivation in the Western development-oriented meaning of the word (McClelland, 1961).

Indeed, neither high salaries nor prestige were adequate incentives to induce the overwhelming majority of our respondents to relocate away from their extended families, to work in the rural areas, or to accept high-risk positions (Table 2). These results indicate that Saudi Arabia faces a substantial problem in motivating its bureaucracy to join battle with the challenge of modernization. Uncomfortable jobs or jobs requiring mobility will continue to be performed by foreign labour, thereby perpetuating the rentier pattern described above. Unfortunately, foreign labour will find it less easy to fill the administrative positions requiring risk-taking, for those decisions must remain, ultimately, in the hands of the Saudis. The less Saudi officials are willing to take risks – and development administration personifies risk-taking – the lower will be the capacity of the Saudi bureaucracy to perform its developmental function.

Change-Related Values

A similar picture emerges in reference to the decision-making strategies pursued by our respondents. An examination of the five questionnaire items relating to decision-making values (Table 3) indicates that 84 per cent of our respondents felt it was best to cancel programmes that might cause social conflict, with

Table 2 Achievement oriented attitudes of Saudi bureaucrats

Items and scales	*Frequency*	*Percentage*
Mobility attitude items		
Item 1:		
Given the option, which of the following would you prefer:		
(1) a high-paying job away from parents and relatives	63	21.8
(2) an adequate-paying job near parents and relatives	226	78.2
Non-response 11	289	100.0
Item 2:		
(1) a position of high authority and responsibility away from parents and relatives	95	33.2
(2) a position of moderate authority and responsibility near parents and relatives	191	66.8
Non-response 14	286	100.0
Scale of mobility attitudes		
High tolerance for mobility	44	15.4
Medium tolerance for mobility	68	23.9
Low tolerance for mobility	173	60.7
	285	100.0
Attitudes relating to work environment		
Item 1:		
(1) a position with high pay in a rural area	86	29.8
(2) a position with adequate pay in a major city	203	70.2
Non-response 11	289	100.0
Item 2:		
(1) a position with high authority and responsibility in a rural area	103	36.1
(2) a position with low authority and responsibility in a major city	182	63.9
Non-response 15	285	100.0

Item 3:		
(1) a low-paying job with a pleasant environment	259	89.6
(2) a high-paying job with an uncomfortable environment	30	10.4
Non-response 11	289	100.0
Scale of work environment attitudes		
High rural tolerance	52	18.3
Medium rural tolerance	82	28.9
Low rural tolerance	150	52.8
	284	100.0
Attitudes toward risk-taking and monetary incentives		
Item 1:		
(1) a low-paying job with high prestige	244	86.5
(2) a high-paying job with low prestige	38	13.5
Non-response 18	282	100.0
Risk-taking		
Item 1:		
(1) a low-paying job with few risks	223	78.0
(2) a high-paying job with high risks	63	22.0
Non-response 14	286	100.0
Scale of attitudes toward monetary incentive		
High responsiveness	25	9.0
Medium responsiveness	69	24.8
Low responsiveness	184	66.2
	278	100.0

90 per cent of the respondents stressing the view that modernization programmes should not pose a threat to traditional values.

The Saudi bureaucrats, then, are predisposed to avoid programmes that might alter the social status quo. This orientation clearly provides a built-in bias against innovative development programmes, for innovation, if successful, can only result in change.

Table 3 Attitudes of Saudi bureaucrats toward social change

Items and scales	*Frequency*	*Percentage*
It is best to change or cancel programmes that cause social conflict:		
(1) strongly agree	71	25.2
(2) agree	165	58.5
(3) disagree	40	14.2
(4) strongly disagree	6	2.1
Non-response = 18	282	100.0
Social change should not be instituted at the expense of traditional values:		
(1) strongly agree	107	37.3
(2) agree	151	52.6
(3) disagree	24	8.4
(4) strongly disagree	5	1.7
Non-response = 13	287	100.0
Scale of attitudes toward development programmes		
High resistance	231	82.0
Medium resistance	37	13.0
Low resistance	14	5.0
	282	100.0

While it is reasonable to assume that the bureaucrats surveyed firmly believe in the maintenance of traditional values, one must also note that the social conservatism of our respondents was clearly reinforced by their pervasive concern for job security. To change is to take risks. Rather than to take risks, it is far better that development programmes should be implemented with extreme caution. This sentiment is also inadvertently reinforced by a Saudi Government which has sought to merge its development programmes with the vigorous reinforcement of traditional religious and family values. It is not always easy for middle-range bureaucrats to divine whether the programmes with which they have been entrusted will ultimately be praised as development or condemned as violating social tradition.

Table 4 Routinization of Saudi bureaucrats

Items and scales	*Frequency*	*Percentage*
One should be very careful in making routine decisions		
(1) strongly agree	48	16.7
(2) agree	144	50.2
(3) disagree	78	27.2
(4) strongly disagree	17	5.9
Non-response = 13	287	100.0
It is best to consult with one's superior before making a decision		
(1) strongly agree	76	26.4
(2) agree	165	57.3
(3) disagree	43	14.9
(4) strongly disagree	4	1.4
Non-response = 12	288	100.0
In making decisions, no one should violate rules and regulations		
(1) strongly agree	61	21.3
(2) agree	158	55.2
(3) disagree	61	21.3
(4) strongly disagree	6	2.1
Non-response = 14	286	100.0

Routinization

Finally, the questionnaire also contained several items relating to routinization or inflexibility, the text and percentage distributions for which appear in Table 4. It is virtually an axiom of development administration that innovative programmes require administrative flexibility. The more rigid and routinized the behaviour of the bureaucrats, the less likely it becomes that innovative programmes will see the light of day.

In line with the other behaviour patterns examined, our respondents emerged as a cautious, routinized group. Particularly problematic was the belief of 84 per cent of our respondents that their supervisors should be consulted before decisions were taken. This pattern conforms to informal interviews with Saudi bureaucrats, the majority of whom consistently stressed the unwillingness of their colleagues to take the responsibility for even minor decisions. The best way to avoid such responsibility is to shift the responsibility upward where it is ultimately diffused by being sent to a committee. Whether the Saudi bureaucracy is any more routinized than other bureaucracies is open to question. The point remains, however, that the Saudi bureaucracy is hardly disposed to cope with the awesome responsibilities placed upon it by recent five-year plans.

In sum, then, the group portrait of the Saudi bureaucracy is one in which the majority of the Saudi bureaucrats lead relatively contented lives, residing in the relative comfort of Saudi Arabia's major cities. Surrounded by relatives, they process routine paper work, avoiding decisions or policies that might rock the boat or cause them undue stress. Money, being plentiful in the Kingdom, provides little incentive for added exertion or risk-taking. The major concern of most Saudi bureaucrats is job security. Uncomfortable tasks or tasks requiring mobility are performed by foreigners. Risk-taking, to the extent that it occurs, is a function of the endless succession of committees that characterizes the Saudi bureaucracy.

A group portrait, it must be stressed, does little justice to the small group that seems to do most of what gets done. The fact remains, however, that bureaucracy is a group endeavour and the efforts of single individuals are often overwhelmed by the lethargy of the whole. Given the responses surveyed above, we would suggest that the Saudi bureaucracy is minimally adequate to perform its maintenance function and ill prepared to perform its developmental role. It may, in future years, be judged to have been a major impediment to Saudi development programmes.

Some Explanations of Non-Innovative Behaviour in the Saudi Bureaucracy

Having found the Saudi bureaucracy to be a less-than-aggressive force in the development process, the remainder of the paper will attempt to evaluate the basis for this lethargy and to suggest obstacles that must be overcome if its development potential is to be enhanced. This evaluation will involve two steps. The first step will examine the influence of age, education, income and place of origin on the bureaucratic behaviour patterns reviewed above. The second stage of the analysis will search for explanations of Saudi bureaucratic behaviour in the broader context of Saudi culture and society.

The objective of controlling the patterns of bureaucratic behaviour, surveyed in the body of the article, for demographic variables such as age, income, education and place of birth was to ascertain the extent to which these crucial background variables, either individually or collectively, shaped the administrative behaviour of Saudi public servants. If younger or more educated bureaucrats were more innovative in their outlook toward bureaucratic problems than their older or less educated counterparts, for example, one could then derive optimism from the fact that the Saudi bureaucracy is experiencing a clear influx of younger, better-educated members. Overcoming bureaucratic lethargy, in this case, would merely be a matter of time. If, on the other hand, the behaviour of younger, more educated members of the bureaucracy varied little from that of their peers, the future outlook for a more vital and innovative Saudi bureaucracy would be considerably dimmed. Parallel arguments could also be made in reference to the income or place of birth, with respondents from wealthier, urban families presumably being more innovative than respondents from poorer rural backgrounds. The logic of this argument would be that individuals from wealthier backgrounds might feel more secure than poorer civil servants and, accordingly, would be more predisposed to try new ideas. Similarly, urban respondents might be presumed to be somewhat less wedded to tradition than their rural counterparts and would have, presumably, become more receptive to modern values.

Multiple regression analysis was used to assess the individual and collective impact of the four control (independent) variables on each of the various forms of bureaucratic behaviour under consideration.

The results of the regression analysis were not optimistic in terms of the future innovative thrust of the Saudi bureaucracy. The bureaucratic behaviour of the younger and more educated members of the bureaucracy did not differ significantly from that of their older, less educated colleagues. The income and place of origin variables also failed to produce significant variations in bureaucratic behaviour.

This suggests that the lethargy of the Saudi bureaucracy is deeply rooted in Saudi society and that entrenched bureaucratic attitudes are not easily transformed by education, urbanization, or increased prosperity. We would also recall our earlier statement that change is a group phenomenon. Placing a minority of reform-minded servants in a group milieu characterized by lethargy and non-innovative behaviour is far more likely to dampen the zeal of the reformers than it is to ignite the passions of the majority. The analysis turns next, therefore, to explanations of Saudi bureaucratic behaviour to be found within the broader confines of traditional Saudi culture.

Bureaucratic Behaviour and Cultural Values

In this regard, one must note that the Saudi bureaucracy is of recent origin, having achieved substantial size and complexity only during the last twenty years. The oil boom of the post-war era, particularly the 1970s, precipitated a concurrent bureaucratic boom. Individuals from all segments of Saudi society, many with minimal educational or bureaucratic skills, were enticed into the bureaucracy with generous salaries and the promise of job security. Many, it seems, felt that this was their right. It was their share of the new prosperity. Be this as it may, the Saudi bureaucrats are very much a product of their social and cultural origins.

The newness of the Saudi bureaucracy, then, suggests that Saudi bureaucratic behaviour will differ little from Saudi social behaviour in general. Thus, the lack of innovation and achievement motivation manifested by our respondents merely reflects the absence of a strong sense of achievement motivation within Saudi society itself. In Saudi society respect is more likely to be accorded on the basis of age, family background or piety than on the basis of monetary success. One need not be successful in the monetary or material realm to enjoy social status. This is not to suggest that money is disdained, but merely to indicate that money is merely one and not necessarily the best route to status. In contrast with the United States and other Western states, the link between material achievement and self-esteem in Saudi Arabia is not automatic. Moreover, in recent years those bureaucrats most concerned with financial incentives have migrated to the more financially lucrative private sector.

Similarly, the unwillingness of Saudi bureaucrats to relocate away from their extended families is that direct bureaucratic expression of perhaps the most fundamental of all Saudi social values, loyalty to the family. The Saudi family has traditionally been the centre of the individual's world, caring for all of his needs ranging from child rearing to old-age security. Individual status remains poorly differentiated from family status. To move away from one's family thus represents far more than an inconvenience. It means a total restructuring of an individual's social environment and, in many instances, it may require a disavowal of parental authority. Few Saudi parents appreciate the need of their sons to leave the family confines for long periods of time. Family ties, in addition to placing a severe restraint upon mobility within Saudi society, have also resulted in manifest tendencies towards nepotism and related forms of family-centred favouritism. This subject was skirted in the questionnaire owing to its sensitive nature.

Turning to other forms of bureaucratic behaviour surveyed, we also find a link between the desire for prestige and the reluctance of bureaucrats to work in the countryside or to fill positions culturally defined in the category of *aib* or shame. Having an urban, white-collar job is prestigious within the Saudi context. Having a rural or dirty job, regardless of the salary, is not.

The above behaviour patterns are common to most developing areas and have been widely observed throughout the Arab states. Beyond this, however, all of the questionnaire items relating to the social behaviour patterns discussed in this section were also used by Dr Ibrahim Alghofaily in a study of some 600 Saudi youth of high-school age. Alghofaily's results were virtually identical with ours (Alghofaily, 1980).

The roots of lethargy in the Saudi bureaucracy have also been shaped by the absence of a viable innovative incentive system. Money, simply stated, has become too plentiful. It has ceased to be a viable incentive for shaping desired behaviour among government employees. Three dimensions of this problem would appear to be particularly important. First, because of its awesome dependence upon foreign labour, the Saudi leadership has been particularly anxious to draw an ever-increasing number of Saudi nationals into the government service. Wages are thus quite high and good positions are relatively easy to come by. Using salaries as an incentive to draw Saudis into the workforce has dulled the edge of money as an incentive for job performance.

A second and closely related point is the desire of the Saudi government to use bureaucratic positions as a means of allowing the maximum number of Saudis to share the nation's wealth. As in many countries, the bureaucracy is used to perform a social-welfare function in addition to its maintenance and developmental functions. The welfare function, unfortunately, runs counter to the developmental function by drawing individuals into the bureaucracy with low skill levels and with little incentive other than to draw their salaries and pursue the interests of their family. Many also pursue second occupations. The presence of a low-incentive/low-skill group clearly contributes to the group-dynamic or group-environment problem introduced at the beginning of our data analysis.

Finally, a quixotic offshoot of Saudi Arabia's oil prosperity has been the emergence of a very vigorous private sector in the areas of real estate, construction, and hotels. The private sector pays salaries well in advance of those paid by the government. Although the risks are higher and the job security is lower, the ability to make a sizeable fortune is clearly available to the most energetic and ambitious Saudis. Thus, the Saudi bureaucracy has witnessed a migration of its most entrepreneurial and achievement-oriented members to the private sector. The bureaucracy is thus being deprived of those individuals most likely to spur it into becoming a more viable agent of change and national development.

Those individuals who remain, by and large, are far more concerned with job security and risk avoidance.

References

Alghofaily, I. F., *Saudi Youth Attitudes Toward Work and Vocational Education: A Constraint on Economic Development*, dissertation, The Florida State University, 1980.

Caiden, N. and A. Wildavsky, *Planning and Budgeting in Poor Countries*, New York: Wiley-Interscience, 1975.

Cartwright, D. and A. Zander (eds.), *Group Dynamics: Research and Theory*, 3rd edn., New York: Harper & Row, 1968.

Heady, F., *Public Administration: A Comparative Perspective*, 2nd edn., New York: Marcel Dekker, 1979.

Mahdavy, H., 'The patterns and problems of economic development in rentier states: the case of Iran', in M. A. Cook (ed.), *Studies in the Economic History of the Middle East*, London: Oxford University Press, 1970.

McClelland, D. C., *The Achieving Society*, Princeton, NJ: D. van Nostrand, 1961.

Meyer, A. J., *Middle Eastern Capitalism: Nine Essays*, Cambridge, Mass.: Harvard University Press, 1959.

Montgomery, J. D. and W. J. Siffin (eds.), *Approaches to Development*, New York: McGraw-Hill, 1966.

Waldo, D., 'Comparative and development administration, retrospect and prospect: a symposium', *Public Administration Review*, 36, November 1976, 615–54.

Egyptian Management at the Crossroads

S. A. Zahra

From *Management International Review*, Vol. 20, 1983, 118–24

In 1974, President Sadat announced his new economic 'open door' policy to attract foreign capital, remedy the ailing public-enterprise system, revive capitalism, and achieve a set of socio-economic goals. Ever since, Arab and international investors who visited Egypt have found it to be a frustrating experience to negotiate a deal with Egyptian management.[1]

This paper explores the major societal dimensions which define the role of Egyptian management. Also, it provides some insights about its major characteristics, its challenges, and available options.

The Setting

Ideological ambiguities, constant political shifts, and unfavorable economic and social conditions impose severe limitations on the role of management as follows:

The Political Dimension

Some years ago, Westfall observed that management in Egypt is, without doubt, political. Appointments are made to key positions by political leaders, and a major consideration is the political loyalty of individuals selected.[2] The relationship between management and politics since has grown stronger and more complex.

With waves of nationalization in the early 1960s, the State has come to play a most significant role in the economy. This was deemed necessary to achieve development, improve the standard of living, and ensure control over the means of production. Consequently, the pre-1952 capitalism was duly replaced by a large and powerful public sector which accounted for 90 per cent of total investment, some 75 per cent of manufacturing value added, and almost the whole of foreign trade.[3] Only very small and insignificant projects were left to private ownership.

'Arab socialism' was proclaimed the only way out of poverty and underdevelopment. This new doctrine was assumed to reconcile the demands of Islam and Socialism. However, its boundaries have never been operationally well defined. For instance, it was described as '. . . a complex *mélange* of Islamic egalitarianism, Eastern political tradition, modern social democracy, latter-day anti-colonialism, and a dash of socialist orthodoxy.'[4]

This ideological ambiguity has resulted in the absence of a well-articulated economic framework or theory to guide plans of development. The problem, however, is that this ambiguity has become an integral part of Egyptian political thinking.

Another feature of Egyptian politics is its unpredictability and instability. This is explained by the existence of rival power centers seeking legitimacy, and the fact that major policy decisions are indeed the direct result of one man's preference – the President.[5] On numerous occasions, these preferences have proven to be radical departures from long-standing policies. Examples include Nasser's nationalization of the Suez Canal in 1956, Sadat's 1973 October war, and his trip to Jerusalem which stunned even his closest cabinet members. The point is there were no signs of any coming change.

Egypt also faces the common Middle Eastern problem of difficulty in establishing real political institutions which will foster or at least permit public participation in policy decisions.[6] Nasser's one party was doomed to failure for corruption and abuse of power. Sadat's new multi-party system is young and fragile. Moreover, it concentrates the powers in the hands of the President.[7]

Absence of true public participation results in a noticeable alliance between the military and political leadership. In fact, political survival is contingent upon this very relationship.

Within such a framework it has been impossible for managers to secure an independent base as professionals. Instead, they serve completely at the discretion of the political élite.[8] As a result, the managers' role has been degraded to that of civil servants.[9]

The Economic Dimension

Egypt is plagued by an ever-increasing population, and shortages of natural resources, skilled labor, managerial talents and capital.

During the transformation into 'socialism', a subsidy system was created and enhanced to reach over a billion dollars a year. With falling productivity in agriculture and industry and increasing population, the balance-of-payments deficit has risen sharply. Meanwhile, food prices have been rising at an average of 10 per cent annually throughout the 1970s. As a result, inflation has reached an annual rate of 25–30 per cent during the same period in spite of the subsidy system and the large army of price controllers.

The noted expansion of government's role in the economy has caused public expenditure to increase from only 19 per cent of the GNP in 1956 to above 28 per cent in 1973. Combined with the noted propensity of Egyptians to consume, the country has been unable to provide needed capital for programs of development.

Several plans of development were implemented over the past two decades. However, lack of coordination among sectors, absence of policy guidelines, and neglect of agriculture contributed greatly to the failure of these plans.[10] Also, war interrupted these plans causing scarce resources to be diverted to finance military expenditures which were estimated at nearly 30 per cent of national income. During the period from June 1967 to October 1973 the country suffered an estimated loss of at least $40 billion in the form of national waste and unused industrial capacity due to war conditions.[11]

Throughout the 1970s, Egypt became dependent on foreign aid which amounted to $2,508 million in 1977. However, the country's capability to absorb and effectively use this substantial amount of economic assistance was restrained by lack of adequate managerial talents to plan and implement programs of relief and development.

It is undebatable that the peace treaty between Egypt and Israel will have a profound impact on the future course of Egypt and the Middle East. Egypt needed peace and stability to cope with its ailing infrastructure and large debts which amounted to more than $13 billion in 1977.

Some observers contend that things are already improving.[12] They noted that the GNP had risen by 9 per cent in 1979 compared to 1978, and cash is flowing from the Suez Canal and other unexpected sources such as oil. While this is a remarkable achievement under the circumstances, one should not allow a temporary optimism to mislead the analysis. The problems facing Egypt are so real, so deep, and so diverse. The per capita income in 1978, for instance, was only $280 and millions still live under inhuman conditions. Furthermore, the noted rise in the GNP does not reflect a real gain in productivity. Rather, it is due, in the major part, to transfers made by the Egyptians working abroad. In short, the spurs of development are widely lacking.

The Social and Cultural Dimensions

Existing norms and the value system contradict the demands of modern management in several ways. Most important of these are:

1. Most Egyptians are illiterate. With less than 35 per cent of the population who can read or write, it is very difficult to direct the labor force.

   The Educational System is increasingly playing an important role in society, particularly in the case of the younger generations.

   Indeed it is the only hope for Egypt in the long run. Yet its emphasis on rote learning and conformity to existing political leadership rather than to the state has fatally injured creativity and individuality. This is perhaps the cardinal sin that has been committed in modern Egypt.

   The present leadership seems determined to enhance the long-standing tradition of educational excellence, and reorient the educational system to make it more responsive to the needs of modernization. This attempt is endangered by lack of facilities, resources, and educators to cope with massive numbers.
2. The values system encourages dependency on the State for employment and services. This has been a traditional feature of the government–public relationship since the dawn of history. The result is the lack of personal initiative.
3. Egyptians, like many other nations of the Middle East, are fatalists. Their appreciation of the value of time, planning, organization, and discipline is widely absent. Moreover, it has been particularly difficult to orient workers to an industrial environment.
4. The social order is riven by a gap which separates a small westernized élite and the mass of people. Despite claims of equality asserted by some, it is increasingly recognized that transformation into socialism has created a new élite of professionals and technocrats who now reside atop the social and economic pyramid. In fairness, it should be stated that mobility between classes has become possible.
5. Another gap exists between the two 'cultures' of rural and urban Egypt. The behavioral differences between the two are widespread, with different aspirations and outlooks.

Urbanization of Egypt has been slow. In 1968, about 41.2 per cent was urban compared to only 43.9 per cent in 1976. The greatest challenge is to enhance regional planning so that rural Egypt may be brought to modernity.

6. Women remain marginal in their role although their number is rising among students and professionals. This is not to belittle either women's quest for equality or their achievements. Some have risen to the ranks of cabinet members.

Major Characteristics

Management is by nature culture bound, and Egyptian management is no exception. Therefore, it reflects the interplay between the various dimensions explored above. Among its most significant features are the following:

Bureaucratic

This is perhaps the best known of all features. Daily newspapers and magazines are filled with stories about the delay in making simple decisions. Yet less known are the reasons behind this phenomenon.

With nationalization of major economic activities, political leadership was confronted with a severe shortage of well groomed, yet loyal, managers to run the newly created public organizations. Thus, some bureaucrats from government were selected to assume managerial leadership in industry and other sectors. While this proved to be a successful means to control the economy, bureaucratic mentality proved to be fatal to the economic order. They tended to emphasize centralized decision making, management by extensive procedures, and undue red tape.

Another source of bureaucracy is the multiplicity of controls inside and outside the organizations. This multiplicity was the result of mistrust of managers' intentions by the political élite. This was reflected in the hierarchy which prevailed prior to 1975. All public firms were controlled by 35 general (holding) organizations which, in turn, were grouped under the relevant ministries. Ministries and holding organizations made major decisions regarding investment, productions, pricing, and employment. Very little, indeed, was left to the discretion of the company's management.

Under Law III of 1975, the 'General Organizations' were redistributed into 23 sectors. Each sector is headed by a 'Higher Council' made up of ministry and company officials and outside experts. The main function of the 'council' is to provide overall planning and coordination while leaving decisions regarding production, investment, and the like to the Boards of companies.[13]

A third source of bureaucracy is overstaffing, which has become a prominent challenge to the Egyptian manager since the 1960s. The State has committed itself to employ high-school and college graduates. The pressure for jobs has been alleviated only by artificially expanding the already swollen public sector. A recent study by the Central Agency for Organization & Administration (CAOA) found that about 450,000, i.e. two-thirds of government employees have little or nothing to do.[14]

This bureaucratic nature of Egyptian management prevents it from meeting the demands of progress. It is also the source of huge national waste in the use of resources. More seriously, it breeds corruption by creating interest groups within the government and encouraging bribery.

Ill Trained

In view of sluggish economic growth, it has become clear that Egyptian managers lack needed talents to lead programs of development. Several attempts have been made to remedy this situation. Business and Public Administration programs were incorporated into almost every University's curriculum. Professional institutes and associations were established with a special focus on management development. Also, several programs to reform managerial practices were introduced by the State. However, absence of a clear concept of management development and overdependency on foreign theories are often cited as the reasons behind the failure of these efforts. Also, more recently the most capable of Egyptian managers left the country to work in rich Arab States to escape frustration.

Lack of proper training led the Egyptian manager to be subjective and opinionated and reinforced his bureaucratic tendency. Also, it led to many problems in setting production and pricing policies in a wide range of activities.

Disoriented

The quintessential example of disorientation is the everchanging priority system. During the 1960s and the 1970s, industry was given the lion's share of investment. Confronted with food shortages, Egyptian planners are now conceding that agriculture should have been the focal point in planning for development. While many other underdeveloped nations committed the same mistake, the question remains why did it take Egyptian planners more than 25 years to realize this simple fact?

Absence of a long-run vision of the country's future and the relative instability of the political paradigm contribute greatly to disorientation of management. Together they result in the transitory manager phenomenon which, admittedly, has never been thoroughly studied. However, it seems to be a common feature of Arab management in general.[15]

As indicated earlier, political shifts often resulted in parallel changes in managerial leadership. Realizing that their position may be short-term and that they may be replaced at any time, these managers tend to emphasize short-run choices to show the political leadership that they are indispensable. In the process, laws are frequently changed and procedures are bent. In fact, they tend to superimpose their personalities on organizations by restructuring the decision-making process around themselves. Hence, organizations are unable to respond to the needs of their environment because they are constantly occupied with internal politics.

Neglect of Human Resources

Egypt's labor force of 9.7 million is very large and relatively well skilled compared to those of other Arab and Third World Countries. Undoubtedly, it represents a great asset for development.

Workers have achieved remarkable gains over the past two decades. These include better pay, reduction of work hours, employment of profit-sharing schemes, compulsory social insurance, the right to unionize, and representation on the Board of Directors. Since October 1963, every nine-member Board includes four representatives of workers. However, several studies concluded that management pays little or no attention to the Industrial Relations functions in their organizations. An appreciable percentage of managers surveyed had no knowledge of the existence of such functions within their own firms. Moreover, as a 1977 study concluded, there is indeed a wide gap between management and the work force. Each party blamed the other for falling productivity and each suspected the real intentions and methods of the other.[16]

Mistrust between management and the labor force seems to be deeply rooted in politics. Managers were stereotyped as being an 'idle intellectual élite' who have no place in a truly socialist society. On the other hand, managers believe that most laws enacted in the 1960s were ideologically and politically motivated and did not take into account the demands of efficiency. For instance, managers had no power to fire an incompetent employee except in very extreme and rare cases. Also, it was argued that the gains workers achieved were the result of their political strength since they are the largest well-organized group in the country.

Some scholars argued that manpower in Egypt is not a problem of surplus or shortage. Rather, it is essentially a problem of improper preparation, estimation, distribution, and use; and here lies a great task for the Egyptian manager.[17]

At the Crossroads

Egypt approaches the future burdened by numerous past mistakes and very few options.[18] The government and the public alike have come to realize that unless effective steps are taken to control population, attract more investment, fight bureaucracy, increase real productivity, and adopt strategic planning Egypt will continue to suffer.

A key factor in Egypt's future is peace and political stability. Without both, economic and human resources will continue to be wasted. Yet it seems that peace is far away; at least for the time being. Meanwhile Egypt is spending more on the military than before. In fact, it has become the most fertile ground for US arms sellers.[19]

Another key factor is the role played by the private and public sectors in the economy. It is clear by now that Egypt is truly witnessing a great transition into a mixed economy.[20] There are also some indications that the newly established private firms helped ease Egypt's financial troubles, enhanced productivity, introduced some new technology, created more than 85,000 new jobs, allowed transfer of some modern managerial practices, and stimulated the public sector.[21]

The question regarding the future of the public sector remains unanswered, adding to the uncertainty facing Egypt. It is almost certain, however, that it will not be disposed of soon, at least for political, and perhaps symbolic, reasons.

It is the contention of this paper that allowing private enterprises to flourish will not only quicken the speed of transformation but will help Egypt create a modern State and achieve development. In conjunction with that, the role of the State has to be clearly redefined. Not only did it prove to be a bad owner and manager but it also killed every reason to excel on the part of the individuals.

Economic progress is meaningless in the absence of basic freedoms and loss of human dignity. Therefore, the most formidable task awaiting Egypt is to enhance democracy.

The future of management itself is an uncertain one. As Baker observed, 'until fundamental ideological and institutional ambiguities of the Sadat transition are resolved, the already flawed performance of industrial managers can only worsen.'[22]

Egyptian management is faced with the greatest challenge of all – rebuilding the individual to participate in development plans. A creative approach, with a prime emphasis on Egyptian personality, is needed, for both culture and demography defy most known western development mechanisms. This should be an overriding concern of Egyptian planners since an accepted concept of man will help define appropriate social technology of change. Man is, and should be, the center of development.

Rebuilding the individual necessitates a new era of industrial relations where all work for a common goal. This entails changes in labor laws and practices to allow more freedom for managers in making decisions, and the use of firm measures to ensure accountability.

Amid this chaos, management has to be realistic. Change needs time and resources. Also, it has to foster self-development and higher levels of professionalism among its members. Without both, sluggish economic growth will continue.

Notes

The author wishes to thank Professor D. L. Howell, and Dr D. Blevins, Assistant Professor, Department of Management and Marketing, The University of Mississippi, and Mr M. J. Sena for their comments and encouragement.

1. Berry, John, 'Hell paved with good intentions', *Forbes*, 120, 1977, 39–40.

2. Westfall, Ralph, 'Business management under Nasser', *Business Horizons*, 7, 1964, 73–84.

3. Mabro, Robert and Samir Radwan, *The Industrialization of Egypt, 1939–1973: Policy and Performance*, p. 40, Oxford: Clarendon Press, 1976.

4. Amuzegar, Jahangir, 'Ideology and economic growth in the Middle East', *The Middle East Journal*, 28, 1974, 2.

5. Heikal, Mohamed Hassanein, 'Egyptian foreign policy', *Foreign Affairs*, 56, 1978, 714–27.

6. Burrell, Michael and Abbas R. Kelidar, *Egypt: The Dilemmas of a Nation: 1970–1976*, p. 6, Georgetown University, Washington, D.C.: The Center For Strategic and International Studies, 1977.

7. Kondrake, Morton, 'The impotence of being Anwar', *New Republic*, 179, 1978, 15–19.

8. Baker, Raymond William, *Egypt's Uncertain Revolution Under Nasser and Sadat*, p. 81, Cambridge, Mass.: Harvard University Press, 1978.

9. Mabro and Radwan, *Industrialization of Egypt*, p. 74.

10. Sayigh, Yusif A., *The Economics of the Arab World: Development since 1945*, pp. 317–73, New York: St Martin's Press, 1978.

11. El Sobky, Abdel Mon'em, 'An interview with the Egyptian Minister of Commerce and Finance', *Arab Review for Management*, 1, 1977, 48 (Arabic).

12. Tinnin, David B., 'Egypt's touch-and-go war on poverty', *Fortune*, 101, 1980, 48–75.

13. Button, Kenneth R., *Marketing in Egypt*, p. 7, GPO, Washington, D.C.: US Department of Commerce, September 1978.

14. 'Teaching Bureaucrats That "Time Is Money" ', *Business Week*, 2618, 1979, 48–51.

15. Pezeshkpur, Changiz, 'Challenges to management in the Arab World', *Business Horizons*, 21, 1978, 47–55.

16. Abdel Wahab, Ali Mohamad, 'Human relations in management: a field study', *Arab Review For Management*, 1, 1977, 11–17 (Arabic).

17. Ashmawy, Saad, 'Problems of manpower in Egypt and suggested solutions', *Management Quarterly Review*, 3, 1971, 94–103 (Arabic).

18. Waterbury, John, *Egypt: Burdens of the Past, Options for the Future*, pp. 85–124, Bloomington: Indiana University Press, 1978.

19. 'The hot race to sell arms to the Arabs', *Business Week*, 2614, 1979, 52–53.

20. Abdelwahed, Farouk, 'Egypt's road to a mixed economy', *Management International Review*, 18, 1978, 23–32.

21. El Banna, Ragab and Osama Gheith, 'What did the economic open door policy achieve till now?', *Al Ahram*, 6 February 1980, p. 3.

22. Baker, *Egypt's Uncertain Revolution*, p. 196.

8

Developing Countries

The Need for Indigenous Management in Developing Countries

Rabindra N. Kanungo and Alfred M. Jaeger

Chapter 1, pp. 1 – 15 in Alfred M. Jaeger and Rabindra N. Kanungo (eds.), *Management in Developing Countries* (London and New York: Routledge, 1990)

Introduction

Organizations are socio-technical systems with specific objectives of producing goods and services for their clientele. In order to manage such organizations effectively, it is necessary to understand how these systems work. Social scientists working in the field of organizational behaviour have proposed many theories and techniques that have helped management practitioners not only to understand the complexities of organizational systems but also to manage them effectively in order to achieve their production and service objectives.

Most widely dispersed management theories and techniques have their origin in the industrialized countries of the West. Many organizations in these industrialized countries have benefited from their prescriptions. As a result, Western management thought and practice have turned into 'sacred cows' for industrial development. Countries in the developing world are advised, and feel themselves, that they must strive to adopt Western thought and practices to achieve economic prosperity within the shortest possible time. Hence many organizational practices and management training programmes in the developing countries in modern times are based on 'an uncritical emulation and extrapolation from the experiences of the economic growth model of Western countries, grossly disregarding the fundamental differences in socio-cultural constraints and local conditions and circumstances' (Sinha and Kao, 1988: 11). Uncritical transfer of management theories and techniques based on Western ideologies and value systems has in many ways contributed to organizational inefficiency and ineffectiveness in the developing country context.

Managing organizations is a complex act. It requires a thorough understanding of the dynamic relationships within the socio-technical system (the internal environment) and the relationship to the external environment with which the system is in constant interaction. Since the external environment of organizations in the developing countries is different from that of the Western industrialized countries, management theories and practices developed in the developed country context may have only limited applicability in the context of the developing world. If one accepts the above premise, it becomes clear that there is a need to develop indigenous management theories and practices for use in the developing country context. This chapter represents an effort at exploring this perspective and an attempt at providing some outlines of management approaches appropriate for the environments found specifically in developing countries.

The Need for Indigenous Management

Every organization must deal with the management of its internal and external environments, i.e. the management of the people and technology within the organization as well as the management of relations with the environment external to or outside the organization.

Every organization has the basic purpose of achieving two sets of objectives with respect to the management of its human resources. The first set has to do with improving the performance of organizational members to deliver goods and services for which the organization is formed in the first place. Productivity of a given organization – whether it is measured in terms of units produced, volume of sales accomplished, quality of services rendered, amount of profit margin, or cost effectiveness of the operation – is largely dependent on the performance of organizational members, be they managers or rank-and-file workers.

The second set of objectives has to do with developing and maintaining the human potential that serves as the backbone of the organization. The capacity of an organization to survive and to respond to competitive challenges from time to time can only be sustained and mobilized when the organization has highly competent and motivated manpower. Thus the effectiveness of the management of an organization is very much dependent on the nature of the human resources it possesses. In other words, an effective organization is one that has members who exhibit high levels of both work-related motivation (job and organizational commitment) and work performance.

Viewing organizational effectiveness in this way presupposes the existence of a system of management practice and employee behaviour that is conducive to high levels of work motivation and performance. Furthermore, such management practice and employee behaviour within an organization in large part results from managerial and employee values, attitudes, and beliefs regarding work and organizations. In other words, every organization has an internal work culture of its own which influences the behaviour or practices of both the management and the workers. The organizational work culture represents a form of organizational reality that shapes both the micro-level individual processes (day-to-day practices and behaviours of organizational members) and macro-level organizational processes (design of organizational structure, technologies employed, and strategic activities).

As a set of shared values, beliefs, and norms about the nature of work and organization, the work culture is constantly influenced by the environment in which the organization operates. In fact, the survival and growth of an organization depends on its developing an appropriate corporate culture that can adequately respond to external environmental forces. Just as the effectiveness of an individual depends on how adequately he or she copes with the surrounding environmental demands, the effectiveness of an organization also depends on how it adapts to its environmental demands by developing an appropriate corporate culture. In developing the appropriate coping strategies, organizations must be sensitive to environmental constraints and opportunities. Such sensitivity implies identifying and responding to three major aspects of the environment: (a) economic and technological; (b) political and legal, and (c) socio-cultural.

The economic-technological environment provides constraints and opportunities with respect to the technological, material, monetary, and human resource procurement necessary for the organization to function effectively. For instance, organizations must respond adequately to the prevailing labour market conditions. Management must plan the manpower needs of the organization according to the availability and flexibility of labour. Manpower planning effectiveness depends on whether management has a free hand in hiring, firing, retraining, or retrenching workers with minimal legal and political interference. Effectiveness in manpower planning for increased productivity and better service also depends on wage levels and the flexibility with which wages can respond to existing realities. For example, if economic or market conditions necessitate lower wage levels, or a moderate increase in wages, or even a wage freeze or reduction, then organizational effectiveness is enhanced to the extent that the ethos governing wages permits a flexible response to these conditions. The success of the organization would also depend on its adequate response to the challenges to its financing activities posed by economic conditions such as the availability of investment capital, inflation rates, interest rates, taxes, etc. Furthermore, the level of technology available for carrying out the organization's tasks is an important consideration for the organization's success. Important also is the development of an infrastructure which facilitates the procurement of materials, the location of suppliers, and distribution outlets. When the prospects of financing the organization, of obtaining the appropriate technology, and of finding the right markets are either inadequate or uncertain, organizational effectiveness suffers.

Besides the economic and technological environment, the political and legal environment also provides either facilitatory or inhibitory conditions for the successful operation of organizations. For instance, the stability of governments (local, regional, and/or national) creates business confidence. Legal systems which provide protection from foreign competition and establish specific labour mores and practices either promote or inhibit healthy organizations. Political interference in the management of organizations and the bureaucratic hurdles that management often encounters are widely known to contribute to organizational failure.

Finally, the socio-cultural environment provides challenges for dealing with human resources (a product of the socio-cultural environment) within the organization and for dealing with the clients (customers, community served) outside the organization. The socio-cultural environment of any given society determines collective norms and values, and individual beliefs, attitudes, and action preferences. Since organizational functioning depends on the behaviour and attitudes of people within a given society, organizational behaviour is profoundly influenced by the socio-cultural environment within which the organization operates. Sensitivity to the socio-cultural environment is particularly important for effective human resource management in organizations. The preceding discussion is summarized in Figure 1, which depicts the external environmental and internal organizational forces that influence organizational effectiveness with respect to human resource management.

Both international business and cross-cultural management studies recognize the importance of environmental variables, particularly those relating to the socio-cultural environment as a major determinant of organizational effectiveness both within a given country (Kanungo, 1980) and across various countries in the world (Kanungo and Wright, 1983; Adler, 1986). However, in the context of developing countries, systematic explorations of what these environmental and cultural variables are and how management can deal with them for greater organizational effectiveness are just beginning to take place (Kiggundu *et al.*, 1983; Sinha and Kao, 1988).

Most of our knowledge and technology about how best to manage human

Figure 1 External and internal environmental factors influencing organizational effectiveness

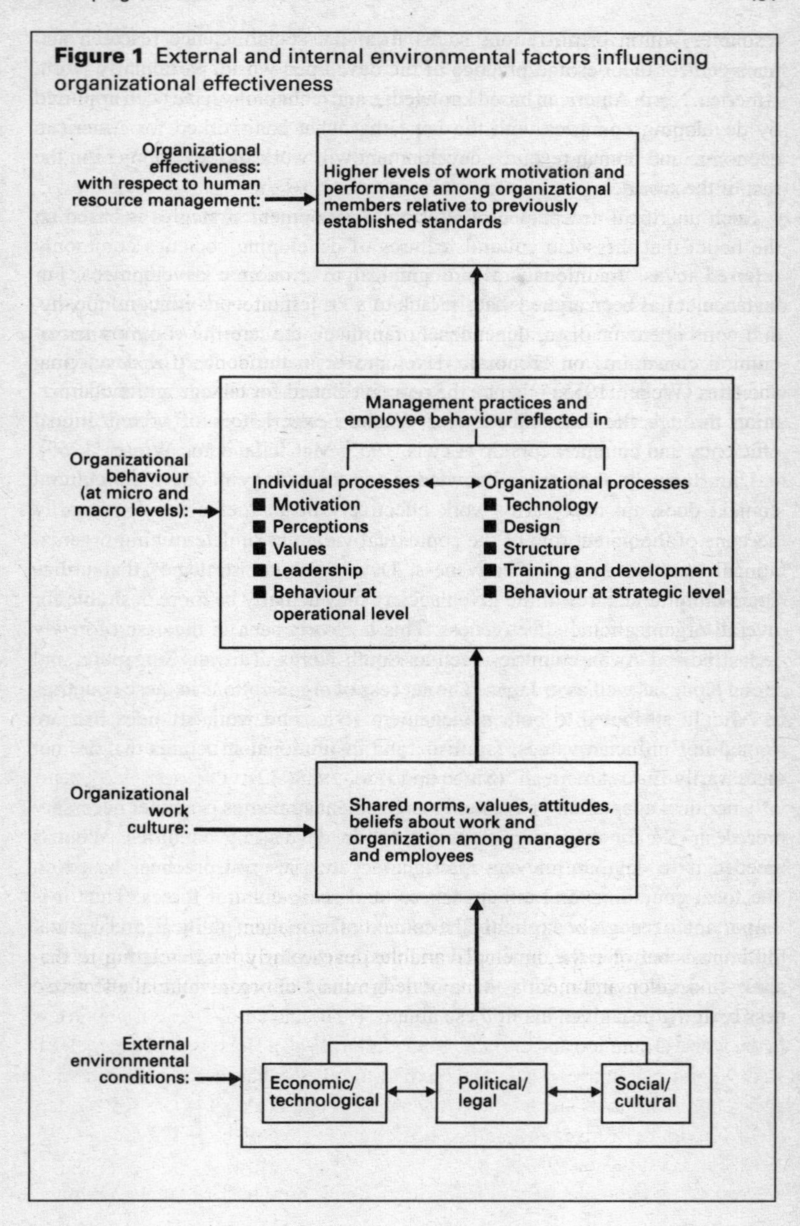

resources within organizations stems from the social science research and management theories and practice of the developed world, particularly North America. North American based knowledge and technology have been imported by developing countries with the hope that what has worked for American economic and human resource development will work for development in the rest of the world.

Such uncritical acceptance of Western development strategies is based on the belief that the socio-cultural features of developing societies commonly referred to as 'traditionalism' are inimical to economic development. For instance, it has been argued that the lack of a Protestant work ethic, religiosity, and consequent fatalism, dependence, familism, etc. are the common socio-cultural constraints on economic development in the context of developing societies (Weber, 1958) – hence the perceived need for change and modernization through the emulsification of Western experiences of organizational efficiency and entrepreneurship (Lewis, 1955; McClelland and Winter, 1969).

Unfortunately, the proven knowledge and technology in one socio-cultural context does not necessarily work effectively in another context, primarily because of the potent role of the contextual variables in determining organizational functioning and effectiveness. Developmental strategies that utilize socio-cultural features of the given society may actually be more desirable for overall organizational effectiveness. This is clearly seen in the case of newly industrialized Asian countries such as South Korea, Taiwan, Singapore, and Hong Kong, as well as in Japan. The success of organizations in these countries is 'widely attributed to both management styles and work attitudes that are rooted in Confucian values, familism, and institutional structures that are not necessarily Euro-American' (Sinha and Kao, 1988: 12).

Uncritical adaptation of Western management strategies is neither necessary nor desirable for managing organizations in developing countries. What is needed is to develop relevant management theories and practices based on the local conditions and circumstances, and socio-cultural forces. Thus it is important to recognize explicitly the context of economic, political, and cultural differences between the developed and the developing countries and appropriately to develop and modify the knowledge and technology that is best suited to managing organizations in these areas.

Characterization of Environments of Developed and Developing Countries

At this point one might ask: how can we characterize the economic, political, and cultural differences between the developed Western industrialized and developing Third World countries? How do these differences impact on the internal work culture and the management practices and employee behaviour in organizations in developing countries? What can managers do to improve the handling of human resources within the specific environmental and cultural constraints? What are the facilitating and inhibiting conditions inherent in the environmental contexts for the effective utilization of human resources? These are some of the complex issues that have no easy solutions. However, some general notions with respect to such differences can give a better appreciation of the need for indigenous management in developing countries and may provide some clues as to what forms it might take.

Although organizations in each country of the world have to adapt to the unique features of their own environment, for the convenience of analysis we shall look at the environment of organizations in two commonly understood clusters: those located in Western industrialized countries and those located in Third World or developing countries.

Organizations found in each cluster have some commonalities. The two clusters differ on several dimensions with respect to their external environment and internal work culture which influence both micro- and macro-level organizational behaviour. These dimensions can be grouped into three categories: dimensions relating to the economic and political environment, dimensions relating to the socio-cultural environment, and dimensions relating to the internal work culture. A listing of the dimensions on which the two clusters differ is presented in Table 1.

Economic and Political Environment

The economic–technological and the political–legal environments with which organizations interact can be characterized in terms of two critical factors suggested by Triandis (1984): (a) the predictability of future environmental events and (b) the difficulty in obtaining resources from the environment. Variations in the environment on these dimensions have a significant impact on overall organizational behaviour as well as on the behaviour of individuals and groups within the organization. As Triandis points out, 'predictability has implications for the difficulty of the environment. Very predictable environments

Table 1 Dimensions on which organizations in developed and developing countries differ

Dimensions	*Developed countries*	*Developing countries*
A *Characterization of economic and political environment*		
Predictability of events	Relatively high	Relatively low
Difficulty of obtaining resources from environment	Relatively easy	Relatively difficult
B *Characterization of socio-cultural environment*		
Uncertainty avoidance	Relatively low	Relatively high
Individualism–collectivism	Relatively high individualism	Relatively low individualism
Power distance	Relatively low	Relatively high
Masculinity–femininity	Relatively high masculinity	Relatively low masculinity
Abstractive–associative	Relatively high abstractive/low associative thinking	Relatively low abstractive/high associative thinking
C *Characterization of internal work culture (management values and climate of beliefs and assumptions)*		
Descriptive assumptions about human nature		
Causality and control of outcomes	Internal	External
Creative potential	Unlimited	Limited
Malleability	Malleable	Fixed
Time perspective	Future oriented	Past and present oriented
Time units for action	Long term	Short term
Prescriptive assumptions about guiding principles of behaviour within organization		
Task orientation	Proactive	Passive/reactive
Success orientation	Pragmatism	Moralism
People orientation	Collegial/participative	Authoritarian/ paternalistic
Environment orientation	Context independent	Context dependent

are easier than very unpredictable, and both very simple and very complex societies live in very predictable environments' (p. 83).

The Western industrialized environment represents a high degree of complexity: a multitude of firms are engaged in producing a vast array of products and services. Their characterization as 'developed' means that the infrastructure is developed, the supply of a trained labour force is developed, the capital markets are developed, and business–government relations are developed to the point of facilitating commerce or at least not hindering it. Thus the difficulty of obtaining resources is comparatively low and predictability is on average relatively high.

The developing-country environment represents complexity of a different kind. Developing countries no longer represent the traditional agrarian society but are on the way to industrialization and modernization. Very often, the developing-country environment becomes complex because of the non-availability of resources to meet the high aspirations for development. Thus, complexity is the result not just of what is, but what 'is not'. Organizational means and goals tend to be incongruous and create difficulties for effective management. Furthermore, the developing-country environment can be characterized as being on average relatively more unpredictable. The political and legal climates in most developing countries are perceived to be relatively less stable. Very often they also represent certain characteristics of 'loose societies' where 'norms are not well developed', and where lawless corrupt practices are more the rule than an exception. This type of environment also poses problems for obtaining the required economic, technological, and skilled human resources. Thus the challenge facing the manager in a developing country is qualitatively very different from that facing his or her counterpart in the developed world. Hence, managing organizations in a developing country requires some very different approaches and skills in order to be successful.

In response to difficult and unpredictable economic and political environments in developing countries, organizations adopt various coping strategies such as lack of planning for the future with a long-term goal perspective, lack of time management, lack of entrepreneurship and moderate risk taking, and behaviour reflective of a lack of trust 'in the system'. These dysfunctional coping strategies act as barriers to organizational effectiveness. Indigenous management theories need to address this issue.

In the context of development, significant changes in the environment are necessary to make it more predictable and easy. These include the supply of adequate financing, vocational training programmes, technology development, political non-interference, judiciary and executive reforms, etc., and in the realm of organizational behaviour, management training and development, time management, reward-system reforms to reinforce appropriate behaviour, etc.

Socio-Cultural Environment

By differentiating developed and developing countries along cultural lines, one can say that they comprise two distinct cultural groups. To understand better what this means, one must examine what is meant by culture. Most management researchers subscribe to a view of culture which sees it as a set of ideas shared by members of a group. A useful definition of culture from this perspective is provided by the anthropologist Roger Keesing (1974). He describes culture as being an individual's theory of what his fellows know, believe, and mean, his theory of the code being followed, the game being played. Culture is therefore not an individual characteristic but rather denotes a set of common theories of behaviour or mental programmes that are shared by a group of individuals.

To connect culture to management, it is helpful to look to an empirical model of culture developed by Hofstede (1980a) along with a dimension from Glenn and Glenn (1981) suggested by Kedia and Bhagat (1988). These dimensions provide us with a framework for understanding cultural variation in an organizational context.

Hofstede carried out an empirical analysis that resulted in a concise framework of dimensions for differentiating national cultures. Although the framework has some limitations, it is most widely used by researchers and is recognized as a significant landmark in cross-cultural research (Triandis, 1982).

Hofstede used a forty-country questionnaire survey of employees of one multinational organization; 116,000 questionnaires were administered in two waves (1968 and 1972). From these data, four dimensions were found to differentiate national cultures: power distance, uncertainty avoidance, individualism (collectivism), and masculinity (femininity). These were described by Hofstede as follows:

- Power distance is 'the extent to which a society accepts the fact that power in institutions and organizations is distributed unequally' (1980b: 45).
- Uncertainty avoidance is 'the extent to which a society feels threatened by uncertain and ambiguous situations. If it does, then it may cope by providing career stability, establishing more formal rules, not tolerating deviant ideas and behaviours, and believing in absolute truths and the attainment of expertise' (1980b: 46).
- Individualism 'implies a loosely knit social framework in which people are supposed to take care of themselves and their immediate families only, while

collectivism is characterized by a tight social framework in which people distinguish between in-groups and out-groups; they expect their in-group (relatives, clan, organizations) to look after them, and in exchange for that they feel they owe absolute loyalty to it' (1980b: 45).

- Masculinity expresses 'the extent to which the dominant values in society are "masculine", that is, assertiveness, the acquisition of money and things, and not caring for others, the quality of life, or people' (1980b: 46).

The cultural dimensions manifest themselves in organizations in a number of ways. For example, associated with high masculinity is a performance rather than a people orientation. The existence of low uncertainty avoidance implies a willingness to take risks and accept organizational change. An individualist believes that involvement with organizations is calculative, whereas a collectivist believes involvement with organizations has a moral basis. If power distance is low, subordinates consider superiors to be 'people like me' and vice versa.

A fifth dimension, that of abstract versus associative thinking, is also particularly useful in understanding cultural differences between developed and developing countries. This dimension can be summarized as follows: 'In associative cultures, people utilize associations among events that may not have much logical basis, whereas in abstractive cultures, cause–effect relationships or rational Judeo-Christian types of thinking are dominant' (Kedia and Bhagat, 1988: 566). Associative and abstractive cultures also tend to differ on the predominant mode of communication and persons' relationship to their context. In associative cultures, the context plays an important role in determining an individual's perceptions, attributions, and behaviours. In contrast, in abstractive cultures these tend to be influenced more by abstract rules and principles applied equally to every situation. In addition, in associative cultures communication tends to be more face to face and is between people who share a large body of historical information from their culture and society. In contrast, in abstractive cultures, communication through technological mechanisms such as the mass media as well as individual electronic media such as telephone and electronic mail tends to be emphasized (Kedia and Bhagat, 1988).

Most importantly, we should point out the ways in which culture affects the interaction of individuals. On the one hand, culture *facilitates* certain behaviours. Members of a cultural group share complementary behavioural programmes which regulate their interaction. Associated with these programmes are values and ideology which provide a guide and a meaning to what they are doing. Implicit in this view is the fact that a culture also *inhibits* other behaviours, behaviours which run counter to the values or practices of the culture. A culture also provides a guide for perception and attribution of others' behaviour. Thus, within a cultural group, certain behaviours will generate a feeling and response that is positive while others will generate a negative feeling and response.

One example which can illustrate these phenomena in an organizational context is the behaviour of 'bypassing', i.e. a subordinate making direct contact with the superior of his boss. In a situation of low power distance, this behaviour would be more likely to occur and would not be viewed very negatively. In a situation of high power distance, this behaviour would be unlikely to occur and, if it did, would be viewed very negatively. Thus, in the latter situation, bypassing behaviour would not only be inhibited, but would in effect be punished, and thus be unlikely to recur.

Work Culture within Organizations

The preceding discussion on the influences of the external environment and the dimensions of national cultures suggests that people's assumptions, beliefs, and values about different aspects of their world are shaped by these environmental forces. Members of an organization in a given environment therefore would share a common set of assumptions, beliefs, and values that in turn would guide their modal pattern of behaviour in the organization. In other words, the external environmental forces shape the internal work culture of an organization.

Analysing culture from a broader perspective, Schein (1985, 1988) has described three levels of culture: basic assumptions and premises; values and ideology; and artefacts and creations. The first level includes such things as the relationship of man to nature, time orientation, beliefs about human nature, the nature of man's relationship to man, and man's concept of space and his place in it. These are usually taken for granted by members of a cultural group and are 'preconscious'. But it is these taken-for-granted assumptions that determine values and ideologies (indicating ideals and goals as well as paths for 'getting there') and the cultural artefacts and creations (such as manifest behaviour, language, technology, and social organization). Schein therefore argues that, in order to understand how organizations work, one needs to understand the internal work culture, particularly the taken-for-granted assumptions of organizational members.

In Table 1, part C, we can see the contrast between the developing countries and developed countries on the dimensions of work culture. The various culture-determined assumptions that affect the work behaviour of organizational members can be broadly categorized under two headings: descriptive assumptions about human nature and prescriptive assumptions about guiding principles of human conduct. The two sets of assumptions are different in the sense that the former describes what human beings are like whereas the latter provides normative guidelines for engaging in and judging the appropriateness of behaviour.

The work cultures of organizations in developed and developing countries differ with respect to the assumptions regarding the nature of causation and control over outcomes (pleasant and unpleasant) which one experiences in life. Rotter (1966) suggested that individuals differ in this respect. Some tend to believe that they are responsible for the outcomes, or their behaviour causes and controls the outcomes (internal locus of control). Others tend to believe that the outcomes they experience in life are determined by forces outside themselves (external locus of control). The locus of control beliefs in developing countries tends to be more external, indicating more of a sense of fatalism in the internal work culture.

Another difference in work culture can be traced to the difference in beliefs about human potential and malleability. Within organizations in developing countries, human capabilities are often viewed as more or less fixed with limited potential. Hence career planning and progression with supporting training facilities are extremely limited. In the developed countries, however, organizations emphasize the malleability and unlimited creative potential of human resources. Thus the internal work culture in the developing countries is more conducive to the Theory X (carrot and stick) model of management (McGregor, 1960), whereas in the developed countries the Theory Y (participative) model is relatively more suitable.

The unpredictable and difficult environment in developing countries has created a time perspective that excludes future orientation and long-term planning (Triandis, 1984). In a predictable environment, being future oriented or having a long-term perspective favours planning, whereas in an unpredictable environment a short-term past and present orientation seems more desirable and hence would not favour planning.

With regard to the normative assumptions guiding one's day-to-day behaviour, several interesting differences are noticed. For example, organizations in developed countries value and encourage a proactive stance while dealing with a given task. This reflects high masculinity of the socio-cultural environment and internal locus of control beliefs. In developing countries, however, a passive stance in relation to tasks is judged to be more desirable. Individuals are encouraged to change themselves to meet environmental pressures (or task demands) rather than to bring about changes in the environment (or the task) to meet their own needs (see Rothbaum *et al.*, 1982, for an interesting discussion on the issue of controlling self versus controlling the environment). Organizational members therefore seem to reflect non-assertive and non-aggressive task orientations.

The success in task-related behaviour is often judged by pragmatic considerations in the developed countries. The individualistic achievement orientation of the Western world coupled with high masculinity has encouraged the use of pragmatic norms. In the developing countries, on the other hand, high collectivism and femininity have encouraged the use of moralism based on traditions and religious beliefs as the norm for judging the success of an individual's behaviour. People are judged successful not because of their entrepreneurship or material prosperity, but because of their nurturant and moral stand to serve interpersonal well-being (rather than personal well-being).

The characterization of people orientation in developing-country organizations as authoritarian and paternalistic indicates a high power distance, whereas the collegial–participative nature of relationships in developed countries is indicative of a relatively lower power distance. In the superior–subordinate relationship, paternalism and dependence are valued and encouraged in developing countries. The trend is quite the opposite in developed countries. Finally, the behaviour orientation towards the environment reveals context dependence in developing countries. This is indicative of the associative mode of thinking. The context independence of the developed countries reflects an abstractive mode of thinking. Abstract principles, rules, and procedures are considered absolutes and transcend contextual forces in guiding behaviour in the developed-country context. In developing countries, such principles are only relative and contextual forces override principles when the two are in conflict.

Indigenous management theories need to address the impact of these cultural factors on individual behaviour in organizations. One assumption implicit in most work in the area of comparative or cross-cultural management, and one shared by the authors, is that the organization is indeed an 'open system' and cultural values from the environment are brought into the work place and have a very strong impact on the organization's work culture.

Future Prospects

Two conclusions are apparent from what has been discussed so far. First, organization theories and practices advocated in the Western industrialized world context can have serious limitations when applied to organizations in the developing countries. For instance, most theories of management originating in the developed world make the assumption that individuals will hold the values of relatively low uncertainty avoidance, relatively high individualism, relatively low power distance, relatively high masculinity, and relatively high abstractive thinking (Hofstede, 1980b; Jaeger, 1986). One example of a management practice which fits with these values of the developed world is management by objectives (MBO). Hofstede (1980b) describes MBO as 'perhaps the single most popular management technique "made in USA" '. He states that MBO presupposes the following underlying value orientations:

1. that subordinates are sufficiently independent to negotiate meaningfully with the boss (not-too-large power distance);
2. that both are willing to take risks (weak uncertainty avoidance);
3. that performance is seen as important by both (high masculinity).

These values are in line with those found in North America, but are clearly at odds with what is often the case in developing countries. As a result, one would expect any attempts at using MBO there to be less than successful. In fact, one can imagine a situation where the use of MBO would be clearly dysfunctional, ultimately causing mistrust and suspicion between a superior and his subordinates, the former essentially trying to force the latter to interact in a manner distinctly foreign to the local culture while at the same time not really willing to accept that type of behaviour.

The second conclusion that follows from the discussion of environmental and cultural differences in the developed and developing countries is the need for indigenous theories and techniques to manage organizations in the Third World effectively.

References

Adler, N. J., *International Dimensions of Organizational Behavior*, Boston, MA: Kent Publishing Co., 1986.

Glenn, E. S. and C. G. Glenn, *Man and Mankind: Conflict and Communication Between Cultures*, Norwood, NJ: Ablex, 1981.

Hofstede, G., *Culture's Consequences: International Differences in Work-related Values*, Beverly Hills, CA: Sage, 1980a.

— 'Motivation, leadership, and organization: do American theories apply abroad?', *Organizational Dynamics*, 9, 1, 1980b, 42–62.

Jaeger, A. M., 'Organization development and national culture: where's the fit?', *Academy of Management Review*, 11, 1, 1986, 178–90.

Kanungo, R. N., *Biculturalism and Management*, Toronto: Butterworths, 1980.

Kanungo, R. N. and R. W. Wright, 'A cross-cultural comparative study of managerial job attitudes', *Journal of International Business Studies*, Fall 1983, 115–29.

Kedia, B. L. and R. S. Bhagat, 'Cultural constraints on transfer of technology across nations:

implications for research in international and comparative management', *Academy of Management Review* 13, 4, 1988, 559–71.

Keesing, R., 'Theories of culture', *Annual Review in Anthropology* 3, 1974, 73–97.

Kiggundu, M. N., J. J. Jørgensen, and T. Hafsi, 'Administrative theory and practice in developing countries: a synthesis', *Administrative Science Quarterly* 28, 1, 1983, 66–84.

Lewis, W. A., *Theory of Economic Growth*, London: Allen & Unwin, 1955.

McClelland, D. C. and D. G. Winter, *Motivating Economic Development*, New York: Free Press, 1969.

McGregor, D., *The Human Side of Enterprise*, New York: McGraw-Hill, 1960.

Rothbaum, F. M., J. R. Weisz, and S. S. Snyder, 'Changing the world and changing self: a two process model of perceived control', *Journal of Personality and Social Psychology* 42, 1982, 5–37.

Rotter, J. B., 'Generalized expectancies for internal versus external control of reinforcement', *Psychological Monographs* 80, 1966 (1, whole no. 609).

Schein, E. H., *Organizational Culture and Leadership*, San Francisco, CA: Jossey-Bass, 1985.

— 'Innovative cultures and adaptive organizations', Working Paper, Sloan School of Management, Massachusetts Institute of Technology, Cambridge, MA, 1988.

Sinha, D. and H. S. R. Kao, 'Introduction: value-development congruence', in D. Sinha and H. S. R. Kao (eds.), *Social Values and Development: Asian Perspectives*, New Delhi: Sage, 1988.

Triandis, H. C., 'Review of culture's consequences: international differences in work-related values', *Human Organization* 41, 1982, 86–90.

— 'Toward a psychological theory of economic growth', *International Journal of Psychology* 19, 1984, 79–95.

Weber, M., *The Religions of India: The Sociology of Hinduism and Buddhism*, Glencoe, IL: Free Press, 1958.

Africa

Managerial Work in Africa

Peter Blunt and Merrick L. Jones

Chapter 2, pp. 30–41 and Figure 1 in Peter Blunt and Merrick L. Jones, *Managing Organisations in Africa* (Berlin and New York: Walter de Gruyter, 1992)

Empirical Evidence

A major study conducted in 1984 by a multinational group of researchers under the direction of John Montgomery of Harvard University gathered 1,868 reports of management events – involving 'effective' and 'ineffective' behaviour – from nine countries in Southern Africa (Angola, Botswana, Lesotho, Malawi, Mozambique, Swaziland, Tanzania, Zambia, and Zimbabwe). The events reported presented data that described the actual behaviours of managers from government, parastatal, and private organizations. In addition, 40 permanent secretaries or their deputies or equivalents completed diaries describing their activities over a period of 7–10 days which produced a total of 1,187 entries that were then coded in terms of Mintzberg's ten managerial roles (outlined in Figure 1).

The study was designed to provide empirical evidence to test the validity of five common complaints about African administration: (1) that African administrative systems operate like personal fiefdoms because the notion of service to the public is much less of an incentive to perform than the economic responsibilities of managers to their immediate and extended families, and because of their inability to meet these demands from their meagre salaries; (2) that African organizations and managers are too concerned with operational issues ('fire fighting'), and questions of 'territory' and status, and too little with policy and strategy; (3) that (party) politics and ideological rhetoric interfere with the functioning and effectiveness of African organizations; (4) that high-performing managers are much more likely to be found in the private sector; and (5) that African organizations and managers are conservative and change

Figure 1 The Manager's Roles

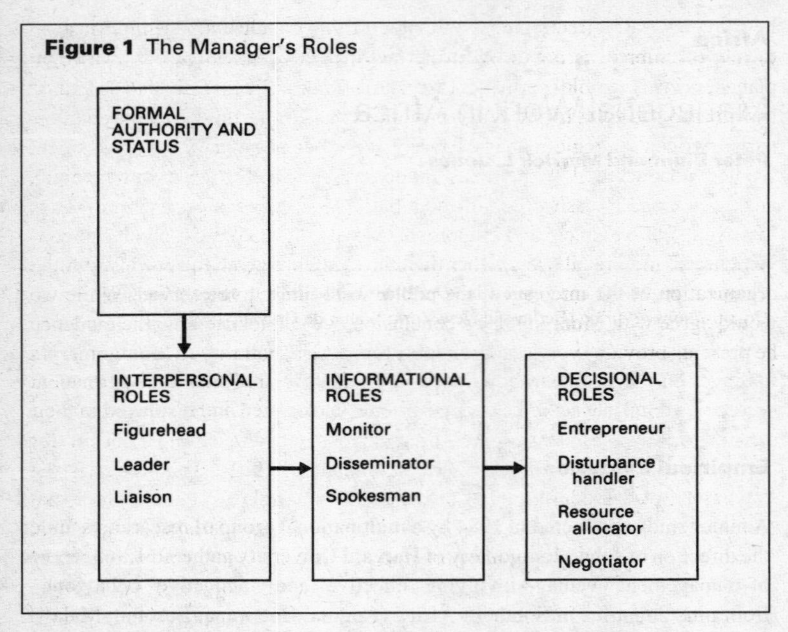

resistant, 'preferring the unacceptable present to the unpredictable future' (Montgomery, 1987: 913).

A later study, in part a replication, used the same categories of management actions or 'skills', but gathered data in a Francophone country, the Central African Republic (CAR), to compare with the seven Anglophone countries studied by Montgomery, 'to see what commonalities exist between different bureaucracies on the continent' (Vengroff *et al.*, 1991: 98). Data gathered on public bureaucracies in Senegal, Chad, and Zaire produced very similar findings on items common to these studies. Montgomery found that the roles of high-ranking officials included all those described by Mintzberg, and Vengroff *et al.* found a very similar closeness of fit with Mintzberg and even more so with the findings of those studying public sector managers (Vengroff *et al.*, 1991: 101).

These images of managerial work in Africa are encountered so frequently in the literature, in the thinking of development management experts, and in their evaluations of development projects that they merit our close attention, for practical development reasons as well as for scientific ones.

With regard to the first proposition, Montgomery (1987: 914) concludes that 'the personalistic interpretation of African bureaucracy is perhaps oversimplified, but turns out to be a recognisable explanation of observed realities'. But he provides little direct evidence to support this conclusion, seeming instead to rely on inferences drawn from the fact that the behaviour of the strategic managers in his sample (permanent secretaries) was different from that described by Mintzberg (1989). In particular, he noticed that, unlike their Western counterparts, African strategic managers rarely served as organizational spokesmen, seemed unconcerned with issues involving the public, dealt with a much narrower range of issues, and in negotiations or disputes over public goods (e.g., housing, vehicles, and equipment) were concerned most about the convenience of individual users rather than the extent to which the purposes of the organization or the interests of the public were likely to be served. While we would agree with Montgomery's conclusion, we cannot see how the evidence he presents provides very strong support for it. Also, contrary to Montgomery's findings, our own recent experience in Zimbabwe indicates that permanent secretaries regularly served as organizational spokesmen and displayed in their statements – and in some cases their actions too – a strong concern for the public (Gustafsson, Blunt, Gisle, & Sjolander, 1991). This indicates the importance of considering carefully national, cultural, economic, and social variables, and organizational ones, in any analysis of managerial work in Africa.

In other respects, however, the permanent secretaries studied by Montgomery engaged in all ten of the managerial roles described by Mintzberg (1989). The balance between the different roles played by the African managers emphasized for Montgomery the inward looking nature of their activities, and 'displayed a kind of collective personalism' (1987: 915). The most frequently performed roles of permanent secretaries were those of resource allocator, liaison, monitor, spokesman, entrepreneur, and disseminator. Routine office chores, which were not included in the ten Mintzberg roles, came next and clearly constituted a category of some significance for permanent secretaries. Evidence of fraud, negligence, corruption, and uncooperativeness, all of which are associated with personalistic, or particularistic, systems – was found, 'but not necessarily in the expected order of intensity or frequency' (Montgomery, 1987: 916). Moreover, many of the reported incidents were trivial:

- My boss told me one thing and wrote another. My expectations had been raised higher and this disappointed me immensely.
- By using personal contacts, a colleague got a scholarship out of turn.
- A road examiner favoured a girl by giving her a driving licence improperly. I prepared a case for his dismissal, but my permanent secretary liked the girl and recommended no punishment.
- The draft report I prepared was circulated by my superior as his own work.
- For political reasons, a colleague of mine had me sign an apparently routine

form which he was later able to use to discredit me. (Montgomery, 1987: 916)

The later study, by Vengroff *et al.* (1991), showed that the technical expert role, added to Mintzberg's list in other studies of public sector managers, was very strong in the Central African Republic. Otherwise there was strong confirmation of Mintzberg's description of managerial activities, although there was some consolidation of the roles. For example, in the interpersonal group, the figurehead and motivator/leader roles seemed to merge, and there were strong similarities between the liaison role from the interpersonal category and the spokesman role from the informational category. 'Each of his (Mintzberg's) other roles is clearly represented by a single factor in the CAR data' (Vengroff *et al.*, 1991: 101). Comparisons were made with Montgomery's work in the SADCC countries, although it was decided that since only two of these countries, Zimbabwe and Lesotho, accounted for more than half of all the data in the 1984 study, more emphasis should be given to comparisons with these countries.

The second image of African managers – that they are more concerned with internal matters than other issues – was confirmed by Montgomery's data. His strategy for testing this proposition involved classifying the reported management events into 20 categories of activities that could be considered instrumental to national development. Examples of these development categories included: (1) 'introducing a new agricultural, industrial or commercial enterprise in the country; (2) discovering a solution or a more promising approach to a significant development problem; (3) introducing a new service or programme; (4) raising standards of products or services provided; (5) securing a material advantage or resource by negotiation; (6) developing more effective working relationships with local agencies or sources of external aid' (Montgomery, 1987: 917), and so on. A surprisingly high proportion (44.5 per cent) of the management events collected by Montgomery could not be coded as having any of the 20 development purposes, and even those which were coded as having such purposes tended to be inward-looking rather than directly relevant to the development goals of the organization. Montgomery argues that these findings might be explained partly by the African practice of 'rotating personnel among jobs and sectors to advance their career prospects' (Montgomery, 1987: 917). This of course limits managers' ability to come to terms with their jobs in a way which permits them to contribute significantly to organizational goals. The problem is made worse by their particularistic inclinations, as indicated above.

But as with the previous image of African managers, there is a danger of over-generalizing from the data. We can think of a number of cases in Africa where these generalizations would not be valid and where the activities of senior and middle managers accord with many of the development-related activities described by Montgomery (e.g., Gustafsson *et al.*, 1991).

Where management events were coded by Montgomery as being development related, they had to do mostly with staff training and development, the improvement of management systems and discipline, and organizational design. All of these are important elements of institution building which are accorded high priority by aid organizations (e.g., Collins, 1989; SIDA, 1990; Johnston & Dyrssen, 1991; Palmlund, 1991), and by public service review commissions (e.g., ZPSRC, 1989).

In terms of the Mintzberg managerial roles, the most time consuming for African managers was that of internal resource allocator. This was true of managers in all of the disparate countries from which data were collected: socialist Tanzania, capitalist Botswana, Zimbabwe and Lesotho. The diary recordings of the permanent secretaries revealed a high degree of involvement in resource allocation activities such as the following:

- I met with other permanent secretaries to figure out how to reemploy young pensioners while training their replacements.
- I chaired a meeting of a standing interministerial committee to consider applications from private investors in the hope of promoting productive employment.
- I chaired a meeting to consider ways the government could help the cooperative movement out of its present financial difficulties.
- I initiated a cabinet memorandum on the further reorganization of the National Agriculture Marketing Board.
- Discussed with my deputy the issue of solving the problem of a blood transfusion team marooned in a mountain district hospital because of bad weather.
- Telephoned the superintendent of the national referral hospital about sending medical help to a village hit by a tornado.
- Dealt with the case of a subordinate who absented himself from work for the whole month and appeared on payday to collect his salary. (Montgomery, 1987: 918)

Another area of considerable activity was that of internal politicking, usually involving money, jurisdiction, people, and policy in that order. As we might expect, internal politics was concerned most with funding and 'territorial' disputes as the following examples illustrate:

- I wrote a memo to the accounts department asking them to make a payment. They refused, saying I had misinterpreted the rules, and I appealed to the Minister of Manpower Development to get the payment made.

- It took a year after the approval by the donor to get the money for a project through bureaucratic channels.
- We were charged with the task of collecting money from all the departments for damages caused by their vehicles. Those of the Defence Department frequently are at fault, but they do not bother to pay the accounts due.
- When I gave instructions to my subordinates, they sometimes shelved them to work first on my superior's instructions, causing delay and frustrations. (Montgomery, 1987: 920)

The suggestion that African administrative systems are adversely affected by party political interference and rhetoric, which constituted the third image of African management tested by Montgomery, was not confirmed by the data. Even at the most senior levels in the public service, he could find little evidence of such interference. Montgomery reports that permanent secretaries have managed to remain politically neutral.

Our own recent experience in Africa again points to the dangers of accepting this generalization too easily. In Zimbabwe, for example, the newly established Ministry of Political Affairs has recently 'poached' a whole cadre of trainees from the Ministry of Local Government Urban and Rural Development, thereby causing a considerable disturbance to that Ministry's activities (Gustafsson *et al.*, 1991). This is a clear example of the strength of influence of party politics in the functioning of public organizations. A further example, involving high levels of party political interference in an urban development project in Liberia, is supplied by Werlin (1990). In relation to public enterprise performance, Nellis (1986) is another who points to the general problem of 'excessive political interference in issues and decisions that should – from an efficiency standpoint – be taken by enterprise managers . . . that is, specifying who should be hired, who cannot be fired, where contracts must be awarded, who should receive credit, what bills should be paid and which can safely be ignored, and where services will be provided and maintained, despite insufficient revenues' (pp. 35–6).

The fourth image of African management suggests that although the private sector in many African countries is relatively small, its effectiveness and management know-how is superior to that of government organizations. Montgomery's study produced little or no evidence to confirm this suggestion. When we think of the small-scale entrepreneur, who typically lacks management skills, and may often be semi-literate, this finding is unsurprising. What is more surprising – at least on the surface – is that Montgomery's findings indicated little or no difference between the management styles and skill requirements of large public and private organizations (e.g., multinational mining companies).

For example, permanent secretaries frequently carried out activities which could be classified as entrepreneurial, as revealed in the following:

- Chaired a meeting to formulate a strategy for sustained economic viability of a town that is wholly dependent on a mine for its economy.
- Met the Director of Information and Broadcasting to consider the possibility of introducing a regular radio programme to educate the public on economic issues.
- Participated in a meeting to consider what guarantees should be given to a potential investor in a hotel development project.
- Chaired a meeting to consider ways of improving the housing situation in the country. (Montgomery, 1987: 922)

Managers in public, parastatal, and private organizations gave priority to the same broad areas of activity, namely, upgrading the calibre, capability, or morale of staff and imposing structures and controls on staff or vendor performance. Also, identified skill requirements for managers in the three sectors were very much the same; in particular, motivational, interpersonal relations, and personnel management skills were needed.

The final image of African organizations investigated by Montgomery – that they are very resistant to change – received some support from his findings. There were very few reports of organizational change introduced by managers on their own initiative. Even when it came to fairly low-level change managers were reluctant to take the risk without having first sought (much) higher level approval. The rigidity of the administrative systems sometimes called for the exercise of 'brute force' to get something done; on other occasions a certain amount of ingenuity was required:

- I consulted the under secretary about the appointment of a retired colleague. I told him that we should inform the personnel commission that he was retired; he advised me to obtain approval for the appointment first, and then inform the commission. It worked; if we had put the two together the request would have been denied.
- I took a proposal to the Finance Ministry, fully justified by facts and figures, for a loan for a road service . . . The officer flatly refused . . . I then went straight to the Finance Minister and got the loan sanctioned.
- When I was PS (Finance) I encountered a controversy over the implementation of a policy. I briefed the President and convinced him that my position was correct and the Ministry of Agriculture was wrong.
- I led a delegation abroad to negotiate a loan. The deputy minister complained that I had gone without permission. I collected information to justify

> the necessity of my trip and submitted it to the Cabinet Minister. Things calmed down ultimately. (Montgomery, 1987: 925)

One very significant additional factor, not previously identified in any of the other studies, 'stands alone' in the opinion of Vengroff and his associates. This factor is 'operating rules and procedures', which 'appears to be very important in African bureaucracies, being rated extremely high in the CAR as well as in the SADCC countries' (Vengroff *et al.*, 1991: 101). They say that, given the orientation and context of French colonial administration, this is not a surprising finding. However, as they note, this emphasis is found by Montgomery (1987) to be almost as great in former British colonies. Vengroff *et al.* in a significant observation say:

> This may indicate something generic about administration and administrative practice in colonial and post colonial regimes in Africa or in developing nations whose policies are dominated by the bureaucracy. (1991: 101)

The greatest disparity between managerial roles in the Francophone and Anglophone African countries studied by Vengroff *et al.* was in the monitor role, which was much more important in the Francophone Central African Republic (but this may be related to differences between the samples in the two studies, as Vengroff *et al.* observe), and in leadership and supervision, which was much more important in Anglophone Zimbabwe and Lesotho, ranking right at the top. The correlations *between* the two Anglophone countries on these factors were very strong. However, the areas of greatest similarity between rankings of managerial roles in the two countries were in the spokesman (disseminator) role, in the concern for operating rules and procedures, and in the technical expertise and executive (policy analysis) roles.

The high levels of resistance to change observed in African organizations in conjunction with the preference for centralized forms of decision making mean that appeals to higher authority are still more likely to bring about change than the more fashionable forms of decentralization favoured by some students of administration. As Montgomery (1987) rightly concludes, the changes most needed by African administrative systems – especially those involving the devolution of power – are the most difficult to bring about. Such changes will need to be based on modified values and leadership styles, as well as the more conventional and widespread recourse to management training and development (Blunt & Jones, 1991a; Collins, 1989). Making managers more risk-taking, more experimental, more outward-looking, and more client-oriented will also require the creation of institutional environments and organizational cultures which are supportive of such behaviours. There is some encouraging evidence that this is beginning to take place already in certain parts of Africa. In Zimbabwe, for example, the government has recently approved more than 100 recommendations aimed at improving the effectiveness and efficiency of the Zimbabwean public service (ZPSRC, 1989); and it has set up an implementation unit to bring about and facilitate recommended changes (Gustafsson *et al.*, 1991).

This section has provided a reasonable description of managerial work in Africa which is directly comparable to accounts of managerial work in the West and in other developing countries. It has also tested the validity of a number of widely held assumptions regarding the behaviour of African managers and organizations. Tentative explanations for some of these findings have also been advanced. Drawing largely on the work on Leonard (1987), the next section extends the discussion of possible causes.

Influences on Public Policy

The starting point for Leonard's (1987) discussion of what he refers to as 'the political realities of African management' is that many of the differences in managerial and organizational behaviour between Africa and more industrialized parts of the world are attributable not so much to managerial or organizational failures as to 'fundamental dissimilarities in the value priorities that encapsulate them' (p. 901). We share this general view (see Blunt, 1990; Blunt & Jones, 1991b). It is clear also that African managers are linked to extensive networks of social obligation (Price, 1975); and that values of reciprocity and social exchange that characterize African social systems still impinge directly on the working lives of African managers (Blunt, 1983; Hyden, 1983). This means that:

> African [managers] are unusual . . . in the extent of their patronage obligations to poorer peoples and the strength of the moral pressures which they feel to fulfil them. For these reasons and for selfish ones that are far more universal, state organisations in Africa are extensively used to pursue informal, personal goals of their managers rather than the collective ones that are formally proclaimed. (Leonard, 1987: 901)

According to Leonard (1987), this tendency finds expression at a number of different levels of organizational behaviour. At the level of public policy, he argues that the seeming economic irrationality of investment decisions and marketing strategies conceals a political rationality whose logic politicians and senior managers follow to the detriment of development. As an example, the provision of jobs, and credit and subsidized inputs to farmers is first and foremost an act of political rationality designed to cement support and strengthen patronage networks. Any national economic benefits which might flow from such actions are of secondary consideration, and are treated as a bonus.

Under these circumstances, it is difficult to see how a recourse to market forces will have the desired effect. In this view, it is not the mechanisms of the market that are at fault, but more the rationality of the economic actors (policy makers etc.) who guide them. It is widely recognized that the survival of African states and political regimes of all political persuasions hinges on their ability to produce and distribute visible benefits to their constituencies, yet this fact does not enter explicitly – or often – enough into the calculations of development workers or governments. The prospects of achieving economic development in Africa are considerably reduced if this fact is ignored. African development is impeded all too frequently by public policies which, for political reasons, produce overvalued currencies, low prices, and monopolistic and ineffective marketing boards. The heavy burden so often imposed on agriculture is the result of deliberate policies 'designed to provide the resources for the public employment and patronage which . . . fragile political regimes need for their survival' (Leonard, 1987: 903).

The rationality which guides such political and economic activity at the macro level not surprisingly lights the way for the activities of managers in public organizations at lower levels, as we demonstrate in the next section.

Leadership and Management

Leadership has reemerged as one of the key issues of effective organization in the industrialized economies of the West (e.g., Keys & Case, 1990; Kotter, 1990; Zaleznik, 1990). Unlike management which can be said largely to be concerned with the maintenance of consistency and order in organizations, leadership produces movement and change. There is wide agreement in Western industrialized nations that the effective leader of the new age shapes and shares a vision which provides direction, focus, meaning, and inspiration to the work of others (Conger, 1989, 1991; Handy, 1989; Kirkpatrick & Locke, 1991; Kotter, 1990). He or she must project a visible role model that embodies, and conveys in actions and words, desirable attitudes, values, and beliefs which act as catalysts for the development of an effective organizational culture. An essential ingredient of such leadership is the establishment of a set of organizational values which provide a foundation for the development and sustenance of commitment and trust. Mistrust undermines and prevents effective performance

(Bartolome, 1989; Blunt, 1990, 1991). Another critical element is the leader's vision which, in order to mobilize and persuade others, should possess the following qualities (after Handy, 1989):

- It should be different, that is, reconstitute or reconceptualize the known and familiar.
- It should make good sense to others, or create what Handy (1989) calls the Aha Effect – 'Aha – of course, now I see it'. It should therefore be clearly connected to people's day-to-day working reality, but at the same time be 'mind expanding', challenging, but within the bounds of reason.
- It should be succinct and easily understood; vivid and memorable; and not too long or laden with numbers and jargon.
- It should recognize that its own realization depends upon the contributions of others, and that without them the vision will simply remain a dream.
- It should be a vision which the leader lives, one which he or she believes in and is seen to believe in. Leaders must have integrity. Their visions and values must be authentic. People must be able to believe in this authenticity.

These qualities are easy to list, but much more difficult to realize in practice. One of the most critical qualities of effective leadership, and one that is difficult to feign, is authenticity. 'I believe in a kind of psychic law of management here: that workers, customers, everyone involved with a management, no matter how physically distant, can tell when it is genuine in its beliefs and when it is just mouthing the right words' (Mintzberg, 1989: 275).

As we have argued elsewhere (Blunt, 1991), these qualities are as important in Africa as they are anywhere else. It is clear that many of these qualities cannot be taught; and it is equally clear that values constitute the core of effective leadership. Kotter (1990) also argues that intelligence, drive and high energy, mental health, and integrity are essential ingredients of effective leadership. Kirkpatrick and Locke (1991) have added a number of important traits to this list, namely, persistence, motivation to lead (leaders must clearly want to do the job), self-confidence, knowledge of the business, charisma, creativity and flexibility. Kotter suggests that these qualities are not often found together in sufficient degrees in the same individual: 'despite the ordinariness of the key attributes, remarkably few people share all (of them)' (Kotter, 1990: 108). Leonard (1987) is of the same opinion: 'in all parts of the world it frequently takes an exceptional person to be able to revise or set the goals and values which an organisation is going to embody' (p. 903). Nevertheless, Leonard (1987) suggests that the prospects of finding such an individual in the industrialized countries are greater because career advancement is more important to individuals in such contexts. In Africa, on the other hand, the links between a manager's career and organizational and individual effectiveness can be said to be much less reliable due to internal and external political influences. One implication of this is that 'to a much greater extent than is true in the West . . . commitment must be internally generated by the manager' (Leonard, 1987: 903).

Another perceived problem is that indigenous morality – and many African managers are deeply ethical, holding strong feelings of attachment and responsibility to their families and villages of origin – does not accord with bureaucratic impersonality or universalism. It may be necessary, as Leonard suggests, to work *with* this sense of morality rather than against it if the small pool of people with leadership talent are to be employed in the interests of organizational effectiveness and development. For example, 'a geographically-focused project is likely to get far better leadership from an official who is from the region than from an "objective" outsider' (Leonard, 1987: 904). Leaders with the qualities outlined above are more crucial to project success, and much scarcer, than technically qualified personnel.

Neither is it necessarily the case that patron–client relationships be dysfunctional, depending on the ultimate purposes for which they are employed (Blunt, 1980; Leonard, 1987). Functional relationships of this kind are common in Western organizations. The difference between such relationships and other forms of patronage is that the former are used to advance, rather than retard, the attainment of organizational objectives. It is worth quoting Leonard (1987) at some length on this point:

> Managers become patrons to those of their subordinates whom they believe can best help them achieve the objectives according to which they themselves will be judged, and junior staff seek to become clients of managers who can best help them with their careers, not on the basis of some ascriptive or political tie. The resulting informal networks of obligation give flexibility and commitment to relationships that would be much less productive if they were only formal. Thus where (but only where) managers are using their patronage to reward those who are committed to the organisation's objectives, there is good reason to assist them with control over scholarships, foreign trips, and off-scale appointments. The result will be better performance from their subordinates. (p. 904)

Implications for Managers and Management Development

We can infer from the above that people who possess the potential to become good leaders are few in number – Kotter (1990) estimates less than one in fifty – and much less numerous than people who possess the potential to become good managers. As Kotter (1990) observes: 'the world is full of smart people with emotional problems, mentally healthy people with only an average motivation level, people high in integrity who have average intelligence, and so on' (pp. 108–9). The good leader 'species' can therefore be said to be rare everywhere, but in Africa it is endangered by:

- the obligations of African managers to networks of kin and ethnic affiliates which may detract from their commitment to organizational objectives;
- the fact that public-policy making in Africa – perhaps to a greater degree than would be true in industrialized countries – is driven by issues of political survival involving the uneven distribution of visible resources – development projects, jobs, credit, and so on;
- the difficulties associated with developing leadership qualities themselves, which mostly cannot be taught easily because they involve values such as integrity;
- the absence of clear connections between organizational and individual behaviour and effectiveness, and career advancement;
- the apparent reluctance of donor agencies and other 'social engineers' to acknowledge the rationality of accommodating indigenous codes of ethics into development and institution building strategies so as to satisfy *both* individual and organizational objectives;
- the tendency of institution strengthening activities to focus on transference of management skills – or the 'technology' of management – and to place too little emphasis on value change, the identification and development of leadership talent, and other aspects such as organizational design and culture building.

Good managers are also hard to find: 'the scarcity of experienced managers is absolutely greater in Africa than in the Middle East, Asia or Latin America, reflecting both the poor human resource base inherited at independence, and the appointment policies followed by a number of governments, which have stressed political loyalty over operational skills' (Nellis, 1986: 36).

Clearly, *both* leaders and managers are necessary for effective organization: that is, *managers* whose activities and roles can be said largely to be concerned with the maintenance of an acceptable degree of consistency and order within organizations, and *leaders* who are concerned with establishing the direction and pace of change, aligning people, and enlisting their commitment and effort.

The material presented in this chapter also demonstrates that in many important respects the actual behaviours of African managers are quite similar to those observed among managers in other countries, although there are important differences, too. This confirms the view that there are 'striking similarities between the bureaucracy of developed and developing countries' (Vengroff *et al.*, 1991: 96). But does it also confirm the view that management is generic, and that Western management can be applied in different cultural settings? We would agree with Vengroff *et al.* that 'while the roles may be similar, the impact of the environment on the decision processes associated with those roles is significantly different' (1991: 107). Historical factors, particularly administrative structures and practices bequeathed by colonial governments, still influence the bureaucracies of Africa, and Asia. The much stronger desire of developing-country managers than of Western managers to avoid uncertainty was originally demonstrated by Hofstede (1980, 1987) and has since been confirmed with reference to Africa (e.g., Seddon, 1985), and South East Asia (e.g., Blunt, 1988; Richards, 1991).

Explanations for such behaviour and its meaning differ widely however. Most management training programmes in Africa would appear to operate on the assumption that the basic tenets of management – meaning planning, organizing, controlling etc. – are universal and that management technology can therefore simply be transferred wholesale. We have tried to demonstrate in this chapter why this approach is wrong, and why it is that in Africa much closer attention needs to be paid – in the development of both effective leaders and managers – to values, especially those of integrity, and commitment to organizational objectives (Blunt, 1990; Nellis, 1986; Washington, 1988), and in public-service organizations, an ethic of service to the wider public.

References

Bartolome, F., 'Nobody trusts the boss completely – now what?', *Harvard Business Review*, 67, 1989, 135–42.

Blunt, P., 'Bureaucracy and ethnicity in Kenya: some conjectures for the eighties', *Journal of Applied Behavioural Science*, 16 (3), 1980, 336–53.

— *Organisational Theory and Behaviour: An African Perspective*, London: Longman, 1983.

— 'Cultural consequences for organisation change in a Southeast Asian State: Brunei', *Academy of Management Executive*, 2 (3), 1988, 235–40.

— 'Strategies for enhancing organisational effectiveness in the Third World', *Public Administration and Development*, 10, 1990, 299–313.

— 'Organisational culture and development', *International Journal of Human Resource Management*, 2 (1), 1991, 55–71.

Blunt, P. and M. Jones (eds.), 'Management development in the Third World', special issue of *Journal of Management Development*, 10 (6), 1991a, 1–83.

— 'Human resource management in developing countries', special issue of *International Journal of Human Resource Management*, 2 (1), 1991b, 1–111.

Collins, P., 'Assessing and meeting the management development needs of the public sector in Africa, Arab States, Asia and Latin America', paper presented at Civil Service Improvement Workshop EDI/World Bank, Washington DC, 4–8 December 1989.

Conger, J. A., 'Leadership: the art of empowering others', *Academy of Management Executive*, 3 (1), 1989, 17–24.

— 'Inspiring others: the language of leadership', *Academy of Management Executive*, 5 (1), 1991, 31–45.

Gustafsson, L., P. Blunt, P. Gisle and S. Sjolander, *The Future of Swedish Support to the Public Administration Sector in Zimbabwe*, Stockholm: SIDA, 1991.

Handy, C., *The Age of Unreason*, London: Hutchinson, 1989.

Hofstede, G., *Culture's Consequences: International Differences in Work-Related Values*, London: Sage, 1980.

— 'The applicability of McGregor's theories in Southeast Asia', *Journal of Management Development*, 6 (3), 1987, 9–18.

Hyden, G., *No Shortcuts to Progress: African Development Management in Perspective*, London: Heinemann, 1983.

Johnston, A. and H. Dyrssen, 'Cooperation in the development of public sector management skills: the SIDA experience', *Journal of Management Development*, 10 (6), 1991, 52–9.

Keys, B. J. and T. L. Case, 'How to become an influential manager', *Academy of Management Executive*, 4 (4), 1990, 38–51.

Kirkpatrick, S. A. and E. A. Locke, 'Leadership: do traits matter?', *Academy of Management Executive*, 5 (2), 1991, 48–60.

Kotter, J. P., *A Force for Change: How Leadership Differs from Management*, New York: Free Press, 1990.

Leonard, D. K., 'The political realities of African management', *World Development*, 15, 1987, 899–910.

Mintzberg, H., *Mintzberg on Management*, New York: Free Press, 1989.

Montgomery, J. D., 'Probing managerial behaviour: image and reality in Southern Africa', *World Development*, 15 (7), 1987, 911–29.

Nellis, J., *Public Enterprises in Sub-Saharan Africa*, Washington, D.C.: World Bank, 1986.

Palmlund, T., 'UNDP's management development programme', *Journal of Management Development*, 10 (6), 1991, 58–61.

Price, R. M., *Society and Bureaucracy in Contemporary Ghana*, Berkeley: University of California Press, 1975.

Richards, D., 'Flying against the wind? Culture and management development in Southeast Asia', *Journal of Management Development*, 10 (6), 1991, 19–33.

Seddon, J. W., 'The development and indigenisation of Third World business: African values in the workplace', in V. Hammond (ed.), *Current Research in Management*, London: Frances Pinter/ATM, 1985.

SIDA, *Guidelines for SIDA Support to the Development of Public Administration*, Stockholm: SIDA, 1990.

Vengroff, R., M. Belhaj and M. Ndiaye, 'The nature of managerial work in the public sector: an African perspective', *Public Administration and Development*, 11, 1991, 95–110.

Washington, R., 'Development and deviance: a situational perspective on African governmental corruption', in H. Glickman (ed.), *The Crisis and Challenge of African Development*, Westport, Connecticut: Greenwood Press, 1988.

Werlin, H., 'Decentralisation and culture: the case of Monrovia, Liberia', *Public Administration and Development*, 10 (3), 1990, 251–61.

Zaleznik, A., 'The leadership gap', *Academy of Management Executive*, 4 (1), 1990, 7–22.

ZPSRC, *Report of the Public Service Review Commission of Zimbabwe*, (2 vols.), Harare, Zimbabwe, 1989.

India with England

Contingency Theory and Culture: A Study of Matched English and Indian Manufacturing Firms

Monir Tayeb

From *Organization Studies*, Vol. 8/3, 1987, 243–52

Research Design

Fourteen organizations in England and in India (from the state of Maharashtra) were selected which were matched in pairs between the two countries with respect to their major contextual variables. These variables were industry, product, production technology, size, status, ownership and control, age and market share. Because a perfect match on all these variables proved to be practically impossible, the level of control over certain factors, such as market share and age, had to be traded-off against control of others, such as size, technology and industry. For instance, two pharmaceutical companies were comparable on all contextual factors except age, and two computer firms on all except age and status. The trade-off was made on the basis of the importance and emphasis that other researchers have placed on these variables as predictors of structure.

Moreover, the samples were chosen in such a way as to offer variations in terms of contextual factors within each country and thus enable the author to observe the effects of different contexts on structure. The firms which were eventually selected in each country operate in the following industries: electronics, chemicals, pharmaceuticals, confectionery, and brewery, with electronics being the highest in terms of technological change and complexity and the brewery and confectionery, the lowest. The size of the organizations (numbers employed) ranged from 133 to 1,670, and their age from 15 to 144 years. Ownership and control varied from family owned and managed firms to those owned by general public shareholders and managed by salaried managers. Market share ranged from 1 per cent to over 60 per cent.

In order to decrease the complications in matching the two sets of organizations, the sample in each country was selected from among companies which (i) were engaged in manufacturing, (ii) were profit-oriented, (iii) operated in the private sector, and (iv) were totally owned, managed and largely manned by people from their respective countries.

In order to compile the samples, various directories and relevant sources were consulted. In England a list of 30 selected companies was drawn from among 200 entries in *Kompass 1981, Key British enterprises 1981* and the Archive of the National (Aston) Study conducted by Child (1972). The initial correspondence and preliminary meetings with the managing directors of these companies led to the selection of the seven English firms which were included in the study. For the Indian sample, an initial list of 295 companies in the relevant industries was prepared from among the entries in *The Times of India directory 81–82* and *Kothari's economic and industrial guide of India 1982*. The initial correspondence with the chief executives of these companies reduced the number of the organizations comparable to the English sample to 18. After a preliminary meeting with each of the senior managers in India, the most appropriate seven firms were selected within which the Indian study was conducted.

The main structural parameters studied were centralization, functional specialization, formalization, chief executive's span of control, height, and communication pattern. The working definitions and scales measuring the first five dimensions were adopted from the Abbreviated Aston Schedule (Inkson *et al.*, 1970) with some modifications. The centralization scale consisted of items covering financial, operative, marketing and other strategic decisions. As a modification to the original scale, 10 new items were included to cover further decision areas. Also, financial items distinguished between allocated and unallocated expenditure. Each category was broken down to smaller brackets, ranging from less than £50 to above £20,000 – making a scale with 60 items in all. Two additional scores, delegation and joint decisions, were also computed using the answers to the centralization items to determine the degree to which the chief executive delegated authority down the hierarchy and the degree to which decisions were taken jointly. A delegation score for each decision was computed by a count of the number of levels down from the chief executive to the level at which the decision was taken. The sum of the scores for all decisions made up the total delegation score for the organization. The joint decisions score was computed on the basis of the number of decisions made in each organization described by the interviewees as 'in conjunction with . . .', 'in consultation with . . .', 'jointly with . . .' and the like.

The functional specialization section consisted of 19 items covering activities that could potentially be carried out by specialists. Three items in the scale were new and were concerned with policy-making, strategic planning and information processing. The formalization scale also consisted of 19 items and measured the extent to which written rules, procedures, and instructions were used to define roles and describe jobs. The chief executive's span of control was a count of the people who reported directly to him. Height was a count of the levels in the main production hierarchy between chief executive and direct workers, inclusive of both.

The communication-pattern section measured the degree to which vertical and lateral communication and consultation took place within the organization and between the organization and people from outside. The pattern was determined on the basis of the amount of time spent by employees with (1) their boss, (2) their subordinates, (3) their colleagues, (4) people from other areas/sections in the organization, and (5) people from outside the organization. Five items corresponding to these communication channels were included in an attitude survey questionnaire which, as part of another phase of the study, was administered among a sample of employees of all the 14 organizations which participated in the study. The number of respondents in the English sample was 343 and in the Indian sample 337. The results of that survey were reported extensively elsewhere (Tayeb, 1984).

The contextual factors studied were industry, product, degree of change in production technology, number of full-time employees, age, status, market share, and ownership and control.

In each organization the product or a group of very similar products which accounted for more than 50 per cent of its turnover was considered as the main product. The degree of change in dominant technology was measured using information about the following matters: (1) frequency of change in manufacturing technology; (2) frequency of change in product technology; (3) frequency of introduction of modified products and change in the ingredients; (4) frequency of introduction of a brand new product or design; and (5) the percentage of annual turnover spent on R and D.

The status measure distinguished between an independent organization with production unit(s), an independent organization without production unit(s), and a wholly-owned autonomous subsidiary. Four categories of ownership were used to classify the fourteen organizations: (1) a family, (2) private shareholders, (3) general public shareholders, and (4) a parent group. The control variable distinguished between (1) members of a family, (2) members of a family and salaried managers, (3) owner chairman and salaried managers, and (4) salaried managers. The levels at which the assessment was made were chairman, managing director/chief executive, and board of directors.

Information about organizational structures and contexts was collected through a structured interview programme conducted in English. The main participant in each company was the managing director (or his/her equivalent). In almost all the firms other senior managers, such as technical director, finance director, sales/marketing director and manufacturing/production manager, were also interviewed to obtain complementary information, where necessary. On average, three senior managers in each organization were formally interviewed. The interviews were complemented by company documents and informal discussions and meetings.

The study was piloted both in England and Maharashtra. The main English study was carried out between September 1981 and May 1982 and the Indian study in February and March 1983. It should be said that this study is of England and the English, and these terms are not used casually to mean Britain and the British as is often – wrongly – done.

Finally, some discussion is necessary of the sample size used in the present study. The importance of obtaining relatively large samples of data in field surveys rests on the need to guard against the risk of detecting spurious differences between populations where sampling strategy cannot be precisely controlled. In this study, the alternative strategy of tightly controlling the nature of the firms comprising the sampling frame was used. By controlling eight aspects of the organizations sampled, it was expected that the risk of spuriously detecting differences between English and Indian samples would be controlled. Whether or not this was in fact accomplished must ultimately be judged in terms of whether the differences which were actually found are coherently explicable in terms of known aspects of the two cultures or whether they are more plausibly seen as random error.

Before presenting the results of the study, it would be useful at this stage to compare briefly the cultural settings of the participating organizations.

There are very few reported studies which have compared cultural attitudes and values of Indian and English peoples. Parekh's (1974) and Elizabeth Child's (1982) works are the only major ones whose findings are relevant to the present study.

Parekh, observing the English as an Indian scholar living in England, compared the two peoples and remarked that the English were more individualistic, less emotional, more concerned about other people, more self-contained, more rule-governed and spatial, more resourceful and more disciplined, and valued their privacy more than did the Indians.

Child, in a comparative study of play behaviour among English and Asian (Indian and Pakistani) children living in England found that English children were more independent, more aggressive, had less respect for people in authority,

Figure 1 Indian Person – English Person

An Indian person is:	An English person is:
more emotional	less emotional
fearful of people in position of power	respectful of people in position of power
more obedient to seniors	less obedient to seniors
more dependent on others	less dependent on others
more fatalist	less fatalist
submissive	aggressive
more open to bribery	less open to bribery
less able to cope with new and uncertain situations	more able to cope with new and uncertain situations
less concerned for others outside own community	more concerned for others outside own community
accepts responsibility less	accepts responsibility more
less disciplined	more disciplined
more modest	more arrogant
less reserved	more reserved
more collectivist	more individualistic
caste conscious	class conscious
law-abiding	bends the law if necessary
opposed to change	opposed to change
less self-controlled	more self-controlled
less trustworthy	more trustworthy
more friendly	less friendly
less tenacious	more tenacious
more clan oriented	less clan oriented
less willing to take account of other people's views	more willing to take account of other people's views

and maintained more physical distance between themselves and others compared with the Asian children.

The present author, in a study of English and Indian cultures by questionnaire survey and analysis of public media and literature conducted as part of a comparative research project, some of whose findings are presented here, found that, among other things, Indians were more obedient to their seniors, more afraid to disagree with powerful people, had less resentment of being commanded, and were more dependent on their parents compared to the English. The latter were more reserved, preferred more to work on their own and valued independence

Table 1 Structural Dimensions of English and Indian Organizations

Dimensions	*English*			*Indian*			*p*
	mean	*sd*	*range*	*mean*	*sd*	*range*	
Centralization	210	15.29	190–227	214	20.76	175–236	.48
Delegation	167	24.44	140–227	153	20.41	132–181	.08
Joint Decisions	19	14.27	3–45	17	9.80	4–35	.84
Communication with:							
– boss	2.40	.17	2.1–3.4	2.23	.22	2.0–2.6	.09
– subordinates	3.00	.19	2.6–3.2	2.49	.38	2.0–3.0	.01
– colleagues	3.36	.20	3.0–3.7	2.32	.23	1.8–2.5	.001
– people from other areas of work	2.34	.37	1.8–2.7	2.02	.18	1.7–2.2	.09
– people from outside the company	1.96	.35	1.4–2.4	2.24	.18	1.9–2.5	.09
Specialization	10	4.91	3–15	8.71	5.34	3–16	.65
Formalization	12	2.57	9–17	4.71	1.11	3–6	.001
Job-description sub-scale	3.28	.48	3–4	1.00	1.29	0–3	.001
Chief Executive's span of control	7	1.15	5–8	9	5.18	4–20	.001
Number of hierarchical levels (height)	6	.81	5–7	5.57	1.51	4–8	.43

Note: 'p' is the Mann-Whitney two-tailed p.

more than did the former. Figure 1 draws a brief cultural 'picture' of an English person and an Indian person in comparison with one another, on the basis of the findings of the survey (Tayeb, 1984, Chapters 6 and 7).

It is argued that if, on the one hand, culture were irrelevant to the way that organizations are structured and/or respond to their environments, the English and Indian organizations studied here would have similar structural configurations and similar relationships with their contexts regardless of the cultural traits attributed to the English and Indians. On the other hand, if these cultural characteristics had significant implications for the participating organizations and for their interaction with environment, then one would assume that contingency theory and culture-free models are inadequate and need to be qualified – for the present samples at any rate. For this to be the case, given the Indian and English peoples' cultures, one should find English organizations to be less centralized and more formalized than their Indian counterparts. There should be more communication and consultation among employees in the former than in the latter. Indian managers should have more people report to them than would the English managers. The following section examines the results of the study against these expectations.

Results and Discussion

Table 1 compares the two samples on their structural dimensions. As can be seen, English and Indian organizations scored similarly on centralization, joint decisions, specialization and number of hierarchical levels and were different in all other aspects. However, these similarities and differences *per se* do not either support or refute the contingency model. What is crucial is whether the structural configurations of the organizations are consistent with their respective task-contexts or with their cultural settings, or perhaps even with both. The analysis which follows attempts to unravel some of the complexities which might lie behind the similarities and differences observed between the two groups of organizations.

Centralization, Delegation, Joint Decisions and Communication

Although the two samples scored similarly on centralization, a closer examination of the scale and other measures related to it reveals some interesting differences between the two groups of organizations.

First, a breakdown of the items comprising the scale, following Yasai-Ardekani (1979), shows that, on the whole, English organizations are more centralized on financial decisions and less so on operative decisions compared to their Indian counterparts. This, on the one hand, may reflect the financial hardship and more competitive environments that the English organizations were experiencing at the time the study was conducted. This might have caused the managers to tighten their grip over financial and strategic decisions. In the Indian case, on the other hand, their higher centralization of operative decisions reflects their own industrial relations climate. Most of the operative decisions concern appointment, promotion and dismissal of shopfloor employees. Indian government regulations are very stringent and 'pro' workers in this respect. For example, managers cannot easily dismiss workers or punish them in any way even if they breach their terms of contract. Also, workers' representatives are very powerful in negotiating promotion and wage increases and other working conditions. If a manager wishes to promote or reward a worker, he may have to do the same for all his workmates. The senior managers therefore are very careful as to who should be recruited, promoted or dismissed, and they are personally involved in the decisions concerning these matters.

Second, in both countries, expenditure of money on capital items is more centralized than on revenue items, and the expenditure of unallocated money is more centralized than allocated money. This strongly suggests the operation of a contingent factor, namely *perceived risk* attached to the decision, including its having longer term consequences.

Third, as Table 1 shows, English managers delegate some of their authority lower down the hierarchy (the higher the score the more levels below the chief executive through which decisions are delegated) and also have a smaller number of subordinates directly reporting to them than do their Indian counterparts (narrower spans of control).

Fourth, the patterns of communication and of consultation processes which take place before decisions are finally made are very different for the two samples and are highly consistent with their respective cultural backgrounds.

A constant feature of English organizations is that, on average, they score higher than Indian organizations on lateral communication with colleagues (mean 3.36 in Table 1) and with people from other areas (2.34). This is consistent with their employees' cultural characteristics. The English are known to be class conscious and that this has strained communication between people from different social strata (Terry, 1979; Tayeb, 1984). Their higher lateral communication can further be interpreted as a reflection of their culturally rooted democratic values and interest in participation, consultation, and collective action by peer groups. In Indian organizations, vertical communication takes place more than lateral communication. This is consistent with their 'authoritarian' culture in which command is given by seniors and submission is expected from juniors (Kakar, 1971; Tayeb, 1984).

On the whole, more time is spent on communication in the English firms than in their Indian counterparts. This is not only consistent with the cultural differences between the two nations, but also with their respective political-economic environments. Many of the English firms had a much smaller market share compared to their Indian counterparts. This is to a great extent a direct result of their respective governments' economic policies. Although the economic system in both countries is based on a capitalistic mode of production with both private and public enterprises, Indian capitalism was much more protectionist and the government intervened in the economy much more directly. For example, local industries were protected against foreign competition by the government's strict import policies. English capitalism, especially under the present Conservative government, is rooted in the concept of reduced direct government intervention and on the stimulation of industry through monetary policies which aim to facilitate the free play and interaction of market forces. In pursuit of this aim, import controls have been dismantled and, in consequence, manufacturing companies face fierce competition from foreign firms.

In short, Indian organizations, with their more stable environment, spend less time on communication and consultation than English organizations with their more unstable environment.

Specialization

The two samples scored similarly on this dimension. But here too one must note a few points. First, although the aggregate scores on specialization are similar, the specialized functions are different. For instance, in the Indian company in the chemicals pair, environmental pollution and medical matters are dealt with by a specialized department, whereas the English counterpart has a specialized section for its printing and publishing requirements. Second, some of the firms have contracted out a number of their functions, but their counterparts have not done so. Third, a number of the functions of some of the English organizations, which are part of a parent group, are carried out either at the group headquarters or in central pools, whereas their Indian counterparts perform them themselves. Fourth, all the English firms except the brewery and confectionery companies have specialized departments for R and D activities to meet, in the words of their managers, their competitors' challenge; whereas none of the Indian firms felt the need for such a specialist function, mainly because they do not face any serious competition. At the most, they would send their senior officers to attend international exhibitions and conferences in order to learn and come back with new ideas.

Formalization

Here there is a major difference. Indian organizations scored considerably lower on this dimension than did their English counterparts. A few explanations for this can be offered. First, the Indian organizations' lower score may be because they are much younger than the English ones – the average age for the two samples is 28 and 63 years respectively. Older organizations are said to use more written rules and documentation (Inkson *et al.*, 1970). However, even when a control is introduced for age, the Indian firms still score much lower than the English firms.

A reason for this may be that the Aston formalization scale employed in the present study does not adequately represent the degree of procedural control in the organizations investigated. The scale measures the extent to which *written documents* are used in the companies. There may also be unwritten rules and directives which regulate employees' activities. This may be especially so in the Indian organizations, where most of the shopfloor manual workers are illiterate (a political economy-type factor).

Second, formalization is, in effect, a means to control employees and to improve their performance (Child, 1984). There are other ways in which control can be exerted. The managers who participated in the interview programme mentioned a variety of methods that they employed, such as training courses, personal supervision, time-keeping, verbal contact, and the like. My discussions with these managers suggest that the Indian managers employed direct supervision and personal contact with shopfloor employees as well as with their immediate subordinates to a larger extent than did the English managers.

Moreover, the degree of formalization may also have something to do with the cultural traits of employees. A closer examination of the scores of English and Indian organizations on this dimension, and of some aspects of their cultures, leads to interesting observations. Four of the items which comprise the formalization scale are concerned with job descriptions. Job descriptions can be argued to reflect, among other things, people's preferences for clear-cut territorial boundaries around their jobs and the spatial and social distance they may wish to maintain between themselves and others. As Table 1 shows, Indian organizations scored considerably lower on the job-description sub-scale than did their English counterparts, which means that they had fewer written job descriptions. This difference of scores is quite consistent with the respective cultures of the two nations. The Indian and English peoples have been depicted as being diametrically opposite with regard to such concepts as spatiality, privacy, and independence. Indian culture is characterized by a lack of concern with privacy, and by close physical and emotional proximity and dependence; whereas English culture is characterized by the love of privacy, independence, and the maintenance of a certain physical and emotional distance (Parekh, 1974; Terry, 1979; Tayeb, 1984).

So far, the findings of the study lend support to both contingency and cultural models for organizational structure. Some aspects of the structural configurations of the English and Indian organizations studied are highly consistent with the task-specific environments within which they operate. For instance, the greater centralization of financial decisions in the English organizations was consistent with the economic hardship which they were experiencing at the time, and the Indian organizations' greater centralization of operative decisions with the strict industrial regulations governing recruitment and dismissal of manual workers in India. The equally high centralization scores for unallocated money and capital expenditure in both groups reflect the similar stand taken by the senior managers in both samples *vis-à-vis* the risks involved in such matters. Functional specialization is another dimension which is associated with contextual factors such as status and technology.

Some aspects of the structures of the participating organizations appear to be more consistent with their respective cultural settings. English people in general are more tolerant of other people's views, and believe in the participation of all concerned more than do the Indians. Also, the former are more willing to accept responsibility. This is reflected in a greater delegation of authority down the hierarchy and smaller span of control in English organizations compared with their Indian counterparts.

The extent of formalization, too, is influenced by cultural factors such as love of privacy and autonomy, and also social conditions, such as illiteracy of the majority of Indian manual workers, which has led to more use of personal supervision by their managers compared to their English counterparts.

Communication pattern displays an interesting blend of cultural and contextual influences. On one hand, the direction of communication in both samples is consistent with the cultural traits of the employees: vertical in Indian organizations, lateral in the English organizations. The amount of time spent in communication and consultation, on the other hand, is more consistent with contextual and environmental factors, such as competition and government policies.

References

Ayoubi, Z. M., 'Technology, size and organizational structures in a developing country: Jordan' in David J. Hickson and Charles J. McMillan (eds.), *Organization and Nation: the Aston Programme IV*, pp. 95–114, Westmead: Gower, 1981.

Badran, Mohamed, and Bob Hinings, 'Strategies of administrative control and contextual constraints in less-developed countries: the case of Egyptian public enterprise', *Organization Studies* 2, 1981, 3–21.

Child, E., 'Individual and social factors associated with the behaviour of children in a play setting', unpublished Ph.D. thesis, University of Aston in Birmingham, 1982.

Child, John, 'Organization structure and strategies of control: a replication of the Aston study', *Administrative Science Quarterly* 17, 1972, 163–77.

— *Organization: A Guide to Problems and Practice*, 2nd edn, London: Harper and Row, 1984.

Conaty, Joseph, H. Mahmoudi, and G. A. Miller, 'Social structure and bureaucracy: a comparison of organizations in the United States and the prerevolutionary Iran', *Organization Studies* 4, 1983, 105–28.

Fayol, Henri, *General Industrial Management*, Bath: Pitman, 1949.

Hickson, David J., C. R. Hinings, C. J. McMillan, and J. P. Schwitter, 'The culture-free context of organization structure: a tri-national comparison', *Sociology* 8, 1974, 59–80.

Hickson, David J., C. J. McMillan, K. Azumi, and D. Horvath, 'Grounds for comparative organization theory: quick sands or hard core?' in Cornelis J. Lammers and David J. Hickson (eds.), *Organizations Alike and Unlike*, pp. 25–41, London: Routledge and Kegan Paul, 1979.

Inkson, J. H. K., D. S. Pugh, and D. J. Hickson, 'Organization context and structure: an abbreviated replication', *Administrative Science Quarterly* 15, 1970, 318–29.

Kakar, Sudir, 'The theme of authority in social relations in India', *Journal of Social Psychology* 84, 1971, 93–101.

Khandwalla, Pradip N., 'Viable and effective organizational designs of firms', *Academy of Management Journal* 6, 1974, 481–95.

Kimberly, John R., 'Organizational size and the structuralist perspective: a review, critique, and proposal', *Administrative Science Quarterly* 21, 1976, 571–97.

Kuc, Bolec, D. J. Hickson, and C. J. McMillan, 'Centrally planned development: a comparison of Polish factories with equivalents in Britain, Japan and Sweden', *Organization Studies* 1, 1980, 253–70.

Lawrence, Paul R., and Jay W. Lorsch, *Organization and Environment: Managing Differentiation and Integration*, Boston: Harvard Business School, 1967.

McGregor, David, *The Human Side of Enterprise*, New York: McGraw-Hill, 1960.

Marsh, R. M., and H. Mannari, 'Technology and size as determinants of the organizational structure of Japanese factories', *Administrative Science Quarterly* 26, 1981, 33–57.

Maurice, Marc, 'Introduction: theoretical and ideological aspects of the universalistic approach to the study of organizations', *International Studies of Management and Organization* VI, 1976, 3–10.

Maurice, Marc, A. Sorge, and M. Warner, 'Social differences in organizing manufacturing units: a comparison of France, West Germany, and Great Britain', *Organization Studies* 1, 1980, 59–85.

Mayo, Elton, *The Social Problems of an Industrial Civilization*, Boston, Mass.: Harvard University, 1945.

Parekh, Bikhu, 'The spectre of self-consciousness' in Bikhu Parekh (ed.), *Colour, Culture, and Consciousness*, pp. 41–85, London: Allen and Unwin, 1974.

Schoonhoven, C. B., 'Problems with contingency theory: testing assumptions hidden within the language of contingency "theory" ', *Administrative Science Quarterly* 26, 1981, 349–77.

Shenoy, S., 'Organization structure and context: a replication of the Aston study in India' in David J. Hickson and Charles J. McMillan (eds.), *Organization and Nation*, pp. 133–54, Westmead: Gower, 1981.

Tayeb, Monir H., 'Nations and organizations', Ph.D. thesis, University of Aston in Birmingham, 1984.

Taylor, Fredrick W., *Scientific Management*, New York: Harper and Brothers, 1911.

Terry, Pat, 'An investigation of some cultural determinants of English organization behaviour', Ph.D. thesis, University of Bath, 1979.

Yasai-Ardekani, Masoud, 'A multivariate analysis of structure, context, strategy and style', Ph.D. thesis, City University Business School, 1979.

9

Overview

Organizational Behaviour and National Cultures

Peter B. Smith

From *British Journal of Management*, Vol. 3, 1992, 39–51

The difficulties of studying management across cultures have been frequently noted (Adler, 1983; Peng, Peterson and Shyi, 1991). They are matched by the growing urgency of the need to find ways of carrying through such studies effectively. The increasing dominance of multinationals and the globalization of world markets ensure that those who do address the question of culture will gain substantial advantages. This review will focus mostly upon studies which make cross-national comparisons rather than those which cover only a single country, since these provide a firmer basis upon which to rest conclusions as to whether there are substantial differences and whether they matter.

Roberts and Boyacigiller (1984) suggest that the most fundamental problem in this area has been the lack of any agreement as to how to define culture, and the consequent lack of a currency within which to conduct studies. They propose that we need to move away from the meanings given to the concept by anthropologists, whom they see as laying too much stress on the physical artefacts which characterize different cultures. Some organizational researchers have also emphasized the physical artefacts, that is to say the technological determinants of organizational behaviour, but it is likely that these are the aspects of organization which vary least around the world. In arriving at a definition useful to both organizational researchers and practitioners, Roberts and Boyacigiller suggest we should do better to start by looking open-mindedly at what it is that may cause organizations to function differently in different parts of the world.

The concept of culture has recently proved attractive not only to those who seek to understand world-wide variations in organizational behaviour (e.g. Ronen, 1986; Adler, 1990), but also those who attempt to delineate contrasts between different organizations in the same part of the world (Schein, 1985). Smircich (1985) goes further than most in asserting that organizations *are* cultures. While this may indeed prove a fruitful line of thinking, Hofstede's (1980) pioneering study, which will be discussed shortly, found large variations around the world within the culture of a single organization. All of the world's largest multinationals are now said to have more employees outside of their home-base country than within it, so that this dispersion is at least in competition with company culture, even if it does not entirely over-ride it. Furthermore, Laurent (1983) has found that contrasts between the attitudes of employees who were from different nations but working within the same multinational were stronger than were overall contrasts between national samples on the same measures.

Contemporary organizations differ from the types of society to whom the concept of culture was originally applied by virtue of the massive amounts of information available to them. This information is quite often equally and contemporaneously available in all parts of the world. A definition of culture valid for our purposes is thus more likely to be based on how organizations receive, interpret and act on information than on their physical location or specific hardware. Within this framework, *the most crucial aspect of a particular contemporary culture is the manner in which it encourages culture members to assign shared meanings to events.*

If one were to work from such a definition, it would be possible to develop a classification of national or organizational cultures, depending upon what proportion of specific organizational events were assigned shared meanings within each grouping of respondents. This would no doubt be a task of some magnitude, and it remains to be done. In the meantime, within the existing literature the dominant approach has been to equate nations with cultures, and thus to study culture and management by comparing samples of managers from different countries. Such an approach is not entirely indefensible. Managers within a single national culture work under a unified legislative system, with substantial impact upon their manpower planning and industrial relations, as well as a shared context of infrastructure and climate. Shared history does thus predispose members of nations to assign shared meanings to at least some events, though they may well differ about others. If nations are to provide our unit of analysis, then a priority for researchers must be whether some justifiable way can be found of classifying the 150 or so countries in the world along dimensions which can guide more detailed study.

Classifications of National Cultures

Most classifications of national cultures have been based upon surveys of work attitudes conducted in a variety of countries. The first substantial study of this kind was that by Haire *et al.* (1966), who surveyed the work goals of 3,641 managers in 14 countries, using semantic differential rating scales. Comparison of the responses yielded five clusters: an Anglo group (USA and Britain); a North European group (Norway, Sweden, Denmark and Germany); a 'Latin European' group (Spain, Italy, France and Belgium); a Developing Countries group (India, Argentina and Chile); and a group containing only Japan. The nature of the groupings likely to emerge from such procedures is obviously heavily dependent upon which countries are included. Haire *et al.* included mostly European countries, and consequently finish up with improbable combinations such as putting India with Argentina and Chile.

Ronen (1986) provides a synthesis of nine studies, starting with Haire *et al.* and adding others which have compared work attitudes in a similar way, but which have used different samples, a varying range of countries and different measures of attitude. Ronen and several of the other investigators use the statistical procedure of smallest space analysis to find the most parsimonious clustering of countries. Ronen (1986) finds eight clusters and four countries which will not fit into those clusters, namely Brazil, Japan, Israel and India. The clusters accord well with common-sense expectation, yielding Anglo, Nordic, Germanic, Latin European, Near Eastern, Arab, Far Eastern and Latin American clusters, including a total of 42 countries. Ronen concedes that inclusion of more Far Eastern countries, as well as those from Africa and the former Communist bloc, would most probably extend the number of clusters.

The difficulty with this type of study is that it yields no information as to what precisely it is that causes the data to cluster in the way that it does. Historical, religious and political factors are no doubt among the more important causes, but the analysis treats the clustering of countries as an end in itself, rather than using it to provide information which may be managerially useful. Furthermore, Griffeth and Hom (1987) show that different clustering methods tend to yield somewhat different groupings of countries.

An alternative method of data analysis was that employed in Hofstede's (1980) well-known study, which was also among those incorporated into Ronen's synthesis. Hofstede analysed 88,000 responses to a questionnaire survey conducted among employees of a single US multinational working in 66 countries. The size of his sample enabled him to average the scores for each questionnaire item for each country. Factor analysis of these means yielded four dimensions along which variation between countries was found to occur. It was then possible to plot the position of each country's data up on each of these dimensions. The initial sample was large enough for this to be done for 40 countries, but Hofstede (1983) extended this to 53.

Hofstede's four dimensions were named as Individualism, Power Distance, Uncertainty Avoidance and Masculinity. The first of these, Individualism, distinguishes countries in which employees see their individual identity as determined by their own continuing individual choices as to how to act. This is contrasted with the situation in countries where identity is collectively defined, that is to say, defined by one's obligations to the groups to which one belongs. Group membership in a collectivist culture is much less a matter of choice than in an individualist culture, whether that choice be determined by one's family of origin or by the organization for which one works. Of all the 53 countries in the survey, the USA ranked highest on individualism, with Australia second and Britain third. The representation of these three countries as thus atypical should give us cause to reflect on how applicable may be ideas emanating from these countries to others who are more collectivist. Among other major industrial nations, France ranked tenth, Germany fourteenth, Japan twenty-second and Hong Kong thirty-fourth.

Hofstede's second dimension, Power Distance, distinguishes countries where relations between superior and subordinate are relatively close and informal or more distant and formal. The countries with the most informal, low power distance relations were Austria, Jamaica and Denmark, while those with the highest power distance were Malaysia, Panama and the Philippines. Although Hofstede found the dimensions of Individualism and Power Distance to be separate, comparisons of the country means on these two scales shows them to be strongly and negatively correlated (−0.75). If the data for two countries (France and Costa Rica) is discarded, then the correlation becomes even more strongly negative. In other words, Hofstede's results suggest that it may be fruitful to distinguish countries which are individualist and low on power distance from those which are collectivist and high on power distance. According to his data, this separates the European and Anglo countries from the rest of the world. However, groupings of countries are less important within his approach. Its value is more that it provides a specific data point for each country upon a range of theoretically interesting dimensions.

Possibly because the collectivism and power distance dimensions are linked to one another, they have provoked rather more interest among researchers than Hofstede's remaining two dimensions, Uncertainty Avoidance and Masculinity/Femininity. This is unfortunate, since it is most unlikely that a single dimension, or pair of linked dimensions, will account for a substantial amount of all the ways in which organizational behaviour may vary across cultures. The dimension of Uncertainty Avoidance, according to Hofstede, distinguishes national cultures who emphasize meticulous forward planning from those in which risk-taking and leaving things to chance are more positively valued. Organizations in high uncertainty avoidance cultures, of which Japan proved to be one, are therefore likely to have longer time perspectives and more structured decision-making procedures. Hofstede's final dimension distinguished 'masculine' cultures, in which values such as assertiveness, challenge and ambition are strongly endorsed, from 'feminine cultures', in which cooperation and security are more highly valued.

Hofstede's findings have been criticized on a variety of grounds. The most important of these are that the data are all derived from the employees of a single corporation, that it was collected more than 20 years ago, and that mean scores for whole countries necessarily obscure substantial within-country variations. Furthermore, it is very likely that there are additional dimensions of cross-national variation which did not emerge because they were not represented in Hofstede's questionnaire. Despite this, Hofstede's concepts continue to provide the best available basis for thinking about cross-national differences in many aspects of organizational performance. In particular, the distinction between individualist and collectivist cultures will recur at a number of points in the sections which follow. We must consider first how substantial and how robust over time might be the size of the differences found.

Are There Organizational Universals?

Hickson *et al.* (1974) propose that there are certain organizational imperatives which require organizations to take on particular configurations if they are to survive. For example, as they grow in size, they will need to specialize activities, formalize procedures and decentralize control. The resulting series of 'Aston' studies has included not only Western countries, but also Japan, India, Jordan, Egypt, Algeria and Iran. Donaldson (1986) reviews the studies and reports that the Aston hypotheses are supported, albeit not so strongly in the non-Western data. However, none of the non-Western countries included in Donaldson's analysis score much above the midpoint for collectivism in Hofstede's survey. It is possible that, as organizations become more and more collectivist, Hickson's imperatives become attenuated as alternative solutions are employed. Redding and Pugh (1986) found substantial differences in the structure of Hong Kong, Japanese and British firms of similar size. Furthermore, 90 per cent of Hong Kong firms have less than 50 employees, so that one could argue that the problem of growth is solved in Hong Kong, and probably in other highly collectivist cultures, by schism rather than by formalization, decentralization and specialization. Formalization in Japanese firms was much greater than in Britain, whereas in Hong Kong it was much less than in Britain. In a study comparing Aston measures in Japanese and American firms, Lincoln and Kalleberg (1990) found a strong correlation between decentralization and use of the *ringi* system of group decision-making in Japan. In the USA, there was no relation between decentralization and the use of group decision-making. Thus the availability of alternative decision processes attenuates the potency of the link between size and decentralization.

There is further reason to be sceptical about the universality of relationships between organizational structures such as formalization and centralization. The Aston studies focus upon the existence of particular structures. Structures may be put in place, not least because of the world-wide diffusion of the ideas of Western management theorists, but they will only be put to use in ways which are culturally compatible. Tayeb (1988) compared a matched set of British and Indian firms. She found some support for the Aston hypotheses, but reported that decision-making in the two cultures was none the less carried through in quite different ways. For example, the Aston measure of centralization indicates *who* shall make certain decisions. However, Tayeb found that British managers tended to consult their subordinates before reaching decisions, while Indian managers did not.

It is very probable that there will prove to be numerous other instances whereby the existence of organizational structures are rather more generally dispersed around the world than are the organizational processes by which these structures are implemented. A related issue of considerable importance concerns whether or not current global industrialization can be expected to push all countries toward the more individualist, low power distance structures which characterize the countries which industrialized longer ago. While such a large question cannot be fully discussed here, the best current tests of such predictions are provided by the rapid growth of countries such as Japan and Korea. Dunphy (1987) surveys the considerable changes in Japanese managerial practice over the past few decades. He concludes that while there have been enormous changes, these are not simply changes toward Western practice, but rather a series of pragmatic changes within a context which continues to be much more collectivist in orientation. Equally, there is no sign of a diminution in Japanese emphasis upon uncertainty avoidance through long-term strategic planning (Kagono *et al.*, 1985). Lincoln and Kalleberg's (1990) comparative survey of Japanese and US workers found that there are still substantial differences, both in work motivations and in the relationship between motivations and organizational structures in the USA and Japan. Korea, whom Hofstede ranks much higher on collectivism than Japan, also continues to reinterpret Western ideas into a more collectivist format (Kim *et al.*, 1985).

Effective Leader Styles

Substantial research has been undertaken into the effectiveness of managerial leadership styles in different parts of the world. There is a considerable irony about the findings. The best-known models of managerial style have been developed in the USA, where the notion of one 'best way' of leading has received little empirical support. US theorists have consequently devised a series of increasingly complex contingency theories to account for the way in which different styles are appropriate to different settings (Smith and Peterson, 1988). However, in a range of more collectivistic countries, including Japan, Taiwan, Iran, India and Brazil, the notion of a single effective leader style has received much stronger support (Smith and Tayeb, 1988). In all these countries, studies have shown that the most effective managers are those who attend well to both task concerns and the needs of their work team. Results from more individualist European countries and from the Soviet Union (Zhurvalev and Shorokhova, 1984), which was not included in Hofstede's survey, show that effective leader style varies with the situation, as in the USA.

There are several possible explanations for this interesting contrast in findings. Firstly, it can be expected that superior–subordinate relations will be different in individualist and collectivist cultures. The collectivist workgroup is more strongly committed to the preservation of overt harmony, and the perspectives of superior and subordinate are less likely to be in conflict. Hence the appropriate balance of task and relationship behaviours may be self-evident to all parties. A second possibility stems from the fact, already noted, that countries high on collectivism are frequently also high on power distance. In a high power distance country, members of successful work-groups may be inclined deferentially to attribute their success to their superior. Conversely, in a low power distance country, a team member is much more likely to attribute credit to him or herself and to feel aggrieved if the superior does not do likewise. The third possibility, that the result is based on artefact due to the use of different research measures in different countries, is discounted in a recent study by Smith *et al.* (1992). This compared leadership of work teams in a matched sample of electronics assembly plants in USA, Britain, Japan and Hong Kong, and did, as expected, find differences in effective leader styles between Japan and the Western countries, although some common effects were also found.

A number of other researchers have used US-derived leadership measures in various countries around the world. For example, Bryman *et al.* (1987) found that construction site managers in Britain were highly task-oriented on Fiedler's (1967) Least Preferred Coworker scale (LPC). However, the most effective managers were those who were relatively less task-oriented. Bennett (1977) found that bank managers who were effective in the Philippines were those who were more task-oriented on the LPC scale. In contrast, he found that relationship-oriented bank managers in Hong Kong were the more effective. There has been some debate as to the meaning of high and low LPC scores on Fiedler's measure, even in Western countries. It is still more difficult to interpret the meaning of such studies where they are undertaken in more collectivist cultures, because Fiedler's measures, and those of other US theorists such as Vroom and Yetton (1973), offer a dichotomy between more autocratic and more participative leader styles. As has been argued earlier, in collectivist cultures effective leadership is frequently both autocratic and participative at the same time.

Earlier comparisons of leader styles in different countries, such as those summarized by Bass and Burger (1979), pose the same problem. Greater reliance can be placed on those leadership studies which look at the correlates of measures *within* countries, not treating autocratic and participative styles as mutually exclusive, and then compare results across countries. The detailed study by Heller *et al.* (1988) of decision-making in Holland, Britain and Yugoslavia provides a valuable example. They found differences within countries to be as great as those between countries.

Human Resource Management Policies

Differences in human resource management policies between countries are a little easier to establish, since it is often possible to assess the existence of policies on the basis of expenditures, rather than the more subjective criteria involved in characterizing the meanings placed on managerial behaviours. The problem here is one of sampling, since there is substantial variance in policies within countries also. Studies using large samples have tended to find rather fewer differences than were expected.

Several studies, for instance, have shown that the policy of life-time employment, thought to be so central to Japanese management practice, is in fact only characteristic of front-rank Japanese companies (Smith and Misumi, 1989). Among the overall Japanese workforce, a slightly lower percentage of employees experience life-time employment than occurs in Western countries.

None the less, Pascale and Maguire's (1980) comparison of a sample of matched pairs of US and Japanese firms did detect a range of differences, e.g. twice as much expenditure on social and recreational facilities in Japan. Even these differences must be qualified by Pascale's (1978) findings that plant location was more important than ownership. There were, in fact, rather more differences between Japanese firms in the US and Japanese firms in Japan than between Japanese and US-owned firms. In a similar way, White and Trevor (1983) concluded that the personnel policies of Japanese firms in Britain were surprisingly similar to those of other firms nearby. Although relations with the unions were often on a different basis, White and Trevor saw the main reason for the Japanese firms' success as being meticulous attention to production management.

A broader survey of US, Japanese and European firms was conducted by Kagono *et al.* (1985). Data were obtained from 277 US firms and 291 Japanese firms, but the response rate from European firms was much lower, with only 50 European responses obtained. The Japanese firms reported flatter hierarchies, less precise job descriptions, longer-term performance evaluation, control systems based upon self-discipline, and more promotion from within.

Child (1981) summarizes a detailed study of decision-making in 71 British companies and 51 West German companies. It was found that decision-making in the German firms was centralized at more senior levels. Senior managers were also more likely to be recruited from outside the organization. In contrast, in the British firms there was more internal promotion, more concern for employees' rewards and benefits, and for the development of young executives. Thus, even within two European countries with relatively similar national cultures, consistent differences were found in certain aspects of human resource development.

Jaeger and Kanungo (1990) provide a variety of perspectives upon the applicability of human resource development strategies in the context of the developing countries. They argue that, while frequent attempts are made to replicate Western policies and procedures in non-Western settings, these practices will only be effective where they fit in with the assumptions of the local cultural context. They single out such concepts as planning, organizational structure and management by objectives for specific critique. Planning is likely to be difficult in low uncertainty avoidance cultures. The construction of organizational structures also requires a conception of individualist roles separable from existing social relationships. Management by objectives requires, among other things, the notion that it is acceptable for superior and subordinate to bargain with one another. Many other examples are given, with particular attention to India and Africa. These cautions must be tempered by the findings of Negandhi (1979). Negandhi and his colleagues undertook a series of studies of US-owned and locally-owned firms in Brazil, Uruguay, Argentina, India, Taiwan and the Philippines, all of which are countries rated relatively high on collectivism by Hofstede. The US firms consistently used more Western human resource management policies and were also more effective, by a variety of criteria. However, Negandhi's broad brush studies do not provide detail of the extent to which particular US-owned firms adapted their policies to specific settings, so that Jaeger and Kanungo's point of view may well retain considerable validity.

Negotiating Across Cultures

The matter of cross-cultural negotiation provides one of the most acute problems in the whole field of culture and organizational behaviour. Negotiations quite often bring together, for relatively short periods of time, those who are not necessarily familiar with the cultural background of those with whom they are dealing. While it may frequently be in the interest of both parties to reach agreement with one another, the process of arriving at that point requires that there is a shared view of *how* it is to be accomplished, and of what is the meaning or implications of any agreement which is reached. Under what conditions may a contract be renegotiable, for instance?

A difficulty in this field is that many of the more detailed studies concern simulated negotiations, whereas accounts of real-world negotiations are covered more sketchily. The major distinction between styles of negotiation turns upon the level of directness employed by negotiators. Graham (1985) portrayed the contrast particularly clearly by observing pairs of US, Japanese and Brazilian businessmen acting as negotiators in a buying and selling game. The Brazilians took much longer, both spoke at once more frequently, said 'No' nearly 10 times as often and touched one another from time to time. The Japanese made more modest initial bids, looked at each other less, said 'No' less often, and had more frequent periods of silence. The Americans were intermediate on most of these criteria, but they expressed their more forceful demands earlier in the negotiations than did the Japanese.

Most commentators characterize the behaviour of more individualist Western negotiators as 'rational and task-centred', in contrast to those from more collectivist national cultures, where the state of relationship between the negotiating parties becomes an increasingly important factor (Glenn *et al.*, 1977; Leung and Wu, 1990; Mead, 1990). Perhaps for this reason, Harnett and Cummings (1980) found that bargainers from the USA and from four European countries drove harder bargains than did those from Japan and Thailand. Negotiators from non-Western countries might well argue however that the maximization of short-term benefit is not always the most rational strategy.

Where the avoidance of long-term conflict is a major priority, indirect communication may consequently be preferred. The Japanese avoidance of saying 'No', and the use of extended periods of silence to communicate failure to agree, provide examples. In a similar way, explicit contracts will be thought undesirable as they may imply the absence of trust in the other party (Sullivan *et al.*, 1981). Indirect negotiations are also likely to take longer and to involve more extended preliminaries during which the parties establish how trustworthy each may be through conversation on more neutral topics.

Differences in the pace at which negotiations are carried through reflect variations in preferences as to how to handle the process of uncertainty avoidance. Negotiators from a high uncertainty avoidance culture, such as Japan, are likely to see the major priority as establishing whether or not the other party is trustworthy on a long-term basis. If they do prove to be so, then the assumption is that any differences of opinion which arise during the implementation of a contract can be ironed out on the basis of goodwill. Negotiators from low uncertainty avoidance cultures, such as Britain or America, will more usually focus on quickly gaining agreement for a set of specific actions during a finite period of time. They anticipate that the other party can then be held to the contract which has been agreed.

The difficulties of bridging such differences in negotiating goals and style are not necessarily insuperable, and a number of case studies are available, for example, of successful US–Japanese and US–Chinese negotiations (Tung, 1984; March, 1988). The cases illustrate the way in which successful cross-cultural negotiations include an understanding by either party as to how the other party prefers to negotiate, and what meanings they put on key words such as 'agreement' and 'contract'.

Multicultural Management

Shenkar and Zeira (1987) report that joint ventures are increasingly displacing wholly owned subsidiaries as the most widespread form of overseas investment. Both subsidiaries and joint ventures may be expected to experience distinctive problems, as well as some that are shared. The most general issue in either case is likely to be relations between the parent company and the local company.

Child's (1990) review of 30 joint ventures within the People's Republic of China reveals distinctive differences in the approach of parent companies from each country. US-owned ventures were found to attempt most strongly to introduce the procedures and policies obtaining within the parent company. This accords with Negandhi's findings concerning US companies in other countries, discussed earlier. Child reports that within China this raised substantial difficulties within a number of ventures, particularly in the fields of informal communication, training and decision-making. Japanese companies were found to discard many practices characteristic of home-based Japanese organizations, and to adopt a much more centralized and autocratic system of decision-making. Japanese willingness to adapt to whatever they judge to work best in local circumstances has been noted in many other studies, including Fruin (1983) for the USA, White and Trevor (1983) in Britain, and Yoshino (1976) in South-East Asia. This flexibility has led to much more autocratic practices in Japanese plants in South-East Asia than in Japanese plants in Europe or North America. The same contrast between American and Japanese policies abroad is noted by Putti and Chong (1985), who compared 12 subsidiaries in Singapore. In this setting, US personnel management practices were reported to work well.

The joint ventures in Child's study in China which were Hong Kong-owned experienced the fewest difficulties, partly at least because language problems and differences in cultural expectations would be at a minimum. The European-owned joint ventures were reported to be intermediate between the Japanese- and American-owned ventures, insofar as they frequently attempted to introduce Western procedures, but were more likely to compromise with Chinese expectations in situations where their attempts went astray.

Shenkar and Zeira's (1987) review concludes that the most widespread problems of joint ventures include communication and decision-making failures between parent company and local organization, unequal participation where there is more than one parent company, difficulties contingent upon time-limited joint ventures, and a variety of issues which also characterize other types of multinational venture.

Earlier studies by Zeira (1975) and Zeira and Banai (1981) examined the personnel problems faced by leading multinationals. The principal problem identified was that of conflict over appointments to senior positions within overseas subsidiaries. Where parent country nationals were appointed, their leadership was frequently resisted by local staffs, who saw them as advancing their own careers at the expense of locals and frequently failing to understand the nuances of local cultural norms. The expatriate managers, for their part, most frequently saw themselves as trying to sustain comparability with practice in other parts of the multinational.

Such problems may be handled either through a policy of maximizing the appointment of local managers, or through stringent attention to selection and training of parent country managers. Either policy has contingent problems, but the choice between them may also be influenced by cultural factors. Tung's (1982) survey showed that Japanese multinationals retained a substantial presence of Japanese as senior managers in all parts of the world. US and European multinationals tended toward the use of local managers at all levels in industrialized countries, but relied on parent country senior managers in developing countries. In an earlier study, Tung (1981) examined the selection criteria said to be important by multinationals for making appointments at various different levels. Maturity, emotional stability, communicative ability and managerial talent were the qualities cited most frequently for senior appointments.

The difficulties faced by parent country senior managers indicate that their selection and training for assignments are crucial to success. Ronen (1986) proposes that there is (or at least has been in the past) a substantial gap between the selection criteria often employed and those which the researches of Zeira and of Tung have suggested are most strongly required. While technical and managerial expertise are clearly important, other attributes, such as emotional maturity, willingness to learn about new environments and respect for others' views, also have great importance.

An alternative way of clarifying the attributes most required has been developed by Ratiu (1983), who examined the characteristics of managers rated as internationally effective by their colleagues while attending business schools in France and Britain. Effective international managers were said to be those who were adaptable, flexible, open-minded, speaking in foreign languages, and making friends with those of many nationalities. Further group interviews suggested that the effective international managers were more intuitive, more provisional in their judgments, more open in discussing their experience of culture shock and how they handle it, and more concerned to understand specific experiences rather than make global generalizations. The propositions advanced are plausible, but need testing against more valid criteria of international effectiveness.

Adler (1990) points out that organizations selecting managers for overseas assignments neglect the views of the selected manager's spouse at their peril. Failure to adapt to the new environment by the spouse is a not infrequent contributor to failed assignments, and the costs of such failures can be very substantial. Tung (1982) reports that in her survey of US multinationals, three-quarters of the companies had failure rates of 10–20 per cent or higher. Failure was defined as the premature termination of an assignment by either party. The reason most frequently cited for failure within both US and European firms was failure of the spouse to adapt. In Japan the most frequent reason given was inability of the manager to cope with the more complex work. This difference probably tells us as much about the types of excuses for failure apparently thought to be most acceptable in different parts of the world as it does about real decision processes. Gregerson and Black (1990) found that the intention of US expatriates to leave their assignments early was not related to the work itself, but was related to their own and their spouses' interactions with host country nationals and the host country culture. In considering these problems it is important to note that European and Japanese firms have substantially lower reported failure rates than US firms, and we shall consider why this might be so in the next section.

Training and Career Development

The studies reviewed in the preceding section highlight a number of issues which face joint ventures, and multinational firms in particular. The fallibility of existing selection procedures for international assignments means that a particular burden rests upon multinationals to manage effectively the career transitions within which such assignments figure, and the training processes designed to optimize the chances of their success.

Tung (1982, 1987) and Miller *et al.* (1990) have reported a series of comparative surveys of the policies of multinationals in this field. Tung notes a particularly strong contrast between US and Japanese policies, which reflects the more general preoccupation of the Japanese with uncertainty avoidance through long-term planning. Japanese placements abroad quite often last 5 or more years and are rather frequently preceded by substantial training input, often with a more extensive emphasis on language training. US placements are more typically for 1–2 years, and 68 per cent of those placed received no training. US firms quite often also expressed the view that training could not be justified, because the employee might not stay with the firm. Peterson and Mueller (1989) surveyed US multinationals based in Florida and also found that very few referred to the need for any kind of country-specific training. Tung found that, in her sample, lack of training was significantly related to failure rates. European firms had failure rates below 5 per cent and also used more training than US firms. This was most frequently focused upon relatively short briefings about a country or region and its cultural patterns.

Tung attributes the relatively low failure rates of European and Japanese firms to their more substantial reliance upon internal promotion and career planning. Many European firms also have a rather longer history of overseas operation and, as Child's (1990) study in Beijing illustrated, are more open to adapting their procedures to local practice. We have seen already that Japanese organizations have also been found to be flexible in their personnel practices, depending upon local circumstance.

The US executive abroad is seen as necessarily preoccupied with future career prospects at home and not likely to wish to step out of line with headquarters policies. Adler's (1981) study indicates that this concern is well-founded. Few organizations in her North American sample made any explicit provision for the management of the expatriate's return. While departure was clearly seen as requiring some preparation, return was often treated as a return to 'normality'. Returnees reported finding their employers not interested in making use of the experience which had been gained abroad. Many of the differences reported between US, European and Japanese experiences abroad thus appear to derive rather directly from differences in time perspective.

The varieties of training which are used have rarely been subjected to systematic evaluation (Black and Mendenhall, 1990), and most of the studies published use students rather than managers as subjects. However, Earley (1987) compared documentary briefings and experiential exercises for 80 US managers preparing to spend 3 months in Korea. Ratings of overall performance while in Korea showed that both forms of training had a significant effect, and that the managers who did best of all were those who received both forms of training. Control subjects who received neither form of training performed worst.

The effectiveness of different forms of training will depend upon how well they are matched to the specific locations to which assignments are made and how long is to be spent there. The range of options is fully explored by Ronen (1989). Generalized programmes such as the 'culture assimilator' (Brislin *et al.*, 1986) seek to induce awareness of cultural differences and of the importance of trying to understand their meaning. This is done by presenting 100 vignettes of cross-cultural interactions, each one accompanied with four possible explanations. Trainees work through these at their own pace, together with details presented subsequently as to why each explanation is more or less plausible. There is good evidence of the positive effects of this approach (Cushner, 1989), although it has rarely been employed with managers. A variety of country-specific culture assimilators have also been developed (Bhawuk, 1990).

The value of language training is widely agreed, but not always implemented. The journal issue edited by Lambert and Moore (1990) underlines substantial progress in this field in Europe and Japan, but opportunities lost by British and American firms who give language training lower priority. The increasing integration of language and business training in continental European countries is a notable advance.

There is also scope for attention to the inevitability of a period of culture shock following arrival at a new location (Furnham and Bochner, 1986). Prior discussion of the issues and of the variety of coping mechanisms available (Mendenhall and Oddou, 1985, 1986) is likely to be invaluable. Where a visit is to be short, didactic forms of 'briefing' may be adequate. For longer stays, it becomes increasingly crucial that trainees are aided in developing ways of learning from their ongoing cross-cultural experiences. What is required is the development of an ability to see what meanings locals are putting upon particular events, and to relate these meanings to one's own reactions to those same events. A variety of more experiential forms of training, many of them derivable from Kolb and Fry's (1975) model of 'learning how to learn', are favoured for this purpose (Landis and Brislin, 1983).

Conclusions

This review indicates that, while there may be some universality to the organizational structures required around the world, the differing national cultures within which organizations are located frequently give those structures substantially different meanings. Working effectively across cultures is therefore not simply a matter of applying the skills found to be most effective within the culture of one's country or organization. It requires also that one can understand and cope with the processes of communication and decision-making in settings where these are achieved in a different manner.

The studies referred to in this review mostly focus upon the same small groupings of countries, particularly USA, Japan and a conglomerate of European countries. There is a clear need to extend the range of countries included in research designs. However, the value of conceptual frameworks such as that provided by the work of Hofstede (1980) is that they do now provide a better basis for choice as to which countries to include. Concepts such as collectivism, power distance and uncertainty avoidance may be used not simply to classify countries, but also to organize data concerning human resource management from single-country studies and to guide the design of selection procedures and training programmes.

Overall measures of cross-cultural effectiveness such as 'failure rates' are exceedingly blunt instruments. The knowledge that by such measures Japanese organizations appear to handle the problem of working across cultures rather more effectively is of little help to Western organizations. Japanese organizations start from a different and culturally rooted point. Furthermore, while Japanese organizations do well at preparing staff for overseas assignments, there is evidence that Japanese returnees do have substantial difficulty when returning to tightly-knit Japanese society.

We have at present only a very partial understanding of how cross-cultural problems are best addressed. Within the industrialized nations of Europe and North America, which were all classified by Hofstede as relatively individualist and low on power distance, it may be that language proficiency is the principal (though by no means the only) barrier to cross-cultural effectiveness. When we consider links between individualist and more collectivist cultures, a much broader range of issues become salient, and it is here that the potential gains and losses are greatest.

The validity of many of the selection and training methods currently in use remains to be established. The importance of remedying this situation is illustrated by the fact that, in the surveys conducted by Tung and others, a frequent reason given by organizations for not providing more training was that they did not expect that it would be effective. As in other fields, a precondition for validation studies will need to be the provision of more adequate data as to what are the requirements for effective work in each specific cross-cultural setting, whether that work be short-term negotiation or longer-term managerial responsibilities. To inspire confidence, the validity criteria would need to reflect rather more of the subtleties which make for managerial success or failure in cross-cultural settings. This could most probably only be achieved by closer attention to the meaning of success in particular organizations and locations, rather than by use of global measures such as failure rates.

The difficulties experienced by those returning from foreign assignments also points to the need for many organizations to give more systematic attention to this aspect of career planning. Those who have acquired cross-cultural experience frequently have an asset of value to the organization, and to fail to use it, or even to lose the employee altogether, incurs a further avoidable cost.

Provision of firmer information on the difficulties currently encountered by expatriates, and on effective ways of handling those difficulties, should provide the basis upon which future policies can rest. Where this is accomplished, organizations may have greater confidence that the planning and execution of their operations in multicultural contexts benefits their overall effectiveness.

Acknowledgement

I am grateful to John Harper, David Hickson and Mark Peterson for comments on an earlier draft.

References

Adler, N. J., 'Re-entry: managing cross-cultural transitions', *Group and Organizational Studies*, 6, 1981, 341–56.

— 'Cross-cultural management research: the ostrich and the trend', *Academy of Management Review*, 8, 1983, 226–32.

— *International Dimensions of Organizational Behavior*, 2nd edn, Boston, MA: Kent Publishing, 1990.

Bass, B. M. and P. C. Burger, *Assessment of Managers: An International Comparison*, New York: Free Press, 1979.

Bennett, M., 'Testing management theories cross-culturally', *Journal of Applied Psychology*, 62, 1977, 578–81.

Bhawuk, D. P. S., 'Cross-cultural orientation programs', in R. W. Brislin (ed.), *Applied Cross-Cultural Psychology*, Newbury Park, CA: Sage, 1990.

Black, J. S. and M. Mendenhall, 'Cross-cultural training effectiveness: a review and theoretical framework for future research', *Academy of Management Review*, 15, 1990, 113–36.

Brislin, R. W., K. Cushner, C. Cherrie and M. Yong, *Intercultural Interactions: A Practical Guide*, Beverly Hills, CA: Sage, 1986.

Bryman, A., M. Bresnen, J. Ford, A. Beardsworth and T. Keil, 'Leader orientation and organizational transience: an investigation using Fiedler's LPC scale', *Journal of Occupational Psychology*, 60, 1987, 13–20.

Child, J., 'Culture, contingency and capitalism in the cross-national study of organizations', in B. M. Staw and L. L. Cummings (eds.), *Research in Organizational Behavior*, Vol. 3, pp. 303–56, Greenwich, CT: JAI Press, 1981.

— *The Management of Equity Joint Ventures in China*, China-EC Management Institute, Beijing, 1990.

Cushner, K. H., 'Assessing the impact of a culture-general assimilator', *International Journal of Intercultural Relations*, 13, 1989, 125–46.

Donaldson, L., 'Size and bureaucracy in East and West: a preliminary meta-analysis', in S. R. Clegg, D. C. Dunphy and S. G. Redding (eds.), *The Enterprise and Management in East Asia*, Centre for Asian Studies, University of Hong Kong, 1986.

Dunphy, D., 'Convergence/divergence: a temporal review of the Japanese enterprise and its management', *Academy of Management Review*, 12, 1987, 445–59.

Earley, P. C., 'Intercultural training for managers: a comparison of documentary and interpersonal methods', *Academy of Management Journal*, 30, 1987, 685–98.

Fiedler, F. E., *A Theory of Leadership Effectiveness*, New York: McGraw-Hill, 1967.

Fruin, W. M., *Kikkoman: Company, Clan and Community*, Cambridge, MA: Harvard University Press, 1983.

Furnham, A. and S. Bochner, *Culture Shock: Psychological Reactions to Unfamiliar Environments*, London: Methuen, 1986.

Glenn, E., D. Witmeyer and K. Stevenson, 'Cultural styles of persuasion', *International Journal of Intercultural Relations*, 1, 1977, 52–66.

Graham, J. L., 'The influence of culture on the process of business negotiations: an exploratory study', *Journal of International Business Studies*, 16, 1985, 81–96.

Gregerson, H. B. and J. S. Black, 'A multifaceted approach to expatriate retention in international assignments', *Group and Organization Studies*, 15, 1990, 461–85.

Griffeth, R. W. and P. W. Hom, 'Some multivariate comparisons of multinational managers', *Multivariate Behavioral Research*, 22, 1987, 173–91.

Haire, M., E. F. Ghiselli and L. W. Porter, *Managerial Thinking: An International Study*, New York: Wiley, 1966.

Harnett, D. L. and L. L. Cummings, *Bargaining Behavior: An International Study*, Houston, TX: Dame Publications, 1980.

Heller, F., P. J. D. Drenth, P. Koopman and V. Rus, *Decisions in Organizations: A Three-Country Comparative Study*, London: Sage, 1988.

Hickson, D. J., C. R. Hinings, C. McMillan and J. P. Schwitter, 'The culture-free context of organization structure', *Sociology*, 8, 1974, 59–80.

Hofstede, G., *Culture's Consequences: International Differences in Work-related Values*, Beverly Hills, CA: Sage, 1980.

— 'National cultures in four dimensions', *International Studies of Management and Organization*, 13, 1983, 46–74.

Jaeger, A. M. and R. N. Kanungo (eds.), *Management in Developing Countries*, London: Routledge, 1990.

Kagono, T., I. Nonaka, K. Sakakibara and A. Okumura, *Strategic vs. Evolutionary Management: A US–Japan Comparison of Strategy and Organization*, Amsterdam: Elsevier, North Holland, 1985.

Kim, B. W., D. S. Bell and C. B. Lee (eds.), *Administrative Dynamics and Development: The Korean Experience*, Seoul: Kyobo, 1985.

Kolb, D. A. and R. Fry, 'Towards an applied theory of experiential learning', in C. L. Cooper (ed.), *Theories of Group Processes*, pp. 33–58, Chichester: Wiley, 1975.

Lambert, R. D. and S. J. Moore (eds.), 'Foreign language in the workplace', *Annals of the American Academy of Political and Social Science*, 511 (whole issue) 1990.

Landis, D. and R. Brislin (eds.), *Handbook of Intercultural Training*, Elmsford, New York: Pergamon, 1983.

Laurent, A., 'The cultural diversity of Western conceptions of management', *International Studies of Management and Organization*, 13(1–2), 1983, 75–96.

Leung, K. and P. G. Wu, 'Dispute processing: a cross-cultural analysis', in R. W. Brislin (ed.), *Applied Cross-cultural Psychology*, Newbury Park, CA: Sage, 1990.

Lincoln, J. R. and A. Kalleberg, *Culture, Control and Commitment: A Study of Work Organization and Work Attitudes in the United States and Japan*, Cambridge: Cambridge University Press, 1990.

March, R. M., *The Japanese Negotiator: Subtlety and Strategy Beyond Western Logic*, Tokyo: Kodansha, 1988.

Mead, R. G., *Cross-Cultural Management Communication*, Chichester: Wiley, 1990.

Mendenhall, M. and G. Oddou, 'The dimensions of expatriate acculturation: a review', *Academy of Management Review*, 10, 1985, 39–47.

— 'Acculturation profiles of expatriate managers: implications for cross-cultural training programs', *Columbia Journal of World Business*, 21(4), 1986, 73–79.

Miller, E. L., R. L. Tung, R. W. Armstrong and B. W. Stening, 'A comparison of Australian and United States management succession systems', *International Human Resource Management Review*, 1, 1990, 123–39.

Negandhi, A., 'Convergence in organizational practices: an empirical study of industrial enterprises in developing countries', in C. J. Lammers and D. J. Hickson (eds.), *Organizations Alike and Unlike: International and Inter-Institutional Studies in the Sociology of Organizations*, London: Routledge, 1979.

Pascale, R. T., 'Communication and decision-making across cultures: Japanese and American comparisons', *Administrative Science Quarterly*, 23, 1978, 91–109.

Pascale, R. T. and M. A. Maguire, 'Comparison of selected work factors in Japan and the United States', *Human Relations*, 33, 1980, 433–55.

Peng, T. K., M. F. Peterson and Y. P. Shyi, 'Quantitative methods in cross-cultural management research', *Journal of Organizational Behavior*, 12, 1991, 87–108.

Peterson, M. F. and R. Mueller, 'University and in-house management education of multinational business and bank employees', *Journal of Teaching in International Business*, 1, 1989, 47–75.

Putti, J. M. and T. F. H. Chong, 'American and Japanese management practices in their Singapore subsidiaries', *Asia Pacific Journal of Management*, 2, 1985, 106–14.

Ratiu, I., 'Thinking internationally: a comparison of how international executives learn', *International Studies of Management and Organization*, 13, 1983, 139–50.

Redding, S. G. and D. S. Pugh, 'The formal and the informal: Japanese and Chinese organization structures', in S. R. Clegg, D. C. Dunphy and S. G. Redding (eds.), *The Enterprise and Management in East Asia*, Centre for Asian Studies, University of Hong Kong, 1986.

Roberts, K. H. and N. A. Boyacigiller, 'Cross-national organizational research: the grasp of the blind man', in B. M. Staw and L. L. Cummings (eds.), *Research in Organizational Behavior*, Vol. 2, pp. 423–75, Greenwich, CT: JAI Press, 1984.

Ronen, S., *Comparative and Multinational Management*, New York: Wiley, 1986.

— 'Training the international assignee', in I. Goldstein (ed.), *Training and Development in Organizations*, pp. 417–51, San Francisco: Jossey-Bass, 1989.

Schein, E. H., *Organizational Culture and Leadership*, San Francisco: Jossey-Bass, 1985.

Shenkar, O. and Y. Zeira, 'Human resource management in international joint ventures: directions for research', *Academy of Management Review*, 12, 1987, 546–57.

Smircich, L., 'Is the concept of culture a paradigm for understanding organizations and ourselves?' in P. J. Frost, L. F. Moore, M. R. Louis, C. C. Lundberg and J. Martin (eds.), *Organizational Culture*, Newbury Park, CA: Sage, 1985.

Smith, P. B. and J. Misumi, 'Japanese management: a sun rising in the West?' in C. L. Cooper and I. T. Robertson (eds.), *International Review of Industrial and Organizational Psychology 1989*, Vol. 4, pp. 330–69, Chichester: Wiley, 1989.

Smith, P. B., J. Misumi, M. H. Tayeb, M. F. Peterson and M. H. Bond, 'On the generality of leadership style across cultures', *Journal of Occupational Psychology*, 62, 1989, 97–110.

Smith, P. B. and M. F. Peterson, *Leadership, Organizations and Culture*, London: Sage, 1988.

Smith, P. B., M. F. Peterson, J. Misumi and M. H. Bond, 'A cross-cultural test of the Japanese PM leadership theory', *Applied Psychology: An International Review*, 41(1), 1992.

Smith, P. B. and M. H. Tayeb, 'Organizational structure and processes', in M. H. Bond (ed.), *The Cross-cultural Challenge to Social Psychology*, Newbury Park, CA: Sage, 1988.

Sullivan, J., R. B. Peterson, N. Kameda and J. Shimada, 'The relationship between conflict resolution approaches and trust: a cross-cultural study', *Academy of Management Journal*, 24, 1981, 803–15.

Tayeb, M. H., *Organizations and National Culture: A Comparative Analysis*, London: Sage, 1988.

Tung, R. L., 'Selection and training for overseas assignments', *Columbia Journal of World Business*, 16(1), 1981, 68–78.

— 'Selection and training procedures of US, European and Japanese multinationals', *California Management Review*, 25(1), 1982, 57–71.

— *Key to Japan's Economic Strength: Human Power*, Lexington, MA: Lexington Books, 1984.

— 'Expatriate assignments: enhancing success and minimizing failure', *Academy of Management Executive*, 1, 1987, 117–26.

Vroom, V. H. and P. W. Yetton, *Leadership and Decision-Making*, Pittsburgh, PA: University of Pittsburgh Press, 1973.

White, M. and M. Trevor, *Under Japanese Management: The Experience of British Workers*, London: Heinemann, 1983.

Yoshino, M. Y., *Japan's Multinational Enterprises*, Cambridge, MA: Harvard University Press, 1976.

Zeira, Y., 'Overlooked personnel problems of multinational corporations', *Columbia Journal of World Business*, 10(2), 1975, 96–103.

Zeira, Y. and M. Banai, 'Attitudes of host country organizations towards MNC's staffing policies: cross-country and cross-industry analysis', *Management International Review*, 21(2), 1981, 38–47.

Zhurvalev, A. L. and E. V. Shorokhova, 'Social psychological problems of managing the collective', in L. H. Strickland (ed.), *Directions in Soviet Social Psychology*, New York: Springer-Verlag, 1984.

READ MORE IN PENGUIN

In every corner of the world, on every subject under the sun, Penguin represents quality and variety – the very best in publishing today.

For complete information about books available from Penguin – including Puffins, Penguin Classics and Arkana – and how to order them, write to us at the appropriate address below. Please note that for copyright reasons the selection of books varies from country to country.

In the United Kingdom: Please write to *Dept. EP, Penguin Books Ltd, Bath Road, Harmondsworth, West Drayton, Middlesex UB7 ODA*

In the United States: Please write to *Consumer Sales, Penguin USA, P.O. Box 999, Dept. 17109, Bergenfield, New Jersey 07621-0120.* VISA and MasterCard holders call 1-800-253-6476 to order Penguin titles

In Canada: Please write to *Penguin Books Canada Ltd, 10 Alcorn Avenue, Suite 300, Toronto, Ontario M4V 3B2*

In Australia: Please write to *Penguin Books Australia Ltd, P.O. Box 257, Ringwood, Victoria 3134*

In New Zealand: Please write to *Penguin Books (NZ) Ltd, Private Bag 102902, North Shore Mail Centre, Auckland 10*

In India: Please write to *Penguin Books India Pvt Ltd, 706 Eros Apartments, 56 Nehru Place, New Delhi 110 019*

In the Netherlands: Please write to *Penguin Books Netherlands bv, Postbus 3507, NL-1001 AH Amsterdam*

In Germany: Please write to *Penguin Books Deutschland GmbH, Metzlerstrasse 26, 60594 Frankfurt am Main*

In Spain: Please write to *Penguin Books S. A., Bravo Murillo 19, 1° B, 28015 Madrid*

In Italy: Please write to *Penguin Italia s.r.l., Via Felice Casati 20, I–20124 Milano*

In France: Please write to *Penguin France S. A., 17 rue Lejeune, F–31000 Toulouse*

In Japan: Please write to *Penguin Books Japan, Ishikiribashi Building, 2–5–4, Suido, Bunkyo-ku, Tokyo 112*

In South Africa: Please write to *Longman Penguin Southern Africa (Pty) Ltd, Private Bag X08, Bertsham 2013*

READ MORE IN PENGUIN

BUSINESS AND ECONOMICS

In with the Euro, Out with the Pound Christopher Johnson

The European Union is committed to setting up the Euro as a single currency, yet Britain has held back, with both politicians and public unable to make up their minds. In this timely, convincing analysis, Christopher Johnson asserts that this 'wait and see' policy is damaging and will result in far less favourable entry terms.

Lloyds Bank Tax Guide Sara Williams and John Willman

An average employee tax bill is over £4,000 a year. But how much time do you spend checking it? Four out of ten never check the bill – and most spend less than an hour. Mistakes happen. This guide can save YOU money. 'An unstuffy read, packed with sound information' – *Observer*

The Penguin Companion to European Union
Timothy Bainbridge with Anthony Teasdale

A balanced, comprehensive picture of the institutions, personalities, arguments and political pressures that have shaped Europe since the end of the Second World War.

Understanding Offices Joanna Eley and Alexi F. Marmot

Few companies systematically treat space as a scarce resource or make conscious efforts to get the best from their buildings. This book offers guidance on image, safety, comfort, amenities, energy-efficiency, value for money and much more.

Faith and Credit Susan George and Fabrizio Sabelli

In its fifty years of existence, the World Bank has influenced more lives in the Third World than any other institution, yet remains largely unknown, even enigmatic. This richly illuminating and lively overview examines the policies of the Bank, its internal culture and the interests it serves.